Back Door to War

The Roosevelt Foreign Policy

1933-1941

Other Books
by CHARLES CALLAN TANSILL

The Canadian Reciprocity Treaty of 1854, 1921

Robert Smith (in *The American Secretaries of State and Their Diplomacy*, 1927)

Documents Illustrative of the Formation of the Union of the American States, 1927

Proposed Amendments to the Constitution, 1889–1927, 1927

The Purchase of the Danish West Indies, 1931

The United States and Santo Domingo, 1798–1873, 1938

America Goes to War, 1938

The Diplomatic Relations Between the United States and Hawaii, 1885–1889, 1940

The Foreign Policy of Thomas F. Bayard, 1885–1889, 1940

Canadian-American Relations, 1875–1911, 1944

The Congressional Career of Thomas F. Bayard, 1869–1885, 1946

Back Door to War

The Roosevelt Foreign Policy
1933-1941

by

CHARLES CALLAN TANSILL

Professor of
American Diplomatic History
Georgetown University

HENRY REGNERY COMPANY
Chicago · 1952

TO

MY STUDENTS OF
MORE THAN THREE DECADES

PREFACE

THE armistice of November 11, 1918, put an end to World War I, but it ushered in a battle of the books that continues to the present day. Responsibility for the outbreak of that conflict was glibly placed by Allied historians upon the shoulders of the statesmen of the Central powers. German historians replied with a flood of books and pamphlets that filled the shelves of many libraries, and the so-called "revisionists" in many lands swelled this rising tide by adding monographs that challenged the Allied war-guilt thesis. While this historical argument was still being vehemently waged, World War II broke out in 1939 and academic attention was shifted to the question of the responsibility for this latest expression of martial madness.

There was little doubt in most American minds that Hitler had deliberately provoked World War II by his attack upon Poland. Since 1933 he had been caustically criticized in the American press. His unrestrained manner of speech, his dubious program for the regeneration of Germany, and the mad antics of some of his fanatical followers had created in numerous American circles a personal hatred of him that far exceeded the strong antipathy felt for Kaiser Wilhelm during the first decade of the twentieth century. There is no doubt that, as far as America was concerned, Hitler was a liability that all the good intentions and the best brains of Germany could never liquidate. The immediate blight that he inflicted upon German-American relations can be readily appreciated when we contrast the friendly press notices of the Brüning government with the sharp attacks made upon the Nazi political groups after February 1933.

Each item in the Hitler program of expansion evoked columns of recriminations in many American newspapers. Distrust of Germany went so deep and spread so far that every vestige of American good will vanished from the pages of periodicals that once had been friendly. Streams of refugees of different races and different creeds gave detailed testimony of widespread injustice and the denial of the freedoms that seemed so essential to the American way of life.

From 1933 to 1939 multitudes of Americans were being slowly conditioned for war along some foreign frontier. As Hitler rearmed Germany and prepared to put force behind his bold announcements, large numbers of persons in this hemisphere began to feel that his bid for power was a menace to them as well as to his European neighbors. The old followers of Woodrow Wilson had never renounced their allegiance to a one-world ideal, and they were fervent in their belief that America should take an active part in the preservation of world peace. They received strong support from many "liberals" and "intellectuals" who believed that modern science had banished the old barriers of time and space and had brought the peoples of the world into such close communion that some form of world government was an international imperative.

Some scholars like Charles A. Beard have pointed out that presidential pronouncements from 1933 to 1937 gave scant encouragement to ardent one-worlders, but they underestimated the importance of the Chief Executive's conversion to the explosive nonrecognition doctrine so strenuously advocated by Henry L. Stimson. This was a bomb whose long fuse sputtered dangerously for several years and finally burst into the flame of World War II. It was entirely fitting that Stimson became Secretary of War in 1940; no one deserved that title quite as well as he. The entry in his *Diary* for November 25, 1941, is illuminating. With regard to Japan "the question is how we should maneuver them into the position of firing the first shot without allowing too much danger to ourselves." On the following day Secretary Hull answered this question by submitting an ultimatum that he knew Japan could not accept. The Japanese attack upon Pearl Harbor fulfilled the fondest hopes of the Roosevelt Cabinet. It was easy now to denounce Japanese perfidy and to exult in the fact that the shock of the tragedy had erased all divisions of opinion in America. It was several years before inquiring minds began seriously to question the background of Pearl Harbor. When the report of the Army Pearl Harbor Board boldly pointed out the questionable conduct of General George C. Marshall, the Chief of Staff, Secretary Stimson rushed to his defense. On the convenient ground of ill-health he later refused to appear before the Joint Congressional Committee that investigated the tragedy of Pearl Harbor.

In preparing this record of American foreign policy during the prewar years I have been fortunate in securing access to the copious correspondence in the confidential files of the Department of State. Up to this time no other historian has fully utilized the same materials. I wish to express my appreciation of the helpful courtesies shown me by Dr. C. Bernard Noble, chief of the Division of Historical Policy Research in the Department of State, and his able assistants, Mr. Richard Humphrey and Dr. Taylor Parks.

In the Library of Congress I have immensely profited by the traditional helpful courtesy now personified by Dr. Luther Evans. I wish also to record my indebtedness to Mr. Verner W. Clapp, chief assistant librarian, Mr. David C. Mearns, chief of the Division of Manuscripts, Mr. Archibald B. Evans, Dr. Charles P. Powell, Dr. Elizabeth McPherson, Mr. John de Porry, Miss Katherine Brand, and Mr. David Cole.

In the National Archives I am indebted for assistance to the National Archivist, Mr. Wayne Grover, Dr. Philip Hamer, and Dr. Carl Lokke. I wish to record a particular debt of gratitude to Mrs. Kieran Carroll whose ability and gracious spirit have made the National Archives a most pleasant place in which to work. I wish also to mention Dr. Almon Wright, Mrs. Natalia Summers, and Mrs. William A. Dowling whose beauty and charm make it a little difficult to keep one's mind upon archival research.

In Georgetown University my colleague, Dr. Tibor Kerekes, has assisted me in innumerable ways, while the librarian, Mr. Phillips Temple, has bent every effort to secure the documentary data on which some of my chapters have been based.

To my old friend, Dr. Harry Elmer Barnes, I am deeply indebted for inspiration and assistance in every stage of the preparation of my manuscript.

There are many personal friends who have been of great assistance: ex-Senator Burton K. Wheeler, Judge Bennett Champ Clark, Dr. Walter A. Foote, Captain Miles DuVal, Rev. Henry F. Wolfe, Dr. Louis M. Sears, Dr. Reinhard H. Luthin, Dr. Rocco Paone, Dr. Carmelo Bernardo, Colonel Joseph Rockis, Dr. John Farrell, Dr. Eugene Bacon, Mr. Edwin H. Stokes, Mr. Anthony Kubek, Mr. Louis Carroll, Miss Mary Ann Sharkey, Miss Susan Sharkey, Mr. William R. Tansill, Mr. Charles B. Tansill, Mr. Raymond T. Parker, Mrs. B. R. Parker, Miss Grace Lee Tansill, Mrs. Mary Ann Sharkey, Mrs. C. Bernard Purcell, Mr. Fred G. Tansill, Mrs. Grace M. Carpenter, Miss Hazell Harris, Miss Amy Holland, and Rev. Herbert Clancy, S.J.

I cannot forget the inspiration of my dear friend, Dr. Gerald G. Walsh, S.J., whose wide scholarship has often kept my feet on the path of objectivity.

I have dedicated this volume to my students of more than three decades. They have been a strong bridge that has carried me over many deep waters of discouragement.

Last, and most of all, I wish to thank my wife, Helen C. Tansill, who has walked with me along all the paths of research, interpretation, composition, and bookmaking which could have been inexpressibly dreary without the proper companionship.

CHARLES CALLAN TANSILL

Georgetown University

TABLE OF CONTENTS

Back Door to War

HISTORICAL INTRODUCTION

a. *The Rise of Anglo-American Friendship*

THE MAIN OBJECTIVE in American foreign policy since 1900 has been the preservation of the British Empire. Intimate ties between Britain and the United States were first forged in 1898 when Britain realized that her policy of isolation had deprived her of any faithful allies upon whom she could depend in the event of war. The guns that brought victory to Admiral Dewey at Manila Bay sounded a new note of authority in the Far East and made the British Government aware of the fact that America could be made into a useful guardian of the life lines of empire. With John Hay as Secretary of State it was not difficult for the Foreign Office to arrive at an understanding with the United States that was as intimate as it was informal.

The first Open Door note of September 6, 1899, was an exercise in Anglo-American co-operation, with Alfred E. Hippisley giving an interesting demonstration of how helpful a British official could be in the drafting of American diplomatic notes. Theodore Roosevelt was evidently impressed with this growing Anglo-American accord, and when certain European powers threatened to intervene in the war Britain waged against the Boers in South Africa, he sounded a note that became very familiar in the eventful years that preceded the outbreak of World War II: "Real liberty and real progress are bound up with the prosperity of the English-speaking peoples. . . . I should very strongly favor this country taking a hand . . . if the European continent selected this opportunity to try and smash the British Empire."[1]

b. *Japan Is Given a Green Light to Expand in Manchuria*

In the Far East this Anglo-American parallel policy had a definite pro-Japanese inclination, with the Anglo-Japanese alliance of January 30, 1902, as the cornerstone of an imposing imperialistic structure. It was inevitable that the Department of State would favor Japan in a struggle which it assumed would result in the emancipation of North China from Russian shackles. The American press was equally pro-Japanese.

[1] John H. Ferguson, *American Diplomacy and the Boer War* (Philadelphia, 1939), pp. 208–9.

On the night of February 8, 1904, Japan launched a surprise attack upon the Russian fleet in the harbor of Port Arthur and thus started the war upon the same pattern she employed against the United States in December 1941.

It was a "sneak attack" upon the Russian fleet, but in 1904 the American press had no criticisms of this Japanese stratagem. The *New York Times* praised "the prompt, enterprising and gallant feat of the Japanese,"[2] while the *St. Louis Globe-Democrat* warmly commended the "dash and intelligence" of the resourceful sons of Nippon.[3] The *Cleveland Plain Dealer* grew lyrical in its description of this Japanese exploit: "As Drake in the harbor of Cadiz singed the beard of the King of Spain, so the active island commanders have set the Czar's whiskers in a blaze."[4] Other American newspapers expressed similar sentiments and public opinion moved swiftly to the support of Japan. This support remained unswerving until the peace conference at Portsmouth revealed the ambitious character of the Japanese terms.

Although Japan gained substantial advantages through the terms of this treaty which established her as the dominant power in the Far East, the Japanese public was indignant that no indemnity had been secured. Rioting broke out in several Japanese cities, and Americans had to be carefully guarded against violence.[5] Britain had been too astute to lend a helping hand to Roosevelt in arranging peace terms. The role of peacemaker had no attractions for the British Foreign Secretary.

President Roosevelt soon discovered that his policy of "balanced antagonisms" in the Far East was a flat failure.[6] Japanese statesmen were too clever to keep alive their diplomatic differences with Russia. The British Foreign Office, moreover, smiled upon an understanding between Japan and Russia. Britain was girding for an eventual conflict with Germany and it was to her obvious advantage to have strong allies whose assistance could be paid for in terms of Chinese territory. On July 30, 1907, Japan and Russia concluded important public and secret treaties which delimited their respective spheres of influence in Manchuria and Mongolia.[7] As political control over these two Chinese provinces was gradually extended by Russia and Japan, the Open Door began to creak on its rusty hinges. President Roosevelt had no desire to keep them well oiled with American support. Indeed, as far as he

---

[2] February 10, 1904.   [3] February 10, 1904.   [4] February 11, 1904.

[5] Tatsuji Takeuchi, *War and Diplomacy in the Japanese Empire* (New York, 1936), pp. 155-57.

[6] Edward H. Zabriskie, *American-Russian Rivalry in the Far East 1895-1914* (Philadelphia, 1946), pp. 101-60.

[7] Ernest B. Price, *The Russo-Japanese Treaties of 1907-1916 Concerning Manchuria and Mongolia* (Baltimore, 1933), pp. 34-38.

was concerned, the Open Door was largely a fiction. In order to confirm this fact, he concluded with Japan the Root-Takahira Agreement (November 30, 1908). The most important article in this agreement was dedicated to the maintenance of the "existing *status quo* . . . in the region of the Pacific Ocean." In Manchuria the status quo meant only one thing to Japan—eventual political and economic control. To President Roosevelt this expansive phrase must have had a similar meaning, and it is the opinion of an outstanding scholar that the Root-Takahira Agreement gave Japan "a free hand in Manchuria" in return for a disavowal of aggressive intentions towards the Philippines.[8]

It is obvious that the President, gravely concerned over our dispute with Japan relative to immigration into California, was ready to purchase peace by acquiescing in Japanese domination of a large area in North China. In a letter to President Taft in December 1910 he frankly stated that the Administration should take no step that would make Japan feel that we are "a menace to their interests" in North China. With special reference to Manchuria he remarked: "If the Japanese choose to follow a course of conduct to which we are adverse, we cannot stop it unless we are prepared to go to war. . . . Our interests in Manchuria are really unimportant, and not such that the American people would be content to run the slightest risk of collision about them."[9]

The Theodore Roosevelt viewpoint in 1910 with reference to Manchuria was a realistic one which could have been followed with profit by the Taft Administration. But Taft had his own ideas about what should be done in the Far East. As a firm believer in "dollar diplomacy" he adopted an ambitious program for increasing American interest and prestige in the Orient by building a firm financial flooring under American policy. He endeavored to push "big business" into placing large investments in China, and as one important item in this plan he proposed in November 1909 to put the railways in Manchuria under international control with the United States as one of the powers in this consortium.[10]

This proposal put the British Foreign Office "on the spot" and Sir Edward Grey's polite rejection of it clearly indicated that the so-called Anglo-American parallel policy in the Far East could be invoked only when it helped to achieve British objectives. But the British Foreign Secretary had to make some gestures of conciliation. America was too

[8] A. Whitney Griswold, *The Far Eastern Policy of the United States* (New York, 1938), pp. 129–34.

[9] Theodore Roosevelt to President William H. Taft, December 22, 1910. Knox MS, Library of Congress.

[10] John G. Reid, *The Manchu Abdication and the Powers, 1908–1912* (Berkeley, 1935), chaps. 4–10.

strong to be continually rebuffed. In 1909, after a series of notes in which Grey moved from one position to another with equal impudence, the British Government finally accepted arbitration of the age-old quarrel with America concerning the North Atlantic fisheries. Two years later he responded to American pressure and helped to write a profitable conclusion to the long story of the fur-seal dispute.[11] Apparently he was clearing the decks of the British ship of state for a possible conflict with Germany. Friendly relations with the United States became a national necessity.

c. *Sir Edward Grey Scores a Diplomatic Success*

In his relations with the United States, Sir Edward Grey was singularly successful. He did not owe his brilliant record to any fluency of speech or unusual ability to draft cogent diplomatic notes. He moved right into American hearts because he seemed to have honesty written in large letters across his pleasant face. There was no trace of subtlety in his open countenance; no lines of cunning that pointed to a scheming mind. He made an instant appeal to most Americans who thought they saw candor and character in eyes that seldom wavered during long diplomatic conversations. To Theodore Roosevelt he appeared as a fellow naturalist who cared more for the pattern of wild life on his country estate than for the intricate web of international intrigue that covered so many of the walls in No. 10 Downing Street. To Colonel House he seemed to be a man of simple tastes and quiet pleasures. In the eyes of the American public he was a man who could be trusted. When the great storm of 1914 blew across the fields of Europe he was widely regarded as a fearless figure who boldly defied the Kaiser's lightning even though its bolts might blast all Britain. But the British people grew tired of a glorified lightning rod, so in 1916 he was retired from his perilous position.

During the early years of the Wilson Administration he was an astounding success with amateur diplomats like Bryan, Secretary Lansing, and Colonel House. He was quick to see the importance of extending British support to the Bryan conciliation treaties and thereby he not only won the admiration of the "Great Commoner" but he also placed a large anchor to windward in case of a heavy American blow at some future time.[12] In this regard he was immeasurably smarter than the German Foreign Secretary who had little liking for the Bryan "cooling off" treaties. If such a convention has been concluded by the Ger-

---

[11] Charles Callan Tansill, *Canadian-American Relations, 1875–1911* (New York, 1944), chaps. 1–4, 10–12.

[12] Merle E. Curti, "Bryan and World Peace," *Smith College Studies in History*, XVI (Northampton, 1931).

man Foreign Office, there would have been no American intervention in 1917 and the history of American foreign policy would not have been marred by the many mistakes of President Wilson before and during the conference at Versailles.

It was fortunate for Britain that the Germans were so inept as diplomats, and it was doubly fortunate that Sir Edward Grey was a great favorite with so many Americans. This cordial regard paid good dividends in the summer of 1914 when the shadows of war began to fall across the European landscape. It was obvious that American public opinion was friendly to both Britain and France while Germany was regarded with deep distrust. The many ties that bound us to Britain were easily discernible to multitudes of Americans. The political concert of recent years, even though on British terms, was a factor that could not be disregarded. Political accord was supplemented by intimate business connections that drew thousands of Americans into profitable relations with Britons throughout the vast regions of the Empire. The American political system traced its roots to British practices, and our legal institutions bore a definite British imprint. But the intellectual ties were far more potent than connections of any other character. Shakespeare, Milton, Scott, Dickens, Burns, Wordsworth, and a host of other British men of letters had knocked on the door of the American heart and had received a warm welcome. There had never been an American tariff on British intellectual goods nor any embargoes on British ideals. In the American mind in 1914 there was a deep substratum of British thought and it was easy for British propaganda to convince the average American that Britain's war was "our war."

Skillfully using this friendly American attitude as a basis for far-reaching belligerent practices, the British Government, after August 1914, began to seize American vessels under such specious pretexts that even our Anglophile President lost his patience and called for some action that would protect American rights. In 1916 legislation was enacted that provided for the construction of a navy second to none, but President Wilson had no real disposition to employ our naval strength as a weapon that would compel Britain to respect the historic American principle of the freedom of the seas. Instead of exerting pressure upon Britain, the President drifted into a quarrel with Germany over the conduct of submarine warfare.

d. *The Department of State Strikes a False Note*

It is apparent that the United States drifted into war with Germany because the Department of State condemned German submarine warfare as inhuman and illegal. It is not so well known that Robert Lansing, the counselor of the Department of State, was badly confused in his controversy with the German Government concerning this submarine warfare. On February 4, 1915, the German Foreign Office announced the establishment of a war zone around the British Isles. In this war zone after February 18 all "enemy merchant vessels" would be destroyed without much regard for the safety of the passengers and the crew. In a sharp note of February 10, 1915, the Department of State protested against the sinking of any merchant ships without the usual preliminary visit and search, and it gave a distinct warning that the German Government would be held to a "strict accountability" for every injury inflicted upon American citizens.[13]

Professor Borchard has clearly demonstrated that this acrid note of February 10 was based upon an incorrect interpretation of international law. After discussing the background of the submarine controversy, he remarks: "It is thus apparent that the first American protest on submarines on February 10, 1915, with its challenging 'strict accountability,' was founded on the false premise that the United States was privileged to speak not only for American vessels and their personnel, but also on behalf of American citizens on Allied and other vessels. No other neutral country appears to have fallen into this error."[14]

It is remarkable that Mr. Lansing, as the counselor of the Department of State, should have drafted a note that was so patently incorrect in its interpretation of the law of nations. Before entering upon his official duties in the Department of State, he had for many years been engaged in the practice of international law. He was quite familiar with American precedents and practices, and it is quite mystifying to find that at one of the great crossroads in American history a presumably competent lawyer should give the President and the Secretary of State a legal opinion that would have shamed a novice.

Having made a fundamental error in his interpretation of international law with reference to submarine attacks upon *unarmed* merchant vessels of the Allied powers, he then hastened to make another error with regard to attacks upon *armed* merchantmen. It was Mr. Lansing's contention, and therefore that of President Wilson, that German submarines should not sink Allied armed merchant ships without first giving a warning that would permit the passengers and crew ample time to disembark with safety. The German Foreign Office hastened to point out that armed merchantmen would take advantage of this procedure to fire upon and destroy the undersea craft. For a brief period in Janu-

---

[13] Charles Callan Tansill, *America Goes to War* (Boston, 1938), chaps. 2–6.

[14] Edwin Borchard and William P. Lage, *Neutrality for the United States* (New Haven, 1937), p. 183.

ary and February 1916, Mr. Lansing, Secretary of State since June 1915, accepted the German contention and the Department of State was ready to insist that Allied merchant ships either go unarmed or take the consequences. But Lansing, upon the insistence of Colonel House, retreated from the sound position he had temporarily assumed and once more asserted with vehemence that armed merchantmen were not vessels of war that could be sunk at sight.[15] Thus, by reason of Secretary Lansing's final opinion, the President "and the House and Senate also, were misled into taking a position which had no foundation either in law or in common sense. Yet on that hollow platform Wilson stood in defending the immunity from attack of British armed merchantmen and of American citizens on board."[16]

It is thus clear that America drifted into war in 1917 either because the chief legal adviser in the Department of State made fundamental errors of interpretation which a mere student of international law would have easily avoided, or because the adviser wanted a war with Germany and therefore purposely wrote erroneous opinions. These facts completely destroy the old popular thesis that America went to war in protest against German barbarities on the high seas.

American intervention in World War I established a pattern that led America into a second world war in 1941. If we had not entered the war in Europe in 1917, World War I would have ended in a stalemate and a balance of power in Europe would have been created. Our intervention completely shattered the old balance of power and sowed the seeds of inevitable future conflict in the dark soil of Versailles. We had a deep interest in maintaining the political structure of 1919. Thousands of American lives and a vast American treasure had been spent in its erection. We could not see it demolished without deep concern. When dictators began to weaken its foundations, the Roosevelt Administration voiced its increasing disapproval of these actions. The bungling handiwork of 1919 had to be preserved at all costs, and America went to war again in 1941 to save a political edifice whose main supports had already rotted in the damp atmosphere of disillusion. The dubious political structure of 1919 is the subject of the next section of this chapter.

[15] Tansill, *op. cit.*, pp. 459–60.
[16] Borchard and Lage, *op. cit.*, p. 88. It is interesting to note that in the eventful days that just preceded America's entry into the World War, President Wilson had so little regard for Secretary Lansing that he complained bitterly to Colonel House about his shortcomings: "I [House] was surprised to hear him [the President] say that Lansing was the most unsatisfactory Secretary in his Cabinet; . . . that he had no imagination, no constructive ability, and but little real ability of any kind. He was constantly afraid of him because he often undertook to launch policies himself which he, the President, had on several occasions rather brusquely reversed." House *Diary*, March 28, 1917. House MS, Yale University Library.

e. *The Allies Violate the Pre-Armistice Contract*

In the period immediately preceding the outbreak of World War II it was the habit of President Roosevelt and Secretary Hull to talk constantly about the sanctity of treaties. They were international contracts that should never be broken. In this regard they were merely repeating an essential part of the ritual that became quite popular *after* 1919. But in Germany numerous persons could not forget the fact that the Treaty of Versailles was the cornerstone of a structure that had been built upon the dubious sands of betrayal. Lloyd George and Clemenceau had reluctantly agreed to a pre-Armistice contract that bound them to fashion the treaty of peace along the lines of the famous Fourteen Points.[17] The Treaty of Versailles was a deliberate violation of this contract. In the dark soil of this breach of promise the seeds of another world war were deeply sown.

It should be kept in mind that Woodrow Wilson acquiesced in this violation of contract. His ardent admirers have contended that he was tricked into this unsavory arrangement by Lloyd George and Clemenceau who were masters of the craft sinister. Ben Hecht, in his *Erik Dorn,* accepts this viewpoint and pungently refers to Wilson in Paris as a "long-faced virgin trapped in a bawdy house and calling in valiant tones for a glass of lemonade."[18] In truth, Wilson ordered his glass of lemonade heavily spiked with the hard liquor of deceit, and the whole world has paid for the extended binge of a so-called statesman who promised peace while weaving a web of war.

The story of this betrayal began on October 5, 1918, when Prince Max of Baden, addressed a note to President Wilson requesting him to negotiate a peace on the basis of the Fourteen Points. Three days later the President inquired if the German Government accepted these points as the basis for a treaty. On October 12, Prince Max gave assurance that his object in "entering into discussions would be only to agree upon practical details of the application" of the Fourteen Points to the terms of the treaty of peace. Two days later President Wilson added other con-

[17] President Wilson did not have a clear idea of the actual meaning of the Fourteen Points. In his *Diary*, December 20, 1918, Secretary Lansing makes the following significant comments: "There are certain phrases in the President's 'Fourteen Points' [Freedom of the Seas and Self-Determination] which I am sure will cause trouble in the future because their meaning and application have not been thought out. . . . These phrases will certainly come home to roost and cause much vexation. . . . He [the President] apparently never thought out in advance where they would lead or how they would be interpreted by others. In fact he does not seem to care just so his words sound well." Lansing Papers, Library of Congress.

[18] Oscar Cargill, *Intellectual America: Ideas on the March* (New York, 1941), p. 504.

ditions. No armistice would be signed which did not insure "absolutely satisfactory safeguards for the maintenance of the present military supremacy" of the Allied and Associated armies. Also, a democratic and representative government should be established in Berlin. When the German Government accepted these conditions, the President informed Prince Max (October 23) that he was now prepared to discuss with the Associated governments the terms of the proposed armistice. This discussion led to an agreement on their part to accept the Fourteen Points with two exceptions. With reference to "freedom of the seas" they reserved to themselves "complete freedom" when they entered the Peace Conference. In connection with the matter of reparations they understood that compensation would be made "by Germany for all damage done to the civilian population of the Allies, and their property, by the aggression of Germany by land, by sea, and from the air." These terms were conveyed to the German Government on November 5 and were promptly accepted by it. On November 11 an armistice placing Germany at the mercy of the Allied powers was signed in the Forest of Compiègne. With the cessation of hostilities the question of a treaty of peace came to the fore.[19]

The good faith of the Allied governments to make this treaty in conformity with the Fourteen Points had been formally pledged. But hardly was the ink dry on the Armistice terms when Lloyd George openly conspired to make the pre-Armistice agreement a mere scrap of paper. During the London Conference (December 1–3) the wily Welshman helped to push through a resolution which recommended an inter-Allied Commission to "examine and report on amount enemy countries are able to pay for reparation and indemnity." The word "indemnity" could easily be stretched to cover the "costs of the war." Although such a move was "clearly precluded by the very intent of the Pre-Armistice Agreement," Lloyd George showed an "apparent nonchalance about principle and contract," and started on a slippery path that "led rapidly downhill into the morasses of the December British elections."[20]

f. Reparations and Rascality

In his pre-election promises Lloyd George revealed a complete disregard of the pre-Armistice contract. His assurances to the British electorate were in direct contradiction to his pledge to Colonel House that he would be guided by the Fourteen Points. At Bristol (December 11, 1918) he jauntily informed his eager audience that "we propose to de-

[19] The correspondence dealing with the pre-Armistice agreement is printed in full in *Foreign Relations, 1918, Supplement,* I, *The World War,* I (Washington, 1933), 337–38, 343, 357–58, 379–81, 382–83, 425, 468–69.
[20] Paul Birdsall, *Versailles Twenty Years After* (New York, 1941), pp. 35–36.

mand the whole cost of the war [from Germany]."[21] The spirit that
animated the election was stridently expressed by Eric Geddes in a
speech in the Cambridge Guildhall: "We shall squeeze the orange until the pips squeak."[22]

At the Paris Peace Conference, Lloyd George (January 22, 1919)
suggested the appointment of a commission to study "reparation and
indemnity." President Wilson succeeded in having the word "indemnity" deleted but it was merely a temporary victory. The French gave
ardent support to the position assumed by Lloyd George. Their schemes
for the dismemberment of Germany would be promoted by an exacting
attitude on the part of Britain. This concerted action against the pre-
Armistice agreement was strongly contested by John Foster Dulles, the
legal adviser of the American members on the Reparation Commission.
He insisted upon a strict adherence to the pre-Armistice promises and
was supported by President Wilson who unequivocally stated that
America was "bound in honor to decline to agree to the inclusion of war
costs in the reparation demanded. . . . It is clearly inconsistent with
what we deliberately led the enemy to expect. . . ."[23]

But Lloyd George and Clemenceau quietly outflanked the American
position by the simple device of expanding the categories of civilian
damage so that they could include huge sums that properly belonged to
the categories of "war costs." Lloyd George insisted that pensions and
separation allowances should be included in the schedule of reparations, and Clemenceau hastened to his support. It was evident to both
of them that these items were excluded by the express terms of the pre-
Armistice agreement. If President Wilson adhered to the assurances he
had given to his financial experts he would immediately reject this
transparent scheme to violate the pledge of the Allied powers. But when
these same experts indicated the obvious implications of the Lloyd
George proposals and stated that they were ruled out by logic, Wilson
profoundly surprised them by bursting out in petulant tones: "Logic!
Logic! I don't give a damn for logic. I am going to include pensions."[24]

Not content with adding an undeserved burden that helped to break
German financial backs, Wilson followed the lead of Lloyd George
along other roads of supreme folly. At the meeting of the Council of
Four (April 5, 1919), the British Prime Minister suggested that in the

[21] David Lloyd George, *Memoirs of the Peace Conference* (New Haven, 1939), I,
306–9.

[22] Harold Nicolson, *Peacemaking, 1919* (New York, 1939), p. 18.

[23] *The Intimate Papers of Colonel House*, ed. Charles Seymour (Cambridge, 1928),
IV, 343.

[24] Philip M. Burnett, *Reparation at the Paris Peace Conference* (New York, 1940),
I, 63–64.

treaty of peace the Allies should "assert their claim" and Germany should recognize "her obligation for all the costs of the war." When Colonel House remarked that such an assertion would be contrary to the pre-Armistice agreement, Clemenceau reassuringly murmured that it was largely "a question of drafting."[25]

This experiment in drafting turned out to be the bitterly disputed Article 231 which placed upon Germany the responsibility "for causing all the loss and damage to which the Allied and Associated Governments and their nationals have been subjected as a consequence of the war imposed upon them by the aggression of Germany." This so-called "War Guilt Clause" aroused a deep and widespread hatred in all classes in Germany against a decision that was regarded as fundamentally unfair. And then to add insult to injury, Article 232 repeated the language of the pre-Armistice agreement with its fake formula which limited reparations to civilian damages. The ease with which this language had been twisted to Allied benefit had clearly indicated that it would be no protection to Germany.

These two American surrenders were followed by a third which meant a complete abandonment of the position that no "punitive treaty" should be imposed upon Germany. The American experts had placed much reliance upon the creation of a Reparation Commission which would have far-reaching powers to estimate what Germany could afford to pay on Allied claims and to modify the manner and date of these payments. But Clemenceau wanted this commission to be nothing more than a glorified adding machine designed merely to register the sums Germany should pay. It was to have no right to make independent judgments. The American contention that the payment of reparations should not extend more than thirty-five years was vetoed by the French who thought that fifty years might be required.[26]

During the heated discussions in the meeting of the Council of Four (April 5, 1919), Colonel House was so obtuse that he did not realize that the French were storming the American position until one of the French experts informed him of that fact. Norman Davis shouted to him that the French banners bore the legend: "Allied claims and not German capacity to pay should be the basis for reparations." Although this French slogan was in direct violation of the principles which the American experts had been fighting for during three long months, the confused Colonel tore down the American flag and hoisted the dubious French tricolor. By this action he flouted "both the letter and the spirit

[25] *Ibid.*, p. 69.
[26] *Ibid.*, pp. 832–33.

of the Pre-Armistice Agreement."[27] When President Wilson confirmed this surrender he thereby extended a favor to Adolf Hitler who warmly welcomed illustrations of Allied bad faith as one of the best means of promoting the Nazi movement.

The financial experts at Versailles failed to fix any particular sum as the measure of German liability for having caused the World War. In 1921 the Reparation Commission remedied this omission by computing the amount to be approximately $33,000,000,000. One third of this sum represented damages to Allied property, "and one-half to two thirds, pensions and similar allowances. In short, Wilson's decision doubled and perhaps tripled the bill."[28] Germany might have been able to pay a bill of not more than ten billion dollars, but when Wilson consented to play the part of Shylock and helped perfect a plan that would exact a pound of flesh from the emaciated frame of a war-wasted nation, he pointed the way to a financial chaos that inevitably overwhelmed Germany and Europe. He also helped to write several chapters in *Mein Kampf*.

g. *The Colonial Question*

The colonial question was dealt with in the fifth of the Fourteen Points. It provided for a "free, open-minded and absolutely impartial adjustment of colonial claims." At the Paris Peace Conference there was no attempt to arrive at this "absolutely impartial judgment." Long before the conference convened there had developed in the minds of prominent publicists in Britain, France, and the United States the opinion that Germany had forfeited all rights to her colonial dominion that had been conquered by Allied forces during the war. The usual argument in favor of this forfeiture was that German colonial administrators had cruelly mistreated the natives. Professor Thorstein Veblen wrote on this topic with his accustomed pontifical certitude: "In the [German] colonial policy colonies are conceived to stand to their Imperial guardian or master in a relation between that of step-child and that of an indentured servant; to be dealt with summarily and at discretion and to be made use of without scruple."[29] In Britain, Edwyn Bevan argued that the return of her colonies would not "be to content Germany but to keep up

---

[27] Birdsall, *op. cit.*, p. 258.

[28] Thomas A. Bailey, *Woodrow Wilson and the Lost Peace* (New York, 1944), p. 240.

[29] Thorstein Veblen, *The Nature of Peace* (New York, 1917), p. 261. Secretary Lansing did not share the viewpoint that the Germans had forfeited their colonies through maladministration. In his *Diary*, January 10, 1918, he remarked: "This purpose of the retention of conquered territory is *prima facie* based upon conquest and is not in accord with the spirit of a peace based upon justice. . . . It is necessary for peace that the adjustment should be equitable." Lansing Papers, Library of Congress.

her appetite for colonial expansion; it would be to restore a condition of things essentially unstable."[30]

In 1917 the American Commission of Inquiry, under the direction of Dr. Sidney E. Mezes, asked Dr. George L. Beer to prepare a series of studies on the colonial question with special reference to German colonial policy. Beer had long been regarded as an outstanding expert on the commercial policy of England during the sixteenth, seventeenth, and eighteenth centuries. In an imposing series of volumes he had "presented the English point of view" with regard to colonial administration.[31] After the outbreak of the World War "his sympathies were very decidedly with the Allies, and particularly with the British empire."[32]

It was only natural that Dr. Beer, despite his alleged historical objectivity, should strongly condemn German colonial policy. In February 1918 he turned over to Dr. Mezes his manuscript on the *German Colonies in Africa*. After weighing a considerable amount of data he came to the conclusion that Germany had totally failed to "appreciate the duties of colonial trusteeship."[33] Therefore, she should lose her colonial dominions.

Dr. Beer accompanied the American delegation to the Paris Peace Conference as a colonial expert and it is evident that he influenced the opinions of President Wilson who stated on July 10, 1919, that the German colonies had not "been governed; they had been exploited merely, without thought of the interest or even the ordinary human rights of their inhabitants."[34]

This accusation of the President was quite groundless. A careful American scholar who made a trip to the Cameroons in order to get an accurate picture of the prewar situation, summarizes his viewpoint as follows: "My own conclusion is that Germany's colonial accomplishments in thirty short years constitute a record of unusual achievement and entitle her to a very high rank as a successful colonial power, a view quite different from that reached in 1919. . . . I feel that if Germany had been allowed to continue as a colonial power after the war, her civil rule would have compared favorably with the very best that the world knows today."[35]

---

[30] Edwyn Bevan, *The Method in the Madness* (London, 1917), pp. 305–6.

[31] Arthur P. Scott, "George Louis Beer," in the *Marcus W. Jernegan Essays in American Historiography*, ed. W. T. Hutchinson (Chicago, 1937), p. 315.

[32] *Ibid.*, p. 319.

[33] George L. Beer, *African Questions at the Paris Peace Conference*, ed. L. H. Gray (New York, 1923), pp. 58–60.

[34] Bailey, *op. cit.*, p. 163.

[35] Harry R. Rudin, *Germany in the Cameroons, 1884–1914* (New Haven, 1938), pp. 11, 414, 419.

The Germans were deeply incensed because the Allied governments refused to count the colonies as an important credit item in the reparation account. Some Germans had estimated the value of the colonies at nine billion dollars. If this estimate had been cut in half there would still have been a large sum that could have been used to reduce the tremendous financial burden imposed upon weary German backs. Such action would have "spared Germany the additional humiliation of losing all her overseas possessions under the hypocritical guise of humanitarian motives."[36] These needless humiliations prepared the way for the tragedy of 1939. It is obvious that the revelations in the Nürnberg documents concerning Hitler's design for aggression are merely the last chapter in a long and depressing book that began at Versailles.

h. *The Problem of Poland: Danzig—The Polish Corridor—Upper Silesia*

In the discussion of questions relating to Poland, President Wilson had the advice of Professor Robert H. Lord, whose monograph on the *Second Partition of Poland* was supposed to make him an authority on the problems of 1919. His lack of objectivity was as striking as that of Professor Beer. It was largely a case of hysterical rather than historical scholarship.[37]

While the President was formulating his Fourteen Points, some of the experts on the American Commission of Inquiry suggested that an independent Polish state be erected with boundaries based upon "a fair balance of national and economic considerations, giving due weight to the necessity for adequate access to the sea."[38] In the thirteenth of the Fourteen Points, President Wilson changed the phraseology of this suggestion so that more stress would be laid upon ethnographic factors: "An independent Polish State should be erected which should include the territories inhabited by indisputably Polish populations, which should be assured a free and secure access to the sea."

(1) DANZIG

If Poland were to be given access to the Baltic Sea the port of Danzig would be of fundamental importance. In order to guide the President in this difficult matter of Polish boundaries, the American experts pre-

36 Bailey, *op. cit.,* p. 167.

37 It is significant that most of Professor Lord's colleagues on the Inquiry thought that his zeal for Poland was "excessive." Birdsall, *op. cit.,* p. 178. See also, Hunter Miller, *My Diary at the Conference of Paris* (privately printed, 1928), I, 289.

38 Ray S. Baker, *Woodrow Wilson and World Settlement* (Garden City, 1922), III, 37–38.

pared two reports (January–February 1919).[39] In dealing with Danzig they granted it to Poland because of economic considerations. They conveniently overlooked the fact that from the viewpoint of population Danzig was 97 per cent German. On February 23, while Wilson was in the United States, Colonel House cabled to him concerning the disposition of Danzig: "Our experts also believe this [the cession of Danzig to Poland] to be the best solution."[40] But the President was unwilling to confirm this suggestion, so the question of Danzig was postponed until March 17 when Lloyd George carried on a brisk exchange of opinions with Colonel House and Clemenceau. Two days later the British Prime Minister flatly refused to accept the proposal to cede both Danzig and the German Kreis of Marienwerder to Poland. He was not greatly impressed with the fact that the members of the Polish Commission and a large array of experts were in favor of this decision.[41]

Despite pressure from Colonel House and Dr. Mezes (the brother-in-law of Colonel House), President Wilson (March 28) rushed to the support of Lloyd George. On April 5 he and Lloyd George reached an understanding that the city and area of Danzig should become a free city with local autonomy under a commissioner of the League of Nations but connected with Poland by a customs union and port facilities. The foreign relations of the free city were to be under Polish control.[42]

To the Germans this large measure of Polish control over the city of Danzig was profoundly irritating, and at times the actions of the Polish authorities in connection with foreign relations and the establishment of export duties seemed unnecessarily provocative. From the viewpoint of economics, Polish control over Danzig had the most serious implications. By altering the customs tariff Poland could adversely affect the trade of the free city, and through control over the railways could extend important favors to the competing port of Gdynia.[43]

This situation led Gustav Stresemann, one of the most moderate of German statesmen, to remark in September 1925 that the "third great task of Germany is the . . . recovery of Danzig."[44] In 1931 the quiet, unaggressive Centrist leader, Heinrich Brüning, sounded out certain European governments in order to ascertain whether they would favor territorial revision at the expense of Poland. But this pressure to recover lost territory suddenly ended in Germany on January 26, 1934, when Marshal Pilsudski concluded with Hitler the well-known non-

[39] Miller, op. cit., IV, 224–26.
[40] Seymour, op. cit., IV, 334–35.
[41] Lloyd George, op. cit., II, 637–42.
[42] René Martel, The Eastern Frontiers of Germany (London, 1930), pp. 49–50.
[43] William H. Dawson, Germany Under the Treaty (London, 1933), pp. 149–52.
[44] Diaries, Letters and Papers (London, 1935–37), II, 503.

aggression treaty.[45] The price Poland paid for this agreement was an immediate acquiescence in a German program aimed at the nazification of Danzig. When Polish statesmen, after Pilsudski's death, tried to reverse this movement by courting British and French favor, they opened the floodgates that permitted the Nazi-Soviet tide to inundate all of Poland.

(2) THE POLISH CORRIDOR

A Polish Corridor through German territory to the Baltic Sea was distinctly forecast in the thirteenth point of the Wilson program which expressly declared that Poland should be granted "free and secure access to the sea." This wide "right of way" was to go through territory inhabited by "indisputably Polish populations." The American experts in their reports of January–February 1919, outlined a broad Polish path to the sea through the German provinces of Posen and West Prussia. They admitted the hardships this action would entail upon some 1,600,-000 Germans in East Prussia but they regarded the benefits conferred upon many millions of Poles as of more significance.[46]

When the reports of these experts were accepted by the Polish Commission and were written into the text of the Treaty of Versailles, it meant that the valley of the Vistula had been placed under Polish control. In order to shut the Germans of East Prussia away from any contact with the Vistula, "a zone fifty yards in width along the east bank was given to Poland, so that along their ancient waterway the East Prussians have no riparian rights. Though the river flows within a stone's throw of their doors, they may not use it."[47]

The Corridor itself was a wedge of territory which ran inland from the Baltic Sea for 45 miles, with a width of 20 miles at the coast, 60 miles in the center, and 140 miles in the south. Transportation across it was made difficult by Polish authorities who "instead of maintaining and developing the existing excellent system of communications by rail and road, river and canal . . . at once scrapped a large part of it in the determination to divert the natural and historical direction of traffic." With reference to conditions in the Corridor in 1933, Professor Dawson wrote as follows: "It is true that a few transit trains cross the Corridor daily, but as they may neither put down nor pick up traffic on the way, this piece of now Polish territory, so far as provision for communication and transport goes, might be unpopulated."[48] Traffic along the

[45] Documents on International Affairs, 1934, ed. John W. Wheeler–Bennett and Stephen Heald (New York), p. 424.

[46] Miller, op. cit., IV, 224–28; VI, 49–52.

[47] E. Alexander Powell, Thunder Over Europe (New York, 1931), p. 62.

[48] Dawson, op. cit., pp. 102–9. See also, I. F. D. Morrow and L. M. Sieveking, The Peace Settlement in the German Polish Borderlands (London, 1936).

highways crossing the Corridor was also very unsatisfactory. In 1931, Colonel Powell discovered that only the main east-and-west highways were open for vehicular traffic and this was "hampered by every device that the ingenuity of the Poles can suggest. Here I speak from personal experience, for I have driven my car across the Corridor four times."[49]

In 1938 and 1939, Hitler tried in vain to secure from the Polish Government the right to construct a railway and a motor road across the Corridor. Relying upon British support, the Polish Foreign Office in the spring of 1939 rejected any thought of granting these concessions. This action so deeply angered Hitler that he began to sound out the Soviet Government with reference to a treaty that would mean the fourth partition of Poland. Polish diplomats had not learned the simple lesson that concessions may prevent a catastrophe.

(3) UPPER SILESIA

During the sessions of the Paris Peace Conference the decision with reference to Upper Silesia was one of the clearest indications that hysteria and not objective history guided the conclusions of some of the American experts. This was particularly so in the case of Professor Robert H. Lord. He was strongly of the opinion that Upper Silesia should go to Poland without a plebiscite to ascertain the desires of the inhabitants. When the treaty was turned over to the German delegation the Upper Silesian article was subjected to a great deal of cogent criticism. Lloyd George was convinced by the German arguments, but President Wilson still gave some heed to Professor Lord who complained that Germany had been sovereign over Upper Silesia for only two centuries. Even though Mr. Lamont countered with the remark that this territory had not "belonged to Poland for 400 years," the President retained a lingering faith in the vehement protestations of Professor Lord. But this faith received a further shock when the learned professor opposed the holding of a plebiscite in Upper Silesia. Lloyd George then pertinently inquired why plebiscites were to be held in "Allenstein, Schleswig, Klagenfurt but not in Silesia."[50] There was no real answer Professor Lord could give to sustain his position so a provision was inserted in the treaty with reference to a plebiscite in Upper Silesia.

But this plebiscite was held in an atmosphere of terror. The International Commission that took over the administration of the voting area consisted of three members: General Le Rond (France); Colonel Sir

[49] Powell, op. cit., p. 66.
[50] Baker, op. cit., pp. 482–84. Apparently, Henry White did much to give President Wilson the correct view of the situation in Upper Silesia. See Allan Nevins, Henry White (New York, 1930), p. 423.

Harold Percival (Britain); and General de Marinis (Italy). France immediately sent 8,000 troops to maintain French domination over Upper Silesia and then procured the appointment of General Le Rond as the head of the civil administration. Although the Allied governments had assured the German delegation at Paris (June 16, 1919) that the International Commission would insist upon the "full impartiality of the vote," they broke faith in this regard as well as in others. Every possible concession was given to the Poles in the plebiscite area, but when the votes were taken on March 20, 1921, the results were a great shock to the French and Poles: 707,554, or 59.6 per cent, voted to remain under German control, while 478,802, or 40.4 per cent, voted to be placed under Polish administration.[51]

When one considers the indefensible tactics of the French before the plebiscite was held, it is surprising that the vote was so pro-German. One of the best accounts of the situation in Upper Silesia in 1919–1920 is given in the monograph by Professor René Martel, *The Eastern Frontiers of Germany:*

On April 4, 1919, the Polish Supreme National Council of Upper Silesia got into touch with Korfanty. Adelbert Korfanty, a former journalist and a popular leader, was the man of action for whom Dmowski was looking to prepare and organize the rising. . . . On May 1, 1919, the Polish secret societies . . . demonstrated their patriotic sentiments by pursuing the Germans. The Terror had begun. . . . The secret organizations which he [Korfanty] had built up . . . continued to exist until the plebiscite. . . . The Germans were tortured, mutilated, put to death and the corpses defiled; villages and châteaux were pillaged, burnt or blown up. The German Government has published on the subject a series of White Papers, illustrated by photographs. . . . The scenes which have thus been perpetuated pictorially surpass in horror the worst imaginable atrocities.[52]

When these bloody Polish outbreaks were finally suppressed, the League of Nations entrusted the task of partitioning Upper Silesia to a commission composed of representatives of Belgium, Brazil, China, Japan, and Spain. The unneutral composition of this commission is worth noting, and their decision reflected their prejudices. Under its terms Poland received nearly five-sixths of the industrial area in dispute. She also was granted "80 per cent of the coal-bearing area . . . besides all the iron ore mines; nearly all the zinc and lead ore mines and a large majority of the works dependent on the primary industries."[53]

[51] In the learned account written by Georges Kaeckenbeeck, *The International Experiment of Upper Silesia* (London, 1942), p. 6, the vote is given as 707,605 for Germany; 479,359 for Poland.
[52] (London, 1930), pp. 79–88.
[53] Dawson, *op. cit.*, pp. 206–9.

In commenting upon the farce of this plebiscite, Sir Robert Donald remarks: "Harder to bear than the material loss were the exasperating and cruel moral wrongs and injustices inflicted upon the German community. It is possible enough that had the Allies transferred Upper Silesia to Poland, basing their action upon no other law than brute force, Germany would have resigned herself to the inevitable. . . . But to inflict upon her the tragic farce of the plebiscite, with all its accompaniments of deceit, broken pledges, massacres, cruel outrages, carried out in an atmosphere of political putrescence, was to add insult to injury, moral torture to robbery under arms."[54]

Despite Wilson's reassuring words about a peace that should not be punitive, Germany had been stripped and severely whipped. After these impressive examples of Allied ill faith it was not difficult for Nazi statesmen to plan for expansion without much thought about the usual principles of international law. Law is based upon logic, and, at Versailles, Woodrow Wilson had frankly condemned the science of right reasoning: "Logic! Logic! I don't give a damn for logic." Hitler could not have made a more damning pronouncement.

i. *The Occupation of the Rhineland*

President Wilson was not always on the wrong side of the diplomatic fence at Paris. In the matter of the Rhineland occupation he adopted a vigorous role which completely blocked the execution of an ambitious French program. One of the main French objectives in 1919 was the separation of the entire left bank of the Rhine from Germany and the establishment of autonomous republics friendly to France. Wilson refused to accept this program even though it was ardently advocated by Colonel House.[55] With the support of Lloyd George he was able to write into the Treaty of Versailles a moderate provision: "German territory situated to the west of the Rhine, together with the bridgeheads, will be occupied by Allied and Associated troops for a period of fifteen years from the coming into force of the present treaty."[56]

The last contingent of the American Army of Occupation left the Rhineland in February 1923; some of the Allied troops remained until 1930. The mere fact that German soil was occupied for a decade aroused resentment in most German minds. This resentment was turned

---

[54] Sir Robert Donald, *The Polish Corridor and the Consequences* (London, 1929), pp. 197–98. See also, Sarah Wambaugh, *Plebiscites Since the World War* (Washington, 1933); W. J. Rose, *The Drama of Upper Silesia* (Brattleboro, 1936); Colonel E. S. Hutchinson, *Silesia Revisited—1929* (London, 1930).

[55] Seymour, *op. cit.*, IV, 347, 349, 383.

[56] Articles 428–432 of the Treaty of Versailles, *The Treaties of Peace, 1919–1923* (New York, 1924), I, 254–55.

into a feeling of outrage when France quartered a considerable number of her Negro colonial troops in private residences in parts of the Rhine territory. Their insulting and at times brutal conduct towards the German women was regarded as an indication that France would go to extreme lengths to humiliate Germany. In December 1921, General Henry T. Allen sent to Secretary Hughes a complaint that had been filed with the High Commision by a delegation of German workingmen: "We fear to leave our homes and go to work leaving our wives and daughters in our houses with these men. This question troubles us more than houses and more food."[57] Felix Morley, during a vacation in France, was sharply critical of French behavior: "If England and America would leave France to herself, there wouldn't be a Frenchman on German soil after a week."[58] Three years later the American consul at Cologne wrote to Secretary Hughes a bitter indictment of French practices in the Rhineland. He reported that once in a while German officials were handcuffed and the German police "beaten and kicked." At Aachen civilians and officials were "horsewhipped."[59] Memories of these insults lingered in German minds and helped to produce a climate of opinion that justified many of the items in Hitler's program of expansion and revenge.

j. *The Starvation Blockade*

The armistice of November 11, 1918, did not put an end to the Allied blockade of Germany. For many months after the war was over the Allied governments did not permit food shipments to the millions of hungry persons in Germany. This callous attitude on the part of the Allied delegations in Paris shocked the Labour Party in England which sponsored the humane "save the children" movement. Funds were raised to buy food "when owing to the blockade, starvation stalked gaunt and livid through the streets of thousands of German towns."[60]

In Paris, President Wilson appealed "again and again for a free exportation of foodstuffs to the half-starving populations of Central Europe, but always the French Government thwarted him. This French policy filled [Henry] White, who had small grandchildren in Germany and heard much from his daughter of the desperate plight of the people, with futile indignation."[61]

[57] General Henry T. Allen to Secretary Hughes, December 22, 1921. 862T.01/346, MS, National Archives.
[58] Ambassador Wallace to Secretary Hughes, Paris, April 27, 1920. 862.00/921, MS, National Archives.
[59] Emil Sauer to Secretary Hughes, Cologne, February 16, 1923. 862.00/1215, MS, National Archives.
[60] Dawson, *op. cit.*, p. 84.
[61] Nevins, *op. cit.*, p. 372.

The impact of the blockade upon the German people was described by George E. R. Gedye who was sent in February 1919 upon an inspection tour of Germany:

Hospital conditions were appalling. A steady average of 10 per cent of the patients had died during the war years from lack of fats, milk and good flour. . . . We saw some terrible sights in the children's hospital, such as the "starvation babies" with ugly, swollen heads. . . . Our report naturally urged the immediate opening of the frontiers for fats, milk and flour . . . but the terrible blockade was maintained as a result of French insistence.[62]

This graphic description by Gedye receives strong confirmation in a recent account written by ex-President Hoover who, in 1919, had been placed by President Wilson in charge of food distribution to the needy population of Europe. When Hoover arrived in London he suffered a severe shock:

I met with Allied ministers to discuss programs and organization. The session was at once a revelation in intrigue, nationalism, selfishness, heartlessness and suspicion. . . . Much as I am devoted to the English, they had one most irritating quality—they were masters at wrapping every national action in words of sanctity which made one really ashamed not to support it all. . . . Within a few hours I found that the greatest famine since the Thirty Years' War did not seem to be of any great immediate concern. . . . They [the Allied governments] were determined to keep the food blockade not only on Germany and the other enemy states but also on the neutrals and liberated nations. . . . On February 1st [1919] . . . I gave him [President Wilson] the following: "Dear Mr. President: There is no right in the law of God or man that we should longer continue to starve people now that we have a surplus of food." . . . The President duly took up the question . . . [and] the Big Four ordered my proposed agreement with the Germans applied forthwith.

To present the formula to the Germans they appointed a delegation to be headed by a British admiral, Sir Rosslyn Wemyss. . . . He said to me arrogantly, "Young man, I don't see why you Americans want to feed these Germans." My impudent reply was: "Old man, I don't understand why you British want to starve women and children after they are licked." . . . When the door for food to Germany opened, I promptly found hate so livid on the Allied side and also in some parts of America as to force me to issue a statement justifying my actions. . . . We had lost four months' time, and the problems in Germany had in the meantime multiplied. . . . The maintenance of the food blockade until March, 1919—four months after the Armistice—was a crime in statesmanship, and a crime against civilization as

[62] G. E. R. Gedye, *The Revolver Republic* (London, 1930), pp. 29-31.

a whole. . . . Nations can take philosophically the hardships of war. But when they lay down their arms and surrender on assurances that they may have food for their women and children, and then find that this worst instrument of attack on them is maintained—then hate never dies.[63]

Finally, under the terms of the Brussels Agreement (March 14, 1919) provision was made for the shipment of food to Germany, but before these supplies were made available thousands of Germans had gone through the tortures of slow starvation. At Versailles the beads in a long rosary of hatred and despair had been forged for the Germans by the Big Four. After 1919 they were counted over numberless times by large groups of unfortunate persons whose health had been wrecked by malnutrition. They neither forgot nor forgave.

k. *German Reaction to the Treaty of Versailles*

On May 7, 1919, the German delegation in Paris was formally presented with the terms of the Treaty of Versailles. When Johann Giesberts read through the long bill of indictment he burst out with vehemence: "This shameful treaty has broken me, for I had believed in Wilson until today. I believed him to be an honest man, and now that scoundrel sends us such a treaty."[64] On May 12 at a great mass meeting in Berlin, Konstantin Fehrenbach, one of the leaders of the Centrist Party, alluded to the attitude that future generations in Germany would adopt relative to the treaty and ended his speech with words of warning that later were implemented by Hitler: "The will to break the chains of slavery will be implanted from childhood on."[65]

These chains were confirmed by the Kellogg-Briand Pact which bestowed a formal blessing upon the injustices of Versailles. They could be broken only by force. When Hitler began to snap them, one by one, the noise was heard round the world and the American public was solemnly informed by Secretaries Stimson and Hull that a wild German bull was breaking the choicest dishes in the china shop of world peace. At Nürnberg men were hanged because they had planned to break these vessels filled with national hatreds. Nothing was said of the pseudo-statesmen who prepared at Paris the witches' brew that poisoned German minds. The results of their criminal bungling will be told in succeeding chapters.

[63] Herbert Hoover, "Communism Erupts in Europe," *Collier's*, CXXVIII (September 8, 1951), pp. 26–27, 68–71.

[64] Alma Luckau, *The German Delegation at the Paris Peace Conference* (New York, 1941), p. 124.

[65] *Ibid.*, pp. 98–100.

I

American Relations with the
Weimar Republic

a. *America Rejects Trials of War Criminals*

IN THE YEARS immediately after the close of the World War the attitude of the American Government towards the Weimar Republic was one of watchful waiting. In the Department of State there was a definite fear that sparks from Soviet Russia might find an easy lodgment in the broken structure of Germany and thus start a fire that would consume all the landmarks of the old German way of life. This fear was increased by the remarks of certain Germans who had held important diplomatic posts under the Kaiser. In October 1919, Count von Bernstorff stressed the importance of establishing close connections between Germany and Russia: "Russia is the country which we can most conveniently exploit. Russia needs capital and intelligence which our industry can provide. Above all, now that Bolshevism is beginning in Germany we are becoming 'cousin germains' of the Russians. We must come to terms with the Bolsheviks."[1]

The mounting unrest in Germany had many unpleasant expressions. In November 1919 there was a large demonstration in Heidelberg in which anti-Semitism and a spirit of excessive nationalism were clearly in evidence.[2] By April 1921 anti-Semitism reached a peak in certain German cities, although it was strongly opposed by Catholic prelates like the Cardinal of Munich.[3] After 1933, Hitler merely played upon prejudices that had long existed in Germany.

Fervid expressions of nationalism were in part caused by the loud talk of certain Allied statesmen with reference to holding trials for many prominent German leaders as war criminals. This talk led the ex-Kaiser, Wilhelm II, to write to President Wilson and offer to serve as a victim in place of other Germans: "If the Allied and Associated Governments want a victim let them take me instead of the nine hun-

[1] American Embassy (Paris) to the Secretary of State, October 24, 1919. 862.00/754, MS, National Archives.
[2] Dyar to the Secretary of State, Berlin, December 31, 1919. 862.00/776, MS, National Archives.
[3] R. D. Murphy to the Secretary of State, January 5, 1924. 862.4016/12, MS, National Archives.

dred Germans who have committed no offence other than that of serving their country in the war."[4] There was no real need for the ex-Kaiser to make this offer. The American Government was strongly opposed to any war-criminal trials. On February 6, 1920, Secretary Lansing sent a significant instruction to the American Embassy in Paris: "This Government has not yet ratified the Treaty; it is not joining in the demand of the Allies, and it is in no way backing the insistence of the Allies in the immediate carrying out of the demand [for the delivery of German war criminals]."[5]

b. *The Allies Balk at the Payment of American Army of Occupation*

The Allies soon abandoned the project of trying Germans as war criminals. Apparently they strongly resented the attitude of Secretary Lansing in this matter because they showed a most non-co-operative spirit with regard to the payment of the costs of the American Army of Occupation. The Wilson Administration had expected the payments to be made promptly out of German reparations, but this action was blocked for several years. In 1923 the British representative on the Reparation Commission expressed a doubt whether the United States, having rejected the Treaty of Versailles, could assert any just claim to be paid for the Rhineland occupation.[6] Similar statements deeply angered George B. Lockwood, secretary of the Republican National Committee, who wrote to Secretary Hughes to express his indignation at the situation. He was certain that the "haggling and pettifogging, duplicity and downright dishonesty that has characterized the attitude of Great Britain and the other Allied Powers in their treatment of America's claims" indicated a strong desire to "bilk" the United States out of any payment for occupation costs.[7]

On May 25, 1923, the governments of Belgium, Britain, France, and Italy signed an agreement with the United States providing for the reimbursement of the costs of the American Army of Occupation. This reimbursement was to be paid out of German reparations over a period of twelve years.[8] Although the Allied governments had finally consented to this long-range schedule of payments, Secretary Hughes

[4] Ex-Kaiser Wilhelm II to President Wilson, February 9, 1920. 763.7219/9116, MS, National Archives.

[5] Secretary Lansing to the American Embassy in Paris, February 6, 1920. 763.7219/8941a, MS, National Archives.

[6] Mr. Wadsworth to Secretary Hughes, Paris, May 16, 1923. 462.00R294/210, MS, National Archives.

[7] George B. Lockwood to Secretary Hughes, May 24, 1923. 462.00R293/232, MS, National Archives.

[8] *Foreign Relations, 1923,* II, 180.

noted that in their own case they had insisted that the payments for occupation be "met practically in full as they fell due." It seemed to him that "they should have distributed the money received for these arms costs equitably; instead, they kept these moneys and left us out."[9]

c. France Moves into the Ruhr

In the matter of reparations the French Government proved exceedingly difficult to satisfy. Under the terms of the Treaty of Versailles provision was made for the appointment of a Reparation Commission which should determine the amount owed by Germany and prepare a schedule for "discharging the entire obligation within a period of thirty years from May 1, 1921." Up to that date the German Government was to pay the equivalent of five billion dollars. Early in 1921, Germany claimed that she had completed this payment in the form of gold, securities, coal, and other commodities, but the Reparation Commission declared that less than half of the required sum had really been paid. The German Government then appealed to the United States to "mediate the reparations question and to fix the sum to be paid . . . to the Allied Powers."[10] Secretary Hughes refused to be drawn into this dispute, but he did admonish the Weimar Republic to make "directly to the Allied Governments clear, definite and adequate proposals which would in all respects meet its just obligations."[11]

On April 28, 1921, the Reparation Commission announced that the total German indemnity had been fixed at 132,000,000,000 gold marks or approximately $33,000,000,000. The schedule of payments was forwarded to Germany on May 5 and was promptly accepted.[12] Although the first installment of $250,000,000 was paid on August 31, the decline in the value of the mark indicated fundamental financial difficulties in Germany. During 1922 the German Government asked for a moratorium extending two and one-half years. Britain was inclined to favor this request; France was bitterly opposed to it. Under French pressure the Reparation Commission finally declared that Germany was in default and Poincaré insisted upon reprisals.

The American Government was deeply interested in this German problem. Peace between Germany and the United States had been ef-

[9] Secretary Hughes to Ambassador Herrick, February 23, March 15, 1924. 462.00R-296/176, 212, MS, National Archives.

[10] Commissioner Dresel to Secretary Hughes, Berlin, April 20, 1921. 462.00R29/649, MS, National Archives.

[11] Secretary Hughes to the American Mission in Berlin, April 22, 1921. 462.00R29/684, MS, National Archives.

[12] Foreign Relations, The Paris Peace Conference, 1919, XIII, 862–67.

fected under the terms of a joint resolution signed by President Harding on July 2, 1921.[13] This action had been followed by a treaty (August 25, 1921) which went into effect on November 11 of that year.[14] Under the terms of these instruments all the rights, privileges, indemnities, and reparations to which the United States was entitled under the Armistice and the Treaty of Versailles were "expressly reserved." Separate peace with Germany would not mean the loss of any of America's hard-won rights.

These rights would have no value in a Germany whose economic structure was destroyed. Therefore, American representatives abroad looked with strong disapproval upon Poincaré's determination to press for prompt payment of impossible reparations. In Rome, Ambassador Child talked the situation over with Barthou, the mouthpiece of Poincaré. He reported to Secretary Hughes that this conversation revealed that Barthou had "an anti-German prejudice so strong as to vitiate sound judgment." He thought it might be necessary for the "world to weigh the necessity of acting independently of the French Government in joint appeals to public opinion."[15]

The following month Ambassador Herrick, who was usually quite Francophile, wrote to Secretary Hughes and deprecated the attitude of Poincaré with reference to pressure upon Germany: "There is now definitely no hope of making any impression on Poincaré personally. He has learned nothing and forgotten nothing, not from lack of intelligence but rather from definite purpose. . . . He has staked his political life and reputation on his aggressive policy. If you want to do anything effective to stop this, you must in my judgment make some public utterance with the idea of helping reasonable French opinion."[16] But Hughes replied that an appeal to the French people over the head of their government was a dangerous proceeding: "Previous efforts of this sort have caused more trouble than they cured."[17]

In January 1923, French troops moved into the Ruhr as far east as Dortmund. The British Government regarded this action as illegal and refused to support it. Occupation of the Ruhr would paralyze German industry and seriously affect reparations and British trade with Germany. In order to counter this French policy of pressure, German workers in the Ruhr laid down their tools. Mines and factories shut down

---

[13] *Ibid.*, pp. 18–19.

[14] *Ibid.*, pp. 22–25.

[15] Ambassador Child to Secretary Hughes, Rome, October 24, 1922. 462.00R296/5, MS, National Archives.

[16] Ambassador Herrick to Secretary Hughes, Paris, November 22, 1922. 462.00R-29/2184, MS, National Archives.

[17] Secretary Hughes to Mr. Boyden, November 24, 1922. 462.00R29/2187, MS, National Archives.

and telephone, telegraph, and railways services were discontinued. All reparation payments to the Allied governments ceased.

The American commercial attaché in Berlin looked at this French invasion of the Ruhr as an attempt permanently to "emasculate Germany as a Great Power."[18] The American Ambassador reported in a similar vein: "The people have been treated as a subject and alien race; their trade has been harassed and largely destroyed; ineffectual troops have been quartered here and there in their villages. Apparently everything that would arouse hostility, and nothing that would conciliate, has been done. As a result, the Rhineland population today is savagely anti-French."[19]

To Herbert Hoover the repressive policy of the French had a world impact. French interference with the coal trade of the Ruhr would upset "the entire coal market of the world and would make life more difficult everywhere."[20] The most graphic description of French terrorism in the Ruhr is given by George E. R. Gedye in *The Revolver Republic:*

In Essen I saw a boy, one morning, sobbing bitterly after being thrashed by a French officer for failing to yield the pavement to him, and in Recklinghausen the French pursued with their riding-whips into the theatre some men who had taken refuge there, stopped the performance of "King Lear," and drove out the whole audience. . . . On the night of 11th March the bodies of a French chasseur subaltern and a *Régie* station master were found near Buer. . . . The next morning a seven o'clock curfew was proclaimed in Buer. . . . The order to be indoors by seven had been issued on a Sunday after many people had gone off on excursions for the day. On their return, all-unwitting, they were beaten with riding-whips, struck with rifle butts, chased through the streets by French soldiers, and shot at. A workman named Fabeck was shot dead as he stood with his young wife waiting for a tram.[21]

These repressive tactics finally bore fruit in the agreement of September 26, 1923, when Germany promised to abandon the policy of passive resistance. But the price of victory had been high. The British Government had not looked with favor upon the occupation of the Ruhr with the consequent collapse of Germany's economic structure, and opinion in neutral countries was sharply critical. In France the fall in the value of the franc caused milder counsel to prevail. The way was thus prepared for discussions that led to the adoption of the Dawes

[18] C. E. Herring to Secretary Hughes, Berlin, September 10, 1923. 462.00R29/3333, MS, National Archives.

[19] Ambassador Houghton to Secretary Hughes, Berlin, July 27, 1923. 462.00R29/2923, MS, National Archives.

[20] Interview between W. R. Castle and Herbert Hoover, March 7, 1923. 862T.01/687, MS, National Archives.

[21] *Ibid.*, pp. 102, 119–21.

Plan. The Inter-Allied Agreement providing for this plan was signed
in London, August 30, 1924, and the evacuation of French troops from
the Ruhr began immediately.[22]

d. *President Hoover Suggests a Moratorium on Reparations*

The Dawes Plan was merely a financial sedative and not a cure for the
ills of Germany. It was silent with reference to the total reparations bill.
Therefore, in a technical sense, the old total bill of $33,000,000,000
fixed by the Reparation Commission was still in force. But it should
have been evident to the so-called financial experts that Germany could
not continue making huge annual reparations payments for an indefinite period. They should also have realized that no great power would
be content to remain in the financial and political chains that were
riveted upon Germany under the terms of the plan. In this regard the
Commercial and Financial Chronicle made some highly pertinent remarks:

Nothing like the proposed procedure is to be found in history. Germany is
to be taken over and administered in the same way as a corporation no longer
able to meet its obligations is taken over by the law and transferred to the
hands of the bankruptcy commissioners. . . . In reality a foreign control of
internal affairs has been imposed such as never before existed either in our
times or in the past. . . . Never before has it been proposed to take such
complete possession of the wealth of a nation.[23]

Payments under the Dawes Plan increased each year until they
reached (in the fifth year) 2,500,000,000 marks. The German Government was able to make them only because of the large volume of foreign
loans. These loans began in 1924 when American financial promoters
were scouring Europe in a fervid search for borrowers. According to
Dr. Koepker-Aschoff, Prussian Minister of Finance during the years
1925–26, every week some representative of American bankers would
call at his office and endeavor to press loans upon him. German officials
were "virtually flooded with loan offers by foreigners."[24] It made little
difference whether a loan was actually needed. In Bavaria a little hamlet
wished to secure $125,000 in order to improve the town's power sta-
tion. An American promoter soon convinced the mayor that he should

[22] *Foreign Relations, Paris Peace Conference*, XIII, 899–902. See also, Charles G.
Dawes, *A Journal of Reparations* (London, 1939).

[23] Quoted in Max Sering, *Germany Under the Dawes Plan* (London, 1929), pp.
64–65.

[24] Max Winkler, *Foreign Bonds, An Autopsy* (Philadelphia, 1933), pp. 86–87.

apply for $3,000,000 which would provide not only for the expansion of the power plant but would also finance the construction of various nonproductive projects. The possibility of repayment was given little thoughtful consideration.[25]

But reparation payments had to be made and this was possible only through foreign loans. From 1924 to June 30, 1931, the following loans were advanced by American bankers:

	Reichsmarks
The Dawes and Young loans	875,000,000
States and Municipalities	860,000,000
Public utilities	1,073,000,000
Municipal Banks	188,000,000
Private borrowers	2,269,000,000
	5,265,000,000

These large American loans represented 55 per cent of the total amount loaned to Germany during these years. It is obvious that American businessmen had a very important stake in continued German solvency, and they scanned with deep interest the manner in which these loans were used in Germany. Her greatest achievement in the sphere of reconstruction was the entire remodeling of her iron and steel industry. Significant technical progress was made in the coal industry, and enormous strides were made in the production of coke and gas and the utilization of by-products. The chemical industry increased its prewar output by at least 25 per cent, and the electrical industries had a similar mushroom growth.[26]

But the tremendous burden of reparation payments and interest charges on foreign loans was too much for the shaky German financial structure.[27] Another financial palliative was now tried. On June 7, 1929, a group of financial experts headed by Owen D. Young handed to the Reparation Commission, and the governments concerned, a financial agreement that was conveniently called the Young Plan. Under its terms the total indemnity bill was reduced to $8,032,500,000 and was capitalized at 5½ per cent. The period for its payment was limited to fifty-eight and one-half years. The Reparation Commission was abolished in favor of a Bank for International Settlements which would enjoy broad powers. As a concession to Germany, the extensive financial

[25] *Ibid.*

[26] On the whole matter of the financial situation in Germany in the pre-Hitler period see C. R. S. Harris, *Germany's Foreign Indebtedness* (London, 1935).

[27] J. W. Angell, *The Recovery of Germany* (New Haven, 1932), pp. 170 ff.

and political controls outlined under the Dawes Plan were abandoned.[28]

The Young Plan went into effect in 1930, but it was a panacea that failed to cure the ills of a world that was on the brink of a breakdown. Some ascribed this desperate situation to an inadequate gold supply; others thought in terms of a surplus of silver. Technology was blamed because it had enabled man to multiply the output of industrial and agricultural products to the point where the world market was flooded with cheap commodities. Aristide Briand pointed to an economic federation of Europe as the best means of surmounting the difficulties that threatened to engulf the Continent, but the Austrian Foreign Minister, Dr. Johann Schober, expressed the opinion that it would not be expedient to push things too fast. Perhaps the best step along the road to eventual European federation would be an Austro-German customs union! In March 1931 this proposed union was formally announced by the governments of Austria and Germany with a cogent explanation of its objectives.

Although Britain was not opposed to this arrangement, France affected to see political motives back of it and expressed vehement disapproval. Her refusal to grant a much-needed loan to the principal bank in Austria (the Kredit Anstalt) helped to undermine confidence in the stability of that institution. This, in turn, had its effect upon the German economic structure that was already tottering under the weight of a large unfavorable trade balance.[29]

Realizing that Austria and Germany were going through a period of frenzied finance, President Hoover (June 20) proposed a one-year world moratorium, from July 1, with reference to "all payments on inter-governmental debts, reparations and relief debts, both principal and interest . . . not including obligations of governments held by private citizens." He made it clear, however, that this action would not mean "the cancellation of the debts" due to the United States.[30]

When France delayed acceptance of this proposal the situation in Europe grew rapidly worse. During the seventeen days "that France held up the Hoover Plan, a run on the German banks and the calling in

---

[28] John W. Wheeler-Bennett and H. Latimer, *Information on the Reparation Settlement* (London, 1930).

[29] P. Einzig, *The World Economic Crisis, 1929–1931* (New York, 1932); F. W. Lawrence, *This World Crisis* (London, 1931); League of Nations, *World Production and Prices, 1925–1933* (Geneva, 1934). The following table will indicate the rapid decline in German exports:

Monthly average	(Rm. Millions) Imports	Exports	Balance
1931	560.7	799.8	239.1
1933	350.3	405.9	55.6
1934	371.0	347.2	−23.8

[30] *New York Times*, June 21, 1931.

of short-term credits drained the country of some $300,000,000. All banks in Germany for a time were closed. The Hoover Plan would have saved Germany $406,000,000 this year."[31]

e. *Chancellor Brüning Is Compelled to Resign*

With Germany in financial chaos, Secretary Stimson decided to pay a visit to Berlin in order to get a close-up of the situation. The German press, "without a single discordant note," gave him a "hearty welcome and the occasion was seized to express in front-page editorials the gratitude felt for America's . . . friendliness towards Germany."[32] Stimson had a long conversation with Dr. Brüning, the German Chancellor. It was not long before they discovered that they had fought along the Western Front in opposing forces that had repeatedly clashed. The warrior tie drew them at once close together and with President Hindenburg it was much the same thing. To Stimson, the President of the Weimar Republic was an "impressive, fine old man."[33]

But it required more than Stimson's good will to save the Weimar Republic. The failure of the Allied governments to carry out the disarmament pledges of the Treaty of Versailles, the heavy burden of the Young Plan with its consequent crushing taxation, and the difficulties in securing a market for manufactured goods made the situation in Germany seem almost hopeless. In the spring of 1932, Brüning realized that generous concessions on the part of the Allies were badly needed in order to check the tide of National Socialism that was beginning to rise in a menacing manner.

The only way to banish the shadow of Hitlerism was to strengthen the supports of the Brüning Government. But France refused to see this plain fact. Indeed there is evidence to indicate that certain French statesmen conspired to destroy the Brüning Government. According to Brüning himself, "one major factor in Hitler's rise . . . was the fact that he received large sums of money from foreign countries in 1923 and later [France, Poland, and Czechoslovakia], and was well paid for sabotaging the passive resistance in the Ruhr district. . . . In later years he [Hitler] was paid to excite unrest and encourage revolution in Germany by people who imagined that this might weaken Germany per-

[31] Sherwood Eddy to Secretary Stimson, Berlin, September 1, 1931. GK 862.00/2616, MS, Department of State.

[32] Frederick M. Sackett to Secretary Stimson, Berlin, July 30, 1931. 033.1140 Stimson, Henry L./144, MS, Department of State.

[33] Memorandum of a conversation between Secretary Stimson and President von Hindenburg, Berlin, July 27, 1931. 033.1140 Stimson, Henry L./142½, MS, Department of State.

manently and make the survival of any constitutional, central government impossible."[34]

In partial support of this statement by Dr. Brüning there is the following paragraph from Louis P. Lochner's intriguing book, *What
About Germany?:*

If there was one foreign statesman who thoroughly misjudged Hitler and
his movement, it was André François-Poncet, the French Ambassador to
Berlin. From what I know of behind-the-scenes activities towards the end of
the Bruening era in 1932, I am forced to conclude that no other diplomat is
more directly responsible for the elevation to power of Adolf Hitler than
this brilliant, forever-wisecracking French politician. According to François-
Poncet, the incorruptible Chancellor, Heinrich Bruening, was too brainy and
experienced in the wily game of international politics. Hitler, on the other
hand, was a fool and a political dilettante. . . . With the Nazi leader in power,
he thought it would be much easier to effect deals which would be favorable
to France.[35]

At any rate, the French Government in the spring of 1932 greatly
helped to bring about Brüning's fall. When the Disarmament Conference met in Geneva in February 1932, Brüning presented a program
that he thought would find favor in Germany. Ramsay MacDonald and
Secretary Stimson expressed their approval of the Brüning proposal,
but Tardieu, of France, resorted to the usual French tactics of delay.
When Brüning returned to Berlin with empty hands, Hindenburg summoned him to the President's office and criticized him so sharply that
resignation was the only course left open to him.[36]

When Brüning fell the fate of the Weimar Republic was sealed. And
the fault did not lie solely on the shoulders of France. Walter Lippmann
summarized the situation in a lucid commentary:

Now that he [Brüning] has fallen, tributes will be paid . . . all over the
world, and everywhere there will be great regret that so experienced and
upright a statesman is no longer the German spokesman. He is the best liked
and most trusted man in Europe. . . . He has lacked only men of equal stature
in other countries with whom he could work. . . . Though it appears that he
has fallen because of intrigues by the Nationalists [in Germany], what undermined him and made the intrigues possible was the failure of France,
Great Britain and the United States to take a single constructive step toward

---

34 Dr. Heinrich Brüning to Rev. Edward J. Dunne, S.J., cited in E. J. Dunne, *The
German Center Party in the Empire and the Republic,* MS, dissertation for the degree
of Doctor of Philosophy, Georgetown University library.

35 (New York, 1942), pp. 42–43.

36 John W. Wheeler-Bennett, *Hindenburg: Wooden Titan* (New York, 1936),
pp. 368–85.

the restoration of international confidence and of the trade and credit which would depend upon it.[37]

f. *The Disarmament Problem Remains a Challenge*

The fall of the Brüning Government emphasized the difficulties surrounding the problem of disarmament. It was the same old story of broken pledges by the Allied governments. They had the plausible excuse that the phraseology of Article 8 of the Covenant of the League of Nations was ambiguous: "The Members of the League recognize that the maintenance of peace requires the reduction of national armaments to the lowest point consistent with national safety and the enforcement by common action of international obligations." In discussing this phraseology, Lord Davies makes the following pertinent comment: "Here is an attempt to compromise, to square the circle, to combine as a basis for reduction two incompatible principles, namely the old doctrine of absolute self-defence . . . and the alternative idea of a police function."[38]

It was inevitable that statesmen would differ with reference to the interpretation of this article. André Tardieu asserted that its language did not bind France to any plan for disarmament. Although there was a "legal obligation" to which Germany had subscribed, there was nothing to which France was bound except a "desire" to reduce her armaments.[39] Aristide Briand did not agree with Tardieu in this matter. He argued that France was bound by Article 8 to agree to some plan for disarmament. She had partly carried out this pledge by making substantial reductions in her armaments, but was unable to go any further unless other nations took adequate steps to insure French security.[40]

The American view relative to disarmament was clearly stated by Professor James T. Shotwell: "Germany had been disarmed with the understanding . . . that the other signatories would also voluntarily limit their armaments with due regard to what Germany was forced to do."[41] In 1933 the American position was given cogent expression by Norman H. Davis, who told the Conference for the Reduction and Limitation of Armaments that

it would neither have been just or wise, nor was it intended, that the Central Powers should be subject for all times to a special treatment in armaments.

[37] *New York Herald-Tribune*, June 1, 1932.
[38] *The Problem of the Twentieth Century: A Study in International Relationships* (London, 1934), p. 227.
[39] Léon Blum, *Peace and Disarmament* (London, 1932), pp. 88–89.
[40] *Ibid.*, pp. 90–91.
[41] James T. Shotwell, *On the Rim of the Abyss* (New York, 1936), p. 269.

There is and has been a corresponding duty on the part of the other Powers, parties to the peace treaties, that by successive stages they too would bring their armaments down to a level strictly determined by the needs of self-defence.[42]

In March 1933, Prime Minister Ramsay MacDonald presented his plan to the Disarmament Conference. The proposed size of European armies was bound to arouse resentment in Germany: Czechoslovakia, 100,000; France, 200,000 for home country, 200,000 for overseas; Germany, 200,000; Italy, 200,000 for home country, 50,000 for overseas; Poland, 200,000; Russia, 500,000.[43]

In order to ascertain with precision the viewpoint of Chancellor Hitler on the matter of disarmament, President Roosevelt decided to send Norman H. Davis to Berlin for a conversation that would explore the situation. On the afternoon of April 8, 1933, Davis had a long conference with Hitler who immediately referred to the provisions of the Treaty of Versailles which he regarded as "designed to keep Germany forever in a state of inferiority and to discredit them in the eyes of the world." He thought it was ridiculous for France to have any fear of Germany. France was the most heavily armed nation in the world; Germany had the pitiful force allowed her under the terms of Versailles. The only reason why "France could have any apprehension of Germany was because she knew she was doing an unjust thing in trying to force Germany forever to live under treaty conditions which no self-respecting nation could tolerate." In conclusion Hitler remarked that while he did not want "war, the Germans could not forever live under the terms of a Treaty which was iniquitous and based entirely upon false premises as to Germany's war guilt."[44]

With these ominous words ringing in his ears, Davis hurried to the Disarmament Conference at Geneva to discuss the MacDonald Plan with its proposed army limitations that Germany would never accept. On April 25 he received definite instructions from Secretary Hull:

Please be guided by the broad policy of United States in consistently pressing for immediate and practical actual disarmament. Our ultimate goal is two-fold: First, reduction of present annual costs of armament maintenance in all national budgets and, Second, arrival at a goal of domestic policing armaments in as few years as possible. . . . We regard the MacDonald Plan as a

42 John W. Wheeler-Bennett, *Documents on International Affairs, 1933* (London, 1934), p. 209.

43 *Foreign Relations, 1933,* I, 45.

44 Memorandum of a conversation between Norman H. Davis and Chancellor Hitler, Berlin, April 8, 1933. *Ibid.,* p. 107.

definite and excellent step towards the ultimate objective, but that it is a step only and must be followed by succeeding steps.[45]

In hurried attempts to expedite a solution of the disarmament problem, Prime Ministers MacDonald and Herriot paid visits to Washington, but they accomplished little. On April 26, President Roosevelt had an extended conference with Herriot during which many important topics were discussed. Herriot expressed the opinion that the most "dangerous spot in Europe" was the Polish Corridor. The President immediately observed that he could "not understand why some mechanical arrangement could not be made by which Germany and East Prussia could be more closely united either by air communication, by elevated train service or, if necessary, by underground tunnels." But Herriot quickly responded with warm praise of the existing train and highway service between the two frontiers. He then, unwittingly, put his finger upon the real difficulty in arriving at any understanding between Germany and Poland by discussing the "artistic qualities of the Poles, how difficult they were to negotiate with and how even the French . . . found them exceedingly difficult to restrain and quiet whenever they became excited." At the end of the conference Herriot "did not offer any suggestion for overcoming the Polish Corridor danger spot nor did he seem to feel that there was any solution to the problem."[46]

It was this "danger spot" that in 1939 was one of the prime causes of conflict. In 1933, Herriot realized that the "artistic qualities" of the Poles made it impossible to suggest to them a realistic solution of the Corridor question. These same qualities were even more in evidence in the summer of 1939 when the Polish Ambassador in Paris was not on speaking terms with either Bonnet or Daladier. Whom the Gods wish to destroy they first make mad!

In 1933, Hitler regarded the Polish demands for an army of 200,000 as an evident indication of madness. He remembered only too well the bloody forays carried on by Korfanty's irregulars both before and after the plebiscite in Upper Silesia. A Polish army of 200,000, together with a Russian army of 500,000, constituted a most dangerous threat to Germany's Eastern Front. The MacDonald Plan was not welcomed in Berlin. It would have to be amended in favor of a larger German army.

But any arguments for an increase in Germany's military forces met with instant opposition in Washington. On May 6, Dr. Schacht had a conference with President Roosevelt who quickly informed him that the "United States will insist that Germany remain *in statu quo* in

[45] Secretary Hull to Norman H. Davis, April 25, 1933. *Ibid.*, p. 107.
[46] Memorandum of a conversation between President Roosevelt and Prime Minister Herriot, April 26, 1933. *Ibid.*, pp. 109–11.

armament." At the same time he was informed that the American Government would "support every possible effort to have the offensive armaments of every other nation brought down to the German level." At the conclusion of the conference the President intimated "as strongly as possible" that he regarded "Germany as the only possible obstacle to a Disarmament Treaty and that he hoped Dr. Schacht would give this point of view to Hitler as quickly as possible."[47]

Hitler responded by calling a meeting of the Reichstag on May 17 to hear his address on the question of disarmament. In order to influence the remarks of the German Chancellor upon that occasion, President Roosevelt hurriedly issued (May 16) a statement to the "Chiefs of State of all countries participating in the General Disarmament or International Monetary and Economic Conferences." He stressed the hope that peace might be assured "through practical measures of disarmament and that all of us may carry to victory our common struggle against economic chaos." These practical measures included the "complete elimination of all offensive weapons." In addition to this momentous step all nations "should enter into a solemn and definite pact of non-aggression."[48]

On May 17, Hitler answered the Roosevelt proposals in a very general manner. He professed to find in the suggestions of the President some items he could support as a means of overcoming "the international crisis." Although Germany would still insist upon "actual equality of rights as regards disarmament," she would not resort to force in order to achieve her objectives."[49]

These conciliatory remarks of the Führer brought instant relief to many Americans. The *Cincinnati Enquirer* thought that Hitler had thrown upon other shoulders the responsibility for real disarmament,[50] while the *Christian Science Monitor* expressed the belief that the movement for world peace had been greatly strengthened.[51]

Encouraged by these signs of agreement, Norman H. Davis announced on May 22 that the American Government was ready to consult with other nations in the event of a threat to world peace and would take no action to hinder the efforts of other nations to restrain the activities of aggressor nations.[52] America was moving down the road to collective security.

[47] *Ibid.*, pp. 130–31. Secretary Hull to the ambassador in Great Britain (Bingham), May 8, 1933.

[48] President Roosevelt to various chiefs of state, May 16, 1933. *Ibid.*, pp. 143–45.

[49] *New York Times*, May 18, 1933.

[50] May 18, 1933.

[51] May 18, 1933.

[52] Department of State, *Press Releases*, May 22, 1933.

g. *American Press Opinion of Hitler in 1933*

While the Department of State was moving down the road of German-American relations with great caution, the American press was divided in its comments upon Hitler. After the Führer had been elevated to the office of Chancellor (January 30, 1933), some papers expressed the opinion that the conservative elements in the German Cabinet would dampen Hitler's ardor for any radical action. In this regard the following excerpt from the *New York Times* is typical:

It would be useless to try to disguise the qualms which the news from Berlin must cause to all friends of Germany. At the head of the German Republic has been placed a man who has openly scorned it and vowed that he would destroy it as soon as he could set up the personal dictatorship which was his boasted aim. A majority of the Cabinet, which he, as Chancellor, has been forced to accept would be strongly opposed to him if he sought to translate the wild words . . . of his campaign speeches into political action. . . . Best assurance of all is that President Hindenburg will retain supreme command and be prepared to unmake Hitler as quickly as he made him.[53]

The *Boston Evening Transcript* leaned toward the view that responsibility had already sobered the new Chancellor: "The more power passes into Hitler's hands, the more sobriety enters his mind."[54] The eagerness to see a silver lining to the clouds over Germany was evident in many newspaper editorials after the German election of March 5 had assured Hitler of a majority in the Reichstag. The New York *Sun* believed this majority was an indication of the yearning of the German people for a ruler with a "strong hand."[55] The Philadelphia *Public Ledger*[56] and the *Los Angeles Times*[57] sought comfort from the fact that Hitler would suppress any internal disorder, while the *Milwaukee Journal* inclined toward the view that the Hitler majority might be a good thing for "the German people."[58] The *Atlanta Constitution* was disposed to think that the Hitler victory at the polls might help stabilize conditions on the continent of Europe.[59]

But there were many papers that expressed deep misgivings. Paul Block's *Pittsburgh Post-Gazette* gloomily commented on the passing of

[53] January 31, 1933.
[54] February 2, 1933.
[55] March 6, 1933.
[56] March 7, 1933.
[57] March 7, 1933.
[58] March 7, 1933.
[59] March 7, 1933.

democracy in Germany.[60] The Nashville *Banner* rejected the view that the election of March 5 was a true reflection of German sentiment,[61] and the *Washington News* flatly declared that the election was a "fake."[62]

The hope that President Hindenburg might prove a restraining force that would curb any radical moves by Hitler was soon dissipated when the Führer pressed for the enactment of an Enabling Bill that would transfer the legislative power to the Chancellor and thus permit him to relieve "the President of unnecessary work." On the morning of March 23 (1933) this Enabling Bill came before the Reichstag, then sitting in the Kroll Opera House. While the bill was being discussed the incendiary chant of the Storm Troopers who surrounded the building came clearly to the ears of the anxious legislators: "Give us the Bill or else fire and murder." When the bill was finally passed by an overwhelming majority in the Reichstag, Hindenburg was prevailed upon to sign it and thus he gave clear evidence of his willingness to destroy the Weimar Republic he had sworn to uphold.[63]

The reaction of certain newspapers to the passage of the Enabling Bill was immediate and bitterly critical. Their viewpoint was trenchantly expressed by the Baltimore *Sun:* "There is no escape from the conclusion that the Hitler dictatorship is an evil, sadistic and brutal affair, with most of whose declared aspirations it is impossible to sympathize."[64]

h. *American Diplomats Regard Germany with Misgivings*

Some of the dispatches from American representatives in Berlin confirmed the dark suspicions of pessimistic American newspapers. The consul general in Berlin was George S. Messersmith who wrote many long accounts that were critical of the Nazi regime. On the evening of May 10 some twenty thousand books by "Jewish and Marxistic authors" were burned in the great square between the State Opera House and the buildings of the University of Berlin. This pyrotechnic display was followed by pressure that compelled large numbers of persons with Jewish blood to retire from important public and semipublic positions. Authors, artists, educators, physicians, and scientists began to flee from Germany in increasing numbers. Concentration camps for political prisoners made their appearance in certain parts of Germany, but Mr.

60 March 7, 1933.
61 March 6, 1933.
62 March 15, 1933.
63 Wheeler-Bennett, *Wooden Titan*, pp. 446–49.
64 March 25, 1933.

Messersmith hastened to add that there was "no reason to believe that the persons in these camps were . . . mistreated."[65]

These critical comments of Mr. Messersmith were supplemented by the less acidulous remarks of George A. Gordon, the American chargé d'affaires in Berlin. Mr. Gordon feared that the German Foreign Office was due for a "shakeup" which might have some unpleasant aspects. He then commented upon the *rapprochement* between Nazi Germany and Fascist Italy. Both Goebbels and Göring were working hard to make this accord firm and lasting. With reference to Russia the situation was quite different. There was a fundamental antagonism between

Hitlerism and Bolshevism. Bolshevism is essentially an *international* movement, based on a single class—the Proletariat—and on the international solidarity of the Proletariat. Its final goal is world revolution and the establishment of a communistic world-state. Hitlerism is an essentially *national* movement. . . . It believes that friendly international relations and universal peace cannot be secured by co-ordinating all nations on a proletarian basis and by wiping out their national differences.[66]

By the middle of June the dispatches from Mr. Gordon took on a distinctly somber tinge. There were indications that the Nazi leaders believed that the time had arrived "for the complete absorption of all political parties in accordance with their philosophy of a 'total state' in which there can be no room for any party other than the Nazi Party. . . . Arrests of Catholic leaders and the suppression of Catholic journals have been reported from various parts of the country."[67]

On the evening of June 22, Dr. Brüning paid a visit to the American Embassy and expressed his profound concern at the "recent events and especially by the apathetic attitude evinced by President Hindenburg and his immediate entourage." The President had "done nothing whatever" about numerous outrages and it was Brüning's fear that the lawless elements in the Nazi Party would always "prevail over Hitler in the long run."[68]

But the Führer soon showed surprising strength in his resistance to the clamor of the Nazi clique that was trying to speed the movement of the revolutionary tide that was sweeping over Germany. He rebuked Goebbels "who had recently been indulging in more than the usual in-

[65] George S. Messersmith to Secretary Hull, Berlin, May 12, 1933. 862.00/2984, *Strictly Confidential,* MS, Department of State.

[66] George A. Gordon to Secretary Hull, Berlin, May 22, 1933. 862.00/2985-86, MS, Department of State.

[67] George A. Gordon to Secretary Hull, Berlin, June 17, 1933. 862.00/3010, MS, Department of State.

[68] George A. Gordon to Secretary Hull, Berlin, June 23, 1933. 862.00/3017, MS, Department of State.

flammatory talk concerning the imminence of a Second Revolution."
Hitler was strongly opposed to such a movement which he believed
would lead to nothing but "chaotic results." It seemed apparent that he
had "decided to take the bolder and more statesmanlike line of trying
to curb the illegalities and excesses of his followers."[69]

Mr. Messersmith shared Gordon's opinion that Hitler was determined to check the excesses of his restless followers. His assurances to
German businessmen had been definite and forceful. The dissolution of
political parties might have some good results. One could only say "that
for the present time the outlook is decidedly more optimistic and encouraging than it has been at any time since March 5."[70]

i. *President Roosevelt "Torpedoes" the World Economic Conference*

After the fall of the Brüning Government the Allies realized that the
system of reparations was at an end. At the Lausanne Conference (June
16–July 8, 1932) this fact was frankly recognized. The new German
Chancellor, Franz von Papen, offered to pay a reasonable sum in order
to liquidate all reparation claims. This suggestion was adopted with certain reservations, and the amount was fixed at $714,000,000.[71]

After this important item had been settled, the German Government
next turned to the task of finding some means of meeting the payments
on the large public and private debts contracted before the banking
crisis of July 1931. The "reflationary policy" of Hitler had resulted in
an impressive increase in the production of coal and iron, and an equally
impressive decline in unemployment, but despite these favorable factors
the German export surplus was constantly dwindling, thus destroying
any possibility of making payments on foreign loans. As the economic
situation in Germany grew worse, Dr. Schacht, president of the Reichsbank, on May 29, 1933, had a conference with the representatives of
Germany's creditors in six countries.[72] After five days of discussion
these representatives issued a statement which agreed that a continued
decline in the Reichsbank's reserves might impair its functions and that
an increase in reserves was required to strengthen the bank "in its successful endeavors to maintain the stability of the German currency."

---

[69] George A. Gordon to Secretary Hull, Berlin, July 10, 1933. 862.00/3028–29,
MS, Department of State.

[70] George S. Messersmith to Secretary Hull, July 10, 1933. 862.00/3033, MS, Department of State.

[71] *The Final Act of the Lausanne Conference,* July 9, 1932 (London, 1932),
Cmd. 4126.

[72] The countries represented at this conference in Berlin were France, Great Britain,
the Netherlands, Sweden, Switzerland, and the United States.

The statement concluded with a strong expression of hope that the permanent solution of the German transfer problem would be made "one of the most important and most urgent objectives of the World Economic Conference" soon to be held in London.[73]

It was apparent to banking circles that Dr. Schacht was about to take some temporary step to protect the reserves of the Reichsbank. He could then wait and see what solution would be offered by the World Economic Conference. On June 9 he finally issued a regulation which decreed a transfer moratorium on the interest and sinking fund payments on foreign debts estimated at approximately 17,000,000,000 reichsmarks.[74] John Foster Dulles, as the representative of American bankers, sent Dr. Schacht a telegram of sharp protest.[75] Schacht, in turn, waited to see what the World Economic Conference would do with reference to the economic ills that were plaguing Europe. He did not have to spend much time in contemplation. When the conference convened on June 12, the representatives of Britain, France, and Italy were anxious as an initial step for President Roosevelt to agree upon a mild declaration of financial policy. Raymond Moley regarded the declaration as "wholly innocuous." It was merely a statement that "gold would ultimately be reestablished as a measure of international exchange value, but that each nation reserved the right to decide when it would return to a gold standard and undertake stabilization."[76]

When this declaration was placed before President Roosevelt he abruptly declined to accept it and thereby "torpedoed" the conference. All Europe "exploded with resentment and wrath" at the President's action,[77] and the delegations of experts dejectedly left London. On July 27 the conference formally adjourned without having reached any agreement on the important questions of credit policy, price levels, limitation of currency fluctuations, exchange control, tariffs, quotas, subsidies, and the resumption of foreign lending.[78] If one may borrow a familiar phrase of Woodrow Wilson used in a different connection, President Roosevelt "broke the heart of the world" and spent the rest of his life trying to put it together again.

After the failure of the World Economic Conference to find some

---

[73] New York Times, June 3, 1933.

[74] The United States was deeply concerned about this transfer moratorium because about 40 per cent of the German external debt, approximately $1,800,000,000, was owed to American creditors. For a different estimate see Cleona Lewis, America's Stake in International Investments (Washington, 1938), p. 414.

[75] New York Times, June 21, 1933.

[76] Raymond Moley, After Seven Years (New York, 1939), p. 247.

[77] Ibid., pp. 261–62.

[78] The documents dealing with the London Economic Conference are given in great detail in Foreign Relations, 1933, I, 452–762.

answer to the questions that clamored for settlement, Dr. Schacht carried on negotiations with the representatives of American bankers and finally reached a compromise whereby the Dawes loan (1924) and the Young loan (1930) would be exempted from the scope of the moratorium he had announced on June 9. Other concessions were made to American banking interests, but the situation remained distinctly unsatisfactory. The collapse at London was a serious blow to the plans of European statesmen for a satisfactory adjustment of political and economic difficulties.

j. *The Four Power Pact Proves a Failure*

The collapse of the London Economic Conference had an immediate effect upon the political situation on the Continent, because it helped to sabotage the political accord arrived at in the Four Power Pact signed at Rome on July 15, 1933. The concept of this Four Power Pact appears to have originated with Prime Minister MacDonald who talked the matter over at Geneva in March 1933. Mussolini then took up the matter and on March 18 transmitted to the British, French, and German ambassadors at Rome a tentative outline of a Four Power agreement. The draft not only provided for the collaboration of the powers in the preservation of European peace but recognized the need for a revision of the peace treaties concluded at the close of the World War. Particular reference was made to the need of some settlement of the colonial aspirations of Germany and Italy. With reference to the Polish Corridor the draft provided for the return to Germany of a strip of territory which would connect East Prussia "with the rest of the Reich." The British Government frowned upon these provisions and they were finally deleted.[79]

As the negotiations for the Four Power Pact slowly proceeded at the different European capitals, the Italian Ambassador in London (Grandi) had a conversation with Norman Davis, with reference to the problem of disarmament. He expressed the opinion that the best way to speed an accord on the matter of disarmament and other questions was to have a meeting between Daladier, Hitler, MacDonald, and Mussolini. This could be brought about only on the initiative of the United States.[80] The President failed to respond to this overture, but the negotiations proceeded so rapidly that the Four Power Agreement was initialed in Rome on June 7. Its provisions were a confirmation of the

[79] Memorandum by the chief of the Division of Western European Affairs (Moffat), March 24, 1933. *Ibid.*, pp. 396–98.

[80] *Ibid.*, pp. 409–11. Atherton to Secretary Hull, London, May 12, 1933.

Kellogg-Briand Pact. The four powers would "consult together as regards all questions which appertain to them," and would "make every effort to pursue, within the framework of the League of Nations, a policy of effective co-operation between all Powers with a view to the maintenance of peace." The high contracting parties would also "make every effort to ensure the success of the Disarmament Conference and, should questions which particularly concern them remain in suspense on the conclusion of the Conference, they reserve the right to re-examine these questions between themselves in pursuance of the present agreement." This consultative arrangement also included "all economic questions which have a common interest for Europe and particularly for its economic restoration."[81]

A week after the agreement had been initialed in Rome, Lord Tyrrell, the British Ambassador in Paris, had a conversation with Ambassador Jesse Straus. After an extended eulogy of Daladier, Tyrrell then expressed "great fear of the future." Hitler was faced with a tremendous task in Germany and would "lose out, unless he found means of carrying out his many promises which were to result from an Organized Germany. . . . Then the great danger of a communistic uprising might threaten the peace of Europe." He was distressed over the fact that a dictatorship existed in Germany because the only stable form of government was "the democratic form, and that the sort of medieval rule that Germany was now suffering from could not last. . . . He expressed the opinion that . . . both England and the United States are responsible for the rise of Hitlerism."[82]

The fears of Lord Tyrrell were felt by many other statesmen who did not have much faith in the Four Power Pact that was formally signed at Rome on July 15, 1933. In confirming the Kellogg-Briand Pact, it merely guaranteed the provisions of the Treaty of Versailles which few recognized as a perfect treaty. Mussolini had been realistic in including in his first draft provisions to deal with the Polish Corridor and the colonial aspirations of the German and Italian governments. The refusal of Britain and France to agree to this draft made the Four Power Pact a scrap of worthless paper.

k. *William E. Dodd Goes to Germany as U.S. Ambassador*

There is ample evidence in the Colonel House Papers in the Yale University library that the selection of William E. Dodd as the American

81 *Ibid.*, pp. 417–19. Agreement of understanding and co-operation.

82 Memorandum by the ambassador in France (Straus) of a conversation with the British Ambassador in France (Tyrrell), June 15, 1933. *Ibid.*, pp. 420–21.

Ambassador to Germany was made upon the strong recommendations of Colonel House and Daniel C. Roper, one-time commissioner of internal revenue.[83] Also, there is no doubt that this selection was an unfortunate one. The Colonel did not realize that Dodd knew little about American foreign policy and even less about the problems of Europe. His knowledge of the German language was so limited that his conversations in that tongue were as full of pauses as a hesitation waltz. In Berlin he was always uncomfortable. As an American liberal he had a deep-seated dislike for every aspect of the Nazi movement. If he had been as fluent as George Bancroft he would have had to watch his words so that some sharp edge of criticism did not thrust its way through the wide-spaced texture of his discourse.

It is evident that a bigger man would have done a better job. Diplomacy is a profession that requires keen eyes that read between the lines of international relations, and sensitive ears that quickly detect the undertones of intrigue. With his second-rate mind that had mastered merely the dubious fundamentals of how to get ahead in the historical profession, Dodd was really a babe-in-the-woods in the dark forests of Berlin. Colonel House had moved with safety through those same deep shadows, but the Nazi wolf was far more dangerous than the Hohenzollern eagle. In the pages of Dodd's diary one gets occasional glimpses of the torments that flitted through his mind as he endeavored to size up a situation that defied definition. He was constantly hoping to discover some common denominator of culture that would solve all difficulties without seeming to realize that he and the Nazi leaders looked at culture through very different eyes. He was a tragic misfit in Berlin in the prewar years, and his selection as ambassador was one of the first mistakes of the Roosevelt Administration.

1. *The President Tells a Spurious Story*

Inasmuch as Ambassador Dodd would have to have frequent conferences in Berlin with reference to the payment of American loans, President Roosevelt thought it expedient to invite him to the White House and regale him with an anecdote that Dodd did not suspect was spurious. He was informed that in the spring of 1933, Schacht had paid a visit to the United States to confer with American officials concerning the matter of the repayment of loans that had been extended to the German Government, German municipalities, German corporations, and

---

[83] Ambassador Dodd's *Diary, 1933–1938*, pp. 9–10. For July 4, 1933, Dodd records a conversation with Colonel House in which the aging colonel remarked: "I sent two nominations to the President, your's and Nicholas Butler's, but I felt that you ought to be given precedence."

German nationals. When Schacht called at the White House to talk with the President, he was treated with Hyde Park courtesy. After detailing with relish that example of boorishness, the President told the following story which was patently untrue:

He described the arrogant bearing of Dr. Hjalmar Schacht in May when he was threatening, as head of the German Reichsbank, to cease paying interest and principal on debts of more than one billion dollars due to American creditors next August. The President said he had told Secretary Hull to receive Schacht, but to pretend to be deeply engaged in looking for certain papers, leaving Schacht standing and unobserved for three minutes, with Hull's secretary watching the German's nervous reactions. Then Hull was to discover a note from the President which indicated serious opposition to any such defaults of German debtors. He was to turn to Schacht and hand him the document and watch the changing color of the German's face as he, Hull, greeted him. This, the President said, was to take a little of the arrogance out of the German's bearing, and he added that the effect was even more marked, as reported from Hull, than had been expected.[84]

In the *Memoirs* of Cordell Hull this story is repeated with some additions. It is easy to demonstrate its falsity.

On May 8, Dr. Schacht, head of the German Reichsbank, who was in Washington on an official visit . . . announced that his Government would cease payments abroad on Germany's external debts, totaling $5,000,000,000, of which nearly $2,000,000,000 were held by Americans. The following day I called Dr. Schacht into my office, determined to speak some bare-fisted words. I found Schacht simple and unaffected, thoroughly approachable. . . . The moment Schacht sat down alongside my desk, I went right to the point and said, with some anger: "I was never so deeply surprised as I was yesterday afternoon by your announcement. My Government is exercising every ounce of its power to bring the nation out of the depths of awful panic conditions. . . . Just as real progress is being made, you come over here and, after sitting in confidential conferences with our officials . . . suddenly let it be given out from our doorstep that Germany has suspended these payments. . . ." I felt outraged at such a bald attempt to involve this Government in so odious an act by Germany. I said: "Any person ought to realize the serious possibilities of such steps." Dr. Schacht kept protesting that he had not foreseen or grasped these reactions. "I am extremely sorry," he said. I gave Dr. Schacht a written memorandum which stated: "The President has directed me to say to you in regard to your communication as to the decision of the German Government to stop transfers on obligations externally sold or externally payable, that he is profoundly shocked."[85]

[84] *Ibid.*, p. 5.
[85] Cordell Hull, *Memoirs* (New York, 1948), I, 237–38.

As one reads the *Memoirs* of Secretary Hull, it is noticeable that he makes no reference to the "arrogant bearing" of Dr. Schacht as described by the President to Dr. Dodd. Instead, he speaks of Dr. Schacht as "simple and unaffected." There is no confirmation of the President's story of the discourteous manner in which Schacht was supposed to be treated in the office of Secretary Hull. But the *Memoirs* of the Secretary are just as fictional, in places, as the story of President Roosevelt. As a matter of fact, Secretary Hull, or his genial "ghost," Lieutenant Colonel Andrew Berding, became badly confused when writing about this "Schacht incident." First of all, Dr. Schacht did not announce on May 8 that "his Government would cease payments abroad on Germany's external debts." That announcement came a month later (June 9). As early as January 19, 1933, Herr Wambold, Minister of Economics in the Reich, announced that repayments "of the principal of foreign private debts will be impossible in 1933."[86] Dr. Schacht countered this statement by an assurance that all "foreign commercial debts will be fully paid."[87] On May 8 an announcement appeared in the American press to the effect that the German "debt service is imperiled by drop in exports."[88] A similar announcement had been previously made on January 19 and April 10. Schacht was not ready to take any definite action until he returned to Berlin and had a conference with the representatives of the principal creditor countries (May 29–June 2).

On May 9 there was no reason for Secretary Hull to call Dr. Schacht to his office and assault him with some "bare-fisted words" with reference to Germany's default on her obligations to American creditors. There had been no announcement of such a proposed default, and the highly colored stories told by President Roosevelt and Secretary Hull are mere flights of imagination.

Ambassador Dodd was not sufficiently acquainted with the President to be able to draw the line between truth and mendacity, so he duly recorded the story for posterity and thereby afforded another illustration of the moral make-up of the Chief Executive. After listening to the President's dubious discourse on Dr. Schacht, Dodd went to New York City (July 3) for a conference with a group of prominent bankers who had no glib prescription with reference to a settlement of financial difficulties with Germany. They merely expressed the hope that the American Ambassador might be able to keep the German Government from "defaulting openly." As an inducement to this end they were

[86] *New York Times*, January 19, 1933.
[87] *New York Times*, March 19, 1933.
[88] *New York Times*, May 8, 1933.

willing to reduce the rate of interest on their loans from seven to four per cent.[89]

After receiving these official and unofficial instructions with regard to proposed German defaults on American loans, Dodd then had to listen to advice on many other problems that vexed the course of German-American relations. One of the most important irritants that pointed to future trouble was the anti-Semitic campaign that had been launched by the Nazi Government. During his conversation with Dodd at the White House the President had remarked: "The German authorities are treating the Jews shamefully and the Jews in this country are greatly excited. But this is . . . not a governmental affair. We can do nothing except for American citizens who happen to be made victims. We must protect them, and whatever we can do to moderate the general persecution by unofficial and personal influence ought to be done."[90]

On the following day Dodd met Raymond Moley who apparently held "entirely different views from the President about the American attitude toward the Jews in Germany." After listening to Moley's remarks for some moments, Dodd countered with an unrelated question about the operation of the Walker tariff of 1846. Moley was thrown off mental balance by this sudden shift in subject, and when he fumbled around for an answer that was not on the tip of his tongue, Dodd decided that he was an intellectual lightweight who "could not long hold his confidential relations with Roosevelt."[91]

In the first week in July, Dodd was in New York City preparing to take the boat for Germany. He had a long conference with some outstanding Jews, including Rabbi Stephen S. Wise and Felix Warburg. They strongly urged him to press for an immediate change in the repressive policy that had been adopted by the Nazi Government towards the Jews, and Dodd assured them that he would "exert all possible personal influence against unjust treatment" of that unfortunate minority.[92]

Dodd then hurried to keep an engagement with Colonel House at Beverly Farms near Boston. With reference to the Jewish question, the Colonel remarked: "You should try to ameliorate Jewish sufferings. They are clearly wrong and terrible; but the Jews should not be allowed to dominate the economic or intellectual life in Berlin as they have done for a long time." In New York City, at the home of Charles R. Crane, Dodd listened to a new viewpoint concerning anti-Semitism in

[89] Dodd, *op. cit.*, p. 9.
[90] *Ibid.*, p. 5.
[91] *Ibid.*, pp. 6–7.
[92] *Ibid.*, p. 9.

Germany. Crane, though old and feeble, showed surprising animation against all Jews. His concluding words to Dodd were sharply sanguinary: "Let Hitler have his way."[93]

One of Dodd's last visitors before his departure for Berlin was George Sylvester Viereck. Viereck was known to Dodd as a German propagandist during the years from 1914 to 1917, and he was held at arm's length as a "curious sort of journalist with whom one would best not be too free." After leaving Viereck he was driven to the steamboat pier where insistent reporters kept clamoring for photographs. Reluctantly, Dodd posed for a picture. Perhaps the "curious" personality of Viereck pursued him, for unfortunately, "unaware of the similarity of the Hitler salute . . . we raised our hands."[94] In months to come, in Berlin, he would frequently raise his hands, not as a salute to Hitler, but by way of imprecation against a regime he quickly grew to loathe.

[93] *Ibid.,* pp. 10–11.
[94] *Ibid.,* p. 11.

II

The Far East in Ferment

a. *A Triple Offensive Is Launched against Japan*

WHILE the Roosevelt Administration was putting its diplomatic house
in order with reference to Nazi Germany, the situation in the Far East
constantly threatened to get out of hand. The heritage of the Stimson
policy was an unfortunate one. But the policy of pressure upon Japan
antedated Stimson some two decades. Dollar diplomacy under Taft
challenged Japan's position in Manchuria, and under Woodrow Wilson a three-pronged offensive was launched against Nippon. The first
phase of this offensive began when Japan presented to China in January 1915 the famous Twenty-One Demands. In connection with these
demands the American Minister at Peking, Paul Reinsch, sent to the
Department of State a series of dispatches so critical in tone that they
helped to create in American minds a fixation of Japanese wickedness
that made eventual war a probability.[1] This probability was increased
when Secretary Bryan (May 11, 1915) sent to Tokyo a nonrecognition
note that was later exhumed from the old files of State Department
correspondence by Secretary Stimson and fashioned into a hand grenade
that shattered all hope of peaceful relations between Japan and the
United States.

In 1917, when America intervened in World War I, the single-track
mind of President Wilson was directed towards Europe. Japan suddenly became our little brown brother in a crusade against the sinister
designs of the Central Powers. She was to be courted instead of criticized and her help to the Allies could be paid in terms of a new understanding of Japan's special position in North China. Britain, France,
and Russia had already in the early months of 1917 signed secret treaties with Japan which pledged their support of her claims to the retention of the German rights in Shantung and the German islands north
of the equator.[2] When America entered the war Balfour paid a visit to
Washington and informed both President Wilson and Secretary Lan-

[1] Paul W. Reinsch, *An American Diplomat in China* (New York, 1922), chap. 12;
Thomas E. La Fargue, *China and the World War* (Stanford, 1937), chap. 3.

[2] F. Seymour Cocks, *The Secret Treaties and Understandings* (London, 1918), pp.
84–88; J. V. A. MacMurray, *Treaties and Agreements with and Concerning China*
(New York, 1921), II, 1168–69.

sing of the terms of the secret treaties.[3] As Professor Griswold sagely remarked: "It is hard to escape the conclusion that those [treaties] relating to Shantung were among Balfour's revelations."[4] As a matter of fact, Lansing, in his *Diary,* frankly admits that he knew the terms of the secret treaty between Britain and Japan: "The problem of the final disposition of Germany's colonial possessions should be considered as unsettled. . . . In the case of the Pacific islands I learned last summer that Japan and Great Britain have a secret agreement by which Japan shall retain after the war the German territories north of the equator."[5]

On November 2, 1917, Lansing and Viscount Ishii signed the well-known Lansing-Ishii Agreement which specifically stated that "territorial propinquity creates special relations between countries, and consequently, the Government of the United States recognizes that Japan has special interests in China, particularly in the part to which her possessions are contiguous." With reference to this agreement, Professor Griswold makes the following comment:

Established diplomatic usage has endowed the phrase "special interests" with political as well as economic connotations. . . . The situation in world politics at the time the agreement was being negotiated was such as to suggest that Lansing realized the political character of his concession and concealed it. . . . The fact is, Lansing knew of the existence of the secret treaties, with which his phrase was pale in comparison and which rendered fantastic the expectations implicit in the rest of the agreement. . . . Given Lansing's knowledge of the Allied commitments to Japan, even the phrase "special interests" implied at least tentative recognition of them.[6]

When one keeps these facts in mind, it is evident that the policy of the President at Paris was a most dubious one. During the sessions of the Peace Conference he led a determined assault upon the Japanese position in Shantung in the face of his acquiescence in the secret treaty that bound Britain to support the Japanese claims to economic domination of that province. The Lansing-Ishii Agreement had formally recorded this acquiescence. Wilson's action, therefore, and his subsequent denial of any knowledge of the secret treaties must have con-

[3] Blanche E. Dugdale, *Arthur James Balfour* (New York, 1936), II, 145–46. See also, Balfour to President Wilson, January 31, 1918, File 2, Box 135. Wilson Papers, Library of Congress; and Secretary Lansing to President Wilson, November 18, 1918, File 2, Box 156. *Ibid.*

[4] A. Whitney Griswold, *The Far Eastern Policy of the United States* (New York, 1938), p. 219.

[5] Lansing *Diary,* January 10, 1918. Lansing Papers, Library of Congress.

[6] Griswold, *op. cit.,* pp. 218–19.

vinced Japanese statesmen that he was implementing the maxims of Machiavelli.

Another aspect of the President's offensive against Japan had to do with Allied intervention in Siberia in 1918. During the spring of that year the Allied governments kept urging the United States to consent to a proposal to have Japan send an expeditionary force into Siberia as "a mandatory of the Powers." On March 19, Lansing opposed this intervention in a strong memorandum: "In view of the almost certain hostility of the Russian people to Japanese occupation of Siberia and the pro-German sentiment which would result . . . it would seem unwise and inexpedient to support the request for Japanese intervention."[7] On April 10, Lansing states in another memorandum that "I am entirely responsible for the present policy which is opposed to intervention by the Japanese in a mandatory capacity."[8] Two months later Lansing continues to remark: "It would be a grave error for Japan to send an expedition alone. I feel that it ought not to be permitted if it can be prevented."[9]

It was soon apparent, however, that it would be necessary to send some type of expeditionary force into Siberia to co-operate with Czechoslovak troops who were making their way to Vladivostok. Inasmuch as Japan was close to that port it was obvious that she should be asked to contribute a considerable number of troops. On July 6 an important conference was held at the White House with the President, the Secretary of State, the Secretary of War, the Secretary of the Navy, General March, and Admiral Benson in attendance. After a detailed discussion of the situation in the Far East it was decided that a "military force" should be assembled at Vladivostok composed of "approximately 7,000 Americans and 7,000 Japanese to guard the line of communication of the Czecho-Slovaks proceeding toward Irkutsk."[10]

On the same day Colonel House had a conversation with Viscount Ishii with regard to the Siberian situation. At the close of this conference House wrote a letter to President Wilson in which he made the following comment: "It has been my opinion for a long time that unless Japan was treated with more consideration regarding the right of her citizens to expand in nearby Asiatic undeveloped countries, she would have to be reckoned with—and rightly so."[11]

As a result of numerous conferences dealing with the Far East it was

[7] Lansing, op. cit. Memorandum by Secretary Lansing, March 18, 1918.
[8] Ibid., April 10, 1918.
[9] Ibid., June 12, 1918.
[10] Lansing, op. cit. Memorandum of a conference at the White House, July 6, 1918.
[11] Colonel House to President Wilson, July 6, 1918. House Papers, Yale University Library.

finally decided to send General William S. Graves with a small army (9,014 officers and men) to Siberia to co-operate with an Allied expeditionary force. The duties assigned to this force were to assist the Czechs, help steady genuine Russian efforts at self-government and self-defense, and to guard Allied military stores. The force under Graves stayed in Siberia from August 1918 until April 1920. Its sole achievement was to save the maritime provinces of Siberia for the ruthless rule of Red Russia.[12]

The third thrust of the Wilson offensive against Japan took the form of financial pressure. During the Taft Administration certain American banks were high-pressured into participating in the Chinese Hukuang Railways loan. This action meant American membership in a four-power banking consortium. The status of this participation was carefully defined in the agreements of November 10, 1910, and May 20, 1911.[13] In 1912 (June 18–20) Japan and Russia joined this banking group making it a six-power consortium. But American bankers were "disgruntled" that they were "not yet in a position to make any profit out of their endeavors." They made it clear to the Wilson Administration in the early days of March 1913 that they would not be satisfied with the "mere approval" of the Department of State. As a necessary condition "to their staying in the business with China they must be asked to do so by the American Government."[14] Instead of extending this invitation, President Wilson favored American abstention from the consortium on the ground that concerted banking pressure "might conceivably go to the length in some unhappy contingency of forcible interference in the financial, and even the political affairs of the great oriental State [China]."[15]

The outbreak of the World War eliminated Germany and Russia from the consortium, and Britain and France were so heavily burdened by the costs of war that they were unable to extend any loans to China. Japan quickly moved into this financial vacuum and loaned to China more than 320,000,000 yen.[16] The political implications of these loans were so evident that the British and French governments intimated to the Department of State that it would be advisable for the

---

[12] General William S. Graves, *America's Siberian Adventure* (New York, 1931); Pauline Tompkins, *American-Russian Relations in the Far East* (New York, 1949), pp. 47–141; John A. White, *The Siberian Intervention* (Princeton, 1950), pp. 270–74.

[13] Frederick V. Field, *American Participation in the China Consortiums* (Chicago, 1931), pp. 14–66; John G. Reid, *The Manchu Abdication and the Powers, 1908–1912* (Berkeley, 1935), pp. 36–241, 258–99.

[14] MacMurray, *op. cit.*, p. 1024; Griswold, *op. cit.*, pp. 172–73.

[15] *Foreign Relations, 1913*, pp. 170–71.

[16] *Ibid., 1918*, pp. 167–68.

United States to re-enter the consortium.[17] Secretary Lansing countered with an important suggestion. In a letter to President Wilson he outlined the financial straits of China and then remarked that, "in view of the present circumstances and of the situation in China," it was probably wise to organize a new four-power banking consortium.[18] On the following day the President approved this suggestion with the proviso that care should be taken to prevent the possibility of any "unconscionable arrangements" like some of the ones that had been contemplated under the terms of the former consortium.[19]

On June 22, Secretary Lansing invited the representatives of important banking groups to discuss with him the formation of a new consortium. They promptly accepted this invitation and on October 8 the Department of State formally outlined to the governments of Britain, France, and Japan a detailed proposal for a new consortium.[20] On March 17, 1919,[21] the British Government accepted the American proposal, but France and Japan delayed favorable action. The Japanese press was opposed to the new consortium on the ground that it would mean the loss by Japan of the "fruits she had amassed" in the past few years.[22] The Japanese Government entertained similar fears and Mr. Odagiri, the Japanese financial representative at Paris, was instructed to inform Mr. Thomas W. Lamont, chief American financial representative, that "all rights and options held by Japan in the regions of Manchuria and Mongolia, where Japan has special interests, should be excluded from the arrangement."[23]

Lamont immediately informed Odagiri that any attempt to exclude Manchuria and Mongolia from the scope of the new consortium would be "inadmissible."[24] He also wrote to J. P. Morgan and Company and expressed the opinion that there was no hope that Japan would recede from her position unless "the United States and Great Britain will

[17] *Ibid., 1917,* pp. 144–45; 154–55. British Embassy to Secretary Lansing, October 3, 1917; Ambassador Jusserand to Secretary Lansing, November 19, 1917.

[18] Secretary Lansing to President Wilson, June 20, 1918. 893.51/2512, MS, Department of State.

[19] President Wilson to Secretary Lansing, June 21, 1918. 893.51/2513, MS, Department of State.

[20] Secretary Lansing to Ambassador Jusserand, October 8, 1918. 893.51/2042e, MS, Department of State.

[21] British Foreign Office to the American Embassy, London, March 17, 1919. *The Consortium, The Official Text of the Four-Power Agreement for a Loan to China and Relevant Documents* (Washington, 1921), No. 5, p. 15.

[22] Ambassador Morris to Secretary Lansing, Tokyo, May 28, 1919. 893.51/2241, MS, Department of State.

[23] J. W. Davis to Acting Secretary Polk, London, June 18, 1919. 893.51/2268, MS, Department of State.

[24] J. P. Morgan and Company to Dept. of State, June 25, 1919. 893.51/2282, MS, Department of State.

assume a very rigorous position in the matter."[25] From Peking the American Minister warned that the Japanese were playing their "usual game" of deceit. Probably "you are being assured that they are favorable to the consortium and will join it in due course. Meanwhile influence is exerted to stir up the Chinese against it."[26]

In order to exert pressure upon the Japanese Government the Department of State toyed with the idea of a three-power consortium, but Britain and France were opposed to such a move.[27] Undue pressure upon Japan might propel her into an alliance with Germany.[28]

In an endeavor to explain their desire to exclude Manchuria and Mongolia from the scope of this proposed consortium, the Japanese Government pointed out that those regions were of vital interest from the viewpoint of national defense. Recent developments in Russia were a matter of "grave concern." The situation in Siberia might take a sudden turn that would threaten "the safety of Japan," and ultimately all eastern Asia might become the victim of the "sinister activities of extremist forces."[29]

Secretary Lansing could understand this Japanese fear of the onward tide of bolshevism. With reference to Japan's desire to station adequate forces in Siberia for the purpose of checking that tide he made the following comment in his diary:

My belief is that they [the Japanese] will send reinforcements to Siberia and attempt to strengthen Seminoff's force [of White Russians]. I cannot see how the Japanese Government can adopt any other policy in view of the very real peril to Japan if the Bolsheviks should gain a foothold in Manchuria and co-operate with the Korean revolutionists. Certainly in the circumstances we ought not to raise any objection to Japan sending a sufficient force to check the Bolshevik advance, for the spread of Bolshevism in the Far East would be a dreadful menace to civilization.[30]

During the very months while the consortium negotiations were going on, Lansing made another illuminating entry in his diary:

I have little patience with these people who are forever on the verge of hysterics about the deep and wicked schemes of Japan. They imagine some

25 T. W. Lamont to J. P. Morgan and Company. 893.51/2268, MS, Department of State.

26 Reinsch to Secretary Lansing, Peking, June 26, 1919. 893.51/2284, MS, Department of State.

27 Ambassador Wallace to Breckinridge Long, Paris, July 13, 1919. 893.51/2308, MS, Department of State.

28 Ambassador Wallace to Secretary Lansing, Paris, September 16, 1919. 893.51/2425, MS, Department of State.

29 Japanese Embassy to the Department of State, March 2, 1920. 893.51/2695. MS, Department of State.

30 Lansing, *op. cit.*, November 30, 1918.

of the most preposterous things and report them as facts. I would be inclined to think that some of these enemies of Japan were mentally unbalanced but for their sanity on all other subjects. Unfortunately, they are listened to by many Americans whose reason ought to warn them against believing such tales without better evidence.[31]

Ambassador Morris, in Tokyo, joined with Secretary Lansing in lending a sympathetic ear to Japanese representations concerning their need to build strong bastions of defense in North China. He believed that the "strong, fundamental, tenacious purpose" of the Japanese Government was to assure protection of their lines of communication with sources of raw materials and foodstuffs. America should give "consideration" to the Japanese viewpoint: "Unless we do so the likelihood of solving the existing problems is scant."[32]

Financiers talk more abruptly than diplomats. Mr. Lamont thought that it would be

poor policy to give the Japanese Government any further leeway in this matter. In my judgment they ought to be down on their knees in gratitude to the American, British and French groups for inviting the Japanese group to become a partner and for being so patient in the matter. My associates and I are agreed that the best thing is to bring them up with a round turn and if they do not like it, let them go their way.[33]

The Department of State swung round to the viewpoint of Mr. Lamont and the British Foreign Office did the same. In the face of this pressure the Japanese Government made some concessions and the new consortium agreement was finally signed on October 15, 1920.[34] The number of exceptions that Japan insisted upon were significant and this fact made the Chinese Government lukewarm in its attitude towards the consortium. In January 1921 the Chinese Foreign Office was notified of the new consortium agreement but no answer to this notification was ever sent from Peiping. In his *Preliminary Report on the New Consortium for China,* Mr. Lamont spoke in his usual blunt fashion:

[31] *Ibid.,* July 31, 1919.

[32] Ambassador Morris to Acting Secretary Polk, March 11, 1920. 893.51/2707, MS, Department of State.

[33] Ambassador Morris to Secretary Colby, Tokyo, April 8, 1920, with inclosures. 893.51/2765, MS, Department of State.

[34] In a letter to Nakaji Kajiwara, president of the Yokohama Specie Bank, May 11, 1920, Mr. Lamont listed the terms agreed upon: "(1) that the South Manchuria Railway and its present branches, together with mines which are subsidiary to the railway, do not come within the scope of the Consortium; (2) that the projected Taonanfu-Jehol Railway and the projected railway connecting a point on the Taonanfu-Jehol Railway with a seaport are to be included within the terms of the Consortium."

If . . . the leading Powers, under whose approval the New Consortium has been organized, should make to the present Peking Government, to the Southern Government and to all factions in China including the Tuchuns, strong diplomatic representations stating that all this nonsense of an *opera bouffe* warfare must be dropped and the Government must get down to business, I am inclined to believe that the result would be surprising in its effectiveness.[35]

But the four powers represented in the new consortium were not inclined to accept the forthright advice of Mr. Lamont. They were content to remain on the sidelines while rival factions in China feverishly undermined the national structure. If Mr. Lamont's bold words had been implemented by some form of effective intervention there may have been some chance for Chinese salvation, but the consortium Powers merely waited for opportunities that never came. Shunned by the rapidly changing governments in China, the consortium accomplished nothing. Nationalist China rejected with hot contempt any thought of surrendering the slightest portion of her sovereignty to international bankers. Moreover, a powerful communist leaven was busily working in China, and the most powerful leader in turbulent Canton was Sun Yat-sen who had a strong leftist inclination. The Kremlin lost no time in exploiting this inclination.

b. *Sun Yat-sen Gives the Chinese Revolution a Red Tinge*

When the Washington Conference (1921–22) refused to accept the program presented by the Chinese delegation, a feeling of deep resentment became manifest in many parts of China. The political division between the north and the south did not mean that Canton and Peking had different viewpoints relative to the demands that should be pressed upon the powers. There was a common denominator of hostility towards America and Europe that could be used by skillful statesmen to solve the problem of Chinese disunity. Moscow quickly perceived this fact and sent able agents to exploit the situation for Russian benefit. In August 1922, Adolf Joffe was dispatched to China with instructions to cultivate intimate relations with the intellectuals and to thunder against the "capitalistic Powers" and the "imperialistic nations." He pledged Russian assistance whenever China thought that the moment had arrived to get rid of "foreign imperialism."[36] Joffe met Sun Yat-sen in Shanghai in January 1923 and soon had the credulous Chinaman

[35] Pp. 14–15.
[36] Lyon Sharman, *Sun Yat-sen: His Life and its Meaning* (New York, 1934), p. 247; M. T. Z. Tyau, *China Awakened* (New York, 1922), chap. 9.

in his control.[37] It was a part of the Soviet technique to blame China's woes upon the wickedness of Western imperialism. Sun Yat-sen quickly learned this lesson and on July 22, 1923, during an interview with Fletcher S. Brockman, he vehemently denounced the ways of the West.[38]

Joffe's propaganda was seconded by another astute communist agent, Mikhail Borodin, who arrived in Canton in October 1923. His keen intellect compensated for his unprepossessing personal appearance, and his career as a communist agitator in Scotland and as a teacher in a commercial college in Chicago had given him an insight into Western habitudes of thought. In China he was intent upon increasing the authority of Sun Yat-sen by converting the unwieldy Kuomintang into an effective and centralized political machine. Party membership would be a restricted privilege and party discipline would be rigidly enforced. The real reins of authority would be in the hands of the Central Executive Committee which would organize and control the national government.

The creed of Sun Yat-sen and his circle of followers was given inflammatory expression in the "Declaration of the First National Congress" issued in January 1924. It read like a real Muscovite memorandum. Armed plundering and shameless exploitation by foreign imperialistic nations had reduced China to a semicolonial status. The main instruments of subjection had been the unequal treaties, foreign control of the customs, the practice of extraterritoriality, and the division of China into spheres of influence. All these special privileges would have to be abandoned and the unequal treaties abrogated.[39]

With the aid of Russian rubles and Russian military instructors Sun Yat-sen established the Whampoa Military Academy for the training of officers to lead his projected army. As a first step in this direction he created "Labor bands" that crushed in a ruthless manner the merchant volunteer organizations in Canton. From Russia he learned that proletarian reforms move faster when they ride on the wings of bullets. His debt to his Soviet masters he freely acknowledged in the fulsome phraseology of ardent converts to communism: "Russia believes in benevolence and righteousness, not in force and utilitarianism. She is

[37] Secretary Lansing had little regard for Sun Yat-sen. In a letter to President Wilson, November 25, 1918, he remarked: "I would not go further than this in regard to this man [Sun Yat-sen] as there are some very ugly stories about him in regard to his acceptance of bribes and his readiness to serve the highest bidder. I believe that the evidence on this subject . . . is of a very conclusive sort." Wilson *op. cit.*, File 2, Box 157.

[38] *New York Times*, July 22–23, 1923.

[39] T. C. Woo, *The Kuomintang and the Future of the Chinese Revolution* (London, 1928), *Appendix* C.

an exponent of justice and does not believe in the principle that a minority should oppress a majority."[40]

This flamboyant expression of faith in Moscow did not prevent Soviet agents from having relations with Peking. Their activities in the North led to the treaty of May 31, 1924, in which Russia renounced the special rights and privileges enjoyed in China by the Czarist Government, including Russia's share of the Boxer indemnity and the right of extraterritoriality.[41]

But this treaty of May 1924 with Peking was merely an empty gesture. While representatives of Moscow were negotiating a treaty with Peking, other agents were grooming Sun Yat-sen for an invasion of the North. Borodin was feverishly pushing plans for a unification of China through the armed forces of the Kuomintang. Red Russia and Red China would soon be able to face the Western powers and compel compliance with their demands. This close association between Borodin and Kuomintang leaders was clearly indicated in Sun Yat-sen's "Message to Soviet Russia," written shortly before Sun's death: "I leave behind me a Party which, as I always hoped, will be bound up with you [Soviet Russia] in the historic work of the final liberations of China and other exploited countries from the yoke of imperialism. . . . Therefore I charge the Kuomintang to continue the work of the revolutionary nationalist movement so that China . . . shall become free. With this object I have instructed the Party to be in constant contact with you."[42]

After the death of Sun Yat-sen on March 12, 1925, the influence of Borodin increased to a point where he largely directed the course of the revolutionary movement in South China. In September 1925 he inspired a coup which placed Chiang Kai-shek in command of the Kuomintang military forces. In 1923, Chiang had been sent to Moscow to study bolshevist ideology and revolutionary techniques. He had returned to China as a protégé of Sun Yat-sen and later was a close associate of Borodin. This meant that in 1925 he was both antiforeign and anti-Christian. During 1926–27 as the Kuomintang armed forces moved northward, this anti-Christian inclination became more manifest in Nationalist attacks upon Christian institutions and converts.

40 Harley F. MacNair, *China in Revolution* (Chicago, 1931), p. 77.

41 Harriet L. Moore, *Soviet Far Eastern Policy, 1931–1945* (Princeton, 1945), pp. 156–64.

42 Sharman, *op. cit.*, pp. 308–9. The close connection between Sun Yat-sen and the Communists was indicated in a dispatch from Consul John K. Davis, United States consul at Nanking to Secretary Kellogg, July 6, 1925: "There is little doubt that but for Sun's illness and death he and Feng Yu-hsiang would have shortly sprung a coup in the capital with Soviet assistance, and once in power instead of asking for treaty revision would have simply announced that all of the so-called 'unequal treaties' had been abolished." 893.00/6465, MS, Department of State.

Missionaries were denounced as "imperialists" while their converts were cursed as the "running dogs of the imperialists."[43] This language of vituperation was the specialty of Eugene Ch'en, the Soviet-Kuomintang Minister of Foreign Affairs, whose active tongue never tired of flaying foreigners.

The tinder of resentment at foreign privileges in China was ignited into flames by the communist-incited Shanghai Incident, May 30, 1925. This was precipitated by student agitators who entered the International Settlement to file a protest against the alleged harsh treatment of Chinese employees in Japanese mills. When the mob got out of hand it was fired upon by Sikh and Chinese constables under the orders of the police inspector at the Louza Station. The small number of casualties indicated the restraint of the police, but communist elements magnified the incident into major proportions.

The background of the incident was sketched by the American consul at Nanking in a dispatch to Secretary Kellogg:

A few weeks prior to the incident of May 30th an American college professor, who had just completed a tour in Russia, delivered a series of lectures in Nanking upon Bolshevism in which he pictured Communism in the most roseate hues and virtually stated that while the system has as yet not been perfected, it gives evidence of being the most ideal from an economic and social standpoint that has yet been evolved by the human race. . . . As he was introduced under American missionary auspices and gave many lectures to, and had conferences with, numerous Chinese, his pronouncements had a very unfortunate effect.

In his final pronouncement on the causes of the May 30th incident, Consul Davis remarks: "The present movement is believed to have been directly and deliberately caused by Soviet Russia fanning into flame the smoldering embers of antiforeign feeling in China, which, but for their nefarious activity, would in all probability have gradually tended to become more and more quiescent."[44]

In London the financial circles were alarmed at this outbreak of violence and Sir Charles Addis, who was the head of the British group of the Chinese consortium, thought that "immediate concerted action by the Powers" was "imperative."[45] Mr. Lamont was not so positive in writing a prescription for the occasion. He assured the representative of the Morgan interests in London that he had been maintaining "fairly

[43] McNair, *op. cit.,* pp. 100–107.

[44] Consul John K. Davis to Secretary Kellogg, Nanking, July 6, 1925. 893.00/ 6465, MS, Department of State.

[45] E. C. Grenfell to T. W. Lamont, London, June 25, 1925. 893.00/6364, MS, Department of State.

close contact with Washington" but he had made no "specific suggestions, for while we agree that the situation is grave, we do not feel
competent to indicate a way out."[46]

c. *Senator Borah Attacks Foreign Imperialism in China*

Close students of Far Eastern affairs were just as hesitant as Mr. Lamont
in writing and recommending broad prescriptions that would fit every
contingency in China. Thomas F. Millard, who had served for a while
as an adviser to the Chinese Foreign Office, was fearful that the Chinese
radicals were pushing things too fast. In a letter to W. W. Yen he outlined his viewpoint:

I arrived in China in December and at once began to study the situation. I
had hoped before leaving America that the reorganization at Peking which
followed the coup d'état of last autumn would provide a chance for something constructive to be done; but after I was out here a while I perceived
that was not the case. . . . Now it appears that political tendencies in China are
toward something like an estrangement with America, whereby all that was
accomplished at Washington will be lost, and perhaps the American Government will be forced by circumstances to alter its China policy in some particulars. . . . I am somewhat puzzled as to what China's intellectual men are
thinking of—where do you think you are going? . . . I find that many Chinese
intelligentsia seem to have gone over to the idea of abrogating the special
position (extraterritorial) treaties by ultimatum, hoping to "get away" with
it as Turkey did. . . . I ask you men who ought to be able to see a little ahead
to ponder the situation. If you repudiate of course you need not be concerned
about your credit, for that will absolutely vanish with such action. But if you
intend to try to stay inside the ring of responsible governments you require
considerable financial help from abroad. Where can that be obtained now?
Only in one place—America.[47]

Mr. Millard then wrote to Senator Borah and advised him against
supporting the idea of abolishing at once extraterritorial rights in
China. He felt that China was

now unprepared for this change, and it is almost certain that a sudden transition will add to the existing confusion. . . . It is doubtful now if the radical
elements here will be willing to stop short of complete and immediate abrogation: they are smart enough to know that just now they have the Powers
by the short hair. . . . The present diplomatic body at Peking is almost pitiable
in its bewilderment and fatuity.[48]

[46] T. W. Lamont to E. C. Grenfell, June 26, 1925. 893.00/6364, MS, Department
of State.

[47] Thomas F. Millard to W. W. Yen, Shanghai, June 11, 1925. Borah MS, Library
of Congress.

[48] Thomas F. Millard to Senator Borah, Shanghai, June 18, 1925. *Ibid.*

Borah wrote back that he was merely in favor of "relinquishing extraterritorial rights in China as soon as practicable. . . . I realized, and realize now, that this cannot be accomplished outright and over night."[49] But Borah was fundamentally opposed to foreign imperialism in China and he embraced every opportunity to denounce it. When the Hankow Chamber of Commerce cabled to the Department of State that the Moscow Third International was "admittedly concentrating in the East with a view to creating chaos," he vehemently expressed the opinion that the trouble in China stemmed from Western imperialism: "The American Chamber of Commerce in China is a part of the imperialistic combine which would oppress and exploit the Chinese people."[50]

On August 21, Secretary Kellogg wrote to Senator Borah and reviewed the background of the May 30th incident in a competent and comprehensive manner. In conclusion he observed: "The shooting was, of course, a very unfortunate affair. It is impossible for me to say at this distance exactly where the responsibility lies. It was not, of course, entirely on the police authorities as, undoubtedly, the mob was bent on mischief."[51] Borah sharply dissented from this view: "From the facts which have been presented to me, I feel the shooting cannot in any sense be justified. It seems to me that this whole affair was treated at first with regret and disregard, and finally with brutality."[52]

While Senator Borah kept closing his eyes to the activities of Soviet agents and continued to belabor the wicked nations of the West for the sins of imperialism, the Shanghai Municipal Council issued a manifesto which stated that the riot of May 30 had been inspired by students and other "disaffected persons" who had made inflammatory speeches. At the trial held in Shanghai the prosecution charged that the students who had started "all this trouble all came from a Bolshevik University —the Shanghai University of Seymour Road."[53] Ferdinand L. Mayer, the chargé at the American Legation in Peking, also emphasized the dangers of Soviet intrigues. He was confident that the situation in China was being "exploited in every manner possible" by "the Soviets."[54] On one point all American observers were in agreement—the antiforeign

[49] Senator Borah to Thomas F. Millard, Boise, Idaho, July 20, 1925. *Ibid.*

[50] *New York Times,* June 16, 1925.

[51] Secretary Kellogg to Senator Borah, August 21, 1925, *Strictly Confidential.* Borah, *op. cit.*

[52] Senator Borah to Secretary Kellogg, Boise, Idaho, August 26, 1925. *Ibid.* In a letter to Bishop William F. McDowell, August 18, 1925, Borah makes the following critical comment: "I think the course of conduct of the Western nations in China [is] indefensible." *Ibid.*

[53] Dorothy Borg, *American Policy and the Chinese Revolution. 1925–1928* (New York, 1947), pp. 24–25.

[54] Ferdinand L. Mayer to Secretary Kellogg, June 19, 1925. *Foreign Relations, 1925,* I, 667.

movement was rapidly spreading in China and it carried implications of grave danger to the vested interests of the Western powers.

d. *Causes of the Antiforeign Movement in China*

Minister MacMurray, after a survey of the situation in China, came to the conclusion that much of the unrest in China was produced by an "inferiority complex" that afflicted large numbers of the intellectuals. They are aware of the "failure they are making in the organization of their national life and morbidly conscious of the poor showing that they have made in the eyes of foreign nations."[55]

Senator Borah thought that this "inferiority complex" came from the fact that the Western powers had imposed "unequal treaties" upon China with special reference to extraterritoriality and tariff autonomy. This situation should be rapidly remedied by sweeping concessions to China. In a letter to the editor of the Baltimore *Sun,* August 11, 1925, he outlined his position with vigor:

Extraterritoriality is contrary to the spirit of the age and in conflict with the principles of sovereignty. . . . What is proposed and what is to be seriously urged is that the foreign powers shall in good faith . . . aid in bringing about a condition wherein extraterritoriality may be abolished. These steps should be taken at once and unmistakably. . . .

Foreign interests in China are exploiting human life . . . beyond the power of human language to portray. There is no place where the blood of helpless children is coined into dollars and cents as in China.[56]

In a letter to the Foreign Minister of the Nationalist Government, Borah expressed the opinion that the "situation in China is not due to temporary causes but to the nationalistic feeling upon the part of China that she is entitled to equal treatment among the nations."[57] In order to pave the way for the best expression of this nationalistic feeling, Senator Borah thought that the American Government should adopt an independent policy and no longer be a member of the concert of powers:

In my opinion the objects and aims and standards of the United States on the one hand and Great Britain and Japan upon the other are so different and diverse that it is utterly impossible to move in accord with them and at the same time protect our own interests and do justice to China. On the other

---

[55] Minister MacMurray to Secretary Kellogg, July 28, 1925. *Ibid.,* pp. 799–802.

[56] Borah, *op. cit.*

[57] Senator Borah to the Minister of Foreign Affairs, Canton Government, September 26, 1925. *Ibid.*

hand, by a bold, independent course, based upon sound principles of justice and fair dealing, the United States can mold public opinion to such an extent as to force a reasonable policy in the Far East.[58]

It is difficult to estimate the influence of Borah upon the Chinese intellectuals who were making a strong fight for tariff autonomy and the abolition of extraterritoriality. There is no doubt that many of them read his statements with deep interest and took courage from his sharp denunciation of the "unequal treaties." Chungting T. Wang, of the Directorate-General of Sino-Russian Negotiations, wrote to assure Borah that the "voice of a great statesman of a great country, advocating international justice and humane principles cannot but be a tremendous encouragement in our fight to recover our lost rights."[59] In a similar vein Harry Hussey, prominent architect in Peking, sent a very appreciative letter to Borah: "Your remarks did more than anything else to restrain the Chinese when things looked very dangerous here in China. Until you spoke the Chinese were desperate. . . . Your speech showed them that they had a friend in America and this fact was so used by the conservative element that they were able to control the others."[60]

e. The Kuomintang Demands Tariff Autonomy

The Shanghai Incident was merely the first of a series of antiforeign riots that broke out in China in the summer of 1925. Along with this violence the Kuomintang leaders organized a boycott against British goods which lasted from June 1925 to October 1926.[61] The Governor of Hong Kong believed that a great deal of the unrest directed against the British was caused by "Bolshevik intrigue."[62] It was certainly true that the left-wing element of the Kuomintang was especially active in the South at this time, and the conservatives in the party began to grow apprehensive with regard to the future in China.

In order to provide a popular basis for their drive to secure control over China, the Kuomintang leaders adopted a program whose chief items were a demand for tariff autonomy and the abolition of extraterritoriality. In 1928 the American Government concluded an agreement with China whereby tariff autonomy would go into operation on January 1, 1929. With reference to the abolition of extraterritoriality

[58] Senator Borah to Thomas F. Millard, September 15, 1925. Ibid.

[59] Ibid. Chungting T. Wang to Senator Borah, Peking, September 28, 1925.

[60] Harry Hussey to Senator Borah, Peking, June 23, 1925. Ibid.

[61] C. F. Remer and William B. Palmer, A Study of Chinese Boycotts with Special Reference to their Economic Effectiveness (Baltimore, 1933), pp. 95–102.

[62] China Year Book, 1926–27, p. 982.

the record was one of failure and this fact added volume and violence to Chinese denunciations of Western imperialism.

f. *American Missionaries Help to Mold United States Policy*

In 1925 there were nearly five thousand American Protestant missionaries living in China. The annual expenditures of American mission societies in that country was approximately $10,000,000 and the lowest estimate of mission property holdings was $43,000,000.[63] It was evident that this important group of very vocal Americans had a definite influence upon the policy of the Department of State. During the Coolidge Administration, missionary opinion was strongly pro-Chinese, and numerous memorials were sent to Washington for the purpose of molding official viewpoints. The religious press was also active in this pro-Chinese campaign.

On August 20, 1925, the *Christian Century* deprecated the alleged fact that the Far Eastern policy of the Department of State was largely controlled by a "little coterie of professional experts." It was hoped that the Coolidge Administration would finally reject the counsel of this small band of biased experts and adopt the pro-Chinese policy of Senator Borah.[64] In September the same magazine came out strongly in favor of the abolition of extraterritoriality which was the "fruit of western imperialism" and which could be maintained only by armed force.[65] Rev. J. L. Stuart, president of Yenching University, gave this viewpoint immediate support.[66] Soon the Federal Council of the Churches of Christ in America and most of the large mission boards were ardently advocating action to end the ancient practice of extraterritoriality.[67]

This pro-Chinese missionary opinion evoked sharp criticism in some quarters. In June 1926, George Bronson Rea, the editor of the *Far Eastern Review*, expressed the opinion that missionary influence in America was so strong that the "selection of our Minister to Peking is determined by qualifications that meet the endorsement of missionary Boards." He was certain that these boards exerted at Washington an "influence that no President, statesman, or politician would dare to antagonize. The successful development of their plans can be attained

[63] *China Year Book, 1928*, p. 4; Julean Arnold, "The Missionaries' Opportunity in China," *Chinese Recorder*, October 1925, p. 639; C. F. Remer, *Foreign Investments in China* (New York, 1933), p. 308.

[64] Pp. 1041–43.

[65] *Ibid.*, September 10, 1925, p. 114.

[66] *American Relations with China: A Report of the Conference Held at the Johns Hopkins University, September 17–20, 1925* (Baltimore, 1925), p. 39.

[67] Borg, *op. cit.*, pp. 76–82.

only by maintaining a sympathetic atmosphere in America towards China, for should popular opinion . . . become hostile, it would automatically shut off the stream of voluntary contributions upon whose continuous and increasing flow depends the very existence of the movement." This missionary influence had not only been a decided detriment to American trade but it was really responsible for the antiforeign unrest that was spreading throughout China: "Every close student of Chinese affairs traces the present outburst of anti-foreign sentiment to the emotional hysteria set in movement by overzealous missionary and educational uplifters."[68]

Rodney Gilbert, a well-known American newspaperman in China, shared Mr. Rea's viewpoint. A change in the missionary attitude from one of friendship to one of a more critical character would quickly mean that the "tide of unspeakable drool which has been going home for a year about China's rights and aspirations" would be "abruptly stemmed in both America and England."[69]

g. *Evolution of U.S. Policy towards Nationalist China*

As political, economic, and social conditions in China grew progressively worse after 1925, it became more difficult for pro-Chinese missionary opinion to have an important influence upon the policy of the Department of State. The political factor was particularly disturbing in the Chinese equation. When the Special Tariff Conference met in Peking on October 25, 1925, the regime of President Tuan Ch'i-jui was distinctly shaky. The Peking Government was largely controlled by Chang Tso-lin and Marshal Fêng Yü-hsiang. Chang was master of Manchuria while Fêng was dominant in Northwest China. But other war lords soon challenged their position when it became evident that any favorable decisions of the Special Tariff Conference would mean increased revenues for the Peking Government. Wu P'ei-fu and Sun Ch'uan-fang promptly protested against the negotiations between the powers and the "illegal" Peking Government. Chang Tso-lin was compelled to retreat to Mukden and, despite the provisions of the Boxer Protocol, communications between Peking and the sea were severed by the troops of the contesting war lords. The military situation in China, however, remained remarkably fluid. In March 1926, Chang Tso-lin joined forces with his recent bitter foe Wu P'ei-fu and soon their armies were in occupation of Peking. The President, Tuan Ch'i-jui, promptly retired from office and for several months there was no

[68] *Far Eastern Review,* June 1926, pp. 242–43.
[69] *North China Herald,* July 10, 1926.

semblance of a central government in China. Faced with this political uncertainty, on July 3, 1926, the Special Tariff Conference adjourned and the powers were warned by contending factions against any attempt to resume discussions.[70]

The minatory message from the Foreign Minister of the Canton Government was an acrid attack upon the "phantom government in Peking," which he described as the creation of "a brace of medieval militarists and a bunch of Mandarin statesboys and statescoolies."[71] Two weeks later he turned his guns upon American policy because it had failed to recognize the fact that the situation in China was "revolutionary" and not "evolutionary." Remedies in China would have to be drastic. The old "unequal treaties" would have to be abrogated and new agreements negotiated which would be "consistent with the real independence and sovereignty of China."[72]

In reply to these blasts from the excitable and impudent Ch'en, the American Minister in Peking sent to the Department of State a long note which carefully reviewed the situation in China. Since 1918 there had been at Peking "no regime asserting an even plausible claim to being a legitimately constituted government." Nevertheless the powers had found it advantageous hitherto to grant "at least *de facto* recognition to each group succeeding to control of the capital and offering to carry out the obligations of the Government of China." It had obviously been worth while to deal with a "central government which we clearly understood to be a fiction," so long as it continued to be a "conservative force" which safeguarded legitimate foreign interests. But the situation in China had recently disintegrated to the point where the powers could not expect "that a conservative or even friendly influence will characterize any new regime." The Central Administration in Peking was nothing more than a "pawn used in a fantastic game being played among military rivals having no loyalties and no principles." It would be idle, therefore, to expect anything from a Special Tariff Conference. The decisions of such a conference could not be carried out by a "central administration which is and for years must be a political nonentity."

It should also be kept in mind that the Red shadow of Russia was encroaching upon North China. Marshal Fêng Yü-hsiang, "freshly schooled in Moscow in revolutionary methods," might at any time return to Peking, and his first move would be to have all existing treaties

---

[70] Robert T. Pollard, *China's Foreign Relations, 1917–1931* (New York, 1933), pp. 275–79.

[71] Eugene Ch'en to the American Consul General Jenkins, Canton, July 14, 1926. *Foreign Relations, 1926,* I, 845.

[72] Eugene Ch'en to the American Consul General Jenkins, Canton, July 28, 1926. *Ibid.,* pp. 851–53.

with the United States and other "capitalistic Powers" canceled by "a declaration he would cause to be made." It would probably be wise for the American Government frankly to "discard the fiction that a central government exists in Peking."[73]

Secretary Kellogg was not inclined to accept MacMurray's suggestions that the Department of State should abandon any hope of results from a Special Tariff Conference. Moreover, he believed that it would be a mistake to issue a "public notification to China that she has no government." Such action would "bring the hostility of the Chinese people upon us and give to other nations an opportunity to lay the blame upon us for the failure of the Conference and furnish them . . . with a sought-for excuse for abandoning the Conference. . . . The action you suggest, I feel certain, would fail to be understood in the United States and would meet quite likely with disfavor."[74]

h. *The Kuomintang Armies Employ Red Advisers*

While Secretary Kellogg and Minister MacMurray were exchanging notes with reference to American policy in China, the rapid advance of Kuomintang armies promised a profound change in the political picture in the Far East. By October 1926 the important cities of Hankow, Hanyang, and Wuchang had been captured, and in December preparations were pushed for a drive against Shanghai.

It was significant that the plan of campaign of the Kuomintang military forces had been prepared by the Bolshevik General Blücher (called General Ga-Lin by the Chinese) and his staff. In each of the ten corps of the armies "one or more Russians held strategic positions for military or propaganda purposes." The advance of the soldiers was preceded by "plain-clothes propagandists who preached to peasants and townsmen the principles of Dr. Sun and Lenin; scattered vast quantities of placards, pamphlets, and handbills; organized the people, willing and unwilling, into peasants' and workers' unions; and set up soviet local governments."[75]

This Red complexion of the Kuomintang's northward thrust seemed to give the British Government little real concern. As early as February 1926 the Foreign Office appeared to be "gravitating in the direction of the early recognition of the Canton Government." MacMurray thought that this inclination was due primarily to commercial considerations. By placating the Red regime at Canton the "strike and boycott" against

---

[73] Minister MacMurray to Secretary Kellogg, Peking, August 14, 1926. *Ibid.*, pp. 671–80.

[74] Secretary Kellogg to MacMurray, August 24, 1926. *Ibid.*, p. 682.

[75] McNair, *op. cit.*, pp. 108–9.

British goods would be "terminated."[76] In September, when the British Foreign Office raised this question of recognition, Secretary Kellogg replied that the American Government was ready to enter "into relations and negotiate with any Government representing China which appears to be capable of fulfilling the obligations which it may undertake." It had no intention, however, of initiating negotiations with "individual provinces or groups of provinces."[77]

i. *Peking and Canton Demand Revision of Existing Treaties*

In the summer of 1926 the Canton Government was ready to take far-reaching action against the so-called "unequal treaties" with the Western powers. In September 1926 it was learned that the first move in this direction would be the levying of surtaxes on foreign goods imported into South China. MacMurray thought that such a measure should produce concerted and "resolute action" by the powers against this "method of indirect repudiation of treaties."[78] The American chargé at Peking was in agreement with MacMurray. Perhaps a "naval blockade or some feasible measure of force" might bring the Canton Government to its senses.[79]

But Secretary Kellogg was opposed to any collective intervention to compel adherence to existing treaties. He would go no further than a formal protest to the Canton Government.[80] Even this protest would have to be lukewarm because the British Government, continuing its appeasement of the Red Nationalist administration at Canton, favored the acceptance of the Kuomintang decision to collect surtaxes. Downing Street proposed that the notes from the powers should merely insist upon guarantees against any increase in the rates of taxation. This was going too far for even the pacific Department of State, which refused to adopt the British suggestion. On November 3 the American consul general at Canton was instructed to file a protest against the legality of the new surtaxes. The other Western powers promptly followed suit.[81]

This bold action by Canton was followed by a similar move on the part of the Peking Government, which in October 1926 informed both Belgium and Japan of its determination to demand a revision of exist-

---

[76] Borg, *op. cit.*, p. 120.

[77] The Department of State to the British Embassy, October 5, 1926. *Foreign Relations, 1926*, I, 855.

[78] Minister MacMurray to Ferdinand L. Mayer, September 30, 1926. *Ibid.*, p. 868.

[79] Ferdinand L. Mayer to Secretary Kellogg, October 3, 1926. *Ibid.*, p. 869.

[80] Secretary Kellogg to Mayer, October 5, 1926. *Ibid.*, p. 871.

[81] Ferdinand L. Mayer to Secretary Kellogg, November 3, 1926. *Ibid.*, pp. 896–97.

ing treaties with those powers. On November 6, Peking announced that the Sino-Belgian Treaty of 1865 was abrogated.[82]

To MacMurray in Peking it was evident that this procedure would be invoked against existing treaties with the United States unless in the "meantime our intention not to tolerate such treatment of our rights has been made very clear."[83] MacMurray then developed the thesis that in China there were two rival schools of thought with reference to a revision of the "unequal treaties"—one evolutionary, the other strongly revolutionary. The first school adhered to the belief that treaty revision should be carried out through joint action by China and the Western powers, and its members also thought that China should prove to the world that it was capable of bearing the responsibilities of a sovereign nation. This had been the theory upon which the Washington Conference had acted and it was the "inspiration of the Special Conference on the Tariff and of the Commission on Extraterritoriality." But the failure of China to use her "opportunities effectively," combined with the reluctance of the powers to implement the Washington treaties, had opened the way "for the Soviet's disruptive influences" with the revolutionary school of thought. China had already taken a significant step along the Russian road to repudiation of treaty obligations. Before she took another step down this dubious path it would be expedient for the United States to speak "some friendly words of warning."[84]

Secretary Kellogg was not disposed to direct any real threat either to Canton or Peking, with the result that the matter of surtaxes was not settled by conferences between representatives of the two governments in China and the ministers of the Western powers. The Peking Government then showed its contempt for Western thought by dismissing Sir Francis Aglen from the office of inspector-general of Customs. This action spurred MacMurray to send a cablegram to Secretary Kellogg in which he stressed the dangerous implications that lay behind this dismissal. It should be apparent that further weak protests against treaty violations would be "fruitless; and foreign commerce will henceforth have no safeguards against the arbitrary exactions of the local authorities."[85]

This dark prospect was not deeply disturbing to Secretary Kellogg. The Department of State had already realized the "increasing difficulty of obtaining complete recognition of the rights of United States na-

[82] *China Year Book, 1928*, p. 782.

[83] MacMurray to Secretary Kellogg, November 12, 1926. *Foreign Relations, 1926,* I, 996–97.

[84] MacMurray to Secretary Kellogg, November 16, 1926. *Ibid.*, pp. 897–99.

[85] MacMurray to Secretary Kellogg, Peking, February 7, 1927. *Foreign Relations, 1927*, II, 379–81.

tionals in China." Moreover, it was not possible to employ the "military and naval forces of the United States to enforce the rights guaranteed under existing treaties." The only policy for America to follow with regard to China was one of "patience and watchfulness."[86]

j. Britain Challenges American Leadership in China

The Canton and Peking governments wanted more from Washington than mere patience and watchfulness. They desired effective mediation between the powers and China in the direction of large concessions relative to tariff autonomy and the abolition of extraterritoriality. The British Foreign Office perceived the direction of political winds in China and decided to engage in an experiment in diplomatic kiteflying. On December 24, 1926, the British Ambassador in Washington handed to Secretary Kellogg a copy of a telegram that had been sent to the British Minister in Peking. This telegram contained a statement of principles that the British Foreign Office thought should in the future guide the policy of the Western powers in China. The first item emphasized the importance of abandoning the idea "that the economic and political development of China can be only secured under foreign tutelage and [the powers] should declare their readiness to recognize her right to the enjoyment of tariff autonomy as soon as she herself has settled and promulgated a new national tariff." After this deep bow to the irresponsible elements that then made up China, the memorandum went on to say that the powers should "expressly disclaim any intention of forcing foreign control upon an unwilling China." A final injunction was to the effect that the powers should also "modify their traditional attitude of rigid insistence on the strict letter of treaty rights."[87]

The Department of State was painfully surprised at this British attempt to steal the "American thunder" with regard to China,[88] and it was fearful of American criticism of the failure of the Secretary to outline and follow an effective policy. MacMurray, in Peking, was caustic in his comments on the British memorandum. While it might be advisable for the powers to adopt towards China a less "querulous and petty attitude," yet the broad formula proposed by the British with regard to "condoning disregard of their obligations by the Chinese in all matters which the Powers may not unanimously consider vital, is . . . an invitation to the Chinese to carry the principle of repudiation to what-

86 Secretary Kellogg to MacMurray, February 15, 1927. *Ibid.*, pp. 382–83.

87 British Secretary of State for Foreign Affairs to the British Ambassador in China, December 2, 1926. *Foreign Relations, 1926*, I, 923–29.

88 London *Times*, January 5, 1927.

ever may prove to be the limit of tolerance on the part of the Powers."
But the mere fact that such radical concessions had been proposed by
the nation which was still predominant in the trade of China would
compel the United States to adopt a similar attitude.[89]

In this estimate of the situation MacMurray was soon proved to be
entirely correct, for Secretary Kellogg immediately fell in line with
British action. Peking was informed that the British recommendations
had "formed part of the United States Government's policy for a long
time." The Department of State was ready to embrace the first opportunity to "negotiate with a Government representing China for the
purpose of revising the existing American treaties in the directions of
relinquishing the extraterritorial privileges of Americans in China and
of granting China the right to establish her own tariff rates on products
of American origin."[90]

MacMurray begged Secretary Kellogg not to move so fast in the matter of granting important concessions to irresponsible political groups
in China. Such a policy would "gain us no consideration or respect on
the part of the [Chinese]. . . . Indeed it would give them courage to
deprive us and other foreigners of all special privileges and ordinary
rights as well."[91] Kellogg rejected this wise counsel and formulated
American policy in strict conformity with Chinese desires as expressed
to him in daily conferences with Dr. Alfred Sze, the Chinese Minister
in Washington. On January 27, 1927, he finally announced that the
American Government was fully prepared to "continue the negotiations on the entire subject of the tariff and extraterritoriality" and to
begin these negotiations "on behalf of the United States alone."[92] Discussions were expected to be with the representatives of both the Canton and Peking governments. It was not long, however, before the
success of the northern thrust of the Nationalist armies made it unnecessary to consider the desires of Peking.

k. *Congress Supports a Policy of Treaty Revision*

The pro-Chinese policy of Secretary Kellogg received strong support
in congressional circles. The Porter Resolution of January 1927 requested the President forthwith to enter into negotiations with the
"duly accredited agents of the Republic of China" with a view to concluding treaties that would establish relations between the two countries

---

[89] MacMurray to Secretary Kellogg, Peking, December 22, 1926. *Foreign Relations,
1926*, I, 919–21.

[90] Secretary Kellogg to Minister MacMurray, December 23, 1926. *Ibid.*, p. 922.

[91] MacMurray to Secretary Kellogg, December 28, 1926. *Ibid.*, p. 929.

[92] Secretary Kellogg to the American chargé in China (Mayer), January 25, 1927.
Foreign Relations, 1927, II, 350–53.

upon an "equal and reciprocal basis." Members of both political parties favored this resolution. Mr. Connally, of Texas, expressed the opinion that the unrest in China went back "as far as the Opium War in 1842. . . . From that day until this . . . the Powers of the world have imposed their will on China."[93] Mr. Carroll L. Beedy, of Maine, was equally sympathetic towards China: "I want my country to do her utmost to free China from the curse of unequal treaties and foreign misrule."[94] On February 21, 1927, the resolution passed the House of Representatives by the overwhelming vote of 262 ayes to 43 nays.[95] It was then sent to the Senate where it languished in a pigeonhole in the office of the Committee on Foreign Relations.

While the Porter Resolution was being debated in the House of Representatives, American press opinion in many quarters was vehemently in support of its adoption. The Baltimore *Sun* was especially active in pressing for immediate and favorable consideration of the resolution. The people of China had been "bullied and outraged" in every possible manner by the Western powers. The long day of oppression was now over and China would at last secure her just position among the nations of the world.[96] The *Washington Post* thought that the only honorable course for America to follow was to "befriend the Chinese nation and deal with it as an equal."[97] The New York *World,*[98] the Louisville *Courier-Journal,*[99] and the *Kansas City Star,*[100] echoed these sentiments of friendship. But the *Chicago Tribune* challenged these pro-Chinese attacks upon the "unequal treaties." The outcry against "foreign exploitation" of the Chinese was "largely a matter of domestic politics and a dangerous device." The Porter Resolution indicated either an "abysmal ignorance of the notorious facts of Chinese conditions" or it was a "play of cheap politics to conciliate a sentimentalism in this country which has no respect for the facts."[101]

The *Chicago Tribune* was particularly concerned over the Red tinge of the Canton Government. The Cantonese had the "closest relations with Moscow," and Americans should realize that Sun Yat-sen in his last years had been closely associated with communist agents.[102] The *New York Times* was equally critical of Canton. Foreign domination

---

93 *Congressional Record,* January 26, 1927, LXVIII, pt. II, 2324.
94 *Ibid.,* LXVIII, pt. II, 4388.
95 *Ibid.,* February 21, 1927, LXVIII, pt. III, 4389.
96 January 8–10, 23–24, 29, 1927.
97 January 9, 1927.
98 January 25, 1927.
99 March 17, 1927.
100 January 21, 26, 1927.
101 January 23, 28, 30; February 3, 5, 9, 1927.
102 March 22, 1927.

in China was a myth except "in so far as the Cantonese are under the influence of Soviet Russia."[103]

1. *The Nanking Incident and Its Repercussions*

As the armies of the Canton Government under Chiang Kai-shek moved northward in the spring of 1927, the antiforeign spirit that had been developing for some years broke through all barriers of restraint. On March 24, 1927, at Nanking, a major incident occurred. As some of the Nationalist soldiers passed by the American Legation, John K. Davis, the American Consul, addressed them. They replied by cursing him in the "most savage manner," and a petty officer shouted: "You are all alike. . . . You Americans have drunk our blood for years and become rich. We are busy now killing Fengtien soldiers but we will soon begin killing all foreigners in Nanking regardless of what country they are from."[104]

This threat was soon carried out. Dr. John E. Williams, the vice-president of the University of Nanking, was "wantonly" shot through the head and instantly killed. Seven American missionaries arrived at the consulate with grim stories of unprovoked attacks. Consul Davis decided to lead the Americans at the consulate to the Standard Oil property known as Socony Hill where some measure of protection could be given by gunboats in the river. Shortly after they arrived at their destination, a band of Nationalist soldiers arrived and were appeased with some difficulty. Other bands opened fire upon the refugees on Socony Hill who would soon have been killed if the gunboats had not been able to protect them with a "curtain of shells." The following morning the entire group was able to board vessels waiting in the river and was taken to safety.

The number of foreigners killed during the Nanking Incident was six: one American, three Englishmen, one Italian, and one French priest. Ten mission buildings were burned and the residences of the missionaries were looted. The American, British, and Japanese consulates were ruined.

The American Consul at Nanking reported to the Department of State that the soldiers responsible for the attacks were "regular Kuomintang troops who were operating under orders." Minister MacMurray was "absolutely convinced" that this "campaign of terrorism and insult to foreigners was not only officially countenanced by and directed but even prearranged" by the Canton Government.[105]

[103] January 25, 1927.
[104] Consul John K. Davis to Secretary Kellogg, Nanking, March 28, 1927. *Foreign Relations, 1927*, II, 151–63.
[105] MacMurray to Secretary Kellogg, Peking, March 28, 1927. *Ibid.*, p. 151.

From Tokyo came word that the outrages at Nanking were merely an item in an extended radical program designed to ruin Chiang Kai-shek. The Japanese Minister for Foreign Affairs expressed to Ambassador MacVeagh the belief that it would be inexpedient for the powers to take "oppressive measures" against Chiang because such action would play into the hands of the "radicals among the Cantonese."[106] The British Foreign Office agreed with this Japanese viewpoint. Support should be given to Chiang in the hope that he would be able to form a "nucleus of a moderate element directed against the extremist faction of the Nationalist Government." Demands for redress should first be presented to Eugene Ch'en, the leftist Minister of Foreign Relations of the Canton Government. This move would necessitate previous consultations among the representatives of the powers with reference to the application of sanctions against Canton.[107]

When the shadow of sanctions fell across the desk of Secretary Kellogg, he was instantly alarmed at the possibility of a real storm in the Far East. His first reaction was to instruct MacMurray that the Department of State was not in favor of applying "drastic sanctions to the Nationalists."[108] He would go only so far as to present to Ch'en identic notes of protest from the American, British, French, Italian, and Japanese governments concerning the outrages committed in Nanking. These notes were finally presented simultaneously on April 11 by the consuls of the five powers at Hankow. In the event that the "Nationalist Authorities" failed to "comply promptly" with these terms, the powers would find themselves compelled to take "such measures" as they considered "appropriate."[109]

When the powers agreed that the replies of Eugene Ch'en were not "satisfactory," the question of sanctions once more came to the front. Secretary Kellogg recoiled before such a suggestion and anxiously sought some alternative. The Japanese Foreign Office supplied one by asserting a belief that the time was ripe for promoting a split between Chiang Kai-shek and the belligerent Eugene Ch'en. Kellogg quickly grasped this diplomatic lifesaver and announced that the best policy

[106] Ambassador MacVeagh to Secretary Kellogg, Tokyo, March 28, 1927. *Ibid.,* p. 164.

[107] British Ambassador (Howard) to Secretary Kellogg, April 5, 1927. *Ibid.,* pp. 179–81.

[108] Memorandum by the Secretary of State, April 6, 1927. *Ibid.,* pp. 182–83.

[109] Consul General at Hankow (Lockhart) to Eugene Ch'en, April 11, 1927. *Ibid.,* pp. 189–90. These demands included the following items: (1) adequate punishment of commanders of the troops responsible for the murders, personal injuries, and indignities and the material damage done as also of all persons found to be implicated; (2) apology in writing by the Commander in Chief of the Nationalist Army including an express written undertaking to refrain from all forms of violence and agitation against foreign lives and property; (3) complete reparation for the personal injuries and material damage done.

to follow would be to let "Eugene Ch'en's note remain unanswered and await developments." No action should be taken that would embarrass Chiang.[110]

MacMurray hoped that these fears of the Department of State would not lead to any break in the collective policy of applying pressure upon the Canton Government. If America withdrew from the concert of powers, the inevitable result would be a new Anglo-Japanese alliance which would dominate the situation in the Far East.[111] Kellogg replied that he had not decided to "withdraw entirely" from co-operation with the powers in the matter of dealing with the Nationalist Government. The Department of State would still honor the commitments made at the Washington Conference concerning extraterritoriality and the revision of the Chinese tariff, but it would also insist upon a policy of "moderate action" in China. The time had passed when foreign countries could "take over Chinese territory or maintain by force special spheres of influence in trade."[112]

When the representatives of the powers in Peking prepared a memorandum which still voiced acceptance of the "principle of sanctions" in connection with the proposed policy to be followed in China, Secretary Kellogg lectured them upon the folly of considering the employment of force to compel the Canton Government to agree upon reparations. America was opposed to "drastic action" and would not even go as far as joining with the powers in the presentation of another identic note to Eugene Ch'en.[113]

In the face of this American policy of inaction the plans of the powers for vigorous action against the Nationalist Government quickly collapsed. This was the signal for Chiang Kai-shek in April 1927 to break with the communist elements in the Kuomintang and to lay plans for the establishment of a more conservative government that would be more favorably regarded by the Western powers.

m. *Secretary Kellogg Is Indifferent to Red Menace in China*

Until April 1927 when Chiang Kai-shek rejected the leadership of Mikhail Borodin and other communist leaders, the Nationalist Party in China had been following a line laid down by Moscow. This was apparent to seasoned observers in the Far East, but President Coolidge and the Department of State appeared indifferent to the communist menace. The President himself continued to sound the note of friend-

110 Memorandum by the Secretary of State, April 20, 1927. *Ibid.,* 204–5.
111 MacMurray to Secretary Kellogg, Peking, April 23, 1927. *Ibid.,* pp. 209–10.
112 Secretary Kellogg to MacMurray, April 25, 1927. *Ibid.,* pp. 210–11.
113 Secretary Kellogg to MacMurray, April 28, 1927. *Ibid.,* pp. 215–16.

ship towards China no matter what complexion the leading faction assumed. On April 25, 1927, at a dinner of the United Press Association, he insisted that his Administration did not "wish to pursue any course of aggression against the Chinese people." Ultimately the turmoil in China would "quiet down and some form of authority will emerge which will no doubt be prepared to make adequate settlement for any wrongs we have suffered."[114]

This "Pollyanna" attitude was distinctly distasteful to American businessmen in Chinese treaty ports. In April 1927, the American Chamber of Commerce at Shanghai issued a statement that called attention to the union of Chinese nationalism and Russian communism:

Militarism, brigandage and Bolshevism have destroyed all semblance of law and order throughout the greater part of China. . . . We believe that immediate concerted action by the Powers to restore a condition of security for foreign lives and property in all treaty ports . . . will have a far-reaching influence throughout China to the ultimate benefit of the Chinese people.[115]

Rodney Gilbert agreed with the views of the American Chamber of Commerce at Shanghai and lamented the fact that the Coolidge Administration had abandoned the policy of collective pressure upon China. Writing from Peking he remarked: "This whole community, official as well as commercial, is disgusted and discouraged beyond expression."[116]

In October 1927, George Bronson Rea, in a speech before the Chamber of Commerce of the United States, presented the specter of bolshevism stalking through large parts of China: "If we admit that Soviet Russia has a right to intervene in the internal affairs of China and use the Chinese armies . . . to carry forward its warfare against the interests of other Powers, then the Powers . . . have the same right to intervene in the internal affairs of China for the protection of their interests."[117]

The American Chamber of Commerce at Shanghai was confident that the Chinese Nationalist movement had been "Soviet-managed and engineered."[118] The same opinion was expressed by the *North China Herald* in its special supplement entitled *China in Chaos:* "Whoever calls for negotiations [between the Powers and China] calls forward self-appointed representatives who are the notorious wreckers and looters of this wretched land, while immediately behind them stand the Bolshevist agitators."[119]

[114] *United States Daily,* April 26, 1927.
[115] *North China Herald,* April 30, 1927.
[116] Borg, *op. cit.,* p. 344.
[117] *Ibid.,* p. 351.
[118] *Bulletin* of the American Chamber of Commerce of Shanghai, August, 1927.
[119] *China in Chaos,* p. 2.

Because of Chiang's bolshevist background, the *North China Herald* was deeply suspicious of his break (April 1927) with the Communists:

Those foreigners who see in the revolt against Soviet dictation or in the ruthless suppression of Communist labor groups, evidence of a sincere change of heart . . . are blind to the fundamental motives behind these changes. Neither in the forwarding of the Bolshevist program nor in the revolt against it have we ever been able to see anything but cold, calculating hypocrisy.[120]

But these charges of hypocrisy against Chiang Kai-shek received little support in the United States. The Coolidge Administration was determined to believe the best of him and in the spring of 1928 it was ready to recognize his government. On March 30, 1928, by an exchange of notes, the Nanking Incident was settled. The next step would be formal recognition. MacMurray warned the Department of State against such a move: "As to the probability of establishment by the Nationalists of a responsible government, in the sense of having a serious capability of fulfilling its responsibilities, domestic and international, it is my opinion that this is extremely problematical, nor do I expect it within any predictable future."[121]

Secretary Kellogg seldom paid any attention to the advice of Minister MacMurray. In this case he merely moved ahead and on July 25, 1928, he concluded a treaty with the government of Chiang Kai-shek in which definite provision was made for Chinese tariff autonomy.[122] When MacMurray requested instructions concerning the status of Chiang's Government, Secretary Kellogg promptly informed him that the "signing of the treaty of July 25 with representatives of the Nationalist Government constitutes technically recognition of that Government and ratification by the Senate is not necessary to give effect to the recognition."[123]

The bitter struggle to achieve Chinese unification and to secure the recognition of the Nationalist Government by the Western powers had won apparent success. But the Red leaven that Chiang himself had planted deep in the heart of the Chinese political loaf never ceased its work of fermentation. In the end it would destroy not only Chiang but all China.

[120] June 18, 1927.
[121] MacMurray to Secretary Kellogg, Peking, June 20, 1928. *Foreign Relations, 1928*, II, 184–85.
[122] *Ibid.*, pp. 475–77.
[123] Secretary Kellogg to MacMurray, August 10, 1928. *Ibid.*, pp. 192–93.

III

Continued Friction with Japan Points
towards Inevitable War

a. *Congress Enacts an Exclusion Law Which Angers Japan*

As AMERICAN STATESMEN looked from the troubled scenes in China to the quiet landscapes in Japan, it was not with relief but with suspicion that they viewed the placid picture of Old Nippon. The orderly ways of empire grated upon the sensibilities of many Americans who preferred the uneasy atmosphere of democracy to the regulated rhythm of the Mikado's Government. Since 1913, Japan had been under almost constant attack by the Department of State. The Wilson Administration had led a sustained assault against Japan along several fronts, and the inauguration of a Republican Administration in 1921 had led to the calling of the Washington Conference for the express purpose of checking Japanese plans for expansion. The climate of opinion in the United States was definitely hostile to Japan, and it was inevitable that clouds of misunderstanding between the two countries should gather along the diplomatic horizon. The first threat of a storm came in connection with the immigration question.

After the close of the World War there was an increasing fear in the United States that the war-impoverished countries of Europe would send a huge wave of immigration to American shores. On May 19, 1921, in order to prevent such a contingency, Congress enacted a law that limited the number of aliens of any particular nationality that would be granted admission to the United States in any one year to 3 per cent of the "number of foreign-born persons of such nationality resident in the United States" in the year 1910. Some months later a new act was framed which reduced the annual admission of any nationality to 2 per cent of the foreign-born population of that nationality resident in the United States in 1890.[1] A high dyke had been erected against the expected wave of immigration.

It was soon apparent that this new legislation would not be used merely to supplement the gentlemen's agreement with Japan which since 1907 had controlled the immigration of laborers from that country. In 1921 a movement began in the Far West to exclude by legislation

[1] A. Whitney Griswold, *The Far Eastern Policy of the United States* (New York, 1938), pp. 369–70.

any further immigration of Japanese laborers. This could be accomplished by employing a phrase suggested in 1922 by the Supreme Court when it ruled that Japanese were ineligible for citizenship by naturalization. Federal legislation could be framed so that it would apply solely to Japanese immigrants.[2]

In December 1923, bills were introduced in Congress prohibiting the admission of aliens ineligible for citizenship. The Japanese Ambassador promptly voiced a strong protest. In the eyes of the Foreign Office it was necessary to know "whether Japan as a nation is or is not entitled to the proper respect and consideration of other nations."[3]

On February 8, Secretary Hughes sent a long letter to Representative Albert Johnson, chairman of the House Committee on Immigration, in which he criticized the proposed legislation as inconsistent with the treaty of 1911. It would also "largely undo the work of the Washington Conference on Limitation of Armament, which so greatly improved our relations with Japan." He was certain that it was not "worth while thus to affront a friendly nation with whom we have established the most cordial relations."[4]

While this letter of protest was resting quietly in a pigeonhole in Mr. Johnson's desk, Secretary Hughes and Ambassador Hanihara were exchanging notes on the immigration issue. Hanihara insisted that his country had no intention of "questioning the sovereign right of any country to regulate immigration to its own territories." He could not, however, understand the need for a measure that would "not only seriously offend the just pride of a friendly nation . . . but would also involve the question of the good faith and therefore of the honor of their government." The enactment of the proposed legislation might lead to "grave consequences" which he hoped might be avoided by another type of restriction.[5]

When Secretary Hughes sent this correspondence to Congress, Senator Lodge declared that the phrase "grave consequences" was a "veiled threat" which should be answered by the immediate passage of the exclusion law. When this suggestion was acted upon by both houses of Congress, Hanihara wrote to Secretary Hughes and asserted that he was "unable to understand how the two words, read in their context,

---

[2] *Ibid.,* p. 369.

[3] The Japanese Embassy to the Department of State, January 15, 1924. 711.945/1063, MS, Department of State.

[4] Secretary Hughes to the chairman of the Committee on Immigration and Naturalization of the House of Representatives, February 8, 1924. 150.01/778, MS, Department of State.

[5] Ambassador Hanihara to Secretary Hughes, April 10, 1924. 711.945/1043, MS, Department of State.

could be construed as meaning anything like a threat."[6] Hughes agreed
with the ambassador's viewpoint and then wrote to Senator Lodge to
express the opinion that an irreparable injury had been done, "not to
Japan but to ourselves." It had been most unwise to arouse in the minds
of large numbers of Japanese a feeling of bitter resentment against the
United States: "I dislike to think what the reaping will be after the
sowing of this seed."[7]

b. *Japan Invites United States Capital to Invest in Manchuria*

Many American newspapers were not deeply concerned about the crop
of hatred America was sowing in Japanese minds by the passage of the
exclusion law. According to the *San Francisco Examiner,* California
felt an "intense and triumphant satisfaction" that the interests of the
West Coast had apparently secured protection.[8] Other papers in the
West and in the Rocky Mountain states expressed similar sentiments.
This feeling of hostility towards Japan was so deep and so widespread
that it colored Japanese-American relations down to the tragedy at
Pearl Harbor. A good indication of how this adverse public opinion
helped to continue tension between the two countries was clearly revealed in the negotiations between the Japanese Government and the
House of Morgan with reference to a loan to develop the facilities of
the South Manchuria Railway.

On October 29, 1927, there was a report in the *New York Journal
of Commerce* that the South Manchuria Railway was seeking an American loan of $40,000,000. The proceeds of this loan would be applied
to the enlargement of the Fushun colliery and to the improvement of
certain fertilizer projects. It would also assist in certain refunding operations. Arthur N. Young, in the Office of the Economic Adviser to the
Secretary of State, wrote at once to Mr. Kellogg and to Nelson T.
Johnson, chief of the Division of Far Eastern Affairs, to call their attention to this item in the *Journal of Commerce.* He then remarked
that the

Department has taken a position previously of objecting to such financing on
the ground that it amounted to the utilization of American capital to promote Japanese penetration in Manchuria, and that we stated that we did not

---

[6] Ambassador Hanihara to Secretary Hughes, April 17, 1924. 711.945/1051, MS,
Department of State. President Coolidge signed the Exclusion Act on May 26, 1924.
[7] Secretary Hughes to Senator Lodge, April 17, 1924. Calvin Coolidge MS, Library of Congress.
[8] April 17, 1924.

view with favor the use of American funds for promoting in third countries activities that might be disadvantageous to American interests.[9]

Nelson Johnson made an immediate reply to Mr. Young. He had seen Secretary Kellogg who had assured him that he had "remembered quite clearly the attitude which we had taken with regard to the question of financing the South Manchuria Railway and that if the matter should come up we would continue to take this attitude."[10]

T. W. Lamont, of the House of Morgan, believed that the Department of State should revise its practice concerning the approval of loans for the development of the facilities of the South Manchuria Railway. In a letter to Mr. Olds, the Under Secretary of State, he discussed his recent trip to Manchuria and the general outlook in that province:

My own observation . . . is that today Manchuria is about the only stable region in all China and that with the Japanese there it is likely to be more of a stabilizing force in Chinese affairs than it is to be a disturbing element. The Japanese are developing Manchuria not chiefly in the military sense but in an economic way. They are doing this not for the benefit of the Japanese colonists who go to Manchuria in only small numbers. As a matter of fact, development is working out in the interest of the Chinese. With the unsettled and belligerent conditions covering so large a part of China, the Chinese are now pouring by the thousands into South Manchuria in order to escape the banditry, looting and despoiling to which they are subjected elsewhere.[11]

When Chiang Kai-shek heard of the proposed loan for the development of the facilities of the South Manchuria Railway, he was deeply disturbed. Mayer, the counselor of the Embassy in Peking, was informed that the "Chinese generally would consider a loan of the above description as a departure from American traditional attitude toward China since this action would be of direct assistance to Japan in her efforts to dominate in Manchuria." Chiang then indicated that he would "more than welcome American capital seeking proper investment in Manchuria for which he would afford every possible facility."[12]

Inasmuch as Chiang Kai-shek had no control over Manchuria, his offer to welcome the investment of American capital was a little premature. It was significant that Mr. Lamont discovered that Manchuria

[9] Arthur N. Young to Secretary Kellogg and to Nelson Johnson, November 1, 1927. 894.51 So 8/1, MS, Department of State.

[10] Nelson T. Johnson to Arthur N. Young, November 1, 1927. 894.51 So 8/1, MS, Department of State.

[11] T. W. Lamont to R. E. Olds, the Under Secretary of State, New York, November 11, 1927. 894.51 So 8/48, MS, Department of State.

[12] Ferdinand L. Mayer to Secretary Kellogg, Peking, November 19, 1927. 894.51 So 8/1, MS, Department of State.

was the only province in China where lives and property were safe. How quickly this situation would deteriorate under the rule of Chiang the events at Nanking, Hankow, and Tsinan had clearly demonstrated.

On November 21, Secretary Kellogg sent an instruction of inquiry to the American Legation in Peking. He was particularly anxious to ascertain "what the reaction would be in China to the Japanese Government making such a loan in the United States for the Manchurian Railway and any further information you may have in relation to discrimination against American commerce and opposition of Japan to the construction of railways by China in Manchuria." The reply of Mayer was particularly significant. From a

purely humanitarian viewpoint it would be advantageous for China to have America participate indirectly in Japanese development of Manchuria. With our national ideals . . . it seems inevitable that if we had certain creditor controls we would exert upon Japan an influence beneficent for China. . . . I would submit that Japan is going ahead anyway in Manchuria consolidating her position there with an eye to an ultimate conflict with Russia. . . . The Powers cannot, and I firmly believe will not, be able to let China drift on in her present anarchy indefinitely and even more disastrously for them—particularly if the Russian influence is not curbed. It is too dangerous internationally. . . . We cannot oppose Japanese plans in Manchuria ethically in view of measures we have taken in our correspondingly vital zone—the Caribbean.[13]

Three days later, Mr. Mayer sent a second note to Secretary Kellogg. Once more he sounded a note of realism that must have disturbed the sentimental Secretary of State. With specific reference to the reaction in China to the granting of a loan to develop the South Manchuria Railway, he acidly remarked:

There would probably be considerable disillusionment throughout China regarding the United States but after all what has the so-called especially friendly attitude of the Chinese ever meant to us? It has not furthered our commercial interests . . . nor has it saved us from the horrors and insults of Nanking.[14]

From Tokyo, Secretary Kellogg received some more realistic advice. Ambassador MacVeagh feared that the Japanese Government would

consider refusal of Department to pass loan as evidence of distrust of Japan's intentions in Manchuria. . . . Japan is extremely anxious to obtain from America rather than from other sources, financial assistance needed and be-

13 Ferdinand L. Mayer to Secretary Kellogg, Peking, November 22, 1927. 894.51 So 8/4, MS, Department of State.

14 Ferdinand L. Mayer to Secretary Kellogg, Peking, November 25, 1927. 894.51 So 8/8, MS, Department of State.

lieves that to have American people financially interested in Manchuria will help her to develop the country along lines of making it desirable and safe place for all nationals including Chinese. . . . I have long felt that we should use the first opportunity to convince the Japanese of our honest desire to help them when we can legitimately do so. . . . I think that Lamont was impressed with the sincere desire of the Japanese bankers to put their affairs on a sound basis. . . . Lamont also seemed to me to be convinced that Japan was earnestly and sincerely trying to find a way by which she could assist China in solving her own problems.[15]

Some American newspapers openly favored the loan to the South Manchuria Railway. The *New York Times* pointed to the excellent record of railway management and made the comment that few American transportation systems could do any better.[16] Even the *San Francisco Chronicle* could see no reason for the Department of State to oppose the loan.[17]

But the strong protests of the different factions in China against the loan influenced American opinion so adversely that Mr. Lamont informed the Department of State that it would be unwise to continue the negotiations.[18] As an offset to this Chinese opposition the Japanese Government invited international investment in the many industries operated by the South Manchuria Railway. Jotaro Yamamoto, the president of the South Manchuria Railway, expressed the opinion that this move should clearly indicate to the world the sincerity of Japan's assurances that she had no territorial designs upon Manchuria. The time had come when it was important to "translate words into deeds and to dispel suspicion."[19]

Peking entered a prompt protest against this second attempt to secure the investment of American capital in Manchuria.[20] Once again American banking interests were influenced by Chinese official opposition and the opportunity for guiding Japanese policy by means of "credit controls" was allowed to slip by. War-ravaged, revolutionary China still had a potent appeal to American sympathies.

c. *Chinese Soldiers Provoke the Tsinan Incident*

On a few occasions Americans did view China through realistic eyes. This was particularly true with reference to the Tsinan Incident. On

[15] Ambassador MacVeagh to Secretary Kellogg, Tokyo, November 21, 1927. 894.51 So 8/2, MS, Department of State.

[16] November 25, 1927.

[17] November 25, 1927.

[18] Secretary Kellogg to Ambassador MacVeagh, December 10, 1927. 894.51 So 8/20, MS, Department of State.

[19] Memorandum of Division of Far Eastern Affairs, 894.51 So 8/61a.

[20] *New York Times*, October 28, 1928.

May 3, 1928, when Chinese Nationalist soldiers began widespread
looting in the city of Tsinan, Japanese troops went into action against
them. Four days later the Japanese commander in Tsinan sent an ultimatum to Chiang Kai-shek demanding the immediate withdrawal of
Chinese armed forces from the city.[21] When Chiang failed to comply
with this demand, Japanese troops in Tsinan launched an attack upon
the Chinese Army which resulted in considerable loss of life and
property.

The Nationalist Government sent an appeal to the League of Nations declaring Japan to be the aggressor. In reply, Japan indicated her
large interests in Shantung province and the considerable number of
Japanese nationals who needed protection.[22] The Peking and Tientsin
Times was favorably impressed with this Japanese statement: "It is a
model of what such statements should be. . . . China has lost a great
deal of the faith once reposed in her veracity by the false propaganda
in which her immature and excited emissaries indulged."[23]

While the League was considering this dispute, the Japanese Government issued to the powers assurances that as soon as order was restored in Shantung province she would withdraw her troops. Everything depended upon the course of the negotiations between Japan and
Nationalist China. These were carried on with many interruptions until
an agreement was finally signed on March 28, 1929. The result was a
diplomatic victory for China. Japan consented to withdraw her troops
from Shantung within two months and the question of damages resulting from the Tsinan Incident would be settled by a Sino-Japanese Commission.[24]

The attitude of a large section of the American press concerning the
Tsinan Incident was significantly pro-Japanese. The *Washington Post*
thought it would be expedient, before people grew excited over alleged
Japanese aggression in China, to "inquire how and when the Nationalist faction acquired the right to call itself the government of China."[25]
The *New York Herald-Tribune* believed that the incident indicated the
"disappearance in China of even the semblance of national control and
responsible government."[26] The *Philadelphia Inquirer* was of the opinion that "Tsinan had emphasized the lesson taught by Nanking. . . .

[21] Ambassador MacVeagh to Secretary Kellogg, Tokyo, May 4, 5, 1928. 893.00
Tsinan/2–7, MS, Department of State.
[22] Ambassador MacVeagh to Secretary Kellogg, Tokyo, June 6, 1928. 893.00
Tsinan/93, MS, Department of State.
[23] June 1, 1928.
[24] Ambassador MacMurray to Secretary Kellogg, Peking, March 26, 1929. 893.00
Tsinan/127, MS, Department of State.
[25] May 13, 1928.
[26] May 11, 1928.

Every Power concerned should show a firm front."[27] The *San Francisco Chronicle* expressed the view that was commonly held throughout the United States: "Japan was forced to protect her people and property in Shantung."[28]

d. *Russia Teaches the War Lord of Manchuria a Lesson*

The Nanking and Tsinan incidents were produced by the high tide of Chinese nationalism that flowed northward as Chiang Kai-shek endeavored to unify China by means of armed force. Checked by American and Japanese military strength, the tide was diverted towards the Russian position in Manchuria. Once more it was turned back after a small advance.

Friction between China and Russia developed out of conflicting claims concerning the administration of the Chinese Eastern Railway. The Sino-Soviet agreements of 1924 provided for the joint administration of the railway as a commercial enterprise. There was also a clause forbidding the dissemination of propaganda inimical to the political and social institutions of either country. In January 1926 a quarrel broke out between Chang Tso-lin, war lord of the Three Eastern Provinces, and Ivanoff, the general manager of the Chinese Eastern Railway. The dispute at first dealt with Ivanoff's insistence upon the prompt payment by Chang of transportation charges for his troops. In the spring of 1927, Chang was informed that the Russians were breaking the agreement of 1924 by spreading propaganda favorable to bolshevism. On April 6, 1927, his troops raided the Soviet embassy in Peking and discovered a large number of documents that "abundantly proved that members of the Embassy staff" were distributing communistic literature in violation of treaty obligations.[29]

The Soviet Minister left Peking in a rage after this raid but Soviet consulates remained in Manchuria and North China. They continued to be focal points from which communist propaganda could be spread in North China, but before Chang could take further action he was mortally wounded by a bomb on June 4, 1928. His son, Chang Hsueh-liang, nursed deep suspicions of communist activities, so on May 27, 1929, his troops made a raid upon the Soviet Consulate in Harbin and arrested forty-two consular officials. Documents seized in the consular buildings confirmed Chinese suspicions that Soviet officials of the

[27] May 7, 1928.
[28] May 22, 1928.
[29] Robert T. Pollard, *China's Foreign Relations, 1917–1931* (New York, 1933), p. 391.

Chinese Eastern Railway were busily spreading bolshevik literature.[30]

On June 1, 1929, the Soviet Government denied that any meetings of the Third International had been held in the cellar of the consulate. The Chinese police were denounced for their "stupidity and shamelessness" and their actions were declared to be in accordance with "jungle law." The Soviet Government, "with inexhaustible patience" was awaiting a note with the proper explanations.[31] Chang replied with new raids. On July 10 the telegraph system of the Chinese Eastern Railway was taken over, Soviet unions were dissolved, the offices of the Soviet Mercantile Fleet and the Far Eastern Trading Organization were closed, and the Russian general manager of the railway was replaced by a Chinese appointee.

On July 13 the Soviet Foreign Office criticized these raids as an "outrageous violation of the Sino-Soviet Treaty of 1924," and the government of Chang Hsueh-liang at Mukden and the Nationalist Government of Chiang Kai-shek were warned that an "extremely serious situation has arisen." A demand was then made that a conference be called "for the settlement of all questions connected with the Chinese Eastern Railway."[32]

In a note to the Soviet Government (July 16) explaining the reasons for these drastic measures, the Chinese Foreign Office stressed the fact that for years Soviet officials in China had been engaged in spreading communist propaganda in violation of the treaty of 1924.[33] Moscow immediately replied that these Chinese charges were false and the note "unsatisfactory in content and hypocritical in tone." All means had "already been exhausted for settling by negotiation the controversial questions and conflicts concerning the Chinese Eastern Railway." It would be necessary, therefore, for the Soviet Government to recall all representatives from Chinese territory and to "sever all rail links between China and the USSR."[34]

It was now apparent that unless some formula for peace could be quickly found there would be war in North China. To Secretary Stimson, the very thought of war was profoundly disturbing. Both China and Russia had adhered to the Kellogg-Briand Pact outlawing war as an instrument of national policy. Although the pact contained no provision for international consultation and no requirement that any nation or combination of nations should attempt to keep the peace of the world,

---

[30] *China Year Book, 1929–1930*, p. 1217.

[31] *Pravda*, June 1, 1929. For a translation of Russian documents published in *Pravda* I am indebted to Mr. Frederick L. Hetter.

[32] *Pravda*, July 14, 1929.

[33] *China Year Book, 1929–1930*, pp. 1217–20.

[34] *Pravda*, July 18, 1929.

Stimson was determined to infuse a vital spark into its lifeless phrases. He was eager to play the role of policeman in the dark jungles of international intrigue. His club would be the awakened opinion of mankind, which he regarded as one of the most potent sanctions in the world.[35]

On July 18 he called the attention of the Chinese and Russian governments to the obligations they had assumed under the Kellogg-Briand Pact.[36] It was obvious to the rest of the world that Chinese and Russian statesmen could read the text of the treaty as easily as Secretary Stimson, and there was no doubt that they were thoroughly acquainted with all of its implications. The Chinese Foreign Minister quickly assured Mr. Stimson that his Government had "no intention of using force in the present controversy." The Russian answer to the Stimson admonition was equally reassuring. "Our signature of the Kellogg Pact was not just a diplomatic gesture. When we talk peace we mean peace."[37]

But despite this pacific talk there was continued friction concerning the administration of the Chinese Eastern Railway. Finally, after a series of minor incidents, a Russian army marched into Manchuria on November 17 and soon imposed its will upon Hsueh-liang, who received no assistance from Chiang Kai-shek. There had been no declaration of war, but the peaceful play upon the plains of North China had been exceedingly rough even for Red Russians.[38]

Stimson was a stickler for the proper form of international conduct. He was resolute in his refusal to regard the Russian military movements in Manchuria as mere playful pranks. If he were not careful the merry Muscovites might overrun all of North China under the guise of a game. In order to dampen these high spirits and to restrain these wild antics, he entered into consultations with France, Germany, Great Britain, Italy, and Japan in an endeavor to exert collective pressure upon Russia. Germany and Japan declined Stimson's invitation, but France, Great Britain, and Italy consented to follow Stimson's lead and a joint note was presented to the disputants on December 2, 1929.[39] China gave prompt assurance that she had never departed from the letter or the spirit of the Kellogg-Briand Pact. The Russian reply indicated a strong belief that the Stimson action had been much ado about nothing. The dispute with China would be settled by "direct negotiations" be-

[35] Henry L. Stimson, "The Pact of Paris," an address delivered before the Council on Foreign Relations, New York City, August 8, 1932 (Washington, 1932).

[36] Stanley K. Hornbeck, "American Policy and the Chinese-Russian Dispute," *Chinese Social and Political Science Review*, XIV (January, 1930), 56–60.

[37] Russell M. Cooper, *American Consultation in World Affairs* (New York, 1934), p. 91.

[38] Eugene Lyons, *Assignment in Utopia* (New York, 1938), chap. 14.

[39] Department of State, *Press Releases*, December 7, 1929.

tween the two powers. As far as the United States was concerned, the commissar expressed great indignation that Stimson had assumed the right to invoke the Pact of Paris. That treaty did not "give any single State or group of States any rights of enforcement." Moreover, the Soviet Government could not forbear to express its amazement that the "Government of the United States, which by its own will has no official relations with the Soviet, deems it possible to apply to it with advice and counsel."[40]

Stimson refused to permit this Russian rebuff to cool his ardor for peace. He was so anxious for peace that he was ready to fight for it. He clearly realized that his defense of the Pact of Paris was merely a battle of the books. In the near future any further intervention into disputes that were constantly arising in the Far East might mean armed conflict. That contingency could never be overlooked by any statesman, and in 1931 Stimson directed a long verbal barrage against Japanese intervention in Manchuria which sounded to many persons like a call to arms. A decade later these same strident accents found expression in a chorus of war.

e. *Background of the Manchurian Incident*

(1) JAPAN IS WORRIED OVER THE SPREAD OF COMMUNISM IN CHINA

The outcome of the conflict between China and Soviet Russia in 1929 had important implications for Japan. First of all, it was clear that Russia had violated the provisions of the Sino-Russian agreement of 1924 which prohibited the spread of communistic propaganda in China. The vast amount of data seized by Chinese police in the Harbin Consulate left no doubt on this point. Russian denials carried no conviction to Japanese minds, and the fact that Chang Hsueh-liang had to fight alone against Soviet armed forces indicated that Chiang Kai-shek was either too weak to guard the frontiers of Manchuria effectively or was not deeply disturbed by the Russian chastisement of the war lord of the Three Eastern Provinces. The Japanese bastions of defense in North China were in evident danger.

This fact seemed apparent to Japanese statesmen when they looked at the ominous failure of Chiang Kai-shek to cope with communist armies. In December 1930, Chiang mobilized troops from Hunan, Hopeh, and Kiangsi provinces and sent them against the Communists.

---

[40] John Wheeler-Bennett, *Documents on International Affairs, 1929* (London, 1930), pp. 278–80.

The Reds soon annihilated the Eighteenth Corps under General Chang Huei-tsan and caused the rapid retreat of the Fiftieth Corps. In February 1931, General Ho Ying-chin was given three army corps to attack the Reds but by May his forces were compelled to withdraw. In July, Chiang Kai-shek himself led a large army to the Nanchang front but accomplished nothing decisive.[41] The Red menace was daily becoming more formidable and Japanese fears rapidly increased. The only way to insure Japanese security was through adequate measures of defense in Manchuria. These might violate some shadowy rights of sovereignty that China had over Manchuria, but these rights had not been successfully asserted since 1912 and would soon be extinguished by Russia if Japan took no action. For Japan, expansion in Manchuria was a national imperative.

(2) DIFFICULTIES CONCERNING THE RAILWAYS IN MANCHURIA

Expansion in Manchuria might mean war with China and eventually conflict with Russia. These possibilities profoundly disturbed Japanese statesmen, who realized the fact that 75 per cent of the employees of the Chinese Eastern Railway were "Russians and they held all the controlling posts."[42] This firm control over the operation of the railway gave Russia a commercial and military advantage in North China that constituted an obvious threat to Japanese interests. Ultimately the road would have to be purchased or taken by force.

Railroads were the lifelines of empire in North China and this fact had been obvious to Japanese statesmen as early as 1905. Under the terms of the secret protocol to the Sino-Japanese Treaty of December 22, 1905, the Chinese Government promised it would not construct any railway "in the neighborhood of and parallel to" the South Manchuria Railway.[43] For many years Japan claimed that this prohibition prevented the building of any parallel lines closer than two hundred miles on each side of their trunk line. But when the sovereignty of China over Manchuria was reduced to a fiction by war lords like Chang Tso-lin and his son, Chang Hsueh-liang, the Japanese Government abandoned its negative attitude and entered into a transportation deal

[41] *Communism in China, Document A, Appendix No. 3* (Tokyo, 1932), pp. 3–5. This document was published by the Japanese Government as a part of the case of Japan. For a sympathetic account of the struggle of Chiang Kai-shek with the Chinese Communists see T'ang Leang-li, *Suppressing Communist Banditry in China* (Shanghai, 1934), chap. 5.

[42] Max Beloff, *The Foreign Policy of Soviet Russia, 1929–1941* (New York, 1947), I, 71.

[43] J. V. A. MacMurray, *Treaties and Agreements with and Concerning China*, I, 554.

with them. The South Manchuria Railway and certain Japanese banks advanced loans to the Changs and supplied engineers who built railways that produced rich returns.[44] With these funds the Changs then proceeded to construct lines that were parallel to the South Manchuria Railway.[45] In December 1930 the Japanese Government took the position that it would not object to these parallel lines as long as they did not adversely affect their large trunk line.[46]

But this conciliatory attitude was modified after Chang Hsueh-liang, in disregard of Japanese warnings, declared his allegiance to Chiang Kai-shek. Japan was not inclined to welcome any wave of nationalism in Manchuria with attendant outbreaks of violence like those in Hankow, Nanking, and Tsinan. In 1927, Mr. Lamont had reported that Manchuria was "about the only stable region in all China" and that large numbers of Chinese were pouring into that region to escape the "banditry, looting and despoiling to which they are subjected elsewhere."[47] Manchuria had become a sanctuary where multitudes of immigrants found safety under a war lord who obeyed Japanese mandates. When this irresponsible war lord had provoked a Soviet invasion by seizing control over the Chinese Eastern Railway, it was high time that Japan took steps to safeguard her vast economic interests in Manchuria.[48] Moreover, this same war lord had shown no disposition to repay the large Japanese loans (143,000,000 yen) that had made it possible for him and his father to construct the railway lines that brought in much-needed revenue. It was difficult to continue friendly relations with a ruler whose actions were becoming increasingly inimical to Japan.

(3) FRICTION WITH REFERENCE TO THE NISHIHARA LOANS

One of the important factors that promoted friction between Japan and China was the failure of the Chinese Nationalist Government to repay the large loans that had been advanced to China by Japanese financiers. By 1930, Japan's unsecured loans to China had reached the large sum of $953,000,000 (including interest). The Nationalist Government

[44] The Ssupingkai-Chenchiatun-Taonan line (with the Piayantala branch) 264 miles, and the Taonan-Anganchi (Tsitsihar) railway, 141 miles. See K. K. Kawakami, "Manchurian Backgrounds," *Pacific Affairs*, V (February, 1932), 111–30.

[45] The Kirin-Hailung-Mukden lines (295 miles); the Piayantala-Takushan line (134 miles), and the partly-built Taonan-Piayantala line.

[46] *New York Times*, December 10, 1930.

[47] See *ante*, p. 83.

[48] Edith E. Ware, *Business and Politics in the Far East* (New Haven, 1932), p. 213, estimates Japanese investments in Manchuria at 2,147,000,000 yen.

viewed a large part of this indebtedness with indifference. This was particularly true of the so-called Nishihara loans of 1917–1918.[49] These loans were spent by the Chinese Government on the construction of railways, the extension of telegraph systems, the reorganization of the Bank of Communications, the discharge of the military expenses required for China's participation in the World War, and for other similar items. The Nationalist Government refused to recognize this indebtedness and paid little heed to Japanese pressure. Japan was not rich enough to write off a total unsecured Chinese debt of close to a billion dollars ($953,000,000). Official Chinese indifference to this obligation was a source of increasing irritation in many Japanese circles and was bound to lead to serious difficulties.

(4) ANTI-JAPANESE EDUCATIONAL PROGRAMS IN CHINA

The Japanese Government was deeply disturbed by the anti-Japanese educational programs inspired by the Nationalist Government of China. They would lead not only to increasing bitterness between the two nations but to eventual war. It was especially irritating to have this hostile program pushed vigorously in Manchuria. In the primary schools in Shanghai the pupils were indoctrinated by the following method: "(a) *composition:* children shall be required to write anti-Japanese essays and verses; (b) *penmanship:* children shall be required to copy anti-Japanese slogans; (c) *drawing:* children shall be required to draw pictures representing atrocities committed by Japanese and tragic scenes at Tsinan."

With reference to *propaganda* the following prescription was required: (a) teachers and pupils shall organize anti-Japanese patriotic propaganda parties in squads of five to deliver open-air speeches; (b) the masses shall be taught to consider Japan their lifelong and greatest enemy; (c) the masses shall be called upon to pledge themselves to the work of blotting out national disgrace and saving the country.[50]

During the decade 1930–40 this anti-Japanese program was pushed with increasing intensity and Japanese statesmen made its suspension one of the cardinal items in their lists of requirements for better relations between China and Japan. These lists received scant consideration in China.

[49] *Leading Cases of Chinese Infringement of Treaties, Document A, Appendix, No. 6,* (Tokyo, 1932), pp. 105–7. See also, Thomas E. LaFargue, *China and the World War* (Stanford, 1937), p. 112.

[50] *Anti-Foreign Education in China, Document A, Appendix No. 5* (Tokyo, 1932), pp. 28–37. For a different viewpoint see T'ang Leang-li, *The Puppet State of Manchukuo* (Shanghai, 1935), pp. 263–72.

(5) THE LEGALITY OF THE TREATIES OF MAY 25, 1915

The refusal of the Chinese Nationalist Government to accept as legal the treaties that were signed on May 25, 1915, was a fundamental cause of the deep bitterness that finally led to the outbreak of hostilities on September 18, 1931. These treaties which resulted from the Twenty-One Demands had given Japanese interests in Manchuria a firm foundation.[51] Nanking claimed that they were invalid because the government of Yüan Shih-k'ai had signed them under duress. Tokyo insisted upon their legality and cogently argued that German hatred of Versailles as a dictated treaty did not invalidate its stringent provisions.

To Japan it appeared obvious that Manchuria was essential to her as a bastion of defense and as the keystone of her economic structure. Her statesmen hoped that the Department of State would recognize that North China was just as important to Japan as the Caribbean area was to the United States. The American Government had sent military forces to Haiti and to the Dominican Republic for the purpose of establishing administrations that would be responsive to American desires.[52] This armed intervention had been so recent and so effective that it led the American chargé in Peking to send a dispatch to Secretary Kellogg which ended on a significant note: "We cannot oppose Japanese plans in Manchuria ethically in view of measures we have taken in our correspondingly vital zone—the Caribbean."[53]

In 1931, Japan felt that she was being pushed to the wall by Chinese Nationalists in Mukden and Nanking. A concerted attempt was being made to reduce the treaties of 1915 to scraps of paper. These treaties were essential to the defense of her tremendous interests in Manchuria and she would fight rather than give them up. She did not realize how close she was to conflict.

In 1930 a large part (17.7%) of the export trade of Japan went to China, and thus any interference with this trade would seriously affect the national economy of the Japanese Empire. In 1923, 1925, 1927, and 1928, Chinese boycotts were declared against Japan, and after the Mukden Incident in the late summer of 1931 another boycott was

[51] Under the treaties of May 25, 1915, Japan secured the following advantages: (a) the lease of the Kwantung Peninsula, including Port Arthur and Dairen, was extended from 1923 to 1997; (b) the lease of the Antung-Mukden Railway was extended from 1923 to 2007; (c) the lease of the Dairen-Changchun Railway was extended to 2002; (d) the right to lease land in South Manchuria for industrial uses and agricultural purposes was expressly granted.
[52] Hallett Abend, New York Times, November 4, 1931.
[53] Ferdinand L. Mayer to Secretary Kellogg, Peking, November 22, 1927. 894.51 So 8/4, MS, Department of State.

launched.[54] The organizing force behind most of these boycotts was the Kuomintang which made effective use of anti-Japanese propaganda. According to the *Lytton Report,* a large number of "illegal acts" were committed by the Chinese during these periods when trade with Japan was prohibited. Inasmuch as the Kuomintang and the Chinese Government were largely identical, Japan held that Chiang Kai-shek and his advisers were really responsible for the economic pressure that was exerted upon the empire.

The Lytton Commission in weighing the evidence concerning the use of boycotts did not deny the right "of the individual Chinese to refuse to buy Japanese goods, use Japanese banks or ships, or to work for Japanese employers," but it did raise the question whether the use of these economic weapons was "consistent with friendly relations."[55] It is certain that Chinese economic reprisals against Japan helped to widen the breach between the two countries.

(6) THE MURDER OF CAPTAIN NAKAMURA

In the hostile atmosphere that had developed in the summer of 1931 it required merely a spark to start an explosion. This spark was provided by the murder of Captain Nakamura on June 27, 1931. The captain, accompanied by three interpreters and assistants, was sent into Manchuria, during the summer of 1931, on a military mission. At Harbin, where his passport was examined by Chinese authorities, he represented himself as an agricultural expert. After proceeding some distance on the Chinese Eastern Railway, he was "placed under detention by Chinese soldiers under Kuan Yuheng, the Commander of the Third Regiment of the Reclamation Army." On June 27 he and his companions "were shot by Chinese soldiers and their bodies were cremated to conceal evidence of the deed."[56]

The Japanese insisted that the

killing of Captain Nakamura and his companions was unjustified and showed arrogant disrespect for the Japanese Army and nation; they asserted that the Chinese authorities in Manchuria delayed to institute official enquiries into the circumstances, were reluctant to assume responsibility for the occurrence, and were insincere in their claim that they were making every effort to ascertain the facts in the case.[57]

[54] On the general subject of Chinese boycotts see C. F. Remer and William B. Palmer, *A Study of Chinese Boycotts* (Baltimore, 1933).

[55] *Report of the Commission of Enquiry Appointed by the League of Nations on Manchuria* (Washington, 1932), (hereafter referred to as the *Lytton Report*), p. 120.

[56] *Ibid.,* pp. 63–64.

[57] *Ibid.,* p. 64.

It is certainly true that long delays did occur in trying to "ascertain the facts in the case," and there is no doubt that they "put a severe strain on the patience of the Japanese." It is also true that this Nakamura case, "more than any other single incident, greatly aggravated the resentment of the Japanese and their agitation in favour of forceful means to effect a solution of outstanding Sino-Japanese difficulties in regard to Manchuria."[58]

While the Lytton Commission was studying the situation in China, it noted with concern the increasing strength of communism. In 1930 armies of the Nationalist Government had been unsuccessful in operations against communist forces, and during the following year Chiang Kai-shek was reported to be driving the Communists back in full retreat towards Fukien when the Mukden Incident occurred. But they were elusive and resourceful antagonists. During the autumn of 1931 they resumed their offensive and soon "large parts of the provinces of Fukien and Kiangsi, and parts of Kwantung were reliably reported to be completely sovietized."[59]

Japan was well aware of the danger that this Red tide might roll over most of China. In the documents presented to the Lytton Commission in 1932, emphasis was placed upon this communist menace and upon the apparent inability of the Chinese Nationalist Government to control it.[60] It seemed to Tokyo that Japanese interests in North China were about to be crushed between the millstones of Chinese nationalism and Russian bolshevism. An appeal to the League of Nations would accomplish little. Chinese nationalism had found a sympathetic audience in the Western powers. Most of them were inclined to accept the fictions and pretensions put forward by the Nanking Government. The Japanese position in North China was in grave danger of being infiltrated by Reds or successfully attacked by fervent Chinese Nationalists whose patriotism had turned into a "flame of hatred."[61]

The dilemma that faced Japan is clearly and cogently stated by George Sokolsky who was used as an intermediary between China and Japan in 1931:

It needs to be recalled here that in 1931 the last efforts were made to reconcile these countries [China and Japan]. Actually, I was an instrument in that attempted reconciliation, going to Japan from China to hold meetings with Baron Shidehara, Minister of Foreign Affairs, and others. I can say that the Japanese attitude was conciliatory; the Chinese, on the whole, antagonistic.

58 *Ibid.*, p. 65.
59 *Ibid.*, p. 22.
60 *Communism in China, Document A, Appendix No. 3* (Tokyo, 1932).
61 *Lytton Report, op. cit.*, p. 19.

. . . Two forces were at work to keep China and Japan quarreling: Soviet Russia and the League of Nations. Soviet Russia had been engaged since 1924 in an active program of stirring hate among the Chinese people against all foreigners except the Russians, but particularly against the British and the Japanese. The League of Nations secretariat was developing in China a field of widespread activity through its agent, Dr. Ludwic Rajchmann, who was spending most of his time in China. Rajchmann was violently anti-Japanese, although Japan was a member of the League of Nations and Rajchmann an employee. Rajchmann is a Pole and is now associated with the United Nations.[62]

f. Secretary Stimson Prepares a Path to War

One of the reasons why Japan was "conciliatory" towards China in 1931 was because of the shaky structure of Japanese finance. A war with China might lead to very serious consequences. On September 18, 1931, the American press published a summary of a report made by Dr. Harold G. Moulton, of the Brookings Institution, on economic conditions in the Japanese Empire. This survey had been undertaken upon the invitation of the Japanese Minister of Finance. In conclusion the summary stated that "military retrenchment, continuation of peaceful relations with the United States, and sharp restriction of the present rates of population are all essential if serious economic and financial difficulties in Japan are to be averted. . . . A balanced budget and tax reduction can be accomplished only if military outlays are curtailed."[63]

It was only with the greatest reluctance, therefore, that Japanese statesmen consented to support a program of expansion in Manchuria. After it was apparent that the Japanese Kwantung Army had seized certain cities in North China, Hugh Byas, writing from Tokyo, reported that the sudden movement of troops had not been "foreseen" by the Japanese Government and had not been preventable.[64] Byas, as well as many other veteran observers in the Far East, had great confidence in the pacific disposition of Baron Shidehara, the Japanese Minister of Foreign Relations. Secretary Stimson shared this view and at first he was anxious to refrain from exerting too much pressure upon the Japanese Government because he feared such a policy would play into the hands of the militarists.

Three days after the clash between Japanese and Chinese troops at Mukden, Sir Eric Drummond, Secretary General of the League of Nations, asked Hugh Wilson (the American Minister at Geneva) to ascertain the views of Secretary Stimson with special reference to the "in-

---

62 George Sokolsky, "These Days," *Washington Times-Herald,* March 14, 1951.
63 Ware, *op. cit.,* p. 206.
64 *New York Times,* September 19, 1931.

volvement of the Kellogg Pact in this matter."[65] Stimson gave a cautious reply. He was "insufficiently informed of the facts of the situation," but he did think it was advisable that no steps be taken that would arouse Japanese nationalistic feeling "against the Foreign Office." The Department of State was "watching with concern the development of events" and the relationship of these events "to the Nine-Power Treaty and to the Kellogg-Briand Peace Pact."[66]

On September 23, Norman H. Davis, at Geneva, became a little hysterical over the situation in Manchuria and tried to talk with President Hoover over the trans-Atlantic telephone. Secretary Stimson was placed on the line and Davis expressed his fears that the situation in the Far East was "loaded with dynamite" which might explode any moment if great care were not exercised by the statesmen of the great powers. Davis was full of suggestions. First, he believed that it was important for the "United States to take a very drastic step and to come and sit on the Council of the League and help compose this thing." Next he would have the Department of State support a resolution calling for a committee of investigation to be appointed by the Council for the purpose of looking into the Manchurian incident.

Stimson was cold to both of these proposals. He was not in favor of authorizing an American representative to sit with the Council of the League and he would "not dream" of appointing any representative to sit with the proposed committee of investigation.[67]

Although Stimson was not ready to adopt these far-reaching proposals of Norman Davis, he was anxious to give ample evidence of a co-operative spirit, so on September 24 he sent some identic notes to China and Japan in which the ardent hope was voiced that they would refrain from "activities" that would prejudice a pacific settlement of the Manchurian dispute.[68] After waiting ten days for this note to take effect, Stimson then advised Drummond to see to it that the League used all "the authority and pressure within its competence" to compel Japan to keep the peace in the Far East. On its part the American Government would "endeavor to reinforce League action and will make clear that the American Government's interest in the matter has not been lost."[69]

The bombing of Chinchow by Japanese planes on October 8 pro-

[65] Hugh Wilson to Secretary Stimson, Geneva, September 21, 1931. *Foreign Relations, 1931*, III, 22.

[66] Secretary Stimson to Hugh Wilson, September 22, 1931. *Ibid.*, p. 26.

[67] Memorandum of a trans-Atlantic telephone conversation among Secretary Stimson, Norman H. Davis, and Hugh Wilson, September 23, 1931. *Ibid.*, pp. 43–47.

[68] Secretary Stimson to Minister Johnson and to the United States chargé d'affaires in Tokyo, September 24, 1931. *Ibid.*, p. 58.

[69] Secretary Stimson to the consul at Geneva (Gilbert), October 5, 1931. *Ibid.*, pp. 116–17.

voked Stimson to take more vigorous action to preserve peace. He now began to consider the employment of sanctions against Japan in order to compel her to "respect the great peace treaties."[70] On October 10 he secured the President's approval of a suggestion to have an American representative participate in all the sessions of the League Council which dealt with the enforcement of the Kellogg-Briand Pact. Next, he authorized Prentiss Gilbert, American Consul at Geneva, to take part in these sessions if an invitation were extended to him. Before he could receive an answer from the League in this regard, he requested Gilbert to place before Sir Eric Drummond the suggestion that the Council invoke the Kellogg Pact.[71]

Drummond neatly countered by indicating how effective it would be for the United States to take this step, but Stimson insisted that the League should take the initiative in invoking the pact. The American Government should "keep in the background" and not serve as a lightning rod that would invite the full discharge of Japanese resentment. With reference to Japanese assurances of good will towards the United States, he applied to them the vulgar but descriptive epithet—"eyewash."[72]

On October 17, with Mr. Gilbert in attendance, the Council of the League decided upon a joint invocation of the Kellogg-Briand Pact. After Stimson had been assured that the League would take action he sent (October 20) identic notes to China and Japan reminding them of their obligations under the pact.[73] The Council took the further step (October 24) of calling upon Japan to "begin immediately with the withdrawal of its troops into the railway zone" of the South Manchuria Railway. This withdrawal should be completed by November 16.[74]

Edwin Neville, the American chargé at Tokyo, regarded this directive of the League as inopportune and ineffective and he requested the Department of State to refrain from giving it any support. American co-operation in this particular case would "weaken American influence in Japan" and would not "accomplish anything" in settling the Manchurian dispute.[75]

Stimson paid scant attention to this advice. On November 5, Am-

---

[70] Henry L. Stimson, *The Far Eastern Crisis: Recollections and Observations* (New York, 1936), pp. 51–57.

[71] Secretary Stimson to Consul Gilbert, October 10, 1931. *Foreign Relations, 1931,* III, 154.

[72] Memorandum of a trans-Atlantic telephone conversation between Secretary Stimson and Prentiss Gilbert, October 16, 1931. *Ibid.,* pp. 203–7.

[73] Secretary Stimson to the American Minister in China and to the American chargé d'affaires in Japan, October 20, 1931. *Ibid.,* p. 275.

[74] *Foreign Relations, Japan: 1931–1941,* I, 29–30.

[75] Chargé in Japan (Neville) to Secretary Stimson, Tokyo, November 4, 1931. *Foreign Relations, 1931,* III, 366–67.

bassador Forbes handed to the Japanese Foreign Minister a memorandum which closely followed the phraseology of the League resolution
with the exception that no time limit was set for the withdrawal of the
Japanese troops.[76] On November 19 he fired another shot in this barrage against Japan. In a conversation with Debuchi he warned him
that the American Government might publish the diplomatic correspondence that had passed between the Foreign Office and the Department of State and thus mobilize world opinion against the actions of
Japanese militarists.[77]

After this thrust against Japan, Stimson once more turned to the
League and explained the basis of American action. Pressure from
President Hoover had softened the tone of his notes. When Stimson in
Cabinet meetings began to talk about coercing Japan by all "means
short of actual use of armed force," the President informed him that
"this was simply the road to war itself and he would have none of it."[78]

Stimson, therefore, instructed Ambassador Dawes to tell certain
members of the League Council that, while the American fleet would
not take any adverse action against any embargo that would be enforced
against Japanese commerce, it should be clearly understood that the
United States would not participate in any economic sanctions. America
would assist in mobilizing public opinion against Japan and would refuse to recognize "any treaties that were created under military force."[79]

Under the impact of this American pressure, Shidehara desperately
strove to modify the policy of the militarists in Tokyo and on November 27 he was able to put a brief stop to the Manchurian advance. But
the Japanese Cabinet fell two weeks later and these futile peace gestures
ceased. On January 2, 1932, Chinchow was captured and the Japanese
conquest of Manchuria was complete.

Before this took place Elihu Root, thoroughly alarmed by the active
measures Secretary Stimson was taking to stop Japanese expansion in
Manchuria, wrote the Secretary a long letter of protest. Root had been
Secretary of State from 1905 to 1909 and had negotiated the Root-
Takahira Agreement that had given Japan a green light in Manchuria.
He now warned Stimson about "getting entangled in League measures
which we have no right to engage in against Japan." He also alluded

76 Memorandum of a conversation between Ambassador Forbes (Tokyo) with the
Japanese Minister for Foreign Affairs (Shidehara), November 5, 1931. *Ibid.*, pp. 375–
80.

77 Memorandum by the Secretary of State of a conversation with the Japanese Ambassador (Debuchi), November 19, 1931. *Japan: 1931–1941*, I, 44–46.

78 Ray L. Wilbur and Arthur M. Hyde, *The Hoover Policies* (New York, 1937),
p. 603.

79 Memorandum of a trans-Atlantic telephone conversation between Secretary Stimson and Ambassador Dawes, November 19, 1931. *Foreign Relations, 1931*, III, 488–98.

to Japan's special interests in Manchuria through a long period of years, and spoke of the need for Japan to protect herself in a political sense against "the dagger aimed at her heart."

Root was a realist who did not want war with Japan. Stimson was a pacifist who loved peace so much he was always ready to fight for it. He wholeheartedly subscribed to the slogan—perpetual war for perpetual peace. In his answer to Root he expressed the belief that his intervention in the Manchurian muddle was necessary to save the whole structure of the peace treaties. He was the Atlas on whose stooping shoulders world peace was precariously balanced. A "new advance by Japan" would "undoubtedly create much adverse and even hostile sentiment in this country and much pressure upon us for some kind of action." As a man of action he was not inclined to draw back into any shell of neutrality.[80]

Perhaps his best policy would be to strive for some kind of tripartite (Britain, France, and the United States) pressure upon Japan. After acquainting the governments of these powers with the outline of this new offensive against Japan, and without waiting for formal replies to his overture, he dispatched identic notes (January 7) to China and Japan in which he developed the theory of nonrecognition. The American Government would not recognize any agreement that "would impair the treaty rights of the United States or its citizens in China, including those which relate to the sovereignty, the independence, or the territorial and administrative integrity of the Republic of China or to the international policy relative to China, commonly known as the Open-Door policy."[81] This nonrecognition would also extend to any changes in the Far East which had been effected by "means contrary to the covenants and obligations of the Pact of Paris."

After firing this sharp volley in the direction of Japan, Stimson waited for the response of the British Government. He was confident that the Foreign Office would answer with a shot that would be heard around the world. This expectation was fulfilled but the guns of the Foreign Office blasted at American suspicions of Japanese policy in the Far East: "His Majesty's Government have not considered it necessary to address any formal note to the Japanese Government on the lines of the American Government's note."[82] The attitude of the Foreign Office was praised by the London *Times* which remarked: "Nor does it seem the immediate business of the Foreign Office to defend the 'administra-

[80] Secretary Stimson to Elihu Root, December 14, 1931, Strictly Personal and Confidential, Box 129, Root Papers, Library of Congress.

[81] Secretary Stimson to Ambassador Forbes, January 7, 1932. *Japan: 1931–1941*, I, 76.

[82] The chargé in Great Britain (Atherton) to Secretary Stimson, London, January 9, 1932. *Foreign Relations, 1932*, III, 19.

tive integrity' of China until that integrity is something more than an ideal. It did not exist in 1922 and it does not exist today."[83]

Delighted with this latest demonstration of the absurdity of the idea that Britain and the United States usually followed a parallel policy in the Far East, the Japanese Foreign Office, on January 16, 1932, sent a note to Stimson which used "almost literally" the phraseology of the critical paragraphs in the London *Times*.[84]

Stung by these words of calculated impudence, Stimson reached for the trans-Atlantic telephone and began a series of conversations with Sir John Simon, the British Foreign Secretary. He was exceedingly anxious to secure British co-operation in a joint invocation of Article 7 of the Nine-Power Treaty.

Sir John was not accustomed to discuss state secrets over the telephone, and at Geneva he had to "receive one of the calls in a booth at the League of Nations." He had not been able to "arrange for stenographic notes to be taken of the conversations, and so could not study the precise words of what had been said and weigh their implications."[85] The whole thing was so informal and unusual that Sir John refused to respond to Stimson's strongly worded importunities, and the Secretary of State finally realized that the old slogan "Hands across the Sea" is the exclusive property of the Foreign Office. It is properly used only when Uncle Sam can give John Bull a lift.[86]

For the next two months Stimson had to stand responsible for the nonrecognition policy without any help from Great Britain, but there were certain factors that slowly pushed the Foreign Office into line with the Department of State. Britain had extensive business interests in Shanghai, and when the Japanese, on January 28, 1932, opened an offensive against the Chinese Nineteenth Route Army stationed in that city, the situation took on a new aspect. The Foreign Office, however, did not at once take action to avert this threat to British big business. Stimson for a while had to continue his one-man offensive against Japan. On February 23 this took the form of a long letter to Senator Borah, chairman of the Senate Committee on Foreign Relations. Once more the nonrecognition theory was given vehement expression and it was extended to cover violations of the Nine-Power Treaty as well as of the Kellogg-Briand Pact.[87]

---

[83] January 11, 1932.

[84] Robert Langer, *Seizure of Territory* (Princeton, 1947), p. 60.

[85] Raymond Gram Swing, "How We Lost the Peace in 1937," *Atlantic Monthly,* CLXXIX (February 1947), 34.

[86] Memoranda of trans-Atlantic conversations between Secretary Stimson and Sir John Simon, February 15, 24, 1932. *Foreign Relations, 1932,* III, 335–40, 341–45, 432–36.

[87] Secretary Stimson to Senator Borah, February 23, 1932. *Japan: 1931–1941,* I, 83–87.

The Stimson letter met with a cool reception in Tokyo. Ambassador Forbes reported that the British and French ambassadors felt that its effect had been "extremely injurious." It had certainly tended to silence "for the present the influences working from within for the correction of this difficult situation." Many newspapers looked upon the letter as "distinctly provocative," and in the talk of "another world war" the United States was regarded as "the probable enemy." The British and French ambassadors expressed the strong hope that Stimson would cease writing letters of such a "provocative nature," and Ambassador Forbes frankly indorsed their viewpoint.[88]

But Stimson, clad in his usual armor of righteousness, gave little heed to this sharp shaft from his own ambassador in Tokyo. Time and British big business were working on his side. On February 16 the League Council sent an appeal to Japan for the purpose of dissuading her from making a full-scale attack upon Shanghai. In this appeal Japan was pointed out as the responsible party in the Far Eastern conflict, and she was reminded of her obligations under the Covenant of the League of Nations and under the provisions of the Nine-Power Treaty.[89] On March 11 the Assembly of the League took a bolder step when it adopted a resolution which declared that it was "incumbent upon the members of the League of Nations not to recognize any situation, treaty or agreement which may be brought about by means contrary to the Covenant of the League of Nations or to the Pact of Paris."[90]

Secretary Stimson had at last maneuvered the League of Nations into a formal approval of the nonrecognition theory. It was a fateful step along a "dead-end" street of fear and frustration, and its inevitable consequence was America's involvement in World War II.[91]

---

[88] Ambassador Forbes to Secretary Stimson, Tokyo, February 27, 1932. *Foreign Relations, 1932,* III, 457–58.

[89] Irving S. Friedman, *British Relations With China, 1931–1939* (New York, 1940), p. 33.

[90] The consul at Geneva (Gilbert) to Secretary Stimson, Geneva, March 15, 1932. *Foreign Relations, 1932,* III, 585–86. Westel W. Willoughby, *The Sino-Japanese Controversy and the League of Nations* (Baltimore, 1935), pp. 299–301.

[91] The dangers that were inherent in the Far Eastern situation were discussed at length by the British Prime Minister (Ramsay MacDonald) in a conversation with Mr. Atherton, the American chargé d'affairs at London, on April 4, 1932: "In substance the Prime Minister said that it was foreseen some time ago by critics of the League that members might well be actually in a state of war without a formal declaration of war, in order to escape the penalties placed upon war by the Covenant. This was in fact what had happened in the present instance, although the Chinese had almost 'put the fat in the fire.' During the last Far Eastern discussions in Geneva the Chinese had drawn up a resolution which a League representative agreed formally to present. This resolution declared that Japan by her actions was in fact in a state of war with members of the League.

"The League representative showed this resolution to Sir John Simon who said that he would have nothing to do with it and that if it were presented he would deny all knowledge of it. Eventually the resolution just escaped presentation, but the Prime Minister said that this showed how near Japan had been to open conflict with members of the League." 793.94/4965. *Confidential file,* MS, Department of State.

IV

Secretary Stimson Produces a Pattern of War

a. *American Press Opinion of the Stimson Doctrine*

WHEN SECRETARY STIMSON boldly announced on January 7, 1932, his nonrecognition policy, he felt confident that he could rely upon a large section of the American press for support. The old tradition of isolation had been slowly and steadily undermined by ardent one-worlders who were desperately anxious for America to bear a larger share of the burdens that the World War had thrust upon the weakened back of Europe. The New York press had led the assaults of these journalistic saboteurs with the *Times* as the leader of the offensive. Stimson had carefully watched this conflict and had come to the conclusion that the old American order had collapsed. His nonrecognition note would serve as a stirring call to all internationalists to build a new political edifice whose ample dimensions would require enormous supplies of American materials and whose maintenance would impose a staggering load upon the American taxpayer.

The *New York Times* was quick to answer the summons of Mr. Stimson. It candidly admitted that in former years "frank communication by Mr. Stimson would have been regarded as indelicate and undiplomatic."[1] In the new international era that had just been ushered in, the Stimson note was a cordial invitation for concerted action against the wickedness that had raised its ugly head in Manchuria. The Richmond *Times-Dispatch* gave expression to this sentiment and was certain that the doctrine of nonrecognition would make Japan a "pariah nation."[2] The *Pittsburg Post-Gazette* echoed this viewpoint[3] with the *Los Angeles Times* humming the same blithe melody.[4] The *Indianapolis News* stressed the "timeliness" of the Stimson note,[5] while the *Boston Daily Globe* burst into ecstasy that Stimson had given voice to the sentiment that "every friend of peace throughout the world has been awaiting."[6]

The *Cleveland Plain Dealer* was outspoken in its praise of the policy expressed by Secretary Stimson,[7] while the *Chicago Daily News*[8] and the *Kansas City Star*[9] added their voices to this chorus of approval. But

[1] January 9, 1932.
[2] January 12, 1932.
[3] February 18, 1932.
[4] January 9, 1932.
[5] January 9, 1932.

[6] January 8, 1932.
[7] January 9, 1932.
[8] January 9, 1932.
[9] January 8, 9, 1932.

the *Chicago Tribune* could not approve the manner in which the Secretary of State had moved in concert with the League of Nations, and it feared that we had given "Japan a grievance which could have been avoided."[10] The *Philadelphia Record* and the *Washington Post* also recorded apprehensions concerning any intimate association with the League.[11]

In the South the *Atlanta Constitution* threw out a hint of warning. "The United States is treading on dangerous ground in becoming involved in the Manchurian situation to the extent of joining other nations in notes of warning to Japan which are tantamount to threats. It is none of our business until some of our rights have been infringed upon."[12]

The Hearst press was quick to point out the dangers of the knight errantry of Mr. Stimson: "The Asiatic treasure house need not agitate us or the State Department. Japan is only doing in Manchuria what the United States did when it took Texas away from Mexico.[13] The *New York Daily News* was equally critical: "When Frank B. Kellogg was Secretary of State he used to be known as Meddlesome Mattie. In justice to Mr. Kellogg it must now be admitted that never in his palmiest days did he equal Secretary of State Henry L. Stimson as a giver of advice."[14]

Some periodicals representing the so-called "liberal elements" in the East were sharply critical of the Stimson note. The *New Republic* thought that the doctrine of nonrecognition would be as "effective as saying to a man who has burned down his neighbor's house: 'I refuse to take cognizance of the conflagration and shall continue to send letters to the old address.' " The implication of war was clearly recognized. "If Mr. Hoover and Secretary Stimson persist in this course and Japan does not yield, we are likely to be faced with the bald choice of fighting or suffering a thumping diplomatic defeat."[15]

The Communist Party organ, the *Daily Worker,* was certain that the Stimson policy had the ultimate aim of crushing the communist movement in China. On February 22 the *Daily Worker* published a manifesto addressed to the American working class: "Workers! War in the Far East means a war against the toiling masses of the world! It means the danger of a world war in the interests of the profiteers! Hands off China! Defend the Soviet Union!"[16]

When the crisis in the Far East became more acute with the Japanese

[10] January 9, 1932.
[11] January 9, 1932.
[12] January 9, 1932.
[13] The *San Francisco Examiner*, January 10, 1932.
[14] January 8, 1932.
[15] January 27, 1932.
[16] January 9, February 20–23, 1932.

attack upon Shanghai (January 28), American press opinion reached a higher pitch of excitement. College professors who are so often invincible in peace and invisible in war, rushed to the linotype front and began firing verbal barrages at the Japanese Government. At Harvard this professorial pugnacity was especially apparent. President Lowell and twenty members of his faculty organized a sniping party which raked the Japanese position from every angle. Lowell was especially anxious to have the League of Nations impose economic sanctions upon the wayward men of Nippon, and he nursed the hope that the American Government would support this action with enthusiasm and efficiency.[17] From Princeton came a demand that President Hoover take appropriate action "regardless of material cost or political position."[18] Cornell and Johns Hopkins universities added to this babble for a boycott,[19] and then President Lowell and Newton D. Baker sponsored a giant petition of college presidents and professors in which a strident note was sounded in favor of collective economic pressure upon Japan.[20]

It was not long before the Committee on the Far Eastern Crisis took an active part in this pastime of heckling Japan. Their main contribution was a petition with some ten thousand signatures, and Professor Tyler Dennett became their spokesman in a statement that contained a dire warning that unless the Japanese march into Manchuria was effectively checked, civilization itself would be dragged back "toward the Dark Ages."[21]

In the South the Louisville Courier-Journal and the Raleigh News and Observer were strongly in support of these petitions for economic sanctions.[22] In other sections of the country the Boston Herald, the Milwaukee Journal, and the Cleveland Plain Dealer stressed the same viewpoint.[23] The Scripps-Howard chain of newspapers expressed "hearty agreement" with the spirit of these petitions but issued a warning that the Department of State should secure definite assurances of Anglo-French co-operation before taking any positive steps towards the application of economic pressure upon Japan.[24]

It was soon evident, however, that these voices in favor of economic sanctions were lost in the chorus of disapproval that swelled throughout the land. The New York Sun denounced sanctions as an "invitation to

[17] Christian Science Monitor, February 18, 1932.
[18] New York Times, February 4, 1932.
[19] Ibid., February 28, 1932.
[20] New York Times, February 22, 1932.
[21] Ibid., February 26, 1932.
[22] February 21, 24, 1932.
[23] February 18, 20, 21, 1932.
[24] New York World-Telegram, February 22, 1932.

war."[25] The *Herald-Tribune* compared the proposed boycott to poison gas which could be aimed in the direction of the enemy but which might be blown back in the faces of its sponsors.[26] Walter Lippmann, writing in the *Herald-Tribune,* feared that further pressure upon Japan might lead to war: "The idea of war should be renounced clearly and decisively, even to the point of evacuating American citizens from the theater of war if that is deemed necessary."[27]

The *New York Daily News* was vehement in its denunciation of the petitions in favor of sanctions: "We hope that the American people will insist that their government . . . pay no attention to this foolish and provocative petition of Mr. Baker and the assorted college presidents."[28] The New York *Evening Post* struck a similar note: "There seems to us something wrong in the fact that a handful of doctrinaire citizens can thus go about framing diplomatic proposals that may get the rest of the United States into war."[29]

In Philadelphia the *Evening Bulletin* entered a spirited protest against the boycott;[30] the *Record* expressed the view that there had never been a more "thoughtless and dangerous movement" in the long record of American history;[31] while the *Public Ledger* pointed out that an effective boycott would be a prelude to war against Japan.[32] The *Boston Evening Transcript* was fearful that President Lowell would have the United States assume the role of policeman "of the universe,"[33] and the *Washington Post* emphasized the perils of such a role: "The proposed commitment would involve the United States in foreign entanglements that might cost the lives of an untold number of American sons."[34]

The Frank E. Gannett chain of newspapers in upstate New York was sharply hostile to the idea of economic sanctions,[35] with the Hearst press warmly supporting the same viewpoint.[36] In the Middle West the *Chicago Tribune* feathered some sharp shafts for American pacifists who were "running amuck." The "Ph.D.'s and the Pacifists" were getting America into a most dangerous position.[37] The *Detroit Free Press*

[25] February 23, 1932.
[26] March 19, 1932.
[27] February 26, 1932.
[28] February 21, 1932.
[29] February 22, 1932.
[30] February 23, 1932.
[31] February 27, 1932.
[32] February 24, 1932.
[33] February 18, 1932.
[34] February 24, 1932.
[35] Rochester *Democrat and Chronicle*, February 26, 1932.
[36] *Washington Times*, March 7, 1932.
[37] March 9, 1932.

regarded the boycott movement as "futile, criminal and dangerous,"[38] while the *Cincinnati Enquirer* thought that the "United States should attend strictly to her proper business."[39] In the Far West the Spokane *Spokesman Review* had an editorial with the descriptive title: "Are They Itching for Another War?"[40] The *San Francisco Examiner* matched this editorial with a flashy one of its own: "Baker's Japanese Boycott a Sure Way to War."[41]

The "liberal press" was openly hostile to the imposition of economic sanctions against Japan. The *Nation* believed that a boycott was "too explosive a device to be trifled with,"[42] and it carried in its columns an able article by Professor Edwin M. Borchard who expressed the firm conviction that "there is no peace in such a program.[43] The *New Republic* had nothing but sharp criticism for anything approaching a boycott. America could not "co-operate with the League in an effort to discipline Japan without going to war."[44]

The business press had no hesitation in joining this outcry against economic pressure upon Japan. The *Commercial and Financial Chronicle* thought that the demand in certain quarters for economic sanctions was one that should be "both reprobated and deplored."[45] *Bradstreet's* denounced the "loose talk" about a boycott,[46] while other business periodicals like the *Journal of Commerce* and *Commerce and Finance* echoed these critical remarks.[47]

This barrage of criticism made little impression upon Secretary Stimson who continued his policy of baiting Japan. He persuaded the President to send the fleet to the Pacific during the winter months of 1931–32 where it engaged in elaborate maneuvers between California and the Hawaiian Islands. This show of strength apparently nerved the Assembly of the League of Nations on March 11, 1932, to adopt a cautious nonrecognition resolution.[48] But this belated action had slight influence upon Japan's policy in Manchuria. Although the Japanese Government had signed on May 5 an agreement that led to the withdrawal of her armed forces from Shanghai, no effort was made to move out of Manchuria. The Stimson doctrine had not only failed to stem the Japanese tide in North China but it was producing an anti-American sentiment that would make the maintenance of good relations a difficult task. To Japanese statesmen it seemed apparent that the situation in the Far East presaged an inevitable conflict between capitalism and com-

38 February 21, 1932.   43 March 9, 1932.
39 February 21, 1932.   44 February 10, March 9, 1932.
40 February 23, 1932.   45 February 27, 1932.
41 February 25, 1932.   46 March 5, 1932.
42 March 9, 1932.   47 February 24, March 9, 1932.
48 Robert Langer, *Seizure of Territory* (Princeton, 1947), pp. 62–66.

munism, and they could not understand why the Department of State insisted upon following a policy which might preclude Japanese assistance in this struggle. In this regard the words of Admiral Toyoda had special significance. In a letter to Ambassador Forbes he commented on the serious condition of affairs in China and then expressed the opinion that the Pacific area would witness some of the more important clashes between capitalism and communism. The nature of this conflict would exclude any idea of compromise:

We, or our near posterity, will have to decide between Sino-Russian communism or the Anglo-Saxon capitalism. If China should fall under the rule of communism, and if Japan keep up her present policy, which she certainly will, the chance is she will be forced to play the role of Iki and Tsushima as the advance posts of the Anglo-Saxon capitalism.[49]

b. *Stimson Helps to Push Japan out of the League*

Stimson always closed his eyes to any evidence of the real conflict of interests in the Far East, and he completely ignored the wise words of Admiral Toyoda. He was bent upon castigating Japan for her defensive moves in Manchuria which in his eyes were merely part of a program of expansion. On April 4 he had a long talk with the Japanese Ambassador (Debuchi) in which he sharply criticized the manner in which Japan had extended her frontiers in Manchuria. His main purpose in holding this conversation was to "take a pretty stiff position" with Debuchi, so "that he could not report to his government that I had shown any signs of yielding to the steps that they were taking or the arguments they were putting up."[50] Some weeks later (June 10) Debuchi had to listen to another long lecture on the misdeeds of his government in North China. The Foreign Office was evidently laying plans to extend recognition to the puppet government of Manchukuo, and as a preliminary step in this direction it had given orders for the assumption of control over the Chinese Maritime Customs Service within that area. This step was viewed by Secretary Stimson with "great concern."[51]

As one means of coping with the Japanese advance in North China, Stimson sent Joseph C. Grew to Tokyo as the American Ambassador. When Grew arrived in Japan in June 1932, the press was friendly and the Emperor was as agreeable as Mr. Grew's deafness permitted him to

[49] Admiral Tejiro Toyoda to Ambassador William Cameron Forbes, Tokyo, March 3, 1932. 793.94/4877, *Confidential file*, MS, Department of State.

[50] Memorandum by the Secretary of State, April 4, 1932. 793.94/4968, MS, Department of State.

[51] Memorandum by the Secretary of State, June 10, 1932. 693.002 Manchuria/77, MS, Department of State.

be. But the shadows of the Manchurian adventure fell across the threshold of the American Embassy and Grew soon realized that they would probably deepen and lengthen despite all his efforts to banish them with the bright light of some new Japanese-American understanding.

The main barrier across the road to friendly relations was the Stimson doctrine itself. The Japanese Government was determined to recognize Manchukuo in defiance of adverse opinion in the United States and in Europe. Secure control over North China appeared to Japanese statesmen, regardless of party affiliations, as a national necessity. As a source of essential raw materials and as a market for manufactured goods, Manchuria had special importance for Japan. Presidents Theodore Roosevelt and Woodrow Wilson had been willing to regard certain portions of North China as a Japanese sphere of influence, and the language of the Root-Takahira and the Lansing-Ishii agreements was so vaguely fertile that Japanese aspirations had enjoyed a rapid growth. Theodore Roosevelt, after boldly plucking the Panama pear, could not turn a deaf ear to Japanese pleas for a bite of Manchurian melon. And Woodrow Wilson, deep in his preparations for a crusade against wicked Germany, could not look too closely into Japanese motives in Manchuria. Encouraged by these friendly gestures of American Presidents, Japanese armies moved into many parts of North China. When Stimson suddenly flashed a red light of warning against any further advance, the Japanese Government made no real effort to obey the signal. Their Manchurian machine had gained too much momentum to be stopped by an American traffic cop who merely blew a tin whistle of nonrecognition.

The efforts of European statesmen were just as futile as those of Secretary Stimson. The Lytton Commission, appointed under the terms of the League resolution of December 10, 1931, reached Tokyo on February 29, 1932, for a series of conferences with Japanese statesmen and with representatives of various Japanese organizations. From April 20 to June 4 the commission took testimony in Manchuria, and then returned to Tokyo for a brief sojourn. It finally moved to Peiping to complete the task of drafting a formal report.

While the commission was in Tokyo, Major General Frank R. McCoy talked freely to Ambassador Grew. He assured the ambassador that the commission was of the opinion that Japan's action in Manchuria was based on two false premises: the argument of self-defense and the argument of self-determination. The commission was also convinced that the erection of a puppet state like Manchukuo "would result in a festering sore which will inevitably lead to future wars." Although Mr. Grew shared these viewpoints, he warned Secretary Stimson that any protest from the United States concerning Japanese recognition of Manchukuo would play right into the hands of the military clique in Tokyo. Silence would pay good diplomatic dividends.[52]

But the task of silencing Stimson was as difficult as stopping the rush of waters over Niagara Falls. He was so full of righteous indignation that he had to deliver a new blast against Japan on August 8 in an address before the Council on Foreign Relations (New York City). As Grew had anticipated, the reaction in Japan to this latest Stimson attack was widespread and bitter. Its violence caused Grew to warn Stimson that "we should have our eyes open to all possible future contingencies."[53] The policy of constantly pricking Japan might eventually lead to a dangerous outburst.

On September 3, Grew sent another telegram of warning. The Japanese Government firmly intended to see "the Manchuria venture through." The Japanese public was convinced that the "whole course of action in Manchuria is one of supreme and vital national interest," and it was determined to meet, if necessary with arms, "all opposition."[54] After sending this telegram to the Department of State, Grew confided to his *Diary* that Japanese resentment was really focused upon only one American—Secretary Stimson. Everyone he met in Japan was "thoroughly friendly" and his personal relations with Japanese officials were of "the best." But Stimson had enraged all Japan with his policy of constant hostile pressure.[55] It was not hard for a diplomat to see the inevitable result of these tactics.

In some circles in Japan the hope was expressed that a change in the Administration in Washington would bring a change in Far Eastern policy. But Stimson still had some six months to serve as Secretary of State, and there was the ominous possibility that during the period he would so firmly fix the pattern of policy that a new Secretary would be unable to alter it. Of one thing everyone in Japan could be certain— Stimson would not recede from the stand he had taken, no matter what the result. America might not be pushed to the point of actual conflict with Japan, but the road to war would be wide open and an invitation to hostilities would be ready for the anxious consideration of the President-elect.

---

[52] Ambassador Grew to Secretary Stimson, Tokyo, July 16, 1932. *Foreign Relations: Japan, 1931–1941*, I, 93–95. On June 21, 1932, Viscount Ishii had made a speech before the America-Japan Society of Tokyo in which he gave assurances that Japan would leave "no stone unturned in order to remove all possible causes of friction with her great neighbor." Shanghai *Evening Post and Mercury*, June 21, 1932.

[53] Ambassador Grew to Secretary Stimson, Tokyo, August 13, 1932. *Japan: 1931–1941*, I, 100.

[54] Ambassador Grew to Secretary Stimson, Tokyo, September 3, 1932. *Ibid.*, p. 102.

[55] Joseph C. Grew, *Ten Years in Japan* (New York, 1944), p. 40.

In order to make sure that this invitation would be no empty affair, Stimson had consented to have Major General Frank R. McCoy serve as a member of the Lytton Commission of Enquiry. If this commission denounced Japanese aggression in North China in acidulous terms, General McCoy would bear a portion of the responsibility for such an indictment.

On October 1, 1932, the report of the Lytton Commission was published in Geneva. It made some interesting admissions. The rapid growth of the Communist Party was briefly described and the inability of Chiang Kai-shek to suppress it was clearly indicated.[56] But nothing was said about Soviet infiltration of Sinkiang and the absorption of Outer Mongolia. Japan was to be the culprit in China, not Russia. In order to prove this point the report expressed in very positive terms the belief that Japan made use of the Mukden Incident of September 18 to carry out a far-reaching plan of expansion in North China. It was admitted that Japan had "special interests" in Manchuria but these interests did not justify the erection of a semi-independent state like Manchukuo which would be under Japanese control. The report therefore recommended that Manchuria should enjoy "a large measure of autonomy" consistent "with the sovereignty and administrative integrity of China."[57]

The report mentioned the fact that the Japanese had erected the new state of Manchukuo on March 9, 1932, and had installed Henry Pu-yi, the boy Emperor of China, as the regent. It did not indicate who was to dethrone the regent or who was to assume the grave responsibility of pushing the large Japanese Army out of Manchukuo and thus permit Manchuria to resume its former status. Indirectly, this assertion of continued Chinese sovereignty over the Three Provinces was an endorsement of the Stimson nonrecognition principle. The commission conveniently closed its eyes to the fact of Japanese control over Manchukuo and assumed that the farce of nonrecognition would bring Japan to heel. It was a little shocked when Japan formally recognized Manchukuo on September 15, and Secretary Stimson felt outraged at this defiance of his doctrine.

Two months later (November 19) Matsuoka, the head of the Japanese delegation at Geneva, whispered some warning words to Hugh Wilson and Norman Davis. The hostility of the Japanese public towards the United States was "dangerous." There was a growing belief that several attempts had been made by the American Government to "check Japanese development in Manchuria and to get control of the

---

[56] *Lytton Report* (Washington, 1932), pp. 20–23.
[57] *Ibid.*, p. 130.

railway situation in that area." The large body of influential Japanese opinion that heretofore had been friendly was "rapidly diminishing." The Japanese people had been very patient, but a point had been reached where this quality was no longer a virtue and the repressed irritation against America might break through all bonds with "suddenness and violence."[58]

Matsuoka had spent many years in the United States as a student and was known among the Japanese as "thinking and conducting himself like an American."[59] His words of warning would have had some influence upon the average Secretary of State, but Stimson refused to heed them. He carelessly boasted to Hugh Wilson that he was acquainted with the "personality and methods" of Matsuoka and had anticipated that he would assume the airs of a "clever advocate."[60] If Stimson had been blest with a more perceptive mind, he would have realized that Matsuoka was not indulging in idle threats. His words were freighted with wisdom, but Stimson still clung to the idea that he could beat the Japanese Foreign Minister into submission with the club of nonrecognition. It gave him small concern if the Foreign Minister squirmed under this punishment and if the Japanese press grew violent in its denunciations of his policy. The Japanese would have to take their medicine no matter how bitter it tasted.

To some American publicists the Stimson policy seemed distinctly ill-advised. Raymond L. Buell was sharply critical of the attitude of the Hoover Administration towards Japan. If the United States "in its righteousness attempts to deny Japan the opportunity of obtaining necessary resources by a policy of force, will it lower its tariffs so that Japan may solve its population problems by means of industrialization?" Mr. Buell thought that the government of the United States should take steps to call a tariff "parley" that would consider some adjustment of existing high rates, and as a concession to Japanese opinion it should cease the elaborate naval maneuvers in Pacific waters.[61]

These suggestions of Mr. Buell failed to awaken any favorable response in the Department of State.[62] Stimson was opposed to any cessation of pressure upon Japan. Fortunately, this unfriendly attitude did

---

[58] Secretary Stimson to Ambassador Grew, Washington, November 21, 1932. *Japan and the United States: 1931–1941*, I, 104–5.

[59] Frederick Moore, *With Japan's Leaders* (New York, 1942), pp. 130–31.

[60] Secretary Stimson to Hugh Wilson, November 21, 1932. *Japan and the United States, 1931–1941*, I, 105.

[61] *New York Herald-Tribune,* November 20, 1932.

[62] Memorandum of the Division of Far Eastern Affairs, November 25, 1932. F/G 711.94/751, MS, Department of State. The memorandum expressed the opinion that a revision of tariff duties in favor of Japanese products would have the unfortunate effect of assisting "the Japanese military to retain their power longer."

not evoke in Japan a correspondingly hostile feeling. Quite the opposite! Japan was anxious to be conciliatory. On December 29 the Japanese Ambassador informed Mr. Hornbeck, chief of the Division of Far Eastern Affairs, that "all the bankers, and merchants and industrialists" were intent upon "cordial and friendly relations with the United States." No one in Japan "would dare to think that war with the United States is possible." In conclusion the ambassador remarked that the "new rapprochement between Russia and China causes the Japanese to look more than ever to the United States for friendship and cordial relations."[63]

In the meantime the League of Nations was giving extended consideration to the implications of the Lytton Report. On December 6 the League Assembly referred the report to a Committee of Nineteen. The representatives of several small nations on this committee were profoundly provoked with Japan because of her military operations in Manchuria. They made up for their military weakness in cascades of strong words of criticism. Stimson's quick ear caught these caustic accents and he repeated them to the Japanese Ambassador. On January 5, 1933, he talked with Debuchi, and after reviewing Japanese disregard of certain treaty obligations, he acidly observed that really there was "no other course" for Japan to follow but "to get out of the League of Nations and the Kellogg Pact."[64]

After reading this stiff lecture to the Japanese Ambassador, Stimson found time to visit Hyde Park on January 9 where he found President-elect Roosevelt in a very receptive mood. He had no trouble in convincing Roosevelt that the Stimson doctrine should be one of the pillars of the foreign policy of the new Administration. Three days later he informed Ambassador Debuchi that the President-elect would adhere to the Stimson policy.[65] On January 16 this news was sent to our diplomatic representatives abroad, and on the following day Roosevelt, at a press conference at Hyde Park, insisted that America must stand behind the principle of the "sanctity of treaties."[66] Party lines in America had disappeared when it came to imposing discipline upon Japan.

On the day following this important announcement, the Japanese

[63] Conversation between Mr. Hornbeck and the Japanese Ambassador, December 29, 1932. F/HS 711.94/758, MS, Department of State.

[64] Conversation between Secretary Stimson and Ambassador Debuchi, January 5, 1933. 793.94/5709, Confidential file, MS, Department of State.

[65] Conversation between Secretary Stimson and Ambassador Debuchi, January 12, 1933. Japan and the United States, 1931–1941, I, 108–9.

[66] New York Times, January 18, 1933. Stimson had already assured the British Foreign Secretary, Sir John Simon, that the President-elect was committed to the Stimson doctrine. Sir John replied, January 14, that the British Government would adhere to the same doctrine. Foreign Relations, 1933, III, 89.

Ambassador had a conversation with Under Secretary of State William R. Castle. After the usual exchange of courtesies, Debuchi ventured the statement that he had planned to discuss "the irritation to Japanese feelings over the fact that our [the American] fleet remained in the Hawaiian Islands." Castle had caught the accent of no compromise with Japan so he coldly remarked that "the disposition of the American fleet was a matter solely for the decision of the American Government." Debuchi quickly conceded this fact and then amicably added that his main desire in this matter was to secure a "diminution of anti-American feeling in Japan" and that the presence of the American fleet in Hawaiian waters "kept this feeling going." Castle "ignored this remark" and then fired another verbal broadside at the retreating ambassador: "I told him it seemed to me that the Japanese were doing everything in their power to stir up anti-Japanese feeling in this country."[67]

It is evident that the prevailing mood in the Department of State was one of thinly veiled hostility towards Japan, and this fact is given additional illustration in a memorandum prepared by Mr. Hornbeck. After alluding to the friction between the United States and Japan, Hornbeck then discusses certain suggestions relative to improving this ominous condition of affairs. It had been suggested "that a meeting should be arranged, preferably at some point between the continental United States and Japan, such as Honolulu, between some prominent American statesman and a prominent Japanese, for example, the Secretary of State and the Japanese Minister for Foreign Affairs." These two statesmen could discuss "fully and frankly the relations between the two countries and effect some arrangement which would tend to assure the maintenance of peace."

This suggestion, which inevitably reminds one of the suggestion made by Prince Konoye in the summer of 1941, was rejected by Mr. Hornbeck because it "would in all probability be abortive" and therefore would do more harm than good. But Secretary Stimson was momentarily intrigued with the idea of this suggested meeting. On the Hornbeck memorandum he made the following endorsement, January 28, 1933: "This is a very useful analysis and I agree with most of it. The only point that I am inclined to disagree with is what I consider its rather ultra-conservatism in the latter portion. I am turning over in my own mind the possibility of a gesture to either immigration or a meeting."[68]

Even if Secretary Stimson had been sincere in his desire to make some

[67] Conversation between William R. Castle and the Japanese Ambassador, January 18, 1933. 793.94/6063, *Confidential file*, MS, Department of State.

[68] Endorsement of Secretary Stimson upon the Hornbeck memorandum, January 28, 1933. 793.94/6063, *Confidential file*, MS, Department of State.

gesture of conciliation towards Japan, it was apparent that time was against him. In a few weeks the Roosevelt Administration would take office and it would be most unusual for an outgoing Secretary of State to take a major diplomatic step which might not be in complete agreement with the policy already outlined by his successor in office after March 4, 1933. At any rate Stimson did nothing to conciliate Japanese statesmen who were now determined to take some radical action at Geneva. The Roosevelt statement at Hyde Park on January 17 in favor of the "sanctity of treaties" failed to make much of an impression upon them. They knew that the British and French empires had been built by the blood, sweat, and tears of millions of persons in conquered countries. Why all this sudden show of international virtue? As Matsuoka sagely remarked: "The Western Powers taught the Japanese the game of poker but after acquiring most of the chips they pronounced the game immoral and took up contract bridge."[69] It was obvious to most Japanese statesmen that the conscience of the Western powers barked only at strangers.

c. Matsuoka Marches Out of the League

At Geneva, Matsuoka was not inclined to listen to lectures in the League Assembly on public morals, and Ambassador Grew on February 23, 1933, informed Secretary Stimson that the Japanese Cabinet was in entire agreement with the viewpoint of their chief delegate. They regarded their position in Manchuria as an essential link in the "life line" of the Japanese Empire. They were determined to fight rather than yield to League pressure.[70] In the face of this resolute Japanese attitude, the League went ahead and on February 24 it formally approved by an overwhelming vote the report of the Committee of Nineteen which had implemented the Lytton Report.[71]

This critical action on the part of the Assembly of the League of Nations provoked an immediate response from Matsuoka. After gravely stating that his government had "reached the limit of its endeavors to co-operate with the League," he marched stiffly from the hall of the Assembly. The rest of the Japanese delegation with the exception of

---

[69] Moore, *op. cit.*, pp. 38–39.

[70] *Japan and the United States: 1931–1941*, I, 110–12. On February 7, 1933, with his tongue in his cheek, Stimson instructed Hugh Wilson, United States Minister at Geneva, to make it clear that he was not in any way attempting "to guide or to influence or prejudice the League in its deliberations." *Foreign Relations, 1933*, III, 153.

[71] Russell M. Cooper, *American Consultation in World Affairs*, pp. 268–69.

Frederick Moore followed Matsuoka. Moore remained for a brief period in his seat while members of the Assembly and the spellbound spectators waited to see what he would do. Growing tired of the strain of being the sole representative of Japan in the Assembly, he slowly walked from the room, realizing all the while that a grave crisis had been reached in world affairs.[72]

Hugh Wilson, representing the United States, was also in the Assembly as Matsuoka walked out. Like Frederick Moore he also realized that a crisis had been reached in world politics, and this crisis he knew had been precipitated by Stimson's nonrecognition policy. In his memoirs, Wilson tells the story of that fateful march of Matsuoka:

The final session of the Assembly remains indelibly printed on my mind. . . . Matsuoka's speech on that day in the Assembly was delivered with a passionate conviction far removed from his usual businesslike manner. He pointed out the danger of pillorying a great nation. He warned that the Assembly was driving Japan from its friendship with the West toward an inevitable development of a self-sustaining, uniquely Eastern position. . . . For the first time the gravest doubts arose as to the wisdom of the course which the Assembly and my country were pursuing. I began to have a conception of the rancor and resentment that public condemnation could bring upon a proud and powerful people, and I began to question, and still do question whether such treatment is wise. . . . Condemnation creates a community of the damned who are forced outside the pale, who have nothing to lose by the violation of all laws of order and international good faith. . . . Not only did such doubts regarding arraignment arise in me, but for the first time I began to question the non-recognition policy. More and more as I thought it over I became conscious that we had entered a dead-end street.[73]

Professor Borchard, of Yale, agreed completely with Hugh Wilson. To him, and to Phoebe Morrison, the doctrine of nonrecognition amounted to

a rather churlish refusal to face unpleasant facts, giving to political judgments a fictitious legal justification. International law makes no place for a doctrine so destitute of constructive value. . . . The doctrine of non-recognition would seem to make no constructive contributions to a disordered world, but on the contrary embodies potentialities for further disequilibrium.[74]

[72] Moore, *op. cit.*, p. 133.

[73] Hugh R. Wilson, *Diplomat Between Wars* (New York, 1941), pp. 279–81.

[74] Edwin M. Borchard and Phoebe Morrison, *Legal Problems in the Far Eastern Conflict* (New York, 1941), pp. 157–78.

To President-elect Franklin D. Roosevelt, however, Stimson looked like some modern Lancelot engaged in a desperate combat with the forces of evil and the doctrine of nonrecognition was a most potent spear. Roosevelt regarded himself as a twentieth-century King Arthur, and his Round Table was crowded with knights who were ready to sally forth and impose a New Deal upon a credulous American public. It was not long before Irvin S. Cobb began to whisper ominously about a Double Deal, but there were few ears that cared to listen to such evil accents.

This New Deal was supposed to have a domestic emphasis, and some of the Roosevelt knights were fearful of far-flung adventures along the distant Far Eastern horizon. Rexford G. Tugwell was not a typical knight because he had in his heart both reproach and fear. He violently reproached his associates for not warning Roosevelt about the obvious dangers of the Stimson doctrine, and he greatly feared that war lurked behind every line of the nonrecognition policy.[75]

Raymond Moley was another Roosevelt favorite who warned his chief against any acceptance of the Stimson doctrine. But the President-elect speedily silenced Moley with the remark: "I have always had the deepest sympathy for the Chinese. How could you expect me not to go along with Stimson on Japan?"[76]

When one reads the colorful columns of Westbrook Pegler's "Fair Enough" and ponders the repeated assertions that the wealth of the Delano family was partly gained from dubious smuggling operations along the coasts of China, it would seem all too true that Roosevelt's roots went very deep into the dark soil of the Orient. The Delano money had helped to furnish him with luxurious living, and it had provided him with the social and financial background that was so helpful to a Presidential aspirant. It is possible that he did feel some spark of gratitude towards the Chinese who had been exploited for his benefit. Of one thing we may be certain: he started his first term as President with a definite suspicion of Japan's policy in North China. This fact was given clear expression during a Cabinet meeting held on March 7, 1933, when the possibility of American involvement in war in the Far East was definitely envisaged.[77] The new Administration was already taking its first steps down the road to war with the Stimson banner of nonrecognition flying high.

[75] Rexford G. Tugwell, *The Stricken Land* (New York, 1947), p. 177.
[76] Raymond Moley, *After Seven Years* (New York, 1939), pp. 94–95.
[77] James Farley MSS, in the possession of Walter Trohan.

d. *President Roosevelt Regards with a Friendly Eye the Principle of Collective Security*

In the development of a detailed critique of the nonrecognition doctrine of Secretary Stimson, it is essential that emphasis be placed upon the dangerous implications that he wished to read into the pious phraseology of the Kellogg-Briand Peace Pact. The general principle of nonrecognition may be traced back, as far as the Department of State is concerned, to numerous diplomatic notes which expressed an ideal Pan-American policy. It received its classic formulation in the well-known note that Secretary Bryan sent to Japan on May 11, 1915, which gave warning that the American Government would not recognize any agreement or understanding between China and Japan which impaired the treaty rights of the United States, or which adversely affected the political or territorial integrity of China or the international policy of the Open Door.[78] The Pact of Paris, and the important treaty (January 5, 1929) which provided for an inter-American court of arbitration, had specifically outlawed war and had given definite support to the nonrecognition policy. They were followed by the Stimson note of January 7, 1932, with respect to the Far East, and by the Declaration of August 3, 1932, in which the United States and eighteen other republics in the New World announced that they would not recognize the validity of territorial acquisitions which might be obtained through conquest.[79] The Hoover Administration was prepared to give substance to these declarations by terminating the imperialistic programs of previous administrations with reference to Latin America. After the withdrawal of American armed forces from Latin America, it was merely a short step to the Roosevelt acceptance in 1936 of the doctrine of *absolute nonintervention* in Latin-American affairs.

But the nonrecognition principle announced by Secretary Bryan in 1915 had no implication of war, and in 1928 there were few persons who believed that the Kellogg-Briand Peace Pact could be used as an instrument to propel nations into war. It took the belligerent eyes of Secretary Stimson to see a martial meaning in the pacific phrases of the Pact of Paris, and it took his aggressive mind to twist the inoffensive

[78] Secretary Bryan to Ambassador Guthrie (Tokyo), May 11, 1915. *Foreign Relations, 1915*, p. 146.

[79] Samuel F. Bemis, *The Latin American Policy of the United States* (New York, 1943). Cf. chaps. 12, 13, 16.

statement of Secretary Bryan (May 11, 1915) into a clarion call to arms.

It was apparent to seasoned diplomats that the manner in which Stimson endeavored to apply the nonrecognition formula was so provocative that war and not peace would be the result of his efforts. The world was not ready to purchase future peace at the price of immediate war. In Tokyo, Ambassador Grew became increasingly dubious with regard to the frenzied actions of Stimson to stop the Japanese advance into Manchuria. It seemed to him that the "peace machinery which the world has been trying . . . to erect these last fourteen years" was basically "unsound." How could statesmen really expect to halt the tides of national ambition by the paper dykes of peace treaties like the Pact of Paris? Could such a pact have stopped the movement that pushed America into conflict with Spain in 1898? Moral sanctions would have little effect upon nations that had completed their blueprints for plunder. And if moral ostracism were "ineffective," how could America "implement the Kellogg Pact?" Certainly not by the force of arms which would be "contrary to the very principle for which the Kellogg Pact stands." Neither the severance of diplomatic relations nor the imposition of economic boycotts would check nations that were moving down the broad highway to war. The future peace of the world could be preserved only by removing the causes of conflict and not by trying to restrict its scope or to soften its impact.[80]

At the same time that Ambassador Grew was recording in his diary these sapient observations, he was writing a dispatch to Secretary Stimson in a very different vein. Japan was essentially a wicked nation with no real understanding of moral obligations. This being so it "would seem that the world was hardly justified in taking for granted that Japan would observe the letter and spirit of international agreements." This "callous disregard of the pledged word" was the "growth of centuries" and could be traced to the fact that in Japan "there was nothing to correspond to the rules of abstract justice contained in the old Roman law." As a result of this lack of knowledge of Roman law the "Japanese naturally do not look upon contracts and agreements as do Occidental peoples."[81]

While Mr. Grew was writing this critical commentary upon the "unmoral" Japanese, his counselor of Embassy, Mr. Neville, was writing an equally caustic memorandum upon the faithless Chinese. It was apparent to him that the Chinese Government had failed to carry out

[80] Grew *Diary*, February 23, 1933; *Ten Years in Japan*, pp. 78–80.

[81] Ambassador Grew to Secretary Stimson, February 21, 1933, 793.94/6026. MS, Department of State.

many of the engagements undertaken at the Washington Conference of 1921–22. Moreover, the menace of Red Russia was growing more formidable every day:

In this atmosphere of distrust and suspicion, aggravated by the world-wide economic collapse and internal problems of industrial and social discontent, the Japanese looked about them. In addition to the normal difficulties in China, the Japanese were subjected to an intense boycott; the situation in Manchuria appeared worse than ever as the Chinese had used borrowed money to operate railways to the detriment of the Japanese line; their various agreements with the Chinese remained unimplemented and in the background was Soviet Russia, apparently once more a Power. The Washington undertakings were unfulfilled, and the Conference called to supplement the Naval Treaty had ignored the actual conditions that Japan had to face. So in 1931 Japan acted alone. . . . The British had acted alone in Shanghai and the British and Americans had acted together at Nanking in 1927. . . . After the Japanese action in September, 1931, the Chinese appealed to the League of Nations, alleging aggression on the part of Japan and asking redress under the Covenant. . . . The Chinese are in no position to bring up any of the Washington settlements. They have defaulted on their obligations thereunder and do not come into court with clean hands.[82]

Secretary Stimson would not have agreed with this indictment of the government of China, and the Division of Far Eastern Affairs continued to needle Japan. On his way home from the debacle at Geneva, Matsuoka passed through the United States and hoped to have a conference with President Roosevelt. When this news came to the Department of State, Mr. Hornbeck immediately wrote a memorandum indicating that it "would be undesirable to have the new President grant Mr. Matsuoka an interview." If he [Matsuoka] were "to speak with the President it would be only natural for the public to assume that Matsuoka had endeavored to convince the President of the justice of the Japanese case."[83] For some reason that is not clear, Mr. Hornbeck believed that the American public should not be placed under the strain of having to follow the arguments of Matsuoka. There was a chance that they might be too cogent and thus defeat the repressive policy of

---

[82] Ambassador Grew to Secretary Stimson, Tokyo, February 24, 1933, with inclosure by Mr. Neville, counselor of the Embassy. 793.94/6031, MS, Department of State.

[83] Memorandum by Mr. Hornbeck, Division of Far Eastern Affairs, February 28, 1933. 811.4611 Japan/24, MS, Department of State. On March 31, 1933, Matsuoka had a brief interview with Secretary Hull. He was "very affable" and "urged that Japan be given time in which to make herself better understood." With reference to this conversation, Mr. Hull remarks: "I was courteous but virtually silent while he was offering these parting remarks." *Foreign Relations, 1933*, p. 264.

the Department of State. As a result of Mr. Hornbeck's advice, Matsuoka did not have an opportunity to present in private the case of Japan
relative to Manchukuo.

While the Department of State was striving to check any conciliatory
gestures in the direction of Japan, the student body of Meiji University,
in Tokyo, was extending to the President-elect their "heartfelt congrat-
ulations" upon his election: "The fact that our Japanese public rejoiced
over your victory, we believe is a clear evidence of the great significance
we are placing upon your Administration. . . . We hope that you will
reweigh the Manchurian troubles and try and comprehend that the cause
is not so simple as one might think."[84]

The Japanese press also expressed an ardent desire that the Roosevelt
Administration would take an understanding view of the Manchurian
situation and thereby lay the basis for "a restoration of friendly relations between the two nations." Matsuoka himself was quite optimistic
with reference to Japanese-American relations. He thought that all talk
of war between the two countries was "ridiculous." If Japan went to
war in the near future, it would be with Soviet Russia, and Matsuoka
expressed the view that in that event "he would not be surprised to see
the United States on Japan's side."

There was no doubt that Japan had no wish for a war with the United
States. Matsuoka was correct in his belief that the logical opponent for
Japan in her next war would be Russia, but logic was not the basis for
the foreign policy of the Roosevelt Administration. The wish that was
closest to Stalin's heart was to involve Japan and the United States in a
war that would remove the Japanese barrier that prevented the Red tide
from overflowing the wide plains of China. The way that wish was
gratified is the story of the succeeding chapters on Japanese-American
relations.

[84] Memorial from the editorial staff of the *Sundai Shimpo,* student publication of
Meiji University, Tokyo, Japan, to President Roosevelt, February 22, 1933. 711.94/
792, MS, Department of State.

V

Secretary Hull Spurns a Japanese
Olive Branch

a. *America Makes a Friendly Bow to League of Nations*

JAPANESE gestures of friendship toward the United States did not evoke any similar action on the part of the United States. It was soon apparent that the Roosevelt Administration was prepared for limited co-operation with the League of Nations that had just censured Japanese conduct in North China. Secretary Hull had no hesitation in accepting an invitation from the League to appoint a representative to participate in the deliberations of the Advisory Committee which would deal with questions concerning the Far East. Hugh Wilson, at Geneva, helped the committee to formulate certain recommendations for the application of the nonrecognition policy to Manchukuo. Secretary Hull gave his approval to these recommendations with a few exceptions. In this indirect manner the Department of State indicated its acceptance of the Stimson policy. It was careful not to emphasize this acceptance with a loud fanfare of explosive notes that had been characteristic of the Stimson practice in 1931–32.

In connection with the problem of disarmament, President Roosevelt showed a definite inclination to work with the League he had so publicly scorned in 1932. During his press conference on May 10, 1933, he candidly admitted that his Administration was ready "to take its part in consultative pacts" which would help to insure "the safety of threatened Nations against war." He regarded this move as a "very considerable advance" over the policy of Secretary Stimson. The State Department was now prepared to move forward to the point of "making its obligations quite definite and authoritative."[1]

This revealing Presidential declaration was followed by a statement of Norman Davis, chairman of the American delegation to the Geneva Disarmament Conference, to the effect that the United States was ready not only to make a "substantive reduction of armaments" but was also willing to consult with other states in case of a real threat to world peace. If the League, as a result of these consultations, should decide to invoke economic sanctions against an aggressor nation, the American

[1] *The Public Papers and Addresses of Franklin D. Roosevelt*, ed. Samuel I. Rosenman (New York, 1938), II, 169 ff.

Government would refrain from "any action tending to defeat such collective effort."[2]

b. *Japan Earmarks Jehol as a Part of Manchukuo*

While the Roosevelt Administration was indicating a co-operative attitude towards the League of Nations, Japanese troops began to move into Jehol. This movement had been anticipated by a Japanese attack upon Shanhaikwan which appeared "designed to shut out from Jehol the Chinese forces recently sent North." From the viewpoint of the British Foreign Office the province of Jehol was "covered by the original proclamation of the Manchukuo state, to which the Governor of the Province was a party." For this reason Sir John Simon, the British Foreign Secretary, was not sure whether the formal incorporation of Jehol into Manchukuo would be regarded "by the League as more than part and parcel of their [the Japanese] action in converting Manchuria into a new state."[3]

It was apparent to Sir John Simon and to Secretary Hull that there was no real central government in China. The Lytton Commission could talk in general terms about this government and could condemn Japan for the erection of Manchukuo, but it was evident to realistic observers that Japan was the only stabilizing force in North China. With China in chaos it had been necessary for Japan to protect her interests against the menacing Red tide of communism and against the outrageous demands of competing Chinese war lords. In Peiping, Ambassador Johnson saw the situation in a clear perspective and informed Secretary Hull that China had "no real national army capable either of making effective the Government's writ throughout the country or of effective resistance under unified control against a modern power despite the fact that over two million men are under arms. They are the tools of rival militarists who have repeatedly plunged the nation into civil war and whose most solemn pledges to support the National Government are usually worthless."[4]

When these Chinese militarists, whose armies had brought devastation to large areas in China, moved into Jehol, the Japanese Government decided to expel them. According to Matsuoka there were more than 100,000 Chinese troops stationed in this territory claimed by Man-

[2] *Peace and War: United States Foreign Policy, 1931–1941* (Washington, 1943), pp. 186–91.

[3] Sir John Simon to Ambassador Mellon, London, January 13, 1933. *Foreign Relations, 1933*, III, 88–90.

[4] Ambassador Johnson to Secretary Hull, Peiping, February 13, 1933. *Foreign Relations, 1933*, III, 171–72.

chukuo. If they did not consent to immediate withdrawal, they would have to be ejected by force.[5]

In the Department of State, the Division of Far Eastern Affairs prepared a special memorandum on the "Possibility of Chinese-Japanese Hostilities in Tientsin-Peiping Area." After discussing the activities of Chinese troops along the frontiers of Manchuria, the memorandum remarks: "The Japanese not unnaturally declare that China's activities in that connection are provocative and, if continued, must be met by Japanese military operations in China proper." In answer to the question about what America should do in this situation, the memorandum continued: "It is believed that there is no initiative which the American Government might advisedly take in this connection. The foreign power which has the most at stake in that area is Great Britain."[6]

While British and French interests were seriously affected by the Japanese advance into North China, it seemed very difficult to secure agreement on the bases of a joint policy. Europe continually turned to the United States for leadership in this Far Eastern crisis, but the Roosevelt Administration refused to crawl far out on a diplomatic limb in the manner that was so characteristic of Secretary Stimson. On April 22 the French Foreign Office indicated to Mr. Marriner, the American chargé d'affaires in Paris, that it would be advisable for the United States, England, and France to "confer with a view of determining what should be done" with reference to the Japanese advance in North China. It was "vital" that the three powers should "act together."[7]

Secretary Hull was not ready to subscribe to a joint policy in the Far East and he was definitely opposed to taking the initiative in this regard. In view of "Great Britain's membership in the League and extensive interests in North China, leadership in any action of the powers in capacity of a go-between should advisedly be left to the British."[8] This decision of Secretary Hull was strongly supported by Mr. Hornbeck, chief of the Division of Far Eastern Affairs. In a penetrating memorandum dealing with the crisis in China he showed that chaos continued to prevail in large areas in that unfortunate country. "China's leaders, both political and military," had not yet "given evidence of having arrived at any position of unity or solidarity among themselves." A "five-fold revolution" was in progress throughout the land and this had prevented the officials from showing any "sign of firmness in terms

[5] Hugh Wilson to Secretary Hull, Geneva, February 13, 1933. *Ibid.,* pp. 174–75.

[6] Memorandum prepared by the Division of Far Eastern Affairs, March 16, 1933. 793.94/6065, *Confidential file,* MS, Department of State.

[7] Mr. Marriner to Secretary Hull, Paris, April 22, 1933. *Foreign Relations, 1933,* III, 286.

[8] Secretary Hull to Ambassador Johnson (China), Washington, April 25, 1933. *Ibid.,* p. 290.

of singleness of purpose and centralization of authority and responsibility on their own part." In the face of this official incapacity it was not worth while to attempt mediation.[9]

The European powers with extensive interests in the Far East were not discouraged by the negative attitude of Secretary Hull relative to co-operation. They kept pressing for some international action to stop the Japanese armies from moving ahead in Manchuria, but the Department of State remained noncommittal. In another memorandum Mr. Hornbeck again defined the policy of the Roosevelt Administration:

The material interests most menaced by the Japanese advance in the area now under attention are British interests. Next, French. The initiative toward concerted action, if to be taken by any of the major powers without reference to the League of Nations, might best be taken by the British Government. Next best, by either the French or the Italians. . . . We have repeatedly stated that initiative should come from them rather than from us. . . . From time to time since September 18, 1931, we have . . . taken the initiative toward inducing action. . . . Very seldom have we had favorable responses from the other major powers concerned.[10]

It was obvious that European and Chinese attempts to draw the United States into some form of concerted action against Japan were futile. Having failed even to elicit from the Secretary of State a note denouncing Japanese aggression in North China, the Chinese Government decided to sign the well-known Tangku Truce of May 31, 1933. At the time the truce was signed, Japanese troops were in secure control of Jehol Province and occupied most of Northeast Hopeh. Under the terms of the agreement (1) Chinese troops were to withdraw from Northeast Hopeh Province. The boundary of this area, subsequently referred to as the "demilitarized zone," extended roughly in a north-west-southeast direction some miles "northeast of the railway connecting Peiping and Tientsin." (2) The Japanese Army was to have the right to conduct inspections to ascertain whether the Chinese Government was fulfilling this stipulation. (3) The Japanese Army was to withdraw to the Great Wall and Chinese police organizations were to undertake the maintenance of order in the "demilitarized zone."[11]

[9] Memorandum by Mr. Hornbeck, chief, Division of Far Eastern Affairs, April 26, 1933. *Ibid.,* pp. 293–94.

[10] Memorandum by Mr. S. K. Hornbeck, May 16, 1933. *Foreign Relations, 1933,* III, 327–28.

[11] Memorandum by Mr. S. K. Hornbeck, July 15, 1937. 793.94/9195, MS, Department of State. In a concluding paragraph of this memorandum Mr. Hornbeck remarks: "The Japanese Army has from time to time put forth claims that there were certain secret agreements embodied in or supplemental to the Tangku Truce, such as provision for through postal, railway and airway communications between North China and Manchuria. Although the Chinese have denied the existence of any secret agreements, actually postal, railway and airway communications have been opened between Manchuria and North China."

The result of the Tangku Truce was the extension of Japanese control, not only over Jehol, but also over Northeast Hopeh Province. While nominally the "policing" of this part of Hopeh Province was entrusted to Chinese forces, it was realized that Japanese authority in that area would be paramount. This arrangement was merely a prelude to the creation in the autumn of 1935, under Japanese direction, of the East Hopeh Anti-Communistic Autonomous Government which will be discussed in another section.

c. *Secretary Hull Rejects Idea of Japanese Good-will Mission*

The fact that Secretary Hull did not issue a statement condemning the Tangku Truce was interpreted by some Japanese statesmen as an indication that the Roosevelt Administration would not continue the hostile attitude toward Japan so often assumed by Secretary Stimson. As early as May 2, Ambassador Grew had a friendly conversation with Matsuoka who "observed that in his opinion the development of good relations between the United States and Japan should be the corner-stone of Japanese policy."[12] In the following month there were indications that the Japanese public shared the feelings of the Foreign Office. When Admiral Montgomery M. Taylor, in command of the United States Asiatic Fleet, paid a visit to Japan, he was greeted with unusual cordiality by everyone. This warm welcome was regarded by the American Embassy as strong evidence of the "marked improvement in the Japanese attitude toward the United States." Japan was turning from Britain to America: "For many years the Japanese have apparently considered the British their best friends in the family of nations. Many of them now have . . . decided that a conflict of commercial interests will always prevent a continuance of their friendship and they are consequently looking to the United States to take the place of their former Allies."[13]

In its earnest desire to improve relations with the United States the Japanese Foreign Office as early as December 1932 had been considering the dispatch of a good-will mission to the United States, and in September 1933 when Ambassador Grew had a formal conversation with Hirota, he found the Foreign Minister in a most friendly mood. Hirota had just succeeded the undemonstrative Uchida, and he made a special effort to convince Grew that the polar star of his policy would be the establishment of cordial relations with the United States. Grew was certain that these assurances were sincere. He discovered it was a

[12] Ambassador Grew to Secretary Hull, Tokyo, May 8, 1933. *Foreign Relations, 1933*, III, 307.

[13] Monthly report of the American Embassy in Tokyo, June, 1933. 894.00 P.R./67, MS, Department of State.

pleasure to meet a Foreign Secretary with whom he could "really talk things out."[14]

The opportunity for a frank discussion of affairs came a few days later when Grew called at the residence of the Foreign Minister. Hirota immediately intimated that he was contemplating the dispatch of a good-will mission to the United States as an evidence of his desire to "develop closer relations between the United States and Japan." Grew at once discouraged such a step. He believed that informal visits by distinguished Japanese statesmen like Prince Tokugawa would accomplish far more than the proposed good-will mission.[15] Secretary Hull agreed with this opinion and he suggested that the best way for Japan to win American friendship was through the removal of any possibility of discrimination against American interests in Manchukuo.[16]

d. *Friction in Far East Points to Eventual Russo-Japanese War*

One of the reasons for this Japanese approach to the United States was the belief that war between Japan and Russia was almost inevitable. By 1933, Outer Mongolia was so completely dominated by Russia that it could be used as a base for further Russian infiltration of North China. The Russian menace to Japanese interests in Inner Mongolia and Manchukuo was assuming clearer outlines each day. In order to meet it with assurance, it would be expedient for Japan to cultivate friendly relations with the United States. The American Government should be able to perceive the dangers of expanding communism and present with Japan a common front against the great enemy of capitalism.

The desire immediate to the heart of Joseph Stalin was some means of preventing any close attachment between the United States and Japan. Such a union could erect an effective barrier against the Red tide that had already rolled into Outer Mongolia and Sinkiang. The fate of China would be decided by the attitude of the United States, and Russia knew that a friendly nod from the United States would weight the scales in her favor.

In the early part of March 1933, Ambassador Grew received from "a reliable Soviet source" an outline of Soviet-Japanese relations. The Embassy's "informant" assured Mr. Grew that Japan was pushing preparations for "a war with the Soviets, with the United States, or with

---

[14] Grew *Diary*, September 18, 1933; *Ten Years in Japan* (New York, 1944), pp. 99–100.

[15] Ambassador Grew to Secretary Hull, October 3, 1933. *Japan: 1931–1941*, I, 123–24.

[16] Secretary Hull to Ambassador Grew, October 6, 1933. *Ibid.*, pp. 125–26.

both." As a bulwark against this threatened war the "Soviet Union badly needs the resumption of diplomatic relations with the United States. It is able, but cannot agree, to repay the old Russian debts owing to American citizens, because to repay one set of debts would make it necessary to repay all." The Russian Government was willing, however, to give economic favors in "return for the cancellation of the old debts."[17]

Four months later the Russian Government made another approach to the United States. M. Bogomolov, the Soviet Ambassador to China, expressed to Ambassador Johnson the opinion that the "absence of friendly relations between Soviet Russia and the United States" made the position of Russia in the Far East "very weak." He then confidentially added that this same absence of friendly relations "was also a factor of weakness in the position of the United States in the Far East." The intimation was very clear: America should resume diplomatic relations with Soviet Russia lest the Japanese Government, in the event of war, would be able to persuade the American public that the armies of Japan were "fighting, not Soviet Russia, but the Soviet regime."[18]

In October 1933, Ambassador Grew sent to the Department of State a careful estimate of the situation in the Far East and came to the conclusion that it was "not unlikely" that Japan was determined "to remove the Russian obstruction from the path of her ambitions at an advantageous moment." This moment might occur in 1935. One of the main reasons for this clash between Japan and Russia was the Japanese fear of communism. "Communistic thought" was regarded in Japan with the utmost aversion and drastic measures were being taken "to stamp it out of the country. Japan considers herself as the bulwark against the spread of communism southward and eastward. Given sufficient provocation, the Japanese could readily be aroused to enter Siberia with the intention of completely destroying a regime which it fears and detests."[19]

This fear of communism, which so strongly colored the relations between Japan and Soviet Russia, was not felt by the Roosevelt Administration which decided to court rather than repel the advances from the Russian Foreign Office. Despite the Russian absorption of Outer Mongolia and the infiltration of Sinkiang, the Department of State refused

[17] Ambassador Grew to Secretary Hull, Tokyo, March 9, 1933. *Foreign Relations, 1933*, III, 228-30.

[18] Memorandum by the United States Minister to China (Johnson), Peiping, July 20, 1933. *Foreign Relations, 1933*, III, 377-78.

[19] Ambassador Grew to the Under Secretary of State (Phillips), Tokyo, October 6, 1933. *Ibid.*, pp. 421-24.

to regard Japan as a bulwark against any further Russian movement into North China. Instead, it decided to recognize Soviet Russia and thus give the cause of communism in China a tremendous boost. On November 16, 1933, recognition was formally extended to Soviet Russia with all its wide implications of a joint policy against Japan. The Roosevelt Administration had made it clear that it had turned its back upon a Japanese bid for a rapprochement based upon a common hostility towards communism. Apparently, in the Far East, Japan, rather than Russia, was the nation to be disciplined.

e. *Japanese Gestures of Friendship are Rebuffed by the U.S.*

The President's decision to favor Russia rather than Japan in the Far East was in defiance of the opinions of some American diplomats in that area. Mr. Edwin L. Neville, counselor of the American Embassy in Tokyo, wrote a long memorandum in October 1933 which gave a realistic summary of the situation in China. It was apparent that the

establishment of the present regime in Manchuria is to place the Japanese and Russians face to face over a long frontier. They need no longer consider any Chinese political interest in that region. . . . So long as the Soviet Government was not a military power the Japanese felt that their national interests in Manchuria were not seriously menaced. When, however, Soviet military prowess was added to the problems which the Japanese had to confront on the mainland, they came to the conclusion that Chinese political complications, at least, should be eliminated in that region. . . . So far as the United States is concerned, there seems no probability that the American people would be willing to engage in any new ventures in this part of the world. . . . In the light of Russian activities in Outer Mongolia and the behavior of Soviet agents in intramural China, it is open to question whether a Russian military victory . . . would be of any value in preserving or restoring the political and administrative integrity of China.[20]

Mr. Neville saw clearly the menace of the Russian advance in North China and indicated the fallacy of any belief that a Russian military victory over the Japanese would restore the political and administrative integrity of China. But Ambassador Grew closed his eyes to the implications that lay behind the Roosevelt Administration's policy of extending recognition to Soviet Russia. In his diary he made the following comments which illustrate his narrow vision: "The President has played

---

[20] Memorandum written by Mr. Edwin L. Neville on the situation in the Far East, Tokyo, October 6, 1933. 793.94/6495, MS, Department of State.

his cards well: he said not a word about Manchuria but started building up the fleet and recognized Soviet Russia; as a result he gets an entirely new and more friendly orientation of Japanese policy toward the United States."[21]

It is quite surprising that Mr. Grew could seriously confide to his diary on November 30 that the Roosevelt recognition of Russia had compelled the Japanese Government to adopt an "entirely new and more friendly orientation" in its policy towards the United States. Since March 1933 the Japanese Government had gone out of its way to conciliate America and to win the approval of the Department of State. It is something of a shock, therefore, to find Ambassador Grew refusing to read the abundant evidence that revealed this Japanese good will and to strike a note of unfairness that was soon sounded with more emphasis by Secretary Hull.

But Hirota was so profuse in his friendly gestures that Grew had to admit that the Foreign Minister was "genuinely doing his best to improve Japan's relations with foreign countries all along the line." In the face of this amicable attitude it would be inexpedient for Secretary Hull to issue any new note with reference to the Stimson doctrine of nonrecognition. America would "sacrifice no principle by silently" maintaining its position.[22]

As the weeks went by, Grew became more and more impressed with the pacific dispositions of Japan's leaders. The Emperor was a man of "mild and peaceful character." Prince Saionji, Count Makino, and many members of the Genro were profoundly imbued with the "horrors of war." The Prime Minister was "more peaceful than bellicose," while Hirota was doing all he could to improve Japan's relations with other countries. At a recent dinner at the Tokyo Club, Baron Hayashi, one of the Emperor's favorites, had voiced with impressive earnestness the desire of the Japanese Government to avoid war: "We want peace."[23]

As an important gesture along this line, Hirota sent a new ambassador to the United States. Hiroshi Saito, who began his duties as ambassador on February 13, 1934, had made an intensive study of American history and was certain that he "knew the American people." His previous experience in consulates on the Pacific Coast and as secretary of the Embassy in Washington had given him an intimate acquaintance with American habitudes of thought. According to Frederick Moore, "no American career diplomatist was his equal."[24]

[21] Grew *Diary*, November 30, 1933; *Ten Years in Japan*, p. 108.
[22] *Ibid.*, January 23, 1934; *ibid.*, pp. 115–16.
[23] *Ibid.*, February 8, 1934; *ibid.*, pp. 117–19.
[24] Frederick Moore, *With Japan's Leaders* (New York, 1942), pp. 70–77.

Saito's first task in Washington was to endeavor to persuade Secretary Hull to negotiate a new treaty with Japan. In the course of these negotiations some formula might be found that would eliminate the causes of future friction between the two countries. At least these conversations would afford an opportunity frankly to discuss all questions at issue. They might lead to a Japanese-American understanding of tremendous importance to the preservation of peace in the Orient. Japan was gravely concerned about Russian objectives in North China. Using this Japanese apprehension as a convenient diplomatic tool, Hull would have a chance to shape the situation in the general direction of American desires. Such a procedure would call for diplomatic skill of a high order. It seems probable that Secretary Hull regarded the task as too difficult for him to handle because he flatly refused to open negotiations looking towards a new treaty with Japan[25] that might have led to a friendly accord.

Hull finally consented to an exchange of diplomatic notes which contained the usual aspirations. Hirota tried to show an amicable spirit by referring to the fact that for eighty years Japan and the United States had "always maintained a relationship of friendliness and cordiality." After alluding to the increasingly important trade relations, he expressed the conviction that "all issues pending between the two nations will be settled in a satisfactory manner." It was the sincere desire of the Japanese Government that a "most peaceful and friendly relation will be firmly established between her and her great neighbor across the Pacific, the United States."

The reply of Secretary Hull was cordial on the surface, but behind each paragraph lurked the shadow of the Stimson doctrine.[26] If he had encouraged lengthy diplomatic conversations in preparation for a formal treaty with Japan, he might have found some answer to the questions that found a thunderous expression in the attack upon Pearl Harbor. His note to Hirota was couched in friendly phraseology, but it dodged the issue of Japanese expansion in North China. Hull knew that this issue was like a small cancer deep in the delicate tissue of Japanese-American relations. It could be removed by the radical procedure of war or it could be checked by the X rays of a friendly understanding. He chose to let it grow until war was the only remedy, and his responsibility for that result is obvious to any student who carefully examines the diplomatic correspondence.

[25] *Ibid.*, pp. 85–86.
[26] Hirota's note was handed to Secretary Hull on Feb. 21, 1934; Hull's note was handed to the Japanese Ambassador on March 3, 1934. *Japan: 1931–1941*, I, 127–29.

f. *Japan Proclaims a Monroe Doctrine for the Far East*

The most important question that disturbed the course of Japanese-American relations was the one dealing with the status of Manchukuo. When the Japanese Foreign Office received word from Saito that Secretary Hull would not discuss in detail the outstanding issues pending between the two countries, Hirota reluctantly realized that it was in vain to hope for any understanding that would remove all causes of friction. He still persisted, however, in making friendly gestures in the direction of the United States. One of the most significant of these was his decision to pay a warm tribute to the memory of Townsend Harris, the first American Consul to Japan. On April 22, Grew was taken on a Japanese destroyer to the port of Shimoda where long lines of school children greeted him with loud shouts of "banzai." There were many speeches that stressed the long tradition of cordial relations between Japan and the United States, and the ceremony impressed Grew as a very "moving one."[27]

But this glow of friendly relations was soon extinguished by the reaction produced by a statement issued by Mr. Amau, the chief of the Bureau of Information and Intelligence of the Japanese Foreign Office. On April 17, 1934, Amau issued to the Japanese press a statement of the foreign policy, formulated by the Foreign Office with reference to China. Its terse phraseology sounded like a challenge to all the powers that had large interests in China. After a declaration that Japan had "special responsibilities in East Asia," the statement went on to say that in order to fulfill those responsibilities it might be necessary at times for Japanese armed forces to act on their own initiative and not to seek the co-operation of other nations. It was only natural, therefore, for Japan to "oppose any attempt on the part of China to avail herself of the influence of any other country in order to resist Japan." Loans for political purposes or shipments of munitions of war would be regarded with suspicion.[28]

Ambassador Grew immediately sent a telegram to Secretary Hull relative to the Amau statement, and Maxwell M. Hamilton, of the Division of Far Eastern Affairs, hurriedly prepared a memorandum on the situation. In the event that the Japanese Government sent to the Department of State a copy of the Amau statement, the acknowledgment of the receipt of that document should be "very brief and should indicate

[27] Grew *Diary*, April 22, 1934; *Ten Years in Japan*, pp. 125–27.
[28] *Ibid.*, April 28, 1933; *ibid.*, pp. 128–33.

merely that we purpose to continue in our traditional and consistent course of conducting foreign relations in accordance with the developing principles of international law and the treaties to which the United States is a party."[29]

On April 20, Ambassador Grew sent to Secretary Hull a dispatch dealing with the issuance of the Japanese Monroe Doctrine for the Far East and he inclosed a copy of the unofficial statement issued by the Japanese Foreign Office on April 17.[30] An interpretation of this statement was made by Ambassador Saito in an interview with Constantine Brown on April 21. The Japanese Government would consider extending loans or selling aircraft to China as "an unfriendly act." The Western nations did not have the "remotest idea" of how "to deal with the Chinese. . . . The Japanese Government . . . has decided to prevent the furtherance of the present trouble by the loans which Western nations are giving the various Chinese leaders to further their own ambitions."[31]

These Japanese statements of policy in the Far East rang like an alarm along the quiet corridors of the Department of State, and Under Secretary of State Phillips requested the Japanese Ambassador to pay a formal call and present some explanation of the action by the Foreign Office. Mr. Saito was disturbingly vague in his answers to the questions of Mr. Phillips. He doubted whether the statement made by Mr. Amau had been made in "any precise form" and therefore it was difficult to give any adequate explanation of it. Phillips complained that Mr. Saito was not of "much help" in this situation, and the interview ended on a distinctly unsatisfactory note.[32]

From April 21 to April 24 some British newspapers expressed opinions that were strongly pro-Japanese. The London *Daily Mail* emphatically stated that it was difficult to see "why Japan's preponderance of interest in China should be disputed,"[33] and the London *Morning Post* acidly observed that "the interventions both in Shanghai and in Manchuria, whatever may be thought of the methods employed, were invited by China, if not forced upon Japan through the anarchy and misrule which threatened every foreign interest."[34]

Sir John Simon, the British Foreign Secretary, had been far more

---

[29] Memorandum prepared by the Division of Far Eastern Affairs, April 20, 1934. 793.94/6700, *Confidential file*, MS, Department of State.

[30] Ambassador Grew to Secretary Hull, Tokyo, April 20, 1934. *Japan: 1931–1941*, I, 223–25.

[31] *Washington Evening Star*, April 22, 1934.

[32] Memorandum by the Under Secretary of State (Phillips), April 24, 1934. *Japan: 1931–1941*, I, 225–26.

[33] April 21, 1934.

[34] London *Morning Post*, April 24, 1934.

cautious than the British press in expressing his opinion. His public statement appeared to Mr. Hornbeck, chief of the Division of Far Eastern Affairs, as "somewhat ambiguous," and the British Ambassador, during a conversation with Mr. Hornbeck, admitted that the Foreign Secretary when under verbal fire was "very cagey" in his language. When the ambassador (Sir Ronald Lindsay) made an inquiry concerning American policy, Mr. Hornbeck replied that "we feel that action by the various governments concerned on parallel lines and with the appearance of a common front would have obvious advantages but that we did not intend to assume or be placed in a position of leadership in initiating proposals for joint or concurrent action."[35]

While the Department of State was seeking some formula that would fit the situation in the Far East, Ambassador Grew had an interview with Hirota who tried to quiet any suspicions by giving explicit assurances that there "was no intention on the part of Japan to claim a privileged position in derogation of the rights and responsibilities to which the signatories of the Nine-Power Treaty are entitled." The Foreign Office was endeavoring faithfully to "follow the policy of the Emperor," and was anxious to "achieve with all countries, and especially with the United States, relations of friendliness."[36]

Mr. Grew was not deeply impressed with these friendly words, and he confided to his diary the opinion that the Amau statement "accurately expresses the policy which Japan would like to pursue."[37] Mr. Hornbeck agreed with this viewpoint,[38] but he prepared a memorandum in which he advised the Secretary of State to follow a policy of caution: "In the light of what has happened up to the present, I personally favor making no reply to the Japanese statement. . . . It appears that no other government is prepared to take a strong position against the Japanese statement. . . . American interests in China are not, in my opinion, any more important than, if as important as, the interests of Great Britain, Russia and possibly France. I do not think that the United States should 'stick out its neck' and become the spearhead in opposition to Japan."[39]

Secretary Hull paid little attention to this warning memorandum by

[35] Memorandum of a conversation between the British Ambassador, Sir Ronald Lindsay, and Mr. Hornbeck, April 24, 1934. 793.94/6617, *Confidential file,* MS, Department of State.
[36] Ambassador Grew to Secretary Hull, Tokyo, April 25, 1934. *Japan: 1931–1941,* I, 227–28.
[37] Grew *Diary,* April 28, 1934; *Ten Years in Japan,* p. 130.
[38] Memorandum prepared by Mr. Hornbeck and addressed to Mr. Phillips, April 25, 1934. 793.94/6669, *Confidential file,* MS, Department of State.
[39] Memorandum prepared by Mr. Hornbeck on Amau statement, April 25, 1934. 793.94/6700, *Confidential file,* MS, Department of State.

Mr. Hornbeck. On April 28 he sent to Tokyo an *aide-mémoire* which clearly outlined the viewpoint of those persons in the Department of State who favored exerting constant pressure upon Japan. He referred to the treaties which defined America's rights in China and then bluntly stated that the treaties themselves could be modified or terminated only by "processes prescribed or recognized or agreed upon by the parties to them."[40]

This *aide-mémoire* reached Tokyo on July 29. Although it was Sunday and was also the Emperor's birthday, Grew sent a hurried note to Hirota and requested an immediate audience. The Foreign Minister at once acceded to this request, and after slowly reading the Hull statement, he remarked that Amau's ill-chosen words had caused "great misunderstanding." His manner was "perfectly friendly," and he betrayed no sign of displeasure because the statement of the spokesman of the Foreign Office had been so directly challenged.[41]

It is evident that Hirota was still trying desperately to court American good will in the face of the growing Russian menace to Japanese dominance in Manchuria. Japan was deeply concerned over the communist threat to one of the main life lines of her empire, and she had directed the implications of the Amau statement at Russia and not at the United States. The establishment of bolshevik control over Russia in 1917 had been viewed by Japan with anxious eyes, and her invasion of Siberia had been prompted by the necessity of stemming the communist tide. As the Bolsheviks strengthened their hold upon Russia, Japanese fears deepened. These fears had been readily recognized in the report of the Lytton Commission:

As the Soviet Government and the Third International had adopted a policy opposed to all imperialist powers which maintained relations with China on the basis of existing treaties, it seemed probable that they would support China in the struggle for the recovery of sovereign rights. This development revived all the old anxieties and suspicions of Japan toward her Russian neighbor.[42]

These suspicions were confirmed when Russia and China signed a treaty on December 12, 1932, which restored diplomatic relations between the two nations. This agreement, it was feared, might be the signal for joint Russian and Chinese pressure upon the Japanese position in North China. Uchida, the Japanese Foreign Minister, recognized

---

[40] Secretary Hull to Ambassador Grew, April 28, 1934. *Japan: 1931–1941*, I, 231–32.

[41] Grew *Diary*, April 29, 1934; *Ten Years in Japan*, pp. 133–34.

[42] *Lytton Report*, League of Nations, Geneva, October 1, 1932, pp. 36–37.

this possibility. In a speech in the Diet he ominously remarked: "Should the Red movement in the Yangtze Valley and South China, which have long suffered from the activities of Communists and the depredations of Communist armies, gain in strength as a result of the Sino-Russian rapprochement, that would be a serious menace to peace in the Orient against which Japan must certainly be on guard."[43]

The establishment of the Japanese-controlled state of Manchukuo was one of the means devised in Tokyo to meet this Russian threat. In order to improve her position in Manchuria, Japan raised Henry Pu-yi from Regent to Emperor and formally crowned him at Hsinking on March 1, 1934.[44] This was an obvious bid for international recognition of the government of Manchukuo. The London *Times* responded with a statement that some countries with large business interests in the Far East would soon find it necessary "to reconcile their trading activities in Manchuria with the policy of recognition."[45] The *New York Journal of Commerce* expressed hearty agreement with this viewpoint and praised the government of Manchukuo as the "most stable and efficient that any portion of China has enjoyed for a long time past."[46] Mr. T. J. League, who had spent many years in China, wrote to Mr. Hornbeck to advise him of the exact status of Manchukuo:

Manchuria has never at any time been part of the "Chinese body-politic." It stands now as it has done, as a unit distinct and entirely separate from China. . . . I should like to suggest to you the wisdom of discrediting entirely the Russian propaganda against Japan, which is, and has been for some time past, virulent. . . . Recognition of Manchukuo would alleviate most of this and put the whole situation in an entirely different and more favorable atmosphere. Personally, I believe that Japan is sincere in her presentations and purposes.[47]

While the great powers hesitated about granting recognition to the state of Manchukuo, Russia was rapidly strengthening her position in the Far East. First she adopted special measures to encourage migration

---

[43] *Contemporary Japan*, published by the Foreign Affairs Association of Japan, Tokyo, March, 1933, I, No. 4, pp. 766–67.

[44] *The United States in World Affairs, 1934–35*, ed. W. H. Shepardson and W. O. Scroggs (New York, 1935), pp. 152–53. Henry Pu-yi was appointed regent of Manchukuo on March 9, 1932. He was born in 1906 and was designated by the Empress Dowager of China as the successor to the throne under the title, Emperor Hsuan Tung. After the overthrow of the Manchu dynasty in 1912 he remained for a while in Peking, but in 1924 he went to live in the Japanese concession at Tientsin. During the years from his abdication to his appointment as regent of Manchukuo he assumed the name of Henry Pu-yi.

[45] May 4, 1934.

[46] March 5, 1934.

[47] T. J. League to Mr. Hornbeck, March 23, 1934. 793.94/6572, MS, Department of State.

to the maritime provinces of Siberia. Next, collective farmers were granted exemptions from agricultural taxes; wages for workers were raised to inviting new levels, while prices paid by the government for the products of the fisheries were increased in a significant manner.[48]

Japan regarded these Russian moves with sharp suspicion and she redoubled her efforts to purchase the Chinese Eastern Railway. When the Soviet Government fixed the price at 160,000,000 yen, Hirota spurned that sum and offered only 120,000,000 yen. In August 1934 the negotiations completely broke down and left relations between the two countries seriously strained.[49] Lieutenant-Colonel Seiichi Aoki, in a popular Japanese magazine, published an article which indicated the imminence of war.[50] Stalin answered this challenge with a defiant declaration: "We do not fear threats and are ready to give blow for blow."[51]

In anticipation of actual warfare in the near future, Japan completed in 1933 some 1,060 miles of new railway in North China and then pushed some new military highways to the borders of Manchukuo.[52] In November 1934 the Japanese Cabinet approved the largest military budget on record. Russia met this action by increasing her army appropriation from 1,573,000,000 rubles in 1933 to 1,795,000,000 rubles in 1934.[53]

It was widely recognized that President Roosevelt's recognition of Russia had added considerable strength to the Muscovite position in the Far East, thereby increasing Japan's difficulties in her endeavor to dominate Manchuria. It was apparent to Japan that Russia had long-range plans to communize China and thus eventually to control a large portion of eastern Asia. The very nature of international communism made it impossible to have stable relations with Russia, so Japan again turned to the United States in May 1934 in the hope of erecting a common front against the foes of capitalism. Knowing that the Roosevelt recognition of Russia would make inexpedient any reference to the dangers of communism, the Japanese Ambassador addressed to Secretary Hull a note which explored the bases upon which a Japanese-American understanding could be built. Emphasis was placed upon the importance of adopting a policy which would prevent China from relying upon her ancient stratagem of playing off America against Japan.

[48] *Economic Review of the Soviet Union*, January, 1934, p. 23.
[49] Harriet L. Moore, *Soviet Far Eastern Policy, 1931–1945* (Princeton, 1945), p. 37.
[50] Tyler Dennett, "America and Japanese Aims," *Current History*, XXXIX (March, 1934), 767.
[51] *New York Times*, January 28, February 4, 1934.
[52] H. J. Timperley, "Japan in Manchuria," *Foreign Affairs*, XII (January, 1934), 295–305.
[53] League of Nations, *Armaments Year Book, 1934*, pp. 441, 725.

It was important to have some joint "governmental action" that would dissipate the "suspicion and fear between the United States and Japan." This could take the form of a joint declaration which would stress a desire to "promote trade to the mutual advantage of the two countries and to make secure the principle of equal opportunity of commerce in the Pacific regions." The declaration could also include a pledge binding each nation to "respect the territorial possessions and the rights and interests of the other," and it would "restate their determination that the two countries should ever maintain a relationship of peace and amity."[54]

g. *The State Department Frowns upon an Understanding with Japan*

It was obvious that Ambassador Saito was angling for some joint statement of policy like the Root-Takahira or the Lansing-Ishii agreements of 1908 and 1917, but Hull did not regard Japanese friendship as worth-while bait. He had already rejected formal negotiations looking towards a treaty between the two nations, and he now refused to be drawn into an executive agreement that would announce American acceptance of Japan's special position in North China. Such an agreement would have changed the history of our Pacific relations and would have eliminated the tragedy of Pearl Harbor. But once more the barrier of the Stimson doctrine held the two nations apart and prevented an accommodation that would have pointed towards peace.[55]

Rebuffed for a second time by Secretary Hull, Japan now turned to Germany. In the summer of 1934 a Japanese naval squadron paid a good-will visit to German waters, and this gesture was followed by the dispatch of Japanese military and naval experts to Germany. Trade agreements were the next item in this catalogue of friendship.[56] As the courtesy list lengthened and commercial advantages became manifest, Poland took an active interest in this Japanese-German rapprochement. Trade possibilities with Manchukuo led many statesmen in Europe to ponder whether it was worth while to adhere to the Stimson doctrine of nonrecognition.

There were other economic factors that disturbed the equation of international friendship. In 1933, Japanese textiles began to flood the markets in which British goods had long held a dominant place. This

[54] Ambassador Saito to Secretary Hull, May 16, 1934. *Japan: 1931–1941*, I, 232–33.
[55] Mr. Phillips, the Acting Secretary of State, to Ambassador Grew, June 18, 1934. *Japan: 1931–1941*, I, 237–39.
[56] Moore, *op. cit.*, pp. 38–39.

was particularly true with reference to the markets in India, Egypt, and East Africa. In 1934 the situation was so serious that a conference was held in London between British and Japanese manufacturers for the purpose of allocating the textile trade of the two countries. No agreement could be reached and this impasse led Mr. Walter Runciman, president of the British Board of Trade, to issue a statement that seemed equivalent to a declaration of economic warfare upon Japan.[57] Trade wars are often the prelude to armed conflict.

The United States experienced this Japanese commercial invasion in 1934 when imports of cotton cloth from Japan rose from 1,116,000 square yards in 1933, to 7,287,000 square yards in 1934. In the first three months of 1935 these imports reached the startling figure of 12,771,000 square yards, and the owners of the New England cotton mills saw bankruptcy just around the corner of another year. But the general picture of American commercial relations with Japan was distinctly reassuring. Japan's total exports to the United States in 1934 were considerably less than in the previous year, while American exports to Japan rose from $143,000,000 in 1933 to $210,000,000 in 1934. This rapidly increasing trade with Japan was partly explained by the fact that Japanese mills were consuming a large portion of the American cotton crop. The percentage of the crop that went to Japan rose from 15 per cent in 1929 to 30 per cent in 1934. While many countries were reducing their imports of American cotton, Japan was constantly increasing her purchases of this important raw product, thus adding another link in the economic chain that bound the two countries together. In comparison with this fast-growing trade, the Open Door in China was like the entrance to the cupboard of Old Mother Hubbard.[58]

h. *Closing the Open Door in Manchuria?*

With Japanese markets expanding each year and with Japanese mills consuming American cotton in a constantly increasing volume, it seemed as though the economic basis for a Japanese-American accord had been firmly established. But Secretary Hull could not keep his eyes from the Manchurian scene where, it was widely alleged, the Open Door was being slowly closed by Japanese pressure. Japan regarded Manchukuo as her first line of defense against Russian aggression. This aggression would not come in the immediate future, but the communist currents in China would gradually be merged into a mighty stream that would surge against all Japanese outposts in Manchukuo in a tide that

---

[57] *Parliamentary Debates,* House of Commons, May 7, 1934, CCLXXXIX, 718.
[58] Shepardson and Scroggs, *op. cit.,* pp. 174–78.

would be difficult to stem. If these bastions of defense were not carefully prepared to meet these rapidly rising waters, they would be engulfed and the creative work of several decades would be destroyed.

This pressing problem of national defense was the one that gave Japanese statesmen their greatest concern, and it was the real reason why the Japanese Foreign Office announced in April 1934 its Monroe Doctrine for eastern Asia. Hirota knew that the American Monroe Doctrine had always rested upon the broad basis of national defense. He also knew that the primary reason behind Theodore Roosevelt's predatory policy in Panama was this same factor of defense. Even as late as 1912 the American Government had invoked the Monroe Doctrine as a deterrent against the acquisition, by a Japanese corporation, of a large tract of land in the vicinity of Magdalena Bay. This bay was in Mexican territory, but if it were controlled by a Japanese corporation, it might be used as a naval base for future operations against the United States. Under pressure from the Department of State the Japanese corporation abandoned its project, and the Senate of the United States, as a warning to other Japanese corporations, passed a resolution opposing the transfer of strategic areas in the Americas to non-American corporations which might be acting as agents for a foreign power.[59]

The Japanese Government in 1912 had readily recognized the fact that the American Government could not permit any part of the Mexican borderlands to pass under the partial control of foreign corporations. Considerations of national defense were of paramount importance to every American statesman, and this factor had outweighed any regard for the feelings of Mexican politicians who might resent Yankee dictation with reference to business dealings with the nationals of other countries. In April 1934, Japan merely took a leaf from the book of American national defense and announced indirect control over the petroleum resources of Manchukuo. China would not like this action and neither would other countries that had hoped to exploit the riches of North China, but for Japan this control took on the aspect of a national imperative.

The first item in this program of control was the issuance by the government of Manchukuo of a charter to the Manchuria Petroleum Company (February 21, 1932). This charter provided that the new company would have a monopoly control over the sale and distribution of petroleum in Manchukuo. The capital stock of the company was owned entirely by the government of Manchukuo and by Japanese interests. There was no possibility that any foreign oil company could

[59] Thomas A. Bailey, "The Lodge Corollary to the Monroe Doctrine," *Political Science Quarterly*, XLVIII (1933), 235ff.

share in the management or the profits of the Manchuria Petroleum Company.

This secure control over the oil business in Manchukuo might adversely affect the oil companies of foreign nations by depriving them of the retail trade which they had developed over a long period of years. In 1932 about 55 per cent of the oil imported into Manchuria was handled by the American Standard Vacuum Oil Company and by the Texas Oil Company. British, Russian, and Dutch interests controlled 35 per cent of the remaining oil imports with Japan having only 10 per cent for her share.[60] It is apparent that the Japanese Government was determined to adjust this balance of business so that it would incline in favor of her nationals. Oil is an essential commodity in modern warfare. It was only common sense for the government of Manchukuo to insist upon control over the oil resources within its borders.

Although the restrictive policy of the government of Manchukuo was criticized as being inconsistent with the Open-Door policy, it was soon obvious that American petroleum interests would not be seriously injured. American exports of petroleum to Manchukuo increased from $782,000 in 1936 to $3,436,000 in the following year. In 1938 these exports continued to increase, but the Department of State explained this favorable factor by asserting that Manchukuo was building up reserves for war purposes. This may have been true in 1938, but it was not true in the early thirties. In 1932, American exports to Manchuria were valued at only $1,186,000. After the erection of Manchukuo into a Japanese dependency, American trade rose to $2,691,000 in 1933, and in 1935 reached the respectable figure of $4,188,000. If the Open Door was slowly being closed in Manchukuo, there still remained a crack wide enough to permit a growing American trade.[61]

But the Department of State was not satisfied with these favorable trade statistics. Secretary Hull sent a series of strong protests to Japan with reference to the monopoly given to the Manchuria Petroleum Company,[62] and American public opinion was aroused over the prefer-

[60] Shepardson and Scroggs, *op. cit.*, pp. 156-59.

[61] Department of State, *Press Releases,* April 6, 1939; *Japan: 1931-1941,* I, 155-56. Ralph Townsend, *The High Cost of Hate* (San Francisco, 1939), pp. 24-25, gives the following table based upon official figures:

Total U. S. sales in Manchukuo by years:

1931	$2,176,000
1932	1,186,000
1933	2,691,000
1934	3,398,000
1935	4,188,000
1936	3,542,000
1937	16,061,000

[62] *Japan: 1931-1941,* I, 130-57.

ences given to Japanese nationals in their business enterprises within Manchukuo. Since 1899 many Americans had tickled their fancies with warm visions of a great export trade to China's teeming millions.[63] Although this trade never developed, they continued to cherish their illusions and they overlooked the far larger trade opportunities with Japan. The friction between the United States and Japan over Japanese commercial policies in Manchukuo was entirely needless. Secretary Hull was determined to press for the continuance of a trade principle (Open Door), even when its partial abrogation meant an increased volume of American trade. He seemed to be unaware of the ominous fact that his notes were creating a backlog of ill will that might later burst into the flames of war.

[63] It had long been apparent to realistic diplomats that the trade between the United States and China would never be large. As Dr. Jacob Schurman remarked to Mr. Hamilton of the Division of Far Eastern Affairs: "China has never been a great market for American goods and there is little reason to suppose that she ever will be." 793.94/6686, MS, Department of State.

VI

Moscow Molds the Political Pattern
in the Far East

a. *Secretary Hull Overlooks a Diplomatic Opportunity*

WHEN SECRETARY HULL rejected in June 1934 the proffer of a Japanese olive branch, he clearly indicated his strong disinclination to have it cultivated in the friendly soil of American good will so that it would bear the rich fruit of a permanent accord. But despite this lack of response from the Department of State, the Japanese Government still strove for an intimate understanding with the United States. Hirota remained as Foreign Secretary in the Okada Cabinet which took office on July 8, and Saionji, Makino, and other moderates were "clearly in the saddle." An eminent Japanese liberal expressed to Ambassador Grew the opinion that "if the United States had had the privilege of choosing the Cabinet in its own interest, it could not have done better."[1]

These favorable factors were entirely overlooked by Secretary Hull who at times liked to flavor the ointment of diplomacy with a dash of strong vinegar. This Hull formula finally grew so distasteful to Prime Minister Okada that he decided it was useless to continue to make friendly gestures in the direction of the United States. He might just as well surrender to the demands of a powerful pressure group in Japan that kept clamoring for naval parity with the United States and Great Britain.

b. *Japan Denounces the Washington Naval Treaty*

The Washington Naval Treaty of February 6, 1922, had never been popular with Japanese militarists who deeply resented the ratio of inferiority that had been imposed upon their naval establishment. Moreover, they realized that parity with the United States and Great Britain would greatly reduce the likelihood of armed intervention by either of these powers to block Japanese expansion in North China.

For a decade after the Washington Conference the situation in China had been a big question mark to the statesmen of the great powers. For a while it had appeared that Chiang Kai-shek might be able to

[1] Grew *Diary*, July 6, 1934; *Ten Years in Japan* (New York, 1944), pp. 139-40.

bring some measure of peace to a country that had been in chaos since the last days of the empire. But the whirlwind of nationalism had been too strong for the successor of Sun Yat-sen to harness, and Americans at Nanking in 1927 and Russians along the Chinese Eastern Railway in 1929 had felt its destructive force. In 1931, Japan had decided to convert Manchuria into a glorified cyclone cellar that would be safe against any adverse wind from China or even from the steppes of Siberia. Stimson, however, was unduly suspicious of Japanese weather maps and he sharply protested against the precautions taken by the watchful men of Nippon. Japanese statesmen not only resented his repeated protests but regarded American naval maneuvers in Hawaiian waters as a covert threat to their position in the Far East. If naval parity were attained it might act as a gag upon American secretaries of state who talked of peace while walking down the road to war.

It is interesting to note that while Stimson was engaged in his favorite pastime of sending irritating notes to Japan, American naval construction was permitted to fall far below the limits permitted by the Washington Naval Treaty. On March 4, 1933, the American Navy was approximately at 65 per cent of treaty strength, while the navy of Japan had mounted to 95 per cent of treaty limits. If Japan, by denouncing the Washington Naval Treaty, could eliminate all limitations upon its naval armament, and if the United States continued its policy of indifference to naval construction, it would not be long before actual parity could be reached. In that event the Stimson policy would no longer be invoked by American statesmen.

But President Roosevelt defeated these hopes of Japanese navalists by allocating in June 1933 the large sum of $238,000,000 from the National Industrial Recovery Act appropriations for the construction of new warships. This action confronted Japanese admirals with a formidable dilemma: they now had the "unenviable task of deciding whether to abrogate the treaties next year [1934] and start a hopeless competition with far wealthier nations for naval supremacy, or else accept a continuance of the present ratios and face an outraged public."[2] The naval leaders in Japan felt that they could not "lose face" by continuing to accept the existing ratios. Their pressure upon Hirota grew so strong that on September 17, 1934, he informed Ambassador Grew that Japan had definitely decided "to give notice before December 31, 1934, to terminate the Washington Naval Treaty."[3]

When preliminary conversations began in London in October 1934

[2] Ambassador Grew to Secretary Hull, September 15, 1933. *Japan: 1931–1941,* I, 249–50.
[3] Ambassador Grew to Secretary Hull, September 18, 1934. *Ibid.,* pp. 253–54.

relative to the renewal of the Naval Treaty of 1930, the Japanese delegates promptly introduced their demand for parity. Their arguments
were based upon the grounds of "prestige and manifest destiny." Manifest destiny had been a favorite American watchword during many
decades of the nineteenth century, but Secretary Hull felt outraged
when Japanese statesmen began to apply it to their expansion in Manchuria. He was certain that the real reason for Japanese parity demands
was the desire to "obtain overwhelming supremacy in the Orient" and
thus secure "preferential rights and privileges."[4] He did not share the
"deep concern" of the British Foreign Office to arrive at some solution
satisfactory to Japan, and he was cool to the suggestion of a tripartite
nonaggression treaty to cover the situation in the Far East. It would be
best for the American delegation at Geneva to give no encouragement
to the Japanese to "expect any concessions or to expect the conclusion
of a new treaty in substitution for the Washington Treaty."[5]

Norman Davis discovered that the British were not in favor of the
stand-and-deliver attitude of Secretary Hull. They were anxious to continue the "talks with the Japanese" even though there was no solution
in sight. Hull reluctantly responded to this British pressure and agreed
that the "conversations should not be broken off right away," but he
instructed Davis to "refrain from doing anything which would diminish the embarrassment of the Japanese as the time of the denunciation
approaches." Hull had developed an ardent dislike for the Japanese
and was now conducting relations with them in a thoroughly feudist
manner.[6]

In the face of this uncompromising attitude there was nothing left
for the Japanese Foreign Office to do but inform Hull on December 29,
1934, of its decision to denounce the Washington Naval Treaty of
February 6, 1922. The limitations imposed by that treaty would expire
on the last day of December 1936. There was still a small chance that
conversations at Geneva could lead to some path of accommodation and
cause the Japanese Cabinet to reconsider its decision. British statesmen
favored further attempts to discover some common denominator of
agreement in the matter of naval ratios, but Hull believed that lessons
of diplomacy to the Japanese should be taught to the tune of verbal
spankings rather than by words of encouragement.[7] It is to be regretted
that President Roosevelt felt the same way.

In this regard his viewpoint differed fundamentally from that of his

[4] Secretary Hull to Norman Davis (at Geneva), November 13, 1934. *Ibid.*, pp.
259–60.
[5] Secretary Hull to Norman Davis, November 22, 1934. *Ibid.*, pp. 262–63.
[6] Secretary Hull to Norman Davis, November 26, 1934. *Ibid.*, pp. 266–67.
[7] Cordell Hull, *Memoirs* (New York, 1948), I, 290–91.

cousin, Theodore Roosevelt. In the winter of 1910, after a mature consideration of all the factors in the Far Eastern situation, Theodore Roosevelt gave President Taft some sound, realistic advice relative to the Japanese advance into Manchuria:

Our vital interest is to keep the Japanese out of our country and at the same time to preserve the good will of Japan. The vital interest of the Japanese, on the other hand, is in Manchuria and Korea. It is therefore peculiarly our interest not to take any steps as regards Manchuria which will give the Japanese cause to feel, with or without reason, that we are hostile to them, or a menace, in however slight a degree, to their interests.[8]

c. *Japan Promotes Autonomy Movement in North China*

It had been very clear to Theodore Roosevelt during his administration as President that Japan regarded Manchuria as a bulwark of defense and as the keystone in the economic structure of the empire. Japan could not retire from her position in that province and any attempt to force her withdrawal would lead to open warfare. President Franklin D. Roosevelt and Secretary Hull by adopting the Stimson formula of nonrecognition had opened a Pandora's box of troubles in the Far East. When they applied the formula to Japan and remained silent concerning Russia's absorption of Outer Mongolia, they emptied every evil in the box and led them to stalk along the Manchurian frontier stirring up discontent.

Chaos and communism are close companions and as Japan looked over the unsettled condition of affairs in North China, it was apparent that Russian agents were busily at work in fomenting discord. They would turn the peasants against the tottering regime of Chiang Kai-shek, and when the fires of revolution had destroyed the weak fabric of the Nationalist Government, communist armies under Mao Tse-tung or Chu Teh would quickly extinguish them under a heavy iron curtain. The formula was simple and very effective. If Japan remained inactive in North China, it would not be long before Manchuria and Korea would be closely besieged by great masses of fanatical Reds. Japan must either extend her frontiers in China or see her troops pushed into the sea.

Under the terms of the Tangku Truce, May 31, 1933, Chinese troops had been withdrawn from Northeast Hopeh Province which was converted into a "demilitarized zone" under the nominal control of China. Order in this area had been insufficiently maintained by organizations

[8] Theodore Roosevelt to President Taft, December 22, 1910. Knox Papers, Library of Congress.

"under the control of Chinese" officials who were "not unsympathetic to the Japanese."[9] As conditions continued unsettled the Japanese decided to restore order by force and to extend the area under her control. In May 1935, Japanese armies moved into the demilitarized zone of Hopeh and some weeks later compelled Chinese officials to consent to a new truce. Under the terms of the Ho-Umedzu Agreement, July 6, 1935 (signed by General Umedzu, commander of the Japanese Army in North China and by General Ho Ying-chin, Chinese Minister of War), Chinese troops would be withdrawn from Hopeh Province and this would be followed by the "dissolution and suppression of certain Chinese organizations to which the Japanese objected." Another important item provided for the prohibition "of all anti-foreign and anti-Japanese activities in China generally."[10]

This important agreement was one expression of the policy stressed by Hirota in the late summer of 1935. After having removed one possibility of friction with Soviet Russia by the purchase of the Chinese Eastern Railway (March 23), Hirota concentrated his attention upon North China. In October he announced three basic principles of accommodation with China: (1) recognition of Manchukuo; (2) suppression of anti-Japanese activities; (3) collaboration in an anti-Communistic program. When the Nanking Government refused to give serious consideration to these proposals, Japan announced on November 24 the existence of a strong independence movement that aimed at the autonomy of the five northern provinces of Chahar, Hopeh, Shansi, Shantung, and Suiyuan. The consolidation of these five provinces into an autonomous unit was not accomplished, but the Japanese did organize the "East Hopeh Anti-Communistic Autonomous Government." This was placed under the control of a Chinese named Yin Ju-keng who was sympathetic with Japanese aspirations. Next, the Hopeh-Chahar Political Council was established "under the nominal control of the Chinese Government." The Japanese puppet in this case was General Sung Che-yuan. Finally, the Japanese erected in "Chahar Province north of the Great Wall (about nine-tenths of the Province) an 'independent' Mongolian regime under the nominal leadership of the Mongolian prince Teh Wang."[11] These political moves were ap-

9 Memorandum written by Stanley K. Hornbeck of the Division of Far Eastern Affairs, July 15, 1937. 793.94/9195, MS, Department of State.

10 Memorandum by Stanley K. Hornbeck, chief of the Division of Far Eastern Affairs, July 15, 1937. 793.94/9194, MS, Department of State.

11 *Ibid.* In this memorandum Dr. Hornbeck makes the following comments: "Although the Chinese state that no such agreement [Ho-Umedzu Agreement] exists, our Embassy at Peiping states that 'circumstantial evidence inclines one to believe in the genuineness of the documents' comprising the agreement. Whether or not the Chinese actually accepted the Japanese demands, 'subsequent actions of the Chinese authorities have not run counter to the Japanese desires.' "

parently merely a prelude to the establishment of a real autonomous government in the five northern provinces.

d. *America and Britain Protest against Japanese Policy*

Britain viewed with evident alarm this sudden expansion of Japanese influence in North China. James L. Garvin, noted British political analyst, called attention to the fact that something "significant and sinister" had taken place in the Far East,[12] while Sir Samuel Hoare, speaking for the Foreign Office, lamented that events had taken place "which, whatever the truth of the matter may be, lend color to the belief that Japanese influence is being exerted to shape Chinese internal political developments and administrative arrangements."[13]

Secretary Hull went far beyond the cautious language of the British Foreign Secretary. On December 5 he issued a press release which indicated the attitude of the Department of State:

There is going on in and with regard to North China a political struggle which is unusual in character and which may have far-reaching effects. . . . Unusual developments in any part of China are rightfully and necessarily of concern not alone to the Government and people of China but to all of the many powers which have interests in China. . . . Political disturbances and pressures give rise to uncertainty and misgiving. . . . They make difficult the enjoyment of treaty rights and the fulfillment of treaty obligations. . . . In international relations there must be . . . faith in principles and pledges.[14]

e. *American Purchases of Silver Adversely Affect China*

While Secretary Hull was talking on this high plane with reference to help for China, the actions of United States Treasury officials under the Silver Purchase Act of 1934 were helping to undermine Chinese opposition to Japanese expansion in North China. American purchases of silver caused a large flow of that metal from China to the United States, thus leading to a serious depletion of bank reserves and a consequent decline in commodity prices. The Chinese Government countered with a tax on silver exports, but large quantities were smuggled out of the country and foreign trade was soon demoralized.[15] After vainly waiting for an expected loan, China was finally compelled to issue on November 3 a decree nationalizing silver. All holders of that

[12] *New York Times*, December 1, 1935.

[13] *Parliamentary Debates*, House of Commons, December 5, 1935, CCCVII, 336.

[14] Department of State, *Press Releases*, December 5, 1935. *Japan, 1931–1941*, I, 240–41.

[15] *Parliamentary Debates, loc. cit.* Statement of Sir Samuel Hoare.

metal were ordered to exchange it for legal-tender notes issued by three government banks.

America's silver policy had caused serious economic distress in large areas in China, had weakened her resistance to Japanese encroachments, and had made many of her "responsible business leaders to feel that their economic interests would perhaps be safer if entrusted to Japanese control than they would be if they were left to be played upon by the hocus-pocus of fourteen American Senators."[16] Instead of increasing American exports to China, the Silver Purchase Act led to a sharp drop in this current of trade.[17]

Secretary Hull admits that the operations of the Treasury Department led to a "disastrous flight of silver from China to the United States," and he laments the fact that it was not until May 1936 that any real relief was afforded by Secretary Morgenthau.[18] During these months of financial dislocation in China, Japan moved forward to a more secure control over large portions of North China.

f. *Japan Again Asks for Naval Parity*

Under the provisions of the London Naval Treaty of 1930 arrangements were outlined for a conference to meet in 1935 for the purpose of drafting a convention that would settle all questions relating to naval limitations. When this convention met in London, December 9, 1935, the Japanese delegates presented their usual plea for parity. This stressed the importance of establishing a "common upper limit" by reducing the existing ration of 5–5–3 to one of 3–3–3. This could be accomplished by destroying a large number of American and British warships.[19]

Admiral Nagano defended the Japanese position by asserting that the common upper limit desired did not "envisage giving Japan any opportunity for aggression; on the contrary, Japan wanted to make aggression by any power impossible." Under the 5–5–3 ratio the American Navy, concentrated in Oriental waters, could "threaten Japanese security." Norman Davis replied that he did not think that the Japanese proposals were "very fair." After discussing the reasons for the establishment of the 5–5–3 ratio he then remarked that it was essential to find some *modus vivendi* which would "avoid both the common upper limit and the ratio." Admiral Standley thought that a satisfactory

[16] *The United States in World Affairs, 1936*, p. 78.
[17] Exports from the United States to China in 1934 amounted to $68,667,000. In 1935 they dropped to $38,156,000.
[18] Hull, *op. cit.*, p. 446.
[19] *New York Times*, December 10, 1935.

temporary arrangement might be effected by taking the existing naval establishments with certain qualitative limitations and add a preamble stating that "an adequate navy was the sovereign right of everybody." This suggestion was accepted by the Japanese delegates for further consideration.[20]

During the course of his remarks Norman Davis had expressed his gratification at the "improvement in Japanese-American relations in the past three years." He paid tribute to the Japanese people and to their urge for progress which the United States admired but which it desired to see "exercised in a peaceful manner." Mr. Phillips also adverted to the "rapidly growing friendship" between the United States and Japan and spoke of his fears that "parity would certainly set us back and breed suspicion."[21]

But the Japanese delegates continued to insist upon parity and refused to discuss the new building programs presented by France, Great Britain, and Italy. On January 15, 1936, when the other powers rejected the parity request, Japan formally withdrew from the conference.[22] Collective security in the Pacific was crumbling even before Mussolini's legions in Africa proved that it was hopelessly out of date.

g. President Roosevelt Delivers a Lecture to Wicked Dictators

As the system of collective security was rapidly breaking down in Africa and in China, it occurred to President Roosevelt that he might check this disintegration by some words of warning to dictators in Germany, Italy, and Japan. In 1936 the Nazi regime in Germany was distasteful to multitudes of Americans and Mussolini's march into Ethiopia had given deep offense to a large and influential group of publicists and professors who believed that the frontiers of America had gradually been extended into every continent on the globe. The Japanese movement into North China had been particularly disturbing to these ardent one-worlders who conveniently forgot that Russia had really taken over Outer Mongolia and was rapidly infiltrating Sinkiang. The Department of State in 1935 had protested to Russia against communist propaganda in the United States, but it had evinced no interest in the advance of the Red tide over the plains of North China. Russia, with its vast reservoir of strength in limitless Siberia, was a far more serious threat to China

[20] Memorandum of conversation between the American and the Japanese delegations at the London Naval Conference, December 17, 1935. *Japan, 1931–1941*, I, 285–89.

[21] *Ibid.*, pp. 288–89.

[22] The chairman of the Japanese delegation (Nagano) to the chairman of the conference (Monsell), London, January 15, 1936. *Ibid.*, p. 297.

than the armies of Japan that had to fight a desperate battle to be able
to cling to the fringes of the continent of China. But President Roosevelt and Secretary Hull kept looking at the problems of eastern Asia
through the myopic eyes of Henry L. Stimson who had bedeviled the
situation in 1931–32 and who still muddled the minds of high officials
who held the reins of authority.

On January 3, 1936, the President delivered an address to Congress
in which he sounded a sharp challenge to wicked dictators who were
engaged in aggressions that might lead to World War II. After congratulating his Administration upon the adoption of a "good neighbor
policy," he belabored other national leaders who had failed to "demonstrate that patience necessary to attain reasonable and legitimate objectives by peaceful negotiation or by an appeal to the finer instincts of
world justice." Fully aware that the injustices of Versailles could never
be rectified through any agency of the League of Nations, the President
must have pressed his tongue hard in his cheek when he uttered such
sonorous nonsense. But he relished his role as lecturer to errant nations,
and he hurried on to further words of castigation: "They [Germany,
Italy, and Japan] have . . . impatiently reverted to the old belief in the
law of the sword, or to the fantastic conception that they, and they alone,
are chosen to fulfill a mission. . . . I recognize that these words which I
have chosen with deliberation will not prove popular in any nation that
chooses to fit this shoe to its foot."[23]

In distant Tokyo, Ambassador Grew regarded these minatory words
of the President as an exercise in "courageous statesmanship." He
realized that this pointed admonition would not stop the "Japanese
push into China," but he hoped that it might retard its progress.[24] He
was not honest enough to admit that it was another step in the direction
of war with Japan.

Japanese reaction to the President's address was given significant expression in a speech made by Hirota who deprecated the fact that American statesmen constantly talked as though they had a mandate from
God: "It is to be regretted that there are abroad statesmen of repute
who seemed determined to impose upon others their private convictions as to how the world should be ordered, and who are apt to denounce those who oppose their dictates as if they were disturbers of
peace."[25]

In New York, Ambassador Saito, speaking before the Japan Society,

[23] *Peace and War: United States Foreign Policy, 1931–1941* (Washington, 1943),
pp. 304–7.
[24] Grew *Diary*, January 5, 1936; *Ten Years in Japan* (New York, 1944), pp.
162–63.
[25] *Ibid.,* January 21, 1936, p. 164.

endeavored to justify Japanese policy in China by comparing it with the American Monroe Doctrine.[26] This statement aroused the ready ire of Senator Pittman who vehemently denied the validity of such a comparison. "We are seeking to preserve the republics of Latin America, not to destroy them."[27]

Although Ambassador Grew recognized that the much-quoted utterance of Pittman was "utterly jingoistic," he did not regret it because he believed that "its net result will be helpful." The Japanese Government should be made to realize that there has always been a limit to American patience. Indeed, if they looked into the history of the United States, they would discover that "the American people are among the most inflammable in the world." Some little incident in the Far East might easily ignite the tinder of American resentment and thus produce a long and devastating war. Grew overlooked the fact that utterances like those of Senator Pittman greatly helped to prepare in Japanese minds a pile of ardent dislike that could be enkindled into flames of conflict by sparks of caustic criticism on the part of American officials.[28]

h. *Chinese Nationalism Makes a Common Cause with Communism*

While jingoists in the United States were denouncing Japanese policy in China, the Japanese Cabinet was doing its best to maintain friendly relations with the United States. In the first week in March 1936, Hirota was commanded by the Emperor to assume the post of Prime Minister. This selection pleased Grew who looked upon Hirota as a "strong and safe" man. In response to a series of questions from Grew, the new Prime Minister repeated the items in his policy towards China which he had announced during the preceding October: (1) Chinese recognition of Manchukuo; (2) suppression of anti-Japanese activities; (3) collaboration in an anti-communistic program. In its execution of this policy Japan would not "interfere with foreign rights and interests including the principle of the Open Door." In conclusion, Hirota again emphasized his warm desire to make "good relations" with the United States the most important item in his program of peace.[29]

This same note of friendly feeling for the United States was echoed by Mr. Yoshida, the Japanese Ambassador to Britain who was visiting Washington. At the conclusion of his friendly remarks he expressed the hope that the American people would soon recognize the need of the "immense and rapidly growing population of Japan" for more ter-

---

[26] *The United States in World Affairs, 1936*, p. 66.
[27] *Congressional Record*, LXXX, 1703.
[28] Grew *Diary*, February 11, 1936; *Ten Years in Japan*, pp. 164–65.
[29] *Ibid.*, March 13, 1936; *ibid.*, pp. 179–81.

ritory.[30] This land hunger could best be satisfied by a large slice of North China.

Secretary Hull reduced Yoshida's fervor of expression by coolly remarking that the American people were getting the impression that Japan "sought absolute economic domination, first of eastern Asia, and then of other portions as she might see fit." This would eventually mean "political as well as military domination," and that the upshot of "the entire movement would be to exclude countries like the United States from trading with all of those portions of China thus brought under the domination . . . of Japan." Hull then discoursed at length upon the beneficent aspects of his reciprocal trade program which aimed at breaking down tariff barriers and thus making it possible for "some 20 billions of dollars of international trade by degrees to be restored." If the Japanese Government would abandon its selfish policy of imperialism in North China and follow American tutelage in the matter of reciprocal trade, it would soon be vastly benefited by the strong new currents of rich commerce.[31]

Japanese statesmen were well acquainted with all the items in the Hull program of reciprocal trade, and they had weighed with care most of the arguments in favor of unrestricted trade. But their problem in North China was primarily one of defense against Russia. The importance of Manchuria as a source of raw materials and as a market for Japanese manufactures was obvious. Less obvious was the importance of that province as a bulwark that would stem the Red tide that had already covered the entire province of Outer Mongolia. The Soviet Army in the Far East during the years 1936–38 increased to an imposing force of more than 300,000 seasoned troops.[32] Not only could this army use Mongolia as a springboard for offensive action, but after 1935, Red forces could recruit further strength in the province of Sinkiang. According to Alexander Barmine, who was in charge of the supply of Soviet arms to military forces in that province, it was evident that all vestiges of Chinese control had vanished. In 1935, Sinkiang had become "a Soviet colony in all but name."[33]

It is significant that the American Government never addressed a

[30] Memorandum of Secretary Hull after a conversation with Ambassador Yoshida, June 12, 1936. *Japan, 1931–1941*, I, 241–44.

[31] *Ibid.*, I, 241–44.

[32] General Lushkov, who escaped from Russia to Japan in June 1938, estimated the Red Army in the Far East at 400,000 infantry. Japanese estimates were somewhat lower. *New York Times*, July 3–14, 1938. See N. Hidaka, *Manchukuo–Soviet Border Issues* (Sinkiang, 1938), p. 260.

[33] Alexander Barmine, *One Who Survived* (New York, 1945), pp. 231–32. On January 1, 1936, Russian agents signed an agreement which established a very close political bond between Russia and Sinkiang. See also, Martin R. Norins, *Gateway to Asia: Sinkiang* (New York, 1944).

note to Soviet Russia protesting against the absorption of these provinces. American concern relative to the preservation of Chinese territorial integrity had its sole expression in acrid notes to Japan. Faith in Russia's good intentions was an important item in the Far Eastern policy of the Roosevelt Administration.

Officials in the Department of State not only overlooked the rapid extension of Russian power through control over Outer Mongolia and Sinkiang, but they deliberately closed their eyes to the implications that lay behind the establishment of the Communist Army in the province of Shensi. After the communist debacle in 1927, Mao Tse-tung and Chu Teh retreated to convenient rural areas in Kiangsi and Kwantung provinces and carefully recruited new strength. In August 1931 a mandate was received from Moscow instructing Chinese Communists to create a full-fledged Soviet government: "In the shortest possible period, a central Soviet government must be formed in the most secure region." In accordance with this directive the First Congress of Chinese Soviets assembled in Juichin, Kiangsi, in November 1931 and promulgated a constitution along Russian lines. Before closing its sessions this Congress elected a permanent Central Executive Committee which immediately chose a Cabinet that included such loyal communist leaders as Mao Tse-tung, Chu Teh, and Chou En-lai. This Cabinet was empowered to rule by decrees which were to have the force of law. The program formulated by the Congress had a definite communist inclination: the confiscation of the estates of landlords and the nationalization of all industries belonging to foreigners.[34]

By September 1932 the Communist Party in China proudly reported to the Comintern that it had organized a Red Army of twenty-six corps and fifteen local divisions. It had also introduced a "well-armed GPU detachment" in order to suppress any "counterrevolutionary movements." In the following year the Chinese delegate, Wang Ming, stated that the Red military forces had grown to an army of 350,000 trained troops with an irregular force approximating 600,000. This military establishment had under its domination a total population of nearly sixty million people.[35]

But the Red Army in China felt insecure in the provinces of Kiangsi and Kwantung, so in October 1934 it began the Long March that finally took it into Kansu and Shensi.[36] In northern Shensi a new Soviet area was rapidly organized in 1935. For Russia the new location for the Chinese Communist Army was of great importance. Bordering on

[34] David J. Dallin, *Soviet Russia and the Far East* (New Haven, 1948), pp. 108–9.
[35] *Ibid.*, pp. 111–12.
[36] Edgar Snow, *Red Star Over China* (New York, 1939), pp. 189–218.

Inner Mongolia, it would provide a bulwark against the projected Japanese advance in that region. Close to the territory of Soviet Russia, it could draw from that area much-needed supplies for warlike operations. As an instrument of Russian policy it was admirably located and was ready to strike upon orders from Moscow.

The Kremlin, however, was too canny to use the Chinese Red Army as an offensive force at that time. It would be better strategy to arrange a truce with the Nationalist armies of Chiang Kai-shek and then preach a crusade against the Japanese invaders. When they were turned back the truce could be conveniently broken and the armed forces of Chiang Kai-shek, war-weary and shattered, could be crushed. All China would then be inundated by the Red tide.

It would, therefore, be smart politics for the Chinese Communists to arrange a hurried understanding with the Nationalist Government and use Chiang Kai-shek as an unwitting tool to further their ends. The first move in this game of wits was to implement a motto forged by Mao Tse-tung: "All parties and classes unite to fight the Japanese and the traitors. . . . We are against civil war."[37] Other communist leaders echoed this clarion call of Mao Tse-tung, and when Chiang Kai-shek was taken prisoner at Sian in December 1936 by Chang Hsueh-liang, Moscow quickly intervened and secured his release.[38] For the time being he was an important Soviet asset that had to be carefully exploited. When his usefulness was over he could be shot as a "fascist-militarist."

i. *Japan Draws Closer to Germany*

In the face of this growing accord between Chiang Kai-shek and the communist leaders in China, Japan concluded the well-known anti-Comintern Pact of November 25, 1936. This was a consultative convention which bound the contracting parties to "keep each other informed concerning the activities of the Communistic International."[39] There was also a secret "additional agreement" which provided that in the event "one of the High Contracting Parties" should "become the object of an unprovoked attack or threat of attack by the Union of Soviet Socialist Republics," the other contracting party would "take no measures which would tend to ease the situation" of Soviet Russia. This secret treaty also made provision for consultations between the contracting parties to safeguard "common interests."[40]

[37] Dallin, *op. cit.*, p. 131.
[38] *Ibid.*, pp. 67–70.
[39] The text of the treaty is given in *United States and Japan, 1931–1941*, II, 153–55.
[40] *Documents on German Foreign Policy, 1918–1945*, I (Washington, 1949), 734.

In a statement explaining the purpose of the anti-Comintern Agreement, the Japanese Foreign Office indicated the extent of communist propaganda and the efforts of communist agents to promote world-wide revolution in order to establish Red control over every part of the globe. Attention was called to the devious means by which the Russian Government had acquired a dominant influence in the Chinese provinces of Outer Mongolia and Sinkiang. In order to meet this growing threat to Japanese security, it had been found necessary to enter into the anti-Comintern Pact with Germany. But this step was merely a preliminary move in the direction of attempting to prove to other powers the importance of becoming parties to a general anti-Comintern pact.[41]

During a conversation with the American chargé d'affaires, Mr. Dickover, Horinouchi, the Japanese Vice Minister for Foreign Affairs, gave an assurance that "no secret military . . . arrangement of any kind was included in the agreement."[42] The Russian Government, however, was confident that some kind of a military alliance had been arranged between Germany and Japan, and the Soviet Ambassador in Tokyo informed Ambassador Grew, "with considerable heat," that this alliance was also directed against the rich British and Dutch colonial empires in the Far East. There was no real foundation for this statement, and Ambassador Grew himself discounted such talk.

j. *Japan Seeks an Accommodation with China*

Ambassador Grew was not disturbed by the ominous assurances of the Russian Ambassador that Japan and Germany had signed an agreement which aimed at eventual absorption of some of the choice British and Dutch possessions in the East Indies. He was happy that on New Year's Day 1937 there were no "current controversies of prime importance" between Japan and the United States.[43] A few weeks later Grew had a "long and intimate" conversation with Amau, the spokesman of the Foreign Office. The burden of their talk was the satisfactory state of Japanese-American relations.[44] But Grew was afraid that the situation was too good to last. In Japan one felt a "little like living on a volcano, never knowing when an explosion is going to occur."[45]

Grew believed that Prime Minister Hirota was largely responsible for this improvement in Japanese-American relations. He had made

[41] Statement of the Japanese Foreign Office, November 25, 1936. *Japan, 1931–1941*, II, 155–57.
[42] Grew *Diary*, December 3, 1936; *Ten Years in Japan*, p. 191.
[43] *Ibid.*, January 1, 1937; *ibid.*, p. 192.
[44] *Ibid.*, February 12, 1937; *ibid.*, pp. 205–6.
[45] *Ibid.*, March 19, 1937; *ibid.*, p. 207.

strenuous efforts to curb hostile comments in the Japanese press, and
Amau had struggled valiantly to have the Japanese public see America
in a more friendly light. But the most important factor in this uncertain
equation of good relations was the status of North China. Faced with a
rapidly growing communist menace, Japan had attempted to extend her
influence in some areas of North China, and this had led to increased
friction with the government of Chiang Kai-shek. The situation could
easily develop into armed conflict unless some formula of accommodation could be found. For many months successive Japanese ministries
endeavored to find this formula.

In the summer of 1936, Hirota made special efforts to conciliate
China at a time when Chinese mobs were maltreating Japanese nationals. At Chengtu, on August 24, two Japanese newspaper reporters were
murdered and two other Japanese nationals were "dragged from their
hotel and brutally beaten."[46] It seemed evident to the Japanese Foreign
Office that this mob action was the result of the "anti-Japanese agitation instigated by the Kuomintang and tolerated by the National Government." The Chengtu Incident was soon followed by many other unfortunate occurrences of a similar nature. On September 17 at Swatow
a hand grenade was thrown into a restaurant owned by a Japanese; at
Hankow on September 18 a Manchukuo official "was molested on a
train by a mob and some of his valuables were taken away." On the same
day at the same place a Japanese consular policeman was killed by some
Chinese while he was "patrolling the border of the Japanese concession
at Hankow." A few days later (September 23) at Shanghai one Japanese bluejacket was killed and two were wounded by Chinese gunmen.
As a result of these unprovoked attacks upon Japanese nationals, the
Japanese Foreign Minister issued a statement (September 28) that negotiations with China "could not be left to drift." China was "now at
the cross-roads where it must decide whether or not to shake hands with
Japan."[47]

The Chinese Government responded to this statement by asking
Secretary Hull to request Japan "to be moderate and conciliatory toward
China,"[48] and the British Government instructed its ambassador in
Tokyo to present a similar request to Foreign Minister Arita.[49] The

[46] R. Y. Jarvis to Secretary Hull, Hankow, September 8, 1936. 893.00 P.R./Han-
kow/112, MS, Department of State.

[47] E. R. Dickover to Secretary Hull, Tokyo, October 1, 1936. 793.94/8272, MS,
Department of State.

[48] Memorandum prepared by Maxwell M. Hamilton, Division of Far Eastern Affairs, October 2, 1936. 793.94/8260, Confidential file, MS, Department of State.

[49] Memorandum prepared by Mr. Hamilton recounting a conversation with André
de Laboulaye, the French Ambassador, October 2, 1936. 793.94/8266, MS, Department of State.

Foreign Office endeavored to quiet the situation by announcing on October 2 the decision to send Mr. Kuwashima, director of the East Asiatic Bureau, to China for conferences with Ambassador Kawagoe. In explaining this step the Foreign Office spokesman remarked that it was important for Japan to convey to Chiang Kai-shek its "real intentions."[50]

According to the Chinese ambassadors to France and Great Britain the real intentions of the Japanese Foreign Office were divulged in a series of "demands" or "requests" which were far-reaching in their scope. The Japanese Government attached special importance to the "demands" dealing with action against communism and with the autonomy movement in five northern provinces.[51]

On October 1 the Japanese Minister for Foreign Affairs informed the British Ambassador that "Japan was determined to make North China safe for Manchukuo."[52] Two days later the Foreign Office advised the American Embassy in Tokyo that the "only demand upon which they will insist is the suppression of anti-Japanese propaganda and agitation because of the danger of further incidents."[53] But this agitation against the Japanese grew in intensity, fanned doubtless by Communists who wished to exclude any thought of compromise between Chiang Kai-shek and the Japanese Government. On October 30, David Berger wrote to Secretary Hull to impart stray bits of information he had gleaned from a "local Chinese official of the Nanking Ministry of Finance." According to this official, in Nanking there was "now a desire to bring about what might be called a Soviet orientation in Chinese foreign affairs."[54]

A Soviet orientation in Chinese foreign affairs meant a widening breach between China and Japan. On December 3, Mr. Suma, first secretary of the Japanese Embassy in Nanking, confided to Ambassador Johnson that during the last month he had noticed a "distinct change for the worse in the attitude of the Chinese toward the Japanese, and

---

[50] E. R. Dickover to Secretary Hull, Tokyo, November 25, 1936. 894.00 P.R./107, MS, Department of State.

[51] These so-called Japanese "demands" were listed as follows: (1) autonomy of the five northern provinces; (2) economic co-operation with the whole of China; (3) joint measures for defense against communism; (4) appointment of Japanese advisers to the Chinese Government; (5) establishment of air communications between Japan and China; (6) a preferential tariff agreement; (7) the complete suppression of anti-Japanese propaganda in China. See memorandum by Maxwell M. Hamilton, of the Division of Far Eastern Affairs, October 3, 1936. 793.94/8234, MS, Department of State.

[52] Memorandum of conversation between Mr. Mallet, British chargé d'affaires at Washington, and Mr. Hornbeck, October 6, 1936. 793.94/8254, MS, Department of State.

[53] E. R. Dickover to Secretary Hull, Tokyo, October 3, 1936. 793.94/8218, MS, Department of State.

[54] David Berger to Secretary Hull, October 30, 1936. 793.94/8451, MS, Department of State.

even the soldiers and officers of General Chiang's own troops were now urging a more anti-Japanese attitude."[55]

This belligerent attitude on the part of the Chinese gave deep concern to the British Foreign Office. Anthony Eden called on the Chinese Ambassador in London and requested him to "urge his Government not to overplay its hand." If Nanking proved "completely recalcitrant to all overtures, the result will tend to solidify and unify Japanese public opinion in favor of stronger measures." In Tokyo the Chinese Ambassador talked to Grew in such a boastful manner that he gave the impression that "China is at present 'feeling its oats' and is very likely to overplay its hand in resisting Japanese overtures."[56]

k. *Chiang Kai-shek Welcomes Communist Help against Japan*

One of the main elements in producing this Chinese boastfulness was the union of the Nationalists and the Communists. This union contributed additional military strength to the Chinese position but the initiative would lie with the communist forces. They would fight only on their own terms and only for communist objectives. This fact was clearly perceived in Japan where the advancing Red tide was viewed with increasing alarm. According to Ambassador Grew the idea was taking root that the government required "but one principle in dealing with China: to oppose any movement in China which is definitely Communist and to assist any movement in China which is definitely anti-Communist. Increasingly, policy toward China appears as simply part of the larger question of the Russian and Communist menace."[57]

This viewpoint was understood by Mr. Hornbeck who prepared many memoranda for the Division of Far Eastern Affairs. On January 16 he discussed the situation in Shensi Province and then remarked: "There is serious danger that the rebellious troops at Sian (and Kansu provincial troops) may join forces with the large Communist armies occupying nearby regions and create a formidable Communist front in Northwest China. Such a development would jeopardize internal peace in China and disturb Sino-Japanese relations."[58]

[55] Interview between Ambassador Johnson and Mr. Suma, Nanking, December 3, 1936. 793.94/8481, MS, Department of State.

[56] Ambassador Grew to Secretary Hull, Tokyo, December 14, 1936. 793.94/8437, MS, Department of State.

[57] Ambassador Grew to Secretary Hull, Tokyo, December 31, 1936. 793.94/8501, MS, Department of State.

[58] Memorandum prepared by Stanley K. Hornbeck, January 16, 1937. 793.94/8505, MS, Department of State.

There was little doubt that the Nationalists and the Communists had reached some satisfactory understanding about objectives and procedures. Although Chiang Kai-shek had demanded that the Communists meet his rigorous conditions for joint operations, there were "reliable indications" that a "reconciliation was proceeding along lines privately agreed upon."[59] This fact gave Japanese statesmen further fears of the communist menace.

1. *Japan Tries to Conciliate China*

The Japanese Diet had not been satisfied with the efforts of the Hirota Ministry to find some solution for the impasse in Japanese-Chinese relations. On January 23, 1937, the Hirota Government went out of office, and on February 2 General Hayashi assumed the duties of Prime Minister. In the Diet, Hayashi immediately gave assurances of a pacific policy towards China: "I have no faith in a pugnacious foreign policy." In elaborating his viewpoint he further remarked: "It is greatly to be regretted if China makes the mistake of thinking Japan is wedded to a policy of aggression."

There were indications that the Hayashi Ministry would not press the far-reaching "demands" of the preceding administration. New negotiations with China would stress only two points: (1) the reduction of the Chinese tariff, and (2) the establishment of an air service between China and Japan. This program of conciliation had the support of the Japanese press which insisted that the government had "no wish to infringe on the territorial integrity of China as an independent State. Thus the contrast between the present tone of the press and its former tone is patent."[60]

When Mr. Grew went to talk with the new Japanese Foreign Minister (Naotake Sato) who took office on March 3, he was informed that a special effort would be made to bring about a "marked improvement" in Sino-Japanese relations. As far as America was concerned, Grew knew Sato "fairly well" and believed that relations "will be of the best."[61]

One of the first expressions of this Japanese conciliatory policy towards China was the dispatch of an economic mission under the chairmanship of Kenji Kodama, former president of the Yokohama Specie

[59] Ambassador Johnson to Secretary Hull, Nanking, February 23, 1937. 893.00/14016, MS, Department of State.

[60] Ambassador Grew to Secretary Hull, Tokyo, February 25, 1937. 793.94/8546, MS, Department of State.

[61] Ambassador Grew to Secretary Hull, Tokyo, March 5, 1937. 894.00/706, MS, Department of State.

Bank. Kodama was reputed to be an authority on Chinese affairs and also was popular in China. This Japanese mission spent two days in Nanking (March 16–17) and was received by Chiang Kai-shek who gave assurances that he desired "the friendly help and advice of Japan." Chiang further stated that Chinese industrialists would "unquestionably" accept the advice of Japanese industrial experts and would "follow their footsteps so that China's culture and economy may rise on the same plane with Japan for the stability of oriental peace and welfare."[62]

But these friendly words had little meaning when the Japanese endeavored to have them translated into favorable action. On March 24, Ambassador Johnson reported that the Japanese economic mission had accomplished nothing because the "Chinese appear to have insisted that a readjustment of the political relations of the two countries is necessary before any concrete program of 'economic cooperation' can be agreed upon." [63] In April, Ambassador Johnson was frankly pessimistic about an improvement in Japanese-Chinese relations. The Chinese attitude towards Japan had distinctly "stiffened" in recent months, and the Foreign Office would insist upon a fundamental change in the Japanese political position in North China before conducting negotiations of an economic character.[64]

The Nationalist Government in China knew that Japan was in no position to abrogate the Tangku Truce of May 31, 1933, or to abolish the Hopeh-Chahar Political Council of 1935. These measures had been taken as a means of defense against the rapidly increasing influence of Soviet Russia in North China. To Japan it was significant that the Nationalist Government was not at all worried about Russian control of the provinces of Outer Mongolia and Sinkiang. Why should Chinese nationalism bitterly oppose any Japanese expansion in North China while regarding with apparent indifference Russian imperialism in the same area? If Chiang Kai-shek had fallen under the domination of Russia, it would be highly dangerous for Japan to make any concessions to him.

But Prime Minister Hayashi still hoped for some satisfactory arrangement with China and he believed that economic adjustments might be the prelude to a political understanding. This friendly attitude, however, failed as bait for Chinese good will. As Ambassador Grew reported from Tokyo: "China's attitude has stiffened as a result

[62] Ambassador Johnson to Secretary Hull, Nanking, March 18, 1937. 793.94/8543, MS, Department of State.

[63] Ambassador Johnson to Secretary Hull, Nanking, March 24, 1937. 793.94/8554, MS, Department of State.

[64] Ambassador Johnson to Secretary Hull, Nanking, April 12, 1937. 893.00 P.R./ 135, MS, Department of State.

of Japan's conciliatory gestures."[65] These gestures did not cease when China refused to reciprocate. On May 10, Foreign Minister Sato assured foreign newspaper correspondents in Tokyo that Japan "does not demand exclusive rights, and believes that it can live peacefully side by side [with China] in the economic world."[66]

Ambassador Grew noted in May that the Japanese "conciliatory program met with setbacks during May and the Minister for Foreign Affairs, the chief proponent of the policy, found it necessary to issue statements showing a firmer stand on the part of Japan. . . . There was a recurrence of anti-Japanese agitation in North China and there occurred several incidents which were said to have caused serious concern to the Japanese authorities."[67] These difficulties were magnified by General Sung Che-yuan's non-co-operative attitude with reference to East Hopeh. In the early autumn of 1936 he had promised "the Japanese economic co-operation but has delayed signing a number of Japanese-prepared agreements for such co-operation. The Japanese desire certain preliminary economic developments such as railway construction, iron mining and cotton growing in order to pave the way for Japanese industrial establishments." Chiang Kai-shek himself desired "to maintain the *status quo* in North China" and not challenge the Japanese position there, but the opposition of his "subordinates" was making his position "difficult."[68]

In the last week in May 1937 the Hayashi Ministry went out of office with its program of economic adjustments with China unfulfilled. On June 4, Prince Konoye assumed the duties of Prime Minister and Hirota once more became Foreign Minister. During a conversation with Ambassador Grew on June 7, Hirota stated that his former three points of accommodation with China "were too abstract for present circumstances, and that he therefore proposed to find concrete solutions of the various problems outstanding between Japan and China."[69] Mr. Grew thought that China was in "the fortunate position of being able to refuse the granting of economic concessions which Japan urgently needs but for the attainment of which Japan is apparently not desirous of using armed forces."[70]

[65] Ambassador Grew to Secretary Hull, Tokyo, April 30, 1937. 793.94/8632, MS, Department of State.
[66] Ambassador Grew to Secretary Hull, Tokyo, May 10, 1937. 793.94/8643, MS, Department of State.
[67] Ambassador Grew to Secretary Hull, Tokyo, report on political conditions in Japan for May 1937. 894.00 P.R./114, MS, Department of State.
[68] Ambassador Johnson to Secretary Hull, Peiping, June 17, 1937. 793.94/8721, MS, Department of State.
[69] Ambassador Grew to Secretary Hull, Tokyo, June 24, 1937. 793.94/8725, MS, Department of State.
[70] *Ibid.*

m. *Soviet Russia Promotes a War between China and Japan*

It is apparent from the diplomatic correspondence that came to the Department of State from Nanking and Tokyo that in the summer of 1937 many Chinese officials were spoiling for a fight between Japan and China. In June 1937, Mr. Andrews, second secretary of the American Embassy in Tokyo, had a conversation with Dr. Mar who held a similar position in the Chinese Embassy. After Ambassador Grew read a report of this conversation he noted that Dr. Mar's attitude was "one of truculence and undue optimism, thus reflecting the enhanced sense of security that has been developed in a section of Chinese officialdom as a consequence of the development of the past year."[71] China, and not Japan, was ready for the outbreak of hostilities.

In China the Japanese Ambassador kept speaking in a conciliatory vein which stressed the idea that "the time would come when there would be 'understandings' between China and Japan." As a result of these pacific words Mr. Gauss, the American Consul-General at Shanghai, reported that in informed quarters it was believed that "the Japanese are unlikely to display a strong attitude or to take any aggressive measures in North China while the question of an Anglo-Japanese understanding is being explored."[72]

It is evident that many foreign observers in June–July 1937 regarded an outbreak of war between China and Japan as quite improbable. The Konoye Ministry seemed intent upon carrying out the pacific policy of the preceding administrations. It was with distinct surprise, therefore, that the governments of the major powers heard that armed hostilities had taken place near Peiping. On the night of July 7, in the vicinity of the famous Marco Polo bridge, some Japanese troops became involved in a sharp fight with some units of the Chinese Twenty-ninth Army.[73] A new drama that would end on a curtain line announcing Russian domiation of the Far East, had opened with an ominous fanfare. The whole world became an interested audience with few of the spectators realizing that the progress of the play was pointed towards a Russian conclusion. Chinese, Japanese, and Americans would move across the Far Eastern stage in intricate patterns that finally proclaimed a definite Muscovite motif. The Moscow theater never staged a more effective puppet show.

[71] *Ibid.*

[72] C. E. Gauss to Secretary Hull, Shanghai, June 30, 1937. 793.94/8992, MS, Department of State.

[73] Walter H. Mallory, "Japan Attacks, China Resists," *Foreign Affairs*, XVI (October 1937), 129–33; T. A. Bisson, "Origins of Sino-Japanese Hostilities," *Foreign Policy Reports*, XIII (March 1, 1938), 291–300.

VII

Mussolini Looks upon Ethiopia with Acquisitive Eyes

WHILE JAPAN was moving ahead in Manchuria in a sustained drive to expand the limits of the Japanese Empire, Mussolini was scrutinizing most carefully the map of Africa in order to plan a drive that would give imperial frontiers to Italy. These Italian dreams of empire did not begin with Mussolini. They began in the latter decades of the nineteenth century and they could be realized only if some of the great powers supported Italian aspirations.

a. *Britain Recognizes Italian Aspirations in Northeast Africa*

Italian colonial aspirations found their first expression in the activities of the missionary Sapeto who landed at Massaua in 1838. After a careful examination of the territory near the straits that separate the Red Sea from the Gulf of Aden, he acquired for the Rubbatino Company of Italy a concession on the Bay of Assab (November 15, 1869). In March 1882 this commercial company agreed to sell its rights to the Italian Government, and when this contract was approved by Parliament on July 5, 1882, Italy formally adopted a policy of colonial expansion in Africa.[1]

After the British Government recognized (1882) Italian sovereignty over Assab, the Italian Foreign Office elevated its gaze to other African horizons and in February 1885 the port of Massaua was occupied. Using this port as a wedge for further penetration, the Italian sphere of influence grew rapidly in size until in May 1889, under the terms of the Treaty of Ucciali, a nominal protectorate over Abyssinia was established. The legal basis for this protectorate was Article 17 of the treaty, but the Amharic text of that document differed from the Italian version and did not specifically place Abyssinian foreign affairs under the control of Italy. Inasmuch as the Amharic text was the only one that was actually signed, the Emperor Menelik's vigorous assertions of independence had a firm legal basis.[2]

---

[1] Maxwell H. H. Macartney and Paul Cremona, *Italy's Foreign and Colonial Policy, 1914–1937* (New York, 1938), p. 276; Charles F. Rey, *The Real Abyssinia* (Philadelphia, 1935), p. 139.

[2] William L. Langer, *The Diplomacy of Imperialism* (New York, 1935), I, 109, 272; Elizabeth P. McCallum, "Rivalries in Ethiopia," *World Affairs Pamphlets*, No. 12 (World Peace Foundation, Boston, 1935), p. 28.

The British Government supported Italian claims. On March 24 and April 15, 1891, an Anglo-Italian arrangement was concluded which recognized Italian control over a large portion of Northeast Africa.[3] But the French Government was strongly opposed to the Italian advance in Abyssinia, so they prompted Menelik to protest against the Italian interpretation of the Treaty of Ucciali and to assert his claims to territory as far as Khartoum. This aggressive attitude led the British to conclude another agreement with Italy (May 5, 1894) which placed the Province of Harar under Italian control. This action was in direct defiance of the Anglo-French Treaty of 1888 which related to this same territory.[4]

b. *Italy Deserts the Triple Alliance*

British recognition of Italian aspirations to control large portions of Ethiopia was followed by French and Russian efforts to preserve the independence of that empire. Munitions of war from France began to pour into Ethiopia and Menelik was emboldened in February 1893 to denounce the Treaty of Ucciali. In 1894, Italian troops advanced into Tigre, and for a time were highly successful. But this aggression was merely a prologue to the crushing defeat at Aduwa (March 1, 1896). In the Treaty of Addis Ababa, Italy recognized the independence of Ethiopia. Nevertheless, Italian hopes for eventual control over that vast region were still nursed by ambitious statesmen in Rome. These hopes could be realized only if France and Britain regarded them with friendly eyes. In Paris, Delcassé made some diplomatic gestures that resulted in the secret Franco-Italian convention of December 1900. As far as France was concerned, Tripoli was earmarked as a future Italian colony.[5] Two years later (November 1, 1902) this political flirtation assumed a more serious character when Italy promised to be neutral in the event that France was involved in a war she did not provoke.[6]

In the spring of 1906, during the sessions of the Algeciras Conference, this Franco-Italian entente paid good dividends to both France and Britain. They responded by concluding with Italy (December 13, 1906) a tripartite arrangement which apparently recognized the independence of Ethiopia. But behind a bold façade of diplomatic double-talk, French and British statesmen gave a friendly nod towards the old Italo-British accord of 1891 with its implications of Italian control over

[3] Augustus B. Wylde, *Modern Abyssinia* (London, 1901), chap. 9.
[4] Leonard Woolf, *Empire and Commerce in Africa* (New York, 1920), pp. 211 ff.
[5] A. F. Pribram, *The Secret Treaties of Austria-Hungary* (Cambridge, 1920), II, 227, 240–45.
[6] *Livre-Jaune: Les Accords Franco-Italiens de 1900–1902* (Paris, 1920), pp. 7–9.

Ethiopia. When Russia followed their example by concluding with Italy the Racconigi bargain of October 1909, the road to Tripoli was open.[7] Strengthened by this series of diplomatic deals, Italy provoked war with Turkey in 1911, and in October of the following year she concluded this conflict by securing the cession of Libya.[8]

By balancing the Triple Entente against the Triple Alliance, Italy had been able to gain her diplomatic objectives. But her intervention in the World War failed to bring any rich spoils of victory. In 1919, at Versailles, Allied statesmen unwittingly prepared the way for the subsequent development of fascism in Italy. When Orlando and Sonnino temporarily left the Peace Conference in high dudgeon because of President Wilson's appeal to the Italian people, "the British and French arranged to divide up Germany's African colonies, leaving the Italians completely out in the cold. Italy later accepted these arrangements with the understanding that she would receive compensations elsewhere, but these were never satisfactorily forthcoming. Here we find one basis for Italy's enduring bitterness over the final settlement, for the rape of Ethiopia in 1935, and for Mussolini's 'stab in the back' of 1940."[9]

c. *Britain Moves to Conciliate Mussolini*

In November 1919 the Italian Government made a strong effort to extract from Britain some territorial compensations in Africa that would help to sweeten the bitter draught forced upon Italy during the Paris Peace Conference. In the proposed arrangement Britain would receive a concession to construct a barrage on Lake Tana even though that body of water would be within the Italian sphere of influence in Ethiopia. Britain would also have the right to build a motor road from that lake to the Sudan. For her part of the bargain Italy would be given a right to build and operate a railway connecting Eritrea and Somaliland. This line would run to the west of Addis Ababa. Italy would also have the exclusive right to the economic exploitation of western Ethiopia.

The British Government rejected this Italian proposal because it was opposed to any sort of Italian control over the headwaters of the Nile.[10] But in 1925 the British Foreign Office experienced a change of heart and notes were exchanged between Sir Ronald Graham, the British

[7] Sidney B. Fay, *Origins of the World War* (New York, 1929), I, 406–11.

[8] Macartney and Cremona, *op. cit.*, p. 279.

[9] Thomas A. Bailey, *Woodrow Wilson and the Lost Peace* (New York, 1944), p. 266. Luigi Villari, in his *Expansion of Italy* (London, 1930), p. 41, discusses the Allied division of the spoils of war and points out how Great Britain received some 989,000 square miles of territory, France about 253,000 square miles, while Italy was awarded a small tract amounting to a mere 23,737 square miles.

[10] Macartney and Cremona, *op. cit.*, pp. 289–90.

Ambassador in Rome, and Mussolini (December 14, 20, 1925) in which the Italian proposals of 1919 were accepted. This meant British support of an Italian railway from Eritrea across Ethiopia to Somaliland, and British recognition of Italy's exclusive right to exploit the resources of western Ethiopia. Apparently, the British Government regarded the Anglo-Italian protocols of 1891 as still in force.[11]

The French Government immediately entered a protest against this Anglo-Italian accord. Britain and Italy then hurriedly addressed notes to the Secretary-General of the League of Nations which contained ample assurances of their innocent intentions towards Ethiopia. But it was obvious that the exchange "of Anglo-Italian notes of 1925 . . . remained in force also after the explanations furnished by the two Governments to Abyssinia, . . . and that the exclusive economic rights which Italy claimed in regard to Abyssinia before 1923 . . . were fully confirmed first by Great Britain and subsequently by France."[12]

Encouraged by this British support, Mussolini went ahead and concluded with Ethiopia a pact of friendship (August 2, 1928) and an additional convention which provided for the construction of a motor road from the port of Assab to Dessie. But work on this road was halted when it reached the boundary of Ethiopia. The Italian Government soon discovered that the "1928 Treaty remained . . . an absolutely dead letter except for the clause regarding conciliation and arbitration. . . . The non-fulfillment by Abyssinia of her economic engagements towards Italy has been one of the strongest grievances of the Italian Government against Abyssinia."[13]

d. *Italy's Alleged Need for Colonial Outlets*

Italian interest in Ethiopia was based upon the alleged need for colonies that would serve first of all as outlets for the overcrowded conditions in the Italian peninsula. In 1913 more than 700,000 Italians had left their native land to seek homes abroad, and the average annual emigration approximated half a million. The remittances which these emigrants

---

[11] Robert G. Woolbert, "Italy in Abyssinia," *Foreign Affairs,* XIII (1935), 499–508.

[12] Macartney and Cremona, *op. cit.,* p. 293. With reference to the Italo-British understanding of 1925, Gaetano Salvemini remarks: "It can surely not have escaped the notice of the Foreign Office that Abyssinia would be reluctant to consent to the construction of such a railway [joining Eritrea and Italian Somaliland], which would therefore lead to military occupation and some sort of political control. The 1925 agreement could only mean that the Foreign Office was giving Mussolini a free hand in a large portion of Abyssinia." "Mussolini, the Foreign Office and Abyssinia," *Contemporary Review,* CXLVIII (September 1935), 271.

[13] Macartney and Cremona, *op. cit.,* pp. 294–95; MacCallum, *op. cit.,* pp. 39–40.

sent home had constituted an important item in the Italian balance of international payments. But this large emigration with its golden flood of remittances had been checked by restrictive legislation enacted by the United States and many other countries. With these ordinary outlets no longer available for her surplus population, Italy became vitally interested in acquiring colonies that would not only welcome immigrants but would also produce essential raw materials needed for home manufacture. Ethiopia, with its large population, could be developed into an important market for Italian goods.

e. *The Walwal Incident Points in the Direction of War*

One factor that constantly disturbed the delicate Ethiopian equation was the aggressive attitude shown at times by the tribesmen of Emperor Haile Selassie in their relations with Italian nationals along the frontiers of Eritrea and Somaliland. Even after her entry into the League of Nations in 1923, Ethiopia had "remained a bad neighbour for all the bordering countries and for Italy in particular. . . . That the Italian colonies had suffered from the incursions of Abyssinian bands cannot be doubted."[14] In the event that Italy were involved in a war in Europe, these restive bands could be a real menace to the Italian colonial empire. This danger was emphasized by Mussolini on May 14, 1935, when he stated that he did not wish Ethiopia to be a "pistol that would be eternally pointed against us, and which in the case of European trouble would render our position in East Africa untenable."

From the viewpoint of Italian imperialists the case against Ethiopia was strong enough to justify war, and the profits that would accrue from such a conflict were carefully weighed. It would require only a spark to ignite the tinder that had been accumulating since 1896, and that tiny bit of fire was generated in the friction caused by the Walwal Incident in December 1934.

This incident had its origin in a dispute about the ownership of the wells at Walwal. It is worthy of note that the "Italians had for some years been in possession of Walwal which they had fortified without any protest from Ethiopia."[15] Although the Emperor claimed that Walwal was within the boundary of Ethiopia, it was evident that Italian forces had occupied that strategic spot for at least five years.[16]

Hostilities at Walwal could have led to an immediate outbreak of actual war, but there were several barriers along the road to conflict. As

[14] Macartney and Cremona, *op. cit.*, p. 285.
[15] E. W. Polson Newman, *Italy's Conquest of Abyssinia* (London, 1937), p. 17.
[16] Publications of the League of Nations, *Official Document C. 49, M. 22, 1935, VII.*

far as Italy was concerned these barriers were formidable: (1) the obligations imposed upon her by the League Covenant; (2) the obligations contained in the Pact of Paris; (3) the pledges freely given in the Three-Power Treaty of 1906; (4) the procedures outlined in the Italo-Ethiopian Arbitration Treaty of 1928. But Mussolini was not deeply concerned over these paper blockades. Since 1933 he had contemplated eventual war with Ethiopia and had been making preparations for it.[17] For the time being, however, he would make a bow in the direction of a pacific settlement of the dispute. While he was making ready for conflict, he would find some plausible excuse for it.

The Emperor Haile Selassie was eager to upset Mussolini's plans in this regard, so he promptly offered arbitration in accordance with the terms of the treaty of 1928. When the Italian Foreign Office rejected this offer and demanded immediate reparation, Ethiopia directed the attention of the League of Nations to the implications of the Walwal Incident (December 14). On December 16, Italy supplied the League with her version of the incident. Some three weeks later (January 3, 1935) Ethiopia made a formal appeal to the League and invoked the application of Article 11 of the Covenant.[18] At the next meeting of the Council (January 11) some action would have to be taken on the Italo-Ethiopian dispute.

In order to anticipate League action, and in an effort to secure Italy's support in eventual pressure upon Germany, Pierre Laval made a visit to Rome and arrived at an accord with Mussolini. In agreement with the terms of this treaty of January 7, 1935, Italy made some concessions with reference to Tunis. In return she received 2,500 shares in the Djibouti Railroad, a considerable strip of territory to add to Italian Libya, a similar increase of territory to be joined to Eritrea, and a final gift of the island of Dumeira in the Red Sea. For these favors Mussolini agreed to consult with France in the event of any threat to the status quo in Europe.

But the published terms of this agreement told only half the story. It is evident that a secret understanding was reached between Mussolini and Laval on January 7, 1935. When Mussolini was asked by Ward Price if he had been given a free hand in Ethiopia by his accord with Laval, he gave the ambiguous answer: "It is correct that all disputes between ourselves and France were settled by the agreement of 7 January."[19] The comments of General de Bono were not so Delphic: "The

---

[17] General Emilo de Bono, *Anno XIII* (London, 1937), pp. 1–17, 55–89.

[18] According to Article 11 any war or threat of war was a "matter of concern to the whole League, and the League shall take any action that may be deemed wise and effectual to safeguard the peace of nations."

[19] London *Daily Mail*, August 24, 1935.

conversations with M. Laval led us to hope that, so far as France was concerned, no obstacles would be placed in our path in any eventual action we should take against Abyssinia."[20] The implications of the Franco-Italian treaty were abundantly clear: "In return for Italian co-operation in Europe, Laval was willing to sacrifice anything, even the League of Nations itself, as events proved. Mussolini understood this to be the case and was prepared to exploit all of its possibilities."[21]

When the Council of the League of Nations met on January 11, Mussolini was ready with certain tactics of delay. He adopted a conciliatory tone with reference to difficulties with Ethiopia and appeared to be ready to proceed in accordance with the provisions of the Italo-Ethiopian Treaty of 1928. During the next two months there was a good deal of diplomatic sparring with no real action towards a settlement of the dispute. On March 17, Ethiopia submitted an appeal to the League of Nations requesting a full investigation of the situation under the terms of Article 15 of the Covenant. But the League was gravely disturbed about other matters. On March 16, Germany had abrogated the clauses of the Treaty of Versailles which limited her armed forces. This defiant step led to the conference at Stresa where Britain, France, and Italy sought some formula to preserve the peace of Europe. There was no time for any protracted discussion of the Italo-Ethiopian dispute. But as the weeks passed and no progress was made in connection with the arbitration of the Walwal Incident, the Council of the League was compelled to adopt two resolutions (May 25). One called upon the two powers in dispute to name the Conciliation Council of four arbitrators (according to the provisions of the treaty of 1928) and to arrive at some settlement by August 25. The other resolution provided for a meeting of the Council in the event that the arbitral proceedings failed to arrive at an acceptable result.[22]

As many statesmen had anticipated, the attempt to arbitrate the Walwal Incident ended in a dismal failure on July 9 when the counsel for Ethiopia referred to Walwal as situated within Ethiopian territory. As soon as this statement was made, the Italian representative left the meeting in evident anger and the dispute took on a more serious aspect. For several weeks the Italian Government had been rushing military supplies to Africa in preparation for eventual hostilities. An early outbreak of war was indicated by Mussolini in an address at Cagliari to the Black Shirts leaving for Africa (June 8): "We have old and new accounts to settle; we will settle them. We shall take no account of what may be

[20] Macartney and Cremona, *op. cit.,* pp. 299–300.
[21] C. Grove Haines and Ross J. S. Hoffman, *The Origins and Background of the Second World War* (New York, 1943), pp. 378–79.
[22] *Survey of International Affairs, 1935,* pp. 143–65.

said beyond our frontiers, because we ourselves, we alone and exclusively, are the judges of our interests and the guarantors of our future."[23]

f. *Secretary Stimson Enjoys Friendly Relations with Mussolini*

The progress of the Italo-Ethiopian dispute was followed with great
interest by President Roosevelt and Secretary Hull. In Rome the American attitude towards this African adventure was studied with equal interest, and it was soon evident that the Italian Government was extremely anxious to preserve the friendly relations that had been so carefully
established by Secretary Stimson during the Hoover Administration. In
July 1931, Stimson paid a visit to Rome for talks with Mussolini and
Dino Grandi concerning disarmament. On July 3, Grandi, the Italian
Minister for Foreign Affairs, made a statement to the Associated Press
with reference to this visit: "I met Mr. Stimson in London during the
Naval Conference and our relations were always most cordial. . . .
There is no prearranged program of conversations. There will be a
friendly exchange of ideas. Italy has never been very favorable to the
idea that the world is divided into geographical sectors. . . . Europe cannot get along without America."[24]

Stimson arrived in Rome on July 8, and on the following day he had
a conference with Mussolini in the Venezia Palace. There was the predicted "friendly exchange of ideas." When Stimson emphasized the
importance of pushing a program of disarmament, Mussolini indicated
his ardent agreement with this viewpoint and stated "emphatically that
everybody knew where Italy stood: she was for disarmament and
peace."[25]

After a pleasant week end at Nettuno with Grandi, including a somewhat terrifying speedboat trip with Mussolini, Stimson returned to
Rome for further conversations with Italian leaders. Grandi made it
clear that Italy feared and opposed "French hegemony" in Europe. She
stood for a "balance of power," side by side "with Great Britain."

Mussolini showed to Stimson and his wife "his attractive side" and
they grew to like him "very much."[26] Grandi made an equally good impression upon them, and when Stimson was about to leave Rome, he
issued a very friendly statement to the press (July 14): "We shall bear

---

[23] *Ibid.,* p. 159.

[24] Statement to the press made by Dino Grandi, July 3, 1931. 033.1140 Stimson,
Henry L./137, MS, Department of State.

[25] Memorandum of a conversation with Signor Benito Mussolini, head of the
Italian Government, at Rome, Thursday, July 9, 1931. 033.1140 Stimson, Henry L./
141, MS, Department of State.

[26] Henry L. Stimson and McGeorge Bundy, *On Active Service in War and Peace*
(New York, 1948), pp. 268–69.

away with us a memory of the kindness expressed to us not only by the Italian Government but by her people everywhere which has convinced us of the essential sympathy which exists between the people of Italy and America. This common understanding augurs well for the future relations of the two countries."[27]

In order to confirm these cordial relations, in November 1931, Dino Grandi decided to pay a brief visit to the United States. On the eve of his sailing for New York, the London *Times* published a penetrating survey of Italo-American relations. It pointed out that Grandi had made an "excellent personal impression" when he went to Washington after the close of the World War as a member of the Italian delegation which had been sent to settle the problem of war debts. In 1931 it was fortunate for Grandi that there were "no outstanding disputes between Italy and the United States." Recent restrictions on Italian immigration into the United States might have caused some unfriendly feeling, but Mussolini had prevented this by indicating his opposition to the old system whereby Italy was losing each year a large part of her population. In order to keep Italians home he had launched new projects "for more intensive and scientific farming and land reclamation plans." On the whole, therefore, there was quite a "satisfactory background for that political co-operation which Signor Mussolini, especially since last January 1, is anxious to promote between the two countries."[28]

Dino Grandi informed American press correspondents that he was going to the United States as an "Ambassador of my country, but also as an Italian to interpret to the great American people the sentiments of deep and unchanging friendship of all Italians."[29] He landed in New York on November 16 and was met by Under Secretary of State William R. Castle. On the train ride to Washington, Grandi expressed his viewpoints freely to Castle. With regard to France he remarked that her statesmen wished "absolute security" but that was a goal most difficult to attain. Disarmament was a question with so many complexities that he felt it wise to visit Washington to discover how far the American Government wanted "to go at the [next Geneva] Conference." Italy would go "as far" as America in that regard.

Castle informed Grandi that Secretary Stimson felt that "there is little hope of any success [in disarmament] unless first the political questions of Europe can be settled, beginning with the Polish Corridor." Grandi agreed with this viewpoint but feared that they could not

[27] John W. Garrett to the Secretary of State, Rome, July 16, 1931. 033.1140 Stimson, Henry L./137, MS, Department of State.

[28] London *Times,* November 5, 1931.

[29] Alexander Kirk to Secretary Stimson, November 10, 1931, inclosure No. 2. 033.6511 Grandi, Dino/87, MS, Department of State.

be settled "now without war." Italy took a revisionist attitude towards the peace treaties of 1919, but any important revisions would have to be postponed for some years. He had informed Chancellor Brüning of this fact and had suggested that he enter into a formal engagement with France to that effect, but Brüning said that any such arrangement would mean his speedy fall from office. He (Brüning) would make an effort, however, to stop "the talk about these hoped-for revisions."

Grandi was inclined to "agree with the French that perhaps it might be just as well to have the Nazis in for a time as they would not dare . . . seriously to change the German foreign policy, and if the rest of Germany saw that even they would have to appeal for outside help, the people might settle down and try to make the best of things."[30]

Grandi had a three-hour conference with President Hoover soon after he reached Washington, and they discussed many details concerning reparations and disarmament. The cordial spirit in which these conversations were conducted made a great impression in Italy. Virginio Gayda was certain that this friendly atmosphere was "another proof that Italian and American foreign policy happily coincide on the general matters now at issue." Much satisfaction was felt at the "unlimited scope of the Washington conversations, and the Secretary's phrase, 'the sky is the limit,' is echoed through the Italian press."[31]

When Grandi sailed for Italy on November 27 he could find "no words to express" the "deep impressions and dear remembrances" he took back with him.[32] A brief Italo-American understanding had been established, and during the sessions of the Disarmament Conference in Geneva during the spring of 1932, Grandi played his role according to schedule. But France blocked the agreement so desperately needed and thus prepared the way for the fall of the Brüning Ministry and the eventual elevation of Hitler to the office of Chancellor.[33]

The failure of the Disarmament Conference to settle the pressing problems before it was deeply discouraging to Secretary Stimson, but he had no fault to find with the attitude of Italy. During the last days of Stimson's term of office as Secretary of State, Signor Augusto Rosso, the Italian Ambassador, went to the Department of State to convey farewell greetings. After the usual salutations, Stimson "thanked the Ambassador and said that, in the case of Italy" his satisfaction at the

[30] Memorandum of a conversation between Signor Grandi and William R. Castle, November 16, 1931. 033.6511 Grandi, Dino/99, MS, Department of State.

[31] Alexander Kirk to Secretary Stimson, November 19, 24, 1931. 033.6511 Grandi, Dino/85–86, MS, Department of State.

[32] Dino Grandi to Secretary Stimson, November 27, 1931. 033.6511 Grandi, Dino/88, MS, Department of State.

[33] See *ante*, p. 34–35.

good relations between the two countries was "accompanied by the personal pleasure he had received in his personal contacts not only with Signor Mussolini but with those gentlemen who represented him."[34] Apparently, Stimson never felt any delicacy in meeting and conversing with the Italian dictator, and when he left office on March 4, 1933, American relations with Italy were of a most cordial character. Under the Roosevelt Administration they soon underwent a complete change.

g. *General Johnson Creates Tension in Italian-American Relations*

The Italo-American accord erected by Secretary Stimson quickly dissolved under the warmth of Secretary Hull's idealistic fervor. The first hint of difficulty came when the irrepressible General Hugh S. Johnson delivered a typical speech before the National Association of Manufacturers (December 7, 1933). During the course of his colorful remarks, Johnson told with great zest of an Italian official who approached Alexander Legge (who had charge of Allied purchasing during the World War) with the usual request in mind. Before he could express it, Legge burst out with vehemence: "Good morning, Sunny Italy! When are those wops of yours going to stop running and start fighting?" The official was nonplussed for a moment and then excitedly murmured: "You wait—zey play treek."

The Italian Ambassador regarded this story as a serious reflection upon the record of Italy during the World War and he asked the Acting Secretary of State for an explanation.[35] All that Mr. Phillips could do was to send a lame reply that General Johnson "may not have been accurately quoted." In any event, Mr. Phillips was certain that the ebullient General had not intended to offend the Italian Government or "the Italian people."[36]

These ill-considered remarks of General Johnson had little effect upon the course of Italo-American relations, but the incident reflected a definite change in the climate of opinion in Washington after the inauguration of President Roosevelt. During the Administration of President Hoover there had been no important officials prone to shoot from the lip. After March 4, 1933, something new and crude had been added to the picture in Washington.

[34] Memorandum of a conversation between Secretary Stimson and the Italian Ambassador, Signor Augusto Rosso, February 23, 1933. 711.65/42, MS, Department of State.

[35] Augusto Rosso to William Phillips, Acting Secretary of State, December 8, 1933. 711.65/44, MS, Department of State.

[36] William Phillips to Signor Augusto Rosso, December 12, 1933. 711.65/44, MS, Department of State.

h. *Beginnings of the Rome-Berlin Axis*

In Rome, in the early years of the Roosevelt reign, there were some innovations in the diplomatic picture that matched the changes in Washington. On June 14–15, 1934, there was an important conference between Hitler and Mussolini at Venice. Many observers believed that these conversations had a definite connection with the bloody purge of the Nazi Party two weeks later. The American Ambassador was inclined to the view that "Mussolini had no doubt advised Hitler that it would be necessary to take drastic steps to maintain his authority."[37] It is quite probable that the Duce did advise the adoption of stern measures to enforce party discipline, but it is not likely that he counseled the bloody procedure followed by Hitler. Liquidation can be effected without adverse publicity and without the sanguinary excesses committed by the Nazi leaders.

While some statesmen indulged in speculation about the degree of responsibility which rested upon Mussolini's shoulders for the Nazi purge of June 30, every official in Europe realized that the meeting of June 14–15 signalized the beginnings of an accord that carried a grave threat to the peace of the Continent. In the United States there were many misgivings concerning this new relationship, and they helped to undermine the Italo-American understanding so painstakingly erected by Stimson. American dislike of Hitler had been rapidly increasing since he assumed the office of Chancellor, and it reached a high point after the party purge. Any friendly gestures of Mussolini in the direction of the German dictator would be certain to arouse deep dissatisfaction in many American circles. It would not be long before Mussolini and Hitler were regarded as two peas in the same black pod. The Italo-Ethiopian dispute prepared the way for this change in American opinion.

i. *Anthony Eden Whispers a Few Confidences to Hugh Wilson*

On May 25 the Council of the League of Nations had adopted two resolutions which it had hoped would provide a formula for the settlement of the Italo-Ethiopian dispute. But Anthony Eden had serious doubts about arriving at an early solution of this problem. During the course of a dinner he had with Ambassador Hugh Wilson at Geneva, he and Lord Cranborne (Eden's Parliamentary assistant) became quite voluble. Eden was in a difficult position. British public opinion was in favor

[37] Breckinridge Long to Secretary Hull, Rome, July 5, 1934. 862.00/3308, MS, Department of State.

of a stern attitude towards Italy, but Eden was fearful that vigorous action might endanger the stability of the Stresa accord. Moreover, Eden had to deal with Pierre Laval who could not "understand Eden's insistence in the Abyssinian matter and seemed willing to adopt a formula face-saving for the League and leaving Italy a free hand."

Eden was particularly disappointed in the attitude of Beneš. He had discovered that the Czechoslovakian statesman was "concerned only with the Austrian question, was unwilling to bring pressure upon Italy or to do anything which would run the slightest risk of upsetting the Continental alignment."

Eden's attitude towards Hitler and Germany was significant. While he was imbued with a "profound skepticism" of the program outlined in Hitler's recent speech, he was determined to go ahead and "explore fully" the possibilities for peace. He was anxious to have Germany re-enter the League, and in his conversation with Hitler he had given assurances that "the British were willing to have the Treaty of Versailles separated from the Covenant if the German so desired." This comment, said Mr. Wilson, was so radical that it should be kept "extremely confidential."

From close observation of the scene in Geneva, Ambassador Wilson had come to the conclusion that Laval and Eden were an "excellent team." He had the impression that Laval was "developing into the type of Foreign Minister that Briand was, with perhaps a greater sense of political realism and a more practical method of achieving and applying his policies. Both he and Eden are on the up-grade politically [and] they have a decided esteem for each other."[38]

j. The Walwal Arbitration Encounters a Delay

In Geneva it was evident to Prentiss B. Gilbert that the arbitration of the Walwal Incident would encounter a lengthy delay. The Ethiopian Government had named its representatives on the arbitral board, but these selections had not impressed Mr. Gilbert very favorably. M. de la Pradelle did not enjoy "the best of reputations," while Pitman Potter had little ability to handle "matters having to do with actual foreign affairs in the practical realm." To Gilbert he appeared as the "sort of man who believes in Santa Claus."[39]

[38] Ambassador Hugh Wilson to Secretary Hull, Geneva, May 29, 1935. 862.20/1058, MS, Department of State.

[39] Prentiss B. Gilbert to Wallace Murray, June 1, 1935. 765.84/501, MS, Department of State. It is interesting to note that Professor Pitman B. Potter has written a monograph on the Wal Wal Arbitration (Washington, 1938), which reviews the evidence in the case and presents the more important documents. It is significant that the arbitral commission dodged the essential point at issue in the dispute: in whose territory was Walwal located in December 1934?

This generous attitude should have appealed to the Italian Government but it was soon obvious that the Walwal Incident was given scant consideration by Mussolini. He had larger objectives in mind. These were partially disclosed during a conversation between Ambassador Long and Signor Suvich, the Italian Under Secretary of State for Foreign Affairs. The Italian diplomat freely confided his hope that the "League of Nations, through its powers of arbitration, should see fit to offer Italy a mandate for Abyssinia. This would be the best thing for Abyssinia which was an undeveloped and lawless country. . . . Italy could not afford to withdraw her soldiers from there; as a matter of fact it was necessary to send more soldiers to protect Italian colonists" from the raids of armed Ethiopians.[40]

These raids from Ethiopia into adjacent Italian colonial territory were the subject of some trenchant editorials by Virginio Gayda in the *Giornale d'Italia*, June 18–20. The Italian public was informed that they could not be permitted to continue indefinitely. Apparently, war or a mandate over Ethiopia were the only alternatives.[41]

k. *Mussolini Rejects a Proposal of Anthony Eden*

Anthony Eden did not agree with Virginio Gayda that war or an Italian mandate over Ethiopia were the only alternatives in the Italo-Ethiopian dispute. A mandate over Ethiopia would offer entirely too much incentive to Mussolini to push his far-reaching plans for colonial expansion. Perhaps the Duce would be satisfied with merely a big bite out of the Ethiopian apple. With this idea in mind, Eden had a momentous interview with the Italian dictator in Rome. Under the terms of his proposal, Britain would offer Ethiopia an outlet to the sea at Zeila, in British Somaliland, together with a narrow strip of land that would connect that port with Ethiopian territory. Ethiopia would then cede to Italy a part of the Ogaden and would also grant certain economic concessions to Italian nationals.

Mussolini immediately rejected the proposals of Eden. In any settlement of the dispute with Ethiopia he would insist upon the annexation of all "those parts of Abyssinia which did not form part of Abyssinia proper." In addition he wished to "control Abyssinia." If he had to go to war to attain his objectives he would endeavor "to wipe the name of Abyssinia from the map."[42]

[40] Ambassador Long to Secretary Hull, Rome, June 10, 1935. 765.84/528, MS, Department of State.

[41] Alexander Kirk to Secretary Hull, Rome, June 20, 1935. 765.84/434, MS, Department of State.

[42] Macartney and Cremona, *op. cit.*, p. 303.

The reaction of Eden to these frank statements is not clearly revealed. In Rome, Italian officials attempted to establish the fiction that Eden's visit had been in the nature of a "conciliatory 'pat on the back' intended to assuage any ill-feeling that might have been caused by England's independent negotiations of naval agreements with Germany. . . . The Mussolini-Eden exchange of views is generally believed to have proved satisfactory on both sides."[43]

The American chargé at Geneva hurriedly telegraphed that he had learned from authoritative sources that Mussolini had decided to "establish a protectorate over Abyssinia," and Eden had been informed of that intention. He had also heard a Russian official remark that "while his Government had originally felt Mussolini was 'playing poker' they had now changed their ideas and believed he 'meant business.' "[44]

The Italian press had criticized Eden's proposals as inadequate, while French press opinion was hostile because Zeila would be in competition with the port of Djibouti and this would violate the tripartite treaty of 1906. In Rome, Virginio Gayda complained that Eden's concessions "neither corresponded to the avowed purposes of the British Government nor answered Italy's requirements for security and economic expansion."[45]

Kirk, the American chargé in Rome, discussed the situation with Chambrun, the French Ambassador, who confided that before "leaving for his recent trip to Paris he had been authorized by Mussolini to state to the French Government that he [the Duce] was definitely in favor of a peaceful solution of the conflict with Abyssinia if Italy's prestige and interests could be safeguarded." It was Chambrun's belief that some "gesture was essential to vindicate the honor and prestige of Italy and this could be effected by the cession of Adowa which would enable Mussolini to advertise the triumph of his regime over the defeat of the previous government."[46]

1. *The Emperor of Ethiopia Seeks American Intervention*

While the principal European powers were anxiously seeking some solution of the Italo-Ethiopian dispute, Emperor Haile Selassie handed to the American chargé at Addis Ababa a note which requested the Ameri-

---

[43] Alexander Kirk to Secretary Hull, Rome, June 28, 1935. 765.84/479, MS, Department of State.

[44] Mayer to Secretary Hull, Geneva, June 29, 1935. 765.84/419, MS, Department of State.

[45] Alexander Kirk to Secretary Hull, Rome, July 2, 1935. 765.84/429, MS, Department of State.

[46] Alexander Kirk to Secretary Hull, Rome, July 2, 1935. 765.84/427, MS, Department of State.

can Government to invoke the Pact of Paris as a means of arresting the
Italian advance into Ethiopia. Secretary Hull answered this request in a
note that was cool and cautious: "My Government hopes that the . . .
arbitral agency dealing with this controversy may be able to arrive at a
decision satisfactory to both of the Governments immediately concerned. . . . My Government would be loath to believe that either of the
Powers [Italy and Ethiopia] would resort to other than pacific means
as a method of dealing with this controversy."[47]

This instruction was given to the press on July 6 and it gave birth to
many rumors concerning American policy in Ethiopia. Secretary Hull
was making his viewpoint very clear to the major powers in Europe but
he was not doing it in the spectacular manner of Secretary Stimson.
Some students of international law thought he was being too cautious
in his handling of the matter. Professor Quincy Wright hurriedly wrote
to Hull and expressed the opinion that "a failure on our part to do anything would be such a severe blow to the cause of peace and respect for
the Pact of Paris that I hope you will find it possible to accept an invitation to consult, if offered, by the League of Nations."[48]

Under pressure of enthusiasts like Professor Wright, Secretary Hull
requested the Italian Ambassador to call at the Department of State.
When Signor Rosso arrived he was informed that the American Government was "deeply interested in the preservation of peace in all parts
of the world." For this reason Mr. Hull felt "impelled to impress upon
the Italian Ambassador our increasing concern over the situation arising
out of Italy's dispute with Ethiopia and our earnest hope that a means
may be found to arrive at a peaceful . . . solution of the problem."[49]

On the following afternoon both the British and French ambassadors
paid formal visits to the Department of State and received statements
similar to the one given to Ambassador Rosso. Mr. Phillips, during a
long conversation with the British Ambassador, drew attention to an
article in the *Boston Evening Transcript* which stated that "it is nearly
the unanimous conclusion of London opinion that the Briand-Kellogg
Pact is dead owing to the brusque refusal of the American Government
to invoke that pact." It was important, Mr. Phillips emphasized, for the
British Government to realize that "this impression is entirely contrary
to the sense of our note to the Emperor."[50]

---

[47] Secretary Hull to American chargé at Addis Ababa, July 5, 1935. 765.84/432,
MS, Department of State.
[48] Quincy Wright to Secretary Hull, July 8, 1935. 765.84/469, MS, Department
of State.
[49] Statement of Secretary Hull to the Italian Ambassador, July 10, 1935. 765.84/
479A, MS, Department of State.
[50] Memorandum of a conversation between Mr. Phillips and the British Ambassador, July 11, 1935. 765.84/611, MS, Department of State.

In order to make the viewpoint of the Department of State entirely clear in this regard, Secretary Hull issued on July 12 a statement to the effect that "the Pact of Paris is no less binding now than when it was entered into by the 63 nations that are parties to it. . . . The United States and the other nations are interested in the maintenance of the Pact and the sanctity of international commitments assumed thereby."[51]

Newton D. Baker, former Secretary of War, was delighted with this press statement of July 12. He had long been of the opinion that it would be "highly desirable to have our country notify the League of Nations that the United States would co-operate with it in any measures it found desirable to take, short of war, to enforce its covenants among its own members." It was apparent to him that caution would never save the day for world peace. He was persuaded that "if the world is to be saved, it must be by daring."[52]

m. *Italy Is Anxious to Assume the White Man's Burden in Africa*

It was soon apparent to Secretary Hull that a policy of "daring" might involve the United States in war. Mussolini was determined to enjoy his adventure in Africa no matter how high the cost might run. From London the word came that there was little hope of preserving the peace of Europe. Of course Britain would continue her "efforts to prevent war," but there was small chance that these would be successful.[53] In Paris, Straus saw Laval who gave assurances that he was "anxious to avoid war" between Italy and Ethiopia. This anxiety led him to propose a formula whereby Italy would be given a mandate over Ethiopia. Under its terms the Italian Government would receive not only territorial concessions and economic advantages but would also be given some form of "administrative control" over Ethiopia. If these concessions were not made at once, Mussolini would move towards war. When asked what effect these belligerent moves of Mussolini would have upon Europe, Laval bluntly replied: "That is Mussolini's business— not mine."[54]

From Rome indirect news came from Mr. H. V. Kaltenborn that Mussolini had informed him that there was still a possibility of peace, but this peace must be on his terms. He was really planning a "colonial enterprise on a large scale rather than a campaign of conquest." This

[51] Department of State, *Press Release,* July 13, 1935, pp. 53–54.
[52] Newton D. Baker to Secretary Hull, July 12, 1935. 765.84/626, MS, Department of State.
[53] Ambassador Bingham to Secretary Hull, London, July 16, 1935. 765.84/541, MS, Department of State.
[54] Straus to Secretary Hull, Paris, July 13, 1935. *Urgent and Confidential,* 765.84/524, MS, Department of State.

colonial enterprise might involve some "military operations" to satisfy Italy's "prestige and enable her to weaken the power of the Negus," but after these ends had been accomplished the "process of colonial enterprise will be gradually carried out."[55]

The Japanese Government, apparently impressed with the beneficent aspects of Italian "colonial enterprise," immediately announced an attitude of neutrality with reference to the situation in Ethiopia. The Italian press acclaimed this "unequivocal" declaration as a gesture of friendship towards Italy, and it was widely interpreted as an indication of a new political alignment.[56]

Further news from Rome came in the form of a series of answers that Mussolini gave to some questions that had been formulated by Mrs. William B. Meloney, of the *New York Herald-Tribune*. In his answers Mussolini stated that "good will on the Italian side has been met by Abyssinia with stubborn obstruction. The treacherous attack on Walwal . . . has been nothing but the latest proof of a spirit of persistent hostility which has lasted for half a century." It was obvious that the frontiers of the Italian colonial empire would have to be defended. Italy, moreover, had now arrived at a clear realization of the "mission of civilization that she has to accomplish in Abyssinia, not only on her own behalf but also on that of the whole western world."[57]

Some nations in the Western world were a little suspicious that Mussolini was unduly anxious to bear the White Man's burden in Ethiopia. In order to meet their objections, the Duce gave an interview to one of the correspondents of the *Echo de Paris* (July 16) in which he crisply remarked that he "was seeking for Italy in Abyssinia what British and French colonizers had sought for their countries." Then as a sop to French and British statesmen, he gave the assurance that he would "continue to consider Austrian independence as the dominating factor in his foreign policy."[58] Germany was not disturbed by this thrust at Nazi ambitions, and von Bülow, in Berlin, informed Dodd that he thought that pressure upon Italy "for the application of the Kellogg Pact might do harm." Hitler's Government was careful to take no step that would cause friction with Italy.[59]

[55] Alexander Kirk to Secretary Hull, Rome, July 17, 1935. *Confidential file,* 765.84/556, MS, Department of State.

[56] Alexander Kirk to Secretary Hull, Rome, July 18, 1935. *Confidential file,* 765.84/567, MS, Department of State.

[57] Alexander Kirk to Secretary Hull, Rome, July 18, 1935. *Strictly Confidential,* 765.84/568, MS, Department of State.

[58] Alexander Kirk to Secretary Hull, Rome, July 23, 1935. 765.84/602, MS, Department of State.

[59] Ambassador Dodd to Secretary Hull, Berlin, July 18, 1935. 826.00/3539, MS, Department of State.

n. *President Roosevelt Urges Mussolini to Accept Arbitration*

The League of Nations, like France and Germany, was distinctly cautious in its handling of the Italo-Ethiopian dispute. Although the council adopted a resolution which provided for a general examination of the Ethiopian situation at the meeting scheduled for September 4, it also adopted another resolution which sharply limited the scope of the Walwal arbitration. In order to give some strength to this action of the League, President Roosevelt made a public statement on August 1 in which he voiced the hope "of the people and the Government of the United States that an amicable solution will be found [for the settlement of the Italo-Ethiopian controversy] and that peace will be maintained."[60]

Emperor Haile Selassie was delighted with this Presidential expression of a hope for peace, but diplomatic circles at Addis Ababa were of the opinion that the government of the United States had "adopted a very cautious attitude, calculated to avoid at all cost any action or positive intervention in the Italo-Ethiopian controversy."[61] This viewpoint nettled Secretary Hull who instructed our ambassadors in London and Paris to send "all information possible to enable our Government to determine whether any further action by it . . . as a signatory of the Pact of Paris would . . . have a beneficial rather than a disadvantageous effect."[62]

When the American chargé at Paris responded with a statement that both the French and British governments were of the opinion that some positive action by the United States would be of real assistance in halting the aggressive plans of Mussolini, a conference was held at the White House. The President suggested an immediate message to Mussolini, so on August 18, Hull instructed Mr. Kirk, the American chargé at Rome, to convey to the Duce the earnest hope of the American Chief Executive that "the controversy between Italy and Ethiopia will be resolved without resort to armed conflict."[63]

When Mr. Kirk delivered this message the following day, Mussolini assured him that he appreciated the "character of the message and its expression of friendliness," but he had already mobilized one million men for conflict with Ethiopia which was now inevitable. Regardless of

[60] Department of State, *Press Release*, August 10, 1935, p. 119.
[61] C. Van H. Engert to Secretary Hull, Addis Ababa, August 9, 1935. 765.84/1075, MS, Department of State.
[62] Cordell Hull, *Memoirs* (New York, 1948), I, 421.
[63] Secretary Hull to Alexander Kirk, August 18, 1935; *Peace and War: United States Foreign Policy, 1931–1941* (Washington, 1943), p. 266.

League action, Italy would proceed with her plans. If the opposition of other countries developed to the point of actual intervention, Italy would "take steps accordingly."[64]

In the face of this Italian defiance, France and Britain worked feverishly to find some solution short of war. At Paris, during August 15–18, tripartite negotiations had been carried on with reference to the Ethiopian situation, and proposals had been made to Mussolini which reduced the sovereignty of Ethiopia to a shadow. But the Duce wanted the whole Abyssinian apple, core and all. After he had rejected the patchwork prepared by Eden and Laval, Ramsay MacDonald startled Europe by a statement that the situation was the "most serious we have had to face since 1914."[65]

The verity of MacDonald's statement was not questioned in most European circles, and it was obvious that Britain was the chief disturbing factor in the explosive international situation. The Italians were "unalterably convinced" that Britain was actuated "only by selfish interests," and that her "professed anxiety for the League is pure hypocrisy."[66] Virginio Gayda, in the *Giornale d'Italia,* ran a series of articles accusing Britain of bad faith with reference to the terms of the tripartite treaty of 1906,[67] and the Italian press was filled with similar charges.

o. *The White House Denounces Dollar Diplomacy*

The situation was suddenly made more complicated when news came from Addis Ababa (August 31, 1935) that the Emperor had granted to a subsidiary of the Standard Oil Company (The African Exploration and Development Company) a concession for the exploitation of oil and mineral resources in a large part of his empire. This concession had been secured by a British subject, Francis Rickett, and there were many rumors that British capital would soon be invested in it. Although the officials of several companies of the Standard Oil group disclaimed all knowledge of this concession, the Emperor flatly stated that it had been granted to that company.[68]

The British Foreign Office promptly intervened and instructed its Minister at Addis Ababa to "inform the Emperor that His Majesty's Government, for its part, advise him to withhold the concession."[69]

[64] Hull, *op. cit.,* p. 422.

[65] *The United States in World Affairs, 1934–35,* ed. W. H. Shepardson and William O. Scroggs (New York, 1935), p. 245.

[66] Alexander Kirk to Secretary Hull, Rome, August 23, 1935. 765.84/1032, MS, Department of State.

[67] See particularly the issues of August 16–17, 1935.

[68] *New York Times,* August 31, September 1, 1935.

[69] London *Times,* September 1, 1935.

From London, Mr. Atherton, the American chargé, reported that the Foreign Office considered Mr. Rickett an "unstable adventurer," and it summed up the "reports of such a deal at such a moment as 'truly deplorable.' "[70] This view was confirmed by Mr. Marriner, at Paris, who reported to Secretary Hull that the "general feeling here in press and semi-official circles is that the reported Abyssinian oil and mineral concession, even though British official participation has been disavowed, will nevertheless weaken Britain's position at Geneva, correspondingly strengthen the Italian thesis, and probably put sanctions out of the question."[71]

Secretary Hull was just as concerned over the news of the Ethiopian concession to the Standard Oil Company as was Anthony Eden. On September 3, two of the officials of that company visited the Department of State and had a long conversation with Wallace Murray, chief of the Division of Near Eastern Affairs. Mr. Murray frankly told them that the concession was a "matter of grave embarrassment" not only to the American Government but to other governments which "are making strenuous and sincere efforts for the preservation of world peace which is seriously threatened by the Italo-Ethiopian dispute." After commenting upon the delicate position of the British Government in the pending difficulties, he emphasized the fact that "this Government, no less than the British Government, desires to divest itself of any suspicion of selfish interest when world peace is at stake." After he had insisted to the Standard Oil officials that only "immediate and unconditional withdrawal from the concession would meet the needs of the situation," they finally agreed to accept his advice. Secretary Hull added some words of wisdom about the ethical aspects of foreign policy, and the representatives of one of America's largest corporations left the Department of State with a better understanding of the crosscurrents that affect the conduct of American foreign affairs. Their departure from Washington was speeded by some weighty words from the White House to the effect that "dollar diplomacy" was no "longer recognized by the American Government."[72]

But this high-sounding declaration was somewhat bewildering to Emperor Haile Selassie who had started the diplomatic fireworks by hurriedly granting the concession. He had not responded to any pressure from wicked Wall Street. Indeed, he had pressed his favors upon American big business with the ardent hope that such action might add

[70] Atherton to Secretary Hull, London, August 31, 1935. 884.6363 African Exploitation and Development Corporation/2, MS, Department of State.

[71] Theodore Marriner to Secretary Hull, Paris, September 3, 1935. 765.84/1005, MS, Department of State.

[72] New York Times, September 5, 1935.

strength to American interest in Ethiopia. Secretary Hull had a difficult time explaining the advantages of righteousness over riches in the new code of diplomacy, but the Emperor finally saw the light and regarded with fresh hope the proceedings of the League. These hopes were doomed to early disappointment.[73]

[73] Hull, *op. cit.*, pp. 423–25. It is interesting to note that the news of the oil concession to the Standard Oil Company did not excite any bitterness in the Italian press against the United States. In a dispatch to Secretary Hull, September 4, 1935, Breckinridge Long, the American Ambassador at Rome, remarked as follows: "As to the American angle of the affair, I may state that even at the outset there was no evidence of resentment against the United States, the participation of American capital being considered a blind for British interests. . . . The subsequent statements issued by the Secretary of State and the action of the Standard Oil in renouncing the concession have made a most favorable impression here. . . . It is felt that the American Government has given further and substantial proof of an impeccable attitude of neutrality." 765.84/1216, MS, Department of State.

VIII

Britain and France Fear to Provoke War over the Issue of Ethiopia

a. *France Vainly Seeks Promises of Aid from Britain*

ON SEPTEMBER 2, in preparation for the meeting of the Council of the League, Anthony Eden and Pierre Laval had a long conversation with reference to the Italo-Ethiopian dispute. Eden endeavored to impress upon Laval "in the strongest terms the British point of view, stating how it was backed throughout by British public opinion, by the Church, by the peace and League societies, and by the Labor and Liberal parties." He then remarked that "unless Mussolini altered his projects the question of sanctions would necessarily arise and that these might mean war." If this emergency arose Britain was "prepared to do its part." After this ambiguous statement, Eden expressed the opinion that "if Britain was willing to go so far at this time as to take its share and run the risks incident to sanctions, France must feel that this would be, if not a guarantee, at least a sure precedent for the future in case difficulties should arise with respect to German aggression." Laval replied that he had not as yet decided whether to ask Britain for "specific assurances as to further action in other cases should the affair be pushed to the extremity of sanctions against Italy."[1]

Two days later, Hugh Wilson had luncheon with Eden at Geneva. Eden informed him that a number of the representatives of the "small states" had assured him that they were in favor of "the application of the Covenant" in the matter of the Italo-Ethiopian controversy. When he had endeavored to elicit from them a definite assurance of support, however, they had evaded his efforts. He then referred to the apparent desire of French statesmen to make diplomatic "bargains." In Paris, Laval had asked him what Britain would do in case of trouble in Austria. Eden had merely replied that the "building up of collective action would certainly be a precedent for British future action." When Laval pressed for a more specific statement, Eden countered with the observation: "I am unable to give you an official answer."

Eden then confidentially informed Wilson that, with reference to the Laval-Mussolini conversation on January 7, Laval had told him that "he

[1] Theodore Marriner to Secretary Hull, Paris, September 3, 1935. 765.84/1013, MS, Department of State.

had given Mussolini a free hand as far as France was concerned only in regard to economic measures. On the other hand, Mussolini had told Eden immediately thereafter that the French 'had agreed to accord him complete liberty of action in Ethiopia.' "

At the conclusion of this lunch, Eden "spoke in tones of the deepest appreciation" of the action of Secretary Hull "in having the Socony Vacuum Company withdraw from the concession." This had "cleared the air enormously and made him 'happier than anything in this dreary situation.' "[2]

b. *The Walwal Arbitral Commission Dodges the Issue*

Before the Council of the League opened its sessions on September 4, a report came from the arbitral commission that had been appointed to assess the blame for the outbreak of hostilities at Walwal. On September 3, this commission rendered a unanimous decision which declared that neither Italy nor Ethiopia was responsible for the incident.[3] On the following day the Italian Ambassador had a brief talk with Wallace Murray, in the Department of State, and remarked that the wording of the arbitral decision apparently "excluded altogether Italian responsibility" for the "Walwal incident," while at the same time it indicated that "proof of Ethiopian responsibility is lacking." This phraseology was quite "satisfactory to Italy."[4]

c. *Laval Wishes to Conciliate Mussolini*

The day after the arbitral commission had rendered its decision on the Walwal Incident, Baron Aloisi laid before the League a lengthy indictment against the empire of Haile Selassie which included some items dealing with slavery, cannibalism, and ritualistic murder. The representative from Ethiopia repelled with vehemence these charges,[5] and the League thereupon appointed a committee of five to "examine as a whole Italo-Ethiopian relations with a view to seeking a peaceful solution."[6]

While this committee was making its study, the Council continued its

[2] Hugh Wilson to Secretary Hull, Geneva, September 4, 1935. 765.84/1036, MS, Department of State.

[3] Pitman B. Potter, *The Wal Wal Arbitration* (New York, 1935).

[4] Wallace Murray to Judge Walton B. Moore, September 4, 1935. 765.84/1255, *Confidential file,* MS, Department of State.

[5] Prentiss Gilbert to Secretary Hull, Geneva, September 4, 1935. 765.84/1039, MS, Department of State.

[6] Breckinridge Long to Secretary Hull, Rome, September 4, 1935. 765.84/1026, MS, Department of State.

consideration of the Italo-Ethiopian dispute and conversations were anxiously held between Laval and Anthony Eden. During one of these talks Eden remarked that if "Mussolini were allowed to 'get away' with what he was doing, Hitler would be the next." Laval then evinced his readiness to support British contentions if Eden would give him adequate guarantees against possible German aggression. The statement that the British Government was "prepared to fulfill their share of responsibilities as a member of the League" did not go far enough to satisfy France.

From the British viewpoint the situation in Geneva was far from reassuring, and Lord Vansittart made it clear that "while Britain will be ready to apply sanctions with adequate support on the part of other Powers, she could not undertake to apply them alone. To satisfy British public opinion they might propose sanctions, but should they not be supported he foresaw a possible British abandonment of the League."[7]

This British talk of sanctions was very distasteful to Laval. At a meeting of the committee appointed by the Council to study the Italo-Ethiopian controversy he remarked that

he was convinced that the only manner in which Italy could be handled without risk of grave European complications was to permit Italy to have at least one victory in Abyssinia. At that time, and not until then . . . did he feel that France could join in taking extreme measures. . . . He believed that Italy would then accept an offer based on those which he together with the British had made at Paris. Eden tacitly acquiesced in this point of view.[8]

To Ambassador Wilson this Laval formula seemed likely to be accepted at Geneva. After hostilities were commenced by Mussolini, a compromise would be "worked up between England, France and Italy at the expense of Abyssinia." Of course there was a possibility that a strong front might be maintained against Italy. If sanctions "are adopted and are efficiently enforced by the States of Europe then the results in Europe and indeed in the world may be incalculable. A belief may be acquired in stability; a sense of solidarity and a sense of safety may arise which would go a long way not only to solving political problems but also economic ones."[9]

In Rome the British Ambassador greatly doubted if sanctions would

[7] Prentiss Gilbert to Secretary Hull, Geneva, September 5, 1935. 765.84/1045, MS, Department of State.

[8] Prentiss Gilbert to Secretary Hull, Geneva, September 7, 1935. 765.84/1067, MS, Department of State.

[9] Hugh Wilson to Secretary Hull, Geneva, September 7, 1935. 765.84/1068, *Strictly Confidential*, MS, Department of State.

be applied against Italy in the event of war against Ethiopia. He inclined to the viewpoint, current in diplomatic circles, that Italy might move ahead to victory and then be ready for joint Franco-British mediation.[10]

In Ciano's address to the American people on September 7, there was no intimation that Italy was counting upon a short war with probable mediation by major European powers. He stressed the wide prevalence of slavery in Ethiopia and the desire on the part of Italy to remedy this sad situation. To this humanitarian ideal was joined the belief that Italy had a mission to open the vast resources of Ethiopia for the benefit of the whole world. This would be a titanic task that could not be accomplished in a short time.[11]

But despite Ciano's speech with its high-sounding objectives, Premier Laval still clung to his belief that before peace talks could have any real foundation it would be necessary "that some military operation . . . take place in Abyssinia in order to satisfy Mussolini who was beginning to feel that the world had turned against him, not with reference to the merits of the case in Abyssinia but as opponents of Fascist party policies."[12]

To Breckinridge Long, in Rome, it was obvious that these military operations would soon take place in Ethiopia. Italy had more than 200,-000 troops south of the Suez Canal. To withdraw them would be equivalent to a disastrous defeat. Every indication pointed to a "well-calculated, well-prepared, cold, hard and cruel prosecution of their preconceived plans using the instrumentality of an army and navy almost fanatic in its devotion to . . . one man. . . . I am led to the firm belief that no compromise is possible except on Mussolini's terms. . . .The settled friendship between Italy and England is gone, not to reappear for generations."[13]

This rift between Italy and Britain was very apparent on September 11 when Sir Samuel Hoare, British Foreign Secretary, addressed the Assembly of the League of Nations. He made it very clear that in the emergency then facing the League with reference to difficulties between Italy and Ethiopia, the British Government would support League action with "unwavering fidelity." In conformity with "its precise, explicit obligations the League stands, and my country stands with it, for

[10] Breckinridge Long to Secretary Hull, Rome, September 7, 1935. 765.84/1069, MS, Department of State.

[11] Breckinridge Long to Secretary Hull, Rome, September 7, 1935. 765.84/1072, MS, Department of State.

[12] Theodore Marriner to Secretary Hull, Paris, September 9, 1935. 765.84/1084, MS, Department of State.

[13] Breckinridge Long to Secretary Hull, Rome, September 10, 1935. 765.84/1101, MS, Department of State.

collective maintenance of the Covenant in its entirety and particularly for steady, collective resistance to all acts of unprovoked aggression."[14]

d. Secretary Hull Rejects the Role of Mediator

The day before Hoare threw this challenge in the face of Mussolini, the American Minister at Addis Abada was asked by Emperor Haile Selassie if the United States would be willing "to mediate between Italy and Ethiopia, provided of course Italy accepts such mediation."[15] Hull promptly replied that American mediation was not "practicable, coming as it does at a moment when the appropriate agencies of the League of Nations . . . are occupied in an endeavor to arrive at a solution under pertinent provisions of the Covenant."[16] The following day, in order to assuage Ethiopian sensibilities, Hull issued a press statement setting forth the attitude of the American Government towards unprovoked war. It sounded a note which soon became very familiar to millions of Americans: "A threat of hostilities anywhere cannot but be a threat to the interests, political, economic, legal and social of all nations."[17]

e. Britain and France Seek to Solve the Ethiopian Problem

Secretary Hull's press statement of September 13 had many broad implications that must have greatly pleased some ardent one-worlders, but

[14] Address of Sir Samuel Hoare to the League of Nations Assembly, September 11, 1935; *International Conciliation,* November 1935, pp. 508–18.

[15] Cornelius Engert to Secretary Hull, Addis Ababa, September 10, 1935. 765.84/1094, MS, Department of State.

[16] Secretary Hull to Engert, September 12, 1915. 765.84/1094, MS, Department of State.

[17] Department of State, *Press Release,* September 14, 1935, pp. 194–96. This statement was prepared in the Department of State on September 12 and was released to the press on the following morning. It was not sent to Ambassador Long on September 12 or 13. On the 13th it was evidently cabled by the Italian Ambassador at Washington to the Foreign Office. On the afternoon of September 13 the Italian Under Secretary of State (Suvich) paid a visit to the American Embassy in order to discuss some of its implications. On that day (September 13) the Italian press had "long accounts" of the Hull statement.
    For some strange reason Secretary Hull had not cabled his statement to Ambassador Long. Therefore, when Suvich made his call at the Embassy, Long could not discuss the Hull press statement with him. This oversight on the part of the Department of State caused Long great embarrassment, and he poured forth to "dear Cordell" his injured feelings: "It is not only a question of my personal and official embarrassment at being confronted by another Government with a matter supposed to be within my information, but it is also the fact that it reflects upon your representatives abroad, and it leads to the broad assumption that they are not in the confidence of their Government. . . . I do trust that in the future particular efforts will be made to advise the Embassies at the seat of trouble of any statements made by the Department concerning the Governments to which they are accredited. . . . Anyhow, please don't do it any more to *me.*" Ambassador Long to Secretary Hull, Rome, September 16, 1935. 765.84/1648, *Confidential file,* MS, Department of State.

the British Foreign Office was anxious for the Department of State to be more specific in its declarations of policy. Hoare had arrived at the point where he believed that Britain would have to take some action because the "potentialities of the Italian adventure in Africa are a threat to the Empire." Pressure upon Italy could take the form of "graduated economic sanctions," which would be applied only if several important nations within the League would agree upon common action. In his conversations with Hoare, Laval had remarked that "if something cannot be given to Italy, there is no use offering her anything." He was willing to go so far as to acquiesce in "Italy's occupation of Abyssinia." Hoare's reply was that any acquiescence in "Italy's occupation of Abyssinia was to acquiesce in a war." He could not accept "any such suggestion." When Laval then pressed Hoare for some formal "British commitments in Europe," the British Foreign Secretary vaguely answered that his country would not enter into "any engagements on the Continent beyond the general conception of League action."[18]

Hoare's noncommittal answer placed Laval on the spot. He realized that he "must do nothing in any way to throw cold water on the British attitude toward the League," but at the same time he had "to preach a measure of prudence and sound a warning against plunging too deeply into trouble before it is demonstrated to be inevitable." It was Hugh Wilson's belief that the "British and French are slowly coming together."[19]

This viewpoint seemed confirmed by information that reached the ears of Ambassador Long in Rome. He had learned from some "French diplomatic sources" that Mussolini had been "plainly told that some solution must be found by negotiation, and found before any feat of arms take place." French diplomats favored an arrangement whereby Italy, France, and Britain would "agree upon Italy's legitimate aspirations in Abyssinia and submit their proposal to the Negus." If Haile Selassie "refused, the Italians might then use force." According to the latest news from Geneva, however, Hoare would probably reject this proposal.

In the event that Britain and France continued to remain indifferent to Italian interests in Ethiopia, there was a definite possibility that an Italo-German rapprochement might develop. While most persons in Rome admitted that Italy preferred "the friendship of France for military, historical, racial, religious and psychological considerations," it

[18] Prentiss Gilbert to Secretary Hull, Geneva, September 12, 1935. 765.84/1133, MS, Department of State.
[19] Hugh Wilson to Secretary Hull, Geneva, September 12, 1935. 765.84/1140, MS, Department of State.

was also felt that if Laval turned his back upon Italy, there was a strong possibility that Mussolini would "seek Allies elsewhere."[20]

f. *Ambassador Long Favors Giving Mussolini a Slice of Ethiopia*

The dangerous situation that was developing in Europe relative to the Italo-Ethiopian impasse, prompted Ambassador Long to suggest a possible solution of the difficulty. His plan was based upon the belief that Italy would have to be given some "additions to her territory in Africa" as a bribe to keep her from going to war. Moreover, it seemed apparent that Germany should be made an active partner in a new European concert.[21]

This judicious plan of settlement proposed by Ambassador Long fell upon the very deaf ears of Secretary Hull who does not even mention it in his *Memoirs*. In an effort to exert pressure upon the Department of State for action with respect to his proposal, Ambassador Long sent a lengthy dispatch which emphasized the growing antagonism between Italy and Britain. The former friendly relations had completely disappeared, and it was impossible to "conceive today that Italy and England will in the next few years proceed to a friendly co-operation in any degree consistent with that which characterized their relations for the past decades." It was necessary, therefore, for some bold action to be taken at once by the United States. If the plan presented to Secretary Hull were not soon adopted, a long line of serious "incidents" would soon follow. Mussolini would not be satisfied with the conquest of

[20] Ambassador Long to Secretary Hull, Rome, September 12, 1935. 765.84/1338, *Confidential file*, MS, Department of State.

[21] Ambassador Long to Secretary Hull, September 12, 1935. 765.84/1134, MS, Department of State. Ambassador Long summarized his plan as follows:

"1. Italy, by agreement with England and France, to receive territorial adjustments to include all the lowlands of Abyssinia and some of the uplands as far as Addis Ababa and east of Mia for some miles and south to the British border. The Italian maps of original Abyssinia and its recently conquered dependencies as submitted to the League by Italy as part of her memorial would indicate the extent of territory to be acquired by Italy.

"2. Ethiopia to have a new capital in the confines of old Abyssinia and to be guaranteed as to its territorial integrity and sovereignty by Italy, France and England.

"3. Germany (a) to be brought into the discussions and a tentative agreement arrived at to cede back to Germany certain of its former African colonies on condition that Germany recognize and join as guarantor with the other three Powers the independence of Austria; (b) Germany's assumption of arms on land, sea and in air to be confirmed by the other three Powers; (c) Germany, Italy, France and England agree to attend in sixty days a conference for the reduction of land and air forces in Europe.

"4. The four Powers to subscribe to mutually operative non-aggression pacts and invoke the Locarno Treaty for the air and land, and subsequently open both agreements for the adherence of all European Governments.

"5. The four Powers to open simultaneously with the Arms Reduction Conference, another conference for lowering tariff barriers and obstacles to trade and for monetary stabilization, and open that agreement for signature by all European Governments."

Ethiopia. After he occupied Addis Ababa he would elevate his gaze to other territories in Africa and in Asia Minor. Europe would have to be stabilized at once through mutual nonaggression pacts of real force or a series of wars would ensue. The world was approaching a period of expansion and explosion, and some safety valve of mutual trust and good will was the only alternative to disaster.[22]

g. *Laval Makes a Bow towards Britain*

While Ambassador Long was feverishly seeking some solution of the Italo-Ethiopian controversy, Premier Laval made an important address before the Assembly of the League of Nations during which he made a deep bow in the direction of Britain. With respect to certain obligations of France he was very precise:

France is faithful to the League Covenant. She cannot fail in her obligations. . . . The adhesion without reservation which we have brought to the League has been enthusiastic and the result of considered opinion. . . . From the protocol in 1924 to the conference for the limitation of armaments, France's representatives have supported with the same fervor the doctrine of collective security. This doctrine remains and will remain the doctrine of France. The Covenant endures as our international law.

Let all realize that there exists no discord between France and Britain in their effective seeking for [a] pacific solution [of the Italo-Ethiopian dispute]. Our obligations are inscribed in the Covenant. France will not evade those obligations.[23]

Anthony Eden was greatly pleased with Laval's address. On the evening of September 13 he had dinner with Hugh Wilson and talked quite frankly. He pointed out that

things are shaping up in the direction for which Great Britain is working; that the French are coming around to the British way of thinking. . . . Eden and Cranborne were quite patently profoundly troubled at the extraordinary seriousness of the situation. . . . Discussing sanctions briefly Eden observed that perhaps the simplest form they could take at the outset at least would be that which would not interfere with sea-borne traffic and so not involve fleet action or questions of American war vessels. . . . Regarding the United States Eden said that his Government had determined during this stage not to make any overtures to us regarding questions of neutrality etc.; that the British did not want either to act prematurely or to act in a manner which might em-

[22] Ambassador Long to Secretary Hull, Rome, September 13, 1935. 765.84/1341, MS, Department of State.

[23] Premier Laval's address before the Assembly of the League of Nations, September 13, 1935; *International Conciliation*, November 1935, pp. 521–23.

barrass the American Government and therefore would defer the discussion with our Government until a definite program for the inspection of the American Government [had been worked out] and hoped for a "benevolent" attitude on our part.[24]

Eden's satisfaction with Laval's speech was shared by other members of the British Government and by a large section of the British press. The comment in the London *Times* was typical:

Unless Signor Mussolini has lost all sense of proportion, the firm words of M. Laval, whose eagerness to reach an agreement with him has been so obviously profound and sincere, should answer at once the Italian dictator that far more is to be gained for his country by timely collaboration with Great Britain and France than by an insensate policy which they can have no choice but to oppose.[25]

In Paris, Laval's address received wide support and the press expressed the view that the Premier had "turned a difficult corner, advanced the cause of peace and increased France's prestige."[26]

h. *Britain Wishes the U.S. to Accept Important Responsibilities*

In London the Foreign Office seemed especially anxious to ascertain the American attitude towards the imposition of sanctions upon Italy. During a conversation with Mr. Atherton (the American chargé) at the Foreign Office, Sir Samuel Hoare made many comments upon the current of recent events and indicated a certain degree of distrust of Laval. He had found the French Premier

a loose talker and while there was nothing written between Mussolini and Laval, he did not doubt for a moment that Laval had left very decided impressions with the Italians as to French policy. . . . However, Sir Samuel stated that the French had made this trip up with the British. France had definitely taken the side of the Covenant.

. . . At the time of consulting League Powers after an act of aggression, non-League Powers would also have to be consulted, and while the Foreign Secretary "made no requests" in the present instance, he said that he was keeping me informed since the attitude of the American Government . . . would be asked. Sir Samuel reiterated that the imposition of sanctions would

24 Hugh Wilson to Secretary Hull, Geneva, September 13, 1935. 765.84/1139, *Strictly Confidential,* MS, Department of State.

25 Atherton to Secretary Hull, London, September 14, 1935. 765.84/1159, MS, Department of State.

26 Marriner to Secretary Hull, Paris, September 14, 1935. 765.84/1153, MS, Department of State.

be a gradual one along the lines of the 1921 resolutions. The first question to be posed was whether League members and non-League members would refrain from selling arms and munitions and implements of war to Italy, and secondly, . . . whether they would also agree to cease purchasing from Italy.

After making these statements concerning League policy, Sir Samuel then shifted to possible action under the terms of the Pact of Paris. An early appeal "to all the signatories of the Paris Pact . . . must be envisaged as another decisive method of concentrating world opinion . . . against Italian aggression."[27]

Before the receipt of this telegram from London, Secretary Hull had held several conferences with his advisers in the Department of State and had expressed the view that the American Government should clearly define its position relative to trade with Italy before the League took any action regarding sanctions. In this way it would be apparent that the decision was independent of any course prescribed by the League.[28]

i. *Anthony Eden Expresses Suspicions of Russia*

While the Department of State was considering what course to take with reference to sanctions against Italy, Hugh Wilson sent an interesting and revealing record of his conversations with M. Massigli, the French representative at Geneva, and with Anthony Eden. On September 12, Wilson had luncheon with Massigli. He informed Wilson in strict confidence that the matter of sanctions against Italy went "very much against the grain with Laval, but he had recognized its inevitability and the fact that the course of events might well cause the French to carry on with England in this direction." In the event sanctions were applied, they must be "swift and efficacious." It would be difficult to realize this ideal if the United States would not join this concert. Wilson immediately informed Massigli that he had "no idea of what the temper of the United States would be when the time came and whether such action would be politically feasible."

Massigli then remarked that he greatly feared that France and Britain were dealing with a "mad man." No argument and no threat seemed to have any effect upon Mussolini. When Chambrun, in Rome, had pointed out to the Duce the danger of conflict with the British if he persisted in his course, he replied that "he was ready and willing, if they so desired, to measure strength with them and was convinced that

---

[27] Atherton to Secretary Hull, London, September 16, 1935. 765.84/1197, *Strictly Confidential for the Secretary*, MS, Department of State.

[28] Cordell Hull, *Memoirs* (New York, 1948), I, 426.

he could beat them in the Mediterranean: 'Je m'en fous des Anglais.' "

On the following day (September 13), Wilson lunched with Eden. Eden was profoundly troubled and felt that "it will be too late to stop hostilities." Regarding Russia, he said that "Litvinov was acting pretty 'naughty.' His general impression . . . was that he felt that the recent Soviet interference in support of the League in the Council and general expressions of a strong attitude by Russia were really prompted not so much by love of mankind as in the hope that the embroilment of the situation would eventually bring the enfeeblement of the capitalist States and offer an advantageous terrain for Communistic success."[29]

There was good reason for Mr. Eden's troubled state of mind and for his belief in the inevitability of hostilities. In Rome on September 17, Ambassador Long had an important conference with Mussolini and soon discovered that he was "definitely and irrevocably determined to proceed in Abyssinia with what he insists upon calling a colonial enterprise." The Duce assured Long that he wished to localize the conflict and keep it confined to Ethiopia. He had no desire to see it spread to Europe. But in the event that

anybody interferes with him he is prepared and that he has an army of a million men in Italy and that he has a competent fleet and an air force with a certain superiority and that he will brook no interference. He is much exercised . . . about sanctions and mentioned specifically the action of France in Morocco, the Chaco affair, Germany's violations of the Treaty of Versailles, the British action four years ago in Iraq and Japan's activities in Manchukuo and China, in none of which cases were sanctions involved. He then said with anger: "It is only for me and on account of Italy when we wish to rectify wrong and have a legitimate expansion that sanctions are sanctions."

He was frank in his admissions that he was rapidly moving down the road to war, and he had no hesitation in declaring that he expected to conquer and hold a large portion of Ethiopia. His air of candor was refreshing and his general attitude made a deep impression upon Ambassador Long:

One cannot talk with Mussolini . . . without being fully conscious of the bold determination and the irrevocable nature of the decisions he has already taken. He is calm, his voice modulated, his manner gracious and his friendly attitude toward the United States unmistakable.[30]

29 Memoranda of conversations between Hugh Wilson and M. Massigli, September 12, and Anthony Eden, September 13, 1935, Geneva. 765.84/1429, *Strictly Confidential*, MS, Department of State.

30 Ambassador Long to Secretary Hull, Rome, September 17, 1935. 765.84/1205, *Strictly Confidential*, MS, Department of State.

j. *Ambassador Long Advises against Sanctions*

Ambassador Long was so deeply concerned over the wide ramifications of the Italo-Ethiopian dispute that he cabled to Secretary Hull (September 18) and expressed the hope that "if sanctions are invoked at Geneva . . . the American Government will not associate itself with them. There would be many unfortunate grave repercussions at home and unnecessary complications here." Long was strongly of the belief that America should beware of European entanglements and should act "without reference to the program of any other government or groups of governments."[31]

These telegrams from Ambassador Long caused Mr. Phillips, the Acting Secretary of State, to have a long conversation with Wallace Murray, the chief of the Division of Near Eastern Affairs, with reference to the matter of sanctions against Italy. Mr. Murray pointed out that upon three recent occasions (August 20, 28, and September 16) Sir Samuel Hoare had discussed with the American chargé at London the "question of sanctions and the possibility of either a *conference* of the signatories to the Kellogg Pact or of *consultation* of the [or between the] signatories to the Kellogg Pact." Mr. Murray was of the opinion that the Department of State should adopt an attitude of "great reserve" regarding any suggestions of *conferences* or *consultations*.[32]

While Mr. Phillips was pondering the problems connected with sanctions against Italy, he received a telegram from Geneva which indicated that Mussolini had approached France with specific proposals for an alliance against Germany. This overture had spurred the French Foreign Office to ask Britain for definite promises of aid in the event of war. These sought-for promises included an "undertaking that British land forces be sent to the Continent in the event of a German move, the undertaking to comprehend specific arrangements respecting the number, character and disposition of such forces." Also, a "bilateral air pact." Until this "or something similar be granted the French will not consider sanctions against Italy."[33]

The Italian press soon got wind of these French proposals for an alliance with Britain and the whole matter was dismissed as of little importance. Doubt was expressed "as to the effective commitments

---

[31] Ambassador Long to Secretary Hull, Rome, September 18, 1935. 765.84/1219, MS, Department of State.

[32] Wallace Murray to Mr. Phillips, September 18, 1935, inclosing a memorandum dealing with the question of consultation under the terms of the Kellogg Pact. 765.84/1329, MS, Department of State.

[33] Prentiss Gilbert to Secretary Hull, Geneva, September 19, 1935. 765.84/1261, *Strictly Confidential*, MS, Department of State.

which England will or can make on the Continent and as to the possibility of the French being satisfied with generic assurances." Britain had in the past demonstrated "the uncertain value of her contribution to security on the Continent." Without Italy there "could be no collective security."[34]

k. *Secretary Hull Defines the Position of the United States*

Under the impact of these telegrams Secretary Hull decided that it was important to give a clear formulation of American foreign policy. On September 20 he instructed Ambassador Long that the plan outlined in the telegram from Rome on September 12 was not acceptable to the Department of State. The American attitude towards world peace had received cogent expression in statements already given to the press by the Secretary of State, who would deeply regret "any occurrences which would indicate that we had lost confidence in the agencies which are striving to reach a satisfactory solution of the present dispute."[35]

After rejecting Ambassador Long's solution of the Italo-Ethiopian dispute, Secretary Hull instructed Mr. Atherton, in London, that the American Government would "not join in the imposition of sanctions upon any nation involved in the pending controversy between Italy and Ethiopia." With regard to League action it was impossible for the United States to "arrive at any conclusion with regard thereto before it was placed in full possession of the reasons and bases upon which such collective action by the League was founded and a complete description of the specific measures to be put into effect."[36]

l. *The Committee of Five Makes a Futile Suggestion*

In order to dispel all doubts concerning the proper settlement of the Italo-Ethiopian dispute the League Committee of Five submitted (September 18) to both powers a proposal for careful consideration. It was in substance a League protectorate over Ethiopia, the Emperor being assisted by four advisers appointed by the Council. In this plan there was express recognition of Italy's "special interest in the economic development of Ethiopia."

In order to secure some information about what was going on during the meetings of the Committee of Five, Hugh Wilson had a conversa-

[34] Ambassador Long to Secretary Hull, Rome, September 12, 1935. 765.84/1503, MS, Department of State.

[35] Secretary Hull to Ambassador Long, September 20, 1935. 765.84/1265, MS, Department of State.

[36] Hull, *op. cit.*, p. 436.

tion with Mr. Beck of Poland. He deprecated any strong action against Italy. Sanctions might drive her out of the League, and without Italy the League might disintegrate. Beck then gave Wilson a detailed description of the international situation, including a colorful vignette of Hitler:

In international affairs Hitler is simple, but it is the simplicity of common sense. He had stated, for instance, to Beck: "There is not a single question between Poland and Germany which is worth a war," and he had specifically included the Corridor in this statement. Hitler had also told Beck that by reading his German history and the history of Europe for two hundred years he had found the same mistake repeated *ad nauseam:* the conquest of territory of alien races in every case left a bitter enemy on the flank. . . . "But," I said, "you are sketching the portrait of a very intelligent man." Beck then threw up his hands and said that never as long as he lived would he understand "what the Devil" Hitler was trying to do in Germany. . . . However, when it came to foreign affairs Beck stated emphatically that no one should make the mistake of underrating Hitler: Hitler was a thoughtful, simple-minded, direct man, full of common sense when it came to the question of foreign relations. Beck described Hitler somewhat as Sir John Simon had done: simple, honest, hard-working, with no thought of self or of luxury.[37]

It was apparent that Mr. Wilson elicited from Mr. Beck a great deal of comment about Hitler and very little information concerning the work of the Committee of Five. When the plan of the committee was made public Signor Rosso (the Italian Ambassador) had a conversation with Mr. Phillips about it. He soon made it clear that the Foreign Office believed that it did not go "nearly far enough" in meeting Italian aspirations in Ethiopia. There was little hope for its acceptance.[38]

m. *The Department of State Ponders the Problem of Sanctions*

In the face of probable Italian rejection of the proposal of the Committee of Five, the Department of State hurriedly made a study of the implications of any policy of sanctions. Once more Wallace Murray submitted a report on the political aspects of conferences and consultations. It seemed to him that the Department of State should adopt an attitude of "great reserve" if it "should be asked to call or to attend a conference as a signatory of the Pact of Paris." Inasmuch as the Euro-

[37] Memorandum of a conversation between Hugh Wilson and Mr. Beck, Minister for Foreign Affairs of Poland, Geneva, September 20, 1935. 765.84/1495, MS, Department of State.

[38] Memorandum of conversation between Mr. Phillips and Signor Rosso, the Italian Ambassador, September 20, 1935. 765.84/1410, MS, Department of State.

pean powers were more directly affected by the Italo-Ethiopian situation, it was obvious that it was "up to them rather than to the United States to call a conference if one is required." In the event a conference were called by some European power to consider the question of sanctions, the Department of State should bear in mind the report of the Senate Committee on Foreign Relations concerning the ratification of the Pact of Paris: "The Committee further understands that the treaty does not provide sanctions, express or implied. Should any signatory to the treaty . . . violate the terms of the same, there is no obligation or commitment, express or implied, upon the part of any of the other signers of the treaty to engage in punitive or coercive measures against the nation violating the treaty."

If the American Government decided to adopt a policy of refraining from any purchases of goods from Italy, it could make this effective by the following procedures: (1) private organizations could inaugurate a campaign to boycott Italian goods; (2) the government could request individuals to cease making any purchases from Italy; (3) if Italy attempted to discriminate against American trade it would be possible to deny her the most-favored-nation treatment in the same manner that Germany had been treated; and (4) consideration could be given to employing as a more drastic measure the provisions of Article 338 of the Tariff Act of 1930.[39]

A long report was also prepared by the Office of the Economic Adviser in the Department of State. With reference to the impact of sanctions upon Italy, this report indicated that certain imports occupied a key place in the Italian economic structure. These included machines and apparatus and parts (Germany the principal source); mineral oils (Romania the principal source); coal and coke (Germany the principal source); copper (United States and Chile the principal sources); cotton (60% from the United States); and nitrates (Chile the only source).

The conclusions that were drawn from these figures were that "as long as Italy is able to pay for its imports, economic sanctions could only be decisively effected if (a) they were virtually universal among the principal suppliers of the strategic materials. . . . In the case of the most important strategic materials, Italy has probably been accumulating stocks in anticipation of unusual needs."[40]

After an extended consideration of these reports from his Department of State advisers, Secretary Hull instructed the American repre-

[39] Memorandum prepared by Wallace Murray, chief of the Division of Near Eastern Affairs, for the Secretary of State, September 20, 1935. 765.84/1281, MS, Department of State.

[40] Memorandum prepared by the Office of the Economic Adviser, Department of State, September 20, 1935. 765.84/1706, MS, Department of State.

sentative in London to inform the Foreign Office that the American Government "would not join in the imposition of sanctions upon any nation involved in the pending controversy between Italy and Ethiopia." With reference to collective action under the terms of the Covenant of the League of Nations, it would "of course be obviously impossible" for the United States to join such a concert without first being "placed in full possession of the reasons" for such a measure.[41]

n. *Italy Rejects the Proposal of the Committee of Five*

While Secretary Hull was informing the British Foreign Office that the American Government would not become a member of any concert to impose sanctions upon Italy, Mussolini was speeding his preparations for war in Ethiopia. For a brief time Ambassador Long thought that the concentration of the British fleet in the Mediterranean was causing the Italian press to adopt a "modified tone" in its comments upon British policy,[42] but when he talked with the Under Secretary for Foreign Affairs (Signor Suvich), he learned that the proposal of the Committee of Five would not "be acceptable." Long then ventured the remark that he believed he could detect a "tone of conciliation" in Italian utterances within the past twenty-four hours, but Suvich merely "gave a doubtful shrug of the shoulders and replied that he was not conscious of it."[43]

It was apparent that in Paris the press had not detected any note of conciliation in Italian utterances, and tension was rapidly rising. It was said that Chambrun had spoken plainly to Mussolini, and "Pertinax," in *L'Echo de Paris,* intimated that Laval had informed the Duce that "any feeling that France would not go as far along the road as Britain with Article 16 was incorrect."[44]

But these French assurances did not completely dissolve British suspicions. On September 20, Sumner Welles and Ambassador Bingham had a conversation with Lord Vansittart,[45] who emphasized the strong insistence of British public opinion upon "implementing the obligations of the Covenant." This insistence worried Bingham who feared

---

[41] Secretary Hull to the American Embassy in London, September 20, 1935. 765.84/1197, *Strictly Confidential,* MS, Department of State.

[42] Ambassador Long to Secretary Hull, Rome, September 21, 1935. 765.84/1287, MS, Department of State.

[43] Ambassador Long to Secretary Hull, Rome, September 21, 1935. 765.84/1288, MS, Department of State.

[44] Theodore Marriner to Secretary Hull, Paris, September 21, 1935. 765.84/1289, MS, Department of State.

[45] The British Acting Secretary for Foreign Affairs.

that some "Maine incident" might lead to seriously strained relations between Britain and Italy. It was evident that Vansittart had similar worries and they were given further extension by the uncertainty in British minds as "to the extent the French consider themselves committed to implement the Covenant and incidentally the British thesis thereinunder."[46]

British uneasiness was given additional development on September 21 when the Italian Government announced its rejection of the proposals of the Committee of Five. On the island of Malta preparations were hastily made for possible conflict with Italy, and the situation was viewed "with extreme gravity."[47] At Geneva the British representatives at the sessions of the League of Nations described the tone of the Italian note of rejection as "extremely brusque," but they admitted that it was cleverly phrased and contained "some elements which . . . are embarrassing."[48] Anthony Eden was particularly disturbed by the possible effects of the Italian reply to the Committee of Five, and he confided to Hugh Wilson that "the affair is just as bad as it could be."[49]

On September 23, Emperor Haile Selassie endeavored to place a barrier along the Italian road to war by accepting the proposals of the Committee of Five. This action appeared to have an immediate effect upon the Italian Government. On the following day the Italian press contained "no attacks on England" and the recent bellicose tone was greatly modified.[50] At Geneva the atmosphere suddenly became clearer. A member of the British delegation informed Prentiss Gilbert that Laval had "definitely informed the British . . . that France would adopt any position which the British might take in Geneva and that he [Laval] had also informed Rome." This information probably soon went the rounds in diplomatic circles because Prentiss Gilbert reported that the "whole outward situation here during the day has been that the British and French have agreed on a common policy." As a result of these rumors and confidences "an almost dramatic change has apparently occurred in the inner circles of the three Powers chiefly concerned." Counsels of moderation were now heard and attention was focused on the "disastrous results to finance and trade" which a Euro-

[46] Ambassador Bingham to Secretary Hull, London, September 21, 1935. 765.84/ 1291, *Confidential for the Secretary*, MS, Department of State.

[47] Mr. George to Secretary Hull, Malta, September 22, 1935. 765.84/1306, MS, Department of State.

[48] Prentiss Gilbert to Secretary Hull, Geneva, September 23, 1935. 765.84/1335, MS, Department of State.

[49] Hugh Wilson to Secretary Hull, Geneva, September 23, 1935. 765.84/1314, *Strictly Confidential*, MS, Department of State.

[50] Ambassador Long to Secretary Hull, Rome, September 24, 1935. 765.84/1326, MS, Department of State.

pean war would inevitably cause.[51] As a gesture of conciliation, the British Ambassador in Rome called upon Mussolini and informed him that "Sir Samuel Hoare wanted him to understand that England's entire conduct was not a manifestation of hostility toward Italy or an aggression of any kind but simply an expression of England's attachment to the principles of the League of Nations."[52]

But this British shadowboxing did not greatly impress Mussolini. Ambassador Long believed that it was "impossible to see a success in continued negotiations." He was met "at the end of every hypothesis with the as yet unaltered conclusion that he [Mussolini] will fight his way out and fall if necessary that way rather than by an ignominious surrender to the Power he provoked."[53]

o. *Mussolini Offers a Formula of Peace*

Although Mussolini was bent upon war with Ethiopia he was wise enough to make some gestures in the direction of peace. As a counter-measure to the proposals of the Committee of Five he submitted a new plan which included three major items: (1) the right to acquire territory, "to the west of Addis Ababa," which would establish a connection between the Italian colonies of Eritrea and Somaliland; (2) a stipulation that the proposal to Ethiopia of an outlet to the sea should be arranged to run through Italian rather than through British or French territory; (3) the adoption of a policy that would provide for the disarmament and demobilization of a large part of the Ethiopian Army. The remaining armed forces of Ethiopia should be under the command of Italian officers.

While the Committee of Five were considering these proposals of Mussolini, the situation in Geneva remained tense. The matter of sanctions gave members of the League deep concern. The Swiss representative (G. Motta) pointed out to Hugh Wilson that he considered economic sanctions as "peculiarly dangerous for Switzerland as he feared their consequences. In the event of sanctions would the Powers protect Switzerland against Italy?" In his opinion it would be "impossible that their application would not be followed by bitterness and hatred from

[51] Prentiss Gilbert to Secretary Hull, Geneva, September 24, 1935. 765.84/1336, MS, Department of State.

[52] Ambassador Long to Secretary Hull, Rome, September 24, 1935. 765.84/1344, MS, Department of State.

[53] Ambassador Long to Secretary Hull, Rome, September 24, 1935. 765.84/1342, *Strictly Confidential*, MS, Department of State.

which the mutual relations of the two countries would suffer for a generation."[54]

But Motta's apprehensions were relieved for a brief period by the sudden appearance of a more friendly note in Anglo-Italian relations. In Geneva it seemed apparent that Mussolini had adopted a more reasonable attitude.[55] In Rome the press emphasized the "amicable relations existing between Italy and England,"[56] while in London the tension was "relieved for the moment."[57]

p. *Britain Bids for American Support*

Even in Addis Ababa there were expressions of hope that conflict could be avoided. The Emperor apparently believed that Britain would insist upon a "fair deal" for Ethiopia. Moreover, he had not lost faith in the League of Nations. He informed the American Minister that he had placed the fate of his country in "the hands of the collective conscience of the world and is ready to make any sacrifice that can be reasonably expected of him."[58]

The extent of his sacrifice would depend upon the strength of collective pressure that Britain would be able to muster against Italy. In order to ascertain the exact degree of this strength, the British Foreign Office decided to make inquiries about attitude of the United States concerning joint action. On September 25, Sir Samuel Hoare had an important conference with Ambassador Bingham during the course of which he frankly asked Bingham if Secretary Hull had given any consideration to the "possibility of consultation among the signatories of the Kellogg Pact." Bingham cautiously replied that he had "no information on this subject." Hoare then hastily assured the ambassador that he had no intention of urging "any course of action upon the United States Government," but he hoped it might be possible for it to take steps that "would tend to limit the war between Italy and Abyssinia in scope and time." Bingham expressed the view that he did not "think it probable" that the Department of State would favor joint action with the members of

[54] Hugh Wilson to Secretary Hull, Geneva, September 25, 1935. 765.84/1380, *Very confidential*, MS, Department of State.

[55] Prentiss Gilbert to Secretary Hull, Geneva, September 25, 1935. 765.84/1378, MS, Department of State.

[56] Ambassador Long to Secretary Hull, Rome, September 25, 1935. 765.84/1377, MS, Department of State.

[57] Ambassador Bingham to Secretary Hull, London, September 25, 1935. 765.84/1374, MS, Department of State.

[58] Cornelius Engert to Secretary Hull, Addis Ababa, September 26, 1935. 765.84/1403, *Confidential file*, MS, Department of State.

the League in imposing sanctions upon Italy if war broke out. He knew, however, that Secretary Hull was interested in "reducing the scope and time of the war," and would give consideration to methods of doing so "in the event of unanimous collective action by other Powers." Sir Samuel Hoare listened attentively to this none-too-encouraging statement of the attitude of the Department of State and then remarked that after the outbreak of hostilities the policy of the British Government would be to "invoke economic pressure . . . as far as possible short of actual sanctions." He expressed the ardent hope that the United States would "aid this effort as far as they might deem it proper to do so."[59]

The reply of Secretary Hull to these remarks of Hoare was an indirect assurance of partial support. The American Government "would not decline an invitation to consult through diplomatic channels with a view to the invocation of the Pact [of Paris], but we are of the opinion that consultation . . . might appear to encroach upon the explicit functions of the Covenant of the League . . . and it would therefore appear undesirable." Hull then hastened to indicate how America could be of assistance if the present Italo-Ethiopian crisis deepened into war. Italy, like other European countries, had defaulted upon its large loan from the United States and therefore (under the Johnson Act) could not be granted further loans or credits from American sources. Moreover, no credits would be granted by the Export-Import Bank to finance the export of commodities to Italy. Private institutions in the United States would quickly adopt a policy of "restricting credits to Italian borrowers," and finally, the recent neutrality resolution approved by Congress would require an embargo upon the export of arms, munitions, and implements of war to Italy if she became a belligerent.[60]

It was quite apparent to Hoare and to other members of the British Government that the United States, in an indirect fashion, could exert tremendous economic pressure upon Italy without having to go to the length of actual sanctions. This obvious fact must have given them solace at a time when they badly needed it. Great Britain was having a mild case of "war jitters." Prentiss Gilbert cabled from Geneva that the British Government would soon "inquire" if the American Government had any objection to "an increase in the British naval building program which they plan to present to Parliament." Aroused British public opinion had caused a delay in the acceptance of the "projected

---

[59] Ambassador Bingham to Secretary Hull, London, September 25, 1935. 765.84/1381, *For the Secretary*, MS, Department of State.

[60] Secretary Hull to Ambassador Bingham, September 27, 1935. 765.84/1381, MS, Department of State.

agreement with France which presumably involved British Continental commitments." A widespread "distrust of the French in the present situation and a dissatisfaction at the present situation through them with Rome has impelled the British to re-open direct relations with Rome."

The British Ambassador in Rome had been instructed to call on Mussolini and complain that his program with regard to Ethiopia was too expansive. If he would be more conciliatory and would be willing "to work out an agreement" with the British Government an effort would be made to "find out how much can be obtained from Addis Ababa." In the meantime, the Duce had disturbed the British official mind by indicating that the question of Ethiopia had not been raised during the conference at Stresa even though the British had summoned their African expert for consultation. Therefore, Mussolini had construed the "British attitude at that period as a tacit consent to his undertaking." Some British officials admitted to Gilbert that they found "this assertion of Mussolini to be unanswerable."[61]

q. Mussolini Moves in the Direction of War

To most European observers it was obvious in the last week in September that Mussolini was making his final preparations for war. On September 26 he had a conversation with Jules Sauerwein of Le Matin and informed him that operations would begin in about ten days. He anticipated the imposition of economic sanctions but did not expect them to be "sufficiently effective to interfere with his operations."[62]

In a long dispatch to Secretary Hull, Ambassador Long carefully canvassed the situation in Rome and came to the conclusion that there was "no evidence that the Italians are considering modifying their African program. While it is true that the presence of the British fleet in the Mediterranean has caused in some quarters a feeling of uneasiness, . . . there is as yet no proof that the country as a whole is not prepared to back up the Government's determination to defy all threats rather than submit to a diplomatic defeat which would be fatal to Italian national prestige."[63]

At Geneva the general attitude seemed to grow more resolute against any Italian advance into Ethiopia. It was believed that after the Italian

---

[61] Prentiss Gilbert to Secretary Hull, Geneva, September 26, 1935. 765.84/1384, MS, Department of State.

[62] Ambassador Long to Secretary Hull, Rome, September 27, 1935. 765.84/1408, MS, Department of State.

[63] Ambassador Long to Secretary Hull, Rome, September 27, 1935. 765.84/1700, MS, Department of State.

troops had gained a "bloodless victory" over Ethiopian forces, an effort would be made by the League to "declare Italy the aggressor and to apply sanctions." At that moment a peace offensive could be launched which would have an excellent chance to be successful. The final peace settlement could give the Italians "such territorial concessions and economic privileges as could be gradually developed into an attractive position although not then or ever a control over Abyssinia which would threaten British Empire interests in Abyssinian independence."[64]

These speculations of Ambassador Wilson gave too little heed to the real objectives of Mussolini. Nothing less than complete control over Ethiopia would satisfy the Duce. On September 28 a statement was issued in Rome which clearly indicated the Italian viewpoint. The proposals of the Committee of Five had failed to make provision for "Italy's needs for expansion and security." All persons of "good faith throughout the world have recognized the justice of Italy's rejection of the suggestions of the Committee." The Duce was determined that his own program would be carried out and was ready to face the consequences. Emperor Haile Selassie had recently completed the mobilization of his armed forces with the "declared intention to attack the frontiers of the Italian colonies." Italy would meet force with force.[65]

1. Secretary Hull Offers "Moral Support" to Ethiopia

Apparently the Emperor was more ready to meet peace with peace, and in order to implement this pacific program he once more turned to Mr. Engert, the American Minister at Addis Ababa. Engert made a prompt appeal to Secretary Hull to "go on record by expressing to the Italian Ambassador your disappointment that his country should deliberately turn its back on the whole post-war structure for the maintenance of peace."[66] Hull's reply to this plea for support was a flat refusal to take a bold stand in this Ethiopian imbroglio. All that America was willing to do at this time was to promise the Emperor its "moral support." He should be buoyed up by the assurance that the Department of State would "continue this support by any action which we can properly take in the light of our limitations as occasions arise."[67]

[64] Hugh Wilson to Secretary Hull, Geneva, September 27, 1935. 765.84/1445, *Strictly Confidential,* MS, Department of State.

[65] Ambassador Long to Secretary Hull, Rome, September 28, 1935. 765.84/1452, MS, Department of State.

[66] Cornelius Engert to Secretary Hull, Addis Ababa, September 29, 1935. 765.84/1460, MS, Department of State.

[67] Secretary Hull to Cornelius Engert, October 1, 1935. 765.84/1460, MS, Department of State.

s. *Britain Engages in a Bit of Diplomatic Double Talk*

While Secretary Hull was trying to satisfy the hungry Emperor with scattered crumbs of morality, Sir Samuel Hoare was endeavoring to placate Laval with a similar slim diet. On September 10 the French Government had addressed a note to Sir Robert Vansittart inquiring just what they might expect from Britain in the event of a "violation of the Covenant of the League of Nations and a resort to force" by some European State "whether or not that State might be a member of the League of Nations." The reply of the British Foreign Office was made public on September 29. It was couched in general terms that were far from satisfactory to France. Hoare made specific reference to the assurances he had voiced in his address before the Assembly of the League of Nations on September 11. He then re-emphasized his statement that the "League stands, and this country stands with it, for the collective maintenance of the Covenant in its entirety, and particularly for steady collective resistance to all acts of unprovoked aggression."[68]

The British press was in substantial agreement that Hoare's reply was the "only possible one which any British Government could have made." Most papers were of the opinion that "no British Government can commit itself to specific action in an undefined hypothetical future case."[69] The French press, with the exception of radical papers like the Socialist *République* and Léon Blum's *Populaire,* expressed deep disappointment with the vague promises of the Hoare note. Nothing short of "a hard and fast guarantee in writing of all the clauses of the Versailles Treaty" would satisfy them.[70]

News came from Rome that the French naval attaché had stated "definitely" that Laval would "not agree to military sanctions." The German Ambassador in the same city expressed the opinion that Germany would "not join *any* sanctions against Italy."[71] In Paris the prevailing attitude indicated a "solidifying French public opinion decidedly set against applications of measures of any kind against Italy."[72] By October 3 even the leftist groups in France were opposed to sanctions. Marcel Deat, leader of the Neo-Socialist group, openly declared

[68] London *Times,* September 30, 1935.
[69] Ambassador Bingham to Secretary Hull, London, September 30, 1935. 765.84/1459, MS, Department of State.
[70] Theodore Marriner to Secretary Hull, Paris, September 30, 1935. 765.84/1456, MS, Department of State.
[71] Ambassador Long to Secretary Hull, Rome, September 29, October 1, 1935. 765.84/1453, 765.84/1488, MS, Department of State.
[72] Theodore Marriner to Secretary Hull, Paris, October 2, 1935. 765.84/1498, MS, Department of State.

that his followers would not favor any "proposals for the application of sanctions which might come before the Chamber." Léon Blum's vigorous utterances against Italy had been gradually reduced to weak whispers about "peaceful sanctions." Apparently, there would be no real concert of powers to block the march of Mussolini's legions into Ethiopia.[73]

On October 2, Italian bombing planes began to drop bombs on northern Ethiopian villages, and on the following day the signal was given for a general advance of Italian armed forces into Ethiopia. As the Italian troops crossed the Ethiopian border they broke out into a gay marching tune whose words indicated their supreme confidence: "With the whiskers of the Emperor we will make a little brush to polish up the shoes of Benito Mussolini." This song was a clear indication that the Italian Army had no doubt that Mussolini had given the British Government a brisk brush-off.[74]

[73] Theodore Marriner to Secretary Hull, Paris, October 3, 1935. 765.84/1515, MS, Department of State.

[74] On October 3, Prentiss Gilbert informed Secretary Hull that a member of the Council of the League had inquired if the American Government would care to participate in any flights over Ethiopia by "impartial observers." Reference was made to American participation in the work of the Lytton Commission. Secretary Hull immediately replied that the American Government continued to "watch sympathetically the efforts of the League to find a peaceful solution of the Italo-Ethiopian dispute," but it did not wish to become an "active participant in its administrative activites." Secretary Hull to Prentiss Gilbert, October 4, 1935. 765.84/1529, MS, Department of State.

IX

America Anticipates the League in Exerting Economic Pressure upon Italy

a. *Senator Nye Flusters Foreign Diplomats*

As THE LEGIONS of Mussolini were preparing to march into Ethiopia, many Americans began to press for neutrality legislation that would insulate the Western Hemisphere against the possible outbreak of World War II. The crusade of 1917 had not made the world safe for democracy, and during the early years of the Roosevelt era a tide of disillusion swept over the United States that hid from the public eye the measuring rods that had been used by patriotic historians during the second Wilson Administration. The average American suddenly began to count the cost of the World War and was deeply disturbed to discover that the vast expenditures in human lives and national wealth entailed by that struggle had been in vain. American intervention had completely destroyed the old balance of power that had been carefully constructed by European statesmen, and at the close of the conflict the United States had retired from a position that might have brought stability to a new international edifice that trembled in the winds of uncertainty. When Hitler began to move with earthquake feet along the German frontiers, the continent of Europe had tremors that shook the White House in Washington. But President Roosevelt had no magic formula that would bring prompt reassurance to anxious millions across the Atlantic. He was looking for re-election in 1936 and he did not dare to flout the strong isolationist sentiment that was so evident in most American circles.

One of the isolationist leaders was Senator Nye who was certain that Americans could derive no benefits from sailing on stormy European waters. The great parade of 1917 had shown all too clearly that the paths of glory led but to the grave. The best way to prevent a repetition of that mad scramble with its dire results was to show the American people the sinister forces that had dragged them into conflict. The wiles of Wall Street should be made familiar to the man in the street so that he would shut his ears to the drums of war that beat a cadence of death for the poor and a rhythm of riches for the wealthy.

This viewpoint of Senator Nye received strong confirmation through a sensational article published in *Fortune* in March 1934, entitled

"Arms and the Men." In a long succession of lurid pages the story was told of the shady deals and the devious methods of great munitions manufacturers of Europe in their efforts to incite wars that would make their profits reach dizzy heights.[1] Nye had this article reprinted in the *Congressional Record* so that its full impact would be felt by susceptible members of Congress. There is little doubt that it helped to influence the action of the Senate in its approval on April 12 of the Nye resolution that provided for the appointment of a special Senate Committee to investigate the activities of munitions makers and dealers.[2]

Vice-President Garner appointed Nye to be the chairman of this committee, and Senator Pittman, chairman of the Senate Committee on Foreign Relations, acquiesced in the appointment. It was quite unusual in a Senate controlled by the Democratic Party for a Republican to be named to this important post. Secretary Hull deeply deprecated this action by the Democratic majority: "Had I dreamed that an isolationist Republican would be appointed I promptly would have opposed it. . . . The appointment of Nye was a fatal mistake because the committee . . . proceeded to enlarge the scope of its inquiry into an attempt to prove that the United States had been drawn into the First World War by American bankers and munitions makers."[3]

But despite his dislike for the appointment of Senator Nye, Secretary Hull promised to aid the committee in every possible way, and President Roosevelt urged the Senate (May 18, 1934) to provide ample funds for the use of committee members so that they would be able to execute their task with a thoroughness commensurate with the high importance of the questions at issue.[4] The committee began its hearings on September 4, and it was not long before a sordid story began to unfold. There were some colorful chapters dealing with the malign activities of highly paid lobbyists who used their influence to secure lucrative contracts. Some of the testimony pointed to the fact that manufacturers of munitions ardently believed in a "one world" of business. There were intimate ties that bound these "merchants of death" into an international trust. Within this business circle many trade secrets freely circulated, patents were exchanged, and the volume of trade was diverted into certain favored channels.

It was also brought out that some American army and naval officers had been of great service to armament firms, and that the Army and Navy departments, in order to speed a "preparedness program," had given definite encouragement to the same corporations. This encourage-

[1] IX, (March 1934), 52–57, 113–26.
[2] *Congressional Record,* 73 Cong., 2 sess., 2192, 4323, 6688, 7154.
[3] Cordell Hull, *Memoirs* (New York, 1948), I, 398.
[4] *Ibid.,* p. 400.

ment went so far as to permit manufacturers to copy designs of equipment that had been tested and perfected in government laboratories. Products made from these plans were freely sold to foreign governments.[5]

Some of the revelations that shocked the American public came from the secret files of the Department of State. Secretary Hull had been most generous in making available for the use of the Nye Committee confidential documents whose contents were supposed to be kept hidden from the prying eyes of newspaper reporters. But the inevitable leaks soon occurred. The Argentine Government protested against certain allegations concerning an Argentine admiral; the Chinese Foreign Office denied that a large wheat loan had been diverted into the itching palms of munitions makers, and Lord Vansittart carefully combed his large vocabulary for words that would express the proper pitch of indignation over the insinuation that King George V had exerted pressure upon Poland in order to secure a contract for a well-known British firm.[6] Taking his cue from the Foreign Office, the British Ambassador at Washington denounced the publication of the correspondence of the British Government with the House of Morgan during the years 1914–17. The American public should remain ignorant of the close connections between American big business and Britain.

Secretary Hull was greatly embarrassed by this barrage of protests, and he endeavored to enlist the support of the President in his effort to keep the Nye Committee "within reasonable limits." Anglo-American relations should be carefully coddled lest some incident arise that might lead to seriously strained relations. But President Roosevelt was not interested in preserving the secrecy of the records of the House of Morgan. Although he agreed to meet the members of the Nye Committee in conference on March 19, he refrained from exerting the slightest pressure upon them.[7] Historians will be eternally grateful to him for his silence on this occasion.

Thanks to this lack of Presidential pressure the Nye Committee unearthed a vast amount of data of great value to historians. These documents clearly showed the economic forces that helped to prepare the hostile climate of opinion against Germany that eventually led to American intervention in 1917. An important part of this evidence revealed the rich financial harvest gathered by some business firms as a result

---

[5] *Hearings Before the Special Senate Committee on the Investigation of the Munitions Industry,* 73 Cong., 2 sess., pts. 1–17. See also, William T. Stone, "The Munitions Industry," Foreign Policy Association Reports, No. 20, 1935; H. C. Engelbrecht, *One Hell of a Business* (New York, 1934).

[6] Hull, *op. cit.,* p. 380.

[7] *Ibid.,* pp. 400–402.

of the conflict.[8] These surprising figures accelerated the movement to enact legislation that would insure American neutrality and would take the profits out of war.

b. *The Offensive against American Neutrality*

The movement to insure American neutrality soon encountered the bitter opposition of many American publicists and politicians who believed that the Kellogg Pact had abolished the old concept of neutrality. They expressed their opinions with vehemence and launched a spirited attack upon anyone who adhered to the belief that America could still stay out of Europe's never-ending cycle of wars. Their carefully planned offensive against the continuance of the American practice of neutrality began long before the findings of the Nye Committee deeply disturbed the American mind. It was a carry-over from the fight for the Treaty of Versailles. That treaty was partly American-made, and it had numerous supporters in the United States. Many readily recognized that it contained some glaring injustices, but they would not condemn the whole convention because of these imperfections. After the defeat of the treaty in the Senate, a group of prominent Americans dedicated all their efforts to bring the United States into a close concert with their former allies by means of some innocent-appearing pact whose broad implications could eventually be made to serve their purposes. The Kellogg-Briand Peace Pact was the answer to their prayers.

The British and French governments watched with great care and deep appreciation the work of these international-minded Americans. It was becoming increasingly difficult to preserve the spoils of the World War. If America could be bound to some general treaty for the renunciation of war her moral support would be assured in favor of the status quo. If some nation still crippled by the chains of Versailles attempted to break those bonds, or if some have-not power should by

---

[8] According to statistics presented in the *Report of the Federal Trade Commission on War-Time Profits and Costs of the Steel Industry*, June 25, 1924, p. 29, the profits of some corporations were fantastically high:

Firm	Year	Profits
Bethlehem Steel Corporation	1917	43%
Jones and Laughlin Steel Company	1917	47%
Colt's Patent Fire Arms Company	1917	64%
Savage Arms Corporation	1917	65%

In Richard Lewisohn's *The Profits of War* (New York, 1937), pp. 153–54, the following statement is made: "The Kennecott Company, one of the Guggenheim group, made a profit in 1917 amounting to 70% of the capital invested. . . . The corresponding profits of the Utah Copper Company . . . were 200%. . . . But even this was surpassed by the Calumet and Hecla Copper Mining Company who won the palm with 800% in 1917." See also the Washington *Evening Star*, December 14, 1935.

armed force endeavor to upset the political structure erected in 1919, she would be denounced as a treaty violator and a wicked foe of world peace. The Kellogg Pact was in the making long before 1928.

In order that this pact should be specially shaped to promote British and French imperial interests, the foreign offices of those two countries insisted upon certain reservations to the general terms of the treaty. The French Government made it very clear that the proposed peace pact should not affect the right of legitimate defense or the performance of the obligations outlined in the Covenant of the League of Nations. The same should be true with reference to the obligations contracted under the terms of the treaties of Locarno or under the provisions of treaties of alliance. Secretary Kellogg indicated his approval of these reservations in his speech before the American Society of International Law (April 28, 1928). On May 19 the British Government expressed its acceptance of the French reservations and then seized the opportunity to announce some of its own. There were *certain regions of the world* whose welfare and integrity constituted a "special and vital interest" for the safety of the Empire. *Interference* with these regions could not be "suffered." Their protection against attack was "to the British Empire a measure of self-defence." It should be clearly understood, therefore, that the British Government would not become a party to a new general peace treaty except upon the "distinct understanding that it does not prejudice their freedom of action in this respect [self-defense of certain regions of the world.]"[9]

In commenting upon these British and French reservations, Professor Edwin Borchard trenchantly remarks: "Considering the breadth of these qualifications or interpretations, it would be difficult to conceive of any wars that nations have fought within the past century, or are likely to fight in the future, that cannot be accommodated under them. Far from being an outlawry of war, they constitute the most definite sanction of specific wars that has ever been promulgated."[10]

It was obvious that the British reservations were purposely ambiguous. British statesmen could still meet with armed force any "interference" in vast undefined "regions of the world" whose welfare and integrity the British Government regarded as "vital" to the interests of the Empire. By accepting this significant phraseology Secretary Kellogg underwrote a reservation which reduced the peace pact to a sorry ges-

---

[9] With reference to the effect of these reservations upon the Kellogg Pact see Edwin Borchard, "The Multilateral Treaty for the Renunciation of War," *American Journal of International Law*, XXIII (1929), 116–20; Philip M. Brown, "The Interpretation of the General Pact for the Renunciation of War," *ibid.*, pp. 374–79.

[10] Edwin Borchard and William P. Lage, *Neutrality for the United States* (New Haven, 1937), pp. 292–93.

ture. His previous acceptance of the French reservations gave further overtones of war to a document that was supposed to be a paean of peace.[11]

This situation was given an additional martial twist by Secretary Kellogg's opinion that wars undertaken by nations in pursuance of their obligations under the Covenant of the League of Nations, under the Locarno treaties, or under treaties of alliance were not outlawed by the Pact of Paris.[12] After this broad statement it was only natural for European statesmen to argue that the American Government was now bound by League decisions concerning aggressor nations and could not oppose collective action decreed by Geneva.[13] It is interesting to note that Senator Borah helped to mold this European viewpoint. In an interview with Kirby Page he boldly declared: "Another important result of such a treaty [the proposed Paris pact] would be to enlist the support of the United States in co-operative action against any nation which is guilty of a flagrant violation of this outlawry agreement. . . . It is quite inconceivable that this country would stand idly by in case of a grave breach of a multilateral treaty to which it is a party."[14]

It should be remembered that Borah, as chairman of the Senate Committee on Foreign Relations, took an active part in the negotiations for this Pact of Paris. Before the pact was signed Secretary Kellogg wrote him a letter to thank him for his "co-operation and very great assistance."[15] Borah replied by congratulating Kellogg "not only in securing the Treaty, but in securing it in the form in which it seems now it will undoubtedly be accepted. I look upon the Treaty as a great and distinct achievement in the cause of peace and I regard the manner and skill with which you have conducted the negotiations as an exhibition of the highest statesmanship."[16]

Kellogg now expressed his fears that there was "a significant movement against the treaty in this country and I think we should all bear this in mind."[17] Borah should have been deeply interested in checking

[11] George Wickersham, "The Pact of Paris: A Gesture or a Pledge?," *Foreign Affairs,* VII (1929), 356 ff.

[12] *The General Pact for the Renunciation of War,* pp. 37, 67.

[13] Frank H. Simonds, "America's Second Peace Adventure," *American Review of Reviews,* LXXVIII (1928), 267; Oscar T. Crosby, "The Paris Pact," *Advocate of Peace,* XC (1928), 693.

[14] *New York Times,* March 25, 1928. Some months later, Senator Borah expressed a very different viewpoint. In a speech in the Senate, January 3, 1929, he now stated: "If a nation violates the treaty [Pact of Paris] are we under any obligation, express or implied, to apply coercive or punitive measures? I answer emphatically, NO!" *Congressional Record,* 70 Cong., 2 sess., LXX, January 3, 1929, 1065.

[15] Secretary Kellogg to Senator Borah, July 16, 1928. *Personal and Confidential,* Borah Papers, Library of Congress.

[16] Senator Borah to Secretary Kellogg, July 22, 1928. *Ibid.*

[17] Secretary Kellogg to Senator Borah, July 26, 1928. *Ibid.*

this movement because he was in many ways one of the authors of the pact that would soon be signed in Paris:

I think the people in Europe understand the great assistance you have been. Many of the suggestions as to its form came from you and your first open letter to the New York *Times* explaining the proposed treaty was of immense value.[18]

In the second week in August, Kellogg wrote to Borah with some anxiety about the "insinuations" in certain newspapers:

Just now representatives of certain papers . . . are writing all the insinuations they can think of and Frank Simonds has joined the crowd. He says we have assumed moral obligations. I know of no moral obligations to apply sanctions or take affirmative military action in any case whatever might happen; in fact this is the only kind of treaty, as you have always said, that we can possibly sign. . . . It makes me discouraged when I see such insinuations.[19]

These insinuations had a good basis in fact and Borah's interview with Kirby Page [March 25, 1928] showed that the chairman of the Senate Committee on Foreign Relations firmly believed that "in the event of a grave violation" of the proposed peace pact the United States could "not stand idly by." It would not be long before the next Secretary of State, Henry L. Stimson, would vehemently assert this very viewpoint. Borah was incredibly naïve in his whole attitude towards the proposed Kellogg-Briand treaty for the outlawry of war. He had been one of the outstanding opponents of the Treaty of Versailles in 1919–20 and had played a major part in encompassing its defeat in the Senate. Now he was throwing all his energies in pushing through the Senate a treaty that would "freeze" all the injustices of Versailles. The so-called chains of Versailles could be broken only by armed conflict; Borah was in the strange position of outlawing war and thus perpetuating those chains. The implications of the proposed pact seemed to escape him, even though some distinguished publicists endeavored to warn him. In December 1929, Professor Borchard wrote him a long letter which ended on the following admonition:

I cannot help but feel grateful that we did not succumb to the campaign for joining the League—a campaign now about to be renewed. . . . We should inevitably have become either a party to or an opponent of these transactions [European disputes then pending] and could not have done anything but drag ourselves into the meshes of European politics. If I correctly read the

[18] Secretary Kellogg to Senator Borah, July 27, 1928. *Ibid.*
[19] Secretary Kellogg to Senator Borah, August 10, 1928. *Ibid.*

British White Paper, it is their idea that this result has been accomplished by our signature of the Kellogg Pact. It was always my belief that this was essentially their purpose in signing the Kellogg Pact.[20]

Senator Capper had already given an indication that he believed that the Kellogg Pact fundamentally changed our historic neutrality policy. In February 1929 he introduced a resolution which called for the prohibition of the shipment of "arms and munitions and implements or other articles for use in war" to any country which the President declared was a violator of the Kellogg Pact.[21] Although this resolution was not adopted by the Senate it was strong evidence that some prominent Republicans and Democrats were ready to follow a bipartisan policy with reference to the outlawry of war.

There were numerous academic supporters of this bipartisan policy. Professor Clyde Eagleton was confident that the "Kellogg Pact will be respected only if we deliberately and strongly take sides against the violator of the Pact,"[22] and Professor Charles G. Fenwick praised the pact because it indicated American concern with regard to its observance "by other States" and an intention to depart from our "traditional attitude of neutrality" should others be guilty of a breach of it.[23]

In order to implement this one-world concept of war and peace (with no middle ground of neutrality), certain publicists expressed the opinion that the provisions of the Kellogg Pact contained implications of international consultation. David Hunter Miller was sure of it. In the event of a threat of war, "inevitably the Government of the United States will be consulted, if not at Geneva, certainly by the Powers most influential at Geneva. . . . No Government of the United States could be indifferent to such an appeal [nor] could it refuse to use its influence in such case in co-operation with the League of Nations to preserve peace." Consultation among the signatories of the Pact of Paris was an obligation inherent in the terms of the Pact itself.[24]

Secretary Stimson shared this view of Mr. Miller, and on August 8, in an address before the Council on Foreign Relations, he gave it clear and emphatic expression.[25] Neutrality, he believed, was an outworn American concept: international co-operation was the new slogan of the Department of State and it would command popular support. The

[20] Edwin M. Borchard to Senator Borah, December 27, 1929. *Ibid.*

[21] *Congressional Record,* 70 Cong., 2 sess., February 11, 1929, p. 3198.

[22] *Proceedings of the American Society of International Law,* 1925, p. 133.

[23] "The Implication of Consultation in the Pact of Paris," *American Journal of International Law,* XXVI (1932), 787–89.

[24] David Hunter Miller, *The Peace Pact of Paris* (New York, 1928), pp. 130–31.

[25] Henry L. Stimson, "The Pact of Paris: Three Years of Development," Department of State, Publication No. 357 (Washington, 1932), pp. 11–12.

Roosevelt Administration was too cautious to go as far as Mr. Stimson, but Norman Davis, at Geneva (May 22, 1933), not only promised consultation but also co-operation with other powers to the extent of refraining from any action that would defeat collective effort to punish an aggressor State.[26]

John Bassett Moore, America's leading authority in the field of international law, listened to the words of Norman Davis with deep dismay. The commitment of the United States to any far-reaching consultative pact would "constitute the gravest danger to which the country has ever been exposed, a danger involving our very independence. . . . It would destroy the last vestige of the power to control our own destiny. . . . Of all conceivable devices the 'consultative pact' is the most pernicious."[27]

These words of warning from Judge Moore carried considerable weight in some Democratic circles, and they had a definite influence upon the Department of State in the Italo-Ethiopian crisis. But before the outbreak of that conflict the fight to preserve American neutrality was transferred to the halls of Congress.

c. *The President Accepts a Congressional Program of Neutrality*

It is a trite observation that politics often makes strange bedfellows. This was certainly true of the relations between Borah and Stimson. At times they were poles apart in their attitude towards the problem of world peace, but upon other occasions they stood shoulder-to-shoulder and gave each other strong support. In the summer of 1932, Borah agreed with Stimson that it would be wise statesmanship to cancel the war debts of the nations that had been associated with America during the World War.[28] In the early days of 1933, Borah once more stood close to Stimson. On January 10, 1933, President Hoover sent to Congress a special message requesting authority to declare an embargo upon munitions of war. This request had particular reference to the war then raging between Bolivia and Paraguay. But the message also contained an inclosure from Secretary Stimson (January 6, 1933) in the form of a resolution that had wide implications.[29] Borah was persuaded to introduce this resolution which passed the Senate on January 19 without discussion. On the following day Senator Bingham made a motion to

[26] Department of State, *Press Release*, May 22, 1933.
[27] "An Appeal to Reason," *Foreign Affairs*, XI (1933), 571–73.
[28] Henry L. Stimson and McGeorge Bundy, *On Active Service in War and Peace* (New York, 1948), p. 214.
[29] *Congressional Record*, 72 Cong., 2 sess., January 10, 1933, pp. 1448, 1546.

reconsider the vote on the resolution and thereby erected a barrier that
prevented final favorable action.[30]

Under the wide terms of this resolution, whenever the President
discovered *in any part of the world* a threatening situation which would
be aggravated by shipments of munitions of war to that quarter, he
could, after securing some measure of international co-operation, issue
a proclamation which would take the form of an arms embargo. This
embargo would be put into force against "such country or countries as
he [the President] may designate."

The tremendous powers thus placed within the discretion of the
President were very apparent to the business interests of the United
States. Officials from the Winchester Repeating Arms Company, and
from similar corporations in different parts of the country, rushed to
Washington and strongly argued against the proposed legislation. In
response to this pressure the scope of the resolution was narrowed. The
embargo would apply not to "any part of the world" but merely to
"any American Country."[31] But even in this emasculated form it failed
to secure the approval of Congress.[32]

When Secretary Hull assumed office in March 1933 he quickly disclosed his irritation that Congress had failed to enact neutrality legislation that placed broad powers within the President's discretion. He and
Stimson saw eye to eye in this regard. In April 1935, he frankly informed the President that he did not want the type of legislation "advocated by isolationists like Nye, which would bind the Executive hand
and foot and inform any prospective aggressors . . . that they could
declare war on their intended victim and we would then see to it that
our citizens did not furnish arms to that victim."[33]

But Hull was not able to suppress the enthusiasm of Senators Nye
and Clark who introduced several measures providing for the very neutrality policy that was scorned by the Department of State. The President and Secretary Hull asked Senator Pittman (chairman of the Senate
Committee on Foreign Relations) to "kill" the proposed legislation by
reporting adversely upon it, but he failed to act according to their desires. Norman Davis was then sent to see Pittman who agreed to "stifle"

[30] *Congressional Record,* 72 Cong., 2 sess., pp. 2134–35.

[31] *New York Times,* February 16, 1933.

[32] Judge John Bassett Moore protested vigorously against the passage of any resolution which placed such great powers within the discretion of the President: "The
pending resolution is . . . opposed to the settled policy and the highest interests of the
United States and also to the provisions of our Federal Constitution. If adopted it
would enable the President (1) to make international engagements of the most far-
reaching kind at his will, without the advice and consent of the Senate, and (2) to
carry us into war without the prerequisite constitutional declaration of war by Congress." House Report No. 22, 73 Cong., 1 sess., pt. 2, pp. 5–9.

[33] Hull, *op. cit.,* p. 406.

the Nye-Clark resolutions. After this promise of acquiescence by Pittman, Hull appeared before the Senate Committee on Foreign Relations and expressed his views. Subsequently he sent to the committee a draft of the legislation which he preferred. This, of course, contained a provision which left to the President's discretion the application of an arms embargo in time of war.[34]

The Department of State feared that the strong isolationist bloc in the Senate might be able to postpone the passage of the proposed legislation, so Hull on August 19 asked President Roosevelt to exert pressure upon Senator Pittman so that he would evince the proper fighting spirit against the obstructionists. But Pittman seemed singularly unresponsive to White House advice in this regard, and the resolution he reported from the Committee on Foreign Relations failed to give the President any discretion in the application of an arms embargo. When this resolution passed both houses of Congress and was sent to the President for his approval, Secretary Hull indicated several provisions that were distasteful to him. But the President waved aside these objections and approved the bill on August 31.

On September 24, the National Munitions Control Board held its first meeting, and now every manufacturer, exporter, and importer of arms, ammunition, and implements of war would have to register with the Department of State. The export of their products would be controlled by a license system. In time of war a mandatory embargo proclaimed by the President would put a stop to this trade with belligerent nations. There would be no opportunity for the use of Presidential discretion. It was also provided that the Chief Executive, by proclamation, could extend to American citizens a warning that if they took passage on belligerent ships they did so at their own risk. He could prohibit or restrict the entry of belligerent submarines into American waters and could bar the transport of men and munitions from American ports to belligerent vessels at sea.[35]

d. *American Reaction to the Italo-Ethiopian War*

The Neutrality Act had established a new policy of peace insurance which it was ardently hoped would keep America safe from the ravages of war. A test for this policy soon arose on October 3 when Mussolini's legions marched into Ethiopia. The usual proclamations of war were omitted. This led Secretary Hull to send telegrams to London, Paris, Rome, Geneva, and Addis Ababa requesting news of actual hostilities.

[34] *Ibid.*, pp. 410–11.
[35] Borchard and Lage, *op. cit.*, p. 315.

Bingham, in London, replied that "His Majesty's Government do not consider a state of war to exist."[36] A little puzzled by the cautious attitude of Britain, Hull sent another telegram of inquiry to London: "Is this attitude based upon legal considerations that relate to belligerent rights, or is it the result of practical considerations pending the Council meeting?"[37]

While Hull was waiting for a reply from Bingham, Stanley K. Hornbeck, chief of the Division of Far Eastern Affairs, proposed to Mr. Phillips that a message be sent to the British Foreign Office and to the Secretary-General of the League of Nations to the effect that no request be made of the American Government to co-operate in the imposition of sanctions.[38]

Dr. Hornbeck's proposal was met with "smiles of disapproval" but he nevertheless continued to push it vigorously. He knew only too well that Europe would be eager for America to co-operate in any program of pressure upon Italy and he realized the dangers that would attend such action. While the Department of State was pondering the problems that would inevitably arise out of the war, word came from Paris that Laval and Eden had been holding important conferences concerning the course that should be followed. Laval had expressed the view that "it might be possible to get by with economic measures" of pressure upon Rome. Eden had countered with the statement that "if such measures should be taken they must be strong, firm and complete, and must commence all at once in order to be effective."[39]

As dispatches continued to pour into the Department of State from European capitals it was soon obvious that a state of actual warfare existed between Italy and Ethiopia. In view of this fact President Roosevelt sent to Secretary Hull a wireless message from the cruiser *Houston* that he believed a proclamation should be immediately issued recognizing this state of war.[40] Hull agreed with this viewpoint even though some of his advisers like Hugh Wilson were of the opinion that America should await action by the League. On October 5 the formal proclamation was issued which placed an embargo upon the shipment of arms and munitions of war to belligerent nations. Along with this proclamation a statement was issued warning all American citizens that those

---

[36] Ambassador Bingham to Secretary Hull, London, October 4, 1935. 765.84/1556, MS, Department of State.

[37] Secretary Hull to Ambassador Bingham, October 4, 1935. 765.84/1556, MS, Department of State.

[38] Stanley K. Hornbeck to Mr. Phillips, October 4, 1935. 765.84/1960, MS, Department of State.

[39] Theodore Marriner to Secretary Hull, Paris, October 4, 1935. 765.84/1557, MS, Department of State.

[40] President Roosevelt to Secretary Hull, October 4, 1935. 765.84/1574, MS, Department of State.

"who voluntarily engage in transactions of any character with either of the belligerents do so at their own risk."[41]

This statement went beyond the letter of the Neutrality Act and was drafted by Secretary Hull in order to discourage "trading of all kinds with Italy." The President had agreed with Hull in this particular case, but he broke with him in connection with the issuance of a warning to American citizens to be careful about traveling on Italian ships. Hull thought this warning was not necessary, but the President insisted that it be issued. He feared that if "Americans continue to patronize Italian ships there may very easily occur some untoward episode."[42]

From Germany, Dodd reported that the Italo-Ethiopian War was being carefully studied by the Foreign Office. With reference to the possible imposition of sanctions, Dodd believed that inasmuch as Germany was no longer a member of the League and had no share in "Geneva decisions, it does not propose to be bound thereby." The German Government hoped "to maintain normal trade with Italy."[43]

In Paris there was a growing disinclination to take strong measures against Italy. Even the leftist press was supporting this viewpoint. The communist papers were exclaiming with emphasis: "We refuse to be dragged into a war through Signor Mussolini's folly." In the leading papers there was a marked tendency to "dissuade England from pressing for the adoption of sanctions."[44]

After a careful scrutiny of the French press the Italian Government reached the conclusion that "France had decided to support Italy without alienating England." The consequence was that "Italy will proceed uninterrupted into Ethiopia, in the meantime seeking some advantageous compromise. . . . Military sanctions seem certain to be discarded and such economic sanctions as may be adopted have the prospect of being so restricted as to be ineffective."[45]

Hugh Wilson, in Geneva, hoped that Secretary Hull would postpone any action with reference to the Italo-Ethiopian conflict. The situation was decidedly "ticklish." The issuance of an American proclamation recognizing a state of war "might influence the decision of the Council and involve us in responsibility for the course of action which they adopt."[46]

---

[41] Department of State, *Press Release*, October 5, 1935, pp. 251–55.

[42] Hull, *op. cit.*, pp. 430–31.

[43] Ambassador Dodd to Secretary Hull, Berlin, October 5, 1935. 765.84/1587, MS, Department of State.

[44] Theodore Marriner to Secretary Hull, Paris, October 5, 1935. 765.84/1591, MS, Department of State.

[45] Ambassador Long to Secretary Hull, Rome, October 5, 1935. 765.84/1607, MS, Department of State.

[46] Hugh Wilson to Secretary Hull, Geneva, October 5, 1935. 765.84/1583, *Strictly Confidential*, MS, Department of State.

Prentiss Gilbert, also in Geneva, presented the opposite viewpoint. He had talked with a British official who took the position that the sooner America acted "the better." League action "would not tend to clarify the situation but [would] probably render it more involved and that early action on our part would not only serve to cut through this atmosphere by a recognition of the realities of the situation, but . . . would also strengthen the British position."[47]

It was the British position that Secretary Hull regarded as being of prime importance. On October 5 he directed James C. Dunn to telephone to the Embassy in London and make certain inquiries about the attitude of the Foreign Office. He learned that the British Government believed that "sanctions might not be agreed to immediately at Geneva, but that eventually there would be sanctions." With reference to the existence of war between Italy and Ethiopia, no decision had as yet been made by the British Government.[48]

While the British Foreign Office was wrestling with the juridical problem of war, the British General Staff and the British Admiralty were engaging in important conversations with French military officials concerning possible operations in the event that France was attacked as a result of League measures. During these conversations the question of sanctions was given extended consideration, the view being expressed that "military measures might be evoked by conditions flowing out of the application of economic measures."[49]

These conversations were given added significance by the reply of the French Government to the British query as to French action in the event Britain was attacked by a third power "against whom sanctions were contemplated." French assistance was promised under the following three conditions:

1) The obligation of assistance must be reciprocal. It must bind Britain to help France in similar circumstances.

2) There must be a joint consultation on the proposed measures of precaution.

3) The obligations must apply whether the aggressor State is or is not a member of the League.[50]

e. *The League Names Italy as an Aggressor Nation*

During the period of Anglo-French military conversations concerning the wide ramifications of the Italo-Ethiopian dispute, the League of Na-

[47] Prentiss Gilbert to Secretary Hull, Geneva, October 5, 1935. 765.84/1595, MS, Department of State.

[48] Memorandum by James C. Dunn, October 5, 1935. 765.84/1583½, MS, Department of State.

[49] Prentiss Gilbert to Secretary Hull, Geneva, October 6, 1935. 765.84/1681, MS, Department of State.

[50] London *Times*, October 8, 1935.

tions was grappling with the same thorny problem. Anthony Eden, at Geneva, had no thought of appeasement, and his inflexible attitude was strongly supported by many important groups in Britain. The clergy of the Church of England was particularly insistent that the British Government stand behind the League. The Archbishop of York[51] and the Archbishop of Canterbury wrote letters that vehemently expressed the opinion that loyalty to the League was a moral obligation.[52] Canon F. R. Barry, preaching in Westminster Abbey, struck a similar note and frankly faced the fact that League support in the crisis then disturbing Europe might have grave consequences for Britain.[53] Just before the Assembly of the League declared Italy to be an aggressor state, Eden received a telegram from the Archbishop of York and a number of bishops, deans, and other representatives of the Church of England assuring him that he had their ardent support in "taking whatever action" might be "necessary to uphold the Covenant of the League."[54]

Many members of the Trades Union Congress were outspoken in their advocacy of loyalty to the League, and when the Labour Party Conference began its sessions on September 30 a demand was immediately voiced for the application of economic sanctions.[55] British public opinion was apparently ready to support the League even at the cost of war.

In France there was a very different situation. As the shadow of resurgent Germany began to darken the northern frontiers of France, Laval grew increasingly reluctant to have any serious break with Mussolini. At first the rightist leagues like the Croix de Feu, the Camelots du Roi, and the Solidarité Française were the most outspoken groups in favor of friendly relations with Mussolini's Italy, but slowly the leftist elements moved in the same direction. In most circles there was no fervor for war. The general viewpoint reflected a profound pessimism about British idealism. It seemed to a large number of Frenchmen that the sudden British enthusiasm for the League masked a selfish concern for British imperial interests. They regarded it as distinctly naïve

to allow their feelings to be engaged by the abrupt conversion of a nation which finds itself overcome by so lively an attachment to the League at a moment when the League can be of service to its national interests. Between the previous indulgence and the present severity of the English attitude towards violations of the Covenant, the French see a contrast which strikes them as singular. . . . Is it not exasperating to see England rallying to the Covenant at last after her long detachment has allowed our victory [in the

[51] *Ibid.*, August 20, 1935.
[52] *Ibid.*, August 28, 1935.
[53] *Ibid.*, August 26, 1935.
[54] *Ibid.*, October 10, 1935.
[55] *Survey of International Affairs, 1935,* pp. 61–63.

World War] to fritter itself away and has permitted an expansion of German nationalism?[56]

But French reluctance to press Mussolini in a vigorous fashion did not prevent the League of Nations from taking action to block Italian expansion in Ethiopia. On October 5 the Council of the League met at Geneva and appointed a Committee of Six which was to submit a report on the Italo-Ethiopian dispute not later than the afternoon of the 7th. On that date the Council reassembled and heard the report of this special committee. In conclusion the report made this ominous statement: "After an examination of the facts stated above, the Committee has come to the conclusion that the Italian Government has resorted to war in disregard of its covenants under Article 12 of the Covenant of the League of Nations." The Council accepted this report naming Italy as an aggressor nation, and it referred the matter to the meeting of the Assembly on October 9.[57]

There was little doubt that the Assembly would confirm the decision of the Council, and in Geneva the question of sanctions began to loom large. On October 8, Hugh Wilson had a long talk with M. Coulondre, the French Foreign Office expert on economics, who wanted to know if copper and petroleum could be included under the term "implements of war" and thus be affected by the American arms embargo. Wilson did not believe that these "strategic materials" would fall within the terminology of the neutrality law. Coulondre then remarked that embargoes and quotas could be made efficacious "only on condition that the United States would co-operate." Wilson felt that such co-operation "might be extremely difficult." After a brief consideration of this discouraging statement, Coulondre expressed the optimistic opinion that the French and British governments were moving towards a "real entente."[58]

In London, Sir Samuel Hoare discussed this entente with Ambassador Bingham and was a little dubious about French co-operation. He inclined towards the view that the "French Government would not go as far as actual military sanctions or a blockade, but he was confident that the French would support the British up to that point." Economic sanctions might turn the trick. If there could be arranged some effective collective action in refusing to accept Italian exports, the war would not last more than a few months.[59]

[56] P. Vaucher and P. H. Siriex, *L'Opinion Britannique, la Société des Nations et la Guerre Italo-Ethiopienne* (Paris, 1936), pp. 8, 23, 91.

[57] *League of Nations Official Journal*, November 1935, p. 1223.

[58] Hugh Wilson to Secretary Hull, Geneva, October 8, 1935. 765.84/1680, *Strictly Confidential*, MS, Department of State.

[59] Ambassador Bingham to Secretary Hull, London, October 8, 1935. 765.84/1666, *Strictly Confidential*, MS, Department of State.

The possibility that the Italo-Ethiopian conflict might widen into a general European war was discounted by Mussolini who assured the editor of the Paris *Soir* of his desire to come to an understanding with Britain: "This disagreement which England has with us is indeed senseless and a conflict between the two countries would be unthinkable. Neither directly nor indirectly do we desire to injure any British interest."[60]

But these gestures of conciliation did not affect the attitude of the Assembly of the League of Nations which on October 11 approved the decision of the Council (October 7) to declare that Italy had resorted to war "in disregard of engagements under Article 12 of the Covenant." The Assembly also appointed a Co-ordination Committee to deal with the matter of possible sanctions against Italy.[61]

Ambassador Long reported that in Rome the press was "bitter over the action of the League." It expressed the opinion that "Italy has been condemned at Geneva under methods which no court in any civilized country would use in the prosecution of the most heinous crime."[62] In view of this sharp Italian animosity towards Britain, Long thought that the Department of State should be prepared for a "possible sudden outbreak of hostilities." If a conflict actually took place, it would not be wise to discount the military strength of Italy. The "potentialities of the situation suggest the possibility of our having to deal on a friendly basis in the future with a more important Italy."[63]

f. *Secretary Hull Insists upon an Independent Policy*

The Department of State was fully aware of the implications of the Italo-Ethiopian dispute. On October 9, Secretary Hull sent a telegram to Hugh Wilson in which he emphasized the fact that as far as the American Government was concerned it should be "increasingly clear" to the League that every possible step had been taken to "preserve the peace." An assurance was then given that the Department of State would not overlook "any measures that we may be able to take consistent with our policy." But the League should realize that the American Government was inclined to pursue its course "independently in the light of circumstances as they develop."[64]

[60] Ambassador Long to Secretary Hull, Rome, October 8, 1935. 765.84/1653, MS, Department of State.

[61] *League of Nations Official Journal,* League Assembly, pp. 255–67.

[62] Ambassador Long to Secretary Hull, Rome, October 9, 1935. 765.84/1695, MS, Department of State.

[63] Ambassador Long to Secretary Hull, Rome, October 9, 1935. 765.84/1711, *Strictly Confidential,* MS, Department of State.

[64] Secretary Hull to Ambassador Wilson, October 9, 1935. 765.84/1686, MS, Department of State.

Ambassador Wilson discussed this instruction with Anthony Eden who said that he "had been particularly careful not to take any steps which could embarrass the United States and that he had reached the conclusion before I spoke to him that it might be embarrassing to us to have an invitation issued." When Wilson took the matter up with Laval he received a prompt assurance that "if the matter of an invitation were raised," France would oppose "such a step."[65] Eden then remarked that further pressure could be exerted upon Italy through collective action on the part of the signatories of the Pact of Paris. He could not see that "such a step would cut across the work at Geneva if done through diplomatic channels." In order to illustrate this statement he outlined the plan he had in mind for applying sanctions to Italy in such a way as to bring the war to an early close.

While Eden was thinking in terms of compulsion, Laval still hoped that it would be "possible to make an agreement which could be accepted by Italy." This hope was based upon confidential information to the effect that Mussolini was prepared to accept "something considerably less than he had formerly demanded."[66]

But from Rome word came that the position of Mussolini in Italy was stronger than ever. The feeling was widespread that "the present issue goes beyond any question of internal policies and involves the very existence of Italy. Mussolini counts among his supporters today persons who formerly would gladly have witnessed this downfall or perhaps even had contributed to that purpose."[67]

In Geneva the British continued to press for effective sanctions. This policy would be pursued until the elections. Consequently, "the weight of English pressure at Geneva on the Italo-Abyssinian crisis may be expected to increase rather than diminish until the general election is over."[68]

This British pressure found expression during a conversation between Sir Samuel Hoare and Ambassador Bingham. The Foreign Secretary was extremely anxious that Italy be made to feel the weight of international displeasure because of her aggressive action in Ethiopia. In this regard the signatories of the Kellogg Pact could play an important role. They could be summoned to action by the League, but this procedure might awaken resentment in the United States. A second alterna-

---

[65] Ambassador Wilson to Secretary Hull, Geneva, October 10, 1935. 765.84/1722, MS, Department of State.

[66] Ambassador Wilson to Secretary Hull, Geneva, October 10, 1935. 765.84/1729, MS, Department of State.

[67] Ambassador Long to Secretary Hull, Rome, October 10, 1935. 765.84/2074, MS, Department of State.

[68] Ambassador Bingham to Secretary Hull, London, October 10–11, 1935. 765.84/1721, 1740, MS, Department of State.

tive could take the form of a series of conversations "between the diplomatic representatives of the Pact signatories," but Hoare was silent as to the method of initiating these conversations. The third alternative was the "possibility of action initiated by the President of the United States."[69]

When these suggestions were conveyed to President Roosevelt he was somewhat confused as to procedure. He was enjoying a cruise at sea and he did not have on board his vessel a "complete copy" of the Kellogg Pact. He could not remember any "clause under which any positive action can be taken by signatories against a violating nation except possibly a *pro forma* protest."[70]

Hull immediately replied by wireless that there was no provision in the Pact of Paris which prescribed any method of invocation. But former secretaries of state [including Stimson] had "unofficially expressed the opinion that the Pact impliedly authorized and calls for consultation, and it is our view that consultation at the present stage . . . does not contemplate anything more than a concerted . . . appeal by all the signatories to the belligerent countries to abide by their legal and moral obligations by desisting from further hostilities."[71]

With the President's approval, Secretary Hull sent a long instruction to Ambassador Bingham indicating the attitude of the American Government. The Department of State was "favorably disposed in principle to the idea of calling attention to the obligations of all signatories to the Pact," and this had already been done with reference to the Italo-Ethiopian dispute. With regard to any consultation between the signatories of the pact in relation to this dispute, such action should have been taken before the outbreak of hostilities. Therefore, the "opportune moment for collective invocation of the Pact . . . has gone by." In view of what the "United States has already done, dramatically and emphatically, I doubt whether it would be wise for a renewed initiative to come from this country."[72]

But this negative attitude towards any formal invocation of the Pact of Paris did not prevent the President and Secretary Hull from making strenuous efforts to exert economic pressure upon Italy even before sanctions were actually imposed by the members of the League. At a press conference on October 10, Secretary Hull was asked whether he

[69] Ambassador Bingham to Secretary Hull, London, October 11, 1935. 765.84/1752, *Confidential for the Secretary*, MS, Department of State.

[70] President Roosevelt to Secretary Hull, October 13, 1935. 765.84/1784, MS, Department of State.

[71] Secretary Hull to President Roosevelt, October 13, 1935. 765.84/1784, MS, Department of State.

[72] Secretary Hull to Ambassador Bingham, October 14, 1935. 765.84/1752, MS, Department of State.

would care to elaborate upon what "the President said about American interests trading with belligerents at their own risk." Hull replied that every person should be able to grasp the "implications" of the President's statement. While there was no legal prohibition against Americans engaging in ordinary commercial transactions with the belligerent nations, the President's warning about the risks attending these business relations would probably act to diminish the extent of them.[73]

This mild, indirect way of checking the flow of American goods to Italy did not satisfy the President's desire to help put a stop to the Italo-Ethiopian War. He suggested to Secretary Hull that it might be possible to put an end to all shipments of processed copper and steel by including those articles in the list of "arms, ammunition and implements of war." When Hull informed him that his advisers in the Department of State were of the opinion that the Neutrality Act did not "authorize such additions to the embargo list," he pressed for the publication of the names of all Americans who, even at their own risk, traveled on belligerent ships or traded with belligerents. Hull conferred with Secretary Roper on this point and then advised the President that such publication would be "unwise." It would be expedient to proceed slowly and avoid incurring the "criticism and the certain antagonism of traders and travellers."[74]

g. *Britain Limits Italian Freedom of Speech*

American interest in the imposition of sanctions against Italy was diverted for a short time by British action to limit Italian freedom of speech. On October 12 the Columbia Broadcasting System issued a press release relative to the refusal of the British postal authorities to relay, through the radio-telephonic circuit between London and New York, a speech made by Baron Aloisi at Geneva. Under Article 27 of the Telecommunication Convention of Madrid, any suspension of radio services could be put into effect only after "all the contracting governments" had been notified through the Bern Bureau of such intended action. The British Government had not taken the trouble to send this notification, and their failure to do so was branded by Francis C. de Wolf, of the Department of State, as "somewhat highhanded." This incident was "further proof of the wisdom of establishing a separate telephonic circuit between New York and Paris."[75]

Dr. Irving Stewart, a member of the Communications Commission,

[73] Department of State, *Press Release*, October 12, 1935, pp. 303–4.
[74] Hull, *op. cit.*, pp. 432–33.
[75] Memorandum of Francis Colt de Wolf on the "Censorship by British of Baron Aloisi's Speech," October 12, 1935. 765.84/2026, MS, Department of State.

took the matter more seriously than Mr. de Wolf. He regarded the British action as a direct breach of Article 26 of the Treaty of Madrid (1932). It might, therefore, be necessary for the Federal Communications Commission to write to Secretary Hull and request that the breach be "brought to the attention of the British authorities." This suggestion was shocking to certain officials in the Department of State who were busily berating Italy for violating treaties. Britain must never be put in the same class with Italy in this matter. Dr. Stewart was quickly informed that it would be preferable to keep all discussion of this question upon a "purely informal basis" because its wide ramifications "involved matters of delicate consequence." It was apparent to Dr. Stewart that Britain must not be judged by ordinary standards, so he promised to do "all he could" to keep the commission from sending any protest to the Department of State.[76] The incident could be safely buried in the voluminous government files.

h. *America Refuses to Follow a Parallel Policy with Britain*

While this burial was being safely accomplished by the members of the Federal Communications Commission, many of the experts in the Department of State were wrestling with the very live problem of sanctions against Italy. They were fully aware of the fact that the Covenant of the League imposed no obligations on the League as such in connection with the imposition of sanctions. The enforcement of such measures was the responsibility of the individual members of the League. The obligation of each member to apply sanctions became effective as soon as it had recognized through its vote that Italy "had gone to war in violation of the Covenant."[77] All the members of the Council with the exception of Italy, Austria, Hungary, and Albania had approved the resolution declaring Italy an aggressor nation, thus indirectly making a declaration in favor of sanctions. In the Assembly on October 10, Italy had voted against the resolution of censure, while Austria and Hungary abstained from formal action. Thus the League was almost a unit in its approval of measures to curb Italian aggression.

In Europe the attitude of Germany was of prime importance. Word from Ambassador Dodd was reassuring: "Notwithstanding the suspicions of the French . . . which I gather are in a measure shared in the United States that Germany may shortly be expected to avail herself of

[76] Memorandum concerning conversation with Dr. Irving Stewart, October 15, 1935. 765.84/2028, MS, Department of State.

[77] Memorandum dealing with the League mechanism concerning sanctions, October 15, 1935. 765.84/2002, MS, Department of State.

the conjuncture to break loose, this country is really out of the picture for the present."[78]

News from France struck a note of muted optimism. Henry Morgenthau, Jr., had a conversation with Pierre Laval on October 15. The French Premier still nursed hopes of finding a solution for the Italo-Ethiopian dispute. France had no intention of "acquiescing in either military sanctions or blockade." He was especially anxious for his policy of conciliation to succeed because if matters were pushed to an extreme point and Mussolini fell there was "great danger that Communism might take over the regime in Italy and Europe could ill afford this blow."[79]

In October 1935 there was little danger of Mussolini's fall. The decision of the League to impose sanctions upon Italy had done more "to rally the nation around the Government . . . than any step yet taken toward a 'peaceful solution' of the dispute." Italy was now certain that Britain sought war in order to "cripple" Italian power "permanently."[80] Mussolini, during a conversation with former Senator Allen, of Kansas, expressed the opinion that the British Government was trying to "provoke Italy into war."[81] In Rome it was reported that a telegram had just been received from Dino Grandi recounting a discussion with Neville Chamberlain. Chamberlain had remarked that "it was no longer a question of war in Abyssinia; no longer a question of support from the League of Nations, but it has become a question of England's prestige."[82]

But Britain had no real intention of going to war to preserve her prestige. There was strong hope in London that economic sanctions would bring Italy to her knees. On October 15 the American press published a statement concerning the financial restrictions that the League was ready to impose upon Italy. All loans to or for the Italian Government, or to any person or corporation in Italian territory, were prohibited. Similar prohibitions would be applied to "all banking or other credits." This action was regarded by Herbert Feis, of the Department of State, as "very drastic."[83]

[78] Ambassador Dodd to Secretary Hull, Berlin, October 14, 1935. 765.84/1819, MS, Department of State.

[79] Memorandum of a conversation between Pierre Laval and Mr. Henry Morgenthau, Jr., Secretary of the Treasury, October 15, 1935. 765.84/2065, MS, Department of State.

[80] Ambassador Long to Secretary Hull, Rome, October 17, 1935. 765.84/2241, MS, Department of State.

[81] Ambassador Long to Secretary Hull, Rome, October 16, 1935. 765.84/1888, MS, Department of State.

[82] Ambassador Long to Secretary Hull, Rome, October 16, 1935. 765.84/1870, MS, Department of State.

[83] Memorandum by Herbert Feis on the League of Nations financial sanctions against Italy, October 16, 1935. 765.84/2027, MS, Department of State.

Although the British Government realized that a policy of economic sanctions might eventually lead to war with Italy, it instructed its delegation at Geneva to push "hard and insistently" for its adoption.[84] The Italian Foreign Office was fearful that this British pressure would have immediate effect upon American policy. On October 16 the Italian Ambassador had a conversation with Mr. Phillips and complained that the Federal Reserve Bank had recently circularized the more important banks in New York City asking for data concerning all credit and banking operations with Italian banks and commercial houses. He regarded this action as one of the many manifestations that the American Government was busily engaged in efforts to discourage trade with Italy. While he was certain that the League of Nations was "not dictating" to the United States, it seemed obvious that the Department of State was "very responsive to the situation developing in Geneva." When the ambassador finally remarked that he assumed that the British Government was in close touch with the United States "with regard to its program," Mr. Phillips hurriedly "denied this and told him definitely that we had not been approached by any Government with regard to League activities."[85]

This assurance by Mr. Phillips was distinctly disingenuous. On the very day that this assurance was given by Mr. Phillips, Anthony Eden had one of his usual confidential conversations with Ambassador Hugh Wilson. Once more the old question arose of consultations between countries which were not members of the League. Wilson expressed the opinion that any action or pronouncement by these non-member countries on the Italo-Ethiopian dispute should be issued as a result of diplomatic discussions rather than as a product of a formal conference. Eden replied by suggesting that France and the United States take the initiative in invoking the Kellogg Pact. He was quite "enthusiastic for this idea." He felt that it would be "enormously helpful ... if Germany could be brought into the picture in some way."[86]

Secretary Hull was cool to this suggestion, and on October 17 he cabled to Prentiss Gilbert at Geneva that the American Government was "acting upon its own initiative and proceeding separately and independently of all other Governments or peace organizations."[87]

When Ambassador Wilson was shown a copy of this instruction he

[84] Ambassador Wilson to Secretary Hull, Geneva, October 15, 1935. 765.84/1849, MS, Department of State.

[85] Memorandum of a conversation between Mr. Phillips and the Italian Ambassador, October 16, 1935. 765.84/2176, MS, Department of State.

[86] Ambassador Wilson to Secretary Hull, Geneva, October 17, 1935. 765.84/1916, MS, Department of State.

[87] Secretary Hull to Prentiss Gilbert, October 17, 1935. 765.84/1847, MS, Department of State.

sought an early opportunity to discuss its contents with Anthony Eden. Eden was reassuring. Undoubtedly a communication from the League would be sent to the United States, but it would be in a form that "could not be embarrassing." With reference to the political situation in Europe, Eden remarked that the "whole relationship between France and England was progressively more unsatisfactory." He had received letters from France indicating that England was more unpopular than at any time since Fashoda. Certainly the public temper in Britain was rapidly mounting against France and their "shilly-shallying in carrying out collective action."[88]

The communication from the League to which Eden had referred took the form of some documents dealing with the Italo-Ethiopian dispute. American comment on these data was requested. On October 26, Secretary Hull sent his reply. Once more emphasis was placed upon the "independent policy" followed by the United States with reference to the war in Ethiopia. While the American Government looked with sympathetic interest upon the concerted efforts of other nations to preserve peace, it would not become a member of this concert. It would, however, be ready at all times to exercise "its moral influence in favor of peace throughout the world."[89]

i. *Italy Hopes to Preserve American Friendship*

In France some of the papers like *Le Jour* were frankly disappointed by the tenor of Secretary Hull's reply. M. Bailby expressed the view that "when America promises to exercise moral influence in favor of peace" it is apparent that she has "no desire to go further." This decision leaves "the door open to transportation of products through Germany and Austria, thus placing sanctions nations in a deplorably inferior position."[90]

Prime Minister Laval, however, informed Ambassador Straus that he was "very well pleased with the statement of the American position." He believed that peace could be preserved by granting to Italy "some form of control over that portion of Ethiopia south of the eighth meridian." He likewise felt that it would be necessary to grant a strip of territory in the North bordering on Eritrea. With regard to sanctions he inclined towards the view that they would be applied "almost

---

[88] Ambassador Wilson to Secretary Hull, Geneva, October 18, 1935. 765.84/1952, MS, Department of State.

[89] Statement of Secretary Hull, October 26, 1935, Department of State, *Press Release*, November 2, 1935, pp. 336–37.

[90] Ambassador Straus to Secretary Hull, Paris, October 28, 1935. 765.84/2167, MS, Department of State.

immediately," and would be confined to "economic measures." He thought that it was exceedingly important to "sustain the administration of Mussolini in order to prevent the spread of communism."[91]

In Italy the reply of Secretary Hull to the League was considered a "full confirmation of the policy of neutrality voted by Congress." Italian opinion remained "friendly to America."[92] The hopes of many Italians were given a lift by the remarks of a well-known American newspaper correspondent, Isaac G. Marcosson, who appeared to speak with authority relative to the impossibility of enforcing sanctions against Italy. It was Mr. Marcosson's conviction that the failure of Austria and Hungary to approve the policy of pressure presaged an early breakdown of that system. German exports would have an easy road to Italy, and Russia, despite promises to the contrary, would supply Mussolini with much-needed oil, pig iron, and manganese.[93]

But Italian optimism as to the ineffective nature of sanctions received a blow on October 30, when President Roosevelt and Secretary Hull issued statements which called attention to the fact that they had warned American citizens "against transactions of any character with either of the belligerent nations except at their own risk." The President then expressed the hope that American businessmen would not be attracted by the possibility of rich returns from wartime trade, and Mr. Hull sounded a warning against "temporary and risky war profits."[94]

This counsel of perfection was not received with favor in some important countries. The Japanese Ambassador in Rome informed Ambassador Long that his Government would "not support the sanctions policy" and would not "even answer the recent League communication on the subject."[95] The Spanish Government was not at all certain what policy it would adopt,[96] while the Polish Ambassador informed Mr. Phillips, the Acting Secretary of State, that his Government was opposed to an early enforcement of sanctions against Italy.[97] The holes in the embargo dykes were constantly growing larger.

It was obvious to many American diplomats abroad that the British program for exerting pressure upon Italy was not meeting with the sup-

[91] Ambassador Straus to Secretary Hull, Paris, October 29, 1935. 765.84/2181, Confidential file, MS, Department of State.

[92] Ambassador Long to Secretary Hull, Rome, October 29, 1935. 765.84/2195, MS, Department of State.

[93] New York Herald-Tribune, (Paris edition), October 18, 1935.

[94] Department of State, Press Release, November 2, 1935, pp. 338–39.

[95] Ambassador Long to Secretary Hull, Rome, October 29, 1935. 765.84/2192, MS, Department of State.

[96] Ambassador Long to Secretary Hull, Rome, October 30, 1935. 765.84/2205, MS, Department of State.

[97] Acting Secretary Phillips to American Embassy at Warsaw, November 2, 1935. 765.84/1866, MS, Department of State.

port that had been expected. The possibility of being drawn into a war had acted as a deterrent upon some nations; others were critical of the way British statesmen had handled the matter. Ambassador Long expressed the view that the Italian invasion of Ethiopia had been a violation of the Kellogg Pact, but she was not alone in this movement towards war. Britain's "naval threat against Italy was also a violation of the Covenant of the League and fairly good evidence that she was, and is, ready to disregard her renunciation of 'war as a national policy' taken under the Kellogg Pact."[98]

It was difficult for Ambassador Long to be sharply critical of Italian policy. In Rome he had been treated with such constant courtesy that he found it easy to supply excuses for violations of the Kellogg Pact. Since October 11 the Italian Government had been faced with the threat of sanctions. This economic warfare would start on November 18, and its impact upon the Italian way of life was dreaded throughout the peninsula. It was widely recognized that America, through her arms embargo, through restrictions upon banking credit, and by repeated warnings of the dangers of trade with belligerent nations, had taken steps that might seriously embarrass the Italian war effort. But the Italian Government had not permitted these adverse moves to produce an attitude of hostility towards the United States. While there was some "querulousness in their scrutiny of American policy, they are on the whole generous in their interpretations of it as it affects them and they very generally consider America in a very friendly way." The hope was still cherished that the Ethiopian war would not sacrifice "the friendship of America not only because of the selfish advantage it is to them in this fight but also because the thought is traditional with them." After this careful presentation of many of the factors in the Italo-Ethiopian equation, Ambassador Long closed with the following advice: "I strongly recommend the American Government be neutral and keep out of this war. . . . I recommend that we pursue a course of studied aloofness."[99]

j. *The Department of State Exerts Pressure upon Italy*

These recommendations of Ambassador Long were wasted words as far as President Roosevelt and Secretary Hull were concerned. The Anglo-American entente, whose existence had been vigorously denied

[98] Ambassador Long to Secretary Hull, Rome, November 12, 1935. 765.84/2507, MS, Department of State.

[99] Ambassador Long to Secretary Hull, Rome, November 12, 1935. 765.84/2507, MS, Department of State.

by Mr. Phillips, was functioning in a most effective manner. The Department of State had been making an exhaustive study of economic sanctions and it had come to the conclusion that they could not function properly unless certain essential raw materials and key commodities were excluded from American exports to Italy. The embargo on "arms, ammunition and implements of war" was too restricted in scope to affect the Italian war effort in a major manner. Something new would have to be added to the American program.

In order to be of the greatest possible service to the League in this matter of sanctions against Italy, Secretary Hull issued on November 15 a statement that was really a declaration of economic warfare upon Italy:

The American people are entitled to know that there are certain commodities such as oil, copper, trucks, tractors, scrap iron, and scrap steel which are essential war materials, although not actually "arms, ammunition, or implements of war," and that according to recent Government trade reports a considerably increased amount of these is being exported for war purposes. This class of trade is directly contrary to the policy of this Government as announced in official statements of the President and Secretary of State, as it is also contrary to the general spirit of the recent neutrality act.[100]

It was the purpose of Secretary Hull to place America in the van of a crusade against aggressor nations. Neither he nor the President had the authority to join with other nations in military sanctions that would stop the march of Italian armies into Ethiopia, but they could invoke the "spirit" of the Neutrality Act in an effort to sabotage any rapid advance of Mussolini's war machine. They had moved several steps ahead of the League in this matter. Secretary Hull's statement of November 15 was three days prior to the date when the League sanctions went into effect. Moreover, the list of commodities and raw materials on this non-export list was more extensive than the one subsequently issued by the League members. The American schedule included the important item of petroleum. The League never went that far and the statements issued by it never struck the note of righteousness so strongly sounded by Secretary Hull. To strident supporters of the League this note of righteousness seemed like a summons to peace; to realistic students of international relations it was a clarion call to arms whose overtones kept vibrating along State Department corridors until they were magnified into a chorus of war by the tragedy of Pearl Harbor.

[100] Department of State, *Press Release*, November 16, 1935, p. 382.

X

Mussolini Makes a Mockery out of
Collective Security

a. *Secretary Hull Defends American Policy*

SECRETARY HULL'S press statement of November 15 convinced Mussolini that the United States should really be classed with the nations that favored economic sanctions against Italy. When Ambassador Long reported this shift in sentiment to the Department of State, Hull glibly explained that America was following an "independent policy" based upon the "spirit and intent" of the recent neutrality legislation.[1] On November 22 he used the same explanation during a long conversation with the Italian Ambassador. He assured Signor Rosso that one of the main reasons for the broad suggestions in the statement of November 15 was the obvious fact that the American people were "almost wildly against war and are at all hazards in favor of keeping out of the present war." Contact with belligerent nations might spread the infection of armed conflict, so the Roosevelt Administration had come to the conclusion that it was expedient to isolate America from such contacts as much as possible. "Heavy pressure" had been exerted upon the Department of State to include in its embargo list a "number of prime and essential war materials" out of which implements of war might be made. The Administration had finally decided to make some favorable response to this pressure.

Mr. Hull then directed the attention of Ambassador Rosso to the very considerable sacrifice the World War had entailed upon America. He also alluded to the large loans the Wilson Administration had extended to Italy during that conflict and to the fact that these loans had later been reduced to a "nominal sum." Many Americans were now asking why the Italian Government was embarking upon a costly adventure in imperialism instead of liquidating these overdue financial obligations. As for Mr. Hull himself, he felt constrained to express his great surprise that "the Italian Government would make a complaint against this Government, in all the circumstances, in the severe language it does."[2] The position of the United States was very clear: "It

---

[1] Cordell Hull, *Memoirs* (New York, 1948), I, 436.

[2] Memorandum by the Secretary of State regarding a conversation with the Italian Ambassador (Rosso), November 22, 1935. 765.84/2747, MS, Department of State. On the previous day (November 21), the Marquis Alberto Rossi Longhi, counselor of

opposed abnormal shipments for war purposes of strictly war materials."

These explanations of Secretary Hull were far from satisfactory to the Italian Government. The League of Nations had named November 18 as the day on which economic sanctions would go into effect, and Mussolini had many fears concerning the impact of these restrictions upon the Italian way of life. The sanctions were divided into four categories: (1) an arms embargo upon ammunition and implements of war; (2) an embargo upon Italian exports; (3) a ban upon exports to Italy; (4) a financial boycott against Italy. The financial boycott, though very stringent, did not seriously affect Italy. The embargo upon Italian exports caused a sharp decline in trade with France and Britain, but the United States bought as much in March 1936 as in January 1935, and Germany, Austria, and Hungary came to the rescue of Mussolini. Although the gold reserves of the Bank of Italy shrank rapidly between November 1935 and March 1936, there was a balance sufficient to provide necessary purchases for a short war.[3] The ban on exports to Italy was not as drastic and as extensive as some statesmen had wished. Coal, oil, and copper were not prohibited. For the three-month period, October through December 1935, the American proportion of Italy's oil purchases rose to 17.8 per cent. Copper exports from the United States showed a similar increase, rising from $1,329,000 (November 1934–March 1935) to $2,201,000 (November 1935–March 1936). Despite the ardent admonitions of President Roosevelt and Secretary Hull, American business interests would not embargo exports that brought large profits.[4]

In November 1935 the Italian Government had no assurance that sanctions would fail to cripple its war effort. There was still a strong sentiment in Geneva to place oil on the embargo list, and there was also

the Italian Embassy, had a long talk with Mr. Joseph C. Green, chief of the Office of Arms and Munitions Control. He complained that "certain features of our neutrality policy were unfair to Italy and seemed to indicate a hostile attitude on our part toward his country." Mr. Green gave Signor Longhi the stereotyped reply that the "primary purpose of our neutrality policy was to keep the United States from becoming involved in war and that the measures we had taken to accomplish that end had been taken independently and on our own initiative and were made applicable to both belligerents equally." Green to Secretary Hull, November 21, 1935. 711001111 Armament Control/492, MS, Department of State.

[3] By December 12, 1935, fifty-three nations had agreed to an arms embargo directed against Italy; fifty-two had accepted the suggestion of a credit boycott; fifty had come around to the view that Italian imports should be prohibited; fifty-one believed that certain exports to Italy should be embargoed; and forty-six had adopted the draft of a plan to assist those nations that had been adversely affected by the sanctions program. Only four states had refused to take action under Article 16 of the Covenant–Albania, Austria, Hungary, and Paraguay. See Dwight E. Lee, *Ten Years* (Boston, 1942), p. 150.

[4] M. J. Bonn, "How Sanctions Failed," *Foreign Affairs*, XV (1937), 350–61.

a possibility that Secretary Hull might be able to induce American oil companies to cease their exports. Ambassador Long believed that if the League banned the export of petroleum to Italy, Mussolini would "choose to fight rather than submit."[5]

Laval also feared this possibility and was decidedly "lukewarm toward the enforcement of sanctions." At a reception in Paris, Mme Laval informed the wife of the Italian Ambassador "in no uncertain terms how utterly opposed she was to the creation of any antagonism between France and Italy." Persons "high in Government" felt that she was "echoing her husband's point of view."[6]

In the face of this threat of war from Mussolini, Britain quickly turned to the United States for advice. On December 5 the British Ambassador in Washington asked Secretary Hull if there was any possibility that the American Government would take "effective action" to prevent increased oil shipments to Italy in the event the League imposed an oil embargo or that the British Government embarked upon an independent course along the same line.[7] Hull's reply was quite cautious. While the Department of State was definitely opposed to the shipment "in abnormal quantities" of war materials to the belligerent nations, "those interested must use their own judgment" in attempting to forecast "the probable attitude and action of Congress" towards these abnormal exportations.

This Delphic answer did not satisfy Sir Ronald Lindsay who returned to the Department of State on December 7 to repeat his inquiry. Hull was somewhat annoyed by this persistence. During the course of his conversation with Sir Ronald he asked if the League were waiting for American assurances before taking any action. Before the Ambassador could reply, Hull indicated that the Department of State had "gone as far" as it could. It did not have any "legal authority to impose an oil embargo." If the League was ready to take steps to put oil on its embargo list it would have to do so without reference to American action.[8]

[5] Ambassador Long to Secretary Hull, Rome, November 25, 1935. 765.84/2742, *Strictly Confidential*, MS, Department of State.

[6] Ambassador Straus to Secretary Hull, Paris, November 25, 1935. 765.84/2740, MS, Department of State.

[7] Many British newspapers were loudly calling for an oil sanction. Professor Gilbert Murray wrote to the *Daily Mail*, December 2, 1935, and categorically stated that "Mussolini has got to be defeated. If you can do it by cutting off his supplies of oil, then do it quickly and universally. It will stop the war." The *Daily Telegraph*, December 2, 1935, was certain that oil sanctions would "paralyze the grandiose overseas expedition on which Mussolini has staked the present prestige of Italy."

[8] Hull, *op. cit.*, p. 442. In the diary of Neville Chamberlain there are some comments of interest concerning sanctions: "November 29, 1935. The U.S.A. has already gone a good deal further than usual. . . . We ought to give the lead ourselves rather than let the question go by default. . . . If we backed out now because of Mussolini's threats we should leave the Americans in the air." Keith Feiling, *The Life of Neville Chamberlain* (New York, 1946), p. 272.

Sir Ronald was taken aback by the tone and content of Hull's remarks and finally murmured that he was not "disposed to make any further inquiry." He could clearly see that the Department of State at that moment was not interested in any adventure in Anglo-American parallel policies.

b. *The Hoare-Laval Agreement*

Without Secretary Hull to stiffen his backbone, John Bull was a very pliant person. At times he could lend an ear to counsel of high principle, but upon other occasions had no difficulty in hearing the soft accents of intrigue. At Geneva the British Foreign Office had a mouthpiece in Anthony Eden who talked as impeccably as he dressed. In Paris the British had an expert, Mr. Maurice Peterson, who whispered in such low terms of realism that Pierre Laval regarded him as a kindred soul and assigned M. de Saint-Quentin to be his boon companion. During the early weeks of October when Eden talked of holding firm against Italian aggression, Peterson and Saint-Quentin were busily engaged upon a project that would frankly recognize the claims of Mussolini to a large portion of Ethiopia. These activities became so well known that the London *Daily Herald* published a plan of appeasement which was supposed to represent the viewpoint of this interesting pair. It provided for Italian domination over the empire of Haile Selassie.[9]

This plan was placed in diplomatic moth balls until after the General Elections in Britain. When Mr. Baldwin had been safely returned to office (November 14), Mr. Peterson resumed his work with Saint-Quentin. On December 4, Laval had an important conference with the Italian Ambassador, and on the following day the *New York Times* published the outline of a project for peace in Ethiopia.[10] Apparently, it was difficult for the plans of Laval to remain secret.

On December 7, Sir Samuel Hoare journeyed to Paris for a talk with Laval, during the course of which he expressed the view that unless some platform of peace were soon placed beneath the tottering structure of Ethiopia it would fall under the hammer blows of Marshal Badoglio. Laval quickly concurred in the gloomy predictions of the British Foreign Secretary. Ethiopia suddenly became the "sick man of Africa" and a major operation was necessary to save its existence. This operation was completed on December 8, and the chief surgeons were Hoare and Laval.

Laval's major concern in December 1935 was the danger of a rapprochement between Italy and Germany. This had to be prevented even

[9] London *Daily Herald*, October 30, 1935.
[10] The *New York Times*, December 5, 1935.

though Mussolini's terms were high. It would be far better to place a
large number of backward Ethiopians under Italian administration
than to push Mussolini into Hitler's arms and thus prepare the way
for World War II. Under Emperor Haile Selassie conditions in Ethiopia were distinctly primitive and the lot of the average native was poverty and personal danger. There was a strong possibility that his way
of life would be improved under Italian rule.

The viewpoint of Laval has been given understanding expression by
Winston Churchill in his latest study of the background of World
War II:

The French, therefore, felt very strongly that they should not be drawn into
permanent estrangement from Italy because of all the strong feeling which
had suddenly surged up in England against Mussolini. . . . Two divisions of
troops were all we could send at the outset to France if she were invaded by
Germany. One can certainly understand Monsieur Laval's point of view at
this time.[11]

Fear of Germany was a constant factor in the European equation of
Laval, and after Hoare had been in Paris for a few hours he began to
share this same apprehension. He finally gave his blessing to the labors
of Saint-Quentin and Maurice Peterson, and the joint product soon
became known as the Hoare-Laval Agreement for the settlement of the
Italo-Ethiopian dispute. Under its terms Ethiopia would cede to Italy
some 60,000 square miles of territory and receive in return a slice of
Eritrea with an outlet to the sea. The southern half of Ethiopia, approximating 160,000 square miles, would be reserved as a sphere of
influence where Italy would enjoy certain economic privileges. Along
with these advantages there would also go a definite amount of political
control which would be equivalent to Italian domination.[12] Sir Samuel
was in full flight before Mussolini.[13]

Hoare's retreat was both moral and physical. After the publication
of the Hoare-Laval Agreement the British Foreign Secretary paid a

---

[11] Winston Churchill, *The Gathering Storm* (Cambridge, 1948), pp. 181–83.

[12] *British White Paper*, Cmd. 5044 (1935); *Parliamentary Debates,* House of
Commons, CCCVII, December 19, 1935, 2004 ff. There were varying estimates of
the exact amount of territory that Italy would receive from Ethiopia. The *Manchester
Guardian*, December 12, 1935, in its editorial, "The Peace Proposals," indicated its
belief that under the Hoare-Laval Agreement, Italy would receive 150,000 out of
Ethiopia's total square mileage of 350,000. This would be ten times as much as the
proposal made by the Committee of Five in September.

[13] The British Foreign Office went so far as to instruct the British Minister at Addis
Ababa, Sir Sidney Barton, to use his "utmost influence to induce the Emperor to give
careful and favorable consideration to these proposals, and on no account lightly to
reject them. . . . He will give further proof of his statesmanship by realizing the advantages of the opportunity of negotiations which they afford." London *News Chronicle*, December 16, 1935.

hurried visit to Switzerland for a much-needed rest. Pictures were circulated showing him skating with great zest, but bad luck followed him. While executing a difficult figure on the ice he fell and broke his nose. The fall of man is an old story but to Hoare it seemed to take on new meaning. He should return at once to England and explain to Parliament why he had become a party to a plan for appeasing Mussolini. Prime Minister Baldwin agreed with this decision and for a while intended to fight alongside of Hoare under his well-known banner of "men not measures." But aroused British public opinion compelled him quickly to lower that banner and frankly confess in Parliament that the Hoare-Laval proposals were "absolutely and completely dead." There would be no attempt "to resurrect them."[14]

Baldwin's decision to abandon the Hoare-Laval Agreement was made after a storm of protest broke loose in the British press. The London *Star* called the agreement a travesty which was "horrifying men with a sense of justice"; the Yorkshire *Post* regarded it as a breach of "international morality"; the *Liverpool Daily Post* looked upon its terms as "shocking"; while the *Manchester Guardian* remarked that it was "incredible that the Government has accepted a plan so utterly remote from any it has ever given the country cause to think it would so much as tolerate."[15] The London *Daily Herald,* a leftist Labour organ, was particularly vehement in its denunciation of the agreement which it called a "breach of faith—a conspiracy to enter into a conspiracy with the aggressor in order to defeat the League."[16] The *News Chronicle* (Liberal) scored the arrangement as an "outrageous betrayal of the Covenant,"[17] while the *Daily Telegraph and Morning Post* printed a similar lament.[18] Harold Laski rushed into print with an acrid estimate of Sir Samuel Hoare: "He is simply the average Tory mind in power instead of out of power. . . . Sir Samuel acted in the crisis exactly as the old Tory mind approves. . . . He thinks in terms of power."[19]

On December 16 the secret corollary to the Hoare-Laval Agreement was published. This article would really prevent the Ethiopian Government from building a railroad from the port of Assab into the interior of the country. The London *Times* regarded this corollary as something at "variance with even the most cynical interpretation of the civilizing mission" of Italy.[20]

The chains of newspapers belonging to Lords Beaverbrook and

[14] *Survey of International Affairs, 1935,* II, 314–20.
[15] Quoted in the London *Times,* December 12, 1935.
[16] December 11, 1935.
[17] December 11, 1935.   [19] London *Daily Herald,* December 20, 1935.
[18] December 14,1935.   [20] December 16, 1935.

Rothermere were generally in favor of the Hoare-Laval Agreement, but the majority of the British press was so sharp in its criticism that Hoare was compelled to resign and Anthony Eden was appointed as the new Foreign Minister. Baldwin thus made a bow in the direction of public opinion, but there was no conviction in the gesture. In June 1936, Hoare was brought back into the Cabinet as the First Lord of the Admiralty. It was impressively stated that his unusual talents as an administrator could not be overlooked. Apparently his colleagues thought that his talents, and not high moral principles, were the main requisite for a statesman.

In Italy this bitter British reaction to the Hoare-Laval Agreement was attributed to the "working of antifascism, masonry and communism upon the misguided masses." These forces did not exist in Germany and this fact prepared the way for an understanding with that country. The Italian press candidly admitted that German statesmen had "no love for Italy," but it was felt that Hitler respected the Fascist State as a "stronghold against Communism, and as an indispensable element for the safety of Europe. . . . In a certain sense the fates of the two countries and regimes are considered to be linked, for both have the same powerful foreign and international enemies and both are working toward similar national ends."[21]

With reference to British policy the feeling in Italy grew increasingly hostile. Even the temperate and optimistic *L'Osservatore Romano* expressed the opinion that the situation had become "extremely dangerous."[22] Sanctions had not impeded the Italian war effort, and in Rome there was "plenty of coal and plenty of food." The Italian people were "ready for any emergency" and strongly disposed to "take any steps which their leader might decide for them."[23]

c. *President Roosevelt Chides Italy*

The existence of this martial spirit in Italy was viewed by President Roosevelt with deep misgivings. In an address to Congress, January 3, 1936, he referred directly to Italy and to other have-not nations. These nations had failed to demonstrate the "patience necessary to attain reasonable and legitimate objectives by peaceful negotiation or by an

[21] Ambassador Long to Secretary Hull, Rome, December 18, 1935. 765.84/3357, MS, Department of State.

[22] Ambassador Long to Secretary Hull, Rome, December 31, 1935. 765.84/3485, MS, Department of State.

[23] Ambassador Long to Secretary Hull, Rome, January 3, 1936. 765.84/3481, MS, Department of State.

appeal to the finer instincts of world justice." He then contrasted these impetuous, grasping nations with peaceful and moral America.[24]

This homily on American virtues infuriated many Italian editors who indicated the many years that Mussolini had waited in vain for justice in the matter of a fair distribution of colonial territory:

It is easy for rich nations (like the United States who, through past ways of expansion and conquest in which natives were exterminated, has everything she needs and who to protect her high standard of living has barred immigration and imports to the detriment of poor nations) to condemn autocracies. . . . As to the beauties of democratic regimes . . . how about Roosevelt himself, who has . . . so thoroughly failed to uproot crime as to force America's national hero [Lindbergh] to seek safety for his child on this side of the Atlantic.[25]

This sharp tone of criticism with reference to America was soon toned down as the Italian press began to reflect increasing optimism concerning the efficiency of the war machine. The American naval attaché in Rome reported that the Italian fleet was in a "very high state of efficiency" with a "high morale amongst the men and a calm and unexcited attitude on the part of the officers."[26] Colonel William J. Donovan, returning from a trip to Eritrea, stated that the "service of supplies was excellent, that morale was high, that health and sanitation were splendid, efficiency first rate, and that the military positions now occupied were secure and could be easily held."[27] In Rome there was a growing feeling that the African adventure would have a happy ending because Italian military strength had risen to such a point that Britain would not dare to intervene. This optimism was confirmed by glowing reports of success in the fierce engagements in the Tembyen, January 19 to January 23, 1936.

The message from President Roosevelt to Congress on January 3 was delivered in the evening over a nationwide radio network. After dealing specifically with international relations he turned to the matter of new neutrality legislation. This proposed new legislation would not only retain the mandatory embargo on the export of arms, munitions,

---

[24] *Peace and War: United States Foreign Policy, 1931–1941* (Washington, 1943), p. 306.

[25] Ambassador Long to Secretary Hull, Rome, January 16, 1936. 765.84/3380, MS, Department of State, with inclosures.

[26] Ambassador Long to Secretary Hull, Rome, January 17, 1936. 765.84/3463, MS, Department of State.

[27] Ambassador Long to Secretary Hull, Rome, January 16, 1936. 765.84/3354, MS, Department of State.

and implements of war to belligerents but it would also empower the President to extend the embargo to the export, in excess of "normal commerce," of other articles or materials used "in the conduct of war" when he believed that such action would "preserve the neutrality of the United States" or if he thought that the war would be prolonged if such an embargo were not put into force. The list of materials subject to these restrictions was left to the discretion of the President.[28]

These wide powers conferred upon the President by the proposed Pittman-McReynolds Bill were regarded by some eminent publicists as dangerous to American liberties. Judge John Bassett Moore declared that it was unwise to "give this unlimited power to any man. . . . The bestowal of such power would constitute the worst form of dictatorship ever set up."[29]

A large number of Italian-American organizations reinforced these objections of Judge Moore's to any enlargement of the President's embargo power. Letters and telegrams began to pour into the offices of influential members of Congress. The League for American Neutrality sponsored a meeting in Faneuil Hall in Boston. Governor Curley, in a speech with strong political overtones, praised Mussolini as a lover of peace and a savior of Christianity. Other speakers were equally lyric in their praise of the Duce.[30]

As the attack on the proposed new neutrality legislation gained strength, Mr. Generoso Pope, publisher of the well-known newspaper, *Il Progresso,* rushed to Washington for an interview with President Roosevelt. The Chief Executive was most reassuring: "Gene, America honestly wishes to remain neutral; and I want you to tell the Italians . . . that our neutrality will in no way imply discrimination at the expense of Italy and in favor of any other nation." When Mr. Pope asked if the existing neutrality legislation could not be re-enacted, the President replied: "Perhaps this could be a good solution." Mr. Pope then pressed the same question upon Secretary Hull who "assured him that he had no personal objection to the idea if Congress should decide to accept it."[31]

Whether as a result of this pressure or not, Congress rejected the section of the Neutrality Bill that enlarged the President's embargo powers. It did forbid the granting of loans and credits to belligerents

28 Edwin Borchard and William P. Lage, *Neutrality for the United States* (New Haven, 1937), pp. 325–29.

29 *Pending "Neutrality" Proposals: Their False Conceptions and Misunderstandings* (New York, 1936), pp. 6–7.

30 *Il Progresso,* January 28, 1936.

31 John Norman, "Influence of Pro-Fascist Propaganda on American Neutrality, 1935–1936," *Essays in History and International Relations in Honor of George Hubbard Blakeslee,* ed. D. E. Lee and G. E. McReynolds (Worcester, 1949), pp. 207–8.

and it made mandatory the existing discretionary power of the President to extend the arms embargo to additional states when they became involved in war. It also exempted from the operation of the law any American republic at war with a non-American state and not "co-operating with a non-American State or States in such war."[32]

It is apparent, therefore, that the Italian-American pressure group made strenuous efforts to defeat any neutrality legislation that would seriously affect Mussolini's "African Adventure," and it is the opinion of an able student of the situation in 1936 that this group "noticeably influenced the course of American neutrality."[33]

d. *Josef Beck Loses Confidence in the League*

Italian victories in the spring of 1936 strengthened the efforts of Italian-Americans to prevent any amendments to neutrality legislation that would confer additional powers upon the President. They also indicated to European statesmen that Italian conquest of Ethiopia was inevitable. It was now realized with deep regret that it had been a mistake to abandon the Hoare-Laval Agreement which might have saved for Emperor Haile Selassie a considerable portion of his empire. In London the American chargé reported that it was "increasingly realized by those responsible for British foreign policy that whereas the methods employed by Hoare were faulty, the general aim of his policy was substantially right." The former British Foreign Secretary had recognized the fact that Germany would greatly profit by any break in the Stresa front. His concessions to Italy were based upon the belief that Europe could not afford to alienate Mussolini. Eden was beginning to realize the truth of some of Hoare's assertions, and his zeal for sanctions was fast disappearing.[34]

At Geneva, Hugh Wilson saw the shadow of Germany begin to darken the minds of many delegates to the League of Nations. He was struck with the "fact that nearly everyone with whom I have spoken has treated the problem of Germany with greater gravity than that of Abyssinia. . . . Massigli says that the French are much concerned lest Germany in the near future denounce the servitudes on the Rhineland."[35]

It was not difficult for French statesmen to see that Hitler would

---

[32] *The United States in World Affairs, 1936,* pp. 142–43.

[33] Norman, *op. cit.,* p. 213.

[34] Atherton to Secretary Hull, London, January 18, 1936. 765.84/3470, MS, Department of State.

[35] Ambassador Wilson to Secretary Hull, Geneva, January 23, 1936. 765.84/3521, MS, Department of State.

take advantage of any coolness between Britain and Italy, and Massigli clearly forecast the German movement in the Rhineland. Britain's pressure upon Poland in the matter of sanctions had distressed Colonel Beck in Warsaw who let Laval know that he had "lost confidence in the League of Nations as an instrument for promoting peace."[36] Anthony Eden's insistence upon a firm policy with reference to Italy soon brought many chickens of hatred to roost in the muted halls of the League of Nations.

e. *Implications of the Maffey Report*

The Italian chickens were offered a comfortable roost on the well-known "Maffey Report" which was published in part in the *Giornale d'Italia*. This confidential British document, dated June 18, 1935, was regarded by the Italian press as a justification of the Italian program in Ethiopia. Sir John Maffey, British Permanent Under Secretary for Colonies, was appointed chairman of a special committee to examine into the more important aspects of the Italo-Ethiopian dispute. Eden admitted that the report of this special committee concluded with a statement that "there was no important British interest in Abyssinia with the exception of Lake Tana, the waters of the Blue Nile, and certain tribal grazing rights." During the early months of 1935, British ministers acted as if they agreed with the findings of this Maffey Report, and "what is more, seemed to care little about their obligations toward the League of Nations in relation to the Italo-Ethiopian dispute. . . . It is little wonder, then, if Mussolini concluded that the British Lion was peacefully and purposely dozing."

But this slumber was rudely interrupted by the announcement on June 27, 1935, of the results of the "Peace Ballot" which since November 1934 had been conducted by some private organizations under the auspices of the League of Nations Union. Approximately eleven and a half million persons in Great Britain and North Ireland recorded their opinions on five questions. On the question as to the advisability of using "military measures" to stop aggression, 74 per cent of the vote cast was in favor "of military sanctions."

This large affirmative vote deeply disturbed the Baldwin Government which had just refused to consider sanctions against German rearmament. The policy of the Foreign Office had been governed by expediency rather than principle, and it was difficult for it suddenly to

[36] Report of Lieutenant L. N. Miller, assistant naval attaché in Paris, January 14–23, 1936. 765.84/3879, MS, Department of State.

"stand forth convincingly as the White Knight of collective security."[37] When the attempt was made in connection with Italian expansion in Ethiopia, Mussolini felt that he had been double-crossed and he
refused to be impressed with British recitations of certain formulas of
peace.

In order to justify his suspicions of British policy he had pertinent
paragraphs of the Maffey Report published in the Italian press. They
contained sharp criticism relating to "Ethiopia's unworthiness of belonging to the League, her ill-will toward Italy and her menace to all
neighboring colonies." The Italian Government had in "due time informed the British Government of the situation in Ethiopia," and had
expressed a desire for co-operation. Why was co-operation denied and
why did the British Foreign Office fail to "go into the fact that, as the
Maffey Report showed, Abyssinia was a violator of League principles
and obligations?"

After reading the excerpts from the Maffey Report as published in
the *Giornale d'Italia,* most Italians believed that British action in the
Ethiopian dispute was based upon a "dislike of Fascism; determination
to destroy the Franco-Italian alliance; a desire to maintain absolute
hegemony in the Mediterranean; and Eden's personal ambition and, at
a later stage, the bitter enmity toward Mussolini." Italians were "be-
wildered by what they regard as the criminal, and also suicidal, policy
of England."[38]

From England, Sir Leo Chiozza Money, former Parliamentary Secretary to the British Ministry of Shipping, wrote a brief letter to President Roosevelt and inclosed many documents that placed Italian penetration of Ethiopia in a favorable light. It was evident to him that the
Italians in Ethiopia were "cultivating, teaching and healing, founding
hospitals and dispensaries, sinking wells, freeing slaves . . . and in the
words of Major Fiske (an American, by the way), doing in 100 days
more than had been done in 1,000 years."[39]

In Rome, Ambassador Long realized the significance of the Italo-
Ethiopian impasse with regard to European alignments. The Italian
Government had made it clear that a "continuance of the present policy
of the League under British direction and French backing will make
Italy revise her whole foreign policy." The heavy concentration of the
British fleet in the Mediterranean was deeply resented by Mussolini
who had been giving careful attention to the suggestion that an ulti-

[37] Lee, *op. cit.,* pp. 135–38.
[38] Ambassador Long to Secretary Hull, February 27, 1936. 765.84/3915, MS, Department of State.
[39] Sir Leo Chiozza Money to President Roosevelt, March 3, 1936. 765.84/3939,
MS, Department of State.

matum be sent to London demanding a reduction in the number of
British warships in those waters.[40]

The possibility of such a step was strengthened by the electrifying
news of a series of brilliant victories gained by Italian armies in Ethiopia. On February 15, Marshal Badoglio won a decisive battle at Amba
Aradam, where the forces of Ras Mulugeta were crushed so completely
that it amounted to a national disaster. On February 27, Italian forces
drove the Ethiopian troops from their strongly fortified positions in
the Tembyen, and on April 12 the Italian flag was hoisted on the
northern shore of Lake Tana. Emperor Haile Selassie realized the shat-
tering effect of these defeats, and in a desperate attempt to stem the
Italian tide he attacked the First Italian Army Corps near Lake Ash-
angi on March 31. After five days of bitter struggle the Emperor's
troops fled in wild disorder down the road to Dessie, and the eventual
Italian conquest of Ethiopia was assured.[41]

f. *Britain Wishes Oil to Be on List of Sanctions*

The Italian victories in February 1936 seemed to spur the British Government into a final attempt to tighten economic restrictions upon Italy
and to impose the long-threatened oil sanction. On March 2, Signor
Bova Scoppa, the head of the Italian delegation at Geneva, informed
the French Foreign Secretary (Flandin) that Mussolini would seriously resent the imposition of the oil sanction. When Flandin informed
Eden of this fact, the British Foreign Secretary stated that he had been
instructed by the Cabinet to push this very measure. Flandin opposed
this move so vigorously that Eden talked with Prime Minister Baldwin
over the telephone and secured a postponement of action upon oil.[42]
On the following day (March 3) the Committee of Thirteen adopted
a resolution which called upon both belligerents to open negotiations
for the "definite restoration of peace." It was expected that the Italian
and Ethiopian governments would have their replies ready for the
meeting of the committee on March 10.

Mussolini was not disposed to pay much attention to this request of
the Committee of Thirteen. He would make peace upon his own terms
when Italian armies had crushed Ethiopian resistance. France could
read this military writing upon the wall of Ethiopia and it spelled a
policy of nonintervention. Flandin was determined to conciliate rather

[40] Ambassador Long to Secretary Hull, Rome, February 27, 1936. 765.84/3911,
MS, Department of State. See also Virginio Gayda, "Mediterranean and International
Agreements," *Giornale d'Italia*, February 26, 1936.
[41] *Survey of International Affairs, 1935*, II, 350–409.
[42] See the remarks of Mme Tabouis. *L'Oeuvre*, March 3, 1936.

than irritate Mussolini, and his attitude was praised by Virginio Gayda (March 3).[43] On that same day the Duce, in an address to his Cabinet, commended the American Government for its refusal to heed "League solicitations" with reference to the imposition of a sanction upon the export of oil to Italy.[44]

In Rome the feeling against an oil sanction had been very strong and Mussolini had several times intimated that he would regard such action as almost the equivalent of a declaration of war. He was, therefore, deeply grateful to Flandin for his pressure upon Eden. But this gratitude to France was soon partially diverted to Hitler when the Nazi leader moved his troops into the Rhineland (March 7) and thus liquidated the Locarno Pact. Once more Germany rocked the foundations of the European state system and made France labor desperately in an attempt to maintain the Stresa front. Mussolini must now be courted rather than chided.

g. Mussolini Makes a Peaceful Gesture

In March the Italian Foreign Office saw at a glance that a profound change had suddenly taken place in the European scene. With victory in Ethiopia now assured, Italy could make some slight gesture of peace. On March 8, Mussolini informed the Committee of Thirteen that he accepted in principle their plea for a restoration of peace. But negotiations for a cessation of Italo-Ethiopian hostilities must be based upon a recognition of the alleged fact that Ethiopia was the "aggressor nation." Moreover, in any peace program acceptable to Italy there should be an assurance that "security and treaty rights" would be guaranteed, and it should be made clear that "the military situation" must be the basis for negotiation.[45]

Engert, in Addis Ababa, ridiculed these terms of peace and vehemently denied the reports of Italian military successes. In recent important engagements the Italian plan for encircling the Ethiopian Army had failed and the Italian "forces, especially the Alpinis, suffered heavy losses." The morale of the Ethiopian soldiers was "excellent and has not been affected by Italian lies." Mussolini's legions were in a "precarious situation and their lines of communication are at the mercy of Ethiopian patrols who take the fullest advantage of it. . . .

[43] *Giornale d'Italia,* March 3, 1936.
[44] Ambassador Long to Secretary Hull, March 4, 1936. 765.84/3944, MS, Department of State.
[45] Secretary Hull to Engert (Addis Ababa), March 9, 1936. 765.84/3889, MS, Department of State.

Ethiopia is determined to eject the invader from her territory."[46]

Mussolini knew the situation in Ethiopia far better than the American Minister in Addis Ababa, and he counted upon the fact that time was on his side. In Rome he evinced a co-operative disposition and let it be understood that he was in favor of a settlement of the Rhineland difficulty "with such a show of strength against Germany that it would make the Reich realize the seriousness of any further infractions" of the Treaty of Versailles.[47]

This apparent conciliatory disposition had some effect upon the Committee of Thirteen which reassembled on March 23 in London. After considering the answers of Italy and Ethiopia to its plea for the restoration of peace, the committee requested its chairman to "take such steps as may be called for" in order to "bring the two parties together . . . and to bring about a prompt cessation of hostilities." On this same day Mussolini made a bitter attack upon sanctions.[48] The path to peace was still blocked by barriers that only an Italian victory could remove.

This victory would not be long delayed. Italian armies were on the road to complete military success in Ethiopia, and the fleet was ready to give a good account of itself. Captain L. N. McNair, the naval attaché at Rome, was much impressed "with the physical preparations in the form of equipment and with the moral and spiritual preparations of the men and officers of the Italian Navy." Within the last six months the situation in the eastern Mediterranean had changed distinctly in the direction of Italy's advantage.[49]

h. *Britain Becomes More Friendly with Hitler*

Britain was not happy to see this increase in Italian military strength, and was inclined to court Germany as one means of balancing the new political equation in the Mediterranean. There was a "distinct pro-German attitude among English people including high army circles."[50] Reliance upon some measure of German support relieved the British Government of the necessity of conciliating Italy, and in Paris it was

[46] Engert to Secretary Hull, Addis Ababa, March 17, 1936. 765.84/3935, MS, Department of State.

[47] Ambassador Long to Secretary Hull, Rome, March 12, 1936. 740.0011 Mutual Guarantee/418 (Locarno), MS, Department of State.

[48] *Survey of International Affairs, 1935*, II, 342.

[49] Ambassador Long to Secretary Hull, Rome, April 3, 1936. 765.84/4104, MS, Department of State.

[50] Anthony J. Biddle to Secretary Hull, Oslo, April 6, 1936. 765.84/4042, MS, Department of State.

believed that "relations between Italy and Great Britain are so tense as to be the really grave danger point on the European horizon today."[51] From Berlin, Dodd reported on the possibility of a rapprochement between Germany and Britain. Several well-informed and experienced observers were of the opinion that "the British may have to choose shortly between following French advice and make up with the Italians ... or pursuing the obvious alternative of virtually allying herself with Germany."[52] If Hitler were smart he could, according to Ambassador Dodd, drive an excellent bargain.

British statesmen were well acquainted with the old dictum that he who sups with the Devil must use a long spoon. They feared that Hitler would ask a high price for any diplomatic support he might give to the British position at Geneva, and Neville Chamberlain insisted that "no demand for the transfer of British colonies to Germany would be entertained for a moment."[53] As a friendly gesture towards Germany, however, the British Cabinet would be willing to "remove the 'guilt clauses' from the Treaty [of Versailles] if Germany gives up claims for mandates." Britain would not "permit Germany to be put again in the 'dock.' " An effort should also be made to "grant France necessary security while at the same time Germany must be granted full equality." But no matter what diplomatic deals the situation in Europe demanded it should always be kept in mind that Italy should never be permitted to dominate Ethiopia.[54]

The items in the British Cabinet memorandum which Prentiss Gilbert disclosed to Secretary Hull were given additional confirmation by Ambassador Bingham. It was now very evident that the British Foreign Office was greatly disappointed that the Hoare-Laval Agreement had been defeated. During a conversation with Bingham the British Under Secretary of Foreign Affairs frankly admitted that he was "more than ever convinced that the Hoare-Laval proposals would have been a great advantage primarily to Abyssinia and indeed to the whole world and he thought that in the end public opinion would come around to this belief."[55]

[51] Warrington Dawson to Secretary Hull, Paris, April 7, 1936. 765.84/4124, MS, Department of State.

[52] Ambassador Dodd to Secretary Hull, Berlin, April 9, 1936. 765.84/4066, MS, Department of State.

[53] Ambassador Bingham to Secretary Hull, London, April 7, 1936. 765.84/4045, MS, Department of State.

[54] Prentiss Gilbert to Secretary Hull, Geneva, April 15, 1936. 765.84/4159, MS, Department of State.

[55] Ambassador Bingham to Secretary Hull, London, April 15, 1936. 765.84/4115, MS, Department of State.

i. *The League Attempts to End the Italo-Ethiopian War*

British belief in the advantages of the Hoare-Laval Agreement was induced by Italian military successes in March and April 1936. On April 15, Baron Aloisi appeared in Geneva and proposed to the chairman of the Committee of Thirteen that peace negotiations be opened on the basis of "the actual situation as it presents itself after six months of military operations." The Ethiopian delegation to the League promptly opposed this proposal and instead suggested the imposition of more rigorous sanctions. Anthony Eden listened with favor to these drastic suggestions, and when the Council met on the afternoon of April 20 he indicated the willingness of the British Government to exert more pressure upon Italy through the enactment of "any further economic and financial sanctions that may be considered necessary . . . for the fulfilment of the obligations which we all of us bear in this dispute."

Monsieur Paul-Boncour completely disagreed with the Eden viewpoint. France was determined to adhere to a policy of conciliation. The Italian Government had signified its desire to support the existing political structure in Europe. This attitude should be encouraged and not flouted. The Russian delegate (Potemkin) denounced the tendency in the League to treat aggressors with "tolerance or even indulgence," and Madariaga referred to the difficulty of conciliating a nation which the League had condemned as a violator of the Covenant. At the close of the session on April 20 the Council finally adopted a harmless resolution which renewed the appeal of the Committee of Thirteen to the two belligerents for a "prompt cessation of hostilities and restoration of peace in the framework of the League of Nations."[56]

This action of the Council was an obvious defeat for Eden. As Hugh Wilson reported from Geneva, "the current has changed. Where previously the general desire was to increase the severity of sanctions under British lead and against French restraint, now the ebb has set in and the British realize that they must maneuver carefully if existing sanctions are not to be swept away." The British Government had been gambling "on a time factor. If before the rains in Abyssinia set in towards the end of May, Abyssinia's resistance is fully crushed, it will mean a disastrous defeat to British policy." At the close of the session of the Council, Wilson encountered Eden who wryly remarked: "It is slipping badly. We have done our best but I fear it [the collective effort against Italy] is going to crumble."[57]

[56] *Survey of International Affairs, 1935,* II, 347-55.
[57] Ambassador Wilson to Secretary Hull, Geneva, April 20, 1936. 765.84/4151, *Strictly Confidential,* MS, Department of State.

j. Britain Continues to Court Hitler

Despite the apparent disintegration of the League front against Italy, Eden still worked feverishly to keep it intact. In doing so he once more looked towards Berlin for assistance. In Paris, Straus learned that there were "certain personalities in Great Britain" who were "taking the dangerous course of encouraging Hitler" to stage an "early Nazi coup in Austria." They were playing this reckless role in order to "show Mussolini the error of his ways."[58]

In Berlin these British friendly gestures were welcomed and the Foreign Office deprecated the collapse of collective security at Geneva because it "greatly affected British prestige." The recent Anglo-German conversations in London "were entirely satisfactory, the German officials . . . having found the British as helpful as their treaty commitments could possibly permit. . . . Reference was made to the disadvantage to the British of being tied to the French apron strings. This it was felt worked against British Empire interests, League interests, and the attempt with which England and Germany are both so concerned to bring about better general European relations and conditions. There were clear implications in my conversations with the Foreign Office yesterday of its feeling that sooner or later the British would come to realize the community of Anglo-German interests vis-à-vis Italian imperialism."[59]

While British statesmen were making "friendly gestures to Hitler,"[60] Italian armies were battering on the gates of Addis Ababa. On May 2 the Emperor and his family hurriedly left the capital, and three days later the Italian advance guard entered the city without any opposition. Mussolini at once issued a proclamation announcing to the "Italian people and to the World that peace is re-established."[61]

The capture of Addis Ababa and the flight of the Emperor was an unmistakable indication to the world that the Italian adventure in Ethiopia had been successful. British policy had received a severe defeat and this fact was emphasized in the British press. Britain had backed down before the threats of Mussolini, and according to the London *Daily Herald* "the League might as well be shut up for any

[58] Ambassador Straus to Secretary Hull, Paris, April 21, 1936. 765.84/4158, MS, Department of State.
[59] Mr. Mayer to Secretary Hull, Berlin, April 22, 1936. 765.84/4176, *Confidential file*, MS, Department of State.
[60] Anthony J. Biddle to Secretary Hull, Oslo, May 2, 1936. 765.84/4228, MS, Department of State.
[61] *New York Times*, May 6, 1936.

roaring bully could shut it up by threatening war if it grimaced at him."[62] The London *Daily Mail* believed it was time for a reversal of the Eden policy: "The right course for Great Britain is to clean the slate and give notice as soon as possible that she will have nothing more to do with sanctions or with the penal clauses of the Covenant. Friendship with Italy is of vital importance both to her and to ourselves."[63]

It was significant to note that the Opposition in Great Britain still clamored for the continuance of sanctions. Its attitude was sharply assailed by the *Morning Post:* "The war is over; the Italian armies are in occupation of Ethiopia, but our Socialists say that the sanctions must be continued. . . . They have been clamouring for the closing of the Suez Canal to Italian transport, and yesterday Mr. Eden told them plainly that such a measure would inevitably lead to war with Italy. . . . The Opposition, having done their best to disarm this country, appear to be willing to face that risk and it is a remarkable fact that exactly those people who worked hardest for disarmament are now working hardest to embroil us in war."[64]

In France the Opposition played the same sinister game. The leftist press called for "revenge on Italy and the prevention of the exploitation of her conquest by the preservation and strict continued application of League principles. . . . Certain organs of the extreme Left press rise in indignation and press for a showdown at once in a crisis which the Geneva Powers had hoped to postpone."[65]

British and French statesmen refused to be pushed into conflict with Italy by the loud clamor of the belligerent Opposition. Some of them were beginning to believe that it was high time for a radical change in the direction of British foreign policy. Lord Lothian was one of the prominent spokesmen of this new viewpoint. He expressed the opinion that it was expedient to eliminate from the Covenant of the League of Nations every obligation "to go to war all over the world which neither we nor the Dominions are willing . . . to live up to." The League should be an instrument for internatinal conciliation and not "an international war office." Moreover, a new attitude should be adopted towards Britain's foes in the World War. It should be evident that a "strong Germany will be the best security for peace and stability. There will certainly be no stability in Europe or Africa so long as we connive at attempting to maintain that system of encirclement and inequality against Germany which has been the root of European unrest

[62] May 7, 1936.
[63] May 7, 1936.
[64] May 7, 1936.
[65] Ambassador Straus to Secretary Hull, Paris, May 11, 1936. 765.84/4365, MS, Department of State.

for fifteen years, and the main cause of the rise of the Hitler regime. . . .
Once the system of universal collective security goes, the next best basis
is that of a regional balance, and once Germany has her rightful place
in Europe and is a member of a revised League alongside of Russia,
Italy and France, it may be possible . . . to secure that twenty-five years
of certain peace of which Herr Hitler talks."[66]

k. *America Refuses to Adopt a Realistic Policy*

It was hardly likely that a period of peace would bless Europe if the
principle of nonrecognition were still adhered to by the major powers.
It was some time before British statesmen recognized this fact. On May
9, 1936, the King of Italy signed a decree which proclaimed that the
former Empire of Ethiopia had been conquered by Italian armies and
was therefore under the "full and entire sovereignty of the Kingdom of
Italy." Emperor Haile Selassie replied to this proclamation with a
telegram to the Secretary-General of the League of Nations (May 10)
requesting the formal adoption of the nonrecognition principle with
reference to the Italo-Ethiopian dispute.[67] Faced with this challenge,
the Council (May 12) adroitly postponed the question of nonrecognition until its next meeting on June 15. By that time the war in
Ethiopia would have reached its final stage and a realistic decision
could be reached.

On that same day (May 12), the British Ambassador in Rome informed Mussolini that his Government would "not recognize" the
Italian regime in Ethiopia. It was fully realized in London that the
Duce would deeply resent this step and the British Cabinet felt that
the situation was "extremely grave."[68]

British action on May 12 was needlessly provocative. The Foreign
Office under Eden's guidance was holding fast to a policy that was
decidedly unrealistic. But Mussolini with victory in his grasp was
content to overlook this verbal challenge. The legions of Marshal
Badoglio had proved far more potent than the economic sanctions of
the League of Nations. Italy had scored a major political and diplomatic success, and the frowns of Anthony Eden would eventually
change into the tight smile of acquiescence.

In America, however, there was determined opposition to the adoption of a realistic policy concerning Ethiopia. Secretary Hull gave little
heed to the fact that in Europe the political weight of Italy was badly

[66] London *Times*, May 5, 1936.
[67] *League of Nations Official Journal*, 1936, p. 660.
[68] Prentiss Gilbert to Secretary Hull, Geneva, May 12, 1936. 765.84/4388, MS,
Department of State.

needed to balance the scales against the fast-increasing pressure of Hitler. Hull had a golden opportunity to help maintain the Stresa front by a slight nod of encouragement to Mussolini. Instead he adhered to the old Stimson formula of nonrecognition with a tenacity that was strengthened by a glow of righteousness. He would rather be right than save the world by a touch of realism.

On May 12, the Italian Ambassador paid a visit to the Department of State for the purpose of explaining to Secretary Hull the civilizing mission of Italy in Ethiopia. Hull regarded this explanation as "somewhat rambling" and was not favorably impressed with its content.[69] The ambassador was disturbed by the Secretary's lack of friendly response, so he stopped at the office of Mr. Phillips, the Under Secretary of State, and hesitantly remarked that the annexation of Ethiopia was "by far the best solution of the problem; that he felt in due course Geneva would recognize the facts as they existed." When he inquired "what position the United States would take in the circumstances," Phillips hastily informed him that the American Government had "not yet decided what course" it would pursue.[70] The words of Mr. Phillips were quite indecisive but his manner was friendly so Ambassador Rosso left the Department of State with a slight feeling of hope in his heart.

1. Eden Recommends that Sanctions Be Lifted

With victory assured in Ethiopia, Italian statesmen made strenuous efforts to show how conciliatory they could be towards countries that had looked askance at the Duce's program in Africa. In Addis Ababa, Marshal Badoglio was exceeding cordial to Mr. Engert. He referred in the friendliest terms to his visit to the United States when he had had the good fortune to meet President Roosevelt, then serving as the Assistant Secretary of the Navy. He also spoke of his "dear friend General Pershing."[71]

Mussolini was in similar good form. In an interview published in the *Intransigeant* on May 24 he tried to quiet British apprehensions by stating that he was "asking nothing of England. I am ready to give her all possible assurances."[72] In London, Dino Grandi stressed Mussolini's

[69] Memorandum of a conversation between Secretary Hull and the Italian Ambassador, Signor Rosso, May 12, 1936. 765.84/4397, MS, Department of State.

[70] Memorandum of a conversation between the Under Secretary of State, Mr. William Phillips, and the Italian Ambassador, Signor Rosso, May 12, 1936. 765.84/4413, MS, Department of State.

[71] Engert to Secretary Hull, Addis Ababa, May 14, 1936. 765.84/4421, MS, Department of State.

[72] Ambassador Straus to Secretary Hull, Paris, May 25, 1936. 765.84/4490, MS, Department of State.

desire for a "better understanding with Great Britain and reiterated the assurance that Italy had no designs against British interests."[73]

On May 28, Mussolini granted an interview to Gordon Lennox, the London *Daily Mail* correspondent in Rome. He was profuse in his protestations that "the interests of Great Britain in so far as the waters of Lake Tana are concerned will be strictly respected." When he was questioned about Anglo-Italian relations he replied that not only was a rapprochement between those two countries desirable but was really "necessary." He then stated that he would do everything in his power "to bring it about."[74]

But these assurances had no effect upon ardent advocates of sanctions like Sir Alfred Zimmern, Professor Gilbert Murray, and Lord Hugh Cecil. They did, however, carry conviction to Neville Chamberlain, Chancellor of the Exchequer. In a speech before the 1900 Club (June 10) he condemned the continuance of sanctions as the "very midsummer of madness." British leaders should open their eyes "to realities." The policy of sanctions had been "tried out and it has failed to prevent war, failed to stop war, failed to save the victim of aggression." Such a policy should be abandoned.[75]

It was evident that the British Cabinet was preparing to reverse its attitude towards Italy, and this fact was made even more clear by the "reinclusion" of Sir Samuel Hoare as the First Lord of the Admiralty. On June 18, Anthony Eden announced in Parliament that he would recommend at Geneva that the sanctions in force against Italy should be lifted. The *Morning Post* warmly approved this statement: "The policy of sanctions against Italy had become an affront to common sense and a menace to the peace of Europe."[76] The *Daily Mail* expressed the same viewpoint: "The *Daily Mail* has from the first maintained that the sanctions policy was stupid and disastrous."[77] But the *News Chronicle* criticized the action of the Government as "grovelling submission,"[78] while the *Daily Herald* called the change in front a "complete and unconditional surrender."[79]

Australia and Canada followed the lead of London, and other members of the League scrambled on the British bandwagon. On July 4 the League Assembly voted to end sanctions. Some months later the question of nonrecognition was raised in Parliament (December 16) and Eden announced that the British Government still adhered to that prin-

---

[73] Atherton to Secretary Hull, London, May 29, 1936. 765.84/4532, MS, Department of State.
[74] London *Daily Mail*, May 29, 1936. See also, Kirk to Secretary Hull, Rome, May 29, 1936. 765.84/4544, MS, Department of State.
[75] London *Times*, June 11, 1936; Feiling, *op. cit.*, p. 296.
[76] June 19, 1936.   [78] June 19, 1936.
[77] June 19, 1936.   [79] June 19, 1936.

ciple.[80] Therefore, it was not "the intention of His Majesty's Government to accord *de jure* recognition to the annexation of Abyssinia." In making this announcement he was careful to conceal the fact that the Cabinet had already decided to extend *de facto* recognition to Italian control over Ethiopia. This decision was soon revealed in a law suit before the Chancery Division of the Supreme Court of Judicature,[81] and later it was reluctantly wrung from the British Under Secretary of State for Foreign Affairs during a debate in the House of Commons (March 17, 1938).[82]

On April 16, 1938, an Anglo-Italian agreement was signed in Rome which amounted to a full recognition of Italian sovereignty over Ethiopia.[83] The stage was all prepared for League action. On May 10, Lord Halifax stated to the members of the Council that the Anglo-Italian agreement dealt solely with affairs between the two nations. The verity of this remark was challenged by Litvinov, and an explosive discussion was precipitated by an appeal from Emperor Haile Selassie against any recognition of Italian conquests in Ethiopia. But most of the members of the Council supported the British viewpoint, the Polish delegate going so far as to denounce the nonrecognition principle as a "source of conflict." Although no vote was taken at this session of the Council, it was obvious that a majority of the members were ready to abandon the principle for which Mr. Stimson had fought with vigor and tenacity.[84]

According to Professor Malbone W. Graham, who discussed the situation with Mr. Munters, president of the League Council, it was frankly admitted in Geneva that the decision to abandon the doctrine of nonrecognition was adopted under pressure from Lord Halifax.[85] Impressed with this British example of appeasement, several members of the League granted recognition to Italian rule in Ethiopia by issuing letters of credence accrediting their envoys to "His Majesty the King of Italy, Emperor of Ethiopia."[86]

Everything was now prepared for a complete repudiation of Eden's assurance that it was not the intention of His Majesty's Government to "accord *de jure* recognition of the annexation of Abyssinia." On No-

[80] *Parliamentary Debates,* 318 House of Commons, 2432.
[81] Robert Langer, *Seizure of Territory* (Princeton, 1947), p. 137.
[82] *Parliamentary Debates,* 333 House of Commons, March 17, 1936, 617.
[83] *Documents on International Affairs, 1938,* I, 141.
[84] *League of Nations Official Journal,* 1938, pp. 339–55.
[85] *Proceedings of the American Society of International Law,* May 13–15, 1940, p. 95.
[86] On January 5, 1938, the Italian Government issued a statement which indicated that seventeen states, most of them League members, had granted *de jure* recognition, and eleven of them, including Great Britain and France, had granted *de facto* recognition of the annexation of Ethiopia.

vember 2, 1938, Prime Minister Chamberlain introduced in the House of Commons a motion to the effect that "this House welcomes the intention" to bring the Anglo-Italian Agreement (April 16, 1938) "into force." After a brisk debate the House approved the motion by an overwhelming vote and the House of Lords did likewise.[87] Anthony Eden had to swallow his brave words of December 16, 1936, and there is no evidence that he gagged too violently over this task.

m. *The Principle of Nonrecognition Is Invoked by the United States*

In the United States the action of the British Government was followed with keen interest if not with approval. After Mussolini's proclamation announcing the annexation of Ethiopia, Ambassador Long made a cordial statement that warmed the heart of the Duce and caused the Italian Government and press to be "outspoken in protestations of friendship for the United States."[88] On June 16, Count Ciano, recently appointed Minister of Foreign Affairs, assured Secretary Hull that he would use "every endeavor to further the existing friendly relations between our two countries."[89] Four days later, President Roosevelt issued a proclamation declaring that a state of war no longer existed between Italy and Ethiopia and therefore the arms embargo was no longer in force.[90]

But the Department of State had no intention of recognizing the annexation of Ethiopia by Italy. When Breckinridge Long retired as ambassador to Italy and his successor, William Phillips, was sent to Rome in August 1936, his letter of credence was addressed merely to "the King of Italy." In October, Mussolini sent to the United States a new ambassador, Signor Fulvio Suvich. His letter of credence employed two titles: "King of Italy—Emperor of Ethiopia." But President Roosevelt was careful to receive him only as the ambassador from the "King of Italy."[91]

The British Government was far more realistic. On January 14, 1938, the Prime Minister informed President Roosevelt that he was prepared, "if possible with the authority of the League of Nations, to recognize *de jure* the Italian conquest of Abyssinia (by which Signor Mussolini sets great store), and to take other action if he found that the Italian Government on their side were ready to give evidence of their desire

[87] *Parliamentary Debates*, 340 House of Commons, 331; *Parliamentary Debates*, 110 House of Lords, 1678.

[88] Kirk to Secretary Hull, Rome, May 11, 1936. 765.84/4362, MS, Department of State.

[89] Signor Rosso to Secretary Hull, June 16, 1936. 711.65/73, MS, Department of State.

[90] Hull, *op. cit.*, p. 471.

[91] *Ibid.*, 470–71.

to contribute to the restoration of confidence and friendly relations."[92]
The President promptly replied that he was "concerned" over this statement of Prime Minister Chamberlain. At a moment "when respect for
treaty obligations would seem to be of such vital importance in international relations, . . . and at the time when our two Governments have
been giving consideration to measures in support of international law
and order in the Far East, . . . I cannot help but feel . . . that a surrender
by His Majesty's Government of the principle of nonrecognition . . .
would have a serious effect upon public opinion in this country."[93]

But the British Government paid little attention to this plea of President Roosevelt's. On April 16, 1938, it concluded with Italy an agreement which specifically recognized the Italian annexation of Ethiopia.
The nonrecognition policy had been buried deep in the grave of expediency. But the Roosevelt Administration adhered to the Stimson
doctrine. On April 19, with special reference to the Anglo-Italian
Agreement, President Roosevelt remarked that "this Government has
seen the conclusion of an agreement with sympathetic interest because
it is proof of the value of peaceful negotiations," but with his tongue in
his cheek he added the proviso that he was not making any attempt to
"pass upon the political features" of such an accord.[94] A few weeks
later, Secretary Hull made it clear that the principles governing the
conduct of American foreign relations had not undergone any change.[95]
As a proof of this statement, President Roosevelt sent a birthday telegram of congratulation to Victor Emmanuel III (November 11, 1938)
who was addressed merely as the "King of Italy."[96]

But this consistency was really the hobgoblin of small minds. The
Roosevelt Administration was stubbornly clinging to a formula that
made for war rather than peace. It served no useful purpose. As a distinguished authority in the field of international law aptly remarks: "It
seems safe to conclude that the policy of non-recognition as practiced
today is of slight value either as a sanction or as evidence that the rule
that conquest confers valid title has been superseded. . . . Conceived of
as a solution of the centuries-old problem of the cause and cure of war,
it appears somewhat fatuous."[97]

As one reviews the whole story of the Italo-Ethiopian dispute, it is

[92] Prime Minister Chamberlain to President Roosevelt, January 14, 1938. 740.00/
264a, *Confidential file*, MS, Department of State.
[93] President Roosevelt to Prime Minister Chamberlain, January 17, 1938. 740.00/
264b, *Confidential file*, MS, Department of State.
[94] Department of State, *Press Release*, April 19, 1938.
[95] *Ibid.*, May 12, 1938.
[96] *Ibid.*, November 11, 1938.
[97] Herbert Briggs, "Non-Recognition of Title by Conquest," *Proceedings of the
American Society of International Law* (May 13–15, 1940), p. 81.

evident that the policy of Britain was worse than "fatuous." Fatuity does not necessarily lead to war, but the persistently hostile attitude of the British Foreign Office towards Italian acquisition of Ethiopia pointed definitely in that direction. When Mussolini moved his legions into a country that was hopelessly backward and in dire need of intelligent direction under some highly civilized state, the British Government pretended to be deeply disturbed as a matter of principle.[98] The compromise policy of Sir Samuel Hoare in December 1935 proved that previous protestations of principle were a mere sham.[99] The French Government was never fooled by the pious platitudes of Eden, and Mussolini regarded them as an insult to his intelligence. British insistence upon sanctions completely destroyed the Stresa front. This fundamental change in political relationships in Europe may be laid directly at the door of Eden who posed as a Lancelot lost in a modern world of intrigue. His unfortunate role, and that of the Baldwin Government, is clearly described by Winston Churchill:

His Majesty's Government had imprudently advanced to champion a great world cause. They had led fifty nations forward with much brave language. . . . Their policy had for a long time been designed to give satisfaction to powerful elements of opinion at home rather than to seek the realities of the European situation. By estranging Italy they had upset the whole balance of Europe and gained nothing for Abyssinia.[100]

With the collapse of the Stresa front the way was wide open for the creation and extension of the Rome-Berlin Axis. Hitler was glad to smile when Eden frowned, and Mussolini quickly learned to prefer the friendly atmosphere of Berlin to the chilly fogs of London. These fogs of misunderstanding hid from most British eyes the stark fact that World War II was just around the corner. Thanks to Eden, and others of his ilk, that corner would soon have to be turned.

[98] It had long been recognized by students of African problems that slavery existed on a large scale in Ethiopia. Major E. W. Polson Newman, in an article in the *Contemporary Review*, CXLVIII (December 1935), entitled "Slavery in Abyssinia," p. 650, makes the following comment: "Slavery is the basis of the Abyssinian economic system. . . . The abolition of slavery in Abyssinia involves a complete social and economic reformation, and can only be carried out by external pressure and the exercise of European administration." As Winston Churchill aptly remarked: "The character of the Ethiopian government and the conditions prevailing in that wild land of tyranny, slavery and tribal war were not consonant with membership of the League." *Op. cit.*, p. 166.

[99] One of the important forces that controlled British attitude towards Mussolini's advance into Ethiopia was the grave fear that he might divert the waters of the Blue Nile "into the arid plains of an extended Eritrea" and thereby affect the water supply of the Nile when it reached Egypt. He could convert Eritrea into a rich cotton growing country, but this diversion of waters might severely injure Egypt. Sir John Harris, "Italy and Abyssinia," *Contemporary Review*, CXLVIII (August 1935), 151.

[100] Churchill, *op. cit.*, p. 187.

XI

Ambassador Dodd Finds Berlin an Unpleasant Spot for a Wilsonian Democrat

a. *Nazi Germany Makes a Friendly Gesture towards America*

WHILE the Roosevelt Administration was rapidly dissipating a large fund of Italian good will for the United States, a more serious crisis was developing in German-American relations. During the spring and early summer of 1933 the prospect seemed bright. When Ambassador Dodd arrived in Berlin on July 13 he discovered that the Germans "seemed very friendly."[1] Two days later he was presented to Konstantin von Neurath, the Minister for Foreign Affairs, who proved "most agreeable." It was not long before Louis P. Lochner, of the Associated Press, informed Dodd that one of Chancellor Hitler's friends had extended an invitation to the new ambassador to meet the Führer at a "quiet, secret luncheon" where the relations between America and Germany could be frankly discussed. Dodd repelled this friendly gesture but he did consent to call upon the family of Professor Henry Wood, of Johns Hopkins University. In the Wood circle he found the conversation was "good" although the "tone was quite Hitlerite."[2]

On July 17, Dodd sent to Secretary Hull a long dispatch dealing with economic conditions in the Reich. Dr. Frick, the Minister of the Interior, was sparing no effort to improve the situation. He had issued a "stern order" forbidding irresponsible Nazi officials to interfere in business affairs. It should now be clear that the German revolution was finished. The Nazi Party would devote all future efforts to "lawful constructive work." There was no doubt that Hitler was strongly in support of this conservative movement, and Dodd regarded the Chancellor's program as a "courageous step."[3]

These favorable comments were repeated in a much louder tone by Lord Rothermere whose estimate of Nazi Germany was couched in the friendliest tone:

Of all the historic changes in our time this upset of Germany under Hitler has been the quickest and most complete and significant. The German peo-

[1] Ambassador Dodd's *Diary, 1933–1938* (New York, 1941), p. 12.
[2] *Ibid.*, pp. 14–15.
[3] Ambassador Dodd to Secretary Hull, July 17, 1933. 862.00/3037, MS, Department of State.

ple are filled with the courage of a crusade. . . . It would be fruitless and unfair to regret this rebirth of the German spirit. . . . It is Germany's good fortune that it has found a leader who can bring together all the youthful elements in the country.[4]

The friendly attitude of the Nazi Government was further demonstrated in connection with the arrest of a young American student from New York who had boasted of his communist faith. He was promptly arrested and for a while kept incommunicado despite the efforts of Mr. Messersmith to get in touch with him. Mr. Messersmith was finally successful, and after ascertaining the facts in the case, he authorized Mr. Mowrer and Mr. Knickerbocker to cable the story to their papers in the United States. Ambassador Dodd noted that Mr. Messersmith did not have the courtesy to act in this matter with the permission of the Embassy. It developed that the young Communist was "an indiscreet sort of fellow." When Mr. Dodd intervened in his behalf, he was immediately released and shipped to New York.[5]

On August 3, Dodd was entertained by the ebullient Karl von Wiegand, a veteran newspaper correspondent who disclosed many aspects of diplomacy hitherto unknown to the ambassador. Although von Wiegand was "sympathetic with the Hitler group," he impressed Dodd "most favorably."[6]

Dodd had not yet closed his mind to favorable impressions of Germans and of Germany, and even Mr. Messersmith was at times able to see something in the German scene that was not repellent. In August 1933 it was apparent to Messersmith that the Nazi authorities were anxious to create a more friendly American public opinion. When a group of young American Boy Scouts visited Munich they were given such a friendly reception that the leader remarked that Hitler was "making true socialism a reality." When some cadets of the United States Coast Guard Service passed through Berlin they were made the guests of the city. During a dinner given in their honor, one of the German officials expressed the hope that the cadets, when they returned to the United States, would "disabuse the American mind of the stories of outrages and persecutions of persons not connected with the Nazi movement." Mr. Messersmith also called the attention of Secretary

[4] *Berliner Tageblatt*, July 10, 1933. In commenting upon this statement of Lord Rothermere, Mr. George S. Messersmith, the American Consul General in Berlin, remarked: "Anyone familiar with the lawless acts of the young people of the Hitler movement, particularly of the S. A. and the student body in the universities, could not agree with the above-mentioned statements." Messersmith to Secretary Hull, July 29, 1933. 862.00/3047, MS, Department of State.

[5] Dodd, *op. cit.*, p. 18.

[6] *Ibid.*, p. 19.

Hull to the recent statements of Mr. Joseph E. Ridder in the *Berliner Tageblatt*. Mr. Ridder, owner of the *New Yorker Staats-Zeitung,* had confided to a reporter of the *Tageblatt* that he had found the atmosphere "in Germany one of clear honesty in all things, whether it is in the political, commercial or cultural field."[7]

On August 12, Mr. Dodd sent to President Roosevelt a letter describing the German scene. There was sharp friction between Germany and Great Britain over the disarmament issue. The situation was so strained that the British military attaché in Berlin reported a recent conversation with Winston Churchill "to the effect that their Government is ready, on the request of France, to apply utmost force against Germany." It was evident to Dodd that the Nazi authorities were going out of their way to court American good will. One reason for this conciliatory attitude was the fact that all revolutionary movements, as soon as they are firmly fixed, "swing a little to the right." Because of this growing conservatism in the Nazi Party, Dodd believed that if the President could "restrain" the British and the French, he was confident that the situation in Berlin would "ease off."[8]

b. *Dodd Declines to Attend the Nürnberg Party Congress*

But despite these Nazi gestures of conciliation, Dodd was very cautious about taking any step that would indicate his approval of the Hitler regime. The program of anti-Semitism sponsored by the Nazis had many implications that were deeply distasteful to Dodd,[9] and he was fully aware of the wave of anti-Hitler sentiment that was sweeping over the United States. In view of this situation he decided to ask for instructions with reference to acceptance of the invitation to attend the Nazi Party Congress at Nürnberg during the first week in September.[10] William Phillips, the Acting Secretary of State, promptly informed Dodd that he did not feel "that it would be advisable for the Department to take any initiative or act directly in the matter. The implications of the local situation are better known to you than to the Department and I rely on your judgment to deal with this question with the minimum of

[7] George S. Messersmith to Secretary Hull, August 8, 1933. 711.62/75, MS, Department of State.
[8] William E. Dodd to President Roosevelt, August 12, 1933. 862.00/3085, MS, Department of State.
[9] For a detailed treatment of anti-Semitism in Germany and its effect upon the British mind, see *Survey of International Affairs, 1933,* ed. Arnold J. Toynbee (New York, 1934), pp. 167–74.
[10] Dodd to Secretary Hull, August 18, 1933. 862.00/3056, MS, Department of State.

embarrassment to yourself or to this Government."[11] Mr. Phillips then advised consultation with the French and British ambassadors in Berlin.

But Dodd did not wish to take the responsibility of acting upon his own judgment. He had consulted with the British chargé d'affaires who was undecided as to his course of action; the French Ambassador had not heard from the Foreign Office and could give no indication of the attitude of his Government. After wrestling with this diplomatic indecision Dodd felt constrained to make another appeal to the Department of State for instructions.[12] He found Mr. Phillips distinctly coy. The Acting Secretary felt that "this government should not take the lead in this matter. The British and French have as much if not more at stake than we, and I should not wish to give them an opportunity later to justify a decision by claiming that it was made at the instance of this government."[13] Once more the matter was placed in the hands of Mr. Dodd who finally declined the invitation on the "ground that I could not absent myself from Berlin long enough to have the pleasure of accepting."[14]

c. *American Citizens Are Roughly Handled by Storm Troopers*

Ambassador Dodd's implausible excuse with reference to nonattendance during the exercises of the Nazi celebration at Nürnberg was regarded as a clear indication of his feeling towards the Hitler Government. Some Nazi officials were now ready to show their feeling of hostility for the Roosevelt regime. At times American citizens were roughly handled without the slightest excuse, and despite the protests of the ambassador these incidents were repeated. Even before Mr. Dodd had declined the Nürnberg invitation, Dr. Daniel Mulvihill, an American citizen, had been assaulted by some members of the Storm Troops *(Sturmabteilung)*. Mulvihill was watching a parade of SA men along the Unter den Linden. When he failed to give the Nazi salute to the German colors, he was attacked and beaten. A protest was promptly filed with the Foreign Office and the Prussian Ministry of the Interior. The Ministry gave assurances of "immediate satisfactory action,"[15] Group Leader Karl Ernst of the Berlin SA apologized to Dodd for the offense, and the offending storm trooper was imprisoned.[16]

[11] William Phillips to Mr. Dodd, August 19, 1933. 862.00/3057, MS, Department of State.
[12] Dodd to Secretary Hull, August 20, 1933. 862.00/3058, MS, Department of State.
[13] Phillips to Mr. Dodd, August 20, 1933. 862.00/3058, MS, Department of State.
[14] Dodd to Mr. Phillips, August 23, 1933. 862.00/3061, MS, Department of State.
[15] Department of State, *Press Release*, August 19, 1933.
[16] *Ibid.*, August 23, 1933.

On this particular occasion, Bernhard von Bülow, Under Secretary of State, paid a visit to the American Embassy for a "frank and cordial conversation" with Mr. Dodd. He explained that the Nazi armament and drill work was "purely defensive and in part as a means of training young people to more serious attitudes toward life." When Dodd warned that the "slightest aggression of Germany on any of her frontiers would likely produce a European conflict," von Bülow replied: "That is exactly what I think." He then observed that "whether the Treaty of Versailles forbids or not, we shall build anti-aircraft and anti-tank guns and defences if the Geneva Conference does not bring about a reduction of air armaments in France."

In conclusion von Bülow strongly deprecated the lurid nature of the accounts in American newspapers of alleged German "atrocities." Dodd then explained to von Bülow the "relationship of the press to government and agreed that many articles which appear in our papers are exaggerated, and also said to him that I would endeavor to influence the *Chicago Daily News* in its treatment of the Mowrer case. Both of us agreed that Mowrer had overstepped the proper limitations. I, of course, told him that Mowrer is leaving on August 31, for which he expressed thanks."[17]

d. *Professor Coar Tries to Improve German-American Relations*

In Berlin, Dodd soon discovered that there were many unofficial ambassadors of good will who were constantly working to create better feeling between Nazi Germany and the United States. In the early days of August 1933, Professor John F. Coar called at the American Embassy for a conversation with Mr. Dodd. Coar had been born in Germany, of American parents, and apparently knew a great deal about conditions in the Reich. He was about to leave for a visit to Hitler at Berchtesgaden, and wished to discuss certain problems with Dodd. The ambassador insisted that the Nazi persecution of the Jews was alienating American sentiment, and Coar agreed with this viewpoint. On August 16, Coar returned to Berlin after his conference with Hitler. Apparently Dodd's words of warning had been wasted upon the Chancellor who informed Coar that the Jews were the world's greatest curse which he was determined to lift.[18]

But Hitler did not wish to undertake this task by himself. He authorized Professor Coar to inform President Roosevelt of "his [Hit-

[17] Dodd to Secretary Hull, August 26, 1933, inclosing a memorandum of his conversation with von Bülow on August 26. 862.00/3076, MS, Department of State.
[18] Ambassador Dodd's *Diary, 1933–1938*, pp. 20–24.

ler's] willingness to open diplomatic discussion with our Administration if he can be personally assured of this Administration's attitude in certain matters."[19] The President consented to see Coar but was ill when he arrived in Washington, and Secretary Hull was so "occupied with the Cuban crisis" that he could spare no time for a conference with the anxious Professor. Coar finally had an extended conversation with Mr. Moffat, chief of the Division of Western European Affairs, who reported to Secretary Hull the substance of Coar's remarks.[20] Hull then assured Coar, by mail, that his views had been "of great help" but inasmuch as the situation in Germany was changing from "day to day it is impossible to give you from this end the type of information you desire."[21]

e. *George Sylvester Viereck Offers to Assist the President*

As Professor Coar moved off the Washington stage his place was taken by George Sylvester Viereck. Viereck had been an important American literary figure before 1914. During the years from 1914 to 1917 he had been the editor of *The Fatherland,* a pro-German periodical. After the World War, Colonel House employed him to write an account of the House-Wilson relations during the war and during the troublous sessions of the Paris Peace Conference. While he was preparing his volume for publication *(The Strangest Friendship in History)* he came across the House-Grey Agreement of February 22, 1916. This agreement was a secret understanding between Britain and the United States, and in accordance with its terms America would give diplomatic assistance to Britain and France whenever they issued a call for help. This diplomatic assistance would be gradually transformed into military support at the most favorable moment. House believed that President Wilson had such secure control over Congress that the war-making power really resided in the Chief Executive. When the President indorsed the House-Grey Agreement the American people were secretly bound to share the military fortunes of the Allied powers whenever these powers would invoke the agreement.[22]

Viereck was greatly shocked when he realized all the implications of the House-Grey Agreement. Secret diplomacy had been one of the most important causes of the World War, and apparently it could have

[19] John F. Coar to President Roosevelt, September 12, 1933. 862.00/3082, MS, Department of State.

[20] Memorandum written by Mr. Pierrepont Moffat, September 14, 1933. 862.00/3084, MS, Department of State.

[21] Secretary Hull to John F. Coar, September 22, 1933. 862.00/3084, MS, Department of State.

[22] Charles Callan Tansill, *America Goes to War* (Boston, 1938), pp. 458–86.

plunged America into that conflict in 1916 if Allied leaders had made the most of their opportunities. It was not difficult for Viereck to see that secret executive agreements could easily involve the United States in future wars. Filled with foreboding as to the future of America, Viereck wrote to President Roosevelt and called his attention to the dark side of Wilson's foreign policy during the eventful years, 1915 to 1917. He felt free to write in this intimate manner to the President because he had once served as the ghost writer for three articles that had appeared in *Liberty* Magazine over the signature of Franklin D. Roosevelt.[23]

On October 11, 1933, Viereck wrote another letter to the President in which he once more directed his attention to the House-Grey Agreement:

You may remember some time ago I called your attention to a "gentleman's agreement" which bound the United States to the chariot of the Entente. My article was published in *Liberty* and was subsequently included in my book "The Strangest Friendship in History," a study of the psychic messmateship between Woodrow Wilson and Colonel House. At the time when I sent you the *Liberty* article you asked me to talk the matter over with you. I did not avail myself of that very kind invitation because I had no remedy to suggest.

The more I think about the problem the more I discover that it is impossible to maintain an international policy without some such informal understandings. I discussed the matter with Senator Gore and Senator Borah but neither had any concrete suggestion to make which I could have offered to you.

I have just returned from Germany where I had the opportunity to talk frankly to Chancellor Hitler, Foreign Minister von Neurath, Vice Chancellor von Papen, Minister of Economics Schmitt, to Goebbels, Minister of Propaganda, Finance Minister Schacht and others. I also had some rather interesting talks with the Crown Prince, with Emperor William at Doorn, and with our own Ambassador Dodd.

Colonel House thinks that possibly some of the facts I learned may be of interest to you. If so, I shall be very glad to present these to you. . . . It seems to me that the United States owes a debt of honor to Germany originating with the Fourteen Points. The only way our government can pay this debt is by using its utmost efforts to maintain peace and to restrain the victors of 1918 from pursuing an unfair advantage over Germany.

I am delighted that your Administration, so brilliant in its achievements at home, seems likely to be equally distinguished and brilliant abroad. At any rate, it seems clear that under your regime the United States will not again

---

[23] George Sylvester Viereck to the author, June 12, 1947. With reference to these articles in *Liberty* Magazine, Viereck remarked: "I rewrote three articles he wrote for *Liberty* which were so badly done that they could not be printed."

permit itself to be made the catspaw for other powers in their selfish struggle for predominance.[24]

The President was slow in sending a reply to this letter from Viereck. Finally, on November 3, Louis Howe extended to him an invitation to visit Washington so that he could talk things over with Secretary Hull or with Under Secretary of State William Phillips.[25] Viereck next wrote to Secretary Hull and inclosed a copy of the letter from Mr. Howe. He remarked that he had recently talked with many of the Nazi leaders, including Chancellor Hitler. It was possible that a "stray bit of information or interpretation may possibly be helpful in one way or another."[26] Secretary Hull turned Viereck's letter over to Mr. Phillips who arranged for a conference.[27] What happened at this conference is not disclosed in any memoranda in the Department of State. According to Viereck he had a "pleasant talk with Phillips and with the heads of the various departments [in the Department of State.] I told them that Hitler was 'the over compensation of Germany's inferiority complex.' I also said that 'Anschluss was inevitable and that it was desired even more in Austria than it was in Germany.' Incidentally, Hull gave me a special letter which recommended me to all diplomatic representatives of the United States in Europe."

But this letter from Secretary Hull did not lead to any discussions abroad that helped to improve German-American relations. When Viereck, a little later, became a critic of the New Deal he received from Fulton Oursler, of *Liberty* Magazine, "an ultimatum that I [Viereck] must either write an article, 'Why I Am Ashamed of Germany,' and another endorsing the New Deal or sever my relations with *Liberty*. If I agreed, he promised to restore my name on the cover and feature my articles. I refused."[28]

Mr. Viereck assures me that he did not talk with President Roosevelt during any of his administrations. This assurance makes distinctly doubtful the following statement by Mr. Erwin H. Klaus in a letter to the President in March 1939: "Mr. Viereck took it upon himself to tell the gathering [of the Roland German-American Democratic Society of Greater New York, March 16, 1939] that a few years ago you

[24] George Sylvester Viereck to President Roosevelt, October 11, 1933. 711.62/81, MS, Department of State.

[25] Louis Howe to George Sylvester Viereck, November 3, 1933. 711.62/83, MS, Department of State.

[26] George Sylvester Viereck to Secretary Hull, November 10, 1933. 711.62/83, MS, Department of State.

[27] Vinton Chapin to George Sylvester Viereck, November 14, 1933. 711.62/83, MS, Department of State.

[28] George Sylvester Viereck to the author, August 21, 1948.

[the President] told him personally that you considered it your principal ambition to destroy Hitler and Germany with him if it would be the last thing you did."[29] It is not likely that the President would have expressed himself so bluntly to Mr. Viereck.

f. *Mr. Kaltenborn Receives a Lesson in Incivility*

During these informal negotiations by amateur diplomats, Ambassador Dodd went to the residence of President Hindenburg in order formally to present his credentials. In the course of his conversation with the President he found an opportunity to launch an attack upon the doctrine of economic nationalism which was becoming increasingly popular in Germany. When he found his viewpoint warmly echoed by the great warrior he suspected that Hindenburg might be engaging in some "indirect criticism of the Nazi extremists."[30]

These extremists were constantly upsetting every little applecart that Dodd and the German moderates were trying to push down the rough lanes of German-American diplomatic intercourse. On September 9 the Department of State issued a press release stating that Mr. Samuel B. Bossard and a son of Mr. H. V. Kaltenborn, noted radio commentator, had been assaulted because they had not given the Nazi salute while watching a parade. The German Foreign Office was prompt in expressing its "deep regrets" at such outrages and it promised to take the most "energetic action" against the offenders.[31] On September 14, Dodd had a conference with Baron von Neurath with regard to this matter: "I acknowledged that Americans were negligent but said that was their privilege. . . . He assured me that he had recently gone over the matter with Goering, . . . and also with the Chancellor, both agreeing that a 'stricter enforcement of the law would be made thereafter.' "[32]

Dodd was far more successful than Mr. Messersmith in receiving verbal satisfaction from Nazi officials with reference to these assaults upon American nationals. When the consul general had a long talk with Dr. Funk, the State Secretary in the Ministry of Propaganda, the Nazi official blamed the Kaltenborns for "having turned their backs to the street and for having looked into a show-window" while a parade of Storm Troops passed. With regard to the assault upon Mr. Bossard, Dr. Funk stated that so many courtesies had been showered upon that

[29] Erwin H. Klaus to President Roosevelt, March 17, 1939. 711.62/236, MS, Department of State.
[30] Dodd, *op. cit.*, pp. 30–31.
[31] Department of State, *Press Release*, September 9, 1933, p. 149.
[32] Dodd, *op. cit.*, p. 36.

young man that he had left Germany "quite satisfied that everything was all right here."[33]

Mr. Messersmith was shocked at the callous manner in which Dr. Funk had dismissed the Kaltenborn and Bossard incidents. He was rapidly becoming intensely hostile to the Nazi regime, and he remarked in a letter to Mr. Phillips that the motto of the Nazi revolution should be "brutality, mendacity and loquacity." The campaign against the Jews had been carried on with such "extreme brutality" that suicides were becoming commonplace. While there had been manifested some popular opposition to these outrages upon the Jews, the matter had been so skillfully handled by Dr. Goebbels that the position of Hitler

is stronger than ever. He has been practically deified by a certain part of the population and fits into the extraordinary psychological situation which has been created. He is the center of the present madness. . . . Goering is still the exponent of the physical force of the party. . . . He has shown himself to be what some of us really believed, a simple-minded, enthusiastic soldier who is a good deal of a boy still. . . . In all justice to Goering it must be said that he is the only one of the three primary leaders of the party who is reasonable and can be reasoned with.[34]

The friendly viewpoint of Mr. Messersmith is clearly shown in his estimate of Göring as a "simple-minded, enthusiastic soldier who is a good deal of a boy still." Any capable person who had spent a few weeks in Germany in close contact with Göring would have arrived at a very different estimate of the man and his influence in Nazi ranks. Dodd judged Göring far more correctly than Messersmith, and he rightly held him responsible for the failure of the Nazi Government to take effective action against the outrages perpetrated upon American citizens by German hoodlums. Göring, as President of Prussia and chief of police, could easily have enforced order if he had been disposed to do so. When Dodd complained to the Foreign Office about these assaults by Storm Troops, von Neurath weakly murmured: "The S.A. men are so uncontrollable that I am afraid we cannot stop them."[35] He meant, of course, that Göring was not interested in protecting Americans.

g. *Germany Withdraws from the League of Nations*

Göring was merely the symbol of the exaggerated nationalism that was fostered by the Nazi Government. In Germany this chauvinism was

[33] Mr. Messersmith to Secretary Hull, September 16, 1933. 862.00/3089, MS, Department of State.

[34] Mr. Messersmith to Secretary Hull, September 29, October 28, 1933. 862.00/3097½, and 862.00/3128, MS, Department of State.

[35] Dodd, *op. cit.*, pp. 44–47.

often expressed in attacks upon foreigners who did not give the Hitler salute during parades. In international relations it often took the form of a series of demands for the revision of the Treaty of Versailles and for equality with reference to armaments. The Geneva Conference, in June 1933, had adjourned all meetings until October 16. During the summer Norman Davis engaged in many conversations in London and Paris in an effort to reduce the scope of German demands and to expand French concessions. On October 9, Secretary Hull gave to Dr. Luther, the German Ambassador, a veiled warning that America looked with disfavor upon any acceleration of the European armaments race: "I stated to him [Luther] that the one primary and paramount purpose . . . of the United States Government was the promotion of general disarmament. I said that, naturally, any organized movement for this purpose could not logically contemplate a modified program by which some governments might proceed to rearm."[36]

A few days later (October 14), Sir John Simon presented a plan which provided for the reorganization of continental armies upon a militia basis with a detailed system of international supervision. The powers with existing large armaments should reduce their military might in accordance with a plan which aimed at achieving equality of status in eight years. In the meantime the "Powers now under restrictions of the peace treaties" should make no effort to increase their armament. Germany, however, would be given some concessions with reference to the organization of the *Reichswehr*.[37]

Hitler took a dim view of any plan that would make Germany wait eight years for a status of equality with regard to armaments, and the Foreign Office immediately informed Geneva that Germany would no longer remain in the Disarmament Conference or in the League of Nations.[38] In defense of this action Hitler stated on the radio that the studied refusals of the great powers to acknowledge the "moral and material equality" of Germany had compelled the Nazi Government to adopt a policy of withdrawal from participation in European conferences. In order to quiet any apprehensions of Nazi designs for aggression he adopted a conciliatory tone in his references to France and went so far as to imply a renunciation of any desire for the recovery of Alsace-Lorraine.[39]

[36] *Peace and War: United States Foreign Policy, 1931–1941* (Washington, 1943), pp. 193–94.

[37] Department of State, *Press Release*, October 14, 1933.

[38] Toynbee, *op. cit.*, pp. 301–8.

[39] "Germany and the Crisis in Disarmament," *Foreign Affairs*, XII (1934), 260–70. In an interview with M. de Brinon, published in *Le Matin*, November 22, 1933, Hitler emphasized his desire for peace. With regard to his attitude towards France he said that the Saar problem was the only fly in the diplomatic ointment: "Alsace and Lorraine? I have said often enough that we have definitely renounced them to think that I have made myself clear on that point."

In a confidential dispatch to Mr. Phillips, Mr. Messersmith gave an explanation of the abrupt manner of the German withdrawal from the League:

I think there is little doubt that Goebbels is more responsible than any other person for the quick decision to get out of Geneva entirely. I think it is quite certain . . . that Sir John Simon had a talk with Goebbels and Goebbels was made to thoroughly understand that England could not help Germany in any way as long as they kept on doing here what they were. I understand that Sir John was very plain, very direct and just as energetic and definite as it would be possible to be. I know Goebbels and I know what effect such a conversation would have on him. He would be absolutely furious. . . . He went post-haste to Hitler and as he and Hitler think alike about all these things and are temperamentally so much the same, I think there is every reason to believe that the decision to get out of Geneva was made then and there.

In order to illustrate the pathological state of mind of the Nazi leaders, Mr. Messersmith observed as follows:

I know of no way in which to emphasize the extraordinary mentality here better than by telling you how outraged I was to learn that in circles surrounding Hitler there is a widespread feeling that President and Mrs. Roosevelt have practically nothing but Jewish advisers. . . . They seem to believe that because we have Jews in official positions, . . . our policy is being dictated by the Jews alone and that particularly the President and Mrs. Roosevelt are conducting anti-German propaganda under the influence of Jewish friends and advisers.[40]

The early portraits that Ambassador Dodd painted of Hitler were in more sober color than those of Mr. Messersmith. On October 17, Dodd had an audience with the Chancellor whom he found to look "somewhat better than the pictures that appear in the papers." Dodd discussed two matters of importance: the assaults upon American citizens and the discriminations against American creditors. Every request he made was acceded to and "the Chancellor assured me personally that he would see that any future attack was punished to the limit." When Dodd turned to the matter of German withdrawal from the League, Hitler became "clearly excited." After he completed an indictment of the injustices of the Treaty of Versailles, Dodd remarked: "There is evident injustice in the French attitude." Hitler was instantly mollified by this frank admission, and the interview was concluded in an agreeable spirit.[41]

[40] Messersmith to Mr. Phillips, October 28, 1933. 862.00/3128, *Confidential file,* MS, Department of State.
[41] Dodd, *op. cit.,* pp. 49–50.

But if Dodd was willing to admit the injustice of the French attitude towards Germany he was also quick to criticize the manner in which pressure was exerted upon voters in order to influence their decisions. Opponents of the Nazi regime were "sysematically intimidated. Nazi speakers have openly boasted that, though the ballotting will be secret, a way has been devised of checking upon all the 'traitors' who fail to vote for Hitler."[42]

Dodd's comments had particular reference to the national election of November 12 which was a referendum on Hitler's decision to withdraw Germany from the Arms Conference and from the League of Nations. Thanks to Nazi pressure, the result was that the "Government candidates received 39,500,000 votes out of a total of about 43,000,000."[43]

In his pre-election speeches Hitler constantly claimed that he desired peace and not war. On November 10 he impressively observed: "One should not expect me to be so insane as to desire a war. If anyone in the world can feel menaced it is only we. We want peace and agreement, nothing else!"[44] But these pacific expressions were discounted by Mr. Messersmith who was certain that Hitler was planning for eventual war: "Hitler and his associates really and sincerely want peace for the moment, but only to have a chance to get ready to use force if it is found finally essential."[45]

This desire for war, however, was checked by President Hindenburg who was strongly opposed to any rash military moves. The memory of Versailles still nestled in the mind of the great marshal, and he went out of his way to be conciliatory to foreign diplomats. On January 1, 1934, Dodd drove to the Presidential palace to pay his respects to the aged warrior. Hindenburg courteously inquired about the progress of Dodd's son in the University of Berlin, and he even complimented Dodd himself on his use of the German language. Hitler, "very much subdued," tried to carry on a conversation with Dodd who insisted upon talking about college professors and conditions in German universities. After several attempts to reach this high academic plane, Hitler moved away from the Dodd circle with a feeling that the American Ambassador had tried to "embarrass him a little."[46]

---

[42] Dodd to Secretary Hull, November 4, 1933. 862.00/3131, MS, Department of State.

[43] Dodd to Secretary Hull, November 13, 1933. 862.00/3127, MS, Department of State.

[44] J. C. White, counselor of Embassy, Berlin, to Secretary Hull, November 16, 1933. 862.00/3143, MS, Department of State.

[45] Messersmith to Mr. Phillips, November 23, 1933; *Peace and War, etc.*, pp. 194–95.

[46] Dodd, *op. cit.*, pp. 67–68.

h. *The Debt Problem Embarrasses German-American Relations*

It was not merely with reference to university matters that Ambassador Dodd would "embarrass" Chancellor Hitler. The problem of the debt owed to American creditors was a recurrent one that gave Hitler deep and lasting concern. The German moratorium of June 9, 1933, had at first applied to all public and private debts except short-term obligations to foreign banking institutions. It was modified so as to exempt from its scope the Dawes Plan loan of 1924 and the Young Plan loan of 1930. Provision was also made for the payment of 75 per cent of the interest on other loans through the operation of a plan that involved the use of scrip.

In December 1933 the Reichsbank extended the moratorium through the first half of 1934, and reduced the interest on German bonds from 75 to 65 per cent. American creditors were greatly disturbed by arrangements with the Netherlands and with Switzerland whereby the bondholders of those countries were to be paid full interest in return for commercial concessions.

On January 3, 1934, Ambassador Dodd filed a strong protest at the Foreign Office against this discriminatory treatment of American creditors. Although the Foreign Office was sympathetic, it could do nothing to better the situation, and the only answer Dodd received was a statement that Germany could pay only in proportion as the creditor nations bought German goods. Thanks to a partial American boycott of German manufacturers, only a certain percentage of interest could be paid to American creditors.[47]

President Roosevelt refused to accept this German explanation. On January 22, 1934, he invited Dr. Luther to the White House and insisted that American creditors be placed on the same footing as the creditors of other nations.[48] In response to this pressure, Dr. Schacht held a conference with the representatives of the creditor nations and he finally agreed to a compromise. According to this arrangement a portion of the interest would still be paid in scrip, but it would be redeemed at 76.9 per cent of the full value of the debts instead of the proposed 65 per cent. In carrying out his instructions of protest Dodd pressed the matter strongly but revealed his sympathy with the nearly bankrupt German Government by the following remark: "I shall do what I can but [I] agree with the Germans that rates of interest ought to be reduced to 4 per cent."[49]

[47] *New York Times*, January 25, 1934; Toynbee, *op. cit.*, pp. 93–98.
[48] Department of State, *Press Release*, January 27, 1934, pp. 47–48.
[49] Dodd, *op. cit.*, p. 74.

But this Schacht compromise lasted only a few months. On June 14 all the creditor governments were given notice of an "unavoidable suspension of the service of the medium-term and long-term foreign loans." It was especially significant that the Dawes and Young Plan loans were included in the new moratorium.

On June 16, Ambassador Dodd was instructed to inform the Foreign Office that the American Government "takes occasion to express its strongest regret that new losses are to be imposed upon American citizens" and that new discriminations are to be put into operation against American creditors.[50] Eleven days later Secretary Hull handed to Rudolf Leitner, the German chargé d'affaires, a detailed protest against this latest action of the Reichsbank. In this memorandum "grave regret" was expressed relative to Nazi fiscal policy.[51]

Secretary Hull was never content to file protests with the German diplomatic representative in Washington concerning the debt problem. Within a week or two this complaint would reach Berlin and would be filed in the Foreign Office. No action could be taken upon it because the Reichsbank had no funds available for American debt service. Hull was fully aware of this fact but this knowledge did not prevent him from sending instructions to Dodd to press von Neurath for payment. Apparently he made full use of the nuisance value of the debt difficulty, and his persistence in this goading policy gave Dodd considerable embarrassment: "What more can I say than I have said a score of times? Germany is in a terrible plight and for once she recognizes war is no remedy."[52] It was apparent to Dodd that repressive measures against the Jews in Germany had produced in foreign countries a boycott against German manufactures. This action had seriously reduced Germany's export trade and had adversely affected her ability to meet her foreign obligations. The collapse of the World Economic Conference at London had profoundly disturbed the European economic equilibrium and had postponed any return to normal times. Moreover, the recovery program in Germany, with its expansion of public works and the development of an armaments industry, had greatly increased imports of raw materials but did not produce goods that would create a favorable export balance. In June the reserves of gold in the Reichsbank had decreased to a mere 80,000,000 marks, so Dr. Schacht had felt that some drastic action was imperative.

Many American newspapers appreciated the difficulties that beset the German Government. The *Cincinnati Enquirer* feared that a tide

---

[50] Department of State, *Press Release*, June 23, 1934, pp. 418–19. See also, *Documents on International Affairs, 1934*, ed. John W. Wheeler-Bennett, pp. 244–46.
[51] Department of State, *Press Release*, June 30, 1934, pp. 444–48.
[52] Dodd, *op. cit.*, pp. 111–12.

of inflation was ready to engulf Germany,[53] while the *Springfield Republican*[54] and the Rochester *Democrat and Chronicle*[55] thought the action of the President of the Reichsbank was no worse than the practice of other nations. The *Seattle Daily Times*[56] and the *Atlanta Constitution*[57] inclined towards the view that Germany had merely followed the example given to her by European nations that had defaulted on American loans.

Although several European countries had failed to meet their financial obligations to the American Government, they refused to permit Germany to follow a similar policy towards them. By threatening to impound German balances within their borders they compelled the Nazi Government to meet some of their demands. In July and August 1934, Germany signed agreements with Great Britain, France, Switzerland, Sweden, and the Netherlands which made provision for partial payments of interest and principal on outstanding loans. The following table will indicate Germany's excess of exports to those countries and the reason why she came to a financial understanding with them:

GERMANY'S FAVORABLE BALANCE OF TRADE WITH
CERTAIN EUROPEAN COUNTRIES
(In millions of reichsmarks)

Country	Full year, 1933	January–March 1933	January–March 1934
France	211.0	57.5	34.4
Great Britain	167.2	31.6	38.3
Netherlands	380.8	80.2	75.6
Sweden	88.5	16.3	23.0
Switzerland	269.9	61.9	51.0

The United States had no comparable economic club over Germany's head which could enforce compliance with her wishes.[58] Indeed, America had a favorable balance of trade with the Reich, so there was no possibility of impounding German funds in the United States. All that the Department of State could do was to send a series of protests against German discrimination in favor of European creditor nations.[59] These

[53] June 16, 1934.
[54] June 19, 1934.
[55] June 21, 1934.
[56] June 16, 1934.
[57] June 16, 1934.

[58] America's favorable balance of trade with Germany may be expressed as follows:

	Exports to Germany	Imports from Germany
1934	$108,738,000	$68,805,000
1935	91,981,000	77,792,000
1936	101,956,000	79,679,000
1937	126,343,000	92,468,000

[59] Department of State, *Press Release,* December 1, 1934, pp. 325–28.

complaints were clearly worded and cogently argued, but they made little impression upon the Nazi Government, and thus an old diplomatic sore was broken open again and again.[60] It was a vicious cycle that helped to keep American public opinion hostile to Hitler.

i. New York City Stages a Mock Trial of Hitler

The debt problem was only one item in the long list of irritants that disturbed American relations with the Reich. Severe measures against the Jews aroused indignation in many American circles, and Hitler's attack upon the principle of democracy offended large numbers of Americans who were deeply concerned over the passing of the Weimar Republic. Goebbels added strength to American dislike of Germany when he attempted on February 28, 1934, to explain the reasons why Germany had become great under the guidance of Hitler. After enlarging upon the theme of German genius, he stated that the outstanding difficulty in the relations of Germany with other nations was their insistence upon looking at the Nazi revolution through rationalistic and liberal eyes. The course of events had clearly shown that the "dynamic driving force of the mind and of the heart were stronger than those of reason, that the spontaneous outburst of the German soul could not be fathomed by the rationalistic methods of a liberalist dialectic, and that in the end the immortal genius of the German soul rose triumphant above the forces of decay."[61]

It was soon evident that in America few eyes could see in the Nazi movement the "immortal genius of the German soul" rising triumphant above the forces of decay. Americans were hopelessly rationalistic. A graphic illustration of this fact was the appearance of advertisements in the New York Times and the Herald-Tribune of a mock trial of Chancellor Hitler to be held on March 7 in Madison Square Garden. Hans Luther, the German Ambassador, rushed to the Department of State on February 19 to register a frenzied complaint against this insult to the Nazi Government. Secretary Hull coldly replied that he was "sorry to see these differences arise between persons in his country and mine; that I would give the matter all due attention such as might be possible and justifiable in all of the circumstances."[62]

[60] It is important to note that Dr. Schacht was careful to fulfill the obligations that derived from banking short-term credits. On February 21, 1934, James Gannon, of the Chase National Bank, called at the American Embassy to "report a satisfactory conference with the German Reichsbank. . . . He was quite satisfied and gave Schacht the highest rating for cleverness and honesty." Dodd, op. cit., p. 81.

[61] Dodd to Secretary Hull, March 6, 1934. 862.00/3208, MS, Department of State.

[62] Memorandum of a conversation between Secretary Hull and the German Ambassador, Hans Luther, February 19, 1934. 862.00 Hitler, Adolf/11, MS, Department of State.

On March 1, Dr. Leitner, counselor of the German Embassy, had a hurried conference with Mr. John Hickerson of the Division of Western European Affairs in the Department of State. He presented a strong protest against the proposed mock trial of Hitler and mentioned the names of several persons, "close to the President," who would participate in this demonstration against the Hitler regime. He particularly referred to Mayor Fiorello La Guardia, Alfred E. Smith, Judge Samuel Seabury, and Bainbridge Colby. Mr. Hickerson then pointed out to Dr. Leitner that "no person connected with the Federal Government" was listed as having any role in this proposed mock trial. He closed the conversation with the candid statement that "in view of our constitutional guarantees of freedom of expression" he could see "no action in the matter which the Federal Government could properly take."[63]

On the following day, Dr. Luther registered his second protest against the mock trial of Hitler, but he was brushed off by Secretary Hull with the comment that the Department of State had not been able to "find any legal authority that would enable the Federal Government to instruct or order the participants to refrain from entering upon such mock trial."[64]

The German Foreign Office was not satisfied with these explanations of Secretary Hull and Mr. Hickerson. On March 5, Ambassador Dodd was summoned to von Neurath's office and found the Foreign Minister greatly excited. After the usual heated protest had been made, Dodd merely remarked that he had several times expressed the view that the "Jewish policy of Hitler would bring further trouble if not changed." As far as he could see nothing could be done to "stop the trial."[65]

After his visit to the Foreign Office, Dodd sent a telegram to Secretary Hull describing his conversation with von Neurath and closing with the intimation that if the Department of State felt disposed to "soothe injured susceptibilities" it could express regret for certain "irresponsible expressions of opinion in regard to problems outside our frontiers."[66]

After these repeated protests to the Department of State concerning the mock trial of Hitler in New York City had failed to get any action, the White House began to show some concern over the matter. On March 5, Mr. Early sent a memorandum of inquiry to Secretary Hull. Mr. James C. Dunn replied that the situation had been carefully can-

[63] Memorandum of a conversation between Dr. Leitner and Mr. John Hickerson, March 1, 1934, 862.002 Hitler, Adolf/22, MS, Department of State.

[64] Memorandum of a conversation between Secretary Hull and the German Ambassador, Herr Hans Luther, March 2, 1934, 862.002 Hitler, Adolf/17, MS, Department of State.

[65] Dodd, op. cit., pp. 86-87.

[66] Dodd to Secretary Hull, March 6, 1934. 862.002 Hitler, Adolf/18, MS, Department of State.

vassed and the "precedents indicated that the Department of State has never recognized any duty to suppress public utterances regarded as hostile to friendly States."[67]

Although this reply seemed satisfactory to Mr. Early, it was regarded with evident distaste by the German Ambassador who called at the Department of State on March 7 for an interview with Mr. Phillips. When his final appeal for intervention was denied by the Under Secretary of State, Dr. Luther expressed the hope that "some statement could be issued tomorrow morning indicating that the views expressed at the meeting were not in accord with those of the Federal Government." Mr. Phillips refused to commit the Department of State "in any way," so Dr. Luther's protests elicited no favorable action.[68]

On March 8, Pierrepont Moffat, of the Division of Western European Affairs in the Department of State, had lunch with Dr. Leitner who repeatedly remarked that to him it was incredible that "such an attack on the Chief of a friendly nation was permitted, and that apart from its political repercussions in Germany, it was establishing a very dangerous precedent which might come home to plague us some day."[69]

While the German Ambassador and his staff were busily engaged in filing protests against the mock trial of Hitler, the Chancellor himself had a long conference with Dodd and did not bother to make the slightest reference to that incident. Dodd found Hitler "very cordial" and quite anxious to review the general subject of German-American relations. When Dodd sharply criticized certain propaganda pamphlets which carried an appeal "to Germans in other countries to think of themselves always as Germans and owing moral, if not political allegiance to the Fatherland," Hitler immediately "denounced everything of that sort and went on to say that it was almost certainly put out by Jews." Dodd then directly referred to the Jewish problem in other countries, and the Chancellor frequently interrupted the ambassador's discourse with sharp imprecations against the "damned Jews."

Dodd argued against this anti-Semitism and pointed out that in the United States a "number of high positions . . . are at present occupied by Jews. . . . I explained to him that where a question of over-activity of Jews in university or official life made trouble, we had managed to redistribute the offices in such a way as not to give great offence. . . .

[67] James C. Dunn to Mr. Early, March 6, 1934. 862.002 Hitler, Adolf/126, MS, Department of State.

[68] Memorandum of a conversation with the German Ambassador, March 7, 1934, 862.002 Hitler, Adolf/30, MS, Department of State.

[69] Memorandum of a conversation between Mr. Pierrepont Moffat and Dr. Leitner, March 8, 1934. 862.002 Hitler, Adolf/27, MS, Department of State.

The Chancellor came back with a still more vigorous reply, saying that 59 per cent of all offices in Russia were held by Jews; that they had ruined the country and that they intended to ruin Germany, and, he added, 'if they continue their activity we shall make a complete end of them in this country.' " When Dodd mentioned that the Communists had polled only a few votes in the United States in 1932, Hitler burst out with the exclamation: "Happy country! Your people seem to be so sensible in this respect."

After Hitler had remarked that "Germany wants peace and will do everything in her power to keep the peace," Dodd inquired if it were not possible for European nations to agree upon the following points: (1) "No nation should cross another nation's boundaries," and (2) "all European nations should agree to a supervisory commission [to inspect armaments] and to respect the rulings of such a body." Hitler agreed "heartily" with these points and then surprised Dodd by indicating his cordial support of the proposal to institute more exchange professorships between the two countries.[70]

Although Hitler had made no mention of the mock trial incident in New York, the difficulties arising out of it continued for some weeks to embarrass German-American relations. On March 13, Ambassador Luther delivered another protest against this insult to the Hitler regime,[71] and ten days later he broadened his barrage so that it covered not only the mock trial but the activities of Samuel Untermyer, the Dickstein resolution in the House of Representatives, and the boycott of German manufactures by large department stores in the United States. He was fearful that "satisfactory relations" between Germany and the United States could not be maintained as long as American citizens used such abusive and insulting language with reference to the Nazi Government. Secretary Hull replied that the prime cause of ill feeling in the United States towards Germany was the repressive manner in which the Jews were treated in that country. After discussing anti-Semitism in Germany, Hull asked Luther if he thought the Jews in this nation should "resume buying goods from Germany." Luther's answer was distinctly naïve: "Yes, it would help to restore good relations." Hull realized at once that Luther was purposely obtuse in this matter, so he quickly concluded the interview.[72]

70 Memorandum of a conversation between Ambassador Dodd and Chancellor Hitler, March 7, 1934. 711.62/90, MS, Department of State.

71 Memorandum of a conversation between Secretary Hull and the German Ambassador, Hans Luther, March 13, 1934. 862.002 Hitler, Adolf/33, MS, Department of State.

72 Memorandum of a conversation between Secretary Hull and the German Ambassador, Hans Luther, March 23, 1934. 862.4016/1369, *Confidential file*, MS, Department of State.

While Ambassador Luther was wearing the patience of Secretary Hull very thin by his numerous protests, Chancellor Hitler decided to placate American public opinion by adopting a more lenient attitude towards the Jews. On March 12 he ordered the closing of Columbia House, "the place where the Jews and others had been tortured." He also announced that "warrants must be proved before anyone could be detained for more than twenty-four hours on any charge."[73]

But these steps indicated a mere relaxation and not a cessation of the campaign of anti-Semitism in Germany. The roots of this movement had penetrated very deep and had spread very far in the dark soil of the Reich. There were several factors that promoted this growth. Nazi racial theories helped to spread a hatred of Jews. It should also be remembered that since 1918 there had existed in many German minds the firm conviction that the military and political collapse that came during the last months of the World War was due primarily to "Jewish perfidy." A third reason for anti-Semitism was the belief that "Marxism is firmly bound up with the Jewish people." The Communist Government in Russia was based upon the principles of Marxism, and these principles with their emphasis upon world revolution were regarded as a distinct menace to the safety of the Reich.[74] It was not hard for Hitler to compose a hymn of hate that was sung with great gusto by millions of Germans.

j. *The Nazi Regime Is Placed upon an Uneasy Defensive*

Anti-Semitism was not the only shadow that fell across the German landscape in 1934. Large numbers of Germans had been devoted to the Weimar Republic and they deeply resented the way in which Hitler had slowly undermined its foundations. From Vienna word came to the Department of State that the "financial and economic situation" in Germany was growing rapidly worse and a "crisis" was approaching.[75] From Prague a similar message was received. Mr. Beneš was certain that the Nazi Government was "in a precarious position, and it is difficult to see how [it] can last much longer."[76]

In Berlin, Dodd found that some Germans in important official

73 Dodd, *op. cit.,* p. 100.
74 Dodd to Secretary Hull, March 12, 1934. 862.00/3216, MS, Department of State. For a recent statement of the thesis that "Communism as embodied in the Soviet Union" is "Jewish-inspired," see Hoffman Nickerson, *The New Slavery* (Garden City, 1947).
75 Mr. Messersmith to Secretary Hull, June 14, 1934. 862.00/3306, MS, Department of State.
76 Mr. J. Webb Benton to Secretary Hull, June 27, 1934. 862.00/3306, MS, Department of State.

positions were definitely hostile to the Nazi administration. On May 24 he had luncheon with Dr. Dieckhoff of the Foreign Office. During a lengthy conversation Dr. Dieckhoff "revealed his whole attitude of opposition to Goebbels and his expectation that Hitler would be overthrown soon." He could hardly have said more "if he had been in England or in the United States. . . . I felt the deep concern of a high official who would thus risk his life in criticism of the existing regime."[77]

Dieckhoff was probably reflecting the viewpoint of many of the officials in the Foreign Office. In the last week in May, Dodd had two conferences with von Neurath. The Foreign Minister was greatly concerned about "the decline of German gold reserves to only 4 per cent of German paper money." In a mood of deep dejection he exclaimed: "What shall we do? It is the Jewish boycott, the tariff barriers of all countries and our inability to purchase cotton and rubber or to sell anything abroad." With reference to a moratorium on debts due to American bankers, von Neurath feared there was no other course that could be taken: "Germany has no exports to the United States and only promises of exports to Denmark and other countries." It was apparent that he was "very uneasy but did not say revolution was in waiting."[78]

When Dodd lunched with Herr Kurt Schmitt, the Minister of Economics, he encountered the same spirit of despair and uneasiness. Schmitt took him on a tour of his extensive gardens and poured his laments into the sympathetic ear of the ambassador: "Schmitt talked for an hour about Germany's calamitous situation; a great and threatening drought, no exports to the outside world, intense hostility in the United States and England on account of Hitler's treatment of the Jews, Protestants and Catholics. . . . I have never seen a German statesman so much distressed. . . . He again and again referred to the folly of Hitler's policy."[79]

Schmitt's litany of laments on the folly of Hitler's policy was repeated in many houses which Dodd visited. Even within the ranks of devout Nazis there were murmurs of discontent. They had looked forward to the recovery of the Polish Corridor and had learned with bitterness of a ten-year pact of nonaggression with Poland. Instead of a Germany remolded according to the leveling principles of National Socialism they had discovered that the important industrial leaders and large landowners were still holding the seats of the mighty. And the Storm Troops were in a ferment of revolt because Hitler had revealed plans for a radical reduction of their legions. Röhm was bitterly op-

[77] Dodd, *op. cit.*, pp. 101–2.
[78] *Ibid.*, pp. 103–4.
[79] *Ibid.*, pp. 104–5.

posed to this proposed reduction, and it was rumored that he was plotting with General von Schleicher for a drastic change in the Nazi
organization.

In the meantime von Papen had paid an important visit to President
Hindenburg at Neudeck and secured his assent to a speech that would
stress the importance of preserving in Germany the right of free
speech and constructive criticism. At the University of Marburg, on
June 17, von Papen flung his verbal bombshell full in the faces of the
Nazi extremists like Goebbels:

A free press ought to exist to inform the Government with open and manly
statements where corruption has made its nest, when bad mistakes have been
made, where the wrong men are in the wrong place, and where the spirit of
the German Revolution has been sinned against. . . . If the official organs of
public opinion do not throw sufficient light on the mysterious darkness which
at present hides the spirit of the German people, then a statesman must step
in and call a spade a spade.[80]

In the United States this speech by von Papen received wide attention. The *Chicago Daily News* believed the utterance at Marburg to be
nothing less than a "body blow at Hitler." It was a "manifestation of
the very spirit of individualism which national socialism was supposed
to eradicate."[81] The Springfield *Republican* was shrewd enough to
surmise that the speech was "the signal for some important development in the internal affairs of Germany";[82] while the *New York Times*
hit the nail on the head by a statement that von Papen's ringing words
"unquestionably had the acquiescence of Hitler."[83]

There is little doubt that Hitler was fully aware of the rising tide of
dissatisfaction within the Nazi ranks. He knew of Röhm's determined
opposition to any large reduction in the numbers of the Storm Troops,
and he had heard of von Schleicher's devious schemes. He knew he
could count upon the support of von Blomberg and Göring, and it is
quite possible that he himself lighted the fuse in von Papen's bombshell. One sentence in the Marburg speech prepared the way for Hitler's dynamic entrance upon the German stage prepared to wield new
thunderbolts of power: "If the official organs of public opinion do not
throw sufficient light on the mysterious darkness which at present hides
the spirit of the German people, then a statesman must step in and call
a spade a spade."

[80] John W. Wheeler-Bennett, *Wooden Titan* (New York, 1936), pp. 454–59.
[81] June 20, 1934.
[82] June 19, 1934.
[83] July 1, 1934.

But before he moved out boldly on this German stage Hitler wanted to be certain of his lines. If he should assume the role of stern dictator bent upon a party purge it might be a wise move to get some sage advice from that master Italian actor, Benito Mussolini. Therefore, on June 14–15, Hitler had some lengthy conversations with the Duce at Venice. According to Breckinridge Long, the American Ambassador in Rome, Mussolini "no doubt advised Hitler that it would be necessary to take drastic steps to maintain his authority and exert the power of the Government over the members of his forces who were not disposed to adhere to his policies. Hitler left Italy with the firm determination to take action which up to that time had been foreign to his character."[84]

On June 28, Dodd confided to his diary that in Berlin the atmosphere was more "tense than any time since I have been in Germany." On the following day he gave a luncheon which von Papen attended. After some discussion of the situation in Germany, von Papen left the luncheon with the significant remark: "Anyway I shall not be torpedoed."[85]

Von Papen knew that a party purge was just around the corner, but he was certain that he was safe. The purge came on the morning of June 30 when Hitler, with a party of devoted adherents, raided a villa near Munich and discovered Röhm and Heines in compromising circumstances. Heines was immediately shot, and later Röhm faced a firing squad in his own cellar. General von Schleicher and his wife were shot down in their residence in Berlin. Throughout the period, June 30–July 2, the executions continued until, as admitted by Hitler in his speech on July 13, some seventy-seven persons had been slain. All the diplomats in Berlin paid particular attention to the fact that von Papen escaped this bloody purge. His parting remark to Dodd on July 29 took on additional significance: "I shall not be torpedoed."

In the United States many newspapers believed that Hitler would not be able completely to suppress the strong spirit of opposition that was rising in the Reich. A real showdown would soon come: "Germany and the waiting world will soon see whether they have to do with another Bismarck or a punctured balloon."[86] The Baltimore *Sun* saw in the events of June 30–July 2 the "beginning of an elemental uprising by a people deceived and betrayed";[87] the Richmond *Times-Dispatch* was of the opinion that "much blood will flow before the little Austrian paperhanger consolidates his position or is hurled from power,"[88]

---

[84] Breckinridge Long to Secretary Hull, July 5, 1934. 862.00/3308, MS, Department of State. See also, Toynbee, *op. cit.*, 1934, pp. 468 ff.
[85] Dodd, *op. cit.*, pp. 115–17.
[86] *Washington News*, July 2, 1934.
[87] July 2, 1934.
[88] July 3, 1934.

while the *Buffalo Evening News* capped the situation with the ominous remark: "He [Hitler] is sitting on a powder keg, and the fuse may be burning to an explosion that will skyrocket the whole Nazi plan of Government."[89]

Drew Pearson and Robert Allen predicted a dark future for Hitler: "The State Department has been receiving detailed reports on Hitler's 'purging' of his Nazi party. These indicate that the Austrian house painter may not long remain in power."[90] Paul Mallon, in his syndicated column, expressed the view that Hitler was copying the methods of the American underworld: "It seems that big shot Hitler adopted Al Capone's methods for the same reason that Al did. His own gang was getting restless and the radicals were trying to muscle in."[91]

Some American papers believed that the bloody purge in Germany would be the prelude to the adoption of more moderate policies by the Nazi leaders. The Rochester *Democrat and Chronicle* predicted that "moderation of extreme Nazi policies may now be expected";[92] the *New Republic* thought that Hitler had turned to the Right and had rejected the radical views of some of his former followers,[93] while the *Literary Digest* inclined to the view that the Chancellor had "apparently embarked on a moderate political policy."[94]

Hitler's speech in the Reichstag on July 13, in defense of his party purge, failed to win many converts in the United States, although the Louisville *Courier-Journal* spoke of him as an "almost pathetic figure" who was pleading for support "of his tottering regime."[95] The Rochester *Democrat and Chronicle* thought he had not "succeeded in wiping the blood guilt from his hands";[96] the *New York Times* regarded his speech as an indication that he was "distinctly on the defensive,"[97] while Oswald G. Villard expressed the conviction that it was "impossible to read Hitler's defense of his atrocious murders without taking heart. . . . I cannot but feel that this orgy of blood-letting marks the beginning of the end of Hitler."[98]

The *St. Louis Globe-Democrat* completely disagreed with Mr. Villard. It regarded Hitler's address on July 13 as one of his great oratorical successes: "There need be no surprise if it should develop that he

---

[89] July 2, 1934. For the same viewpoint see also the *Los Angeles Times*, July 3; the Philadelphia *Evening Bulletin*, July 2; and the *St. Louis Globe-Democrat*, July 2, 1934.

[90] *Des Moines Register*, July 10, 1934.

[91] *Atlanta Constitution*, July 3, 1934.

[92] July 2, 1934.

[93] July 18, 1934.

[94] July 7, 1934.

[95] July 15, 1934.

[96] July 14, 1934.

[97] July 14, 1934.

[98] *The Nation*, August 1, 1934.

has by it not only regained the confidence of the people of Germany but strengthened their faith in him."[99] This view was shared by Arthur Brisbane who believed that "Hitler still retains his power in Germany and his grip on the German imagination."[100]

Brisbane was correct in his belief that Hitler still maintained a "grip on the German imagination," but he did not seem to realize the extent and bitterness of the dislike in America for the Hitler regime. The party purge had removed from the Hitler entourage some persons he was glad to get rid of, but it had also removed from most American minds any lingering respect for the Nazi movement and its leaders. When Ambassador Dodd was invited to hear Hitler's speech (July 13) in defense of the purge, he promptly declined to be present at the ceremony. In explaining his absence to Sir Eric Phipps, the British Ambassador, he remarked: "He is such a horror to me I cannot endure his presence."[101]

Before June 30, Dodd had disliked Hitler and was out of sympathy with his objectives, but he had been glad to confer with him and he had helped to prevent a repetition in Chicago of the mock trial of Hitler that had been staged in New York. After the purge, Dodd and a host of other Americans felt that Hitler was capable of any action that would further his selfish interests. It made little difference if this indictment were too harsh. Hitler was now a tremendous liability for the German people to bear, and the burden eventually broke them and the whole German way of life.

[99] July 16, 1934.

[100] *Chicago Herald and Examiner*, July 15, 1934.

[101] Dodd, *op. cit.*, p. 126. On July 25, 1934, Dodd sent a *strictly confidential* dispatch to Secretary Hull with reference to the Hitler purge. He had obtained from an "official personage whose position should enable him to be conversant with the facts," an "inside story" which he hastened to send to the Department of State: "According to this informant, world Jewry having collected large sums to improve the plight of the German Jews, those in charge of the funds decided to devote twelve million marks to monarchistic propaganda in Germany as being one of the best means to achieve the desired end. The Secret State Police got wind of this and learned that the money was to be transferred from Paris to Germany by way of Prague. . . . The necessary surveillance involved large expenditures which Diels . . . finally asserted he was no longer able to supply, and thus the German plan failed for 'want of the last thousand marks.'

"The ex-Crown Prince meanwhile became active in favor of restoration, enlisting the aid of the masonic lodges and monarchistic associations, and also collecting further sums for his purpose. . . . The authorities became aware of his plans, and while not being able to locate and seize the funds, dissolved the aforementioned organizations. In order to exculpate himself, the ex-Crown Prince presented 12,000,000 marks to the SA, and he and his sons donned SA uniforms. Roehm determined to avail himself of this financial windfall to promote his own plans of revolt. Agents of the Secret State police discovered the plot and . . . turned to von Papen who welcomed the opportunity to frustrate Roehm's radical tendencies. . . . Von Papen collected all the material concerning the plot . . . and showed it to Hindenburg. The President . . . sent for Hitler and presented him an ultimatum—either Hitler must immediately suppress the planned revolt or Hindenburg would do so himself. . . . Hitler . . . had a nerve-crisis, and . . . ordered the shootings of June 30." Dodd to Secretary Hull, July 25, 1934. 862.00/3344, *Strictly Confidential*, MS, Department of State.

XII

America Views the Hitler Regime
with Increasing Dislike

a. *Similarities between Nazi and American Fiscal Policies*

THE PURGE of the Nazi Party temporarily disrupted the ordinary processes of government in the Third Reich. It was obvious to the average statesman that important diplomatic problems could not receive due attention until administrative order was completely restored. But Secretary Hull refused to recognize the realities of the situation in Germany: he was determined to press the Nazi Government with reference to financial obligations even though he knew it was in no position to return a satisfactory answer. If he could keep this fiscal sore from healing it might lead to a general inflammation that would spread over the whole body of German-American relations and lead to fatal results. It was somewhat surprising to see how this quiet lawyer from an agrarian state became so intensely interested in safeguarding the investments of Wall Street bankers.

While the embers of the crisis in Germany were still brightly glowing, he sent an instruction to Ambassador Dodd directing him to register a strong protest against the announced decision of the Nazi Government to discriminate in favor of British creditors. When this instruction reached the American Embassy on July 6, Dodd hurried with it to the Foreign Office and had a conference with von Neurath: "Both of us were embarrassed. He knew Germany had done wrong to promise the payment of English debts and not pay American; I knew the same; both of us knew Germany could not pay even the English debt. . . . He asked me to say that he was sorry and would pay, if any reserves were available, but these are not at all probable."[1]

In his telegram to Secretary Hull recounting the interview with von Neurath, Dodd revealed a sympathy for Germany because of her desperate financial plight. Many other nations had passed through similar cycles, and America had been one of them: "Washington, Jefferson and Hamilton gave same excuses in 1790 for failure to pay 'unpayable' Revolutionary debts. English, French and Spanish markets were closed to the United States. . . . Between 1820 and 1850 our States borrowed $400,000,000 when national wealth was ten billions. Nearly all these

[1] Ambassador Dodd's *Diary, 1933–1938*, pp. 119–20.

States defaulted or repudiated. . . . The Federal Government refused to act in any way. . . . All these facts are known to competent officials here if not to some of our eminent men. One cannot banish facts from one's mind no matter how patriotic one may be."[2]

Despite Dodd's clear telegram of July 14 indicating financial chaos in Germany, Secretary Hull sent repeated instructions directing him to continue his protests against Nazi financial discriminations. On July 16 he called at the Foreign Office and once more both he and von Neurath confessed their "embarrassment" at the situation,[3] but there was no remedy in sight and no one knew this better than Secretary Hull. With Germany on the point of financial "collapse,"[4] it was useless to continue a barrage of protests. Diplomatic vinegar attracted no flies of mutual understanding.

b. *General Johnson Denounces the Nazi Party Purge*

While the threatened collapse of the Nazi financial structure was sending tremors through American banking circles and thereby causing evident uneasiness in the Department of State, certain prominent Americans were widening the breach in German-American relations by their bitter denunciations of the Nazi Party purge. On July 12, General Hugh S. Johnson, the chief official in the National Recovery Administration, made a speech in which he vigorously criticized Hitler for permitting the murders that attended the cleansing of the party stables on June 30. These brutalities had made General Johnson "not figuratively, but physically and very actively sick. The idea that adult, responsible men can be taken from their homes, stood up against a wall . . . and shot to death is beyond expression. . . . That such a thing should happen in a country of some supposed culture passes comprehension."

When the German chargé d'affaires made a hurried visit to the Department of State to protest against this vitriolic denunciation of Nazi Germany, Secretary Hull called his attention to General Johnson's statement that he "was speaking as an individual and not for the State Department or for the Administration." After assuring Dr. Leitner that "it was to be regretted that the position in the Government occupied by the speaker made it possible for remarks uttered by him as an individual to be misconstrued as official," Mr. Hull brought the interview to an abrupt close.[5]

[2] Dodd to Secretary Hull, July 14, 1934. 862.00/3307, MS, Department of State.
[3] Dodd, *op. cit.*, pp. 129–30.
[4] Dodd to Secretary Hull, July 21, 1934. 862.00/3320, MS, Department of State.
[5] Secretary Hull to Ambassador Dodd, July 13, 1934. 862.00/3307A, MS, Department of State.

But this official explanation of General Johnson's heated remarks did not please the German press which blazed into indignation. The following remarks from the *Deutsche Allgemeine Zeitung* were typical:

The German protest was to be expected, as the remarks of General Johnson, the head of the NIRA, concerning the events of June 30 were so monstrous that a sovereign state never could stand for such vilification of the head of its government. . . . Secretary of State Hull's reply to the German protest . . . appears to us to settle the incident in a most unsatisfactory manner.[6]

After looking around for some way in which to express its displeasure at the mild manner in which the Department of State had handled the "Johnson incident," the Nazi Government decided to give vent to its deep dissatisfaction by expelling from Germany Mrs. Sinclair Lewis (Dorothy Thompson). On August 24, Mrs. Lewis had called at the American Embassy for a pleasant chat with Dodd. After her return to her hotel she telephoned the Embassy to announce the unpleasant news that she had just received an order from the secret police to leave Germany within twenty-four hours. Her offense consisted of some articles she had written two years earlier that contained some critical comments on Hitler. Dodd immediately bent every effort to prevent the expulsion of Mrs. Lewis, but all his efforts were in vain.

Thoroughly angered by this action of the Nazi Government, Dodd sent a strong telegram to the Department of State and inquired as to the "position of our Government with reference to expulsion of undesirable foreigners from the United States."[7] He was promptly informed that the American Government had always held that "it is the sovereign right of our own country to determine exactly what aliens it may wish to deport from the United States, . . . This Government does not question the right of any foreign government to expel from its territory American citizens whom it considers undesirable."[8]

There was nothing that Dodd could do to stay the expulsion of Mrs. Lewis, but the "solidarity of the foreign press corps of Berlin in escorting Dorothy Thompson to her train of banishment" was an unmistakable indication of the deep and widespread resentment that had been aroused by Nazi attacks upon the freedom of the press.[9]

[6] July 15, 1934.
[7] Dodd to Secretary Hull, August 26, 1934. FW 811.91262/134, MS, Department of State.
[8] J. F. Simmons to Pierrepont Moffat, August 27, 1934. FW 811.91262/134, MS, Department of State.
[9] Washington *Daily News,* August 27, 1934.

c. *The Assassination of Chancellor Dollfuss*

In the summer of 1934 there was a stream of incidents that awakened in the United States a feeling of sharp dislike for Nazi Germany. Some weeks before the expulsion of Dorothy Thompson from Germany a group of Nazi sympathizers in Austria suddenly seized the Vienna broadcasting stations and then murdered the Chancellor, Engelbert Dollfuss. Mr. Messersmith, the American Consul General in Vienna, telephoned at once to the American Consul General in Berlin (Mr. Geist) and told the details of the Nazi *Putsch.* Dodd regarded this action by Messersmith as an "indiscretion" which would do "both of us and our government harm."[10] He had warned Messersmith to be especially careful about using the tapped telephones in Germany.

It was evident to Dodd that the American press would be filled with "bitter denunciations" of the assassination of Dollfuss, and in this regard he was entirely correct. The *Birmingham News* was quick to remark that intuition pointed "unwaveringly toward Adolf Hitler as the primary causative force behind the unspeakable crimes which have blotched the face of Europe this summer."[11] The *Cleveland Plain Dealer* thought that it was clear that the movement behind the assassination was of "Nazi origin."[12] Professor Sidney Fay expressed the view that one of the causes contributing to the crime was the "long announced determination of Hitler and his followers to bring Austria under Nazi rule."[13] The *Seattle Daily Times* dissented from the popular opinion which pinned the guilt upon Hitler: "Hitler, the only ruler against whom suspicion might have been directed, has been as prompt as any to denounce the act; and in sending his conservative critic, von Papen, to Vienna, has spiked the chance to charge him with collusion in Austrian Nazi madness."[14] The *Albuquerque Journal* believed that "the assassination of Premier Dollfuss has brought down the wrath of other Powers and wrecked Nazi hopes for sympathy and control of Austria."[15] The *Milwaukee Sentinel* agreed with this viewpoint: "One thing is fairly certain: the union of Austria and Germany is more remote than it has been at any time since it was proposed."[16]

[10] Dodd, *op. cit.,* p. 132. For an extended account of the assassination of Chancellor Dollfuss and its sequel, see *Survey of International Affairs, 1934,* ed. Arnold J. Toynbee, (New York, 1936), pp. 471–87.

[11] July 30, 1934.

[12] July 26, 1934.

[13] *Current History,* September 1934.

[14] July 28, 1934.

[15] July 28, 1934. For a similar opinion see also the *Los Angeles Times,* July 26, and the *Cincinnati Enquirer,* July 27, 1934.

[16] July 27, 1934.

d. *The Death of President Hindenburg*

The death of President Hindenburg on August 1 was viewed with open dismay by most of the American press which regarded him as a check upon the excesses of Hitler. Hindenburg had been regarded with warm favor in many American circles, and the Hoover Administration had courted his good will. The *Seattle Daily Times* pronounced him "one of the greatest of warriors";[17] the Richmond *Times-Dispatch* was certain that he was the "idol of the German people,"[18] while the *St. Louis Globe-Democrat* looked upon him as one of the greatest men that Germany has ever produced.[19]

But there were some American newspapers that refused to join this chorus of praise. The *Chicago Daily News* complained that Hindenburg had lived too long. If he had died before Hitler became Chancellor his fame would have rested upon a more secure pedestal.[20] The *Milwaukee Sentinel* saw much to criticize in Hindenburg: "History presently will sit in judgment on Paul von Hindenburg and the blame heaped upon his memory may exceed the praise. . . . The onus of a Hitler is a heavy burder for any man to bear."[21]

The heavy burden Germany had to bear with Hitler as Chancellor was greatly increased when Hindenburg's death was made the occasion for Hitler to assume also the office of President of the Reich. This new responsibility seemed to sober him for a little while. On August 6, in the Reichstag auditorium, there was an impressive service in commemoration of the contributions Hindenburg had made to the fatherland, and Hitler delivered an oration on the "military genius" of the late President. On the following day this ritual was repeated at Tannenberg, and it was noticeable that the Chancellor refrained from any remarks that could be regarded as "challenges to the French or English or Americans."[22]

Hitler had his eyes upon the approaching Saar plebiscite in January 1935, and for the time being he wished to conciliate rather than anger public opinion in foreign countries.

---

[17] August 2, 1934.
[18] August 3, 1934.
[19] August 3, 1934.
[20] August 21, 1934.
[21] August 3, 1934.
[22] Dodd, *op. cit.*, pp. 141–43. On August 19, 1934, there was a plebiscite in Germany with reference to Hitler's assumption of the Presidential office. The vote was—Yes: 38,279,000; No: 4,278,808.

e. *American Opinion of the Saar Plebiscite*

In December 1934 the French Government came to an agreement with Chancellor Hitler with reference to the implications of the Saar plebiscite. If the vote favored reabsorption into the Reich the Nazi Government would pay a large sum in settlement of French claims (900,000,-000 francs). This payment would be made partly in cash and partly in future coal deliveries.

On January 13, 1935, the plebiscite was held and 528,541 votes were cast. The results were: 477,119 in favor of union with the Reich; 46,-613 were in favor of a continuance of the existing regime (2,124 voted for union with France). In view of this overwhelming vote in favor of union with Germany (90%), the formal transfer of the territory took place on March 1, 1935.[23] Needless to say, the outcome of the Saar plebiscite was a resounding victory for Hitler.

Many American newspapers were pleased with the outcome of the plebiscite because they regarded it as a form of peace insurance. They were particularly pleased by the fact that the League of Nations had handled the matter in a very efficient manner and had thereby increased its prestige. The Louisville *Courier-Journal* emphasized this aspect of the affair: "The Saar plebiscite adds another accomplishment of far-reaching importance to the credit of the League of Nations. In every way it was a complete success."[24]

Some papers were impressed with the plebiscite as an indication of the strength of the principle of nationalism. The *Boston Daily Globe* regarded it as "one of the most impressive barometer readings on nationalism available in recent European history,"[25] while the *Omaha World-Herald* remarked that the Germans in the Saar seemed to "care not for the risk but gaily, defiantly, enthusiastically follow the dictates of their hearts to become a part again of the Fatherland."[26]

The Rochester *Democrat and Chronicle* voiced a warning that victory in the Saar plebiscite might merely whet Hitler's appetite for more territory. The "peace of Europe still requires careful nursing."[27] The *Chicago Tribune* was confident that the only way to preserve this peace was to give heed to the clear call of nationalism. The one-worlders with their accent upon internationalism were a disturbing factor in the delicate European equation: "The Saar vote ought to remind them . . . that the sentiment of race or nationalism is omnipresent and almost

---

[23] Sarah Wambaugh, *The Saar Plebiscite* (Cambridge, 1940). See also, *Documents on International Affairs, 1935*, pp. 50–98.

[24] January 17, 1935.
[25] January 17, 1935.
[26] January 16, 1935.
[27] January 16, 1935.

omnipotent in international affairs. . . . Except for a very small and in Europe, ineffectual minority, the sentiment of internationalism has little appeal and experiments based upon it . . . have no more chance of standing up against the deep and powerful sentiment of nationalism than a sapling has in a hurricane."[28]

f. *The Anglo-French Declaration Looks towards Collective Security*

This rapidly developing spirit of German nationalism under Hitler had many disturbing implications for the statesmen of Europe. With no general agreement on disarmament in sight the French Government became increasingly worried over the situation. In January 1935, Laval visited Rome for conversations with Mussolini. As a result of his efforts an agreement was concluded to the effect that the two powers would consult in the event of an aggressive act by a third power against Austria. This was the first step in a drive to insure the preservation of peace in Europe. On February 3, a second step was taken when the prime ministers of France and Great Britain issued a declaration which was to form the basis for a "general settlement freely negotiated among other Powers, including Germany." It was in reality an invitation to Germany to join this proposed collective system and thereby give evidence of her desire to maintain peace. There would be a new agreement on armaments under whose terms the military provisions of the Treaty of Versailles would be canceled. In addition to this repudiation of the settlement of 1919 there would be an Eastern pact of mutual assistance, a Central European pact for preserving the independence of Austria, and an air convention which would stipulate that the Western powers would provide immediate help to any of the signatory powers that were the victims of an unprovoked aerial attack.[29]

In the United States this Anglo-French declaration aroused great interest. The Portland *Morning Oregonian* was frankly skeptical of the proposed pact: "We dislike being derogatory towards agreements reached and announced in such an air of excitement, but they are very patently intended to trap Germany by offering her minor concessions. . . . After bolting the League and rearming in the face of a hostile Western Europe, Germany is not likely to be drawn into a trap so thinly disguised."[30]

The *Atlanta Constitution* was hopeful that the proposed treaties would open "the way for a sound readjustment of troublesome condi-

[28] January 17, 1935.
[29] *Documents on International Affairs, 1935,* pp. 119–27.
[30] February 4, 1935.

tions,"[31] and the *Cleveland Plain Dealer* was favorable to them.[32] The *Nashville Banner* believed that Hitler's often repeated declarations in favor of peace would now be put to the test: "He has often proclaimed . . . that he contemplated no aggressive action, but sought only security and peace. The sincerity of those protestations is now to be tested."[33]

On February 14, Hitler gave a conciliatory answer to the French and British ambassadors in Berlin and approved in principle an air treaty. But he showed no disposition to accept the proposed Eastern and Central European pacts. Instead, he suggested further discussion of the matters contained in these conventions. This suggestion greatly annoyed the *Cleveland Plain Dealer:* "The German reply to the French-British proposals is an invitation to talk and more talk."[34] The *Detroit Free Press* pointed out that the "attitude of Berlin isn't precisely peace breeding,"[35] while the *New York Times* was dubious about the sincerity of Hitler: "The Third Reich now looks forward to a long period of negotiation. For her every delay is a gain. Herr Hitler has enjoyed the freedom he gained by withdrawal from the League and the Disarmament Conference. He is in no hurry to sign an agreement sealing Germany within her present boundaries."[36]

It was apparent that Hitler was endeavoring to arrange for a bilateral pact with Britain instead of a general European treaty, and his suggestion that the British Government send a spokesman to Berlin was regarded favorably in London. On February 24, Sir John Simon, the British Foreign Minister, announced that he would visit Berlin on March 7.[37] But this pacific gesture was premature. Suddenly on March 4 the British Government published a White Paper which adverted to armament expenditures in other countries. Then, with special reference to Germany, it remarked that Hitler's plans for rearmament had the unfortunate effect of aggravating the "existing anxieties of Germany's neighbors," and had produced "a situation where peace will be imperiled."[38]

This British blast at Hitler had a depressing effect upon the Chancellor's health. An announcement was made in Berlin that the Führer had contracted a severe cold. Apparently, in Germany, diplomatic negotiations could be conducted only when the top officials enjoyed the best of health. Sir John Simon's visit to the capital of the Reich was indefinitely postponed.[39]

[31] February 5, 1935.
[32] February 4, 1935.
[33] February 7, 1935.
[37] *New York Times*, February 25, 1935.
[38] *Documents on International Affairs, 1935*, pp. 132–34.
[39] *New York Times*, March 7, 1935.

[34] February 16, 1935.
[35] February 17, 1935.
[36] February 17, 1935.

Many American newspapers deprecated the publication of the British White Paper. The *Indianapolis News* thought that it had considerably darkened the hopes for European peace and a general understanding with Germany,[40] while the *Springfield Republican* raised the point as to whether the "British Government is playing a deep game or is merely in the not uncommon position of having its right hand ignorant of what its left is about."[41] The *Christian Science Monitor* expressed the belief that the British action "makes the situation clearer and brings fear closer, but it does little to turn the thoughts of men and women toward the greater friendliness and understanding which must be the real foundation of peace."[42] The *Philadelphia Record* was frankly critical of the British move: "Is the fault all Germany's? What of the promises of the former Allied Powers to disarm? And what of British and other armament firms which have aided Germany in this perilous rearmament?"[43]

g. Hitler Breaks Another Link in the Chain of Versailles

European statesmen anxiously awaited Hitler's response to the British White Paper of March 4. It came on March 16 when he denounced the arms provisions of the Treaty of Versailles. After pointing out how France had recently broken these same provisions by enacting a law raising the term of service in the army to two years, he then referred to the Soviet Union's large army of 960,000 troops. Because of this Franco-Russian threat Germany would have to increase its military strength to 550,000 carefully trained troops. He was aware that this number exceeded by 350,000 the estimate made by the concert of Europe with reference to Germany's military needs.[44]

Hitler's defiance of Europe did not throw the American press into a panic. The *Detroit Free Press* scoffed at the widespread fears of war.[45] The *Dallas Morning News* agreed with this reassuring verdict,[46] and the *Milwaukee Journal* believed that the "essential situation is not greatly different."[47] But in order to maintain peace Germany would have to be surrounded with a "ring of iron."[48]

To the Richmond *Times-Dispatch* it was evident that the real re-

[40] March 7, 1935.
[41] March 7, 1935.
[42] March 5, 1935.
[43] March 7, 1935.
[44] *Documents on International Affairs, 1935,* pp. 141–43.
[45] March 18, 1935.
[46] March 19, 1935.
[47] March 18, 1935.
[48] March 19, 1935.

sponsibility for Hitler's action rested upon the shoulders of the Allied statesmen because of the "revengeful policies" they had followed after the World War.[49] This view was shared by the Portland *Morning Oregonian:* "France and her associates, by their timidity toward post-war republican Germany, and their lack of faith in the matter of disarmament, gave us Hitler."[50]

The *Cincinnati Enquirer* inclined towards the opinion that neither Germany nor the Allies had a strong case, and it called attention to the fact that the British White Paper and the recent French legislation had definitely influenced the action of Hitler.[51] The Raleigh *News and Observer* felt much the same way: "As even the Devil is entitled to his due, it should be pointed out that Hitler's repudiation of the Versailles treaty prohibition against an armed Germany is not the only menace to peace in the modern world. Long before his announcement that Germany would arm again, walls of steel had grown in the increasing armaments of nations about Germany. . . . Certainly, Germany had no reason to do otherwise than fear so heavily armed and ancient enemy as France."[52]

The Hearst press rejoiced that America had no European political ties and was "free to mind her own business without obligations to anybody abroad,"[53] while the *Philadelphia Record* struck the same isolationist note.[54]

William Allen White assumed the role of prophet and his words of warning revealed keen insight into the problems of Europe: "The blunt announcement last week [by Hitler] was not a new departure [but] only another milestone on the road to ruin which Europe has been travelling for several years. . . . In a few weeks . . . certainly not less than a year, Germany will announce that she is fortifying the left bank of the Rhine. . . . Not even this will touch off the powder keg. But the fuse is sputtering, the hissing flame advances along the powder-dusted cord, notch by notch."[55]

h. *Apparent Agreement at Stresa*

On April 11, Mussolini acted as the host to representatives of Great Britain and France during an important conference at Stresa. After a brief period of discussion the three powers issued on April 14 a com-

[49] March 17, 1935.
[50] March 18, 1935.
[51] March 17, 1935.
[52] March 27, 1935.
[53] *New York Evening Journal,* March 19, 1935.
[54] March 18, 1935.
[55] *Emporia Gazette,* March 21, 1935.

muniqué which indicated a common front against Germany's plans for rearmament.[56]

The *Pittsburgh Post-Gazette* took the Stresa declaration quite serious-ly: "The communiqué yesterday on the Anglo-French-Italian confer-ence at Stresa indicates that . . . a united front is to be maintained against Hitlerism. . . . The situation demanded a firm stand in the face of the Hitler defiance, and it is the best hope of peace."[57] The *Detroit Free Press* expressed a similar optimistic viewpoint,[58] but the *Milwaukee Journal* thought that the Stresa announcement was distinctly inade-quate.[59] Many other papers reflected this pessimism. The New Orleans *Times-Picayune* believed that the conference had left "in the air most of the questions that were considered";[60] the *Los Angeles Times* criti-cally remarked that the meeting at Stresa "appears to have changed the situation in no material particular,"[61] while the *Dallas Morning News* was fearful that Hitler had won a diplomatic victory.[62]

i. *France Makes an Important Agreement with Russia*

France was not content with the outcome of the Stresa conference. As the shadow of Germany began to darken the frontiers of France, the Laval Government felt additional fright and hastened to sign on May 2, 1935, a pact with the Soviet Government of Russia. Although this was a treaty of mutual assistance against aggression, this assistance could be extended only after consultations had been held with the Western Locarno powers and with representatives of the League of Nations.[63]

Hitler saw the weakness of this Franco-Soviet pact and he denounced it (May 21) as decidedly dangerous because the ideology of the Russian leaders was fundamentally opposed to the concept of capitalism. Capi-talism and communism had no common ground on which their repre-sentatives could meet with safety. He then indicated his willingness to negotiate treaties of nonaggression and consultation with neighboring powers. He was also ready to become a party to agreements for localiz-ing conflicts and for isolating aggressor nations. After hinting that he would not oppose the re-entry of Germany into the League of Nations on the basis of equality, he stated that the Reich must have air parity

[56] *New York Times*, April 15, 1935. See also, *Documents on International Affairs, 1935*, pp. 156–61.
[57] April 15, 1935.
[58] April 16, 1935.
[59] April 15, 1935.
[60] April 16, 1935.
[61] April 16, 1935.
[62] April 16, 1935.
[63] *Documents on International Affairs, 1935*, pp. 116–19.

with the strongest Western power and a naval force equal to 35 per cent of the British Navy.[64]

To numerous American editors this speech by the German Chancellor seemed so reasonable that it evoked a favorable response. The *Christian Science Monitor* thought it should be welcomed as "tentatively opening several bridges over the chasm that has deepened so alarmingly in Europe in the last few months";[65] the *Chicago Tribune* regarded the speech as an "even-toned discussion" which declared clear purposes with which "very little quarrel can be had";[66] while the Louisville *Courier-Journal* was fulsome in its praise of this Hitler gesture: "Hitler's speech . . . was a full and frank avowal of Germany's foreign policy. . . . As a candid statement of the aims and aspirations of the Third Reich nothing is wanting. As such it offers a basis for reconciliation and understanding provided the other Powers will accept the Fatherland as an equal and not as an inferior. . . . It offers the way to a just and lasting peace."[67]

The *New York Times* was distinctly skeptical of any promise that Hitler might make,[68] and the *Washington News* delivered a sharp blast against the Chancellor and all his devious schemes: "As usual everybody is out of step but Adolf. . . . He proposes to open a systematic attack 'upon the poisoning of public opinion' through the press. This from the arch-poisoner of the press of all time."[69]

j. *Britain and Germany Negotiate a Naval Treaty*

Hitler's address of May 21 with its bid for a bilateral treaty with Great Britain bore fruit in the Anglo-German Naval Agreement of June 18, 1935. In accordance with its terms the strength of the German fleet was fixed at 35 per cent of the total tonnage of the British Commonwealth of Nations. It was obvious that this agreement had far-reaching implications for the other naval powers. France and Italy were sharply critical of the British Government for "conniving with the Reich" in a breach of the Treaty of Versailles.[70] In Germany the agreement gave great satisfaction because it not only permitted the Reich to have a

[64] *Ibid.*, pp. 159–75.
[65] May 22, 1935.
[66] May 24, 1935.
[67] May 23, 1935.
[68] May 23, 1935.
[69] May 22, 1935.
[70] *The United States in World Affairs, 1934–35*, ed. W. H. Shepardson and William O. Scroggs (New York, 1935), p. 235. See also, André Géraud ("Pertinax"), "France and the Anglo-German Naval Treaty," *Foreign Affairs*, XIV (October, 1935), 51–61.

navy three times as large as the naval armament allowed by the peace settlement of 1919, but it also granted eventual parity with Britain in submarines.[71]

In the United States the Anglo-German Naval Agreement was received with general approval. The *Cincinnati Enquirer* was quick to give its blessing to the arrangement: "Wiser than their friends in Paris, the British have made a sane compromise with Germany and have thereby reached a satisfactory agreement on naval ratios without impairing their friendly relations."[72] The *Des Moines Register* was pleased with any accord that "curbed the Nazi craze for maximum armaments,"[73] while the *Albuquerque Journal* looked upon it as an "important foundation stone" in the rebuilding of the "wreck which is now political Europe."[74]

There were some voices raised in sharp disapproval of the British desire to appease Hitler. The *Washington News* hoped that Britain's "present quixotic course will not do more harm than good";[75] the *New York Times* deprecated the fact that Britain "allowed itself to do what in another it condemns as a breach of international law";[76] while the *Chicago Daily News* regarded the agreement as an important German diplomatic victory: "This agreement is the greatest triumph of German diplomacy since its successful repudiation of the disarmament provisions of the Versailles Treaty last March."[77]

k. *Secretary Hull Is Fearful of the Role of Moral Leadership*

The tension in European diplomatic circles in the spring of 1935 made a deep impression upon American observers. But no matter how desperate the situation became in Europe it was believed that America should abstain from taking an active role in an effort to better conditions. Ambassador Bingham, in London, was distinctly of this opinion. In a telegram to Secretary Hull he remarked: "If a . . . European meeting is called in which Germany is to participate, we are now of the opinion that the United States should not attend or send an observer. . . . It is our opinion that if we mingle in the European situation we must be prepared to accept the responsibilities therein entailed; we cannot participate merely on the basis of that specious form of 'moral

---

[71] *Documents on International Affairs, 1935,* pp. 141–152.
[72] June 22, 1935.
[73] June 26, 1935.
[74] July 1, 1935.
[75] June 20, 1935.
[76] June 20, 1935.
[77] June 19, 1935.

leadership' from which the present administration has thus far wisely refrained."[78]

Secretary Hull was not ready to assume any "specious" role of "moral leadership" in the early months of 1935. He knew only too well how badly Europe needed such leadership, but there was no possibility that European statesmen would respond to any clarion call. In order, however, to be ready for any emergency he scanned with great care the dispatches from American embassies in Europe, and during March he became increasingly concerned over the danger of an outbreak of hostilities. On April 4, Ambassador Dodd received a telegram from Hull inquiring whether "war in Europe is imminent." On the following day, Dodd sent a reassuring answer to the Department of State but he confided to his diary that the "irresponsible trio, Hitler, Goering and Goebbels might easily do a wild thing, knowing so little of past history."[79]

The negotiation of the Anglo-German naval pact appeared to Dodd as the first step in a German move to "encircle" Russia. Absolute control "of the Baltic was the major point . . . in the naval agreement. The other means of encircling Russia is the entente with Japan which gives that country an almost free hand in Asia." Germany had to be cautious, however, because the Franco-Italian understanding and the Franco-Russian pact were major obstacles along the road to conflict. Thus "we have Europe stalled in a way which fairly guarantees peace for some years to come."[80]

1. *The* Bremen *Incident*

The course of German-American relations was never permitted to run smoothly even for a brief period. There was always some incident to provoke ill will. In this regard it should be remembered that in 1934 the Communist Party in America was taking an active part in stirring the embers of American discontent with both Germany and Japan. Those powers were barriers against a Red tide that might engulf Europe and Asia. If America could be "needled" into war with those Russian rivals it would be a great victory for Soviet diplomacy. Nothing would suit the Kremlin better than to have the United States fight for Russian objectives. As one reads the diplomatic correspondence of the thirties it is easy to see how communist agents worked untiringly to inject the poison of hatred into German-American relations. A good example of their technique was the *Bremen* Incident.

[78] Ambassador Bingham, London, to Secretary Hull, March 29, 1935. 862.20/798, Personal and Strictly Confidential, *Confidential file*, MS, Department of State.

[79] Dodd, *op. cit.*, pp. 228–31.

[80] Dodd to Secretary Hull, July 15, 1935. 862.00/3539, MS, Department of State.

On July 25 the Third Division Office of the Police Department of New York City received a copy of a circular issued by the Communist Party which called for a "demonstration" on Pier 86 at midnight on July 26 "on the occasion of the sailing of the S.S. *Bremen.*" The wording of the circular is very interesting. It presumed a union of Communists, Catholics, Jews, and Anti-Fascists against Nazi Germany:

All Catholics must immediately come to the aid of their fellow-Catholics in Germany. While you are at mass today, the Hitler fascist government is launching the most brutal attack on religious liberty in modern history. . . . The Communist Party is calling on all anti-fascist individuals and organizations to rally to the defence of the Catholic people of Germany. . . . THOSE WHO TALK AGAINST COMMUNISM WANT FASCISM. LEARN FROM GERMANY. We urge you to flood the pier with anti-fascist workers.[81]

On the evening of July 26 some Communists were able to slip aboard the *Bremen,* and at 11:45 they began to assault the German sailors. When the New York police hurried to quell this disturbance, they were immediately attacked by the belligerent Communists and firearms were freely used. During this pitched battle some Communists were able to reach the "flagstaff of the S.S. *Bremen* and pulled down the German Swastika, throwing it into the river." After a lengthy and spirited contest the Communists were finally subdued and many of them were arrested.[82]

Three days after this incident occurred, Dr. Rudolf Leitner, the chargé d'affaires of Germany, paid a formal visit to the Department of State to make a "most emphatic protest against this serious insult to the German national emblem." In his note addressed to Mr. Phillips, the Acting Secretary of State, Dr. Leitner expressed the expectation that the "guilty persons may be duly punished."[83]

Dr. Leitner was not able to see Mr. Phillips, so he had a long conversation with Mr. James C. Dunn:

He [Dr. Leitner] said that the combination of the La Guardia ruling against granting a masseur's license to a German citizen and the *Bremen* flag incident caused a great deal of resentment in Germany and said that as far as he could see, whenever there is presented an opportunity to do so, all the American press fulminates against the German Government as if they were directed to

[81] A copy of this circular is printed in the Department of State, *Press Release,* August 3, 1935, pp. 104–5.

[82] See reports of Alexander C. Anderson, chief deputy inspector, and James Pyke, acting lieutenant of the New York City Police Department, Department of State, *Press Release,* August 3, 1935, pp. 100–109.

[83] Dr. Rudolf Leitner to Mr. William Phillips, July 29, 1935, *ibid.,* p. 100.

do so by some superior authority. . . . He handed me a page from the illustrated section of the Minneapolis *Sunday Tribune* of July 7, 1935 which is clearly an attack upon Hitler, stating that his father was a drunkard, mistreated his wife and frequently beat his son.

I told Dr. Leitner that we considered the *Bremen* flag incident as most unfortunate. I said, however, that . . . the police of New York had acted promptly and efficiently. . . . As far as concerned the article in the Minneapolis *Sunday Tribune,* there was nothing this Government could do . . . as the press in this country was entirely free to express itself in any manner it desired to on any subject.[84]

On August 1, Mr. Phillips sent a formal note to Dr. Leitner which merely stated that it was "unfortunate" that the "German national emblem should not have received that respect to which it is entitled."[85] There was no assurance that Communists would not be able to repeat their performance of July 26. As far as the Department of State was concerned the incident was closed, but the German Foreign Office was far from pleased with this cool, verbal settlement of the affair, and it remained in their minds as an important item of unfinished business.

m. *American Hostility towards the Hitler Regime*

Some officials in the Department of State were inclined to pass over the *Bremen* Incident lightly because they hoped for an early collapse of the Hitler Government. But Ambassador Dodd dashed these hopes in some of his telegrams. On August 9 he canvassed the strength of Nazi organization and came to the conclusion that there was "nothing to warrant prediction of an early break-down of economic or political regime."[86]

This view was partially confirmed by Mr. Clifton M. Utley, director of the Chicago Council on Foreign Relations. Mr. Utley had a conversation with Mr. R. E. Schoenfeld of the Division of Western European Affairs in the Department of State. During the course of this conversation Mr. Utley voiced the view that the German people were strongly in support of the Hitler Government. This fact was demonstrated in the recent elections: "As for Hitler, personally, Mr. Utley felt that the two referenda held [recently] accurately represented the feeling of the people." Mr. Utley then made some interesting remarks concerning Himmler: "Himmler was personally a completely honest and upright man."

---

[84] Memorandum of a conversation between Mr. James C. Dunn and Dr. Rudolf Leitner, July 29, 1935. 862.002/Hitler, Adolf, MS, Department of State.

[85] Mr. Phillips to Dr. Leitner, August 1, 1935. Department of State, *Press Release,* August 3, 1935, pp. 100–101.

[86] Dodd to Secretary Hull, August 9, 1935. 862.00/3522, *Strictly Confidential,* MS, Department of State.

The concentration camp at Dachau was "well organized." The discipline of the "inmates was excellent and their health was apparently satisfactory." These inmates were largely Communists, and inasmuch as in Germany the officials regarded communism as Jewish inspired, this fact had sinister implications for the large Jewish population.[87]

In the summer of 1935 there was a great deal of discussion in Nazi ranks about the advisability of issuing new decrees that would supplement the anti-Semitic Nuremberg Laws. At this period, however, it was believed that Hitler was opposed to harsher measures:

> It is fairly well established that a sharp conflict has broken out in Party and Government circles respecting the scope of the application of the [anti-Semitic] legislation. According to good authority, Herr Hitler and Dr. Schacht, at a meeting of Gauleiters and Reichleiters held immediately after the [Nürnberg] Congress, drove home to their hearers the necessity for discipline and the avoidance of excesses against the Jews. . . . On the other hand, it appears that the concession was made to radicals that the class to be known as "full Jews" would be subject to severer restrictions.[88]

 The very fact that supplementary anti-Semitic decrees were being projected in Germany helped to increase in the United States the deep-seated hostility that made it difficult to continue diplomatic relations with the Reich. The anti-Jewish rioting in certain German cities in July clearly indicated the insecure status of the Jews. Moreover the projected supplementary regulations were already "being enforced by the Party against Jews and Jewish business concerns."[89] American indignation over these repressive measures aroused the anger of Goebbels who remarked on January 17, 1936, in a speech in Berlin that American public opinion defied understanding. Lindbergh, once a national hero, was now despised by many in America because he refused to ride the anti-German wave that was sweeping over America: "We do not wish to be Pharisees, but a people who would let such a thing happen have every cause to attend to their own affairs. As regards the rest of the world, if it loves the Jews so much, let it take them!"[90] This defiant attitude towards world opinion presaged some new Nazi thrust for power. It was not long before the Führer startled Europe with another repudiation of treaty obligations.

[87] Memorandum of a conversation between Mr. Clifton M. Utley and Mr. Schoenfeld, September 6, 1935. 862.00/3537, MS, Department of State.

[88] John C. White, counselor of the American Embassy, Berlin, to Secretary Hull, October 5, 1935. 862.00/3546, MS, Department of State. 862.00/3552, MS, Department of State.

[89] Douglas Jenkins, consul general in Berlin, to Secretary Hull, November 4, 1935.

[90] Dodd to Secretary Hull, January 22, 1936. 862.00/3569, MS, Department of State.

XIII

Europe Fails to Find a Substitute for Locarno

a. *Hitler Liquidates the Locarno Pact*

As tension in Europe increased as a result of the Italo-Ethiopian dispute there was a fear in some quarters that Hitler would exploit the situation in order to gain some substantial concessions. Hugh Wilson, American Minister at Geneva, wrote to Secretary Hull that it was the "concern regarding Germany which is decisively influencing the action of all the European . . . States today." There was no "real fear of Italy" but many statesmen were "profoundly afraid of Germany."[1]

One of the concessions that Hitler wished to extract from England and France was the return of the former German colonies. In June 1935, Bullitt wrote to Secretary Hull that he had just been told by a British diplomat that his government was ready to "concede as just and reasonable" Germany's claim to colonial territory.[2] In January of the following year he had a different story to report. The British Ambassador in Paris had bluntly informed him that the Foreign Office would "regard with displeasure the raising of the question of colonies."[3] It was during this very month that Ambassador Davies had a conversation with Dr. Schacht who confidentially remarked that his Government had authorized him to submit proposals to England and France that would guarantee the peace of Europe, reduce armaments, and settle the question of international boundaries if the matter of colonies were satisfactorily adjusted.[4]

Schacht made little impression upon the British Government which was in the mood to ask rather than grant concessions. In December 1935 the Foreign Office instructed Sir Eric Phipps, in Berlin, to ask Hitler if he had any objections to the establishment of "British air bases in Northern France and Belgium."[5] This point-blank question as-

---

[1] Minister Wilson to Secretary Hull, Bern, November 13, 1935. 740.00/40½, *Confidential file*, MS, Department of State.

[2] Ambassador Bullitt to Secretary Hull, June 28, 1935. 862.014/106, MS, Department of State.

[3] Ambassador Bullitt to Secretary Hull, January 14, 1936. 751.62/391, MS, Department of State.

[4] Ambassador Davies to Secretary Hull, January 20, 1936. 740.00/100, MS, Department of State.

[5] Ambassador Dodd to Secretary Hull, Berlin, January 9, 1936. 740.0011 Locarno Mutual Guarantee/351, *Confidential file*, MS, Department of State.

tounded the German Chancellor. It indicated either that the Foreign Office had lost all faith in the Locarno treaty of October 1925 or that it regarded him as an easy mark. He told Phipps with considerable vehemence that he was entirely opposed to any indirect repudiation of Locarno, and Paul Scheffer, in the *Berliner Tageblatt,* devoted a long editorial to the "inequitable features of any Franco-British mutual assistance arrangements vis-a-vis Locarno and the general discontent and apprehension in Germany which these alleged arrangements inspire."[6] When other German newspapers acidly commented upon this remarkable British proposal, the French Ambassador objected to such a barrage and it suddenly ceased.[7]

The German Foreign Office was also apprehensive concerning the Franco-British staff conversations which seemed to indicate military preparations against Germany. Ferdinand L. Mayer, the American chargé in Berlin, had a long conversation with Dieckhoff in the Foreign Office and the latter frankly disclosed many doubts relative to the Franco-British attitude towards Locarno:

Dieckhoff said that while the British and French had given most solemn assurances that their recent staff discussions referred only to the Mediterranean, he must state frankly that the value of those assurances was somewhat diminished by the fact that similar assurances given in 1913 and 1914, with regard to staff discussions, had proven valueless. Furthermore, these present assurances were weakened by the rather naive and amazing question Phipps had asked Hitler last December when he requested what would Germany's attitude be if England established air bases in Northern France and Belgium.[8]

The public statements of British statesmen still expressed a determination to adhere to Locarno. In the House of Commons, February 12, 1936, Anthony Eden insisted that His Majesty's Government would "stand by those obligations and . . . faithfully fulfill them."[9] This meant that any German occupation of the demilitarized zone along the

---

[6] Ambassador Dodd to Secretary Hull, Berlin, January 13, 1936. 740.0011 Locarno Mutual Guarantee/352, MS, Department of State. In this telegram Dodd told of a conversation with the editor of an important German paper who informed him "unequivocally that the Phipps-Hitler meeting last month was for the purpose of sounding out the German Government with regard to the question of British air bases in Northern France and Belgium."

[7] Ambassador Dodd to Secretary Hull, Berlin, January 18, 1936. 740.0011 Locarno Mutual Guarantee/353, MS, Department of State.

[8] Ambassador Dodd to Secretary Hull, Berlin, February 6, 1936. 862.20/1102, MS, Department of State.

[9] *Survey of International Affairs, 1936,* ed. Arnold J. Toynbee (New York, 1937), p. 255.

Rhine would be followed by prompt British action according to the terms of the treaty.

In France the situation was complicated by difficulties arising out of the debate upon the Franco-Soviet Pact. On February 11 this treaty had been placed before the Chamber for ratification. Flandin, the Foreign Minister, referred to the possibility of a German repudiation of Locarno but he did not seem deeply concerned about such a contingency. On February 27 the Chamber approved the treaty by a large majority and on March 3 it came before the Senate.[10]

British and French statesmen were carefully watching the diplomatic skies over Germany for storm clouds. They remembered Hitler's speech of May 21, 1935, in which he had promised "scrupulously to maintain every treaty voluntarily signed" by the German Government. But they also recalled his reservation to the effect that German adherence to Locarno would last only "so long as the other partners are on their side ready to stand by that pact." It was known that Hitler regarded the Franco-Soviet Pact as a violation of Locarno, and in February 1936 the German press had expressed bitter resentment over its possible ratification by the French Parliament.

The British and French ambassadors, therefore, should not have been greatly surprised when on March 7 they (along with the ambassadors from Belgium and Italy) were summoned to the Wilhelmstrasse where Neurath informed them that German military reoccupation of the de-militarized zone had already begun. He then handed them a memorandum which explained the reasons for this action. At noon Hitler addressed the Reichstag and then read to it the memorandum that had been handed to the ambassadors representing the Locarno powers. Emphasis was placed upon the need for some new political alignment that would restrain the Red tide of Russia. The best way to erect a strong dyke against the Soviet tide would be the prompt ratification of four agreements: (1) a multilateral treaty which would provide a new de-militarized zone along the frontiers of Belgium, France, and Germany; (2) a twenty-five year nonaggression pact between Belgium, France, Germany, and the Netherlands; (3) an air pact which would insure Western Europe against a surprise attack; (4) a series of bilateral non-aggression treaties with the countries on the eastern frontier of Germany.[11]

[10] *Ibid.*, p. 256. The French Senate ratified the pact on March 12, 1936.

[11] *Documents on International Affairs, 1936*, pp. 35–41. It was estimated that within two weeks after March 7 the German military strength in the demilitarized zone was 90,000.

b. *American Press Opinion Relative to the Rhineland*

In the United States the news of the Nazi occupation of the Rhineland evoked nationwide interest. The Baltimore *Sun*[12] and the Louisville *Courier-Journal*[13] were suspicious of Hitler's proposals, and the *San Francisco Chronicle* was confident that anything that emanated from Hitler was counterfeit: "The world does not trust him at all."[14]

The Oklahoma City *Daily Oklahoman* feared that a general European war was imminent. After this Hitler coup, war would "ensue inevitably."[15] The *Emporia Gazette* shared this view: "The danger of a European war draws nearer."[16] The Portland *Morning Oregonian* refused to be frightened by the specter of war,[17] and the Hearst press put on a similar brave front.[18]

The *St. Louis Post-Dispatch* was inclined to look with favor upon Hitler's peace proposals: it was high time for a New Deal in Europe.[19] The *Omaha World-Herald* expressed a similar opinion: "One can only wait and see—and hope. Hitler presents the possibility that he may become the post-war peacemaker. . . . The Versailles Treaty could well be sacrificed for such positive gains."[20]

The *Cincinnati Enquirer* went so far as to defend Hitler's bold move into the Rhineland: "Great Britain and France, not to mention Russia, Japan and the United States are at work building unprecedentedly great military machines. . . . The Powers, therefore, have no logical objection to Chancellor Hitler's newest move into the Rhineland."[21]

c. *Europe Views the Hitler Coup with Alarm*

Immediately after the news of Hitler's occupation of the Rhineland the French Government favored a call upon the other signatories of Locarno to implement their obligations. After a Cabinet meeting on the evening of March 7 it was decided to follow a more cautious line of action. An appeal would be made to the Council of the League of Nations. If the Council should find that Germany was guilty of a violation of Locarno the signatory powers could rush at once to the assistance of France.[22]

While this procedure was being followed some nations like Russia

[12] March 8, 1936.
[13] March 9, 1936.
[14] March 9, 1936.
[15] March 10, 1936.
[16] March 9, 1936.
[17] March 9, 1936.
[18] The *San Francisco Examiner*, March 11, 1936.
[19] March 8, 1936.
[20] March 9, 1936.
[21] March 8, 1936.
[22] Ambassador Straus to Secretary Hull, Paris, March 7, 1936. 740.0011 Locarno Mutual Guarantee/365, MS, Department of State.

and Czechoslovakia were giving France assurances of support. In Moscow, Ambassador Bullitt talked with Litvinov whose excitement can be read between every line of the dispatch to Secretary Hull:

Litvinov displayed almost violent rage in his comments on Hitler. I asked him if he would not welcome the German-Lithuanian pact of non-aggression proposed by Hitler. . . . He replied that the promise of a dog, liar and blackguard like Hitler was worthless to Lithuania or any other country. . . . I asked Litvinov if he hoped that France would march troops into the Rhineland. He replied that he did not as that would mean immediate war. . . . He said that he was disgusted by the proposal of Hitler to re-enter the League of Nations and even more disgusted by the fact that the British would welcome the re-entry of Germany.[23]

Ambassador Dodd, in Berlin, regarded Hitler's speech before the Reichstag as "impressive," and he noted the "great spontaneous applause" which greeted the statement concerning Germany's willingness to re-enter the League of Nations. Some American newspapermen in Berlin were of the opinion that "Hitler's move may not have been unwelcome to the British particularly as it made such striking concessions with regard to international co-operation with the League."[24]

It was soon evident that Belgium and Italy would take no action that would anger Hitler, and Poland was equally cautious.[25] The British Government held the key to the future. Eden quickly indicated that he was strongly opposed to any "hasty action" and in this course he was supported by a large section of the British press. The *Observer* counseled the British public to keep "cool heads and just hearts." The first need for Britain was "to repair her defenses. The second is to consider Herr Hitler's proposals in a spirit of sympathy and good will." The *Sunday Despatch* made a comment which expressed the sentiment of multitudes of British: "The Locarno Pact is dead. It was a commitment to which the people of Britain never gave their sanction."[26]

The British Foreign Office adhered to the belief that some deal could be made with Hitler that would at least temporarily quiet the situation. It was clear to the American chargé in London that Eden hoped to handle this Rhineland muddle in a "realistic manner." Eventually the

---

[23] Ambassador Bullitt to Secretary Hull, Moscow, March 8, 1936. 740.0011 Locarno Mutual Guarantee/373, MS, Department of State.

[24] Ambassador Dodd to Secretary Hull, Berlin, March 8, 1936. 740.0011 Locarno Mutual Guarantee/375, MS, Department of State.

[25] Ambassador Cudahy to Secretary Hull, Warsaw, March 8, 1936. 740.0011 Locarno Mutual Guarantee/382, MS, Department of State.

[26] Chargé Atherton to Secretary Hull, London, March 8, 1936. 740.0011 Locarno Mutual Guarantee/370, MS, Department of State.

Foreign Office could find some satisfactory formula in which France would have to acquiesce.[27]

In France there was some feeling, "even in official circles," that the Premier had been too abrupt in dealing with Hitler. There was definite skepticism about any prompt British assistance under the terms of the Locarno Pact. It was obvious from Eden's speech in the House of Commons that Britain would go to France's rescue "only in case of invasion of or attack on French territory."[28]

The cautious attitude of the British Foreign Office had its effect upon France. On March 10, Flandin assured Eden that "French policy was one hundred per cent pacific and was not intended to lead to a conflict."[29] But France was eager for British support of economic and financial sanctions against Germany, and Russia was pressing hard for action that would "foster the further encirclement of Germany through the 'most resolute action' by the League Council."[30] When the Baldwin Ministry insisted upon following a conservative course, the French press reflected a growing bitterness "towards Hitler and Baldwin." Tabouis, in L'Oeuvre, claimed that a "strict liaison had been established between London and Berlin and claims to know from an authorized source that it was during Lord Londonderry's trip to Berlin, after King George's funeral, that Hitler made known to him that the military occupation of the demilitarized zone would be accomplished early in March." Ambassador Straus then added this confidential item: "The Embassy has reason to believe that Madame Tabouis' information is in the main correct."[31]

While Belgium and France were showing their deep concern about the final result of the German occupation of the Rhineland, other nations were equally worried over the re-entry of Russia into European politics. In Budapest the Hungarian Foreign Office was particularly concerned about the "construction of air bases in Czechoslovakia especially one near the Hungarian border." Eckhardt told the American Minister that he would soon speak on this subject in Parliament and added: "If Germany should offer to assist Hungary to combat this danger could any Prime Minister take the responsibility of refusing

[27] Chargé Atherton to Secretary Hull, London, March 9, 1936. 740.0011 Locarno Mutual Guarantee/381, Confidential file, MS, Department of State.

[28] Ambassador Straus to Secretary Hull, Paris, March 9, 10, 1936. 740.0011 Locarno Mutual Guarantee/388, 396, MS, Department of State.

[29] Ambassador Straus to Secretary Hull, Paris, March 10, 1936. 740.0011 Locarno Mutual Guarantee/401, MS, Department of State.

[30] Chargé Atherton to Secretary Hull, London, March 11, 1936. 740.0011 Locarno Mutual Guarantee/406, Confidential file, MS, Department of State.

[31] Ambassador Straus to Secretary Hull, Paris, March 11, 1936. 740.0011 Locarno Mutual Guarantee/412, MS, Department of State.

such an offer?" In Hungary it was apparent that the "re-entry of Russia into Europe is generally considered a new Communist menace."[32]

In view of this threatening international situation, Eden anxiously sought some solution that would prove satisfactory. On March 11 he asked the German Ambassador in London if he would not immediately inquire if his Government would be willing to withdraw from the demilitarized zone all but a symbolical number of troops and also to give a promise not to erect any fortifications there during the present emergency. The Nazi Government responded by giving assurances that the number of German troops in the zone would not be increased and would not be stationed near the border.[33] This small concession led the League of Nations on March 14 to invite the German Government to send a representative to sit with the League Council during its consideration of the Rhineland question. Germany accepted this invitation and on March 19, Herr von Ribbentrop presented Germany's case. It was too big a task for a man whose brain was usually on the tip of his tongue. The Council adopted the Franco-Belgian resolution declaring Germany guilty of a breach of the Versailles and Locarno treaties.[34] Inasmuch as the Council made no recommendation for the application of sanctions, this victory for France had little practical value.

Although the British representative on the League Council had voted in favor of the French-Belgian resolution of censure, public opinion in France held to the view that the "tentative London accords" were quite "fragile" and that the importance of the results "so painfully obtained by the French delegation" were only relative.[35] In order to dissipate these French fears Eden made a speech on March 26 in which he stated that Britain would stand behind her obligations under Locarno. This assurance displeased some of the British newspapers like the *Daily Mail* which expressed the opinion that Eden's promises would not "satisfy this country which is fearful of the possibilities of war."[36] In France the language of Eden was criticized as "too moderate and open-minded." The general conclusion "drawn by the majority of the press is that France must henceforth count upon herself only and the strengthening of her own forces."[37]

[32] Minister Montgomery to Secretary Hull, Budapest, March 14, 1936. 740.0011 Locarno Mutual Guarantee/452, MS, Department of State.

[33] Toynbee, *op cit.*, pp. 285–87.

[34] *Ibid.*, p. 304.

[35] Ambassador Straus to Secretary Hull, Paris, March 20, 1936. 740.0011 Locarno Mutual Guarantee/489, MS, Department of State.

[36] Chargé Atherton to Secretary Hull, London, March 27, 1935. 740.0011 Locarno Mutual Guarantee/523, MS, Department of State.

[37] Ambassador Straus to Secretary Hull, Paris, March 27, 1936. 740.0011 Locarno/531, MS, Department of State.

While the League Council was giving careful consideration to the problem of Germany's violation of the Locarno Pact, Hitler ordered a plebiscite to be held on March 29 with reference to German occupation of the Rhineland. The top Nazi leaders worked feverishly to get an overwhelming affirmative vote:

Goebbels spoke seven times in Berlin and vicinity, Goering in the Rhineland, and Hess in Stuttgart, while Hitler made an impassioned address at Frankfort. . . . Hitler's tone is increasingly Messianic, the German people are "His people" and he takes God as his witness and asks to be struck down if he is doing wrong.[38]

Thanks to these strenuous efforts the plebiscite was a one-sided victory for Hitler. Approximately 98.79 per cent of the votes were cast in favor of the march into the Rhineland. This fact gave Hitler "at least the appearance of complete support for his present policy" and it represented a "record vote in his favor and a correspondingly strong springboard for his next international move."[39]

d. *Hitler Offers a New Formula for Peace*

Hitler's next move was the submission to Britain on March 31 of a far-reaching peace plan. In the United States the majority of press comments upon this plan were unfavorable. The *Los Angeles Times* believed that Hitler was trying to "drive a wedge between France and her Allies. She cannot accept these terms without abandoning her Allies to the East."[40] The Rochester *Democrat and Chronicle* was of the opinion that Hitler had assumed "the power of dictating terms of peace to the rest of Europe, and he appears in the phrase of the day, to get away with it."[41] The Salt Lake City *Deseret News* expressed a spirit of pessimism: "If Europe endeavors to check Hitler it will mean war. If Europe fails to do so it will mean unrestrained dictatorship."[42]

[38] Ambassador Dodd to Secretary Hull, Berlin, March 18, 1936. 862.00/3580, MS, Department of State.

[39] Ambassador Dodd to Secretary Hull, Berlin, March 30, 1936. 862.00/3584, MS, Department of State.

[40] April 2, 1936. The main items in Hitler's peace plan of March 31 were: (1) a four-month standstill period during which Germany would not augment her military forces in the Rhineland providing that Belgium and France would not increase their armed forces in the same area; (2) negotiations for an air pact to supplement and reinforce the security agreements; (3) the conclusion of a twenty-five year nonaggression pact between Belgium, France, and Germany; (4) bilateral nonaggression pacts with Germany's neighbors on the east; (5) the assumption by Germany of any special obligations to render military assistance which might arise out of the proposed security treaties; (6) the establishment of a special court of arbitration to which disputes regarding the observance of the various agreements should be referred. *Documents on International Affairs, 1936*, pp. 183–92.

[41] April 3, 1936.

[42] April 2, 1936.

The *New York Times* breathed a spirit of optimism: "Europe has been granted an interval in which the forces of peace may be brought into play with promise of greater success than has for months past seemed possible."[43] The *Springfield Republican* was even more hopeful: "The new proposals, largely based upon the principles of Woodrow Wilson, give a splendid opportunity to force Germany to declare itself for a settled peace on all fronts." Now that the immediate crisis has been passed it was up to the "other Powers and especially for the Locarno group to decide whether they will meet Hitler halfway and attempt to give Europe more security and good will than the present generation has known."[44]

The religious press appeared to view the Rhineland crisis with an open mind. *America* thought it was "hard to condemn the desire of the German people to hold the Rhineland as their own."[45] The *Christian Century* expressed similar sentiments. Versailles was fundamentally wrong. Permanent peace could not be built "upon the theory that one of the [nations of Europe] occupies a lower status and enjoys a smaller degree of independence than any of the others."[46] The *Catholic World*, after an extended critique of Versailles, turned its guns upon Hitler who was denounced as a "cold-blooded, calculating murderer."[47]

e. *Eden Turns with Each New Diplomatic Breeze*

The French Government would have agreed with the *Catholic World* concerning Hitler and it was convinced that it would do no good to give his proposals any serious consideration. On April 6 the French Cabinet approved two documents that had been drafted by the Foreign Office. They constituted a detailed critique of the Hitler program. After presenting a long bill of indictment they finally produced the outline of a plan that would make the League of Nations more effective in preserving the peace of Europe.[48]

On April 8 the Committee of Thirteen met at Geneva to consider the Italo-Ethiopian dispute. The French members of the committee took this occasion to present the French case with regard to the Rhineland problem and they insisted that all efforts to conciliate Germany should cease. Eden refused to accept the thesis that negotiations with Hitler had broken down, and he secured approval of the idea that the British Government should inquire "what was the meaning attached by the German Government to the bilateral treaties which it proposed and

43 April 2, 1936.
44 April 3, 1936.
45 April 4, 1936.

46 March 18, 1936.
47 May 1936, p. 130.
48 London *Times,* April 9, 1936.

how these treaties would fall into the framework of collective security."[49]

On April 15, Ambassador Straus informed Secretary Hull that the French Government did not know the exact form in which the British inquiries would be put to the German Government but he supposed that he would soon receive the text of the document. He had learned that the British Foreign Office had received assurances "in principle" from Germany regarding the "non-fortification of the Rhineland during the proposed four-month period of negotiations."[50]

From London, Ambassador Bingham made a brief report on the indecision that marked the efforts to settle the Rhineland deadlock:

During the course of my interview with the Under-Secretary of State this afternoon he . . . said that in view of the insistent demand of the French that the German forces should withdraw from the heretofore demilitarized zone of the Rhineland, it had been necessary to make such concessions to the French Government as would induce them to arrive at a position where negotiations were possible. It was on this basis that conversations among the general staffs were agreed to by the British Government. As a result the French had moved from an extreme position to a middle ground where negotiations were possible. . . . The German Government apparently felt that they had won a great success and had assumed a completely recalcitrant . . . position. [If Hitler would not recede from this stand] the negotiations had no hope of success.[51]

In Berlin, Ferdinand L. Mayer, the American chargé d'affaires, had a talk with the French Ambassador and found him "quite pessimistic" about arriving at a satisfactory settlement of the Rhineland question.[52] This pessimism was well founded. On May 7 the British Ambassador in Berlin submitted to the Foreign Office a detailed questionnaire which reflected a strong inclination towards the views expressed in the French memorandum of April 6.[53] Eden knew very well that Hitler was not prepared to give a pledge to respect all the remaining operative clauses of the Treaty of Versailles. He was also aware of the fact that the German Foreign Office would not agree to any real limitation of air power and would refuse to enter into a nonaggression pact with Soviet Russia. British policy had suddenly changed from conciliation to challenge.

[49] Toynbee, op. cit., p. 334.

[50] Ambassador Straus to Secretary Hull, Paris, April 15, 1936. 765.84/4101, MS, Department of State.

[51] Ambassador Bingham to Secretary Hull, London, April 15, 1936. 765.84/4115, MS, Department of State.

[52] Chargé Mayer to Secretary Hull, Berlin, April 22, 1936. 765.84/4176, MS, Department of State.

[53] Documents on International Affairs, 1936, pp. 211–16.

There was no expectation that this challenge would soon be answered.

The attitude of the German Foreign Office towards Eden's vacillations was clearly revealed in a conversation between Ambassador Bullitt and von Neurath, the Minister for Foreign Affairs. He assured Bullitt that "the deepest desire of Hitler was to come to a real understanding with France," but every attempt he or Hitler had made to draw closer to the French had "resulted in either no reply from France or a rebuff." With regard to England he said that he regretted

greatly that no really friendly contact had been established between the German and British Governments. I asked him if he meant that he did not talk and could not talk with Eden or the British Ambassador in Berlin as simply and directly as he was talking to me. He replied that he absolutely could not and that it was totally impossible. . . . He went on to say that the entire matter of the British note of inquiry had been mishandled grossly by the British Foreign Office. He said that Sir Eric Phipps had brought him the note with the request to keep its contents absolutely secret. . . . He [von Neurath] said that to his utter astonishment Sir Eric Phipps had then telephoned to him and said that he regretted greatly to inform him that there had been a leak as to the contents of the note and that it would be essential for the British Government to publish it the following morning.

Eden's reversal of policy towards Germany came in the face of certain knowledge that German military strength was the main barrier that held back the tide of bolshevism that constantly threatened to inundate Europe. In this regard the conversation between Bullitt and von Neurath assumes additional importance:

We discussed relations between Germany and the Soviet Government. Von Neurath said that he considered the hostility between Germany and the Soviet Union absolutely irremovable. He asserted that the Soviet Union believed that Nazi Germany was the one obstacle to the conquest of Europe by Communism. This, incidentally, is the view of the Soviet Government.[54]

The German Foreign Office did not bother about making a formal reply to the British memorandum, and Prime Minister van Zeeland, of Belgium, confided to Ambassador Bullitt that he "regarded the future most pessimistically."[55] In order to banish this pessimism, representatives of Belgium, Britain, and France met at London on July 23 and issued a communiqué setting forth their views. The three powers were

[54] Ambassador Bullitt to Secretary Hull, May 18, 1936. 740.00/52, *Strictly Confidential*, MS, Department of State.

[55] Ambassador Bullitt to Secretary Hull, Brussels, May 20, 1936. 740.00/47, *Confidential file*, MS, Department of State.

now ready to meet Germany in conference as soon as possible in order to endeavor to find some formula that would replace Locarno. Germany did not respond to this overture, so the King of Belgium on October 14 made a speech to his Cabinet which clarified the situation as far as his country was concerned. He was anxious for Belgium to return to her prewar status of guaranteed neutrality. Her policy should "aim resolutely at putting us outside the conflicts of our neighbours."[56] Locarno was dead beyond any hope of revival.

Over the ashes of Locarno hovered the shadow of bolshevism. It carried increasing consternation to European minds because of the collapse of collective security. To Ambassador Dodd, in Berlin, this collapse was largely the fault of France:

Under French leadership the League itself became partisan and only emphasized the duration of the dictated peace of Versailles and divided Europe into opposed camps. Germany's refusal in March, 1935 longer to endure this situation shattered the delicately poised artificiality and thereby . . . all of Europe was thrown into a ferment and a scramble for adjustment. . . .

Heretofore the Bolshevik menace in Europe has been typified by the subterranean activities of the Third International rather than by Russian nationalistic militarism. Latterly, however, . . . there seems to have been a significant and aggressive change in Russian sponsorship of World Revolution. We incline to feel that this may have reached a point where the prospect for this revolution, as far as Europe is concerned, . . . has persuaded Stalin and his advisers of the desirability of coming out into the open and aggressively combining Russian militant imperialism with Russian Communism. . . . Through the Franco-Soviet alliance, through the apprehensions felt in many quarters in Europe over Germany's renaissance, and through Russia's adroit diplomatic maneuvers, the Soviets have been able to pose as the saviour to those States in Europe most fearful of the rebirth of a powerful Germany.[57]

f. *Hitler and Mussolini Reach an Important Accord*

In order to meet this mounting menace of communism and at the same time strengthen their position in Europe, Hitler and Mussolini through the summer of 1936 moved towards an accord. The revolution in Spain and the fateful Austro-German Agreement of the same month, accelerated this movement. On July 25, Hitler closed the German Legation in Addis Ababa thereby announcing his readiness to recognize the Italian conquest of Ethiopia.[58]

[56] Toynbee, *op. cit.,* pp. 344–57.
[57] Ambassador Dodd to Secretary Hull, Berlin, September 3, 1936. 740.00/59, *Confidential file,* MS, Department of State.
[58] Elizabeth Wiskemann, *The Rome-Berlin Axis* (New York, 1949), pp. 57–65.

The visit of Lloyd George to Berchtesgaden during the summer of 1936 slightly delayed the German drift towards Italy. For a brief period Hitler revived his interest in a real rapprochement with Britain. Conversations with Lloyd George confirmed his belief in the rising power of Germany and led him to discount the possibility of American intervention in a second world war.[59] But the German Foreign Office was suspicious of Eden who never seemed to know just what his attitude towards Nazi Germany should be.

With London hesitant about improving relations with Hitler, Rome showed a spirit of friendship which led the Foreign Office to send Hans Frank to survey the situation. Frank's visit to Rome was followed by Ciano's trip to Berlin. In his portfolio Ciano carried two documents that had fallen into Mussolini's hands. When Ciano showed Hitler a telegram from Sir Eric Phipps to the British Foreign Office in which the German Government was criticized as one of "dangerous adventurers," Hitler flew into the expected rage. He was eager for a pact with Italy against the "inept creatures" who formulated British foreign policy.[60]

In America the Hitler-Mussolini Pact evoked little comment. The Baltimore *Sun* feared that the "understanding" between Ciano and Hitler had "far-reaching significance for it reveals that the two Fascist dictators have agreed upon a common plan of action in their future diplomatic relations with the other Western European Powers."[61] The Richmond *Times-Dispatch* looked upon the pact as an "exceedingly ominous" portent for the future,[62] but the *Christian Science Monitor* hoped that "sound economic adjustments between these two countries might improve rather than endanger the peace of Europe."[63]

g. *Versailles Undergoes Another Attack*

Shortly after the announcement of the Hitler-Ciano Pact, Hitler produced another tremor throughout Europe by repudiating those clauses in the Treaty of Versailles which placed important German waterways under the control of an international commission.[64] The main question that now plagued American minds was whether he would soon attack the territorial clauses in the dictated pact of Versailles. The *Los Angeles Times* feared that a "war of revenge at Germany's earliest opportunity

[59] De Witt C. Poole, "Light on Nazi Foreign Policy," *Foreign Affairs*, XXV (1946), 130–54.

[60] Wiskemann, *op. cit.*, pp. 66–67.

[61] October 28, 1936.

[62] October 27, 1936.

[63] October 27, 1936.

[64] *Documents on International Affairs, 1936*, pp. 283–84.

is now almost inevitable,"[65] and the *Chicago Daily News* was deeply concerned over the effects of the Nazi unilateral denunciation of important treaties.[66] The *Springfield Republican* expressed a very different viewpoint. The signatories to the Treaty of Versailles should have remedied the situation long ago and thus prevented the development of the fierce nationalism that was "splitting Europe into badly damaged fragments."[67] The *Providence Journal* thought that the whole difficulty stemmed back to the "short-sighted statesmanship" that produced the "impractical" Treaty of Versailles.[68]

h. *Germany and Italy Recognize Franco*

When Hitler and Mussolini recognized the Franco Government (November 18) the Portland *Morning Oregonian* remarked that the "situation in Europe is daily more dangerous."[69] The *Birmingham News* was apprehensive that Russia would soon take some action that would bring on a "general war."[70] The *Atlanta Constitution* took a more hopeful view: "It is more probable that the strengthened alignment against Communism will act as a powerful deterrent against aggressive steps by Russia."[71]

The Rochester *Democrat and Chronicle* was able to distill some sunshine from the grey wash of the news from Europe: "There are too many points of rivalry between Italy and Germany to permit a real military alliance between them. Neither can get along without the co-operation of France and Britain. Together, however, they may help to bring about a four power pact that will serve the interests of all."[72]

i. *The German-Japanese Anti-Comintern Pact, November 25, 1936*

The Baltimore *Sun* was gravely concerned about the implications of the Anti-Comintern Pact: "There is no use in denying that most of the world Powers are rushing pell-mell towards war."[73] The *Cleveland Plain Dealer* feared that the pact might become "the opening wedge of the next war."[74]

The *Des Moines Register* believed that the new German-Japanese treaty was a distinct threat to the historic American position in the Far East: "Shall we abandon, lock, stock and barrel our whole basic policy

[65] November 17, 1936.
[66] November 17, 1936.
[67] November 17, 1936.
[68] November 17, 1936.

[69] November 20, 1936.
[70] November 19, 1936.
[71] November 21, 1936.
[72] November 20, 1936.

[73] November 19, 1936. The Anti-Comintern Pact was a consultative agreement with reference to measures that might be necessary as a safeguard against the intrigues of the Communist Third International. Toynbee, *op. cit.*, pp. 384ff.

[74] November 23, 1936.

as to the far side of the Pacific, or shall we . . . continue to play the balance of power game in the far Pacific?"[75]

The business press had few comments to make on this accord between Germany and Japan, but *Barron's* thought that its purpose was evident: "While the German-Japanese understanding is aimed at Communism and ostensibly has nothing to do with Soviet Russia as a country, the mask is so obviously thin as to be almost deliberately transparent. In effect, these countries are saying to the Spanish Leftists and to the world: 'We now show our strength. If any country wishes to interfere with our plans, that country must take the consequences!' "[76]

j. *Europe Tries to Replace Locarno*

The increase in German military strength through the creation of accords with Italy and Japan aroused great concern in the minds of many European statesmen. Georges Bonnet had a conversation with Ambassador Bullitt during which he stressed the importance of a "reconciliation between France and Germany." He felt that an effort should be made to achieve that objective but he was certain that the "blessing of the United States would be necessary." Bullitt hastened to assure him that any effort to "reach such a reconciliation would have the full benediction of the United States."

Later that afternoon the German Ambassador called at the American Embassy in Paris and confided to Bullitt that he had been instructed by Ribbentrop to discuss the matter of effecting a "full understanding" between France and Germany. His Government "ardently desired" such an understanding and wished to know if Bullitt could propose some steps towards that end. Bullitt assured the ambassador that the French Government "desired intensely to reach an understanding with Germany." The best way to insure this objective would be "through discreet conversations" between representatives of the two countries. The ambassador then said that he had

initiated such conversations by bringing Schacht to Paris; that Schacht's conversation with Blum had been most promising but that the French had then conferred with the British and because of British opposition had not followed up the initiative of Schacht. He then pointed out that England, the Soviet Union and Italy were all opposed to Franco-German reconciliation and that the United States was the only Great Power in the Western world which would regard such reconciliation favorably. I told him that our Government would certainly favor such reconciliation. . . . I asked him what would be the attitude of the German Government if Delbos would say to him that France

[75] November 27, 1936.   [76] November 23, 1936.

would like to enter into such a global negotiation. He replied that the German Government would accept with enthusiasm.[77]

On this same afternoon Bonnet discussed with Bullitt the possibility of "creating a close collaboration between France, England and the United States." The three great democracies should first agree upon some plan for world peace and then offer it to Germany. If Germany could be convinced that the great democracies were standing shoulder to shoulder she would not dare attack in the next eighteen months. Bullitt bluntly informed Bonnet that he felt that there

was not the slightest chance that the United States would participate. I explained to him that while we were deeply and sincerely interested in the preservation of peace, not only in the Western Hemisphere but also in Europe and the Far East, there were certain absolute limits beyond which we could not go. He and all other French statesmen must realize that the United States would not send troops, warships and money to Europe again to support France and England. He should also realize that we would not become involved in the political difficulties of Europe.[78]

But despite Bullitt's blunt words the French statesmen continued to place before him "different variations of a plan for the settlement of the difficulties of Europe." Great international corporations should be established "with capital drawn chiefly from England, France and the United States but with representation on the board of all the leading nations of the world." These corporations would be world clearing houses for the exchange of raw materials for manufactured goods. Coupled with this proposal, which was "designed essentially to relieve Germany of her present economic difficulties, would be a proposal for limitation of armaments." French statesmen hoped that President Roosevelt would "take the lead in making a proposal of this sort."[79]

Although Bullitt had warned the French Foreign Office that the President would not take the initiative in any search for a formula that would insure the peace of Europe, there was still hope in Paris that America would abandon her policy of isolation and assume the burdens of leadership. Dr. Schacht had an important conversation with Ambassador Davies who was passing through Berlin en route to Moscow. He stated that the "present condition of the German people was intolerable" and that he had been authorized to submit to England and

[77] Ambassador Bullitt to Secretary Hull, Paris, December 16, 1936. 751.62/380, *Confidential file*, MS, Department of State.

[78] Ambassador Bullitt to Secretary Hull, Paris, December 16, 1936. 800.51 W89 France/1065, *Confidential file*, MS, Department of State.

[79] Ambassador Bullitt to Secretary Hull, Paris, January 12, 1937. 751.62/386, *Confidential file*, MS, Department of State.

France significant proposals that might save the situation.[80] He had found Prime Minister Blum "surprisingly agreeable," but England had "flatly rejected" the proposals and had refused even to have informal discussions on the subject. Schacht thought the only way out of the existing dead-end street was for President Roosevelt to call an international conference that would discuss the abolition of the numerous barriers to world trade.[81]

Davies was slightly more encouraging than Bullitt. He told Schacht that the President would be indisposed to "become entangled in these matters unless there was some assurance of success." It would, in the meantime, be wise for German leaders to tone down the aggressive spirit that was so manifest in the recent speeches at Nürnberg.

While Schacht in Berlin was putting out peace feelers, Blum in Paris was doing the same thing. He told Bullitt that the French Ambassador had just reported a "most amicable conversation" with the German Foreign Minister who had been profuse "in his assertions that Germany desired nothing but peace." Blum agreed with von Neurath's opinion that any "real conciliation between France and Germany must be prefaced by a settlement of the Spanish conflict." When this was effected there could then be conversations that would "explore the possibilities" of economic co-operation on a large scale.[82]

It was apparent that Blum was in favor of definite concessions to Germany in the hope of building some bridge of understanding between France and the Nazi Government. This inclination towards appeasement was abruptly halted by Anthony Eden who made a visit to Paris for the purpose of giving Blum some blunt advice.[83]

On January 19, Eden made a speech in the House of Commons in which he stressed the opinion that "economic collaboration and political appeasement must go hand in hand." He then referred to Germany as a nation that had "exalted race and nationalism into a creed which is practised with the same fervour as it is preached. All the world is asking . . . whither these doctrines are to lead Germany, whither they are to lead all of us?"[84]

[80] These proposals were: (1) a plan to guarantee European peace; (2) a guarantee of existing European international boundaries; (3) a plan to reduce armaments; (4) the establishment of a new and workable League of Nations; (5) the cession to Germany of colonies that would provide an outlet for surplus population and would be a source of foodstuffs, fats, and raw materials.

[81] Ambassador Davies to Secretary Hull and President Roosevelt, Moscow, January 20, 1937. 740.00/100, *Confidential file*, MS, Department of State.

[82] Ambassador Bullitt to Secretary Hull, Paris, January 20, 1937. 740.00/99, *Confidential file*, MS, Department of State.

[83] Minister Wilson to Secretary Hull, Geneva, January 25, 1937. 740.00/104, *Confidential file*, MS, Department of State.

[84] Toynbee, *op. cit.*, p. 30.

On January 24, Prime Minister Blum, in a speech at Lyons, underlined the British thesis that peace in Europe was indivisible. It would not be preserved by a series of bilateral treaties. No "engagements limited to France would guarantee the security of France."[85]

k. *Hitler's Soft Answers Stir New Hope in Europe*

On January 30, 1937, Chancellor Hitler gave his answer to the speeches of Eden and Blum. First he denounced the "war guilt" clauses of the Treaty of Versailles. Next he expressed a desire for co-operation with other nations and cited as proof of this statement the German agreements with Austria, Italy, Japan, and Poland. Assurances were given of a disposition to guarantee the neutrality of Belgium and Holland. He once more asserted that the Nazi Government had no quarrel with France. His sharp shafts were feathered for only one nation—Soviet Russia. In this regard he referred to the untenability of the British thesis that European peace was indivisible. In fact Europe was divided into two camps and this division had been brought about by the proclamation of the bolshevist doctrine, the chief feature of which is to enforce itself on all peoples.[86] Peace could be preserved only by preparation against the Red menace.

In America about one half the newspapers received Hitler's words with suspicion as to his underlying motives. The *Omaha World-Herald* saw no promise of peace in the speech of January 30: "Europe must wait for more pacific assurances from Germany's leader."[87] The Rochester *Democrat and Chronicle* thought that the "conditions on which Hitler would deal with other nations are impossible unless the world is willing to carry civilization back a thousand years."[88] The *Memphis Commercial Appeal* was certain that Hitler's attack upon Russia was for the purpose of "inflaming the French conservative and peasant opposition to the Pink and Red Blum Government."[89] The *San Francisco Chronicle* attacked Hitler as "still unregenerate." He had "offered to join any sort of a peace movement in Europe that left Russia out. So far, so bad. There can be no peace in Europe unless it includes everybody."[90]

Some American newspapers saw Hitler as a herald of peace. The *Boston Evening Transcript* regarded the speech of January 30 as "re-

---

[85] *Ibid.*, p. 31.
[86] *The Speeches of Adolf Hitler*, ed. and tr. Norman H. Baynes (London, 1942), II, 1334–47.
[87] February 3, 1937.
[88] February 2, 1937.
[89] February 2, 1937.
[90] February 1, 1937.

assuring." What the "Fuehrer said was conciliatory in tone."[91] The *St. Louis Post-Dispatch* insisted that it was an "amiable Hitler the Reichstag listened to,"[92] while the *Des Moines Register* called attention to his "generally conciliatory tone."[93] The *Brooklyn Daily Eagle* made similar comments: "He [Hitler] was surprisingly conciliatory on all of those matters which might add to the tension in Europe."[94]

Louis Einstein, in London, believed that Hitler's speech was "principally designed to influence British opinion towards exercising a greater forbearance in regard to future German expansion eastward."[95] In Paris, Prime Minister Blum told Bullitt that he had heard from the French Ambassador in Berlin to the effect that Hitler had prepared his speech under the influence of Neurath and Schacht but that Göring on his return from Italy had persuaded the Führer "to make it much less positive and conciliatory than the first draft."[96] Hugh Wilson, in Bern, thought that he saw in Hitler's speech some evidence of a "slow evolution in favor of a better understanding with his neighbors. This may eventually make possible a meeting point although I do not believe that the meeting point is yet reached whether in respect to limitation of armaments, economic co-operation or colonial aspirations."[97]

It was obvious to Ambassador Davies that the Soviet Government was concerned about the effect of Hitler's speech upon the British and French governments. Litvinov complained to Davies that he "failed to understand why England and France were continually making overtures to Hitler. . . . Hitler's policy was still that outlined in his book *Mein Kampf* and he continued to be dominated by a lust for conquest." After listening to Litvinov's acidulous remarks, Davies gained the impression that the Russian Foreign Office was "apprehensive lest there should be some composition of differences between France, Great Britain and Germany."[98]

1. *France Is Hopeful of American Support*

The French Foreign Office thought there might be some basis for this Russian fear that Britain, France, and Germany would compose all their

---

91 February 1, 1937.   93 January 31, 1937.
92 February 1, 1937.   94 January 31, 1937.

95 Louis Einstein to Secretary Hull, London, February 2, 1937. 862.002 Hitler/88, MS, Department of State.

96 Ambassador Bullitt to Secretary Hull, Paris, February 3, 1937. 751.62/398, *Confidential file,* MS, Department of State.

97 Minister Wilson to Secretary Hull, Bern, February 4, 1937. 740.00/115, *Confidential file,* MS, Department of State.

98 Ambassador Davies to Secretary Hull, Moscow, February 5, 1937. 740.00/114, *Confidential file,* MS, Department of State.

difficulties. Since January, the Nazi Government had "definitely in-augurated a more moderate policy." The French Ambassador in Berlin had just sent word that "Schacht and the businessmen of Germany once more had rather more influence with Hitler than the leaders of the Nazi party." Delbos, the French Foreign Minister, thought this in-formation so significant that he was "sending the experts of the Min-istry of Commerce to Berlin tomorrow to conduct the negotiations for the renewal of the Franco-German Treaty of Commerce. He had given them orders to act with the greatest liberality."

One important barrier to a Franco-German accord was the opposi-tion of the British Foreign Office. Delbos was certain that Eden was a "good European and would really like to see France and Germany get together. Unfortunately, however, Eden often did not control British foreign policy. The ground was cut from under him by other members of the British Cabinet and even by the permanent officials of the British Foreign Office. He believed that the British would pretend to desire Franco-German reconciliation but would continue to follow their old policy of keeping France and Germany hostile to each other though not at war."[99]

This official French suspicion of Britain did not extend to the United States. In America the working of the radical leaven in France was viewed with sympathetic understanding. Prime Minister Blum confided to Bullitt that he wished to extend his "most profound thanks" to Presi-dent Roosevelt for the support he was giving to the "forces of democ-racy in France." America, alone of the great powers, was "genuinely interested in the same policies" that Blum was "trying to put through." The British Government was conservative and it "disapproved highly" of Blum's radical "domestic policy." Moreover, the British Foreign Office was always "reluctant to see France and Germany begin to ap-proach each other." It was evident, said Blum, that France counted greatly upon "American good will for the preservation of peace in Europe."[100]

No matter how strongly Bullitt admonished French statesmen not to expect American assistance in the event of a European war, Blum and the Foreign Office continued to cherish a hope that President Roose-velt would soon take an active role in world affairs. The President was loath to disappoint those hopes.

99 Ambassador Bullitt to Secretary Hull, Paris, February 20, 1937. 740.00/117, *Confidential file*, MS, Department of State.

100 Ambassador Bullitt to Secretary Hull, Paris, February 23, 1937. 740.00/118, *Confidential file*, MS, Department of State.

XIV

The Shadow of Dictatorship Begins to
Darken the American Landscape

a. *European Statesmen Fumble for a Peace Formula*

WHEN it became apparent to British and French statesmen that President Roosevelt would make no effort to point a path to peace they merely continued their policy of drifting towards the rim of the abyss. Eden mournfully confided to Ambassador Bingham that he "saw little prospect of a western Locarno pact in the near future although he felt such a pact necessary as a beginning towards restoring any bases of confidence in Europe." The crux of the whole European situation was "Germany." The Nazi Foreign Office kept digging up the old issue of colonies which Britain and France had hoped was safely buried in the clauses of the Treaty of Versailles. Ribbentrop had recently stressed the importance of concessions in this regard, but Eden had abruptly informed him that the "British position was unchanged." This curt reply had drawn from Ribbentrop the rejoinder that such news "would be badly received in his country and would be a strong influence against any co-operation towards peace by Germany."[1]

French statesmen did not follow this policy of drift with the calm demeanor affected by Anthony Eden, and they kept trying to pry out of the Department of State some slight assurance of American support. On March 18 the French Ambassador in Washington (Georges Bonnet) had a long conversation with Secretary Hull, during the course of which he remarked that he would be happy to learn of any plans the American Government had in mind relative to a peaceful settlement of the "chief international problems" which were clamoring for a prompt solution. Hull answered this provocative thrust by recourse to his usual platitudes. The American Government was "keenly aware of the numerous problems of an international character which in many respects were now growing more acute and dangerous." It should be kept in mind, however, that any "definite, concrete steps" which the President had in mind towards the solution of these problems were the President's own business and the Secretary of State could not disclose the slightest information concerning them. The ambassador felt

[1] Ambassador Bingham to Secretary Hull, London, March 11, 1937. 740.00/125, *Confidential file*, MS, Department of State.

that he had been firmly put in his place, so he merely murmured that he would continue to look for "opportunities to co-operate" with the Department of State, and the conversation closed with the usual amenities of diplomatic discourse.[2]

But these amenities did not hide the fear that was always present in British and French hearts with reference to the rising power of Germany. In London the Foreign Office still regarded the Nazi Government as the "greatest threat to European peace." It was this fact that made Britain ready to appease Italy by refusing to take any steps that would effectively check Italian intervention in the Spanish Civil War.[3]

This Spanish factor in the international equation seemed particularly significant to Anthony Eden who suddenly informed Norman Davis that the best way to arrive at a satisfactory answer was for the United States "to take the lead or act as mediator." Davis immediately replied that President Roosevelt "had no desire or intention of interjecting himself in the European political situation." It would be futile to "attempt anything until Europe makes up its mind that it wants peace and until the British . . . are prepared to get behind any efforts that may be made by anyone to achieve such a result." The British Government should at once take steps in the direction of close "economic collaboration" with the United States. When Eden expressed the view that Chamberlain wished to achieve this objective, Davis dryly remarked that he hoped British statesmen would not wait "until they missed the boat."[4]

The uneasiness in British and French minds caused by the Spanish Civil War was aggravated by the implications that lay underneath the Belgian situation. The Belgian ambassadors in London and Paris had made it crystal clear that their Government was determined "not to permit her soil to become the battleground of the next war; not to permit either the foot of a German, British or French soldier to be placed on her soil." This neutral position had profoundly disturbed the Polish Foreign Office which quickly informed France that the Franco-Polish alliance was now "virtually useless."

The position of Czechoslovakia was also adversely affected by this sudden change in the European diplomatic picture. When Bullitt asked Léger, in the Foreign Office, about possible French aid to the Czechs in case of need, he received the fantastic answer that French troops "would

[2] Memorandum of a conversation between Secretary Hull and the French Ambassador (Georges Bonnet), March 18, 1937. 500. A 19/70, MS, Department of State.

[3] Ambassador Bingham to Secretary Hull, London, March 31, 1937. 740.00/134, MS, Department of State.

[4] Norman H. Davis to Secretary Hull, London, April 10, 1937. 740.00/143, *Confidential file*, MS, Department of State.

pass through Roumania and Yugoslavia." At the same time Bullitt learned from another source that Russia would not "support Czechoslovakia in case of a German attack" upon that country.[5]

In summing up the situation in Europe, Bullitt remarked that it was generally felt that there would "probably be no war before next spring but that during that period French influence will diminish and German influence will increase throughout Central and Eastern Europe."[6]

As an offset to this increasing German influence on the Continent, some statesmen, like Prime Minister van Zeeland, of Belgium, believed that British power was constantly growing to a point where, in a few years, Great Britain would "very nearly control the trend of international affairs." But the British were now unfortunately retreating within the economic walls of their empire and subjecting other nations to increasing tariff restrictions. For this reason van Zeeland had determined to go on a mission to the United States in an effort to get President Roosevelt to take some effective action in breaking down some of the barriers to world trade. If America would take the lead in this matter, Britain would be compelled to follow her.

Bullitt then warned van Zeeland that the United States would not make "any political commitments and that it was almost inconceivable that European countries would be allowed to float loans in the United States." But despite these pointed admonitions by Bullitt, van Zeeland still hoped that during some "utterly frank conversations" with President Roosevelt and Secretary Hull some new avenue to unrestricted world trade could be opened.[7]

b. *Belgium Breaks Her Bonds with Britain and France*

The announcement of the Belgian Government that it would follow a policy of neutrality in the event of a new European war fell like a bombshell in many Foreign Offices. Czechoslovakia, France, and Poland immediately began to resurvey the situation. On April 30, Bullitt lunched with Delbos and Sir Eric Phipps, who had recently been transferred from Berlin to Paris. Delbos frankly admitted that the ability of France to "come to the assistance of Czechoslovakia . . . had been diminished

[5] Bullitt learned that Coulondre, the French Ambassador at Moscow, and a French general had been "talking recently with Litvinov and the French general had asked Litvinov pointblank: 'If Germany attacks Czechoslovakia will you send support to Czechoslovakia?' Litvinov had replied–'No.' . . . Coulondre said that in his opinion the 'no' was decisive and sincere."

[6] Ambassador Bullitt to Secretary Hull, Paris, April 22, 1937. 740.00/149, *Confidential file*, MS, Department of State.

[7] Ambassador Bullitt to Secretary Hull, Paris, April 29, 1937. 740.00/153, MS, Department of State.

greatly by the new policy of Belgium." In order to give the Czechs adequate support it would now be necessary for the British Government
to make it "clear that in case of a German attack on Czechoslovakia"
she would rush at once to her assistance. The Czech Foreign Office remembered with gratitude the statement of Britain that she was "not
disinterested" in the "fate of Czechoslovakia." But Delbos considered
this statement "insufficient," and he urged Phipps to secure from his
Government a "definite promise to support Czechoslovakia." The British Ambassador quickly replied that his Government "could not make
any such promise in advance." The only formula either Britain or
France could rely upon was for both powers to "show their teeth to
Germany and have behind them the benevolent neutrality of the United
States."[8]

On the same afternoon (April 30) Bullitt had an intimate conversation with Sir Eric Phipps who exhibited a deep-seated hostility towards
Germany. He was particularly annoyed to find in Paris some statesmen
who still believed "that it might be possible for France to come to terms
with Germany." He considered such a rapprochement "totally impossible." After listening to the acrid remarks of Phipps, Bullitt came to
the conclusion that the British Ambassador had been instructed "to
prevent the French from having any tête-à-tête conversations with Germany; that the policy of Great Britain is still to keep the Continent of
Europe divided . . . and that little or nothing is to be expected from
Great Britain in the way of support of the policy of reduction of barriers to international commerce and restoration of the economic life of
the world."[9]

This refusal of Britain to take any real step that would insure the
maintenance of the political structure of Europe was deeply discouraging to Delbos, the French Foreign Minister. He had suggested to the
governments of Austria, Czechoslovakia, Romania, and Yugoslavia to
"take a more decided attitude of opposition to Germany," but they had
replied that it was first necessary to secure from Britain definite promises of support. When Phipps had been sounded out in this regard he
had made it entirely clear that "Great Britain would not guarantee
either Czechoslovakia or Austria to say nothing of Roumania." Phipps
had also revealed that Britain would do nothing towards making van
Zeeland's mission to the United States a success.

When Delbos inquired whether "Britain was prepared as France
was prepared to make concessions to Germany on the colonial field,"
Sir Eric had tersely answered that France "might do what she pleased

8 Ambassador Bullitt to Secretary Hull, Paris, April 30, 1937. 740.00/156, *Confidential file*, MS, Department of State.
   9 Ambassador Bullitt to Secretary Hull, Paris, April 30, 1937. 740.00/158, *Confidential file*, MS, Department of State.

but Great Britain would not give Germany one inch of the territory of the British Empire including mandated territory."

With reference to Austria, Delbos confided to Bullitt that France could make no promise of aid in the event of invasion. Mussolini had made it "clear to Schuschnigg that he would do nothing to keep Austria from falling into Germany's hands." Delbos believed that Schuschnigg would hold out "to the end" against absorption by Germany because he knew that the Pope was doing everything he could not only to support Schuschnigg "against the Nazis" but to influence him to maintain Austrian independence.

Delbos concluded his conversation with an assurance to Bullitt that "if Germany should attack Czechoslovakia, France would immediately declare war on Germany," but his voice carried such a note of irresolution that Bullitt suspected that after Delbos paid his visit to Brussels the "decision of the French Government to go to war on behalf of Czechoslovakia may weaken." It should be obvious to most statesmen that France "could take a strong position only if she should have the absolute support in England."[10]

By the middle of May it was obvious that the search for a new agreement that would replace Locarno had been entirely fruitless. Prime Minister Blum sorrowfully admitted that the "net result of all the recent political conversations in London and Paris would be very small." Litvinov had given assurances that if Germany should attack Czechoslovakia, and *if* France should go to war with Germany to defend the Czechs, the Soviet Union "would make war on Germany at once." But Bullitt pointed out that the aid of Russia could not be very effective in view of the fact that "Soviet planes and armies could not cross Poland or Roumania."

Blum admitted that Hitler had the "political initiative on the Continent of Europe at the moment and he did not see any way to take this initiative out of the hands of Germany." The "single chance of preserving the peace in Europe" would be through the creation of a close entente between England, France, and Russia. When Bullitt expressed the opinion that it would not be easy to convince the British Government to have intimate relations with Soviet Russia, "especially in view of the recent wholesale exilings and shootings," Blum ruefully remarked that there was no alternative. Litvinov had asked him to do his "utmost to bring about a rapprochement between England and the Soviet Union," and under the circumstances he would work towards that end.[11]

[10] Ambassador Bullitt to Secretary Hull, Paris, May 6, 1937. 740.00/164, MS, Department of State.

[11] Ambassador Bullitt to Secretary Hull, Paris, May 10, 1937. 740.00/178, *Confidential file,* MS, Department of State.

c. *Mayor La Guardia Hurls a Verbal Bomb at Hitler*

While European statesmen were groping through the dusk that was settling over the Continent, American relations with Germany were disturbed as a result of some vituperation that Mayor La Guardia hurled at Hitler. On March 3, in an address before the women's division of the American Jewish Congress, La Guardia proposed that the 1939 World's Fair in New York should feature a temple dedicated to religious freedom: "But within that temple I'd have a Chamber of Horrors and as a climax I'd have a figure in it of that brown-shirted fanatic who is now menacing the peace of the world."[12]

Joseph Goebbels countered with the Bowery invective of which he was such a master. After calling La Guardia a ruffian and a gangster, he then opened a barrage against the Roosevelt Administration: "One would think . . . the White House . . . would have sufficient power to curb procurers. . . . It seems, however, that the men of the government are afraid of New York's underworld guns, which obey the chief gangster master as he whistles. They let the Jewish lout utter his abuses as suggested to his dirty mind."[13]

A majority of American newspapers criticized the La Guardia attack upon Hitler as an example of bad taste on the part of an important municipal official. The *Milwaukee Journal* thought that "all decent sentiment in the nation" would regret the mayor's words.[14] The *Brooklyn Daily Eagle* condemned the mayor's outburst as an exhibition of "atrocious bad taste";[15] the *Detroit Free Press* regarded them as "a wretched example of bad manners,"[16] while the Rochester *Democrat and Chronicle* deprecated the mayor's effusion as "foolish and ill-considered."[17]

There were some papers and periodicals, however, which supported the exuberant mayor. To the *New Republic* the mayor's words were an "expression of honest and indignant opinion."[18] The *New York Daily News* agreed with the "Mayor's general criticism of Hitler,"[19] and the Boise *Idaho Daily Statesman* concurred in the sentiment "without apology."[20] The pungent pen of Westbrook Pegler rushed into

[12] *New York Times,* March 4, 1937.
[13] *Newsweek,* March 13, 1937, p. 16.
[14] March 5, 1937.
[15] March 6, 1937.
[16] March 7, 1937.
[17] March 6, 1937.
[18] March 17, 1937.
[19] March 6, 1937.
[20] March 6, 1937.

words of approval: "The little inconvenience to the State Department occasioned by La Guardia's remark that Hitler belongs in a chamber of horrors probably was worth while after all."[21]

d. *Secretary Hull Regrets the Action of La Guardia*

On March 4, the counselor of the German Embassy presented to the Department of State a protest against Mayor La Guardia's verbal assault upon Hitler. Mr. Dunn, chief of the Division of Western European Affairs, assured the counselor that he had no doubt that "Secretary Hull considered it most unfortunate that a city official should express himself in terms which might cause offence to a foreign government." In addition to this assurance, Dunn stated that the Secretary would also "pursue the matter in any manner in which he properly could within the limitations of the lack of authority which existed here to repress or control any free expression of opinion."[22]

On March 5, Secretary Hull made a statement with reference to the La Guardia remarks. After stressing the right of freedom of speech the Secretary then remarked that this fact did not "lessen the regret of the Government when utterances either by private citizens or by public officials speaking in an individual capacity give offence to a Government with which we have official relations. I very earnestly deprecate the utterances which have thus given offence to the German Government."[23]

In Germany the mayor's caustic remarks let loose a flood of abuse directed, not only against La Guardia, but against America as well. Ambassador Dodd was greatly surprised at the "language with which the attack was implemented," but he also noted that the Foreign Office held a conference with the Propaganda Ministry "with a view to muzzling the *Angriff* on its American publicity."[24]

After receiving the Dodd dispatch, Secretary Hull instructed the ambassador to make a formal protest against the "coarse and wholly indecent character" of the German press attacks upon "American womanhood and American institutions." There could be no "human provocation which would justify such language."[25] Dodd immediately

[21] *Chicago Daily News,* March 6, 1937.

[22] Memorandum of a conversation between Mr. James C. Dunn, chief of the Division of Western European Affairs, and Mr. Thomsen, counselor of the German Embassy, March 4, 1937. 862.002 Hitler/107, MS, Department of State.

[23] Statement of Secretary Hull, March 5, 1937. 862.002 Hitler/101, MS, Department of State.

[24] Ambassador Dodd to Secretary Hull, Berlin, March 8, 1937. 862.002 Hitler/116, MS, Department of State.

[25] Secretary Hull to Ambassador Dodd, March 10, 1937. 862.002 Hitler/102, MS, Department of State.

sought an interview with von Neurath who informed him that he had already discussed the matter with Goebbels who had rebuked the editor of *Der Angriff.* When Dodd pressed the matter further, Neurath said that he could "not state that any other paper had been rebuked or that retraction had been published." While not expressing any formal regret, "Neurath's attitude was distinctly understanding and sympathetic."[26]

But von Neurath's understanding attitude completely changed when Mayor La Guardia, on the evening of March 15, made a fresh attack upon Chancellor Hitler. Two days later the German Ambassador called at the Department of State and requested that Secretary Hull make a "strong and definite apology" for this new outburst and offer "new and special regrets." Hull first remarked that the Mayor of New York was denouncing Hitler as a means of building up political capital to help in his race for re-election. This capital would grow much larger if the German Government continued to take formal notice of the mayor's insulting comments. He assured the ambassador that the President was "deeply anxious to preserve suitable relations between our countries and our governments, but that it presented an impossible situation when the German Government took seriously every objectionable utterance of politicians and others of this country who were not under the control of the Federal Government." The ambassador seemed satisfied with this explanation of Secretary Hull and said that he would do his "very best" to induce his Government to view the matter with an understanding heart.[27]

Ambassador Luther was apparently successful in persuading the Foreign Office to overlook the insulting remarks of Mayor La Guardia, although on March 18, Dieckhoff asked Dodd if he could "recommend that the President or the Secretary of State stop the Mayor's talk about Germany and the Chancellor."[28] It was difficult for the Nazi Government to appreciate the fact that the American Federal Government is one of definitely limited powers.

e. *Cardinal Mundelein Creates Tension between the Vatican and Germany*

The last echoes of the La Guardia incident were slowly dying away when certain critical remarks of Cardinal Mundelein concerning Hitler

---

[26] Ambassador Dodd to Secretary Hull, Berlin, March 12, 1937. 862.002 Hitler/104, MS, Department of State.

[27] Conversation between Secretary Hull and Ambassador Luther, March 17, 1937. 862.002 Hitler/122, MS, Department of State.

[28] Ambassador Dodd to Secretary Hull, Berlin, March 18, 1937. 862.002 Hitler/113, MS, Department of State.

aroused such a storm of indignation in Germany that the relations between the Vatican and the Nazi Government were seriously strained.
On May 18, 1937, at a meeting of the Catholic clergy of the arch-
diocese of Chicago, Cardinal Mundelein gave a review of the situation
in Germany and then referred to Hitler in the following language:
"Perhaps you will ask how it is that a nation of 60 million intelligent
people will submit in fear and servitude to an alien, an Austrian paper
hanger, and a poor one at that, and a few associates like Goebbels and
Goering, who dictate every move of the people's lives."[29]

Ambassador Dieckhoff, in Washington, refrained from filing a
formal protest against these remarks because the Cardinal held an
office that had "no connection with the United States Government" and
therefore he was regarded merely "as a private person." But the ambassador did send Herr Thomsen, counselor of the Embassy, to the
Department of State to protest informally against the Cardinal's stric-
tures. Thomsen talked the matter over with Mr. Dunn, chief of the
Division of Western European Affairs, and endeavored to impress upon
Mr. Dunn the unfortunate effect of the Cardinal's outburst upon German-American relations.[30]

Although the Nazi Government refrained from filing a formal protest against Mundelein's biting words, it immediately shifted the attack
to another quarter. The German Ambassador in Rome was instructed
to discuss the matter with the Papal Secretary of State. Rome and not
Washington was to be held responsible for the Cardinal's verbal assault.

The Cardinal Secretary of State was not seriously disturbed by this
German barrage. In his studiously cool reply he first noted that he was
not in the habit of commenting upon speeches until he had before him
the "absolutely correct text" of the speech in question. After this thrust
he asked some very pertinent questions of his own: "What has the German Government done, and what does it intend to do in the future
against the malicious slander and defamation, against the disgraceful
calumnies directed at churches, ecclesiastical institutions, the Pope, the
cardinals, priests, etc., which appear . . . in German newspapers and in
the speeches of prominent personages?"[31]

After recovering from his astonishment at such a tart reply, the German Foreign Secretary instructed the ambassador in Rome to inform
the Cardinal Secretary of State that the "unexpected and incompre-

[29] *New York Times*, May 19, 1937.

[30] Ambassador Dieckhoff to the German Foreign Ministry, Washington, May 21,
1937. *Documents on Germany Foreign Policy, 1918–1945*, Series D (Washington,
1949), I, 969–70.

[31] German Ambassador to the Holy See (Bergen) to the German Foreign Ministry,
Rome, May 25, 1937. *Ibid.*, pp. 970–72.

hensible conduct" of the Holy See in this matter had "eliminated the conditions necessary for a normal state of relations between the German Government and the Curia. The full responsibility for this development rests solely with the Curia."[32]

The German Foreign Office waited for some break in the attitude of the Curia, and on June 9 the chargé d'affaires in Rome reported that there was a "certain inclination towards conciliation" in Vatican circles. *Avvenire d'Italia* had carried an article by a well-known Jesuit priest, Father Yves de la Brière, which had characterized Cardinal Mundelein's words as "somewhat violent and lacking in diplomatic finesse."[33]

On June 24 the Cardinal Secretary of State addressed a long note to the German Embassy in Rome. The Holy See had now received the "complete text" of the Mundelein remarks and was therefore able to comment upon them. In the first place, it should be remembered that the German Ambassador in Washington had presented a protest to the Department of State and had been content that no formal reply had been made to this protest. This official silence on the part of the Department of State had not adversely affected German-American relations. Apparently it was quite different with regard to the relations between the Vatican and the German Government. When the Holy See made no formal reply to a German note of protest, the silence in this case led to a second German note which stated that Papal non-action had "eliminated the conditions necessary for a normal state of relations between the German Government and the Curia." The application of such a "double standard" was more than "unusual." This was particularly true in view of the fact that Cardinal Mundelein was an American citizen "who made use of the right guaranteed him by his country's Constitution to express opinion freely in the sphere of publicly-known facts." It should also be kept in mind that the Cardinal's remarks were made on the assumption that they were not "intended for the public." Their publication was "not according to his intention." Although the Cardinal of Chicago, as a bishop, was under the "authority of the Holy See," he was not "an official of the Holy See such as a nuncio." The "Holy See itself and its representatives" were always scrupulous in "observing the line between objective controversies and those colored by personal factors."[34]

[32] German Foreign Ministry to the German Embassy to the Holy See, Berlin, May 27, 1937. *Ibid.,* pp. 973–74.

[33] Chargé d'affaires of the German Embassy to the Holy See to the German Foreign Ministry, Rome, June 9, 1937. *Ibid.,* p. 975.

[34] The Papal Secretary of State (Pacelli) to the German Embassy to the Holy See, Vatican, June 24, 1937. *Ibid.,* pp. 976–81.

This note from Cardinal Pacelli gave little satisfaction to the German Ambassador to the Holy See who noted four days later that the mood of the Papal Secretary of State was "more irritated than ever."[35] This irritation was soon transferred to the ambassador himself when Pope Pius XI, on July 17, received a group of American Catholics from Chicago. On this occasion His Holiness had words of praise for Cardinal Mundelein, who was so "solicitous and zealous in the defense of the rights of God and of the Church and in the salvation of souls."[36]

Cardinal Pacelli tried to assure the German Ambassador that the Pope's words of praise of Cardinal Mundelein carried no implication of approval of the Cardinal's critical remarks concerning Hitler,[37] but the Reich and Prussian Minister for Ecclesiastical Affairs was not impressed with this explanation. He suggested to the Ministry of Foreign Affairs that all "diplomatic business" with the Curia be suspended. Von Neurath refused to accept this suggestion,[38] but he did veto any thought of making a visit to Rome for the purpose of discussing with Cardinal Pacelli the existing difficulties between the Church and the Nazi Government. Such a visit would have to be postponed until after "a settlement of the Mundelein case satisfactory to us has been made by the Holy See."[39]

It was impossible for the Vatican to settle the Mundelein case in a manner satisfactory to the Nazi Government, so the rift between Rome and Berlin widened. The effect of this friction upon American Catholics was clearly depicted by Ambassador Dieckhoff in a dispatch to the Foreign Office. After referring to the close ties between the Vatican and American Catholics, he remarked:

American Catholics formerly were among the Americans who understood Germany best, and many of them up to four years ago sympathized with Germany as the champion in the struggle against Communism. We cannot ignore the regrettable fact that they have gone over to the enemy camp in increasing numbers during the last few years.[40]

[35] German Ambassador to the Holy See to Counselor Dumont of the German Foreign Ministry, Rome, July 7, 1937. *Ibid.*, p. 988.

[36] German Ambassador to the Holy See (Bergen) to the German Foreign Ministry, Rome, July 20, 1937. *Ibid.*, p. 989.

[37] German Ambassador to the Holy See (Bergen) to the German Foreign Ministry, Rome, July 23, 1937. *Ibid.*, pp. 990–92.

[38] The Foreign Ministry to the Reich and Prussian Ministry for Ecclesiastical Affairs, Berlin, August 5, 1937. *Ibid.*, pp. 995–96.

[39] German Foreign Minister to the Reich and Prussian Minister for Ecclesiastical Affairs, August 13, 1937. *Ibid.*, p. 998.

[40] Ambassador Dieckhoff to the German Foreign Ministry, Washington, November 22, 1937. *Ibid.*, pp. 646–48.

f. *The American Press Is Critical of the Bombardment of Almería*

The American press was not too deeply interested in the case of Cardinal Mundelein but it flared into hot indignation over the news that Almería had been bombarded in reprisal for the bombing of the German pocket battleship *Deutschland* by a Loyalist airplane. The partial destruction of this small Spanish town by a squadron of German warships evoked numberless bitter comments in the periodical and daily press.

The *Providence Journal* was certain that the shelling of Almería had "brought all Europe, indeed the world, face to face with one of its gravest crises in many years."[41] The Spokane *Spokesman-Review* believed that the action against Almería would "revive reluctant memories of German submarine atrocities in the World War."[42] The *Atlanta Constitution* feared that the Almería incident had "precipitated the most serious crisis in Europe since the dawn of the World War,"[43] while the *Seattle Daily Times* felt that "nothing short of diplomatic miracles can avert a full-powered descent of Germany and Italy upon Spain."[44]

Many papers believed that the dangerous implications of the Almería incident had been exaggerated. The Richmond *Times-Dispatch* expressed the opinion that the crisis would soon subside: "No European government wants war now."[45] The *Springfield Republican* was hopeful: "The chances seem to be that not even yet has the edge of the precipice been reached."[46] The *Kansas City Journal-Post* thought that if England and France followed a parallel policy they could make "Hitler 'be nice' about Spain."[47]

As far as German-American relations were concerned, the shelling of Almería was distinctly unfortunate because it convinced many Americans that Hitler's Germany was reviving all the brutal practices of former years. The *Los Angeles Times* condemned the German action as "outright savagery,"[48] while the *Portland Morning Oregonian* directed a heavy blast against German cruelty: "May God have pity on a generation of men which has committed itself, in the prosecution of war, to the use of terrorism! It is obviously the purpose of the war and naval colleges to make the civilian populations the chief victims of the next general war."[49]

[41] June 1, 1937.
[42] June 2, 1937.
[43] June 1, 1937.
[44] June 1, 1937.
[45] June 1, 1937.

[46] June 1, 1937.
[47] June 1, 1937.
[48] June 1, 1937.
[49] June 2, 1937.

g. *Points of Friction along the Economic Front*

This rising tide of American dislike for Nazi Germany was not contained within strong dykes of mutual economic interest. The foreign commerce between Germany and the United States was seriously affected by different theories of international trade. Under the terms of the Trade Agreements Act of 1934, Secretary Hull pushed a program which emphasized the principle of equality of treatment as the basis of commercial relations. He was insistent that the idea of equality should not be defeated by the imposition on the part of other nations of exchange controls, government monopolies, and quotas. He was particularly opposed to barter deals.

In 1934, President Roosevelt named George N. Peek to the Office of Foreign Trade Adviser, and Peek lost no time in negotiating with Germany a barter agreement whereby the Nazi Government would buy 800,000 bales of American cotton through the facilities of the Export-Import Bank. Payment for this cotton would be arranged so that one-fourth of the price would be paid in American dollars and three-fourths in German currency plus a premium of 22½ per cent. The banks would sell this currency to American importers of German goods who could use it for their purchases.

Secretary Hull voiced vehement opposition to this barter deal and was able to secure not only its defeat but also the abolition of the Office of Foreign Trade Adviser.[50] Needless to say, this action was a blow to everyone who had hoped that the development of economic ties with Germany might lead to better political relations.

The difficulties of 1934 expanded into further friction in 1936. Under the terms of a ruling by the Attorney General, the German plan for subsidizing exports was classified as a discriminatory trade practice. The Treasury Department then applied the antibounty provisions of the Tariff Act of 1930 with countervailing duties ranging from 22 to 56 per cent on about a dozen German commodities. The German Government at once sent a group of experts to Washington in an effort to obtain the removal of these high duties.[51] Failing in this endeavor, it then tried to conciliate the Treasury Department by issuing a decree which forbade the use of Aski marks and barter deals in German-American trade.[52]

The Treasury Department refused to look with favor upon these

[50] Cordell Hull, *Memoirs* (New York, 1948), I, 370–74.
[51] *New York Times*, July 6, 7, 12, 1936.
[52] *Ibid.*, August 4, 1936.

gestures of accommodation. Instead, it struck another blow at German-American trade by instructing American consular officials in Germany to require that every invoice of exported German goods should be accompanied by a complete declaration of "any benefits or privileges, including marks subject to special exchange" which had been extended to the shipper by his government. Since under German law the revelation of business secrets to foreigners was strictly forbidden, the new regulation by the Treasury Department was highly effective in depressing the volume of trade between the Reich and the United States.[53]

On August 13 the German Government announced that subsidies on exports to the United States would be discontinued. The Treasury Department cautiously replied that the countervailing duties would be revoked when satisfactory assurances were received that German exports actually did not receive any artificial stimulation.[54] To conserve the small volume of trade that continued despite all these difficulties, the Continental Export and Import Company was established to act as a clearinghouse for German-American commercial exchanges. Exporters of American raw materials were brought into contact with American importers of German goods, and a balance was struck between the respective debits and credits. It was a condition of trade upon weak crutches with the probability that either might slip or break at any moment.[55]

h. *The Department of State Authorizes Attendance at Nazi Parteitag*

In 1937, Ambassador Dodd was determined to follow his usual practice of refusing to attend the Nazi Party celebration at Nürnberg. In order to insure his nonattendance he made a special trip to the United States with the expectation of staying several months. Shortly after his departure from Berlin, the French Ambassador called to see Mr. Mayer, the American chargé d'affaires. He frankly informed Mr. Mayer that it appeared to his Government that it would not be "desirable any longer to continue to 'boycott' the Nuremberg Party rally." To adhere to the "past practice would be conspicuous if not antagonistic." The Nazi

---

[53] *Journal of Commerce,* August 5, 1936.

[54] *New York Times,* August 14, 1936.

[55] The following table will illustrate the fluctuations in German-American trade from 1934 to 1938:

American exports to Germany	American imports from Germany
1935...............$ 91,980,719	1935...............$78,336,330
1937............... 126,342,536	1937............... 91,175,901
1938............... 107,129,899	1938............... 62,532,302

Party had now "become the State and to refuse the invitation would be acting out of accord with realities." The French and British ambassadors had agreed to attend the celebration on September 10 and on the morning of the following day. American agreement on this point would be welcomed as "continuing the identic attitude which the three governments had pursued in the past."[56]

After this conversation with the French Ambassador, Mayer cabled to Secretary Hull and asked for a specific instruction relative to attendance at the Nürnberg rally. The Secretary replied that the matter should be left to the discretion of the Embassy in Berlin.[57] In the end, the American chargé in Berlin accepted the invitation of the Nazi Government and attended the Nazi Party celebration in Nürnberg. This action evoked a strong protest from Congressman Emmanuel Celler who protested that this attendance would subject the Department of State to "severe criticism."[58] But Secretary Hull remained firm and informed Mr. Celler that the American Government was merely following the practice of other governments that maintained relations with Nazi Germany.[59]

On September 4, Ambassador Dodd was surprised to read in the *New York Herald-Tribune* a paragraph taken from his confidential letter to Secretary Hull advising against having an American representative at the Nazi Party celebration in Nürnberg. There was also a reference to a telegram he had recently sent to the Department of State repeating his former advice. The fact that the department permitted the publication of these communications was an indication that the opinions of Ambassador Dodd were not highly regarded in official circles.[60]

i. *Secretary Hull Is Critical of Ambassador Dodd*

When Ambassador Dodd landed at Norfolk on August 4 for an extended vacation in the United States, he made a statement to the effect that the basic objective of "some of the Powers in Europe was to frighten and even destroy Democracies everywhere." These pointed remarks led Ambassador Dieckhoff to pay a prompt visit to the Depart-

[56] Ferdinand L. Mayer, American chargé d'affaires in Berlin, to Secretary Hull, August 11, 1937. 862.00/3664, MS, Department of State.

[57] Secretary Hull to the American Embassy in Berlin, August 13, 1937. 862.00/3664, MS, Department of State.

[58] Emmanuel Celler to Secretary Hull, August 27, 1937. 862.00/3673, MS, Department of State.

[59] Secretary Hull to Emmanuel Celler, August 28, 1937. 862.00/3673, MS, Department of State.

[60] Ambassador Dodd's *Diary*, 1933-1938, p. 427.

ment of State where Secretary Hull assured him that "Dodd's pet hobby was known to be ideal Jeffersonian democracy; on this subject Dodd was 'somewhat insane.' " Hull was also certain that Dodd, in making his statement, had "no particular country in mind."[61]

On August 31, Dodd wrote to the German Foreign Office and explained that his remarks on August 4 had "no reference to Germany at all." If there was any "criticism at all it was of certain things done in my own country."[62] A few weeks later Ambassador Dieckhoff had a conversation with Sumner Welles. When the subject of Dodd's remarks came up, Welles "frankly confessed that Dodd was as incomprehensible to him as to us."[63] On October 1, Welles informed Dieckhoff that the President had decided to recall Dodd as ambassador to Germany. He would soon return to Berlin but "only to arrange his affairs there."[64] Dodd himself urged the President to appoint Professor James T. Shotwell as his successor "because of his university connections as well as his national reputation as a scholar."[65] Dodd seemed confident that only professors could fill satisfactorily the position of ambassador to Germany.

j. *The President Advocates a Quarantine of Aggressors*

It is an age-old axiom that rulers often, in periods of dire economic distress, seek by a bold foreign policy to divert attention from the home front to distant stormy horizons. Some historians believe that, in 1937, President Roosevelt followed this axiom with regard to his famous quarantine speech delivered in Chicago on October 5, 1937. There is no doubt that he was deeply concerned over the severe economic recession in the United States which became manifest in the late summer of 1937. After a conversation with the President on August 11, Ambassador Dodd recorded in his diary that the Chief Executive was "greatly troubled about the danger of war and also the continued depression in the United States."[66]

[61] German Ambassador in Washington (Dieckhoff) to the German Foreign Ministry, August 5, 1937. *Documents on German Foreign Policy, 1918–1945,* Series D, I, 627–28.

[62] Ambassador Dodd to the German Foreign Minister, August 31, 1937. *Ibid.,* p. 628.

[63] German Ambassador in Washington to the German Foreign Ministry, New York, September 27, 1937. *Ibid.,* pp. 630–31.

[64] German Ambassador in Washington to the German Foreign Ministry, Washington, October 1, 1937. *Ibid.,* p. 632.

[65] Dodd, *op. cit.,* pp. 428–29.

[66] *Ibid.,* p. 426.

Between August and December 1937, the index of industrial production declined about 27 per cent, and stock-market averages about 37 per cent. In the last two months of the year more than 850,000 factory workers lost their jobs. The transition from prosperity to economic distress was the "most severe the country had ever experienced in so brief a period."[67] According to Professor Beard, the shock of the "economic collapse was startling to President Roosevelt and his advisers."[68]

But the economic factor was not the only one that disturbed the domestic equation. The appointment of Hugo Black to the Supreme Court and the widespread and bitter opposition that arose when it was discovered that at one time he had hidden beneath the robes of the Ku Klux Klan, made many of the President's advisers look with alarm at the evident dangers that lurked along the political front.

These facts do not prove, however, that the President decided to file a vigorous indictment against aggressor nations in order to divert public attention from the home scene. It should be kept in mind that as early as January 1933 he had regarded with favor the Stimson theory of non-recognition as applied to Japanese expansion in North China. In October 1937, Japan had once more moved ahead in Manchuria, and in Ethiopia the legions of Mussolini had conquered an empire. The Stimson "stop sign" was applicable in both situations, and there were many moralists in America who wished the President to plant it boldly along those far-flung horizons and to call upon the world to stand behind it. Even if the domestic scene had remained perfectly calm there was still a possibility that the Chief Executive would have directed a blast against "aggressor nations."

At any rate, on October 5 at Chicago, the President delivered a sonorous denunciation of all wicked nations who were disturbing the peace of the world. After referring to the destruction of life and property resulting from wars abroad, he then endeavored to show that if these conflicts continued their sparks would fly to America and cause similar havoc here: "Let no one imagine that America will escape, that this Western Hemisphere will not be attacked." The world could not be safe from aggression until moral standards were "adhered to by all." Apparently these standards would be widely accepted if some structure of collective security could be created to enforce them. The easiest measure of enforcement would be an international quarantine against aggressors.[69]

---

[67] *The United States in World Affairs, 1937,* p. 90.

[68] Charles A. Beard, *American Foreign Policy in the Making, 1932–1940* (New Haven, 1946), p. 178. See also *American Year Book, 1937* (New York, 1937), p. 366.

[69] *New York Times.* October 6, 1937.

k. *American Opinion of the Quarantine Speech*

Raymond Leslie Buell, head of the Foreign Policy Association in New
York City, promptly praised the President's speech as a rejection of the
isolationist philosophy which he had followed since 1933. He then expressed a fervent hope that the Department of State would adopt a
"positive foreign policy."[70] Oswald Garrison Villard thought that the
President had "rendered a tremendous service to the world." The time
had come when he should "reassume the moral leadership of the world
which Woodrow Wilson abandoned when he surrendered to the 'peace-
makers' at Paris."[71] Nicholas Murray Butler warmly commended the
President's strong words and hoped they would be followed by the
creation of an international police force that could maintain world
order. The "folly" of an isolationist policy was exceeded only by its
"immorality."[72]

A large section of the American press echoed these sentiments of
Villard and Butler. In New York the *World-Telegram* regarded the
President's words as a "reminder and a warning." They reminded us
"that we cannot live unto ourselves alone" and they warned us "that
mere wishing will not suffice to keep us safe."[73] The *New York Daily
News* had already on October 3 advocated a long-range naval blockade
of Japan in the event she were to threaten the position of the Western
powers in China. On October 6 the quarantine speech was given strong
indorsement, and the principal editorial had the significant heading:
"Shall We Take Them Now or Try It Later?"[74]

The *Washington Post* joined this chorus of approval. The President
had "enormously strengthened his reputation as one of the great leaders
of mankind."[75] The *Washington Evening Star* added its voice to this
acclamation: "Not since Woodrow Wilson's message to Congress in
April, 1917, have more prescient words fallen from the lips of the
President of the United States. . . . They are the words that needed to
be uttered from such a place at this critical hour."[76]

In the Middle West the *Chicago Daily News* had "nothing but praise
for the broad generalities" of the quarantine speech.[77] The *St. Louis*

---

[70] *Foreign Policy Bulletin*, October 15, 1937, p. 1.
[71] *The Nation*, October 16, 1937, p. 405.
[72] *New York Times*, November 12, 1937.
[73] October 6, 1937.
[74] October 7, 1937.
[75] October 7, 1937.
[76] October 6, 1937.
[77] October 6, 1937.

Globe-Democrat praised the President's words of warning and was certain that Secretary Hull could be depended upon to "steer a safe course."[78] The *Cincinnati Enquirer* gave its support to the idea of collective pressure in applying sanctions against aggressor nations but was opposed to unilateral American action.[79]

Along the Pacific coast the *San Francisco Chronicle* had strong and laudatory words for the "soundness" of the views of the Chief Executive on foreign affairs.[80] The *Los Angeles Times* took a similar stand: "This Chicago utterance says forcibly things which need saying and utters warnings which should be uttered."[81] The *Portland Morning Oregonian* believed that the United States should not "shirk its responsibility" if the great powers decided upon sanctions to curb aggressors.[82] In these same sections of the country there was a larger number of papers that dissented from these favorable views of the President's speech.

The *New York Herald-Tribune* sharply criticized any thought of applying sanctions in an effort to stop the so-called aggressor nations: "Presumably we shall soon know what the President intends. One can only hope that the public will at the same time realize the full meaning of whatever course his restless and adventurous nature may now be leading him to adopt."[83]

The New York *Sun* belabored the President with its heaviest sticks of type: "If Mr. Roosevelt had no further thought than to give voice to moral indignation, he chose an unfortunate manner and time. The note he struck was hectoring and supercilious. . . . Surely he does not suppose that the United States can impose its own standards of political morality on other nations by the simple process of slapping them rhetorically on the wrist."[84]

In its criticism of the President's speech the *Boston Herald* struck a loud isolationist note: "Americans must not, knowingly or unknowingly, jointly or alone, embark on another costly attempt to reform the world."[85] The *Boston Post* feared that the road of collective security was a "dangerous one for us";[86] the *Philadelphia Inquirer* warned that the path of an "aggressive peacemaker" is "beset with pitfalls,"[87] while

[78] October 7, 8, 1937.
[79] October 6, 1937.
[80] October 6, 1937.
[81] October 6, 1937.
[82] October 6, 1937.
[83] October 8, 1937.
[84] October 6, 1937.
[85] October 8, 1937.
[86] October 6, 1937.
[87] October 6, 1937.

the Philadelphia *Evening Bulletin* felt that any boycott of Japan would be imprudent and unsuccessful.[88]

In the Middle West the *Chicago Tribune* led the assault: "Does not Mr. Roosevelt's policy invite the coming of the day when he, too, may have no alternative but to resort to arms?"[89] The *Detroit Free Press* was vehement in its opposition to the President's viewpoint: "Certainly at best the President's words are likely to accomplish nothing good that could not be accomplished as well and far less dangerously by the use of quieter methods."[90] The *Minneapolis Tribune* was apprehensive that the quarantine speech might lead to war: "If we do not intend to fight for the underdog . . . we would do well to avoid the dangers which lie in the persistent dramatization of the underdog's predicament."[91] The Spokane *Spokesman-Review* ominously remarked: "That disquieting pronouncement approximates a declaration of war";[92] while the *San Francisco Examiner,* representing the Hearst press, published a strong warning against warlike gestures: "Don't Stick Out Your Neck, Uncle!"[93]

The religious press failed to see any moral imperatives in favor of taking a strong stand against aggressor nations. *America* insisted that "the people of the United States positively are opposed to foreign imbroglios."[94] The *Catholic World* thought it was ridiculous for the President to imagine that he could frighten Germany, Italy, and Japan "with a few explosive phrases!" His language had belligerent overtones but it should be remembered that Uncle Sam was no longer a fool in international relations. The Allied powers had "lured him into one war to make the world safe for democracy," but Sam would not fall for that stale bait another time.[95] *Ave Maria* was equally critical of any drift towards war and alluded to the fact that we had gained nothing from the World War: "We have only unpaid foreign debts to add to our own ones to show for our sacrifices, offered in France, to bring victory to the Allies."[96] The *Christian Century,* the influential voice of American Protestantism, expressed deep suspicions of the President's policy, and it made the remarkable prophecy that in the event of war a victory for China would also result in a victory for Russia.[97]

[88] October 11, 1937.
[89] October 6, 1937.
[90] October 7, 1937.
[91] October 11, 1937.
[92] October 6, 1937.
[93] October 11, 1937.
[94] October 16, 1937.
[95] December, 1937, pp. 257–65.
[96] October 23, 1937, pp. 534–35.
[97] October 20, 1937, pp. 1287–88.

Two important journals representing the business press were outspoken in their opposition to war. The *Wall Street Journal* printed a leading editorial under the arresting headline: "Stop Foreign Meddling: America Wants Peace,"[98] and the *Commercial and Financial Chronicle* sounded the same note: "There should be stern repudiation of any steps that would lead us into another conflict."[99]

1. *The Nazi Regime Is Placed upon an Uneasy Defensive*

On October 11, the German Ambassador called to see Sumner Welles, the Acting Secretary of State. After discussing some aspects of the civil war in Spain, the ambassador directly inquired as to the "exact interpretation" which his Government should give to the President's quarantine speech. Welles replied that

it seemed to me hardly necessary for me to attempt to interpret the President's speech inasmuch as it was in my judgment a speech which spoke for itself. . . . I said that the President sincerely believed that all of the difficult problems with which the countries of the world were today confronted could be solved through a spirit of friendly co-operation and by recognition of each other's difficulties, and that permanent solution could never be found through force.

The ambassador then remarked that "this was exactly the view which he himself had taken of the speech," and that he had "to express his regret that the press in Germany, as well as a portion of the press in the United States, should through erroneous and exaggerated interpretations of the President's statements, endeavor to create further ill-will between the two peoples."[100]

In his dispatches to the Foreign Office, Ambassador Dieckhoff stressed the viewpoint that the Chicago address was "mainly, if not exclusively, directed against *Japan* and that the possibility of assuming a more active role in European questions was not contemplated."[101] A week later, Dieckhoff reported that the "sharp tone" of the quarantine speech had greatly surprised Secretary Hull himself. The first draft of the speech had not contained any "quarantine threat." This passage "originated with the President himself," and was not incorporated into the text of the speech "until immediately before his arrival in Chicago."

[98] October 7, 8, 1937.

[99] October 9, 1937.

[100] Memorandum of a conversation between Sumner Welles and the German Ambassador, October 11, 1937. 711.00 President's Speech, October 5, 1937/99, MS, Department of State.

[101] Ambassador Dieckhoff to the German Foreign Ministry, Washington, October 9, 1937. *Documents on German Foreign Policy, 1918–1945*, Series D., I, 634–35.

The reason for this sharp tone and the incorporation of the quarantine threat was the "intensification of the Far Eastern conflict. . . . It is certain that the Chicago speech was aimed principally at Japan." The reception of the speech in the United States was "overwhelmingly negative; the war cry, which was immediately sounded by some groups, caused considerable reaction, and meanwhile things have become rather quiet."[102]

The ambassador's reports from Washington, stressing the unfavorable reaction in the American press to the President's speech, aroused such a deep interest in Hitler's mind that he suddenly determined to send one of his personal friends, Fritz Wiedemann, on a brief American tour. According to Ambassador Dieckhoff, Wiedemann "looked around very thoroughly," and returned to Germany with "very deep impressions of America."[103] According to Prentiss Gilbert, who talked with Wiedemann in Berlin after his return, Hitler's special agent had been "appalled by his observations of anti-German sentiments throughout the United States," and he was at a "loss what to suggest to the Chancellor," to whom he would report directly, "respecting steps Germany might take looking to a betterment of the situation."[104]

m. *Mussolini Pays a Momentous Visit to Berlin*

One of the reasons for these "anti-German sentiments" in the United States was the fear that Mussolini and Hitler were plotting against the peace of the world. In the event that a second world war would break out there was always a strong possibility of American involvement with its consequent heavy loss in life and mounting national debt. Pacifism was close to the hearts of most Americans who watched with anxious eyes the movements of the restless European dictators.

On September 4, an announcement was made in Rome of an imminent visit of Mussolini to Berlin. On September 23 the Duce began the first stage of his journey, flanked by three ministers and a retinue of about a hundred persons. On September 28, in Berlin, a crowd of some 800,000 gathered on the Maifeld to listen to Hitler and Mussolini exchange courtesies. Halfway through Mussolini's speech a tremendous thunderstorm burst upon the scene of festivities, and the Duce made his disconsolate way to his car almost unescorted, soaked with rain, and

[102] Ambassador Dieckhoff to the German Foreign Ministry, Washington, October 15, 1937. *Ibid.,* pp. 639–41.

[103] German Ambassador in the United States (Dieckhoff) to the head of the Political Department in the German Foreign Ministry, Washington, December 20, 1937. *Ibid.,* pp. 658–61.

[104] Prentiss Gilbert to Secretary Hull, Berlin, December 29, 1937. 811.00 Nazi/330, MS, Department of State.

on the point of collapse.[105] The Berlin adventure already showed its ominous side.

Mussolini and Hitler had been too busy with social activities to pay much attention to political affairs. No treaties or agreements were negotiated, but a rapprochement had been confirmed with all its dangerous implications. It was probably this fact that disturbed President Roosevelt and sharpened the tone of his Chicago address on October 5.

The American press took this meeting between the two dictators very seriously. The *Albuquerque Journal* thought that the world might be "witnessing, in the meeting of these two strong men, one of the important events of contemporary history."[106] The *Los Angeles Times* was fearful that catastrophe might follow this meeting of dictators: "No one knows what has gone on behind the scenes in Berlin. It may be new war, new conquest, new centralizing of power."[107] The *Birmingham News* expressed its evident apprehension of sudden war: "These two blatant gentlemen are today the greatest individual enemies of peace. They are today the greatest threats to the peace and security of Europe and the world."[108] In Chattanooga the *Daily Times* remarked that if "Hitler and Mussolini did not enter into a military alliance, Mussolini achieved a working agreement for any emergency."[109] In the Middle West the *St. Louis Post-Dispatch,* in a vitriolic editorial entitled, "As the Gods Laugh," went to the limit in an invective against Hitler:

The Gods must rock with ironic laughter as they hear Benito Mussolini refer to Adolf Hitler as "the herald and defender of European civilization against subversive activities." Hitler is defending his country against the poetry of Heine and the music of Mendelssohn. . . . In the name of European civilization he has crushed the twin heresies of democracy and liberty. . . . He has wrecked the universities and sent their greatest men into pitiful exile. . . . Yes, Hitler is the defender of European civilization, the civilization of the thumbscrew and rack, the civilization of . . . ignorance and bestiality.[110]

It was no wonder that Fritz Wiedemann was "appalled" at these extreme expressions of American opinion of Nazi Germany. A large portion of the American public was filled with deep suspicion and strong dislike of Hitler and all his works. This hostility reached a peak after Munich and it gave ample support to the Roosevelt policy of moving down the road to war while talking loudly about the importance of peace.

[105] Elizabeth Wiskemann, *The Rome-Berlin Axis* (New York, 1949), pp. 79–82.
[106] September 29, 1937.
[107] September 29, 1937.   [109] October 3, 1937.
[108] September 29, 1937.   [110] September 27, 1937.

XV

Britain Blocks an Effort of Roosevelt
to Find a Path to Peace

WHILE Ambassador Dieckhoff was trying to convince the German Foreign Office that Roosevelt's quarantine speech of October 5, 1937, was aimed at Japan and not at Germany, Secretary Ickes was striving desperately to prove to suspicious Nazis that America was definitely hostile to the Hitler regime.

a. *Secretary Ickes Widens the Breach between the United States and Germany*

In the early months of 1937 the Department of Commerce became deeply interested in promoting commercial travel by airships. This type of travel had been developed to a point of high efficiency by German scientists, with the *Hindenburg* as the test dirigible. On February 2, 1937, Colonel Johnson, the Assistant Secretary of Commerce, wrote to Walton Moore, the Assistant Secretary of State, to inform him that the matter of additional flights for "the *Hindenburg* to and from the United States has been discussed at the White House. The reaction there is favorable." In view of this fact the Department of Commerce was willing to grant a German request for a "reasonable number of flights, say ten or twelve." On February 17 the Department granted "permission for not to exceed eighteen round trip flights by the *Hindenburg* between Frankfort-on-the-Main, Germany, and Lakehurst, New Jersey." The *Hindenburg* was making its first flight under this permission when it exploded and burned on May 6.[1]

Secretary Roper was deeply shocked by this disaster, and on May 12 he issued a statement to the press in which he remarked that "some well-guarded plan will be worked out whereby helium gas from our reserves can be made available for world commercial needs without . . . any sacrifice whatever of our peace policy."[2] The following day Colonel Johnson expressed the opinion that Americans could look forward to a "modification of our national policy with respect to the release of helium for use beyond our own frontiers."[3]

---

[1] Memorandum of L. H. Price, Office of Arms and Munitions Control, Department of State, November 13, 1937. 811.659 HELIUM-AMERICAN ZEPPELIN TRANSPORT, Inc./18, MS, Department of State.

[2] *Ibid.*

[3] *New York Times*, May 14, 1937.

President Roosevelt acted promptly in this matter and appointed a five-member inter-Cabinet committee to "formulate and recommend a policy for the sale and exportation of helium gas." On May 25 this committee consisting of the Secretaries of State, War, Navy, Commerce, and Interior sent a letter to the President stating that the helium reserves of the United States were "adequate for many years." It therefore recommended that the Government be authorized to "make both domestic and export sales for operation of commercial lighter-than-air craft plying between the United States and other countries." It was believed that these sales could be surrounded with safeguards that would "prevent the use of helium by foreign countries for military purposes."[4]

Congress responded to this Executive pressure by passing the Helium Act of September 1, 1937, which permitted the exportation of helium gas for use in "commercial airships operating between the United States and a foreign country." Sales of this gas would have to be approved by the National Munitions Control Board consisting of the Secretaries of State, Treasury, War, Navy, and Commerce. The concurrence of the Secretary of the Interior was added as an extra precaution against any unwise sale of helium gas. Regulations governing the exportation of helium were promulgated on September 3.

In accordance with the terms of these regulations the German Zeppelin Company, through its agent, American Zeppelin Transport, Inc., applied to the Secretary of State for an allotment of 17,900,000 cubic feet of helium gas. On November 23, 1937, this application was granted by the Secretary of State with "the unanimous approval of all the members of the National Munitions Control Board and the Secretary of the Interior." On January 31, 1938, a license was issued to the American Zeppelin Transport, Inc., to export 2,600,000 cubic feet of helium gas. The company then submitted to the Secretary of the Interior a contract for the purchase of 10,000,000 cubic feet of helium gas, and deposited with him a check for $76,850 as required by the sales regulations. All formalities had now been fulfilled and the company was informed "by officers of the Interior Department that the contract would be ready for signature within a few days."[5]

After receiving this assurance, the American Zeppelin Transport, Inc., sent a vessel to Houston, Texas, with empty gas containers for the promised supply of helium gas. But this matter of the sale of helium

[4] Secretaries Hull, Woodring, Swanson, Roper, and Ickes to President Roosevelt, May 25, 1937. 811.659 HELIUM/13½, MS, Department of State.

[5] Memorandum prepared by Joseph C. Green, executive secretary of the National Munitions Control Board and sent to President Roosevelt by Secretary Hull, March 22, 1938. 811.659 HELIUM/96A, MS, Department of State.

gas assumed a political aspect in the early months of 1938 when it became apparent that Germany had aggressive intentions towards Austria. Representatives Bruce Barton, John M. O'Connell, Donald L. O'Toole, Alfred N. Phillips, James G. Polk, and Mark Wilcox voiced objections to the sale of helium to any German agency, their main argument being that such a sale would "exhaust for a year the available supply of helium and thus jeopardize the national defense."

The Secretary of War, Admiral Leahy, and a series of experts in the War and Navy departments testified that it was "almost inconceivable that the German Government could contemplate the use of this helium for bombing purposes or that it could carry out such an intention." After reviewing these facts, the executive secretary of the National Munitions Control Board remarked that "recent developments in the European situation do not affect the fundamental issues involved in this case. . . . This Government would lay itself open to a charge of bad faith if it were now to refuse to permit the proposed exportation or to employ indirect means such as the requirement of an exorbitant bond from the purchaser in order to make the proposed exportation impossible."[6]

This charge of "bad faith" was given definite substance by the very "indirect means" that Mr. Green had feared. On March 31 a new set of regulations was issued which provided "both for the posting of a bond to guarantee the non-utilization of helium for war purposes and for control within Germany by American officers of the disposition of helium." The German Foreign Office complained to Ambassador Hugh Wilson that "both of these conditions were impossible of acceptance for the reason that they cast doubt upon the good faith of the German Government." Wilson himself expressed to Secretary Hull the opinion that the German Government was "sincere in its belief that the new regulations would constitute an unfair departure from the original understanding." He was afraid that they would arouse "so deep a resentment" in the Foreign Office that it would be difficult thereafter to "obtain effective protection and fair treatment for American individuals and interests" in Germany.[7]

As soon as Hugo Eckener, the genius behind the German Zeppelin Company, heard of the regulations of March 31, he sent a telegram to President Roosevelt in which he emphasized the fact that it was the unanimous opinion of all experts in Germany that it was "absolutely impossible" for a helium-inflated airship to conduct military operations.

---

6 *Ibid.*

7 Ambassador Wilson to Secretary Hull, Berlin, April 13, 1938. 811.659 HELIUM/101, MS, Department of State.

He therefore begged the President to take immediate favorable action upon the pending application for the export of helium gas.[8]

It was obvious that a crisis in German-American relations was inevitably approaching, and many important German leaders were apprehensive of what might happen. According to a competent American observer who had recently visited Germany, Hitler was "exceedingly perturbed at the relations between Germany and the United States and the extent of the feeling in America against him personally and to the Nazi regime in general."[9]

Secretary Ickes shared this feeling of deep dislike for Hitler, and it was his refusal to approve any contract for the sale of helium gas to Germany that shattered the hope of Dr. Eckener. Many Americans regarded the action of Secretary Ickes as unfortunate. The periodical *American Aviation* published an editorial which commented upon the new regulation which required the posting of a bond to guarantee the non-military use of purchased helium. How any

domestic bonding agency can guarantee that a foreign government would not confiscate helium in time of war is one of those matters beyond human conception. The irony in the whole helium business is that Secretary Ickes is going on the assumption that helium for lighter-than-air craft is of military value. On the other hand, the Navy Department has refused to recognize any military value in the dirigible. . . . We fear that Secretary Ickes has acquired another one of his publicity phobias.[10]

On April 27 the Office of the National Munitions Control Board prepared a memorandum which frankly stated that all the evidence available to the board indicated that neither the German Zeppelin Company nor the German Government had "any intention whatever of using any of the helium, to be exported under the allotment mentioned above, otherwise than for the inflation of the airship LZ-130 in commercial operations between Germany and the United States."[11]

During a conversation with Ambassador Wilson on April 28, General Göring spoke with "deep emotion and bluntness" about the helium matter. The American reversal of policy concerning the sale of helium gas to the German Zeppelin Company "could only mean deliberate

[8] Dr. Hugo Eckener to President Roosevelt, April 5, 1938. 811.659 HELIUM/102, MS, Department of State.

[9] Memorandum prepared by Pierrepont Moffat, chief of the Division of European Affairs in the Department of State, January 15, 1938. 811.607 New York, 1939/437, MS, Department of State.

[10] April 15, 1938, p. 13.

[11] Memorandum prepared by L. H. Price, National Munitions Control Board, April 27, 1938. 811.659 HELIUM/126, MS, Department of State.

unfriendliness on the part of the American Government." Relations between Germany and the United States had been brought

to the lowest possible point and this over a matter of minor importance to both nations. He said "I cannot understand what leads a nation to earn the enmity of another over such a little thing." . . . If it was impossible to get helium the German people would not forget America's attitude.[12]

In a final effort to secure the delivery of helium gas the German Government, in May 1938, sent Dr. Eckener to the United States to talk with American officials. On May 21, Ambassador Dieckhoff and Dr. Eckener were received by President Roosevelt who was "plainly embarrassed." He greeted them in an "excessively friendly manner" and said that he was "firmly convinced that helium should be delivered to us." Regret was expressed that the stubborn opposition of Secretary Ickes had delayed any decision in the matter. Nothing could be done without his approval. But the question of the sale of helium to Germany was still under consideration, and there was "hope" that it would finally be settled to the "satisfaction" of the German Zeppelin Company.[13]

These hopes were never realized and the helium gas was never shipped to Germany. On May 14, Ambassador Wilson reported that hostile feeling was running "exceedingly high in German circles among those who are aware of our decision respecting helium." It was apparent, however, that restraint had "been exercised on the German press," and the Foreign Office was seemingly anxious to cultivate American good will.[14] A week later Wilson informed Secretary Hull that Hitler was making a personal study of the "current strain in German-American relations" in the hope of finding a basis for a "rapprochement." In this regard it was said that the Chancellor was considering approaching the President directly, proposing a joint effort to liquidate outstanding "controversies."[15] Before making such a proposal he would have to take steps to curb the activities of certain German societies in the United States. He was ready to take these steps.

b. *Hitler Repudiates the German-American Bund*

In 1937 the Roosevelt Administration became increasingly concerned over the activities of the German-American Bund. On October 2 the

[12] Ambassador Wilson to Secretary Hull, Berlin, April 29, 1938. 811.659 HE-LIUM/120, *Confidential file*, MS, Department of State.

[13] Ambassador Dieckhoff to the German Foreign Ministry, Washington, May 21, 1938. *Documents on German Foreign Policy, 1918–1945*, Series D, I, 706–7.

[14] Ambassador Wilson to Secretary Hull, Berlin, May 14, 1938. 811.659 HE-LIUM/136, MS, Department of State.

[15] Ambassador Wilson to Secretary Hull, Berlin, May 20, 1938. 711.62/152, MS, Department of State.

American chargé at Berlin called on Baron von Weizsäcker, the head of the Political Department of the Foreign Office, to discuss with him the "serious and disturbing effects upon German-American relations caused by the conduct of Germans in the United States." Parades by "Germans in brown uniforms" and antidemocratic statements made by German nationals or German-Americans were creating much "uneasiness," and there was widespread alarm at the possibility of "German meddling in American domestic politics."[16]

This was not the first protest against the activities of German nationals in the United States. In 1935 the "Friends of the New Germany" had taken a conspicuous part in promoting a closer understanding between German-Americans and the "New Germany" under Hitler. Their efforts towards this goal had drawn a protest from the Department of State with the result that "German nationals were instructed to resign their membership in that society in order that it might appear to be a purely American organization." After this action the "Friends of the New Germany" dissolved their organization and established another one under the title, the German-American Bund.

The question before the German Foreign Office in 1937 was whether instructions should now be issued to German nationals in the United States to withdraw from the Bund. The North American Division of the Foreign Office prepared a memorandum on October 11 which answered this question in the affirmative. The Bund should be replaced by an organization with "purely cultural aims" like the Italian Dante Alighieri Society.[17]

This suggestion to dissolve all ties between German nationals and the German-American Bund was supported by Jacob G. Schurman, former American Ambassador to Germany. In November 1937, Schurman had a long conversation with Ambassador Dieckhoff during the course of which he expressed the fear that the activities of German nationals in the United States would lead to strained relations. Dieckhoff immediately assured him that the German Government was taking the "utmost pains not to interfere in any way whatever in the political concerns of American citizens, including American citizens of German descent. All that we expected from American citizens of German descent was interest in their German cultural heritage, especially in the German language." Schurman promptly replied that he did not think the German-American societies in the United States limited "themselves to purely cultural matters." In some cases they had "become the

[16] Memorandum of Baron von Weizsäcker, October 2, 1937. *Documents on German Foreign Policy, 1918–1945*, Series D, I, 632–33.

[17] Memorandum prepared by Herr Freytag, head of the North American Division of the Foreign Office, October 11, 1937. *Ibid.*, pp. 635–38.

self-styled champions of German political philosophy on American soil" and had given the impression that "they were acting under German orders." Any American, "regardless of where he stood politically, had to resist such interference."

In reporting this conversation to the Foreign Office, Dieckhoff sharply criticized the "stupid and noisy activities" of the German-American Bund. Unless the German Government clearly indicated that it did not sponsor these activities, the relations between Germany and the United States would be "seriously impaired."[18]

On December 20, Ambassador Dieckhoff wrote again to the Foreign Office concerning German-American relations which had not improved "during the last 7 months." One of the main reasons for this coolness was the fact that in the United States many people were suspicious of the "increasing activity" of the German-American Bund. He thought that it was "incontestable" that American dislike of this organization had made relations between the two countries "more difficult."[19]

Von Mackensen assured Ambassador Dieckhoff that the Foreign Office was following with "great concern the attacks of the press and of American authorities which are directed against alleged German interference in the American domestic situation." All correspondence between "Governmental or Party offices and the German-American Bund" had been stopped, and the ambassador's unfriendly attitude towards the Bund was approved.[20]

In the early part of January 1938, Ambassador Dieckhoff again adverted to the question of the unfortunate influence of the German-American Bund upon diplomatic relations. By its "program, by its uniformed parades, by its flag (identical with that of the German Reich), by its summer camps" and by numerous other activities, the Bund had given numerous Americans the impression that it is trying to "introduce an authoritarian regime in America." The so-called cultural program of the Bund could not achieve any unification of German-Americans to the point where they could be an important political asset for Germany. Indeed, "any political connection between any authorities in Germany and the German-American element, if any such exists, must be broken off." The methods of the Bund were likely to cause "difficulties and discord between the United States and Germany," and its role in Ger-

[18] Ambassador Dieckhoff to the State Secretary in the German Foreign Ministry, (Mackensen), Washington, November 24, 1937. *Ibid.,* pp. 648–51.

[19] Ambassador Dieckhoff to the head of the Political Department in the German Foreign Office (Weizsäcker), Washington, December 20, 1937. *Ibid.,* pp. 658–61.

[20] State Secretary in the German Foreign Ministry (Mackensen) to Ambassador Dieckhoff, Berlin, December 22, 1937. *Ibid.,* p. 662.

man-American relations should be carefully reviewed by the Foreign Office.[21]

In response to these dispatches from Ambassador Dieckhoff, the Foreign Office, through the head of the Auslandsorganization, decided to tell "Reich-Germans and Party members living in America immediately to renounce their membership" in the Bund. It was hoped that this action would "prove to the American Government and the American public that Germany had no intention whatever of interfering in America's domestic affairs."[22] On February 10 the Foreign Office instructed Ambassador Dieckhoff to inform Reich Germans that they could not be members of the German-American Bund or of any substitute organizations. This was regarded as an important gesture of friendship which should win American good will.[23]

In the meantime Prentiss Gilbert, the American chargé in Berlin, had a lengthy conversation with Dr. Schacht. Schacht prefaced his remarks with some words of high praise for Hitler whom he described as a "man of sound principles on whom the German people should pin its entire faith." He then professed great surprise that the activities of members of the German-American Bund should arouse so much concern in the United States. Von Neurath had definitely stated at Stuttgart that the "German Government was only interested in German citizens abroad." Gilbert replied that the "American people were not convinced" that the activities of the Auslandsorganization were "confined to German citizens."[24] It would be expedient for the Nazi Government to clarify this situation.

Shortly after this conversation with Dr. Schacht, Gilbert attended a dinner given by the Foreign Office and was surprised to find that he was sought out by Dr. E. W. Bohle, the head of the Auslandsorganization in the Foreign Ministry. Bohle expressed his concern at "the hostility of American public opinion toward Germany and stated that because of this he was insistent that German citizens should refrain from National Socialist agitation in the United States." Gilbert believed that this action on the part of Dr. Bohle revealed an "anxiety" on the part of German officials to have better relations with the United States. The

---

[21] Ambassador Dieckhoff to the German Foreign Ministry, Washington, January 7, 1938. *Ibid.*, pp. 664–77.

[22] Memorandum of a meeting between Herr Grothe, of the Auslandsorganization, and Consul General Lorenz representing the Cultural Department of the Foreign Office, Berlin, January 26, 1938. *Ibid.*, pp. 685–87.

[23] German Foreign Ministry to Ambassador Dieckhoff, Berlin, February 10, 1938. *Ibid.*, p. 691.

[24] Prentiss Gilbert to Secretary Hull, Berlin, January 27, 1938. 862.002/320, MS, Department of State.

new Four Year Plan of Hitler to strengthen the national economy of
Germany was partly dependent upon a larger volume of trade with the
United States. This objective could be achieved only on the basis of a
friendly accord between the United States and Germany.[25]

But this accord was not possible unless there was a profound change
in American opinion of Germany. Ambassador Dieckhoff wrote to the
Foreign Office on April 14 that anti-German sentiment in the United
States was still "strong" and that the German Government should
"make greater efforts than ever to give it a more favorable turn."[26]
While Ribbentrop was studying this problem he had a conversation
with Ambassador Wilson on April 29. When Ribbentrop complained
of the hostility of the American press, Wilson said that this animosity
was largely confined to the press "on the East coast which was dependent on banks and trusts." Among the American people as a whole
there was still "much sympathy for Germany." This evoked from Ribbentrop the remark that "the American people were regarded with respect and sympathy by Germans."[27]

Ambassador Dieckhoff found little sympathy in America for Germany. In July 1938, on the eve of his departure for Germany, he paid a
visit to the Department of State and sadly confessed to Secretary Hull
that relations between the United States and the Reich had grown
worse since his arrival as ambassador. Hull pointedly remarked that
relations would be better if Germany would adopt the high-level program followed by the United States: equality of opportunity for all
nations, fair play and fair dealing and noninterference in the internal
affairs of other countries. In contrast with American fair play the German Government had recently announced that it did not recognize any
liability for the payment of Austria's "external indebtedness." This
meant that Germany, after absorbing Austria, was repudiating rather
than paying Austria's debts. This example of lack of fundamental
principles, coupled with other examples of bad faith, had produced
such a strong tide of disapproval in the United States that it was difficult
for him and the President to hold it back in the hope that amicable relations between the two nations could be established.[28]

It was apparent to Dieckhoff that the German gesture of conciliation
concerning the activities of the German-American Bund had not created

[25] Prentiss Gilbert to Secretary Hull, Berlin, February 14, 1938. 711.62/138, MS,
Department of State.
[26] Ambassador Dieckhoff to the German Foreign Minister (Ribbentrop), Washington, April 14, 1938. *Documents on German Foreign Policy, 1918–1945*, Series D,
I, 703–4.
[27] Memorandum by Foreign Minister Ribbentrop, April 29, 1938. *Ibid.*, 704–5.
[28] Memorandum by Secretary Hull of a conversation he had with Ambassador
Dieckhoff, July 7, 1938. 711.62/160, MS, Department of State.

a friendly climate of opinion in the Department of State. Germany, if she wished to win American friendship, would have to abandon all hope of expansion through military force or by "interference in the internal affairs of other countries." The Treaty of Versailles had frozen the political structure of Europe. Any attempt to thaw this structure by the friction of armed pressure would awaken strong American disapproval. Peace was the President's passion and he expected other nations to express some of his fervor. He would regard with deep dislike any design for aggression. In November 1937, Hitler had prepared a detailed plan for Austrian absorption. The successful execution of that plan profoundly affected German-American relations.

c. *Austrian Independence Hangs in the Balance*

Hitler's plan for the absorption of Austria was disclosed on November 5, 1937, in the Reich Chancellery to an important group of trusted counselors—Field Marshal von Blomberg, Colonel General Baron von Fritsch, Admiral Dr. Erich Raeder, Colonel General Hermann Göring, Baron von Neurath, and Colonel Hossbach. In his discussion of the problems facing Germany, Hitler stated that the future of the Reich could not be assured either by autarchy or by a wider participation in world economy. There was pressing need for *Lebensraum* and this could be secured only through the conquest of desirable territory: "The German question can be solved only by way of force." The latest period when this war of aggression should be waged was during the period from 1943 to 1945. It was quite probable that war would come long before that date. In the event that "social tensions in France" should seriously reduce the efficiency of the French Army, or if France were engaged in a conflict with another state, Germany could then put her plan for expansion into effect.

The direction of this military thrust was clearly indicated: "It must be our first aim to conquer Czechoslovakia and Austria simultaneously." But this directive was flexible. When the time for action arrived, the absorption of Austria was given priority although Czechoslovakia was regarded as the richer prize.

The opportunity for conflict might develop from an Anglo-French attack upon Italy because of her intervention in the Spanish Civil War and her continued occupation of the Balearic Islands. In this regard Hitler stated that the "date which appeared to him as a possibility was the summer of 1938."[29]

---

[29] Minutes of the conference in the Reich Chancellery, Berlin, November 5, 1937. *Documents on German Foreign Policy, 1918–1945*, Series D., I, 29–39.

d. *Ambassador Bullitt Has Some Important Conversations*

A few days after this important conference in the Reich Chancellery
in Berlin, Ambassador Bullitt decided to pay a visit to Poland and Germany in order to discover if the ship of European peace were likely to
founder upon some hidden rock of misunderstanding. During his visit
to Warsaw, November 14–17, 1937, he had some extended conferences
with important Polish leaders. Colonel Beck, the Polish Foreign Minister, confided to him that he believed that Germany

in the near future would take some action against Czechoslovakia. . . . He
and Marshal Smigly-Rydz both expressed the opinion that France would not
intervene to save Czechoslovakia. . . . I [Bullitt] disagreed with this opinion
as I believe that at the *present moment* the French would mobilize at once
in case of a German attack on Czechoslovakia, either direct or through the
Germans of Bohemia. I do not know how long this state of mind on the part
of the French Government will prevail. . . .

I asked Beck what Poland would do in case France should become involved
in war with Germany because of a German attack on Czechoslovakia. Beck
replied that in the hypothetical case I had presented . . . Poland positively
would not march. . . . Under no circumstances would Poland become involved
in protecting French satellites in Central Europe, especially Czechoslovakia.
. . . In discussing the question of Danzig, Beck said that Hitler personally had
given Lipski, the Polish Ambassador in Berlin, the most absolute assurance
that he cared too much about Germany's good relations with Poland to permit the Germans of Danzig to do anything which would be totally inacceptable to Poland.

From Warsaw, Bullitt went to Berlin where he had several conversations with German officials. He found Baron von Neurath, the Foreign Minister, to be "supremely self-confident" and the atmosphere of
"the Wilhelmstrasse was as cocky as before the war." Neurath gave assurances that

Germany certainly desired peace. So far as France was concerned, there was
absolutely no outstanding question whatsoever between Germany and France.
. . . The national economies of the two countries supplemented each other
perfectly, and there was no reason why their trade should conflict. . . . Furthermore, the French had made it clear that they were ready to return the
German colonies they had been given by the Treaty of Versailles, provided
that England should take a similar course. . . . He feared that the British were
going to be extremely stiff-necked on the subject of the German colonies. . . .

In conclusion, Neurath said to me: "Tell your French friends that we are quite ready to establish the best possible relations with them."

Bullitt found that Dr. Schacht was rather cautious in his comments. He did feel impelled to speak of the "absolute necessity for doing something to produce peace in Europe before the outbreak of war toward which the Continent was drifting." Hitler was "determined to have Austria eventually and to obtain at least autonomy for the Germans of Bohemia." The one way "he could see peace was through direct negotiations between France and Germany."

General Göring was quite voluble. He repeated Dr. Schacht's opinion that there was no real quarrel between France and Germany. With regard to many of the problems that faced Germany, Göring expressed himself in great detail:

I asked Goering if . . . Germany was absolutely determined to annex Austria to the Reich. He replied that this was an absolute determination of the German Government. . . . Germany would tolerate no solution of the Austrian question other than the consolidation of Austria in the German Reich. . . . I asked Goering if the German Government was as decided in its views with regard to the Germans in Bohemia as it was with regard to Austria. He replied that there could be only one final solution of this question: the Sudeten Germans must enter the German Reich as all other Germans who lived contiguous to the Reich.

Goering then went on to say that he deplored greatly the present state of trade relations between Germany and the United States. The trade between the two countries was ceasing to be of any importance which was contrary to all reason. . . . He then asked me why I believed there was such hostility to Germany in the United States. I replied that there were many sources of this hostility. All Americans were devoted to the ideal of democracy. There has been a democratic government in Germany . . . which had been destroyed and replaced by Nazi dictatorship. . . . Furthermore, the German Government had at the same time attacked with the utmost violence the Jews, the Catholic Church and the Protestant Church. . . .

He thought that the violence of the reaction in the United States probably was due to the Jews. I replied that in some measure it was due to the Jews as was only natural. . . . I then added that . . . it appeared that the Nazi Government was engaged in forming Nazi organizations in the United States. Neither the Government nor the people of the United States could tolerate the formation on their soil of any national group . . . directed by any foreign country. . . . Goering said that he considered this entirely reasonable and understandable. . . . The German Government had forbidden any German citizen to participate in any way in the formation of such groups. . . . Goering then said that he hoped I realized there was an intense desire on the part of the German Government to develop better relations with the United States.[30]

e. *Hitler Plays Host to Lord Halifax*

Germany desired "better relations" not only with the United States but also with Great Britain. Göring had been very frank with Ambassador Bullitt with regard to the absorption of Austria. This same candor might pay big dividends with some important British statesman. Göring felt that he and Lord Halifax had a common denominator of understanding that was created by a mutual love of hunting. In the autumn of 1937, Göring, as game warden of the Reich, invited Halifax to Berlin to attend the International Exhibition of Hunting. As a well-known master of foxhounds, Halifax had never accepted Oscar Wilde's tart description of fox hunting: "The pursuit of the uneatable by the unspeakable."

Before Halifax reached Berlin the German Government made a quick survey of the situation. Franz von Papen had left Vienna for a brief visit to Paris where he discussed with French statesmen some of the important problems that required prompt settlement. He was a more devious person than Göring and did not speak as frankly of Hitler's ultimate aims. In a conversation with the French Minister of Finance he expressed the hope that France would "stop calling every extension of German influence in the Danube region a threat to French interests." When Bonnet inquired as to the real objectives of Germany in that region, von Papen answered with the glib lie that Germany wished merely the "closest community of economic and intellectual interests, with the preservation of Austrian independence." Later when talking with Premier Chautemps, von Papen repeated this exercise in mendacity. He did not reveal Hitler's determination to absorb Austria. The Führer desired a "marked extension of German influence in Austria obtained through evolutionary means." When Chautemps heard von Papen's assurance that Hitler's policy in the Danubian region was evolutionary rather than revolutionary, he was so overcome with emotion that he impulsively embraced the Nazi diplomat and exclaimed with delight: "Tell the Führer it would be a milestone in world history if we two were to place European politics on a new and healthier basis."[31]

In London, Halifax had a brief talk with Ambassador Ribbentrop

[30] Ambassador Bullitt to Secretary Hull, Paris, November 23, 1937. 123 Bullitt, William C./382-383, MS, Department of State.

[31] Von Papen's report to Chancellor Hitler of his conversation with Bonnet and Chautemps, November 8, 1937. *Documents on German Foreign Policy, 1918–1945,* Series D, I, 41–45.

with reference to his approaching visit to Berchtesgaden. It was apparent that his conversations with the Führer would deal mainly with the "Austrian and Czech questions," and with the important matter of the restoration of German colonies. Halifax stressed the viewpoint that a war between Britain and Germany would "mean the end of civilization." Ribbentrop agreed with this dire prediction and then observed that "not a single German desired such a conflict."[32]

On November 10, Halifax arrived in Berlin and soon had a talk with General Göring who confided to him that the German Government was bent upon incorporating Austria and the Sudetenland into the Reich. He made the further statement that Hitler also wished the return of Danzig to Germany and a reasonable solution of the Polish Corridor problem.

After hearing Göring's candid statements concerning the aims of the Nazi Government, Halifax went to Berchtesgaden to match wits with Hitler. On November 19 he had his momentous conversation with the Führer. There are four versions of this conversation, three of them from the German Foreign Office,[33] the fourth from the unpublished report Lord Halifax made to the British Foreign Office. A copy of this Foreign Office version was sent to the Department of State in order that President Roosevelt might have an "inside picture" of the European diplomatic crisis.

After the conversation had been formally opened by Lord Halifax, Hitler remarked that an agreement between Britain, France, Germany, and Italy would not be worth much "unless it took account of realities however unpleasant." The status quo "could not last forever. Changes could be brought about by (1) the play of forces—which meant war; (2) settlement by reason. We had had experience of (1) and it was therefore imperative to turn to (2), the way of reasonable solution."

Hitler then complained that "democracies were difficult to do business with owing to the party system and freedom of the press. All his previous efforts except the Naval Agreement had failed owing to this difficulty of doing business with democracies." Lord Halifax drily replied that "if agreement had to wait upon the abandonment of democracy by Great Britain, it was a waste of time to talk of an agreement." Hitler then hurriedly remarked that his reference had been "mainly to French democracy."[34]

[32]Ambassador Ribbentrop to the German Foreign Ministry, London, November 15, 1937. *Ibid.*, pp. 46–47.

[33] The most complete version of the Halifax-Hitler conversation on November 19, 1937, is printed in *Documents on German Policy, 1918–1945*, Series D, I, 55–67.

[34] Conversation between Lord Halifax and Hitler at Berchtesgaden, November 19, 1937. 740.00/238½, *Confidential file*, MS, Department of State.

Halifax then remarked that in England it was believed that it was "perfectly possible to clear out of the way the misunderstandings which existed at the present moment" between Britain and Germany. The solution sought for might be found in an "open exchange of views." These views could possibly lead to an agreement that would include not only Britain and Germany but also France and Italy.

Hitler thought that such an agreement should go much farther than merely "mutually polite relations." Germany should first of all be treated as a nation that "no longer bore the moral or material stigma of the Treaty of Versailles." The nucleus of the problem was the question as to "what active political co-operation could be accorded by a country which in other respects was not even accorded the most urgent necessities of life."

Halifax quickly replied that everyone in England "respected Germany as a great and sovereign country and that it was only upon this basis that she would be treated." The British Government did not necessarily believe that the status quo "must be maintained under all circumstances." Changes, however, should take place only upon "the basis of reasonable agreements reasonably reached."

But Hitler expressed the fear that it would be difficult for democracies to negotiate "reasonable agreements" because of the pressure exerted by demagogues. In the matter of restoring the colonies taken from Germany at the close of the World War he knew that the British Conservatives would vigorously oppose such a measure. The "same was the case in France." Political parties with their constant need to build political fences would erect high barriers along the road to realism.

Lord Halifax sharply challenged the view that the British Government was the "slave" of politicians with demagogic views. In England, no government "which was worthy of the name was under the domination of outside parties." He wished also to make it clear that Britain did not take the position that the question of the return of German colonies must not be discussed. British statesmen, however, were firm in their belief that it was a problem that required a general settlement and therefore negotiations between Britain and Germany should be merely of a preparatory character.

The conversation shifted to the League of Nations and Halifax asked Hitler if he "saw any possibility of leading Germany back to a closer co-operation with the other nations in the League of Nations." In what respect would Hitler want the League to be "altered before Germany could once more become a member?" Hitler expressed the view that the League without Germany, Italy, and Japan was not a real league of nations. Whether Germany would ever return to Geneva was a "question which could not at the moment be answered."

With reference to the disarmament question Hitler confessed that he had no idea how it could be brought "within the realm of practical possibilities." In any case he did not believe in conferences which were "doomed to failure from the start."

As far as Austria was concerned Hitler referred to the Austro-German Agreement of July 11, 1936, and expressed the hope that "it would lead to the removal of all difficulties." In the case of Czechoslovakia the Czechs themselves were in a "position to clear away any existing difficulties." Germany "set great store by good relations with all her neighbours."[35]

In his report to the British Foreign Office, Lord Halifax remarked that the atmosphere at Berchtesgaden and the

whole conversation was quiet and friendly although the Chancellor showed a certain reserve due perhaps to tiredness or perhaps to a feeling that his outlook has so little in common with that of democratic Governments. Herr Hitler said that he hoped we might get away from the atmosphere of "imminent catastrophe." The situation in Europe was not dangerous and of all the nations only Russia might think of war today.

The German Chancellor and others gave the impression that they were not likely to embark on adventures involving force or at least war. . . . Lord Halifax formed the view that they would pursue their objectives in Central or Eastern Europe in a fashion that would be perhaps unlikely to give other nations cause or at least the opportunity for intervention.[36]

On November 29, Prime Minister Chamberlain and Lord Halifax had a conference in London with the French Premier and the French Foreign Minister. Lord Halifax reviewed his conversation with Hitler and expressed the "general conclusion" that Germany thought that it was now up to Britain and France to "propose a solution of the colonial question if they wanted one." In this regard Germany believed that "all her former African colonies should be restored."

Halifax then gave his personal impressions of Hitler and of the European situation. His main impression was

that the Germans intended to press their colonial claim, but that they would not press it to the point of war. Unless the claim could be met in some form

---

[35] Conversation between Lord Halifax and Hitler, November 19, 1937. *Documents on German Foreign Policy, 1918–1945,* Series D, I, 55–65.

[36] Conversation between Lord Halifax and Hitler, November 19, 1937. 740.00/238½, MS, Department of State.

it would be impossible to improve relations in such a way as to make an advance towards the object which we all had in view. The question we had to ask ourselves, therefore, was whether it was possible to use this problem as a lever for getting some of the things both the French and British Governments wanted, such for example, as a contribution by Germany towards European peace. . . .

His [Lord Halifax's] broad impression was that Germany was extremely anxious for friendly relations with us. The Germans to whom he had spoken were also anxious to convince him that Germany had no direct cause of difficulty with France. . . . At the same time, while he [Hitler] desired to be friendly with us, the Chancellor was not prepared to run after us and was conscious of his own strength. He was not bent on early adventures, partly because these might be unprofitable, and partly because he was busy building up Germany internally. . . . General Goering had assured him that not one drop of German blood would be shed in Europe unless Germany was absolutely forced to it.

The Germans gave him [Lord Halifax] the impression of being convinced that time was on their side and of intending to achieve their aims in orderly fashion.

Premier Chautemps broke into the Halifax discourse and asked about the sincerity of Hitler's "reassuring words about Czechoslovakia." Halifax replied that he had been "surprised at the moderation of Herr Hitler's remarks on this point. He could only suppose the degree of permanence would in part depend on Germany's general international position and on the influence which we might exercise on the later developments of German policy." It was obvious, he believed, that Hitler was awaiting for some concrete proposal on the colonial issue before engaging in a discussion of other issues.[37]

Shortly after Premier Chautemps returned to Paris, Ambassador Bullitt had a long talk with him concerning the European situation. Chautemps stated that he

believed any immediate practical developments would be impossible due to the unwillingness of the British to make any concessions in the colonial domain to Germany. During the conversations in London his [Chamberlain's] Government had begun to approach delicately the question of whether France might be disposed to hand the Cameroons to Germany at once without any *quid pro quo*. Chamberlain had not made any direct statement on this subject, but he, Chautemps, had perceived what was in Chamberlain's thoughts and had therefore said at once that France could not place herself in the position of being the only country to make concessions to Germany in the colonial

[37] Conversation among Prime Minister Chamberlain, Lord Halifax, Premier Chautemps, and Foreign Minister Delbos, at London, November 29, 1937. 740.00/241½, *Confidential file*, MS, Department of State.

domain and would do so only if England was prepared to make similar concessions, and if such concessions should be a part of a general settlement. . . . Chautemps said that his declaration had stopped all suggestions which might conceivably have come from the British to satisfy Germany's colonial ambitions by giving her Portuguese, Belgian or French colonies. . . .

Chautemps went on to say that Halifax had made one blunder of the first water in his conversation with Hitler. He had begun by saying to Hitler that he had not come to discuss matters in Central Europe and had accepted without protest Hitler's reply that Great Britain was indeed very little interested in what might happen in Central Europe. . . .

I asked Chautemps if he saw any possibility of using the London conversations as the basis for an improvement in relations between France and Germany. . . . Chautemps said he felt there was a genuine desire in Germany at the present time to develop closer relations with France. It was, of course, impossible for France to rush into the arms of Germany and form overnight an offensive and defensive alliance; but it might be possible to inaugurate a period of genuine search for friendship. . . .

Chautemps went on to say that both he and Chamberlain believed that the Germans were entirely right in their view that Article XVI [dealing with the imposition of sanctions] should be eliminated from the Covenant of the League of Nations. He scarcely dared to say this above his breath because Delbos did not agree with him; and Herriot and Paul Boncour . . . were still quite unaware that their God had died. They were on their knees in front of the altar of the League from which the Deity had long since been removed. . . .

Chautemps said he would also say something else to me which was highly indiscreet. So far as he was concerned he looked with considerable equanimity on the possibility that Germany might annex Austria because he believed that this would produce an immediate reaction of Italy against Germany.[38]

In December 1937 the French Foreign Minister, Delbos, made a hurried trip to Poland and to the countries of the so-called Little Entente. He assured Ambassador Bullitt that he was "well satisfied" with the results of this brief survey. He had been able to "ascertain by personal contact that the Little Entente and Poland were determined to continue to occupy their positions within the orb of French policy." He was fearful, however, of a "German movement against Austria which would meet with little resistance either within Austria or from outside

[38] Ambassador Bullitt to Secretary Hull, Paris, December 4, 1937. 740.00/239, *Confidential file*, MS, Department of State. In a conversation with Foreign Minister Delbos, January 25, 1938, Bullitt heard once more these strong statements concerning Germany's desire for an accord with France: "Delbos said that he was convinced Germany desired genuinely to come to terms with France at the present time." *New York Times*, December 2, 1949.

Powers." He had no "constructive plans for the future but felt compelled to follow a policy of wait and see."[39]

f. *Britain Blocks a Presidential Program for Peace*

President Roosevelt did not accept the Delbos policy of "wait and see." Shortly after his quarantine speech of October 5 he decided to launch a real peace offensive. As President of the United States he would issue an appeal to the nations of the world to attempt to find some path to peace. He would emphasize the necessity for a close adherence to basic principles of international conduct. A suggestion would be made with reference to the problem of disarmament and he would call attention to the importance of breaking down the main barriers to world trade. Because of the horrors of modern warfare, he planned to ask the nations of the world to adopt far-reaching regulations that would conserve the safety and welfare of civilian populations. The detailed plan for carrying out these suggestions should be intrusted to a committee of ten nations whose membership would be representative of all parts of the world.[40]

The President had planned to issue this appeal on Armistice Day at a White House meeting of all the Diplomatic Corps, but he ran into the almost "hysterical opposition" of certain of his "closest advisers." He finally decided to take the matter up first with the British Foreign Office and get their reaction to it. When the Roosevelt proposal arrived at the Foreign Office on January 12, 1938, Anthony Eden was in France enjoying a brief vacation. Prime Minister Chamberlain read the proposal with surprise and immediately sent a strong negative. The British Government was ready to present an appeasement plan to Germany and Italy which might be adversely affected by any American diplomatic intervention. Prime Minister Chamberlain sent a letter to President Roosevelt in which he remarked that the American Government was well aware of

the efforts which His Majesty's Government for their part are making to bring about a measure of appeasement [with reference to Germany and Italy]. He [the President] will be interested to know that recently his Majesty's Government received an enquiry from the Italian Government as to when conversations could be re-opened with His Majesty's Government and that in the last few days I have agreed with the Secretary of State that the

[39] Ambassador Bullitt to Secretary Hull, Paris, December 23, 1937. 740.00/251, *Confidential file*, MS, Department of State.
[40] Sumner Welles, *The Time for Decision* (New York, 1944), pp. 64–66; Keith Feiling, *The Life of Neville Chamberlain* (New York, 1946), p. 336.

latter should on January 16th discuss with the French Minister for Foreign Affairs in Geneva the possibility of making a fresh approach towards reconciliation with Italy that might bring appeasement to the Mediterranean region at least. . . .

Our plan, both as regards Germany and Italy, rests upon the view that we and they are both in a position each to make a contribution towards the objective we both desire to obtain. There would be no need to discuss whether our contribution were greater or less than theirs. . . .

I mention these facts so that the President may consider . . . whether there is not a risk of his proposal cutting across our efforts here. It is probable that the Italian and German Governments, of whom we should have to ask a contribution, . . . will be none too ready to give . . . on the ground that the subjects under discussion, which for the most part will be specific and concrete in character, seem all merged in the wider problems which the President contemplates tackling as a whole. . . .

It would, I feel, be regrettable if what I am sure the President intends to be . . . action taken by him parallel to the efforts which we are making, were found to be capable of being used to block progress in the directions which over recent months we have laboriously worked, and for which we feel the stage has at last been set in not too unfavourable a manner. This leads me to ask the President to consider whether it would not be wiser to consider holding his hand for a short while to see what progress we can make in beginning to tackle some of the problems—see my letter of May 23rd.[41]

In response to this appeal from the Prime Minister, the President abandoned all thought of taking the initiative in proposing to the nations of the world a plan that might insure peace. In his reply to Mr. Chamberlain, the President made the following comments:

In view of the opinions and considerations advanced by the Prime Minister, I readily agree to defer making the proposal I had intended to make for a short while as he suggests in order that His Majesty's Government may see what progress they can make in beginning the negotiations they are contemplating. . . .

I will express the hope that he may be good enough to keep me advised of developments with regard to some aspects of the direct negotiations with Germany and Italy. . . . With regard to the political features of these negotiations, this Government of course has no connection. I feel, however, that it would be most helpful to this Government to be apprised of those features of the negotiations which would have a material effect upon the maintenance of those international principles and upon the policies of world appeasement which this Government endeavors to support.[42]

[41] Prime Minister Chamberlain to President Roosevelt, January 14, 1938. 740.00/264A, *Confidential file,* MS, Department of State.

[42] President Roosevelt to Prime Minister Chamberlain, Washington, January 17, 1938. 740.00/264B, *Confidential file,* MS, Department of State.

Anthony Eden was an ardent advocate of working in close co-operation with the United States. When he heard that Prime Minister Chamberlain had rejected the President's proposal of January 12 he returned at once to England and voiced strong disapproval of this action. As a result of this pressure the Prime Minister soon sent a second letter to the President in which he declared that he would "welcome the President's initiative and that the British government would do its utmost to contribute to the success of the scheme whenever the President decided to launch it."[43]

But President Roosevelt now thought that it was too late for him to embark upon a major adventure on the seas of diplomacy that were growing constantly more rough as the Ides of March approached. It would be expedient for him to follow a policy of watchful waiting. His proposal of January 12, therefore, remains as one of the great might-have-beens of world history. In this regard Sumner Welles remarks:

In November, 1937, the European situation was still fluid. While Hitler had undoubtedly already fully formulated his plans in co-operation with the German General Staff, the policies of Italy were far from crystallized. The full participation by the United States in such a world-wide effort to keep the peace as that envisaged by the President might have given Italy pause. It might have resulted in a radical modification of Japanese policy. . . .

With the annexation of Austria and with the threatened attack upon Czechoslovakia in the spring of 1938, the President had no longer any real opportunity to arrest impending calamity.[44]

The vacillations of Chamberlain were so profoundly disturbing to Anthony Eden that he resigned his office as Foreign Secretary on February 20. Lord Halifax and Chamberlain could now carry on their policy of appeasement which ended abruptly when Hitler's legions made their long-feared entry into Prague.

[43] Welles, *op cit.*, p. 68.
[44] *Ibid.*, p. 69.

XVI

Hitler Takes over Austria as a Long-Delayed Step towards *Anschluss*

THE PLANS of President Roosevelt and Prime Minister Chamberlain for effecting some sort of agreement with Chancellor Hitler were merely expressions of wishful thinking. The Chancellor had plans of his own which partial appeasement would not satisfy.

a. *The Viennese Waltz Takes on Macabre Overtones*

Austro-German relations from 1936 to 1938 afford an excellent example of the devious procedures of Nazi diplomacy. The agreement of July 11, 1936, was the opening wedge in the process of Austrian disintegration. Behind a façade of friendly phrases the Nazi propaganda machine was duly installed and, with the aid of numerous bunds, the gospel of National Socialism was spread far and wide. The agreement explicitly stated that both countries belonged within the German cultural orbit, and all existing restrictions on "cultural exchanges" were to be promptly removed. Both nations should "influence their respective press" so that "its objective criticism of conditions in the other country" should not be "offensive." The Austrian Government should conduct its foreign policy "in the light of the peaceful endeavors of the German Government's foreign policy." It should also appoint in the near future "representatives of the so-called 'National Opposition in Austria' to participate in political responsibility."[1]

Between every line of this agreement stalked the grim fact of eventual Nazi absorption of Austria. Political pressures in Europe would not permit any long postponement of this union. Franz von Papen and other diplomats might indulge in double talk that evaded any clear statement of this fact, but General Göring was quite frank in expressing the real implications of Nazi policy. In October 1936 he had an important conversation with Kurt von Schuschnigg, the Austrian Federal Chancellor, and after sounding him out on the Austrian situation, he reported that he had a certain "confidence" in the "aims" of Schuschnigg.[2]

---

[1] *Documents on German Foreign Policy, 1919–1945*, Series D, I, 278–81.

[2] Memorandum concerning the meeting between Colonel General Göring and the Austrian Federal Chancellor, Kurt von Schuschnigg, October 13, 1936. *Ibid.*, pp. 306–9.

But Schuschnigg destroyed a large part of this confidence when, on November 26, at Klagenfurt, he delivered a speech which opposed any further advance of National Socialism in Austria. Von Neurath instructed the German Legation in Vienna to express "astonishment" at such a tirade. Did the Federal Chancellor "really believe" that he could continue "ruthlessly to take measures against National Socialism?"[3] This hostile attitude of Schuschnigg led Hitler in January 1937 to send a protest to the Austrian Government with special reference to the punitive action that had been taken against persons who were members of a "National Socialist organization."[4] The explanation of the Federal Chancellor was not entirely satisfactory to the German Foreign Office.[5]

It was now entirely clear to Hitler that he could not count upon Schuschnigg to lend any support to Nazi plans for expansion. The Federal Chancellor would have to be eliminated, but it would be expedient first of all to see how close the ties were between Mussolini and the Austrian leaders. In January 1937, Göring was sent to Rome to explore the situation. In his usual blunt way he inquired if the Duce was willing to admit that Austria was within the "German sphere of interest" and therefore "even an Anschluss could be carried out" if Hitler desired it.[6] Mussolini did not rush to grab this bait. He did, however, finally assure Göring that he would exert pressure upon the Austrian Government so that the agreement of July 11 would be faithfully executed. Also, in the event of "a conflict in Austria, Italy would not resume . . . the 'Watch on the Brenner' against Germany."[7]

Göring realized that Mussolini had been too wary to underwrite Nazi schemes for aggression unless he received a substantial *quid pro quo*. This could be given in the form of potent German support of Italian ambitions in Ethiopia. In the face of strong League opposition, this action would soon convince the Duce that German friendship was worth far more than Austrian independence. When he arrived at this point of view the German Army could move into Vienna with confidence.

Germany was careful not to press this matter on Mussolini with too much haste. In May 1937, von Neurath visited Rome and reassuringly told the Duce that Germany still honored the Austro-German Agree-

[3] German Foreign Ministry to the German Legation in Austria, Berlin, November 28, 1936. *Ibid.*, p. 351.

[4] The State Secretary and chief of the Presidential Chancellery to the Foreign Minister, January 13, 1937. *Ibid.*, p. 374.

[5] The German Ambassador in Austria (Papen) to the German Foreign Ministry, Vienna, January 14, 1937. *Ibid.*, pp. 375–76.

[6] Memorandum by the German Ambassador in Italy (Hassell), Rome, January 16, 1937. *Ibid.*, p. 376.

[7] Memorandum by the German Ambassador in Italy (Hassell), Rome, January 30, 1937. *Ibid.*, pp. 384–85.

ment of July 11, 1936, and did not "intend any surprises or rash actions."[8] But Schuschnigg became increasingly hard to handle, and von Papen soon confided to the Italian Minister in Vienna that the actions of the Federal Chancellor were so disturbing that unless the tension were relieved "we might easily find ourselves in a situation highly detrimental to the interests of the Berlin-Rome Axis."[9]

It was soon evident to the German Foreign Office that time and British ineptitude were on the side of Hitler. The Ethiopian adventure and the civil war in Spain had thrown Mussolini deeper and deeper into Hitler's arms while Anthony Eden was lecturing him on the sins of aggression. When Germany moved ahead and recognized the Italian conquest of Ethiopia while also sending armed assistance to Franco, the Duce completely forgot his former interest in Austrian independence. *Realpolitik* became the watchword of the hour in the Wilhelmstrasse.

In London, British diplomats regarded with deep concern this Italo-German rapprochement, and some of them believed that British acquiescence in Hitler's demands for expansion in Central Europe might weaken these recent ties. One of these apostles of appeasement was Sir Nevile Henderson, the British Ambassador to Germany. Shortly after he arrived in Berlin he received an invitation from von Papen to visit Austria. In Vienna he quickly exchanged intimate confidences with the Nazi Ambassador. He entirely agreed "with the Führer that the first and greatest danger to the existence of Europe was Bolshevism and all other viewpoints had to be subordinated to this view." After von Papen outlined the Nazi way of looking at the Austrian problem, he remarked that he was convinced that "England fully understood the historical need for a solution of this question in the Reich-German sense." He was entirely opposed to the efforts of the British Ambassador in Vienna to preserve Austrian independence, and he was certain that his own opinions in that regard would "prevail in London." He hoped, however, that Germany would not "rush the solution of this problem."[10]

Hitler had no intention of seeking an immediate answer to the problem of Austria. During a conversation with General Göring and Foreign Minister von Neurath he stressed the belief that Germany should refrain from causing any "explosion" in Austria in "the forseeable future. We should continue to seek an evolutionary solution."[11] But the processes of evolution soon proved too slow to suit the Nazi program

[8] The German Foreign Ministry to the German Embassy in France and the German legations in Austria and Czechoslovakia, Berlin, May 8, 1937. *Ibid.*, p. 419.

[9] The German Ambassador in Austria (Papen) to the German Foreign Ministry, Vienna, May 26, 1937. *Ibid.*, p. 424.

[10] The German Ambassador in Austria (Papen) to the Führer and Chancellor, Vienna, June 1, 1937. *Ibid.*, pp. 427–28.

[11] Memorandum of a conversation among the Führer, Göring, and Baron von Neurath, October 1, 1937. *Ibid.*, pp. 463–64.

of expansion. In December 1937, von Papen warned Schuschnigg that the relations between Austria and Germany were not "developing favorably." The Federal Chancellor should realize that the German Reich was embarked upon a movement of the "greatest historical significance." Austria, "with heart and soul," should "support this struggle of the German world for its existence."[12]

In order to insure victory in this struggle, the Führer decided to make some changes in important official positions. At the historic meeting in the Reich Chancellery on November 5, 1937, when Hitler's plan of aggression in Central Europe had first been broached, opposition had been voiced by Marshal von Blomberg, Reich War Minister, Colonel General von Fritsch, Commander in Chief of the Army, and Baron von Neurath, the Foreign Minister. On February 4, 1938, an announcement was suddenly made in Germany that all three of these important leaders had been removed from office. Hitler himself became the Chief of the High Command; Ribbentrop replaced von Neurath; Colonel General Walther von Brauchitsch assumed the office recently held by Baron von Fritsch, while Göring was promoted to the office of Field Marshal.[13]

The American chargé in commenting upon these changes indicated that "the underlying causes of these changes" went much "deeper" than the much-discussed unfortunate marriage of Marshal Blomberg to the notorious Eva Gruhn. The sudden shift in personnel might well mean the beginning of a "more radical tendency in the conduct of German foreign affairs." In some quarters there were "strong apprehensions concerning some immediate move with especial reference to Austria."[14]

The German Ambassador in Washington assured Sumner Welles, the Under Secretary of State, that the recent replacement of von Neurath by Ribbentrop implied no change "whatever in German foreign policy." He admitted that Ribbentrop was "young and impulsive," but he would have the experienced von Neurath available for consultation on difficult problems that demanded careful consideration.[15]

From Berlin, Prentiss Gilbert, the American chargé, expressed the

---

[12] The German Ambassador in Austria (Papen) to the Führer and Chancellor, Vienna, December 21, 1937. *Ibid.,* pp. 483–84. The increasing pressure that Hitler was exerting upon Austria was well known to France. On November 22, 1937, Foreign Minister Delbos remarked to Ambassador Bullitt that he was "increasingly apprehensive that Germany in the near future would make some sort of drive against Austria. It was clear that the Germans were determined in one way or another to incorporate Austria in the German Reich." 740.00/225, *Confidential file,* Department of State.

[13] Sir Nevile Henderson, in his *Failure of a Mission* (New York, 1940), pp. 105–9, ascribes the removal of Marshal von Blomberg from office to his ill-fated marriage to Eva Gruhn.

[14] Prentiss Gilbert, the American chargé in Berlin, to Secretary Hull, February 5, 1938. 862.00/3726, MS, Department of State.

[15] Memorandum of a conversation between Ambassador Dieckhoff and Sumner Welles, February 8, 1938. 862.00/3742, MS, Department of State.

opinion that the "influence of Ribbentrop will be largely dominant in the advices in foreign affairs given to the Chancellor." He then alluded to the fact that Ribbentrop's character and the "past expressions of his policy" suggested that Germany had turned to a "more radical, a more active and thus a more 'dangerous' policy."[16]

Ambassador Wilson's first interview with Ribbentrop was brief and not very illuminating. The new Foreign Minister complained that the hostility of the British and French press made it difficult to carry on satisfactory relations with those countries.[17] With von Neurath it was a very different story. The former head of the Foreign Office was friendly and loquacious. He spoke of his desire for retirement and Hitler's refusal to permit him to leave office. This situation had been completely changed by von Blomberg's marriage to Eva Gruhn who had loved too much and too often. When Hitler learned that the door of Eva's heart had been opened to many men long before von Blomberg had rapped his aged knuckles upon its well-worn portals, he summoned von Neurath to the Chancellery. Neurath found the Führer

in tears, very much cut up by the fact that von Blomberg had misled him as to the wedding and put him [Hitler] in a disgraceful position. Von Neurath says that Hitler is extremely sensitive, especially as to what he considers anything that looked like betrayal of his friendship by his friends. He had been deeply fond of Blomberg and felt that the latter had let him down badly. He then said to von Neurath that he needed his post. Von Neurath said: "It is, of course, at your disposition." Hitler went on to say that he wanted to keep Neurath near him, nearer than before, and nearer than was possible when von Neurath was charged with an administrative position; but that he, Hitler, felt that something had to be done to divert public opinion, especially abroad, from the "shameful position" in which the Blomberg wedding had placed the Chancellor.[18]

b. *Schuschnigg Pays a Visit to Berchtesgaden*

Sir Nevile Henderson makes much of the von Blomberg affair and states that it precipitated a "fit of uncontrolled rage" on the part of Hitler which darkened the atmosphere in Berlin for a long period. It was convenient to find a scapegoat on whom much of the load of the Führer's wrath could be unloosed. The sinister von Papen suggested that

[16] Prentiss Gilbert to Secretary Hull, Berlin, February 11, 1938. 862.00/3735, MS, Department of State.

[17] Interview between Ambassador Wilson and Foreign Minister Ribbentrop, February 17, 1938. 762.00/185, MS, Department of State.

[18] Conversation between Ambassador Wilson and Baron von Neurath, February 19, 1938. 762.00/185, MS, Department of State.

Schuschnigg would be just the victim for such an ordeal by verbal fire. The Austrian Federal Chancellor was at once summoned to Berchtesgaden to meet Hitler in one of his nastiest tempers. Schuschnigg arrived on February 12 and was immediately subjected to a long ritual of indignities. He was always addressed as "Herr" or "Doktor" and not by his official title. Although he was an inveterate smoker he was not permitted to indulge in this habit in the presence of the Führer.

He was first scolded because Austria had not left the League of Nations, and his whole policy was condemned as a long betrayal of Germany's interests. It would be well for the Chancellor to realize that Austria's puny armed forces could not stem the advance of Hitler's legions if they should be ordered to march: "I may be in Vienna overnight like a storm in the spring! Then you will experience something!" He was warned that after the entry of German troops in Vienna the SA and the Austrian Legion would take over and no one would be able "to prevent their revenge." It should be obvious to most Austrians that no power in the world could "impede" Hitler's progress.[19]

After some eleven hours of such pressure, Schuschnigg broke down and signed an agreement that was the prelude to the absorption of Austria by Nazi Germany. First of all it was agreed that Dr. Artur Seyss-Inquart would be taken into the Austrian Cabinet as Minister of the Interior and Public Security. Under his constant supervision it would be possible to develop a National Socialist program that would eventually put Austria under German domination. Other items in the agreement had similar implications.[20]

Schuschnigg's return to Vienna marked the beginning of twilight in the Austrian capital. This was apparent to Mussolini who did not approve of the abrupt manner in which Hitler had treated Schuschnigg, and he resented the fact that Italy had not been consulted in the whole affair. Ciano read Philip of Hesse a lecture on German neglect of simple diplomatic courtesy and Mussolini sent some meaningless assurances to Schuschnigg, but it should have been obvious to most Austrian officials that the sands of their country's independence were fast running out. President Miklas made a brief, futile stand against the Nazi demands, but he was finally forced to agree to a new cabinet that con-

---

[19] The story of Austria's downfall is told in Kurt von Schuschnigg, *Requiem in Rot-Weiss-Rot* (Zurich, 1946); Guido Zernatto, *Die Wahrheit ueber Oesterreich* (London, 1938); M. W. Fodor, "Finis Austriae," *Foreign Affairs*, XVI (1938), 587–600; Elizabeth Wiskemann, *The Rome-Berlin Axis* (New York, 1949); G. E. R. Gedye, *Betrayal in Central Europe* (New York, 1939); and Eugene Lenhof, *The Last Five Hours of Austria* (New York, 1938).

[20] Protocols of the conference of February 12, 1938, at Berchtesgaden between Chancellor Hitler and Federal Chancellor Kurt von Schuschnigg, *Documents on German Foreign Policy, 1918–1945*, Series D, I, 513–17.

tained not only Dr. Seyss-Inquart but three other members friendly to Germany.[21]

On February 20, Hitler made a speech to the Reichstag that sounded like a requiem for Austria. There was no assurance of Austrian independence. Instead, Hitler merely expressed his "sincere thanks" to Schuschnigg for his "great understanding and the warm-hearted willingness with which he accepted my invitation [to Berchtesgaden] and worked with me so that we might discover a way for serving the best interests of the two countries." The real meaning of his words was disclosed by his fervid statement that it was "intolerable for a self-respecting world power to be permanently deprived of its entity," and to know that "across the frontier are kinsman who have to suffer severe persecution simply because of their sympathy . . . with the whole German people."[22]

c. *Lord Halifax Learns the Price of Appeasement*

In London there was great indecision concerning the best method of handling Hitler. In December, Chamberlain told Ribbentrop that Britain would be ready to make some proposals to the German Government in February or March with special reference to the colonial question. Ribbentrop then remarked that only a "very generous attitude toward German interests could finally lead to an understanding." Chamberlain, after weighing this statement, remarked that he would give his "full support" to a "German-British understanding."[23]

Chamberlain's conciliatory assurances led the German Foreign Office to prepare a memorandum which summarized British policy as follows: "British policy today proceeds on the thesis that it is possible to do complete justice to German grievances by peaceful means."[24] Ribbentrop, however, disagreed with this Pollyanna interpretation of the situation. In January he prepared a memorandum of his own in which he frankly stated that he placed little faith in Britain's desire for a real understanding with Germany. Britain was merely wearing a mask of friendship so that she could gain time for the preparation of a large armament. It would be unwise to put any dependence upon an "under-

[21] Fodor, *op cit.*, pp. 594–95.

[22] *The United States in World Affairs, 1938*, pp. 35–36; *New York Times*, February 21, 1938.

[23] The German Ambassador in Great Britain (Ribbentrop) to the German Foreign Ministry, London, December 17, 1937. *Documents on German Foreign Policy, 1918–1945*, Series D, I, 131–34.

[24] Memorandum on the diplomatic situation in Europe, December, 1937. *Ibid.*, pp. 148–51.

standing" with England. In reality she was Germany's "most dangerous enemy."[25]

Hitler probably had this memorandum in mind when, on March 3, 1938, he had a fruitless conference with Sir Nevile Henderson. Henderson struck a high note that must have sounded a little ridiculous to Hitler. The British Government, Henderson remarked, believed that any understanding with Germany could be reached if the negotiations proceeded on the "principle of higher reason as distinct from the use of mere force." Hitler listened to this high-level talk with a "ferocious scowl on his face," and then broke out into an impassioned harangue about the "sad fate of Nazi-loving Germans in Austria." After two hours of discussion which covered a multitude of topics, Henderson left the Reich Chancellery without having accomplished anything.[26]

A week later (March 9), the uneasy solution in the Austrian test tube was precipitated by an announcement of Schuschnigg that on the following Sunday (March 13) a plebiscite would be held on the issue of Austrian independence. His announcement was the death knell of Austrian sovereignty.

Hitler was thoroughly angered by any thought of a plebiscite in Austria and he at once began to exert pressure to prevent it. These tactics were regarded with deep disapproval by Lord Halifax. During a conversation with Ribbentrop on March 10 he indicated that His Majesty's Government was greatly disappointed at the attitude

of Herr Hitler towards their conciliatory and constructive approach but at the same time [he pointed out] that this disappointment made no difference to our firm desire for a better understanding with Germany. But if we were to succeed that could not be by unilateral effort on our part and all must make their contribution. . . . With regard to Central Europe we had not tried to "block up" Austria, but had rather tried to steady European opinion shaken by the Berchtesgaden interview [February 12]. . . . But we should be less than frank if we did not make it clear to the German Government the danger we saw in the expression that responsible leaders in Germany were giving in public to German policy and to the spirit in which that policy was being pursued. . . . The last thing we wanted was to see a war in Europe. But if once war should start in Central Europe it was quite impossible to say where it might not end or who might not become involved.

[25] Memorandum prepared by Ribbentrop for Hitler, January 2, 1938. *Ibid.*, pp. 162–68.

[26] Henderson, *op. cit.*, pp. 113–18. In the *Documents on German Foreign Policy, 1918–1945*, Series D, I, 250–49, there is a long memorandum covering this conversation between Hitler and Nevile Henderson. With reference to German minorities in Austria and Czechoslovakia, Hitler emphatically stated that "Germany must and would intervene if Germans in Central Europe continued to be oppressed in the same manner as hitherto, or in any other way."

Lord Halifax then expressed the opinion that the Austrian plebiscite, scheduled for March 13, should

be carried out without interference or intimidation. Herr von Ribbentrop . . . said that . . . he thought the most useful contribution we [the British Government] could make would be to use our influence with the Austrian Chancellor to cancel it. I replied that it seemed astonishing to me to assert that the head of a State should not have a plebiscite if he wanted one. . . .

Subsequently, at 5:15 P.M. I myself saw Herr von Ribbentrop again and spoke to him more strongly. . . . Our approach to Germany was not encouraging. . . . Their brutal disregard for any argument but force shows the difficulty of reasoning with them and must cast doubt upon the value of agreements reached with them. . . . The world has been faced with a *fait accompli:* it is extremely doubtful if any threat could have averted it; and certainly no threat which those making it were prepared to support by force.[27]

On this same day (March 10), Lord Halifax sent two telegrams to Sir Nevile Henderson, in Berlin, in which he used much the same language that he employed in his letter to President Roosevelt.[28] Henderson replied that he thought that German methods were "indefensible," but Schuschnigg's action in calling for a plebiscite was "precipitous and unwise."[29]

With reference to the plebiscite, Schuschnigg at first refused to bend before Nazi pressure and he turned to Britain and asked "what he should do."[30] Halifax replied at once that the British Government could "not take the responsibility" of advising the Chancellor to take a course of action that might lead to war.[31] All that Britain could do in this matter was to file a protest in Berlin against undue Nazi pressure.

A mere British protest to Berlin was too slender a reed for Schuschnigg to lean upon, so he resigned his office as Federal Chancellor. When this news reached London, Ribbentrop blandly remarked to Halifax that this action was "really much the best thing that could have happened." Surely the British Foreign Office would agree that it was "the object of us all to see peaceful solutions arrived at." Ribbentrop had no doubt that Schuschnigg was guilty of bad faith and had "completely gone back on his word from the Berchtesgaden arrangements." This reprehensible conduct had made the situation in Austria "quite impossible."

[27] Foreign Minister Viscount Halifax to President Roosevelt, London, March 11, 1938. 740.00/324½, *Confidential file*, MS, Department of State.
[28] Viscount Halifax to Sir Nevile Henderson, March 10, 1938. *Documents on British Foreign Policy, 1919–1939*, Third Series, I (London, 1949), 4–6.
[29] Sir Nevile Henderson to Viscount Halifax, March 11, 1938. *Ibid.*, p. 8.
[30] Mr. Palairet to Viscount Halifax, Vienna, March 11, 1938. *Ibid.*, p. 10.
[31] Viscount Halifax to Mr. Palairet, Foreign Office, March 11, 1938. *Ibid.*, p. 13.

Lord Halifax refused to look at matters through Nazi eyes. What the world had seen in Vienna was "an exhibition of naked force," and it should be obvious that such a dubious procedure would "seriously prejudice Anglo-German relations." Ribbentrop regarded this Halifax statement as wide of the mark. He was confident that British opinion could be "guided to take a realist view of what had passed and not be unwilling eventually to welcome it."[32]

On the following day Chamberlain had Ribbentrop as a luncheon guest and this meeting afforded another opportunity for conversation. Chamberlain very "emphatically requested" Ribbentrop to inform Hitler of his "most sincere desire for an understanding with Germany." At this point Viscount Halifax brought several telegrams to the Prime Minister. They indicating increasing tension in Vienna and Halifax excitedly remarked that the Nazi threats of force constituted an "intolerable method" of exerting pressure upon Schuschnigg. He then inquired if a plebiscite along "the pattern of the Saar plebiscite" would be held in Austria on a later date. Chamberlain at once interjected the opinion that this procedure did not "seeem to be required by the situation." This negative observation had a sedative effect upon Halifax who declared that he did not "insist" upon his suggestion concerning a plebiscite. Ribbentrop noted that the "usually very calm Lord Halifax" was more excited "than Chamberlain who outwardly at least appeared calm and coolheaded." At the close of the conversation "even Halifax was calm again."[33]

d. *British Appeasement of Italy Is Too Little and Too Late*

The formula of appeasement which Chamberlain worked out in the early months of 1938 was so dear to his heart that he clung to it with tenacity when the rest of the world saw that it could not solve the problems that threatened the peace of Europe. Anthony Eden did not share the enthusiasm of the Prime Minister in this regard and this fact put a strain upon their personal relations. The crisis came on February 18 when Chamberlain and Eden had two detailed conversations with Dino Grandi, the Italian Ambassador in London. According to Grandi, Chamberlain had already entered into an intrigue to oust Eden from office. During these important conversations among Chamberlain, Eden, and Grandi, the Italian Ambassador denied that an understanding had been reached with Germany whereby Hitler had been given a

---

[32] Viscount Halifax to Sir Nevile Henderson, Foreign Office, March 11, 1938. *Ibid.,* pp. 21–23.

[33] Memorandum by the German Foreign Minister, London, March 11, 1938. *Documents on German Foreign Policy, 1918–1945,* Series D, I, 273–75.

free hand in Austria in return for a promise of German support in the Mediterranean and in Europe. He did admit, however, that the Italian Foreign Office believed that a "friendly intimacy and close collaboration" between Germany and Austria was "essential to the peace and tranquility of Central Europe." Grandi also insisted that British recognition of the Italian conquest of Ethiopia be expressly granted as a preliminary step in the direction of an eventual Anglo-Italian rapprochement.[34]

The London *Times* showed that it was in complete agreement with the Italian thesis that close collaboration between Austria and Germany was essential to the peace of Central Europe. In an editorial on February 17, the argument was advanced that Britain should not attempt to block German expansion eastward, and four days later the assertion was made that Britain had no real concern with events in Central and Eastern Europe unless they should develop into a "catastrophic conflict."[35]

With the London *Times* preaching a policy of appeasement, Hitler on February 20 delivered a speech that attacked Anthony Eden with all the fury of long-suppressed hatred. With Chamberlain convinced that appeasement was the only way to quiet the turmoil in Europe and therefore in no mood to resent this Hitler harangue, it was evident that there was no real place for Eden in the British Cabinet. On February 20 he felt constrained to resign as Foreign Minister and his office was filled by Viscount Halifax, who was willing to follow Chamberlain's directions.[36]

With Eden out of the Cabinet, Chamberlain had even stronger hopes for the creation of an Anglo-Italian understanding. He was ready, of course, to pay the price. In a letter to Grandi he made the observation that he had never had the

slightest intention or plan to do anything that might weaken Italian-German solidarity. On the contrary, I consider the Rome-Berlin Axis as a reality which might represent the most valuable pillar of European peace. . . . This con-

---

[34] The German chargé d'affaires in Great Britain (Woermann) to the German Foreign Ministry, London, February 25, 1938. *Documents on German Foreign Policy, 1918–1945*, Series D, I, 218–23; Victor Gordon Lennox, "Anthony Eden," *Foreign Affairs*, XVI (1938), 691–703; *New York Times*, February 19, 20, 1938. Of outstanding value with reference to this episode is Count Ciano, *L'Europa verso la catastrofe* (Milan, 1948).

[35] London *Times*, February 21, 1938.

[36] It had long been apparent to Chamberlain that a rapprochement with Italy was difficult as long as Eden was in the Cabinet. On January 25, 1938, Foreign Minister Delbos told Ambassador Bullitt that "he was very positive of one thing; that Eden hated Mussolini more than any living human being." *New York Times*, December 2, 1949.

viction of mine, I am happy to confirm, is shared by my friend Lord Halifax.
... I want the Duce himself to know that while my immediate aim is a strong
and permanent treaty with the Duce and Fascist Italy, my long range ... aim
is a permanent and as strong as possible a treaty with the Fuehrer and National Socialist Germany.[37]

But these conciliatory words made no deep impression upon Mussolini who had now climbed with great agility upon the Hitler bandwagon. There would be no Anglo-Italian understanding that would
serve in any way to halt Hitler's march into Austria. The Duce had decided that Austria should be delivered into the Führer's eager arms as
the price for German recognition of Italian conquests in Africa. Schuschnigg was slow in grasping this fact. In order to keep alive Italian
dislike for German expansion in Austria, he sent his military attaché,
Colonel Liebitzky, to Rome to recount to Mussolini all the contemptuous remarks that Hitler had poured out against Italy during the famous
Berchtesgaden conversations on February 12. But the Duce shrugged
them off and began to make elaborate plans to welcome Hitler when he
arrived in Rome.[38] The Austrian plum was nearly ready for the picking
and Mussolini realized that no European power could hold back Hitler's hand.

e. *Hitler Marches into Vienna*

Before Hitler moved into Austria he was careful to extract from Mussolini assurance that this action was fully approved. On March 11 he sent
Prince Philip of Hesse to Rome with an urgent letter to Mussolini concerning the Austrian situation. This letter stated that the Austrian Government had in recent months established a close "relationship with
Czechoslovakia" which was a "most serious threat to the security of the
Reich." The Austrian Government was gradually arming "all the frontiers with fortifications" to bar the progress of German military forces.
In the event that war "was imposed upon Germany," the Austrian and
Czech soldiers could attack Germany's flank. The absorption of Austria
by Germany had therefore become a national imperative.[39]

After delivering this letter to the Duce, the Prince telephoned to
Hitler from Rome and announced the glad tidings that Mussolini had

---

[37] Prime Minister Chamberlain to Ambassador Dino Grandi, undated. *Documents
on German Foreign Policy, 1918–1945*, Series D, I, 238.

[38] Wiskemann, *op. cit.*, pp. 97–98.

[39] The Führer and Chancellor to Benito Mussolini, March 11, 1938. *Documents on
German Foreign Policy, 1918–1945*, Series D, I, 573–76.

"accepted the whole thing in a very friendly manner." The impact of these reassuring words upon Hitler was so great that he became hysterical. He asked the Prince to tell the Duce that he would never forget his assistance in this hour of need: "If he should ever need any help or be in any danger, he can be convinced that I shall stick to him whatever may happen, even if the whole world were against him."[40]

In Berlin, Göring telephoned to Seyss-Inquart and other Nazi sympathizers in Vienna in order to put pressure upon President Miklas. When Miklas finally succumbed to this pressure and appointed Seyss-Inquart as Chancellor, the last hour of Austrian independence was at hand.[41] German troops crossed the Austrian border on March 12, and two days later Hitler entered Vienna in triumph.

f. *American Reaction to* Anschluss

American reaction to the absorption of Austria by Nazi Germany was recounted in considerable detail in the dispatches of Ambassador Dieckhoff. On March 12 the ambassador called at the Department of State to discuss the situation in Austria. Although Secretary Hull asked a number of questions, he did not "express any critical or even disapproving attitude." This was also largely true of the American press on March 12 and 13, but the next day a "sudden change took place." The absorption of Austria was now stigmatized as "a breach of treaty, as militarism, as the rape of defenceless little Austria by her big neighbor bristling with arms." As far as the "shaping of the opinion of the American Government was concerned," the ambassador believed that the President himself had "intervened personally and gave instructions to both the State Department and the press." In the Department of State "they were probably, from the very outset, thinking less of Austria than of Czechoslovakia, with all the possible complications." On March 14, Dieckhoff had another conversation with Secretary Hull who maintained a calm and courteous demeanor, but Sumner Welles received the German Ambassador with a sour expression.[42] Indeed, in a dispatch to the Foreign Office on March 15, Dieckhoff complained that Welles

[40] Telephone conversation between Chancellor Hitler and Prince Philip of Hesse, March 11, 1938. *Nazi Conspiracy and Aggression* (Washington, 1946), V, 641–42. With reference to the possibility of using armed force to carry out Hitler's designs in Austria, see *ibid.*, VI, 911–13.

[41] Telephone conversation between General Göring and Nazi sympathizers in Vienna, March 11, 1938. *Ibid.*, V, 628–41.

[42] Ambassador Dieckhoff to the German Foreign Ministry, Washington, April 18, 1938. *Documents on German Foreign Policy, 1918–1945*, Series D, I, 615–20.

"gave expression to a sort of malevolent bitterness" when he alluded to the Nazi absorption of Austria.[43]

In the Department of State there is a copy of the conversation between Dieckhoff and Welles on March 14. After the ambassador had turned over to the Under Secretary of State the texts of the decrees incorporating Austria into the Reich, he evidently expected Welles to make some comments upon them. When Welles remained silent, Dieckhoff, with a show of "very considerable degree of nervous excitement," broke out with the exclamation: "This is a great day, a wonderful day for Germany." When Welles continued to remain silent, Dieckhoff then "embarked upon a tirade" against the critics of the recent *Anschluss*. He was particularly disturbed over the comments in the American press which he condemned as outright "lies." Next he sharply attacked the Jews and asked Welles why they were permitted "to dominate the press and public opinion." The Under Secretary denied the truth of such a statement and then remarked that "the Jewish element in the population of the United States was only a small percentage of our total population, nevertheless, the people of the United States felt that that element among them was as much a part of the United States as any other element of the population." Most Americans had Jewish friends "whom they regarded highly and whom they admired as fellow citizens." The unjust treatment meted out to them in Germany had aroused strong indignation against the Nazi regime. When Welles finished his remarks, Ambassador Dieckhoff hastily concluded the conversation with another brief diatribe against the "malignant and malicious falsehoods" of the American press.[44]

Dr. Goebbels, in Berlin, was also greatly perturbed over the hostile attitude of the American press. He thought that it was

lamentable that this campaign of hatred should be carried on. He did not in any way expect that Germany would escape criticism, but . . . what he did not expect and what he deeply deplored were wilful misstatements of fact and slander and libel against the persons of the Reich Chancellor and those immediately around him. He said that the person of the Fuehrer was venerated by every German. . . . Therefore the Germans deeply resented the personal attacks upon him. . . . He was sure that in the coming months I would have frequent opportunity to talk with and know the Fuehrer, and I could not but be impressed with the singleness of purpose and the undeviating honesty of the man's character. . . .

[43] Ambassador Dieckhoff to the German Foreign Ministry, Washington, March 15, 1938. *Ibid.*, pp. 604–5.

[44] Memorandum of a conversation between Sumner Welles, Under Secretary of State, and the German Ambassador, March 14, 1938. 863.00/1691, MS, Department of State.

Many people in Germany felt that relations with America were so bad through the press that there was no use trying to do anything about it. . . . But he was not one of those and such a point of view was to him a stultifying attitude. He thought there were possibilities of making it better and believed that if we could work with some measure of confidence we could bring about an improved relationship.

Ambassador Wilson expressed the opinion that the

most crucial thing that stood between any betterment of our Press relationship was the Jewish question. . . . Hatreds so deep as those which existed in my country on this question could not be mitigated in weeks or even months. It was a matter of years before such hatreds would lessen or be forgotten, and then only if new incidents did not give fresh fuel to the flames.

Turning from this outstanding question, Ambassador Wilson then remarked that much of the existing American hostility towards Germany was the result of a Freudian complex

by which deep affection which is shattered turns inevitably to hatred. . . . Americans of my age and generation had been accustomed to see the best intellectuals in our country go to Germany for education in medicine, technical matters, arts, and so on; . . . that ten thousands of families had German relatives. Thus the bonds between the two lands went so deep that we could not regard what happened in Germany with indifference.

Goebbels confessed that this was "an entirely new and interesting point of view," and he voiced the hope that the American Ambassador would come often to talk over matters of common interest.[45] There was little doubt that Goebbels was anxious to explore the reasons that lay behind German-American hostility. He had uncovered one of the important causes for friction when he referred to the German veneration for Hitler and the ceaseless attacks in the American press upon the Führer. It was obvious to many close observers of the scene in Germany that Goebbels himself had been indefatigable in his efforts to create this veneration for the Führer. His speech on April 20, in honor of Hitler's birthday, was a typical example of the Goebbels rhetoric in this regard. He was certain that an air of divinity surrounded the Chancellor. He recounted that after Hitler entered Austria his attendants saw a man "rush up to the Führer's car with his hands uplifted in prayer, and we had the feeling that here the emotion of the human soul had

[45] Memorandum of a conversation between Ambassador Wilson and Dr. Goebbels, March 22, 1938. 711.62/145, MS, Department of State.

found its consummate expression.''[46] With vast numbers of Germans sharing this viewpoint it became more and more difficult to maintain friendly relations between the two countries when the American press continued its campaign of criticism and ridicule.

This matter of the hostility of the American press continually thrust itself into the diplomatic picture in Berlin. At the end of April, Ambassador Wilson had a long talk with Foreign Minister Ribbentrop and the familiar topic of press criticism inevitably came up for discussion. Ribbentrop said that he had just been looking through a mass of clippings from American newspapers and they showed

a depth of hostility which had startled and shocked him. There was a lack of comprehension of everything that Germany had done and an immense proportion of complete misstatement of fact. . . . These reports could only be based upon gossip and rumor and usually originated from those who by race or politics were hostile to the regime and therefore inclined to distort facts.

He then observed that he had

spent a long and happy time in the United States as a boy, as well as in Canada; that he had numerous American friends with some of whom he still corresponded; that no one could spend a portion of his youth in a country without leaving a bit of his heart there; . . . hence it was doubly depressing to him that this outpouring of wrath should take place against his country.

Wilson interrupted this discourse to venture the opinion that this American hostility to Germany had many causes. The persecutions of Protestants and Catholics, the intimate relations between Germany and Japan, the Jewish question, and the manner in which the Nazi Government had absorbed Austria were important factors in creating a widespread dislike in America for the Nazi Government.

Ribbentrop then commented upon this factor of German absorption of Austria. Britain and France were far more concerned with the Austrian question than the United States, yet the press in those countries had taken a much more objective attitude than the American press. When the German editors read the vehement criticisms in American newspapers, they promptly "pled for the right to reply to them in their press. So far the German Government had refused to permit it. He defied me [Wilson], for instance, to find a personal criticism of President Roosevelt." Wilson made no attempt to disprove this statement. He merely confessed that he was afraid that the hostility in the American

[46] Ambassador Wilson to Secretary Hull, Berlin, April 22, 1938. 862.002 HITLER/161, MS, Department of State.

press "would not disappear for some years." In the meantime it was obviously the "part of those dealing in foreign affairs to try" to hold "their countries in normal and friendly relationships."[47]

Ambassador Wilson was entirely correct in his belief that the criticisms in the American press of Nazi Germany would "not disappear for some years." As they continued, the reaction in Germany became more pronounced. On the night of August 10 a reception was given in the Italian Embassy in honor of Marshal Balbo. During the course of the evening, Mr. Riddleberger, a member of the staff of the American Embassy, had a talk with Marshal Göring who immediately ascribed much of the hostility in America towards Germany to the machinations of the Jews and then launched into a

discussion of the Jewish problem. He predicted that within "ten years from this night" the United States would have become the most anti-Semitic country in the world. . . . I [Mr. Riddleberger] said to General Goering that this statement respecting the possibilities of anti-Semitism in the United States had interested me although I naturally did not agree with his prediction. I said that without going into a discussion of German policy with respect to the Jews, I was sure he would understand how this policy had caused grave concern to our and other Governments within whose jurisdiction the German Jews were seeking refuge. . . .

General Goering made no answer to this, but went on to declare that the Jews must be eliminated from German economic life. . . . Returning again to the problem of German-American relations, General Goering said that although they were none too harmonious, it was not necessary to despair and that we must hope for better days. . . . He ended his remarks by stating that the combination of Negroes and Jews in the United States, with the latter furnishing the leadership, was a matter that should give rise to considerable anxiety as to our future.[48]

It was apparent to Ambassador Wilson that while the German Government cordially disliked the American press it was nevertheless quite anxious to remain on friendly terms with the Department of State. For this reason Wilson accepted the invitation to attend the Nazi Party celebration in September at Nürnberg. He made plans to be present "during approximately the same period as the French and British Ambassadors."[49] This decision evoked from the B'nai Israel Jewish Centre

[47] Ambassador Wilson to Secretary Hull, Berlin, August 23, 1938. 862.00/3781, MS, Department of State.

[48] Memorandum of a conversation between Mr. James W. Riddleberger, of the staff of the American Embassy, and General Göring, Berlin, August 11, 1936. 711.62/163, MS, Department of State.

[49] Ambassador Wilson to Secretary Hull, Berlin, August 23, 1938. 862.00/3781, MS, Department of State.

of Brooklyn, New York, a spirited protest. Attendance at the Nürnberg celebration would be a "tacit condonance of the Nazi program of racial and minority persecution."[50] The Department of State refused to accept this viewpoint,[51] and Ambassador Wilson went to Nürnberg with his British and French colleagues.

It was the last Nürnberg celebration that any American Ambassador would attend. Underneath the surface of German-American relations there were many points of difference that constantly threatened to pierce the thin texture of political accord. The American press was unceasing in its attacks upon the German way of life and in many parts of the United States there were gestures of contempt that must have infuriated the Nazi leaders. On the amusement pier at Venice, California, there was an archery stand that used a life-size painting of Hitler as a target for a patronage that was "mostly Jewish, Italian and German."[52]

 In other cities Hitler was depicted on toilet paper and on other articles of toilet use. These forms of vulgar ridicule were infuriating to multitudes of Germans and they created a background for eventual war. Hatred is one of the heralds of conflict and already in the summer of 1938 he was busily blowing upon his trumpet all along the German-American front. After Munich his blasts would gain in volume and in tempo, but most Americans closed their ears to his din and continued to cherish the hope that President Roosevelt would keep them out of war. They did not realize that, like Lincoln, he was so fond of peace that he was ready to fight for it.

[50] David Surowitz to Secretary Hull, New York, August 25, 1938. 862.00/3783, MS, Department of State.

[51] Pierrepont Moffat, chief Division of European Affairs, to David Surowitz, Washington, September 8, 1938. 862.00/3783, MS, Department of State.

[52] R. J. Frazer to Secretary Hull, Santa Monica, California, May 22, 1938. 862.002 HITLER/162, MS, Department of State.

XVII

President Beneš Postpones Too Long
a Policy of Appeasement

a. *Czechoslovakia Precipitates the May Crisis*

HITLER'S ABSORPTION of Austria made a fundamental change in British and French plans to appease Germany by restoring some of the colonial domain that had been taken away from her by the Treaty of Versailles. France had long been favorable to the return of some of the German colonies as one means of satisfying the demands of the Nazi Government for *Lebensraum*. In September 1937, Chautemps had informed Ambassador Bullitt that for France the question of colonies was "not insurmountable," but he believed that Britain would "resist to the utmost" any colonial settlement satisfactory to Germany.[1] British opposition to any "deal" with Germany concerning colonies was given vehement expression by Anthony Eden: "The British answer to Germany *in re* colonies should be a vast increase of Britain's armament program."[2] France thought that this British position was too extreme, and Foreign Minister Delbos had tried to argue the question with Eden. He discovered, however, that the British Foreign Minister was "adamant" in his opposition. The British Government was "fully determined not to permit the clauses [of the Treaty of Versailles] with regard to colonies to be changed."[3]

Some weeks later Delbos remarked to Ambassador Bullitt that he believed the

best chance of beginning negotiations which might lead to a peaceful settlement of the situation in Europe or at least postponement of war would be in the colonial domain. France and England could not offer Germany "concessions" in Austria and Czechoslovakia ... [but] in the colonial domain France and England had something to give and could therefore demand something in exchange. He felt, therefore, that through the door of colonial concessions it might be possible to enter into fruitful negotiations. He believed that if

---

[1] Ambassador Bullitt to Secretary Hull, Paris, September 20, 1937. 751.6111/196, MS, Department of State.

[2] Ambassador Bullitt to Secretary Hull, Paris, November 26, 1937. 741.62/202, MS, Department of State.

[3] Ambassador Bullitt to Secretary Hull, Paris, November 6, 1937. 740.00/221, *Confidential file*, MS, Department of State.

some progress could be made in the colonial field it might not be impossible to begin conversations for a new Locarno. . . .

He [Delbos] said that as far as he was concerned, he favored making concessions to Germany piecemeal in order to stave off war, but in a democracy it was intensely difficult to make piecemeal concessions. Public opinion would very much prefer to submit to a *fait accompli* rather than make a concession.[4]

This conciliatory attitude on the part of France continued during the spring of 1938. In March, Flandin, former Foreign Minister, told the German Ambassador in Paris that from the "French standpoint the solution of the colonial question" was not a serious matter.[5] For a while Britain also seemed in the mood for some concessions. With Eden out of the British Cabinet, Chamberlain was ready to discuss the colonial question. In his conference with the Führer, March 3, Sir Nevile Henderson had indicated that Britain "might be prepared to transfer some colonial territory in Africa to Germany." Hitler had replied to this cautious statement by insisting that "all German colonies must be returned."[6] Henderson could give no "definite answer" to this sweeping demand, so the subject was postponed for future discussion.

Lord Halifax kept the matter open by assuring Ribbentrop that Britain "had in mind returning colonial territory to German sovereignty." But he insisted that the British Government could not settle the colonial problem in "isolation from other problems."[7] Some solution was necessary for the questions that constantly threatened the status quo on the Continent. Hitler's sudden absorption of Austria disturbed Halifax and postponed for a while all further conversations concerning colonies. British interest shifted to Italy and plans were made to entice Mussolini back into the arms of British and French statesmen.

In order to sound out Italy in this regard, Churchill was sent to France to survey the situation. He was surprised that the French Government would "place no confidence in an Anglo-French tie-up with the Soviet because of France's doubts as to the value of the Soviet as an Ally." Finally, after talking matters over with the French statesmen, Churchill frankly asked Blum a series of questions as to whether the

---

[4] Ambassador Bullitt to Secretary Hull, Paris, November 22, 1937. 740.00/225, *Confidential file*, MS, Department of State. In December 1937, Franz von Papen left the German Legation in Vienna for a brief visit to Paris. He discovered that French statesmen believed that the "colonial question" could be "easily solved." *Documents on German Foreign Policy, 1918–1945*, Series D, I, 102–3.

[5] The German Ambassador in France (Welczek) to the German Foreign Ministry. *Ibid.*, p. 230.

[6] Memorandum by the German Foreign Minister, Berlin, March 3, 1938. *Ibid.*, pp. 236–38.

[7] Record of a conversation between Viscount Halifax and Foreign Minister Ribbentrop, March 10, 1938. *Ibid.*, pp. 253–61.

French Government would be willing to enter into close relations with Britain and Italy for the purpose of negotiating "a Mediterranean Locarno." The recognition of Franco's government in Spain was an important item in this proposed three-power accord.[8]

After carefully studying all the implications behind these questions, Blum was said to have told Churchill that he was in favor of proceeding with the "preliminary discussions" leading to a new Locarno treaty.[9] While France would be engaged in the first stages of these discussions, Britain was to initiate negotiations with Germany for a pact that would settle not only the question of colonies but would also extract from Hitler some general "guarantees of security" for the status quo in Europe. Chamberlain was said to be ready to "inform Daladier and Bonnet that if the French would agree not to put obstacles in the way of British direct bilateral talks with Germany, and if the French would complete their deal with Mussolini, the British would be prepared to make a defensive alliance with France."[10]

b. *The Sudeten Germans Formulate Demands Which They Know Cannot Be Fulfilled*

It was difficult for Chamberlain or Halifax to realize the impossibility of negotiating a satisfactory treaty with either Germany or Italy. The European structure built upon the Treaty of Versailles was already tot-

---

[8] Ambassador Biddle to Secretary Hull, Warsaw, March 31, 1938. 740.00/340, MS, Department of State. The questions that Churchill asked Léon Blum were listed as follows:

"1. Was Blum prepared and willing that both Blum and Chamberlain should recommend to the League recognition of Italian conquest of Ethiopia?

"2. Would Blum entertain the idea of a pact of non-aggression and economic cooperation between the British, French and Italian colonial empires on condition that Italy would assure France and Great Britain of:
   a. No threat of interference with French and British Mediterranean communications?
   b. No Italian bases to be established and no Italian territorial ambitions in Spain?

"3. In the event of Franco's victory would France join Britain in eventually recognizing Franco in the first stage as a *de facto* government which might lay way open for Franco to negotiate a pact of mutual understanding or non-aggression with Britain and France guaranteeing no Italian or German troops or bases in Spanish territory?

"4. Would France join Great Britain and Italy in negotiating a Mediterranean Locarno to be supported by Franco in certain aspects although Franco would not be expected to be a principal part to the guarantees involved?

"5. In second stage would France join Britain in recommending to League the recognition of Franco government *de jure*?

"6. Would France then conclude an Anglo-French military alliance in support of the above policy with the approval of Italy?"

[9] *Ibid.*

[10] Ambassador Biddle to Secretary Hull, Warsaw, April 28, 1938. 740.00/373, *Confidential file*, MS, Department of State.

tering and Hitler was determined that it should not be repaired by any mortar of appeasement. He was bent upon its destruction and out of the ruins he expected to erect an edifice with the new Germany as the keystone. Such a task would require diplomacy with just the right flavor of force. Needless to say, there would also be the proper amount of deceit which through the centuries has earned for diplomacy the apt description of the "craft sinister."

The assurances that General Göring gave to M. Mastný, the Czech Minister in Berlin, on the night of March 11 were too transparent to be deceptive.[11] The Nazi leaders had worked out a blueprint of aggression that looked towards the absorption of Czechoslovakia as well as of Austria. They would first split the Czech State along the line of the Sudetenland, and the remaining portion would inevitably fall into German hands. The demands for Sudeten autonomy could be given a reasonable appearance, but they would really serve as a screen behind which the drive for the absorption of the Sudetenland could be organized and carried out. This fact was made clear during the conversation between Hitler and the leaders of the Sudeten German Party, Konrad Henlein and Karl H. Frank. The Führer stated that he "intended to settle the Sudeten German problem in the not-too-distant future." He could "no longer tolerate Germans being oppressed or fired upon." Hitler then turned to Henlein and remarked: "I will stand by you; from tomorrow you will be my Viceroy." The purport of the instructions that the Führer gave to Henlein indicated that no compromise with the Czechs was acceptable: "Demands should be made by the Sudeten German Party which are unacceptable to the Czech Government." Henlein replied: "We must always demand so much that we can never be satisfied."[12]

The Karlsbad Programme issued by Henlein on April 24 was prepared in the spirit of Hitler's instructions and was far-reaching in its implications. In the meantime, on April 21, Hitler had an important conversation with General Keitel in which a plan of operations for an attack upon Czechoslovakia was discussed in detail.[13] Hitler's policy of "planned aggression" left little to chance. While Britain and France nursed hopes of finding some formula of appeasement that might lead to a new Locarno, Germany was thinking of peace only upon her terms, and those terms meant Nazi dominance in Europe.

11 The German Minister in Czechoslovakia (Eisenlohr) to the German Foreign Ministry, Prague, March 13, 1938. *Documents on German Foreign Policy, 1918–1945*, Series D, II, pp. 158–60.

12 Memorandum of conversation among Hitler, Konrad Henlein, and Karl Hermann Frank, Berlin, March 28, 1938. *Ibid.*, pp. 197–98.

13 Memorandum on "Operation Green": Summary of the Führer-General Keitel conversation, April 21, 1938. *Ibid.*, pp. 239–40.

c. *Chamberlain Says Britain Will Not Fight for Czechoslovakia*

It was obvious to France that German dominance in Europe would soon be insured unless some way were found to defeat the schemes of Nazi leaders. But any plan that had any real promise of success in checking Hitler would presuppose an intimate association between Britain and France and an evident readiness to meet a Nazi challenge with the answer of immediate mobilization. But Chamberlain feared that such an answer might lead to the outbreak of hostilities. On March 14 he momentarily laid aside these fears and boldly denounced the use of "violent methods" in solving the problems of Europe. Further aggression could not be regarded by His Majesty's Government "with indifference or equanimity."[14] But this show of courage soon disappeared. On March 24 he was much more cautious in his comments. Now he declared that Britain was not prepared to defend Czechoslovakia against unprovoked aggression.[15]

Two days earlier Viscount Halifax had instructed Sir Eric Phipps, in Paris, to inform the French Government that Britain recognized its obligations under the Covenant of the League of Nations and under the terms of the Treaty of Locarno, but the Foreign Office had no intention of enlarging the scope of its responsibilities. A German attack upon Czechoslovakia would not, therefore, bring a British army into the field to defend Czech frontiers, although it was always possible that political pressures might compel the British Government to join a crusade against oppression.[16]

Halifax realized that this statement would be cold comfort to the French Foreign Office, but he was apprehensive about being more specific. His objection to the use of threats arose from his doubt of the ability of Britain, "or the ability of France and Great Britain combined, effectively to enforce them."[17]

Henderson, in Berlin, agreed with Halifax about the "futility of forcible protests unbacked by force or the fear of force." Moreover, one should not underestimate Hitler. He might be a "pathological subject, an introvert, a mystic or anything else which one may choose to call him,

---

[14] Statement by Prime Minister Chamberlain to the House of Commons, March 14, 1938. *Parliamentary Debates,* House of Commons, 5th Ser., vol. 333, cols. 45–52.

[15] John Wheeler-Bennett, *Munich: Prologue to Tragedy* (New York, 1948), pp. 36–40.

[16] Viscount Halifax to Sir Eric Phipps, Foreign Office, March 22, 1938. *Documents on British Foreign Policy, 1919–1939,* Third Series, I, 82–86.

[17] Viscount Halifax to Sir Eric Phipps, Foreign Office, March 23, 1938. *Ibid.,* pp. 86–88.

but in addition to all that, there is no doubt that he is a constructive genius."[18]

With Hitler a big question mark and his policy a threat to the peace of Europe, British and French statesmen decided to hold some conversations in London on April 28–29. During the course of these talks Halifax repeated the warning that Britain's specific commitments of aid were limited to the conditions laid down in the Covenant of the League of Nations and in the terms of the Treaty of Locarno. The British Government was not ready to "assume fresh military commitments." It was, therefore, extremely important for the Czechoslovak Government to realize the gravity of the situation and make "a supreme effort to reach a settlement" with Germany with reference to the autonomy of the Sudetenland.[19]

In order to conciliate Germany, Halifax sent word to Henderson that the Nazi Government should be advised that Britain had "no desire to interfere in what they [the Germans] regard as their own domestic sphere. . . . We are fully prepared to recognize that they have a special interest" in the Sudetenland problem. But it should be kept in mind that the British Government was not "disinterested in a question that may involve an outbreak of war."[20]

Chamberlain, apparently, had some misgivings about these final words of warning to Germany. In order, therefore, to show a most sincere spirit of appeasement he made some revealing statements at an informal luncheon party given by Lady Astor to American and Canadian newspaper correspondents. He was reported to have said that "neither France nor Russia, and certainly not Britain, would fight for Czechoslovakia in the event of German aggression, and that the Czechoslovak State could not continue to exist in its present form."[21]

d. *Tension in Czechoslovakia*

Despite the excessively conciliatory attitude of Chamberlain, Halifax continued his efforts to exert some pressure upon Germany in favor of the acceptance of a reasonable compromise of the Sudetenland problem. He instructed Henderson to convey an indirect warning to the German

[18] Sir Nevile Henderson to Viscount Halifax, Berlin, March 24, 1938. *Ibid.,* pp. 97–100.

[19] Record of Anglo-French conversations, held at No. 10 Downing Street, April 28–29, 1938. *Ibid.,* pp. 198–234.

[20] Viscount Halifax to Sir Nevile Henderson, Foreign Office, May 5, 1938. *Ibid.,* pp. 253–55.

[21] Wheeler-Bennett, *op. cit.,* p. 52; See also "Augur," *New York Times,* May 14, 1938.

Government not to be "stiff" in its attitude towards Czechoslovakia. Ribbentrop should be impressed by the fact that it would be impossible for Britain "to be disinterested in any issue on which the future of European peace might one day be found to depend."[22] This warning appeared to have some effect upon the Nazi Foreign Minister who discussed the problems of Europe with Henderson in an "unusually temperate maner." He was obviously "impressed both by the dangers of the situation" if it were "allowed to drag on and by the necessity of finding peaceful solution in this last opportunity for co-operation with Great Britain."[23]

As the period of tension in Czechoslovakia did "drag on" without any real solution in sight, Henderson expressed to Halifax the fear that in the event of any "serious bloodshed" arising out of clashes between Germans and Czechs it was certain that Germany would intervene. It should be remembered that the Nazi Government regarded Henlein's demands for Sudeten autonomy as reasonable. It would, therefore, be a "grave mistake" for the British Government to count upon its "moderating counsels at Berlin proving effective, even if backed by threat of war, if we support Czech proposals which fail approximately to satisfy Henlein's demands."[24]

As the crisis grew more threatening there were rumors (May 20) of partial German mobilization. Although these were promptly denied there was increasing anxiety about the imminence of war. This deepened when the Czech Government itself (May 20) suddenly decided upon partial mobilization.[25] Matters were made worse when a Czech policeman fired upon and killed two Sudeten German motorcyclists who refused to answer his challenge. Karl Frank, one of the Sudeten leaders, had an audience with Prime Minister Hodža with regard to this incident, and when asked what he wished as a final solution of the Sudeten problem he replied: "Complete federalization, and in the event of its failure, a plebiscite." Hodža agreed "unreservedly and declared that he intended to resign if Beneš did not side with him."[26]

While things in Czechoslovakia remained unsettled, the tension in Berlin rose to such a height that Sir Nevile Henderson found Ribbentrop in a "highly excitable and pugnacious frame of mind." He warned

[22] Viscount Halifax to Sir Nevile Henderson, Foreign Office, May 11, 1938. *Documents on British Foreign Policy, 1919–1939*, Third Series, I, 281–82.

[23] Sir Nevile Henderson to Viscount Halifax, Berlin, May 12, 1938. *Ibid.*, pp. 284–86.

[24] Sir Nevile Henderson to Viscount Halifax, Berlin, May 19, 1938. *Ibid.*, pp. 318–19.

[25] Wheeler-Bennett, *op. cit.*, p. 55.

[26] The German Minister in Czechoslovakia (Eisenlohr) to the German Foreign Ministry. *Documents on German Foreign Policy, 1918–1945*, Series D, II, 304–5.

Henderson that "Germany would not wait much longer and if provocation continued her 75 millions would act as one man."[27]

Halifax responded to this threat by advising Germany to have patience. Britain was exerting all possible pressure upon the Czech Government in order to "promote a peaceful solution" of the Sudetenland question. The Foreign Office in Berlin should remember that in the event of German aggression upon the Czechs, France would be compelled to intervene at once. In such circumstances, "His Majesty's Government could not guarantee that they would not be forced" to become "involved also."[28] On the following day Halifax was more precise and more threatening. He informed the German Ambassador in London that "in the case of a German entry into Czechoslovakia, in whatever circumstances, even in the event of serious acts of provocation by the Czechs, the French would march against us [the Germans]. . . . In the event of a European conflict it was impossible to foresee whether Britain would not be drawn into it."[29]

After sending these clear warnings to Berlin, Halifax then tried to exert a restraining influence upon the French Government. He assured the French Foreign Office that His Majesty's Government would always honor their "pledge to come to the assistance of France if she were the victim of unprovoked aggression by Germany." But the French Government should not assume that the British Government would "at once take joint military action with them to preserve Czechoslovakia against German aggression."[30]

These British warnings to Germany had some influence upon Hitler who was always willing to revise his timetable if some compelling necessity dictated it. The evidence that France was ready to lend armed support to Czechoslovakia, together with the partial mobilization of Czech troops, were additional factors that led Hitler to abandon any thought of ordering his armies to cross the Czech border. On May 23 the Czech Minister in Berlin received assurances as to German intentions towards his country. On the same day Henlein was ordered to return to Czechoslovakia and resume negotiations for the peaceful settlement of the Sudetenland problem.

Czechoslovakia had won a diplomatic victory but her success would

[27] Sir Nevile Henderson to Viscount Halifax, Berlin, May 21, 1938. *Documents on British Foreign Policy, 1919–1939*, Third Series, I, 329–30.
[28] Viscount Halifax to Sir Nevile Henderson, Foreign Office, May 21, 1938. *Ibid.*, pp. 331–32.
[29] The German Ambassador in Great Britain (Dirksen) to the German Foreign Ministry, London, May 22, 1938. *Documents on German Foreign Policy, 1918–1945*, Series D, II, 322–23.
[30] Viscount Halifax to Sir Eric Phipps, May 22, 1938. *Documents on British Foreign Policy, 1919–1939*, Third Series, I, 346–47.

be short-lived. Hitler was now bent upon her destruction. He particularly resented the Czech rumors of German mobilization. The British military attaché in Berlin, Colonel Mason-MacFarlane, had been permitted to ride along 1,100 kilometers of frontier roads and had seen no signs of troop activity.[31] This negative report had been confirmed by certain consular officials, and at Nürnberg, Generals Jodl and Keitel testified that they had not moved "a single soldier" towards the Czech border.[32] To be falsely accused by Czech officials was to Hitler the supreme insult.

It is significant to note that Beneš had decided upon mobilization without first informing France of his decision.[33] He had then suddenly left for his country estate and thus isolated himself from events in Prague.[34] High army officers had seized their cue and had taken over the situation. This action had so disturbed the Czech Cabinet that it had been decided to summon Beneš to return to Prague and choose between the civil government and the General Staff.

It was apparent to Hitler that Beneš had precipitated a crisis in order to humiliate Germany. Such tactics could never be forgiven or forgotten. On May 30, he issued a directive for "Operation Green." The execution of this operation was to be assured by "October 1, 1938 at the latest." The first two paragraphs reveal the Führer's deep hatred for the Czechs and his determination to destroy their country: "It is my unalterable decision to smash Czechoslovakia by military action in the near future." Some "unavoidable development of events within Czechoslovakia, or other political events in Europe providing a suddenly favorable opportunity which may never recur, may cause me to take early action."[35] This action was now inevitable.

e. Germany Prepares a List of Political Imperatives

To a French statesman like Bonnet the approaching Munich crisis was expected and welcomed. He constantly breathed a spirit of defeatism and was entirely ready to acquiesce in German domination of the European continent. He was cordially disliked by Prime Minister Daladier who lacked the courage to dismiss him from office. Daladier's experience in the World War had made him an ardent pacifist. That long con-

31 Sir Nevile Henderson to Viscount Halifax, Berlin, May 23, 1938. *Ibid.*, p. 358.

32 *Ibid.*, p. 359. See also, *Nazi Conspiracy and Aggression*, IV, 363.

33 Sir Eric Phipps to Viscount Halifax, Paris, May 21, 1938. *Documents on British Foreign Policy, 1919–1939*, Third Series, I, 336.

34 German Minister in Prague (Eisenlohr) to the German Foreign Ministry, *Documents on German Foreign Policy, 1918–1945*, II, 308–9.

35 Directive for "Operation Green," Berlin, May 30, 1938. *Documents on German Foreign Policy, 1918–1945*, Series D, II, 357–62.

flict had served as a grindstone that ground him down rather than polished him up. The "Bull of Auvergne" had grown weary of conflict and was longing for peaceful pastures. In a conversation with the German Ambassador in Paris he stressed the "horrors of the last war," and feared that a second world war would end in a Russian triumph that would mean that "Cossack and Mongol hordes" would bring to Europe a hideous new design for living.[36]

With France ready for acquiescence and Britain bent upon appeasement, the future looked bright to Hitler. He was particularly pleased over the rift between Poland and Czechoslovakia. In Paris, Ambassador Biddle talked with the Czech Minister to France (M. Oszuski) and was shocked at his bitterness towards Poland. He was very fearful that there was "little hope of ameliorating Polish-Czech relations on a durable basis."[37] Hitler could make good use of this bitterness.

But the Führer would have to be more careful of appearances because in the United States there was a fast-growing suspicion of Nazi motives. On the last day of May, Ambassador Dieckhoff sent to the Foreign Office a long summary of American opinion of Germany in which there was a curtain line of warning:

I repeat on this occasion, too, that if, as a result of the Czech affair, a large-scale conflict should arise in which Britons became involved, the United States would not permanently stand aside, but would enter the conflict against us. Feeling here has become much more acute and bitter in recent months, and the few friends we still have are so timorous and dumb that there is little to prevent the entry of the United States into a war against us. The propaganda news from Austria has produced a bad impression in the widest circles here.[38]

Dieckhoff's letter evidently made a deep impression upon Weizsäcker who prepared a memorandum which outlined a number of political imperatives that Germany should follow. First of all it should be assumed that in the path of German expansion, France would stand as the "most certain opponent" and Britain as the "most dangerous enemy." But neither country would cross swords with Germany "without the other." In case of war, Germany would have to reckon "as a matter of course that the United States of America and Soviet Russia will associate themselves with the *de facto* alliance against us of these two

36 The German Ambassador in France (Welczek) to the German Foreign Ministry, Paris, May 23, 1938. *Ibid.*, II, 326–28.

37 Ambassador Biddle to Secretary Hull, Warsaw, July 20, 1938. 740.00/437, *Confidential file*, MS, Department of State.

38 Ambassador Dieckhoff to the State Secretary (Weizsäcker), Washington, May 31, 1938. *Documents on German Foreign Policy, 1918–1945*, II, 369–72.

Powers, France and Britain." Germany would have to brush the opposition of "this Entente from her future path by diplomacy or by war."
Only if the "Entente attacks us will the Third Reich consider staking its
existence on a war. Our essential war aims do not lie on their territory.
We have no military recipe for defeating France and Britain." Even
taking into account Italian and Japanese assistance, the war would end
in German "exhaustion and defeat." The task of German diplomacy
was to recognize clearly the limits to which German policy could be
"pushed for the time being without causing the Entente to interfere."
The most immediate problem for Germany to solve was that dealing
with Czechoslovakia. By leaving war out of the question for the time
being, it was then obvious that the Czech State should be destroyed by
"internal disruptive tendencies." This process should be a gradual one
and plebiscites and other peaceful procedures should be employed.
Slogans like "self-determination" could serve a most useful purpose.
But it should never be forgotten that Germany was "not free to choose
the moment when this fruit may be plucked without too great a risk."[39]

f. *Konrad Henlein Asks for Provocative Concessions*

Konrad Henlein was an important factor in this Nazi program for
the gradual disintegration of Czechoslovakia. His list of demands
would include items which he knew the Czech Government would not
accept. But the Foreign Office did not want these demands to be so excessive as to cause "a new crisis."[40] After some pressure had been
exerted upon him he presented to Dr. Hodža (June 8) his new program
which emphasized the importance of dividing Czechoslovakia into racial areas. Each of these areas should enjoy such a degree of autonomy
as to be virtually independent although it still retained an important
voice in the affairs of the central Czech Government. Hodža accepted
this memorandum along with the Karlsbad Programme as a basis for
round-table conferences which should begin on June 23. Ernst Kundt
would serve as the chief representative of the Sudeten Germans during
these conferences.

Prime Minister Hodža assured the German Minister in Prague that
"in the matter of autonomy he was ready to go to the utmost limit,"
and his assurances were accepted at face value.[41] But the negotiations
dragged on without any settlement, and the British Government be-

[39] Memorandum by State Secretary Weizsäcker, June 20, 1938. *Ibid.*, pp. 420–22.
[40] State Secretary (Weizsäcker) to the German Ambassador in Great Britain
(Dirksen), Berlin, June 1, 1938. *Ibid.*, pp. 374–75.
[41] The German Minister in Czechoslovakia (Eisenlohr) to the German Foreign
Ministry, Prague, June 10, 1938. *Ibid.*, pp. 402–3.

came deeply concerned about the situation. These fears were increased when the German Foreign Office expressed to Sir Nevile Henderson the opinion that the "state of the negotiations was highly unsatisfactory."[42] The German Government was critical of the dilatory manner in which the negotiations at Prague were being handled, and when the British Minister pressed this point, Beneš protested that he was anxious to settle everything as "soon as possible."[43] Henderson, in Berlin, was particularly worried about the continued delay in arriving at some solution of the problem. He sharply complained to Lord Halifax that his efforts for peace stood "no chance of success as long as there are no practical results to show for our action in Prague."[44]

This lack of response in Prague to British pressure made the German Foreign Office skeptical of British intentions. Weizsäcker had a conversation with Hugh Wilson, the American Ambassador, and expressed his disgust with the fact that Viscount Halifax had never told the Czechs that they "must not go beyond a certain limit of patience if they did not wish finally to gamble away the support of the Western Powers in the event of a conflict." Ambassador Wilson was in sympathy with the position of Herr Weizsäcker and he criticized the "delaying tactics" of Beneš and his methods of "suppressing facts." The British apparently did not want a European war but they did not do "what was really necessary to avoid it."[45]

g. Lord Runciman Calls Czechoslovakia an "Accursed Land"

It was difficult for the British Government to know what to do to prevent the outbreak of hostilities along the border of Czechoslovakia. Any little incident could be magnified into dangerous proportions. The British Minister in Prague followed with anxiety the conversations between Henlein and Czech officials, and he was disturbed when Hitler summoned the Sudeten leader (July 9) to Berchtesgaden to report on the progress of the negotiations. There was a possibility that this was the first step in a new Hitler program aimed at crushing Czechoslovakia by a surprise attack. British apprehensions were heightened by the surprisingly stiff attitude of President Beneš who appeared determined to "give the Sudeten Germans only a very short time in which to comment on the cut-and-dried indivisible scheme" which he intended to

---

[42] Memorandum by the State Secretary (Weizsäcker) for the Foreign Minister, July 1, 1938. *Ibid.*, p. 449.

[43] Mr. Newton to Viscount Halifax, Prague, June 3, 1938. *Documents on British Foreign Policy, 1919–1939*, Third Series, I, 442–43.

[44] Sir Nevile Henderson to Viscount Halifax, Berlin, June 6, 1938. *Ibid.*, p. 447.

[45] Memorandum by the State Secretary (Weizsäcker) for the Foreign Minister, Berlin, July 8, 1938. *Documents on German Foreign Policy, 1918–1945*, II, 481–82.

present to the Czech Parliament. Lord Halifax thought that it was "obviously unfair" for the Czech Government to take "several weeks to make up their own minds" and then demand that the Sudeten Germans "make up theirs in a few days." In order to stave off a possible war the British Foreign Secretary decided to ask the Czech Government to accept Lord Runciman as an independent arbitrator.[46]

While the Czech Government was pondering the appointment of Lord Runciman, Lord Halifax had a long conversation with Captain Wiedemann who paid a visit to London as a special representative of Hitler. The Captain lost no time in telling Halifax of Hitler's "admiration and friendship" for Britain. The Führer was anxious to preserve friendly relations with England and that was the reason for the Wiedemann mission. He was especially worried about the delays in the settlement of the problem of the Sudetenland Germans. At any moment incidents might occur which a "great State like Germany could not overlook."[47]

These words of warning made Lord Halifax doubly anxious for the success of the Runciman mission, but the Czech Government insisted that the Sudetenland problem could not be the subject of outside arbitration so Runciman was finally sent to Prague merely as a "mediator and adviser."[48] When he talked the situation over with President Beneš he discovered that the Czechs had serious objections to an autonomous Sudetenland which, if it did not soon secede from Czechoslovakia, would at least constitute a dangerous leaven of discontent within the uneasy dough of the Czech State. While Runciman did not meet Henlein for some time after his arrival in Prague, he did have many conferences with other Sudeten Germans and took careful note of their arguments.[49]

It was soon obvious to him that the situation in Czechoslovakia was filled with political dynamite. The National Minorities Statute passed by the Czech Parliament did not meet the demands of Hitler, and the so-called Czech "Plan No. 2," drawn up to meet all Sudeten objections, was rejected on August 17 by the Sudeten leaders. When this action was followed by large-scale German military maneuvers in Saxony and Silesia, the British Foreign Office grew alarmed. But British diplomats in Central Europe had evident sympathy with this German method of pressure. Sir Nevile Henderson, in Berlin, had long realized that the

[46] Viscount Halifax to Mr. Newton, Foreign Office, July 18, 1938. *Documents on British Foreign Policy, 1919–1939*, I, 581–83.

[47] Record of a conversation between Viscount Halifax and Captain Wiedemann, July 18, 1938. *Ibid.*, pp. 548–89.

[48] Mr. Newton to Viscount Halifax, Prague, July 21, 1938. *Ibid.*, pp. 604–8.

[49] Viscount Halifax to Viscount Runciman, Foreign Office, August 18, 1938; Viscount Runciman to Viscount Halifax, August 18, 1938. *Ibid.*, II, 111–16.

only way to keep the Sudetenland out of German hands was to propose to Sudeten leaders a compromise solution that would be so reasonable that European opinion would demand its acceptance. Any delays in this matter would invite Germany to push its own program of complete autonomy for the Sudetenland. President Beneš could never make up his mind how far to go along the road to concessions to the Sudeten Germans, and this indecision cost his country dearly.

In surveying this situation in Central Europe, Sir Nevile Henderson was anxious that the Foreign Office make no misstep. He was particularly anxious that it should discard the Eyre Crowe tradition of inveterate hostility towards Germany. Such a viewpoint might be disastrous. It should also be kept in mind that the Sudeten Germans had a very good case to present to world opinion. Their rights had not been carefully guarded by the Czech Government. In fact, the position of "Beneš and his military enthusiasts" was "quite untenable." Moreover, Beneš himself was a "small man. That is a fact. And now all depends on Lord Runciman."[50]

Chamberlain thought that he might be able to contribute to the success of the Runciman mission by exerting pressure upon Hitler. On August 27, at Lanark, he pushed Sir John Simon into repeating, during a speech, the warning of March 24 to the effect that if war resulted from Czechoslovak complications it would be "quite impossible to say where it would end and what Governments would become involved."[51] The French Government followed this warning by ordering troops to occupy the Maginot line.

Hitler's response to this pressure was a message to the British Legation in Prague that he would "welcome a peaceful solution of [the] Sudeten question if it comes quickly." He was also interested in a general "Anglo-German settlement" whose terms Henlein could bring to Berlin upon his next visit.[52] Lord Halifax quickly vetoed any use of Henlein as an agent who could assist in negotiating a general settlement of Anglo-German problems. That could best be done through regular diplomatic channels. With reference to the Sudeten question he thought it would be expedient for Beneš to publish his latest offer to Hitler immediately, so that the world would appreciate its reasonable character.[53]

When Beneš handed to Mr. Newton his "Plan No. 3" the British Minister was "very much disappointed" in its contents and complained

[50] Sir Nevile Henderson to Viscount Halifax, Berlin, August 22, 1938. *Ibid.*, pp. 131–34.
[51] Viscount Halifax to Mr. Newton, Foreign Office, August 27, 1938. *Ibid.*, pp. 172–75.
[52] Mr. Troutbeck to Viscount Halifax, Prague, August 29, 1938. *Ibid.*, p. 177.
[53] Viscount Halifax to Mr. Newton, Foreign Office, August 29, 1938. *Ibid.*, pp. 180–82.

that instead of amplifying his former proposals he merely "diluted" them.[54] Lord Runciman himself was so deeply disturbed by the way things were going that he began to call Czechoslovakia an "accursed country." As he looked around the signs of "bad government" in Czechoslovakia were accumulating every day and "at any moment Hitler may find an excuse for crossing the frontier in order to maintain order." The new plan of Beneš was distinctly unsatisfactory. It was a "long nine-page memorandum covered with bolt holes and qualifications."[55]

Lord Halifax was greatly upset by this letter from Lord Runciman. If Beneš were "playing fast and loose" was it not time for "taking drastic action?" His behavior would "do incalculable harm" if something were not done to check him. He should be advised immediately to publish his new plan for the settlement of Sudeten difficulties. It should be evident that the German Government would not "stand aside and wait much longer for the present negotiations to produce a satisfactory solution of the Czechoslovak question."[56]

Lord Runciman was now ready to tell Beneš that his "latest memorandum" had made a "bad impression." He was also prepared to have Henlein visit Hitler and place the situation before him. As for Henlein himself, Runciman assured Lord Halifax that he was "courteous, friendly, and (I believe) honest." It might be well for Britain to support the eight points of the Karlsbad Programme as the only way to peace.[57]

While Henlein was in Berchtesgaden discussing the Beneš proposal with Hitler, Prime Minister Chamberlain had a talk with Ambassador Kennedy. Chamberlain admitted that Britain did not have a strong enough army to stop Hitler if he invaded Czechoslovakia and therefore he did not believe in the use of empty threats. Kennedy became somewhat excited as the discussion proceeded and exclaimed that if Hitler seized Czechoslovakia it would "be Hell." He believed that if France went to the aid of the Czechs and if Britain had "to go in too, the United States would follow before long." When Kennedy asked if President Roosevelt could make any move that would be of assistance in this crisis, Chamberlain advised against another speech like the Chicago address of October 5, 1937. Any repetition of the threats contained in that address would "now be bad." Kennedy then broke into the discourse to express the view that President Roosevelt had de-

[54] Mr. Newton to Viscount Halifax, Prague, August 30, 1938. *Ibid.*, pp. 188–89.
[55] Lord Runciman to Viscount Halifax, Prague, August 30, 1938. *Ibid.*, p. 192.
[56] Viscount Halifax to Mr. Newton, Foreign Office, August 31, 1938. *Ibid.*, p. 193.
[57] Mr. Newton to Viscount Halifax, Prague, September 1, 1938. *Ibid.*, p. 199.

cided "to go in with Chamberlain; whatever course Chamberlain desires to adopt, he [Roosevelt] would think right."[58]

Several days after Ambassador Kennedy had so generously promised
Prime Minister Chamberlain American armed assistance in the event
that Britain was drawn into a second world war, Ambassador Bullitt,
in Paris, struck a very different note. In a conversation with Sir Eric
Phipps, the British Ambassador, Bullitt remarked that if any German
troops crossed the Czech frontier, France would "undoubtedly fight on
behalf of Czechoslovakia." Fortunately for France, Bullitt believed
that she had the finest army "in the world today." Bullitt then referred
to the strong anti-German sentiment in the United States. When Phipps
asked him if this meant any "likelihood of United States' participation
in hostilities at an early stage," Bullitt replied in the negative. It should
be kept in mind that the American people had a very definite objection
to being "involved in hostilities in Europe only twenty years after the
last war, with the likelihood that they would again get more kicks than
ha'pence for their help." He had made this fact clear to the French
Government and was certain that they had "no illusions on this score."[59]

On the day of this conference between Bullitt and Sir Eric Phipps,
Henlein returned to Prague. He had talked with Hitler at Berchtesgaden and had told the Führer that the objectives sought by the Sudeten
Germans were either "autonomy within Czechoslovakia" or a "plebiscite which means solidification with the Reich." He had assured Hitler
that he wished to gain either of these objectives in "a peaceable way"
and to this the Führer had "fully assented."[60]

As soon as the British Minister in Prague had this word from Henlein he advised President Beneš to go to the "limit of concession" and
this limit "ought not to stop short of the eight Karlsbad points if a
settlement could not be obtained otherwise." After tendering this advice to Beneš, Mr. Newton then criticized Czech insincerity with reference to former promises that had not been carried out. President Beneš
should understand that the failure of the Czech Government to live up
to its word in these matters had made "a very bad impression."[61]

h. *Sir Nevile Henderson Loses Patience with Beneš*

Sir Nevile Henderson was just as critical of President Beneš as was Mr.
Newton. He thought it should be obvious that Hitler would not permit

---

[58] Viscount Halifax to Sir Ronald Lindsay (In Washington), Foreign Office, September 2, 1938. *Ibid.*, pp. 212–13.
[59] Sir Eric Phipps to Viscount Halifax, Paris, September 2, 1938. *Ibid.*, pp. 218–19.
[60] Mr. Newton to Viscount Halifax, Prague, September 3, 1938. *Ibid.*, pp. 231–32.
[61] Mr. Newton to Viscount Halifax, Prague, September 4, 1938. *Ibid.*, pp. 226–29.

Henlein to accept less than the Karlsbad Programme and that the reluctance of Beneš to use these eight points as a basis for discussion had caused a dangerous delay in settling the Sudeten problem. It was difficult for the Czech President to face "realities." In the end he would probably play the "same role as Schuschnigg and will end by doing incalculable harm to his country and possibly to all of us."[62]

At this point, according to the dramatic story recounted by John Wheeler-Bennett, Beneš suddenly decided to summon the Sudeten leaders and ask them to enumerate in writing their principal demands. When they refused to do so he requested them to dictate their program which he took down and signed. This was later known as "Plan No. 4." It embodied most of the items in the Karlsbad Programme and it indicated the limit of concessions that Beneš felt called upon to make.[63]

It is significant that the text of this "Plan No. 4" was furnished to the Royal Institute of International Affairs by the Czechoslovak Government in Exile in 1942.[64] It may or may not be authentic in all particulars. It is also necessary to call attention to the fact that the colorful account of the meeting between Beneš and the Sudeten leaders, as given in the monograph by Mr. Wheeler-Bennett, was drawn entirely from the interview between Beneš and G. E. R. Gedye as published in the London *Daily Herald* of October 8, 1945. It is quite probable that Beneš gave his story as dramatic a setting as was possible. The admirers of President Beneš may still wish to accept his version of the meeting with the Sudeten leaders.

In the meantime it will be pertinent to notice that Mr. Newton, Lord Runciman, and Sir Nevile Henderson were at times sharply critical of Beneš and were suspicious of his program. In the dispatches of Lord Runciman there is no mention of the meeting of September 4 and the impression is given that Beneš was still negotiating with the Sudeten leaders. Mr. Newton, the British Minister, saw Beneš on September 4 and apparently talked to him "pretty plainly" about his "delays" in presenting terms to Henlein. Runciman regarded these delays as inexcusable: "Nothing can excuse his [Beneš'] slow movements and dilatory negotiations of the past five months."[65]

By the first week in September, Sir Nevile Henderson had lost all patience with Beneš for his interminable delays. On September 6, he expressed to Halifax the opinion that the "moment has come" for

[62] Sir Nevile Henderson to Viscount Halifax, Berlin, September 4, 1938. *Ibid.*, pp. 238–39.

[63] Wheeler-Bennett, *op. cit.*, pp. 89–92.

[64] *Documents on International Affairs, 1938*, ed. Monica Curtis (New York, 1943), II, 178–84.

[65] Viscount Runciman to Viscount Halifax, Prague, September 5, 1938. *Documents on British Foreign Policy, 1919–1939*, II, 248–49.

Britain and France to give "categoric advice" to Beneš to accept "even what the latter describes as Hitler's ultimatum."[66]

Prime Minister Hodža appeared to share some of this Henderson viewpoint because he removed from the hands of Beneš (September 6) the control of the negotiations with the Sudeten leaders. He then told them that the final text of the plan for Sudeten autonomy "was not yet complete" but would soon be drafted. The Sudeten German delegation was impressed with the sincerity of Hodža and expressed the unanimous opinion that the Czech proposals "could not be turned down" because they included the substance of the Karlsbad Programme. But because of certain incidents that had just occurred at Maehrisch-Ostrau, the negotiations would have to be broken off until the matter was "cleared up."[67] They were never seriously resumed.

This decision on the part of the Sudeten German delegation to break off negotiations seemed to Lord Halifax to have so many ominous implications that he instructed Sir Nevile Henderson to inform Hitler that His Majesty's Government was "greatly disturbed" by the situation in Prague and felt impelled to ask for the co-operation of the German Government in averting a "calamitous termination" of the Czech-Sudeten German negotiations.[68] Henderson, at Nürnberg attending the Nazi Party celebration, was very much opposed to a policy of making even an indirect threat for the purpose of checking German action against Czechoslovakia. There would be no aggression against the Czechs but if they continued their "pin-pricking, anything may happen and no threat will deter the Chancellor once he decides that German honour . . . obliges him to act. It is essential to keep cool."[69]

i. *Kennedy Predicts U.S. Intervention in World War II*

In London, Ambassador Kennedy was watching the situation in Prague and Nürnberg with evident apprehension. During a conversation with Lord Halifax he voiced the opinion that it was "essential to take every possible step to avoid a misunderstanding in Herr Hitler's mind." The British Government should be ready for any emergency and he wondered if "it might not be possible for the Soviet Government to make some movement that would compel attention, such as a concentration of aeroplanes near the frontier." As far as America was concerned, he

[66] Sir Nevile Henderson to Viscount Halifax, Berlin, September 6, 1938. *Ibid.*, pp. 250–51.

[67] The German chargé d'affaires in Czechoslovakia (Hencke) to the German Foreign Ministry, Prague, September 7, 1938. *Documents on German Foreign Policy, 1918–1945*, II, 711–12.

[68] Viscount Halifax to Mr. Kirkpatrick, Foreign Office, September 9, 1938. *Documents on British Foreign Policy, 1919–1939*, II, 277–78.

[69] Sir G. Ogilvie-Forbes to Viscount Halifax, Berlin, September 10, 1938. *Ibid.*, p. 280.

had been interested to notice that "American opinion was much more excited against Germany now than he had ever known it." If Britain were drawn into the war now threatening Europe, and if London were bombed, the "history of the last war would be repeated, leading a good deal more rapidly than in the last war to American intervention.[70]

While Ambassador Kennedy was predicting American intervention in a second world war on the side of Britain, the German chargé d'affaires in Washington was writing in the same key. Although President Roosevelt was trying to preserve peace in Europe, it was very likely that if a German invasion of Czechoslovakia caused Britain and France to come to the aid of the Czechs, then America would be "found on their side."[71]

As an offset to these widespread rumors of probable American intervention in any new war that might break out in Europe, President Roosevelt, at a press conference (September 9), blamed American newspapers for creating a war psychosis. Any inference that he was ready to support "the Democracies" against the totalitarian bloc in the event of war was not warranted by his formal or informal remarks. If newspapermen would pay careful attention to his exact words they would discover that they had been "100 per cent wrong."[72]

j. *Chamberlain Decides to Visit Berchtesgaden*

Three days after the President made these statements at his press conference, Hitler delivered a speech (September 12) at Nürnberg. After blasting the Bolsheviks and Jews he turned his attack upon the Czechs who were "torturing three and a half million Germans." He did not, however, offer any solution of the Sudetenland problem although he emphasized the importance of applying the principle of self-determination for the benefit of the hard-pressed Germans in Czechoslovakia.[73]

Hitler's speech seemed to incite serious disorders in the Sudetenland, so the Czech Government promptly declared martial law (September 13). Henderson, in Berlin, believed that "only immediate action" by Czechoslovakia could avert "recourse to force by Germany." The German Government would never put any faith in "the honesty of M. Beneš until something was *done*." Mere words no longer carried any conviction. It seemed apparent that Beneš, even with doom knocking on the door, would "continue to haggle and will be unable to bring himself to make comprehensive, generous and immediate concessions

[70] Viscount Halifax to Sir Ronald Lindsay, Foreign Office, September 10, 1938. *Ibid.*, pp. 284–85.
[71] The German chargé d'affaires in the United States (Thomsen) to the German Foreign Ministry, Washington, September 10, 1938. *Documents on German Foreign Policy, 1918–1945*, II, 735–36.
[72] *New York Times*, September 10, 1938.
[73] *New York Times*, September 13, 1938.

essential to peace" unless the "severest pressure" was exerted upon him.[74] In Paris, Prime Minister Daladier betrayed his apprehension of war so plainly that the British Ambassador believed that his recent bold words might have been only a game of "bluff." During conversations with Sir Eric Phipps both Daladier and Bonnet had been seeking for some scapegoat and had finally settled upon Beneš.[75]

As Prime Minister Chamberlain read these telegrams with their high note of urgency, he decided to send a personal message to Hitler proposing a personal meeting "with a view of trying to find a peaceful solution" of the problems that beset Europe.[76] When the Führer replied that he was "absolutely at the disposal" of the Prime Minister, the stage was set for another momentous meeting at Berchtesgaden.[77] If the meeting had not occurred there were forces in Germany ready to challenge the authority of Hitler and possibly to depose him. Chamberlain's passion for peace ruined the best-laid plans of plotters who might have saved the world from the agonies and destruction of World War II.

k. *British Appeasement Saves Hitler*

Chamberlain's determination to carry appeasement to the bitter end was the salvation of Hitler and his clique who were bent upon a policy that meant inevitable war. In Germany, a large group of important persons were plotting to push Hitler aside and present a program that would preserve the peace of Europe. This group included such outstanding army officers as Colonel General Ludwig von Beck, Chief of Staff; Colonel General Kurt von Hammerstein, Commander in Chief of the German Army from 1930 to 1934; General Erwin von Witzleben; General Georg Thomas, head of the economic division of the planning staff of the Army; General Eduard Wagner, Quartermaster General; Major General Hans Oster; and Colonel Claus von Stauffenberg. Admiral Canaris was especially active in this plot to overthrow Hitler. The civilians included Carl Friedrich Goerdeler, one-time mayor of Leipzig; Hans B. Gisevius; Johannes Popitz, Prussian Minister of Finance; and Ulrich von Hassell, former German Ambassador in Rome.

In the summer of 1938 the plotters were pushed to prompt action by the Sudeten crisis. General Beck sent to the entire General Staff a memorandum which presented the view that hostilities with Czecho-

---

[74] Sir Nevile Henderson to Viscount Halifax, Berlin, September 13, 1938. *Documents on British Foreign Policy, 1919–1939*, II, 306–7.

[75] Sir Eric Phipps to Viscount Halifax, Paris, September 13, 1938. *Ibid.*, pp. 311–12.

[76] Viscount Halifax to Sir Nevile Henderson, Foreign Office, September 13, 1938, inclosing telegram from Chamberlain to Hitler. *Ibid.*, p. 314.

[77] Viscount Halifax to Sir Eric Phipps, Foreign Office, September 14, 1938. *Ibid.*, p. 325.

slovakia would bring about a general European war which Germany could not win. General Brauchitsch approved the main points in the memorandum and took it to Hitler in July 1938 with definite words of warning. The Führer immediately brushed it aside and continued his Sudeten program.[78]

General Beck then informed the British Government of Hitler's bellicose plans with reference to Czechoslovakia and urged an "unequivocal declaration by Britain that any violation of Czech neutrality would mean war." Chamberlain, however, preferred continued appeasement and paid little attention to the significant advice of General Beck.[79]

After an interview with Hitler in which he pleaded against any action that might provoke a European conflict, Beck resigned as Chief of Staff and was succeeded by General Halder. Halder was also in the plot to remove Hitler and was ready to obey any order issued by General von Brauchitsch, who was Commander in Chief of the Army.

These highly-placed plotters were ready to take action when Hitler returned to Berlin which was scheduled for September 14. But at this moment news came that Chamberlain had decided to visit Berchtesgaden in a last attempt to prevent war. Although these tidings were deeply disturbing to the conspirators, it was presumed that Chamberlain would be faced with proposals that he could not accept. In that event, the plot would be carried out as a preventive of war. On September 28, when General von Witzleben went to the office of General Halder to receive the orders that would start the *Putsch,* a message came through to the effect that Chamberlain and Daladier would meet Hitler at Munich on the following day. This news checked the immediate execution of the plot, and the appeasement as recorded in the Munich Agreement so strengthened Hitler's position that all plans to push him aside had to be indefinitely postponed. The "old man with the umbrella" had scared off an immediate shower in favor of the wild tempest of World War II.[80]

[78] Allen W. Dulles, *Germany's Underground* (New York, 1947), pp. 35–44.
[79] *Ibid.,* p. 42.
[80] *Ibid.,* pp. 42–48. See also, Franklin L. Ford, "The Twentieth of July in the History of the German Resistance," *American Historical Review,* LI (July 1946), 609–26, and Hans B. Gisevius, *Bis zum bitteren Ende* (2 vols.; Zurich, 1946). In the Nürnberg trials General Halder gave lengthy testimony with reference to this plot against Hitler. In answer to a specific question about the timing of the plot, Halder replied: "Adolf Hitler was at the Berghof at the time when Schacht was with me. Von Witzleben was ready with his preparations. But they could be put into action only after Hitler had come back to Berlin. On the day . . . I learned that Hitler had come back to Berlin I communicated with von Witzleben at once. . . . He requested that I give him the order of execution. We discussed other details—how much time he needed for the other preparations, etc. During this discussion the news came that the British Prime Minister and the French Premier had come to Hitler for a discussion. . . . Therefore I took back the order of execution because, owing to this fact the entire basis for the action had been taken away." *Nazi Conspiracy and Aggression,* Supplement B (Washington, D. C., 1947–48), pp. 1547–75.

XVIII

Munich: Prelude to Prague

a. *President Roosevelt Extends Monroe Doctrine*

As TENSION developed in Europe over the problem of the Sudeten Germans, President Roosevelt became deeply concerned over the possible outbreak of war. In January 1938 he had vainly endeavored to secure British support of a plan for world peace, but Prime Minister Chamberlain had rejected this appeal on the ground that it might adversely affect his efforts to conciliate Italy and thus dislodge the uneasy Duce from the eager arms of Hitler. In the midsummer of 1938 the President decided to take an independent step in foreign policy which apparently would be along a road familiar to Americans since 1823. He would have his fellow countrymen raise their eyes from accustomed American sights to a distant horizon where a one-world concept could be dimly seen. Since 1932 he had been lustily singing in a chorus of isolationists but had been furtively eyeing the exotic wench of collective security who waited in the wings for the cue that would inevitably come.

In order to give this cue in the most impressive manner, he paid a visit to Queens University in Kingston, Ontario (August 18) for the ostensible purpose of receiving one of his innumerable honorary degrees. As a part of this ritual for securing knowledge by degrees, Roosevelt then made an address which formally placed Canada under the protection of the Monroe Doctrine: "I give to you assurance that the people of the United States will not stand idly by if domination of Canadian soil is threatened by any other empire."

After this broad promise of protection he then began to talk as though the Monroe Doctrine had some far-flung implications. He made it clear that the Dominion of Canada was a "part of the sisterhood of the British Empire." The question then arose: if America would help one of these sisters in distress would she stand idly by if the others were reduced to dire straits? In partial answer to this query he repeated one of the Hull clichés to the effect that "we in the Americas are no longer a far-away continent, to which the eddies of controversies beyond the seas could bring no interest or no harm. . . . The vast amount of our resources, the vigor of our commerce, and the strength of our men have made us vital factors in world peace whether we choose or not."[1]

[1] *New York Times,* August 19, 1938.

Some American newspapers regarded the President's address at Kingston as a "somewhat startling statement" of a familiar fact,[2] but it was admitted that he had given it a "calculated portentousness" by timing it at "a tense moment in international affairs."[3] In London, J. L. Garvin, noted editor of the *Observer,* interpreted the President's words as an "intimation to the dictatorships that at a pinch the United States would be unable to keep out,"[4] while the *Manchester Guardian* was certain that they were "virtually a guarantee of help against aggression."[5]

In France, the Kingston address was received as a definite assurance of support to the "democracies" if a serious crisis arose. Bonnet, the Foreign Minister, was moved to make several suggestions to Ambassador Bullitt. He thought it would be helpful if the American Ambassador in Berlin were instructed to inform the German Foreign Office that the Department of State believed the negotiations at Prague between the Sudeten Germans and the Czech Government "offered substantial possibilities for success." Therefore, the "use of force" to influence these negotiations would be regarded with disfavor. Bonnet also suggested that "in case of dire necessity" the President could offer to serve as a mediator in the difficulties between the Czechs and the Sudeten Germans and thus save the situation.[6]

A few days later, Léon Blum, former Premier of France, urged the President "to address himself to Europe with all the prestige of his person and with all the authority of the State whose moral or material support would be finally decisive in any general war."[7] It was obvious that a large part of the world was looking to the United States for leadership in a crisis that threatened war, and the President was strongly tempted to respond to this pressure. But Prime Minister Chamberlain was once more devising a settlement through appeasement, so the American Chief Executive had to bide his time.

b. *Chamberlain Pays a Visit to Berchtesgaden*

When Prime Minister Chamberlain prepared to visit Berchtesgaden in search of peace he had some very definite ideas in mind concerning the Sudetenland problem. He knew that the Czech State rested upon "weak foundations" of diverse nationalities that had a sharp dislike for one

[2] *Ibid.*
[3] *New York Herald-Tribune,* August 19, 1938.
[4] *New York Times,* August 21, 1938.
[5] *Manchester Guardian,* August 26, 1938.
[6] Cordell Hull, *Memoirs* (New York, 1948), I, 588-89.
[7] *New York Herald-Tribune,* September 19, 1938.

another. Great wisdom, good fortune, and ample time were needed to overcome these nationalistic difficulties, but "even before the death of the wise Masaryk too little of these was vouchsafed." The liberal regime about which Beneš had waxed so eloquent at Versailles slowly disintegrated. The country

was made a centralised State, and later, under stress and strain, in part a police State, exacerbated at every point where conflict always breaks out in a land of antagonistic races,—as to the proportion of officials, allotment of schools, or census statistics. These wrangles were still dragging their length along when the great depression cast the German areas . . . into sudden poverty. . . .

Unemployment was chronic in the German region . . . but unemployment benefit for Germans was wholly inadequate, and much lower than for Czechs. Drastic laws of 1935–6 tightened the Czech hold on government employment, drew a wide frontier zone within which arbitrary imprisonment could be imposed, and imported a Czech police into German areas. . . . While Beneš and Hodza, his Slovak Premier, slowly embarked in 1937 on steps to give Germans a pinch more of office or employment, they stoutly declined to hear of anything "Swiss," or local autonomy. . . .

After six years of warning the British Government, late in 1937, pressed Beneš to make serious concessions. . . . Zero hour was near.[8]

Chamberlain thought that the only way to greet this zero hour with any chance of success would be to invoke the principle of self-determination. But this invocation presented formidable difficulties and he saw this fact clearly during his first conversation with Hitler. When he reached Berchtesgaden on September 15, he noticed that the Führer appeared "very shy" and had some trouble in finding appropriate small talk. It was decided that the conversation between Chamberlain and Hitler should be held in the Führer's sparsely furnished bedroom with only Paul Schmidt to act as the interpreter. This arrangement excluded the presence of Ribbentrop who was visibly excited at being left out of the picture.

The Führer spoke "quietly and in low tones" most of the time, but occasionally he became "very excited and poured out his indignation against the Czechs in a torrent of words."[9] Chamberlain listened attentively and "then, looking Hitler full in the face, he emphasized that he was prepared to discuss every possibility of righting German grievances, but that in all circumstances the use of force must be excluded." At this point Hitler exploded: "Force! Who speaks of force? Herr Beneš applies force against my countrymen in the Sudetenland, Herr Beneš

[8] Keith Feiling, *The Life of Neville Chamberlain* (New York, 1946), pp. 344–46.
[9] *Ibid.*, pp. 366–67.

mobilised in May, not I. . . . I shall not put up with this any longer. . . . I shall take matters into my own hands." This outburst provoked Chamberlain who excitedly exclaimed: "If I have understood you aright, you are determined to proceed against Czecho-Slovakia in any case. . . . If that is so, why did you let me come to Berchtesgaden. . . . It is best for me to return at once."

Hitler now hastened to conciliate Chamberlain. He quickly referred to the troubles in the Sudetenland and calmly remarked: "If you are prepared to recognise the principle of the right of peoples to self-determination, . . . then we can continue the discussion in order to see how that principle can be applied in practice." But Chamberlain suddenly became exceedingly cautious. A plebiscite in the Sudetenland would entail enormous "practical difficulties." It would be best for him to return to London to discuss this matter with the Cabinet. After securing from Hitler a promise that no aggressive action would be undertaken against Czechoslovakia, Chamberlain returned to the Berchtesgaden hotel and on the following day took a plane from Munich to London.[10]

When he reached No. 10 Downing Street he read a telegram from Nevile Henderson warning him that "no discussion of half measures at this stage will serve any purpose whatsoever but merely encourage Herr Hitler to throw discretion . . . to the winds. . . . If the British and French Governments do not agree to the principle of incorporation of the German areas in the Reich, it is absolutely certain that Germany will act by herself."[11]

It was apparent to Chamberlain that it was no time for "half measures." Something far-reaching would have to be done at once. Summoning Prime Minister Daladier and Foreign Minister Bonnet to London, he recounted to them his talk with the Führer and then observed that the issue involved was a "very simple one." It was a question "whether or not to accept the principle of self-determination." If this principle were applied to the Sudetenland problem he did not "anticipate any great difficulties from the German side." But Daladier was full of misgivings concerning the application of the principle of self-determination to the Sudetenland. Lord Halifax shared these misgivings but he asked Daladier to look at the "practical realities of the situation." Neither France nor Russia, and certainly not England, would be able to give "effective protection" to Czechoslovakia in the event of war with Germany. It was obvious, therefore, that both Britain and France

[10] Paul Schmidt, *Hitler's Interpreter* (London, 1950), pp. 92–94, *Documents on British Foreign Policy, 1919–1939*, Third Series, II, 338–41.

[11] Sir Nevile Henderson to Viscount Halifax, Berlin, September 17, 1938. *Documents on British Foreign Policy, 1919–1939*, Third Series, pp. 360–61.

would have to devise some means to save Europe "from destruction." This formula might not be palatable but it would have to be tried.

Finally, after three meetings, Prime Ministers Chamberlain and Daladier, and Foreign Ministers Bonnet and Halifax agreed upon a formula that was submitted to the Czech Government on September 19. The British and French governments were convinced that the point had been reached where it was evident that the Sudetenland districts "mainly inhabited by Sudeten-Deutsch" would have to be transferred to the Reich. This could be effected either by "direct transfer or as the result of a plebiscite." The areas marked for transfer would contain more than 50 per cent "of German inhabitants." The details covering these transfers could be settled by "some international body including a Czech representative." If the Czech Government accepted this Anglo-French proposal, Britain was prepared to join France in an "international guarantee of the new boundaries of the Czechoslovak State against unprovoked aggression."[12] The matter was now up to President Beneš and the Czech Cabinet.

c. *Beneš Accepts the Anglo-French Proposals*

The problems facing Beneš were so complicated that they defied successful handling. If he accepted the Anglo-French proposals, he would have to witness the dismemberment of the Czech State and would have to consent to the surrender of the strategic frontier. If he refused to respond to this pressure, Britain and France might declare that they were no longer vitally interested in the fate of Czechoslovakia and this action would be an invitation to Hitler to take over the whole country. On September 20 the reply of the Czech Government was handed to the representatives of Britain and France in Prague. It was an appeal to them to reconsider the point of view expressed in their joint note of September 19. They should recognize the fact that it was "not merely the fate of Czechoslovakia which is at stake, but that of other nations as well."[13]

This Czech appeal fell upon British and French ears that were not only deaf but were somewhat indignant. Did President Beneš desire a second world war? In Berlin, Sir Nevile Henderson appreciated the fact that the Czech President had "terribly difficult circumstances to contend with," but he had "thrown away his opportunities during the

[12] Record of Anglo-French conversations held at No. 10 Downing Street, September 18, 1938; Viscount Halifax to Mr. Newton, Foreign Office, September 19, 1938. *Ibid.*, pp. 373–99, 404–6.

[13] *Documents on International Affairs, 1938*, ed. Monica Curtis (New York, 1943), II, 214–16.

past four months until it was too late." The only thing Beneš could do was to bow to *"force majeure* and accept the Franco-British plan."[14]

The application of this *force majeure* came during the early morning hours of September 21 when Beneš was informed by the British and French representatives in Prague that he would have to accept the Anglo-French proposals or, in the event of war with Germany, Czechoslovakia could not count upon British and French assistance.[15] Throughout the morning and early afternoon of September 21 the Czech Cabinet gave anxious consideration to these proposals. Finally, at five o'clock, the Czech Government indicated that it had "sadly accepted" them. The way was now open for the second scene in the drama of Munich.

d. *Hitler Formulates New Demands*

This second scene was devoid of the little touches of courtesy that had marked the meeting at Berchtesgaden. Godesberg-on-the-Rhine had been selected because of its convenient location, but that was the only item in its favor. The conference between Chamberlain and Hitler was held in the Hotel Dreesen with its ominous background as the birthplace of the bloody purge of June 1934. In such an atmosphere Hitler dropped any pretense of accommodation and showed the ugly attitude of a highwayman who insists upon beating his victims while robbing them.

At the beginning of the conversation on September 22, Prime Minister Chamberlain rehearsed what had been agreed upon at Berchtesgaden and what the British and French governments had done to implement this agreement. There would be no necessity for a plebiscite but only an agreed cession of territory to the Reich in accordance with some "guiding principle." The details could be settled by a commission consisting of one German, one Czech, and a neutral chairman.

When Chamberlain completed his recital, Hitler asked if this Anglo-French program had been submitted to the Czech Government and had been accepted by it. Chamberlain answered in the affirmative. Hitler paused for a moment and then slowly remarked: "I am exceedingly sorry, but that is no longer of any use."[16] It was evident that the crisis over the Sudetenland had moved to its "most critical stage." There was no time for the usual delays of diplomacy.

[14] Sir Nevile Henderson to Viscount Halifax, Berlin, September 20, 1938. *Documents on British Foreign Policy, 1919–1939,* Third Series, pp. 428–29.

[15] Mr. Newton to Viscount Halifax, Prague, September 21, 1938. *Ibid.,* pp. 431–34.

[16] Sir Nevile Henderson, *Failure of a Mission,* (New York, 1940), p. 158.

When Chamberlain heard Hitler's terse negative observation he ardently argued that the Anglo-French proposals had really met all reasonable demands for the application of the principle of self-determination. Moreover, these proposals had been accepted by the Czech Government. The British and French governments had "got exactly what the Fuehrer wanted and without the expenditure of a drop of German blood." Hitler replied that he had no use for international commissions with their usual interminable delays. A frontier line would have to be drawn "at once." But it would have to be a language frontier based upon "existing reliable maps."

He was insistent that the Czechs should immediately withdraw from the areas that were so delimited and that German troops should occupy them. He expected that the Czechs would claim that this frontier line "did not represent the real minority situation." In that case he was "in favour of holding a plebiscite everywhere" in the disputed areas. Where the result "showed a Czech majority, he would be perfectly prepared to surrender the territory which he had occupied." He would be quite ready to "bow to a majority." And although he had no high opinion of international commissions he would be "perfectly ready for the plebiscite to be carried out" by one. But he insisted that the disputed areas be occupied "by German troops at once." As to a nonaggression pact with Czechoslovakia, the Führer declared that he would be willing to go that far only if the Czechs succeeded in placing their relations with Poland and Hungary "on a proper footing."[17]

These demands overwhelmed Chamberlain who protested that they were in sharp contradiction with the ones that had been agreed upon at Berchtesgaden. Perhaps some better understanding could be reached in tomorrow's conversation! After bringing the conference to a close, Chamberlain walked slowly to the terrace of the Hotel Dreesen where he was suddenly stopped by Hitler who addressed him in soft, contrite tones: "Oh, Mr. Prime Minister, I am so sorry: I had looked forward to showing you this beautiful view of the Rhine . . . but now it is hidden by the mist."[18]

The Prime Minister was startled by this unexpected shift from far-reaching political demands to poignant regrets over hidden natural beauties. A breath-taking vista over the fabulous Rhine might have softened Chamberlain's mood a trifle, but the blanket of mist depressed his spirits to such an extent that he confessed to Lord Halifax that his

---

[17] Notes of a conversation between Mr. Chamberlain and Herr Hitler at Godesberg on September 22, 1938. *Documents on British Foreign Policy, 1919–1939*, pp. 463–73.

[18] André Maurois, *Tragedy in France* (London, 1940), pp. 12–13.

conversation with Hitler had been "most unsatisfactory." It was possible that he would soon return to London.[19]

On the morning of the twenty-third, Chamberlain sent a letter to Hitler in which he pointed out that the chief difficulty in the German proposal was the suggestion that German troops "in the immediate future" should occupy the Sudeten areas that were in dispute. If the soldiers of the Reich moved into any part of the Sudetenland there was "no doubt that the Czechoslovak Government would have no option but to order their forces to resist." This would mean war with all its grim implications. There was, however, a slim possibility that the Czech Government might permit law and order to be maintained by the "Sudeten Germans themselves."[20]

In reply to this letter, Hitler sent a note to Chamberlain in which he made the small concession that German troops could be removed "from doubtful areas when vote is taken in them."[21] But Chamberlain knew that this bait was too small to interest the Czech Government. He would have to talk things over with Hitler once more and try to make him more pliable. On the evening of September 23–24 he had his second conversation with the Führer. Unlike the first meeting, there were now three British and two German officials present. Ribbentrop opened proceedings by handing to Chamberlain a memorandum which stated the "German desiderata" with regard to an agreement. It contained a provision under whose terms the Czech troops were required to begin the evacuation of predominantly German areas in the Sudetenland at 8:00 A.M. on September 26 and to complete their withdrawal by September 28.

Chamberlain read this memorandum carefully and remarked in surprise: "But this is nothing less than an ultimatum." "No, no," exclaimed Hitler, it is "nothing of the sort." It is not "a diktat at all: look, the document is headed by the word, 'Memorandum.'" As the Führer went through this little exercise in mockery, Chamberlain's patience gave way and he broke out into a bitter indictment of the way he had been treated. There had been no real effort to respond to conciliatory proposals.[22] Surprised by this outburst from the Prime Min-

[19] Viscount Halifax to Sir Eric Phipps, Foreign Office, September 23, 1938. *Documents on British Foreign Policy, 1919–1939*, p. 477.

[20] British Delegation (Godesberg) to Viscount Halifax, September 23, 1938. *Ibid.*, pp. 482–83. See also, *British White Paper, Cmd. 5847, Correspondence Respecting Czechoslovakia*, September 1938, No. 3.

[21] British Delegation (Godesberg) to Mr. Newton, September 23, 1938. *Ibid.*, pp. 484–85.

[22] Speech of Prime Minister Chamberlain in the House of Commons, September 28, 1938. *Parliamentary Debates*, House of Commons, CCCXXXIX, 21–22.

ister, Hitler finally agreed to a slight concession. He would postpone the date of the entry of German troops into the Sudetenland until October 1. Then, after making a few other minor alterations in the draft of his memorandum, he presented it to Chamberlain for study and for eventual transmission to the Czech Government.[23]

Realizing that all this bluster must have badly frayed the nerves of Prime Minister Chamberlain, Hitler attempted to soothe them with a few words of flattery. Turning to the Prime Minister he softly remarked: "You are the only man to whom I have made a concession." He then gave an assurance that the annexation of the Sudetenland would satisfy his territorial ambitions in Europe. He had no desire to dismember Czechoslovakia; he did not wish to incorporate into the Reich any peoples other than German. With these conciliatory words and wide promises the conference at Godesberg closed and Chamberlain prepared to leave for London. His anxious efforts for peace had gained such minor concessions that the drums of war resumed their long roll.

e. *Chamberlain Makes a New Appeal to Hitler*

When Chamberlain reached No. 10 Downing Street he found many telegrams of importance awaiting him. Sir Eric Phipps had telegraphed from Paris that "unless German aggression were so brutal, bloody and prolonged (through the gallantry of Czechoslovak resistance) as to infuriate French public opinion to the extent of making it lose its reason, war now would be most unpopular in France. . . . All that is best in France is against war, almost at any price."[24] From Berlin, Sir Nevile Henderson sent a warning that the Germans were now insisting upon actual Czech concessions and would not be satisfied with mere words. Any encouragement "given to the Czechs to hesitate or prevaricate will be disastrous and only immediate surrender of territories which they have agreed ultimately to surrender can save them from complete tragedy."[25] His Majesty's Government might be able to prevent war by making it "absolutely clear at Prague that they must accept [the] German plan or forfeit claim to further support from Western Powers."[26]

After reading this urgent telegram from Sir Nevile Henderson,

---

[23] Notes of a conversation between the Prime Minister and Herr Hitler at Godesberg, September 23–24, 1938. *Documents on British Foreign Policy, 1919–1939*, pp. 499–508.

[24] Sir Eric Phipps to Viscount Halifax, Paris, September 24, 1938. *Ibid.*, p. 510.

[25] Sir Nevile Henderson to Viscount Halifax, Berlin, September 25, 1938. *Ibid.*, pp. 512–13.

[26] Sir Nevile Henderson to Viscount Halifax, Berlin, September 25, 1938. *Ibid.*, pp. 515–16.

Chamberlain turned to a note that had just been received from Prague. The Czech Government had carefully considered the German demands and had rejected them. They were "absolutely and unconditionally unacceptable."[27]

On this same day there was a meeting at No. 10 Downing Street between carefully selected groups of British and French statesmen. After Prime Minister Chamberlain described his conference with Hitler at Godesberg, Premier Daladier spoke some bold words. The French Council of Ministers had rejected any "idea of suppressing the international commission which had been decided upon in principle by the French and British Ministers." It had also been "agreed that the French Government could not recognize Herr Hitler's right to take possession" of Czech territory "by force." It was apparent that the Führer considered all the territory marked red on the map was "his already without a plebiscite in view of the fact that these areas were over 50 per cent [German]." Therefore, in this area "there was no need for a plebiscite." But there were other areas where a plebiscite should be held because "it was uncertain whether there was a German or a Czech majority." If these areas were held by German troops until the plebiscite were held it would mean that the "remaining Czech territory would be cut off from Slovakia" and would be "at Germany's mercy." Hitler should be told that he would have to accept the "Anglo-French proposals agreed upon last Sunday."

When Chamberlain inquired what should be done if Hitler refused to accept these proposals, Daladier boldly answered that in such an event "each of us would have to do his duty." As Chamberlain listened to these defiant words he remembered the telegrams from Sir Eric Phipps stressing the passionate desire in France for peace at almost any price. Therefore, he suggested that it was time to get down to the "stern realities of the situation." If Germany invaded Czechoslovakia, would France declare war? Daladier replied that France would undoubtedly "fulfill her obligations" to the Czech State in case of an "unprovoked aggression." This fulfillment would consist of "offensive operations" against the Siegfried line and bombing raids upon "German factories and military centres." Chamberlain quickly alluded to the fact that the French air force was quite weak. It might happen that German planes would dominate the situation and subject Paris to a "rain of bombs." He also referred to many comments in the French press which certainly did not indicate the existence of a strong and "bellicose spirit" in favor of an unyielding attitude towards Germany. In conclusion, he assured

[27] Note from the Czechoslovak Minister to Viscount Halifax, September 25, 1938. *Ibid.*, pp. 518–19.

Daladier that the British Government would not "exert pressure" upon the Czechs to accept Hitler's Godesberg demands. Neither would it express an opinion as to the course France should pursue. The French Government would have to make its own decisions.[28]

On the following day, Chamberlain had a "personal conversation" with Daladier and General Gamelin. The French Chief of Staff breathed a spirit of confidence and gave assurances that if hostilities broke out the democratic nations would "dictate the peace."[29] The Prime Minister was encouraged by this fluent optimism to make some assurances of his own. The British Government had said "publicly several times" that it could not "afford to see France overrun or defeated by Germany, and that we would come to her assistance if France were in danger." It should be perfectly clear that "His Majesty's Government had no intention of going back on what they had said."[30]

This was an important pledge and Chamberlain made it with some misgivings. Despite the bold words of General Gamelin it was well known that a spirit of defeatism was manifest in many French circles. Moreover, Sir Eric Phipps had definitely warned that "all that was best in France" was opposed to war. The only group in favor of hostilities was a "small and corrupt" clique of Communists who were "paid by Moscow and have been working for war for months."[31]

With this admonition from Phipps clearly in mind, Chamberlain decided to write a last letter to Hitler with the hope that it might stave off the conflict that constantly threatened to break out. On September 26 he entrusted to Sir Horace Wilson a letter that was to be delivered to Hitler immediately. In it he called attention to the fact that the Czech Government had already signified its acceptance of the proposal to transfer a large portion of the Sudetenland to the Reich. Would it not be possible for Hitler to agree that representatives of Germany would meet with representatives of Czechoslovakia and settle by agreement "the way in which the territory is to be handed over?" Surely the tragic consequences of a war "ought not to be incurred over a difference in method."[32]

---

[28] Record of an Anglo-French conversation held at No. 10 Downing Street, September 25, 1938. *Ibid.*, pp. 520–35.

[29] "Pertinax" (André Géraud), *The Gravediggers of France* (New York, 1944), p. 3.

[30] Record of an Anglo-French conversation held at No. 10 Downing Street, September 26, 1938. *Documents on British Foreign Policy, 1919–1939*, p. 537.

[31] Sir Eric Phipps to Viscount Halifax, Paris, September 26, 1938. *Ibid.*, pp. 543–44.

[32] Letter of Prime Minister Chamberlain to Herr Hitler, September 26, 1938. *Ibid.*, pp. 541–42.

f. *Roosevelt Supports Chamberlain's Plea for Peace*

While Prime Minister Chamberlain was wrestling with Hitler at Berchtesgaden and Godesberg, President Roosevelt was kept in close touch with events in Europe by telephone messages from Ambassador Kennedy in London and Ambassador Bullitt in Paris. On September 24, Bullitt urged that "some effort" be made by the American Government to "maintain peace." He suggested that the President direct an appeal to the British, French, German, Italian, and Polish governments to send representatives to The Hague in an effort to find a formula for peace. The United States should also be represented at this conference.[33]

On the following day, the American Minister at Prague sent a message from Beneš to President Roosevelt entreating him to urge Britain and France not to desert Czechoslovakia and thus cause her destruction by Hitler. The President was moved by these urgent requests for aid and he was ready to make some statement in support of the preservation of peace in Europe. After throwing off the restraining hand of Secretary Hull, President Roosevelt directed Sumner Welles and Adolf Berle to draft an appeal to both Hitler and Beneš. He signed them at 12:15 A.M. on September 26 and they were cabled at once to Berlin and Prague.[34]

In these communications to Beneš and Hitler the President pointed out the terrible destruction that a second world war would entail. The economic system "of every country is certain to be shattered," and the "social structure" might well be "completely wrecked." Although America was in a different hemisphere it could not "escape some measure of the consequences of such a world catastrophe." The President therefore felt that he should call attention to the solemn obligations of the Kellogg-Briand Pact to solve "controversies by pacific methods." He was persuaded that there was no problem "so difficult or so pressing for solution that it cannot be justly solved by the resort to reason rather than by resort to force." For this reason, and on behalf of the "130,-000,000 of the people of the United States and for the sake of humanity everywhere," he most earnestly appealed to Beneš and Hitler "not to break off the negotiations looking to a peaceful, fair and constructive settlement of the questions at issue."[35]

[33] Hull, *op. cit.,* p. 590.
[34] *Ibid.,* p. 591.
[35] President Roosevelt to President Beneš and to Chancellor Hitler, September 26, 1938. *Peace and War: United States Foreign Policy, 1931–1941* (Washington, 1943), pp. 425–26.

President Beneš sent a prompt and favorable reply on September 26, but Hitler was too busy to take any notice of the President's appeal. That evening he was scheduled to make a speech in the Sportspalast in Berlin. President Roosevelt would have to wait a while for an answer.

g. *Britain Makes Further Efforts to Preserve Peace*

Although Hitler was engaged upon the task of putting finishing touches to the speech he was to give at the Sportspalast on the evening of September 26, he still found time to see Sir Horace Wilson who had been sent to Berlin with Chamberlain's latest note. Sir Nevile Henderson accompanied Sir Horace. Henderson had received from Viscount Halifax an important instruction: "Since you left, [the] French have definitely stated their intention of supporting Czechoslovakia by offensive measures if latter is attacked. This would bring us in, and it should be made plain to [the] Chancellor that this is an inevitable alternative to a peaceful solution."[36]

Armed with this strong warning, Sir Horace Wilson and Sir Nevile Henderson had a conference with Hitler at 5:00 P.M. He was extremely restive and could be persuaded only with difficulty to listen to the letter from the Prime Minister. At one point he shouted: "It is no use talking any more," and then he moved to the door as if to leave the room. He finally agreed that a meeting between Czech and German representatives could take place "but only on the assumption that the Czechoslovak Government accepted the memorandum including October 1." In view of his "intense emotion" it was thought best not to advise him of the sharp instruction Henderson had received from Lord Halifax.[37]

During this heated conversation Hitler several times exclaimed that Germany was being "treated like niggers; one would not dare treat even Turks like that." Finally he shouted: "On the 1st October I shall have Czechoslovakia where I want her." If France and England "decide to strike, let them strike. I care not a farthing." He would not permit "M. Beneš to lead him any further by the nose." Whether by negotiation or by the exercise of force, the Sudeten territory would be "free on 1st October." He must have an affirmative reply to his demands "within two days, that was to say by Wednesday."[38]

That evening (September 26) Hitler delivered his speech in the

---

[36] Viscount Halifax to Sir Nevile Henderson, Foreign Office, September 26, 1938. *Documents on British Foreign Policy, 1919–1939*, II, 550.

[37] Sir Nevile Henderson to Viscount Halifax, Berlin, September 26, 1938. *Ibid.*, pp. 552–53; Notes of a conversation between Sir Horace Wilson and Herr Hitler at Berlin, September 26, 1938. *Ibid.*, pp. 554–57.

[38] *Ibid.*, p. 554.

Sportspalast. It contained an acidulous attack upon President Beneš and the responsibility for any hostilities that might break out was placed squarely upon his shoulders: "Now let M. Beneš make his choice." His comments upon Chamberlain were friendly and he reiterated his desire for "good relations with England." He declared that after the Sudeten question was settled, Germany had "no further territorial claims to make in Europe." The Reich wanted no Czechs within her borders. But he wished to make it clear that the Sudetenland problem would have to be solved by October 1 or German troops would occupy the disputed territory with "himself as the first soldier of the Reich."[39]

Chamberlain read this vitriolic speech with increasing alarm and at once instructed Sir Horace Wilson to assure Hitler that the promises of the Czech Government relative to the Sudetenland were really made to Britain and France. The British Government was prepared to "undertake that they shall be carried out fairly and fully . . . and with reasonable promptitude," provided that the German Government would agree to "the settlement of terms and conditions of transfer by discussion and not by force."[40]

On the afternoon of the twenty-seventh, Sir Horace had his second conversation with the Führer. With regard to the Czechs and the Sudetenland, Hitler said there were two alternatives: the Czech Government had either to accept the terms of the Godesberg memorandum or to reject them. If they rejected the terms he would "smash the Czechs." This sentence of destruction he repeated several times as though he wished to give proper emphasis to it. At this point Sir Horace conveyed a warning to the Führer: "If, in pursuit of her Treaty obligations, France became actively engaged in hostilities against Germany, the United Kingdom would feel obliged to support her." This threat angered Hitler who shouted in reply: "If France and England strike, let them do so. It is a matter of complete indifference to me. I am prepared for every eventuality. . . . It is Tuesday today, and by next Monday we shall be at war."[41]

After Sir Horace left the Chancellery, Hitler began to have some doubts concerning the abrupt manner in which he had conducted his conference with the British representative. Perhaps he would gain more by adopting a more conciliatory attitude. With this idea in mind he immediately addressed a letter to Chamberlain in which he stated that if he gained his objective with reference to the Sudetenland he was ready

[39] *The Speeches of Adolf Hitler,* ed. and tr. Norman H. Baynes (London, 1942), II, 1487–99.

[40] Viscount Halifax to Sir Nevile Henderson, September 27, 1938. *Documents on British Foreign Policy, 1919–1939,* II, 559.

[41] Henderson, *op. cit.,* pp. 164–65; Notes of a conversation between Herr Hitler and Sir Horace Wilson, Berlin, September 27, 1938. *Documents on British Foreign Policy, 1919–1939,* II, 564–67.

to "give a formal guarantee for the remainder of Czechoslovakia." In view of this fact he left it to the judgment of the Prime Minister whether it would be worth while to continue his much-appreciated efforts to "bring the Government in Prague to reason at the very last hour."[42]

Hitler now had time to answer President Roosevelt's appeal of September 26. His telegram to the President emphasized the importance of the principle of self-determination and adverted to the betrayal of this principle by President Wilson with special reference to the inclusion of the Sudeten Germans in the artificial state of Czechoslovakia. When the President gained a better understanding of the problem of the Sudetenland he would realize that the German Government had not been lacking either "in patience or a sincere desire for a peaceful understanding."[43]

h. *Roosevelt Exerts Further Pressure upon the Dictators*

When President Roosevelt received this telegram from Chancellor Hitler he decided that its dubious tone required a second appeal for world peace. In this second communication to the Führer he stated that the "question before the world today . . . is not the question of errors of judgment or of injustices committed in the past. It is the question of the fate of the world today and tomorrow." Resort to force in the World War had failed to bring tranquility to the nations that had been engaged in that conflict. Victory and defeat "were alike sterile." World War II would be as "unnecessary as it was unjustifiable." Negotiations for a peaceful ending of the present dispute over the Sudetenland were "still open." They could be continued if the Führer would "give the word." Acceptance by the Chancellor of a pacific solution of the Sudetenland dispute would gain for him the gratitude of "hundreds of millions throughout the world."[44]

On this same day (September 27), the President also sent a strong appeal to Mussolini to lend his assistance to efforts for peace. After stating that a second world war would mean the "destruction of millions of men, women and children in Europe," he urged the Duce to help "in the continuation of the efforts to arrive at an agreement of the questions at issue by negotiation or by other pacific means rather than

---

[42] Sir Nevile Henderson to Viscount Halifax, inclosing a letter from Hitler to Prime Minister Chamberlain, September 27, 1938. *Ibid.,* pp. 576–78.

[43] Telegram from Chancellor Hitler to President Roosevelt, September 27, 1938. Department of State, *Press Release,* October 1, 1938, XIX, 221–23.

[44] President Roosevelt to Chancellor Hitler, September 27, 1938. *Peace and War,* pp. 428–29.

by resort to force."[45] Mussolini thus had the eyes of the world trained upon him and he greatly enjoyed this opportunity to stroll across the European stage as the one person who could bring war or peace to countless millions.

i. *Chamberlain Prepares the Basis for the Munich Accord*

While President Roosevelt was sending his appeals to Hitler and Mussolini in favor of a pacific solution of the Sudetenland problem, Prime Minister Chamberlain was making further efforts along the same line. On the night of September 27, Henderson paid a late visit to the German Foreign Office in order to hand to the State Secretary some new proposals, agreed to by France, which would press the Czech Government to consent to the "immediate transfer of the Sudeten territories on the basis of a time-table guaranteed by His Majesty's Government." These proposals were a definite concession to Hitler and they constituted "the main basis of the final settlement at Munich."[46]

On the following morning, Henderson received from the Prime Minister a final letter that was to be presented to Chancellor Hitler. It began by conveying to the Führer an assurance that he could gain all his important objectives "without war and without delay." In order to find some basis for peace it might be expedient to call a conference in Berlin between the representatives of Britain, Czechoslovakia, France, Germany, and Italy for the purpose of discussing the Sudeten problem. Prime Minister Chamberlain himself would be willing to visit Berlin at once in order to help arrange the necessary details. The Führer should have no doubt that Britain and France would see that all Czech promises would be "carried out fairly and fully and forthwith."[47] On this same day (September 28), Chamberlain also sent a personal message to Mussolini in which he recounted his appeal to Hitler and then asked the Duce to support his efforts to prevent the outbreak of war.

Before these letters could evoke any response, the French Ambassador called Ernst von Weizsäcker and asked for an audience with Hitler. Ribbentrop, who thought that war would be the best solution of the Czech problem, was opposed to any parleys between the ambassador and the Führer. According to Weizsäcker, this belligerent attitude of Ribbentrop was the cause of a violent scene: "I said that it was

---

[45] President Roosevelt to the American Ambassador in Italy (Phillips), September 27, 1938. *Ibid.*, p. 427.

[46] Henderson, *op. cit.*, p. 166.

[47] Viscount Halifax to Sir Nevile Henderson, September 28, 1938. *Documents on British Foreign Policy, 1919–1939*, II, 587.

a monstrous thing that he should want to start a war when the real differences between the two sides were so small and were concerned only with the method by which the Sudetenland should be incorporated. . . . In this mood we went together from the Kaiserhof to the Chancellory."[48]

When the French Ambassador arrived for his audience with the Führer he was clear and cogent in his arguments against any precipitate action with regard to the Sudetenland: "You deceive yourself, Chancellor, if you believe that you can confine the conflict to Czechoslovakia. If you attack that country you will set all Europe ablaze. . . . Why should you take this risk when your essential demands can be met without war?" The Ambassador then produced a map which showed the separate phases of the evacuation. Hitler was impressed with the remarks of François-Poncet and later frankly stated that he had been the only one "who made a sensible proposal." At this point there was an important interruption. The Italian Ambassador (Attolico) hurried into the room and announced in excited tones: "I have an urgent message to you from the Duce, Fuehrer!" The Duce, in responding to Chamberlain's plea for pressure upon Berlin, expressed to Hitler the opinion that it "would be wise to accept the British proposal" and voiced the hope that mobilization would not be ordered.[49]

When Sir Nevile Henderson called at the Chancellery some hours later he was greeted by Hitler with the welcome remark: "At the request of my great friend and ally, Mussolini, I have postponed mobilizing my troops for twenty-four hours." The atmosphere in Berlin was noticeably less tense than on the previous day and the Führer, "though a little distrait, was not unreasonable." When Henderson handed him Chamberlain's suggestion concerning a five-power conference he replied that he would have to consult the Duce before making any decision. He had hardly made this remark before Attolico made another breathless appearance and murmured that Mussolini had signified his approval of a five-power conference to deal with the Sudetenland problem.[50]

Hitler had already received a note from the French Foreign Office which was even more conciliatory than the one from Chamberlain. In answer to these gestures of appeasement, the Führer invited Mussolini, Prime Minister Chamberlain, and the French Premier (Daladier) to Munich for a conference on the following day (September 29).

[48] Ernst von Weizsäcker, *Memoirs* (Chicago, 1951), pp. 152–53.
[49] Schmidt, *op. cit.,* pp. 105–7.
[50] Henderson, *op. cit.,* pp. 168–69.

j. *Capitulation at Munich*

The Munich Conference did little more than confirm the program of appeasement that had already been agreed upon by Britain and France. Although Daladier at first showed a combative spirit he was taken in hand by General Göring and soon subsided. Göring was delighted with the Premier's quick surrender: "M. Daladier is the very kind of man I like—he is so elastic."[51] Thanks to the elastic attitude of both Chamberlain and Daladier, the Munich Agreement was signed in the early morning of September 30 after considerable debate which revealed no sharp differences of opinion. The Sudetenland was ceded to Germany, and in order to simplify matters it was divided into four zones whose occupation by German troops would commence on October 1 and continue until October 7. The evacuation of these zones by the Czechs was guaranteed by Britain, France, and Italy; the details were to be carried out by an international commission in Berlin whose membership would include the State Secretary in the German Foreign Office, the British, French, and Italian ambassadors, and a representative of Czechoslovakia.[52] Germany had thus "incorporated the Sudeten Lands in the Reich without bloodshed and without firing a shot."[53]

It was apparent that in this whole matter of Munich, President Roosevelt played a very minor part. His appeals to Hitler were without any appreciable influence, and his message to Mussolini was regarded by the Duce with indifference. American relations with Italy since 1935 had grown steadily worse, so there was no reason why Mussolini should pay any attention to an American President who consistently refused to recognize the Italian conquest of Ethiopia. Chamberlain, on the other hand, had gone out of his way to appease the Duce, and the British Ambassador in Rome was justified in his statement that it was the Prime Minister's plea that moved Mussolini to ask Hitler to muzzle the dogs of war.[54] There is a possibility that Chamberlain was influenced to seek a pacific solution of the deepening crisis by the assurance that had been given to him some weeks earlier by Ambassador Kennedy: "Whatever course Chamberlain desires to adopt, he [Roosevelt] would think right." This amounted to a far-reaching blank check and

[51] John Wheeler-Bennett, *Munich: Prologue to Tragedy* (New York, 1948), p. 173.

[52] Note by Sir Horace Wilson on the Munich Conference, September 29–30, 1938. *Documents on British Foreign Policy, 1919–1939*, II, 630–35.

[53] Henderson, *op. cit.*, p. 172.

[54] The Earl of Perth to Viscount Halifax, Rome, September 30, 1938. *Documents on British Foreign Policy, 1919–1939*, II, 641–45.

Chamberlain undoubtedly had it in mind during the Munich crisis. I was able to discover in the State Department archives, however, no evidence of any real pressure upon the Prime Minister in favor of peace at any price.

In Administration circles there were some persons who were greatly pleased with the Munich Agreement. Sumner Welles hailed it as a pact that promised the possibility of a new world order "based upon justice and law."[55] Secretary Hull was more cautious although he did admit that the agreement afforded "a universal sense of relief."[56] In a letter to Mackenzie King, President Roosevelt remarked: "I can assure you that we in the United States rejoice with you, and the world at large, that the outbreak of war was averted."[57] A week later he expressed his thoughts to Ambassador Phillips in Rome: "I want you to know that I am not a bit upset over the final result [Munich Agreement]."[58]

k. *American Opinion of Munich*

This Presidential indifference to the implications of the Munich Agreement was not shared by the American press. To the *Miami Herald,* on the eve of Munich, it seemed that Europe was about to be "plunged into the mass murder of modern war because of the will of one man."[59] The Richmond *Times-Dispatch* was confident that the "responsibility for war, if it comes, will remain on the shoulders of Nazi Germany, where it belongs,"[60] and the New Orleans *Times-Picayune* voiced a similar opinion: "In the event that the world is thrown again into chaos, the war guilt almost inevitably will be chained to the neck of Adolf Hitler."[61]

When the text of the Munich Agreement was made public many papers had words of praise for Chamberlain. The *New York Herald-Tribune* thought that there could be "only heartfelt applause for the scrupulous integrity and the self-sacrificing devotion with which he [Prime Minister Chamberlain] labored for peace."[62] Other papers were equally laudatory. The *Washington Post* regarded the agreement as a step down the road to peace. The sacrifices of the Czechs would

55 *New York Times,* October 4, 1938.

56 September 30, 1938. *Peace and War,* p. 430.

57 President Roosevelt to Mackenzie King, October 11, 1938. *F. D. R.: His Personal Letters,* ed. Elliott Roosevelt (New York, 1950), II, 816–17.

58 President Roosevelt to Ambassador Phillips, October 17, 1938. *Ibid.,* pp. 818–19.

59 September 28, 1938.

60 September 29, 1938.

61 September 28, 1938.

62 September 29, 1938.

"seem a small price to pay for peace, particularly if the peace thereby obtained is stabilized."[63] The *Washington Evening Star* had no doubt that Hitler had "won a considerable victory," but of "paramount importance is the fact that a bloodless solution has been found for the gravest threat to international tranquility in the last quarter of a century."[64] The *Atlanta Constitution* thought the Munich accord had many imperfections, but "hope has come where only yesterday was despair, and the peoples of the world can take heart anew."[65]

The *New York Times* had words of praise for Munich: "Let no man say that too high a price has been paid for peace in Europe until he has searched his soul and found himself willing to risk in war the lives of those who are nearest and dearest to him."[66] The *Chicago Tribune* was also impressed with the importance of preserving the peace of Europe: "No doubt there were neurotics and hotheads in all the countries concerned who were eager for war, but they were outnumbered a thousand to one by those who were willing to make substantial sacrifices for peace."[67] The *Los Angeles Times* belonged to this large group of papers that had words of praise for the results of the Munich Conference: "There was no doubt that war was narrowly averted at Munich." Therefore, in comparison "with its immediate alternatives it rates among the first diplomatic achievements of history."[68] The *Cleveland Press* had a similar viewpoint. The critics who heaped blame upon Chamberlain and Daladier should pause a moment and think of the horrors of war. Then they would "thank God for the truce thus achieved."[69] The *Boston Evening Transcript* stressed the fact that the "big thing at the moment is that there is still peace in the world. Reason has not abdicated, it is only trampled a bit."[70] This theme was repeated by the *Christian Science Monitor:* "Reason has played a part in the present agreement. . . . It is a peace made without war—possibly the most notable one in history."[71]

These favorable comments in the press were balanced by adverse remarks in many other papers. The *Philadelphia Inquirer* believed there were "aspects of this so-called settlement . . . which thoughtful persons the world over must view with a profound sense of futility and foreboding."[72] The Norfolk *Virginian-Pilot* could see nothing to praise in the Munich negotiations. The net result was an "ill-smelling peace."[73] The *Emporia Gazette* saw the settlement at Munich as only

[63] September 29, 1938.
[64] September 30, 1938.
[65] September 30, 1938.
[66] September 30, 1938.
[67] September 30, 1938.
[68] September 30, 1938.
[69] September 30, 1938.
[70] September 30, 1938.
[71] September 30, 1938.
[72] October 1, 1938.
[73] September 30, 1938.

a stopgap. Real peace had not been achieved: "America may breathe deeply now, but she should tighten-up her belt for tomorrow, gird up her loins for the inevitable strife."[74] The *Portland Oregonian* was openly derisive of a peace with Hitler: "What good is a peace pact with this curser of democracy, torturer of Jews, coercer of minorities, and maestro of brutal prison camps?"[75]

The *Atlanta Constitution* was of the opinion that the Munich Agreement conclusively showed that the United States could "no longer trust Great Britain. The policy of the empire is expediency and the people of this country cannot rely upon England's word under these circumstances."[76] The *Constitution,* however, had warm words of praise for the policy of President Roosevelt. It was he who had "almost single-handedly tugged the world back from the brink. . . . To his eternal credit, Franklin Roosevelt did not falter in his purpose, now so dramatically brought to a fruitful conclusion."[77] The Hearst press had the same surprising viewpoint: "There can be no doubt that if a peaceful adjustment of the crisis in Europe is achieved, as a result of the Four-Power agreement in Munich, President Roosevelt will have contributed enormously to that end. . . . Mr. Roosevelt's second message to Chancellor Hitler ranks with the great state papers of all time. . . . Wishful foreign commentators had read into the first message a hint that the United States might follow its sympathies into another European war as it did in 1917. President Roosevelt left no room for that false interpretation in his second message."[78]

Not to be outdone in passing out words of praise for individuals who supposedly worked for peace in Europe, the *New York Daily News* had some friendly words for Adolf Hitler: "Now is the time for haters of Hitler to hold their harsh words. He has made a significant gesture towards peace; one that nobody but himself could have made at this time."[79]

1. *Diplomatic Straws in the Wind*

In Washington the German Ambassador pursued a policy of conciliation in the late summer of 1938. On the day before Munich he had a long talk with Secretary Hull which covered many topics. When the Secretary mentioned certain rumors to the effect that Chancellor Hit-

[74] September 30, 1938.
[75] October 1, 1938.
[76] October 1, 1938.
[77] September 30, 1938.
[78] *San Francisco Examiner,* September 30, 1938.
[79] September 29, 1938.

ler was seeking "general dominion by force," Ambassador Dieckhoff hastily denied that the Führer had any "world ambitions." He believed that Germany had a right to "interests in the Balkan and Danubian countries," and he saw no reason why they should be "bottled up." Hull pointed out the implications of this German drive to the East by remarking that it was incomprehensible to him why Europe wished "to commit suicide." Dieckhoff quickly changed the subject and began to discuss German-American relations. He had recently talked with Hitler and had discovered that the Führer was taking a "genuine interest" in the United States. He was beginning to realize that "certain readjustments of existing practices or policies by his Government relating to trade and also the Jewish question would be important, if not vital in the restoration of entirely satisfactory relations between our two countries."[80]

From the American Embassy in Berlin information was received to the effect that during the Munich crisis there had existed an intimate understanding between the German and the Polish armies. Lieutenant Colonel Truman Smith, military attaché in Berlin, submitted a report to Ambassador Wilson which left "no doubt of a large measure of military understanding between Poland and Germany. Perhaps the understanding was for *this episode only,* but it raises the possibility of a co-operation of a greater degree of intimacy than has yet been demonstrated between any two of the three points of the Axis."

In his report to Ambassador Wilson, Colonel Smith had remarked:

I believe that in the recent crisis [Munich] the Polish and German Governments had definite and far-reaching military agreements. . . . From the start to the end of the crisis, the German Army indicated not the slightest concern for Russian intervention. Unless the Germans felt sure of Poland and that Poland would resist militarily a Russian attack, it is not thinkable that this indifference would have been so apparent in Berlin. . . . It appears scarcely possible that the above-described German and Polish movements could have taken place on a mere loose oral understanding of the two heads of State.[81]

Ambassador Biddle, in Warsaw, informed the Department of State that he had talked with Polish officials concerning the details in Lieutenant Colonel Smith's memorandum and they had assured him that

---

[80] Memorandum of a conversation between Secretary Hull and the German Ambassador (Dieckhoff), September 28, 1938. 611.6231/1055, MS, Department of State.

[81] Ambassador Wilson to Secretary Hull, inclosing memorandum of Lieutenant Colonel Truman Smith, Berlin, October 26, 1938. 740.00/4961/2, MS, Department of State.

Smith's information was incorrect.[82] But in the documents on German foreign policy there is definite evidence that the Polish Foreign Minister, Beck, gave the German Ambassador in Warsaw some "very confidential information about Polish troops concentrations, in which confirmation of practical co-operation must certainly have been mentioned."[83] On this same day (September 27), the German State Secretary of the Foreign Office showed the Polish Ambassador in Berlin a map prepared by the headquarters of the *Wehrmacht* on which was drawn the demarcation line to be "observed between Polish and German troops if it came to an advance on Czechoslovakia." The ambassador thought it would "be useful" if he had the opportunity to discuss this matter with the German Foreign Office on the following day. After that, the "military authorities should contact one another."[84] It is apparent that there was some definite co-operation between the General Staffs of the German and Polish armies with reference to a possible conflict with Czechoslovakia. The real extent of this co-operation must remain a matter of conjecture.

There was one fact, however, that was beyond all dispute: Hitler had won a most significant diplomatic victory at Munich. The German plan of expansion contained many items that had not yet been disclosed, so realistic statesmen adopted an attitude of watchful waiting. Even Prime Minister Chamberlain at times abandoned his role of Pollyanna and expressed some misgivings about Hitler. It is certain that he felt a definite personal distrust of the Führer. To Lord Halifax he admitted that Hitler was "uncouth and certainly not the kind of a fellow one would like to go around the world with on a two-wheeled bicycle."[85]

It was not long before the Führer made Chamberlain and millions of other Britons hurriedly mount the machines of war and take long rides that would span much of the world. The strain of this unusual exercise meant death for Neville Chamberlain.

[82] Ambassador A. J. Drexel Biddle to Sumner Welles, Warsaw, November 25, 1938. 740.00/520½, MS, Department of State.

[83] German Ambassador in Poland (Moltke) to the German Foreign Ministry, Warsaw, September 27, 1938. *Documents of German Foreign Policy, 1918–1945,* II, 973–74.

[84] Minute by the State Secretary (Weizsäcker) for the Foreign Minister, Berlin, September 28, 1938. *Ibid.,* II, 975.

[85] Ambassador Kennedy to Secretary Hull, London, October 12, 1938. 741.00/202, *Confidential file,* MS, Department of State.

XIX

Hitler Takes Czechoslovakia under Protective Custody

THE AGREEMENT at Munich made provision for an international commission that was to fix the new boundaries of Czechoslovakia. The work of this commission was soon made a tragic farce by Hitler's determination to absorb what was left of the Czech State.[1] This flagrant violation of a solemn pledge and his continued pressure upon the Jews within the Reich converted American opinion of Hitler into open hostility.

a. *International Aspects of Anti-Semitism in Germany*

One of the most unfortunate legacies of the World War was the refugee problem. After February 1920, the League of Nations attempted to handle several aspects of this problem and during the following year Dr. Fridtjof Nansen was appointed to supervise the work done for Russian refugees. Later his duties were expanded so as to include the Armenians, the Assyrians, and the Turks. The League itself did not supply relief. Its main function was to assist in raising necessary funds in several European states and to act as an agent to help in the distribution of food and clothing to the refugees.

After January 1933, Nazi Germany inaugurated a campaign against Jews and political malcontents who hated the harsh measures of the Hitler regime. In order to alleviate the plight of this new stream of refugees the League created the office of High Commissioner. James G. McDonald was appointed to fill this vacancy and he served for two years in a brave attempt to accomplish something worth-while. When he resigned in 1935 he indicated that steps should be taken to remove the causes of the refugee problem rather than extend relief to a growing stream of helpless human beings.[2]

By 1937 some 130,000 Jews had left Germany. Those who remained in the Reich lived under restrictions that made it difficult for them to secure acceptable employment. The *Anschluss* which added Austria to

[1] The meetings of this international commission are reproduced in outline form in *Documents on German Foreign Policy, 1918–1945*, Series D, IV; *The Aftermath of Munich, 1938–1939* (Washington, 1951), pp. 2–4, 9–14, 22–24, 27–29, 34–35, 41–43, 63–66.

[2] Dorothy Thompson, *Refugees: Anarchy or Organization* (New York, 1938); Sir John Hope Simpson, *Refugees: Preliminary Report of a Survey* (New York, 1938).

Germany (March 1938) considerably widened the area of anti-Semitism and made the problem of refugees a more serious one. On March 24, 1938, in answer to this challenge, Secretary Hull issued an invitation to a large number of nations to join with the United States in setting up a special committee "for the purpose of facilitating the emigration from Austria and presumably from Germany of political refugees." It was pointed out that although the members of the committee would be appointed by the co-operating governments, the costs of this enterprise would be met by funds from private organizations. No country would be asked to change its prevailing immigration quota and care would be taken not to interfere with the work that was already being carried out by the League of Nations.[3]

With special reference to the United States it was apparent that there was no need to seek an increase in the existing quotas relative to immigration from Austria and Germany. For the fiscal year ending June 30, 1938, the immigration from those areas was considerably less than the quotas fixed by law.[4] This small number of refugees was due to the restrictions in the Reich with reference to the removal of money or other assets. In 1933, emigrants from the Reich had been permitted to take 75 per cent of their property with them; subsequently, the proportion had been reduced to 15 per cent and in 1938 it had reached the low level of 5 per cent. These restrictions made it necessary for private organizations to finance the emigration of minority groups like the Jews.[5]

The first meeting of the international committee proposed by Secretary Hull was held in France on July 6, 1938, at which a temporary organization was effected. Later the committee met in London and Lord Winterton was appointed permanent chairman with Mr. George Rublee, an American, being selected as director. Estimates were submitted indicating that the number of refugees from Germany would probably total at least 660,000. Upon the broad shoulders of Mr. Rublee was imposed the burden of persuading Nazi officials to liberalize the restrictions upon the removal of property from the Reich and thus make it possible for a large number of refugees to proceed to countries willing to receive them.[6]

While Mr. Rublee was awaiting an invitation from the Nazi Government to visit Berlin for the purpose of discussing the refugee problem, the German Ambassador in Washington (Dieckhoff) had a long conversation with Sumner Welles, the Acting Secretary of State. He seemed

[3] Department of State, *Press Release*, March 24, 1938.

[4] For the fiscal year ending June 30, 1938, the total Austrian and German immigration into the United States was 17,868. The official quota was 27,370.

[5] *The United States in World Affairs, 1938*, p. 94.

[6] *New York Times*, July 16, 31, August 5, 8, 18, 1938.

to be in a "distinctly emotional and nervous condition" and complained that it was very difficult for any "German diplomatic representative" to carry on his duties in the United States without "suffering a very serious nervous strain." After this introduction he launched into a detailed defense of Germany's expansion at the expense of Czechoslovakia. The government of the Reich was merely following out the Wilsonian policy as enunciated in the well-known Fourteen Points. Germany had now "incorporated within its own territory all individuals of German nationality in Central Europe. The present German Reich had not the slightest intention of extending its sovereignty any further within Europe either through force or through any other method. . . . Germany had not only announced but had repeatedly reiterated her desire to live at peace with her neighbors, especially with France and Great Britain, and that the Munich Agreement had made such peace possible."

With reference to the treatment of Jews and other minorities within the Reich, Dieckhoff said that he was of the opinion that no other nation was entitled to criticize the "domestic policy" of Germany. Welles immediately replied that it was

absolutely impossible for American public opinion to think that the policy which Germany had been pursuing these recent years with regard to the Jews within their own borders . . . could be regarded as a purely domestic question. I [Welles] said that any country that forced the emigration from its borders of hundreds of thousands of individuals whom other countries for humanitarian reasons felt it necessary to shelter . . . would hardly expect the rest of the world to regard such a policy as this a domestic policy. . . . The people of the United States . . . were a deeply religious people and a highly idealistic people and the torture of human beings which had been taking place in Germany revolted the best instincts in all of them.

I then went on to discuss the injustices done to our nationals, whether of Jewish origin or not, in Germany by refusing to permit them to take out of Germany the moneys which they possessed and I said I thought it necessary to say in all frankness that public opinion in the United States on this point had reached such a stage that there would inevitably be a general demand in the immediate future for the taking by the United States Government of retaliatory measures against German nationals residing within the United States.

In conclusion Welles remarked that nothing would do more to "ameliorate public indignation" in the United States than an agreement on the part of the German Government to receive Mr. Rublee and negotiate with him some satisfactory agreement. Ambassador Dieckhoff seemed "very much impressed" with the advice of Mr. Welles and promised to do "everything in his power" to persuade his Government to extend an invitation to Mr. Rublee to visit Berlin and settle the refugee problem.[7]

b. *Ambassador Kennedy Toys with the Idea of Acting as an Interlocutor between Hitler and Roosevelt*

While the German Government was pondering the question of inviting Mr. Rublee to Berlin, Ambassador Dirksen, in Rome, sent an important dispatch to the Foreign Office. It dealt with the desire of Ambassador Kennedy to pay a visit to Berlin for the express purpose of a conference with Hitler. Kennedy would talk frankly with the Führer and "try to bring about a better understanding between the United States and Germany." Kennedy hinted that persons who "regarded Germany sympathetically were prevented from seeing the President. . . . For this reason Kennedy believed he could be of general use in the advancement of German-American relations, as he had the ear of the President and approached the Germany of today with understanding and sympathy." Kennedy then "repeatedly emphasized the sympathy which the average American felt for the German and which was greater than his liking for the average Englishman." Moreover, it should be remembered that "very strong anti-Semitic tendencies existed in the United States and that a large portion of the population had an understanding of the German attitude toward the Jews."[8]

In Washington, Ambassador Dieckhoff was not enthusiastic about the proposed Kennedy visit to Berlin. He felt that the argument that the President should be "better informed regarding Germany" was pretty weak. The President was "well informed from the reports of his Berlin Ambassador," but in spite of this fact he still assumed an "unfriendly attitude" towards Germany. Kennedy could not alter this attitude. American public opinion could be "rectified" only by the "rebuilding of Europe through joint, successful action of the European Great Powers."[9]

c. *Ambassador Wilson Is Recalled from Germany*

Any possibility that Ambassador Kennedy might visit Berlin was destroyed by fresh outbreaks of anti-Semitism in Germany. On November 7 a young Jewish refugee from Poland (Herschel Grynszpan) went

[7] Memorandum of a conversation between Sumner Welles, Acting Secretary of State, and Ambassador Dieckhoff, November 1, 1938. 702.6211/929, MS, Department of State.

[8] Ambassador Dirksen to State Secretary Weizsäcker, London, October 13, 1938. *Documents of German Foreign Policy, 1918–1945,* IV, 634–36.

[9] Ambassador Dieckhoff to Ambassador Dirksen, Washington, November 2, 1938. *Ibid.,* p. 637.

to the German Embassy in Paris and shot Ernst vom Rath, the third secretary, who died three days later. Immediately, throughout Germany, Jews were plundered and beaten, their shops were wrecked, and their synagogues were burned. On November 13 the Nazi Government imposed a fine of a billion marks ($420,000,000) upon German Jews as a form of collective punishment. This drastic action was succeeded by a number of decrees which barred all Jews from high schools and universities, and excluded them from many types of business enterprise. They were forbidden to attend cinemas, theaters, museums, public concerts, and lectures, and their permits to drive motor vehicles of all kinds were withdrawn. Far-reaching ordinances of segregation were put immediately into force.[10]

This outburst of anti-Semitism in the Reich aroused deep-seated resentment in the United States which was given partial expression on November 14 in a nationwide radio broadcast featuring critical remarks by leaders of various political and religious faiths. Among these speakers were former President Hoover, Harold L. Ickes, Rev. Robert I. Gannon, S.J., president of Fordham University, and Bishop Edwin Hughes of the Methodist Episcopal Church. At a press conference, President Roosevelt sharply denounced the measures of the Nazi Government: "I myself could scarcely believe that such things could occur in a twentieth-century civilization."[11] He then announced the recall of Ambassador Wilson from Berlin in order to get a "first-hand picture" of the situation in Germany. This action led the German Government to recall Ambassador Dieckhoff from Washington. Relations between the two countries were seriously strained.

Before Ambassador Wilson received his letter of recall he telegraphed to Secretary Hull that Senator Reynolds, of North Carolina, was anxious for him to arrange for an interview with Chancellor Hitler.[12] Hull responded by instructing the ambassador that "in the circumstances as they exist today we feel that it would be inadvisable for the Embassy to request or arrange for an interview with Chancellor Hitler for any American, whether official or otherwise."[13] Apparently he felt that all Americans should be protected from any contact with the Führer.[14]

[10] *Frankfurter Zeitung,* November 11, 30, December 5, 1938.

[11] *New York Times,* November 15, 16, 1938.

[12] Ambassador Wilson to Secretary Hull, Berlin, November 15, 1938. 862.002 HITLER/171, MS, Department of State.

[13] Secretary Hull to Ambassador Wilson, November 18, 1938. 862.002 HITLER/171, MS, Department of State.

[14] Ambassador Dieckhoff was greatly worried about the hostility of American public opinion towards Germany. Men "like Dewey, Hoover, Hearst and many others" had suddenly adopted "a violent and bitter attitude" against the Hitler regime. There was a "general atmosphere of hate" with regard to Nazi excesses. *Documents on German Foreign Policy, 1918–1945,* IV, 639–40.

d. *Dr. Schacht Offers Solution of Refugee Problem*

It was apparent to thoughtful Germans that the strained relations between Germany and the United States might eventually lead to war.
Perhaps a bargain might be made whereby the economic conflict between the two countries could be ended and thus make it possible to
inaugurate a period of milder treatment for the Jews in Germany.

This economic conflict between Germany and the United States had
been heightened by the reluctance of the Nazi Government in March–
April 1938 to assume the obligation of Austria's external debts. After
the close of the World War the American Congress had authorized a
credit to the Austrian Government of $26,000,000 for the purpose of
purchasing flour for relief distribution. American investors had then
moved into the picture by putting their funds into several types of
Austrian external obligations. These private investments had at one
time reached the considerable total of $38,000,000. In April 1938,
after the *Anschluss,* the American Government took up this matter of
the payment of these Austrian obligations and frankly informed the
German Foreign Office that the "welfare of numerous American citizens is directly affected [by the absorption of Austria] and this Government would appreciate prompt assurances on the subject."[15]

The Reich failed to respond to this invitation and then added insult
to injury by concluding with the British Government an arrangement
for a limited service on Austrian external obligations that were payable
in London. This deal was made possible because Germany's trade balance with Britain was favorable and thus British officials had it within
their power to impound German surplus funds and apply them to the
Austrian debt. The Chamberlain Government had no desire to adopt
such rigorous countermeasures, so an agreement was reached whereby
German goods (not cash) would be accepted in payment of these
obligations. This agreement led German newspapers to boast that the
usual Anglo-American parallel policy had been discarded by the British
Foreign Office.[16]

By the end of 1938, Germany had concluded arrangements with
most of the creditor countries for some kind of payment to the holders
of Austrian obligations. The United States was the shining exception.

---

[15] Department of State, *Press Releases,* April 9, 1938, XVIII, 465–67. See also the
"Outline of the Present State of Economic Relations Between Germany and the United
States of America, November 18, 1938," in *Documents on German Foreign Policy,
1918–1945,* IV, 641–643.

[16] *Economist* (London), July 9, 1938, CXXXII, 71.

In the last week of November, Dr. Schacht was anxious to come to some agreement with the Department of State that would partially satisfy American demands. During a conversation with Donald R. Heath, first secretary of the American Embassy in Berlin, he expressed his urgent desire

for a settlement of the economic conflict and difficulties in German-American relations, not because of the mutual economic benefits which would result but because such a settlement would work to prevent further measures against the German Jews. . . . He made a veiled but unmistakable reference to the anti-Jewish measures and demonstrations and said with great feeling that they were scandalous. Returning to the difficulties in the state of German-American economic relations he said: "If I could only sit down with Secretary Hull I know that we could quickly find a way out of our difficulties."[17]

In December 1938, Schacht went to London to visit Montagu Norman, governor of the Bank of England. In London he made it a point to confer with Mr. Rublee with reference to the emigration of Jews from the Reich. He proposed the pooling of all the capital supplies left by the refugees in Germany and the use of this property as collateral for a large international loan. This loan would be used to expedite the movement of refugees from Germany to their new homes. It would be repaid from the proceeds derived from additional German exports to new markets or to old markets that had been partially closed.[18]

On December 20, Mr. Rublee was invited to Berlin for further discussions of the Schacht plan for aiding the emigration of persons from the Reich. During the following month there was an exchange of notes between the Department of State and the German Foreign Office. The Foreign Office refused to acknowledge the $26,000,000 relief loan to Austria as a valid obligation, and it contended that payments on other Austrian external obligations held by American investors should be adjusted in the light of Germany's unfavorable trade balance with the United States. The Department of State rejected these contentions, but it did suggest that Reich officials might initiate conversations with representatives of American holders of Austrian bonds.[19] This suggestion failed to lead to any worth-while results so the Austrian debt question remained as one of the constant irritants in German-American relations.

[17] Memorandum of a conversation between Donald R. Heath and Dr. Schacht, Berlin, November 30, 1938. 711.62/175, MS, Department of State.
[18] London *Times,* December 21, 22, 1938; *New York Times,* December 13, 17, 20, 25, 1938.
[19] Department of State, *Press Release,* January 28, 1939, XX, 53–55.

e. *Secretary Ickes Increases Tension in German-American Relations*

Another important irritant in German-American relations was Secretary Ickes, whose contemptuous remarks deeply disturbed German officials. On December 18, in a speech delivered in Cleveland, he sharply criticized Henry Ford and Colonel Lindbergh for accepting the award of the German Eagle from Chancellor Hitler: "How can any American accept a decoration at the hand of a brutal dictator who, with the same hand, is robbing and torturing thousands of fellow human beings?"[20]

Before Dr. Thomsen, the German chargé d'affaires, could file a formal protest at the Department of State with reference to the pungent remarks of Secretary Ickes, George S. Messersmith, Assistant Secretary of State, sent a memorandum to Sumner Welles dealing with this Cleveland incident. He thought that any "protest from the German Government concerning the relatively innocuous remarks of Secretary Ickes comes with particularly bad grace at this time. The German newspapers have recently contained dastardly attacks on the President and Mrs. Roosevelt. . . . As the complete . . . control of the German press is a declared part of the program of the National Socialist Government, the German Government cannot escape responsibility for such attacks."[21]

Mr. Welles accepted the advice of Mr. Messersmith with reference to answering the protest of Dr. Thomsen. After the German diplomat had recited his complaint, Welles coldly remarked that the criticism that Secretary Ickes had hurled at Henry Ford and Colonel Lindbergh primarily touched American citizens and therefore the German Foreign Office was injecting itself into an American domestic question. Needless to say, the Department of State would not discuss such questions with "the representative of any foreign government." With particular reference to the criticism by Secretary Ickes of the policies of the Nazi Government, Welles acidly declared that

the German Government must surely be familiar with the fact that the recent policies pursued in Germany had shocked and confounded public opinion in the United States more profoundly than anything that had taken place in many decades, and that such references to this state of public indignation as might have been made certainly represented the feeling of the overwhelming majority of the people of the United States. . . . It seemed to him that the

[20] *New York Times,* December 19, 1938.
[21] George S. Messersmith to Sumner Welles, December 21, 1938. 711.62/186, MS, Department of State.

desire of the German Government to make a protest of this character came with singular ill grace. He said that for the past few months he had carefully followed the German press which was completely under the influence and dictation of the authorities of the German Government, and that he had rarely read more unjustifiable criticism or open attacks . . . against the President of the United States and members of his Cabinet.[22]

f. *The Economic Offensive against Germany Is Accelerated*

While political relations with Germany were daily becoming more strained, Secretary Hull widened the breach between the Department of State and the German Foreign Office by pushing with increasing ardor his economic offensive against the Reich. In order for his trade agreements program to be really effective it was necessary for him to enlist the support of Britain. In the early part of 1936, Hull bluntly informed the British Ambassador in Washington that the "clearing arrangements reached by Britain with Argentina, Germany, Italy and other countries were handicapping the efforts of this Government to carry forward its broad program with the favored-nation policy underlying it." The tendency in most of these arrangements was "to drive straight toward bilateral trading and to restrict and obstruct the sum total of world trade." These restrictions and obstructions were milestones along the road to war.[23]

In October 1936, Hull instructed James C. Dunn, chief of the Western European Division, to write a letter to Ambassador Bingham in which the situation was placed squarely before the British Government. No time should be lost in establishing "sound and substantial trade upon a firm basis of equality of treatment and exchange of opportunities for trade to the greatest extent each nation can possibly contribute." Widened trade opportunities would provide a basis for world peace.[24]

Finally, on November 17, 1938, a formal ceremony was held at the White House at which Secretary Hull, Prime Minister Mackenzie King of Canada, and Sir Ronald Lindsay, the British Ambassador, signed important trade agreements on behalf of their respective governments. The capstone was thus placed upon the large economic structure sponsored by Secretary Hull. The most important trading nations were now

---

[22] Memorandum of a conference between Sumner Welles and Dr. Thomsen, German chargé d'affaires, December 21, 1938. 711.62/199, MS, Department of State. In a dispatch to State Secretary Weizsäcker, December 21, 1938, Dieckhoff recounts this conversation with Welles and finally remarks: "I broke off the discussion at this point as hopeless." *Documents on German Foreign Policy, 1918–1945,* IV, 662–63.

[23] Cordell Hull, *Memoirs* (New York, 1948), I, 520–21.

[24] *Ibid.,* pp. 523–24.

lowering barriers while many other countries were raising theirs. The
concessions provided for in these agreements were "generalized" so
that a considerable number of nations could profit by them if they could
supply any of the products affected. American farmers were particularly
benefited by reduced rates on important agricultural exports. Duties
were entirely removed from wheat and lard. Canadian concessions to
the United States included reductions in the duties on fruits, vegetables,
and types of machinery not manufactured in the Dominion. In return,
three of Canada's major exports to the United States were "bound"
to the free list—pulpwood, wood pulp, and newsprint paper.[25] America's answer to Munich was given in strong economic accents which
grated loudly upon German ears that were closely attuned to the dubious harmonies of bilateral agreements.

g. Germany Is Anxious for an Accord with the United States

The actions of Secretary Hull and the acidulous comments of Sumner
Welles seemed to point the way to a definite deterioration in German-
American relations. Mr. Gilbert, the American chargé d'affaires in Berlin, thought that it was possible that Hitler had decided to break off
diplomatic relations with the United States "immediately after Christmas."[26] He had learned that the Führer had become "exceedingly irate"
upon being informed of the reply of Sumner Welles to the protest of
Dr. Thomsen relative to the tart remarks of Secretary Ickes on December 18. Ribbentrop was believed to be preparing a counterblast to the
pungent comments of the Secretary of the Interior.[27]

Although Ribbentrop did not make this expected attack upon American officials, Mr. Gilbert was told that "certain extremists" close to
Hitler were "urging a break with the United States." But such a break
in relations would not be "popular in Germany," and the chargé had
not been able to detect "even a hint" of hostility in his conversations
with German officials.[28]

From Paris, Hugh Wilson reported that Dr. Goebbels had recently
requested the Havas correspondent in Berlin "not to present in his
despatches the future of German-American relations in too gloomy
fashion." The German Government had "no intention of aggravating

[25] Department of State, *Press Releases,* XIX, Supplements A and B.

[26] Prentiss Gilbert to Secretary Hull, Berlin, December 24, 1938. 711.62/178, MS,
Department of State.

[27] Prentiss Gilbert to Secretary Hull, Berlin, December 27, 1938. 711.62/182, MS,
Department of State.

[28] Prentiss Gilbert to Secretary Hull, Berlin, January 3, 1939. 711.62/191, MS,
Department of State.

the present conflict and sincerely desired the re-establishment of normal relations between the two countries."[29]

It was apparent that Goebbels and other Nazi officials awaited with deep interest the President's message to Congress in January 1939. It contained the expected warning that acts of new aggression were all "about us" and that the "God-fearing democracies of the world" could not "forever let pass without effective protest" these threats to their way of life. But it was made clear that democratic protests must be along "peaceful lines." It was also emphasized that there were many methods "short of war" that could be employed to bring home to aggressor nations "the aggregate sentiments of our own people."[30]

The temperate language of this Presidential message to Congress gave reassurance to the German Government and led it to continue the recent gestures of conciliation. These gestures were listed by Mr. Gilbert as follows:

1) A cessation of the unrestrained violence of the press.
2) The invitation to the Evian Committee to come to Berlin.
3) More conciliatory replies to our notes respecting discrimination against certain classes of American citizens together with publicity given to recent exchanges.

The question of whether these actions were "gestures for immediate ends" or whether they represented a "considered change of policy" remained to be seen. It should appear obvious to German leaders that "self-interest would suggest the desirability of better relations with the United States."[31]

This self-interest led General Göring to have a conference with Mr. Rublee on the refugee problem and to arrange for a series of talks between Rublee and Ministerial Direktor Wohltat. Göring then invited Mr. Gilbert to his private residence for a discussion of German-American relations. The atmosphere of the meeting was

most cordial and friendly and Goering stressed repeatedly that he was anxious to find a solution of the Jewish problem. He appeared to be fully conscious of the importance of settling the problem from the point of view of good relations with other countries particularly the United States. . . . He discussed the subject of Jewish emigration generally and particularly emphasized the

---

[29] Ambassador Wilson to Secretary Hull, Paris, January 5, 1939. 711.62/194, MS, Department of State.

[30] *The Public Papers and Addresses of Franklin D. Roosevelt, 1939,* ed. Samuel I. Rosenman (New York, 1939), pp. 1–12.

[31] Prentiss Gilbert to Secretary Hull, Berlin, January 14, 1939. 711.62/201, MS, Department of State.

necessity of moving rapidly. . . . In concluding the conversation, Goering laid
great stress at considerable length on the desirability of good relations between Germany and the United States. Outside of the Jewish problem he
saw no concrete problems which should trouble relations between the two
countries.[32]

Dr. Schacht was equally conciliatory. In a talk with Donald Heath,
third secretary of the American Embassy, he said that he would be interested in "taking over any worth-while project which might be offered him either in Germany or abroad." After this intimation that he
might be willing to accept a position with some large American banking
institution, he stated that he was largely responsible for the invitation
that had been extended to Mr. Rublee to visit Berlin with reference to
the refugee problem. It was due to "his initiative" that the recent conversations between Rublee and Nazi officials had taken place. He had
personally suggested the matter to "Hitler and had his approval before
he started his talks." He had also "gotten Hitler's approval of each stage
of the conversations."[33]

h. *Chamberlain Pays Ardent Court to Mussolini*

While Göring, Goebbels, and Schacht made these gestures of conciliation towards the United States, the basic Nazi policy of expansion made
them so futile that it is difficult to understand why they were regarded
as worth-while. The restless mind of Hitler, despite all his public promises to the contrary, was fixed upon the early absorption of Czechoslovakia. Before he would make any military move in this direction he
wished to expand the Rome-Berlin Axis into a triple German-Italian-
Japanese military alliance. On October 28, Ribbentrop urged this alliance upon Mussolini as a necessary weapon to use against the democracies when the inevitable war with them broke out.[34]

After waiting some months, Mussolini, on January 1, 1939, instructed Ciano to "accept the proposition of von Ribbentrop to trans-
form the anti-Comintern pact into an alliance." He also considered a
clash with the democracies as "inevitable" and wished to "effect a military alignment in advance." On January 2, Ciano informed Ribbentrop
by telephone of the decision of the Duce, and on the following day
Ambassador Attolico returned to Berlin with detailed instructions rela-

---

[32] Prentiss Gilbert to Secretary Hull, Berlin, January 21, 1939. 840.48 REFU-
GEES/1328, MS, Department of State.

[33] Memorandum of a conversation between Donald R. Heath and Dr. Schacht,
February 7, 1939. 862.00/3835, MS, Department of State.

[34] Elizabeth Wiskemann, *The Rome-Berlin Axis* (New York, 1949), p. 134.

tive to the proposed pact. After talking with Ribbentrop, Attolico favored January 28 as "the date for the signing of the alliance." The German Foreign Office promptly prepared an outline of this new triple alliance which was sent to Rome where it gained Mussolini's speedy approval.[35]

While Mussolini and Hitler were planning a triple alliance to face the democracies in an inevitable war, Neville Chamberlain decided to visit Rome in order to secure certain guarantees of world peace. It was a hopeless quest and the fascist leaders were determined that the negotiations should end in nothing more than empty promises. Ciano was anxious that Chamberlain should not receive an "enthusiastic welcome" in Rome and he was disappointed when the populace cheered "the old man with the umbrella."

After a conference at the Palazzo Venezia with Chamberlain and Lord Halifax, Mussolini contemptuously remarked to Ciano: "These men are not made of the same stuff as Francis Drake and the other magnificent adventurers who created the empire. These . . . are the tired sons of a long line of rich men and they will lose their empire." During the conversations on January 12, Lord Halifax talked with such caution that Ciano was certain that the "British do not want to fight." The Duce's contempt for these pacific Britishers grew apace and Ciano told Ribbentrop on the telephone that the visit of Chamberlain was "a big lemonade, absolutely harmless." But Chamberlain still nursed hopes for a continuance of the peace of Europe, and Ciano noted that the Prime Minister's eyes "filled with tears when the train started moving and his countrymen began singing 'For He's a Jolly Good Fellow.' "[36]

The communiqué issued to the press gave an assurance that it was the "will of Italy and Great Britain to pursue a policy aiming effectively at the maintenance of peace."[37] At the same time this optimistic note was being sounded for the anxious ears of the public, Ciano was confiding to his diary that the Italian Foreign Office was planning a campaign of "steadily increasing propaganda against France." When this had its expected effect the news of the new triple alliance could then be announced and the populace gradually prepared for war with the democracies. As for England, Ciano thought that there was little to worry about. Towards the end of January, Lord Perth had submitted for Italian approval the outline of a speech which Chamberlain would soon make in the House of Commons. The comments of the Duce on this gesture of conciliation revealed his growing contempt for the British

[35] *The Ciano Diaries, 1939–1943*, ed. Hugh Gibson (Garden City, 1947), January 1–8, 1939, pp. 3–8.
[36] *Ibid.*, January 11–14, 1939, pp. 9–12.
[37] *New York Times*, January 13, 14, 1939.

Cabinet: "I believe this is the first time that the head of the British Government submits to a foreign government the outline of one of his speeches. It's a bad sign for them."[38]

i. *France Favors a Free Hand to Hitler in Eastern Europe*

While Chamberlain was courting Mussolini, Georges Bonnet, the French Foreign Minister, was planning a new program of appeasement that would please Hitler. His first step was to endeavor to negotiate with Germany an accord similar to the one Chamberlain had signed with the Führer at the time of the Munich Agreement. On October 19, M. François-Poncet, at his farewell audience with Hitler, carefully broached this matter of an arrangement that would build a new understanding between the two countries.[39] The Führer was pleased with this evidence of French naïveté and gave the project his blessing. On December 6, in the famous Salle de l'Horloge where the Kellogg-Briand Peace Pact had been signed, Bonnet and Ribbentrop inscribed their signatures upon a Franco-German Declaration of Friendship. This declaration announced that no question of a territorial nature remained in suspense between France and Germany and it recognized as permanent the frontier line as then drawn. After emphasizing the importance of pacific relations, provision was then made for consultation "in case any complications" arose that "should threaten to lead to international difficulties."[40]

According to Ribbentrop, Bonnet, in the secrecy of personal conversations, assured him that the Four-Power guarantee relative to Czechoslovakia was "something to which no special importance was to be attached." Although Bonnet, some months later, strenuously denied the statements in the Ribbentrop letter, it is quite apparent that in December 1938 he was anxious to give Germany far-reaching assurances with reference to Nazi plans for expansion in eastern Europe.[41]

In December 1938, Jules Lukasiewicz, the Polish Ambassador to France, reported a conversation with Bonnet in which the French Foreign Minister stated that Ribbentrop had "received a French promise not to oppose German economic expansion in the Danube Basin." It was also true that Bonnet had intimated to Ribbentrop that German

---

38 Gibson, *op. cit.*, January 27, 1939, p. 17.

39 M. François-Poncet to Georges Bonnet, the French Foreign Minister, Berlin, October 20, 24, 1938. *French Yellow Book: Diplomatic Documents, 1938–1939* (New York, 1940), pp. 20–29.

40 *Ibid.*, p. 35.

41 Herr von Ribbentrop to M. Georges Bonnet, Fuschl, July 13, 1939. *Ibid.*, pp. 213–15. For the answer of Bonnet, July 21, 1939, denying the statements of Ribbentrop, see pp. 221–24.

"political expansion" in the same region would not "encounter serious French resistance."[42]

In order to provide further development of his schemes for appeasement, Bonnet sent Paul Baudouin to Rome with offers of a share in the directorate of the Suez Canal, of certain privileges for Italians in Tunis, and of important concessions relative to Djibouti and the railway to Addis Ababa. To Berlin he sent Count Ferdinand de Brinon to solicit Ribbentrop's assistance in securing Italian acceptance of these proposals. But Ribbentrop had no desire to compose the difficulties between France and Italy, so he "torpedoed" the Baudouin mission by revealing some of its secrets to the press.[43] The Rome-Berlin Axis was now treating the democracies with open contempt.

j. *The British Foreign Office Has a Case of Jitters*

To Chamberlain these repeated doses of appeasement which he forced down his throat were increasingly bitter but he swallowed them as the price of peace. At least he had been able to preserve the independence of Czechoslovakia. In Parliament, Sir Samuel Hoare glibly expressed the opinion that the Czech State was now as "safe as Switzerland," and Sir Thomas Inskip solemnly declared that in the event of an act of unprovoked aggression against the Czechs, His Majesty's Government would feel "bound to take all steps in their power to see that the integrity of Czechoslovakia is preserved."[44]

By November 1, Chamberlain, impressed with the gravity of the situation in Europe, began to hedge with reference to the scope of the British guarantee of the integrity of the Czech State. He still supported Inskip's statement as to the policy of the British Government, but he frankly confessed that he could not enlighten the House of Commons as to "what the terms of the guarantee will be and who will be the partakers in that guarantee." He could say, however, that Britain had never guaranteed "the frontiers as they existed." Her pledge was merely

[42] *The German White Paper: Full Text of the Polish Documents Issued by the Berlin Foreign Office* (New York, 1940), p. 28.

[43] Gibson, *op. cit.*, January 28, February 2, 3, 6, March 18, 1939, pp. 17, 20–21, 23, 47. The French Foreign Office continued to believe that the ties between Hitler and Mussolini were not very close. Hugh Wilson, at Paris, talked with Léger, Secretary-General of the French Foreign Office, who informed him that "so far as German support is concerned . . . Hitler earnestly desires that France and Great Britain stand firm against any concessions to Mussolini. So long as Britain and France stand firm, Hitler will give Mussolini press and diplomatic support but nothing more. Hitler knows well that in case of war on account of Italian claims, Germany would bear four-fifths of the brunt of the fighting." Ambassador Wilson to Secretary Hull, Paris, January 16, 1939. 740.00/546, *Confidential file*, MS, Department of State.

[44] John Wheeler-Bennett, *Munich: Prologue to Tragedy* (New York, 1948), p. 314.

against "unprovoked aggression and not the crystallization of the frontiers."[45]

He did not hide the fact that this aggression might come at any
time. Indeed, throughout Europe there was increasing fear of the outbreak of war. In January 1939, Coulondre, the French Ambassador in
Berlin, reported that Hitler had uttered a most disturbing threat: "If
Czechoslovakia did not toe the line, he would let loose against her a
lightning action."[46]

The British Foreign Office learned that Hitler was

bitterly resentful at the Munich Agreement which baulked him of a localized
war against Czechoslovakia and demonstrated the will to peace of the German masses in opposition to the war-mongering of the Nazi party. He feels
personally humiliated by this demonstration. He regards Great Britain as
primarily responsible for this humiliation and his rage is therefore directed
principally against this country which he holds to be the chief obstacle now
to the fulfilment of his further ambitions.

In the event of Germany picking a quarrel with Holland, His Majesty's Government was considering

the desirability, as a matter of tactics and precaution, of being ready at once
with a proposal to both Governments for the selection by a neutral Government of a board of three arbitrators. Such a proposal might not prove effective but if arbitration were overriden by Germany the issue would be clear
and His Majesty's Government would have *locus standi* for appropriate
action.[47]

A few days later the British Government decided that the "strategic
importance of Holland and her colonies" was so great that a "German
attack on that country must be regarded as a direct threat to the security
of the Western Powers. Failure to take up such a challenge would
place Germany in a position of overwhelming predominance in Europe
and in such circumstances His Majesty's Government is disposed to
think that it would have no choice but to regard a German invasion of
Holland as a *casus belli*."[48]

On February 7, President Roosevelt received a message from Lord
Halifax to the effect that the British Government had now moved to
the point where "any attempt by Germany to dominate Holland by

[45] *Parliamentary Debates,* House of Commons, November 1, 1938, cols. 80–82.

[46] L. B. Namier, *Diplomatic Prelude, 1938–1939* (New York, 1948), p. 64.

[47] Lord Halifax to President Roosevelt, January 25, 1939. 740.00/555½, *Confidential file,* MS, Department of State.

[48] Chargé Johnson to Secretary Hull, London, January 28, 1939. 740.00/553, *Confidential file,* MS, Department of State.

force or threat of force would also have to be regarded as a menace to the security of the United Kingdom." A German attack "on Holland and an attack on Switzerland are in the same category." Replies from the French Foreign Office to British inquiries as to French policy clearly indicated that the "French Government agree with His Majesty's Government in considering the contingency of an invasion of Holland as a *casus belli*."[49]

On February 17, Ambassador Kennedy had a long talk with Chamberlain who expressed the view that the general outlook in Europe "is much better." He could not see any "definite indication of moves toward Holland, Switzerland, or elsewhere to the West or to the Ukraine and in this he takes issue with the Foreign Office. He still feels that the only hope of doing business with Hitler is to take him at his word." He believed that there was a "very definite chance of arriving at some solution through economics."

Chamberlain discussed at length his visit to Rome to see Mussolini. He contrasted the Duce, "as a man who likes to see the whole picture . . . as against Hitler who looks out of the window at Berchtesgaden dreamingly considering the future prospect of Germany without being very practical." But Chamberlain still thought that he could "do business with Hitler" and that his policy of appeasement could "still be worked out." He remained "very optimistic."[50]

Three days later Kennedy talked matters over with Viscount Halifax who apparently had caught some of Chamberlain's optimism. In a report to Secretary Hull, Kennedy summed up the situation in England as follows:

My observations, and I have talked with Chatfield, Simon, Hoare, Halifax and Chamberlain, in addition to many other people, are that they thoroughly believe that England is on its way; that Germany will not attack; that the problem of last fall, when they were obliged to do things that perhaps they would rather have done otherwise, is gone, and that while England will not go to war if Germany should attack Rumania or the Ukraine, they would declare war at once if Germany moved towards Switzerland or Holland.[51]

The fluctuating atmosphere in the Foreign Office was described by the British Ambassador during a conversation with Sumner Welles:

[49] Lord Halifax to President Roosevelt, London, February 7, 1939. 740.00/569½, *Confidential file*, MS, Department of State.
[50] Ambassador Kennedy to Secretary Hull, London, February 17, 1939. 740.00/588, *Confidential file*, MS, Department of State.
[51] Ambassador Kennedy to Secretary Hull, London, February 20, 1939. 740.00/589, *Confidential file*, MS, Department of State.

The Ambassador said that on January 24 and 26 public opinion in London and the Foreign Office in particular had been in an almost unbelievable state of excitement because of reports that Germany was planning a move in the West involving the invasion of Holland. By February 11, the day he had left London to come to the United States, opinion in general including that of the Foreign Office had swung over to a state of almost unbelievable optimism and of reassurance. The Ambassador said that he thought one state of mind was as disquieting as the other and that the nervous strain under which they were all living in England was appalling. He said that his own Foreign Office was in a very unsatisfactory condition. He said that Lord Halifax was a man of real ability and an "excellent Christian gentleman," but that he did not seem to have any real insight into the European situation. . . . He said that he doubted whether Mr. Chamberlain's colleagues in the Cabinet shared his feeling of reassurance, and that he knew as a positive fact that the Foreign Office was extremely apprehensive.[52]

k. *Germany Fears the U.S. Will Intervene in World War II*

From London, Kennedy sent further information on the threatening situation in Europe. Halifax had asked the Nazi Ambassador in London (von Dirksen) why Hitler, if he really wished to have peace, was continuing his "terrific armament program." Dirksen replied that "they were greatly disturbed in Germany at the almost weekly utterances of the President of the United States and they had become convinced that the United States would come to the aid of England and France not in two years, but probably in two days and they therefore felt that the only thing to do was to keep making themselves strong." It was Kennedy's own belief that the "top-side men" in the British Government asked themselves every night how Hitler, in the face of the tremendous armament program in Germany, could possibly proceed to a peacetime basis. There was little doubt that the "long-term outlook for England was exceedingly dark."[53]

These German fears of American intervention in a possible second world war were confirmed by the statements of American diplomats like Kennedy and Bullitt. Before the Munich crisis, Kennedy repeatedly told Chamberlain that America would rush to the assistance of Britain and France in the event of unprovoked aggression. Bullitt had been more cautious but at times he gave similar assurances. In a conversation with Count Potocki, Polish Ambassador at Washington, he spoke

[52] Memorandum of a conversation between Sir Ronald Lindsay, British Ambassador at Washington, and Sumner Welles, the Under Secretary of State, February 20, 1939. 740.00/595½, *Confidential file*, MS, Department of State.

[53] Ambassador Kennedy to Secretary Hull, London, February 23, 1939. 740.00/592, *Confidential file*, MS, Department of State.

of the possibility of a conflict between Germany and the European democracies. When asked if the United States would enter such a war he replied: "Undoubtedly yes, but only after Great Britain and France had made the first move." Sentiment in the United States was "so tense against Nazism and Hitlerism" that it amounted to a "psychosis" similar to that which existed "before America's declaration of war on Germany in 1917."[54]

After stating that this "psychosis" was partly created by "emigrants from Germany and Czechoslovakia" who incited the American public against Germany by the use of "various calumnies," he finally came to the topic of American sentiment towards Russia:

It is interesting to note that in this extremely well-planned campaign which is conducted above all against National Socialism, Soviet Russia is almost completely eliminated. Soviet Russia, if mentioned at all, is mentioned in a friendly manner and things are presented in such a way that it would seem that the Soviet Union were co-operating with the bloc of democratic states. Thanks to the clever propaganda the sympathies of the American public are completely on the side of Red Spain.[55]

On January 14, Bullitt had a last talk with Ambassador Potocki before leaving for Paris with instructions from President Roosevelt. He stated that he was prepared to assure Britain and France that they could rely upon the fact that the United States would be prepared "to intervene actively on the side of Britain and France in case of war." America was ready to "place its whole wealth of money and raw materials at their disposal."[56] In February 1939, after he reached Paris, Bullitt informed the Polish Ambassador, Jules Lukasiewicz, that if hostilities should break out one could "foresee right from the beginning the participation of the United States in the war on the side of France and Britain."[57]

[54] Ambassador Jerzy Potocki to the Polish Foreign Office, Washington, November 21, 1938. *German White Paper*, pp. 19–21.

[55] Ambassador Jerzy Potocki to the Polish Foreign Office, Washington, January 12, 1939. *Ibid.*, pp. 29–31.

[56] Ambassador Jerzy Potocki to the Polish Foreign Office, Washington, January 16, 1939. *Ibid.*, pp. 32–34.

[57] Ambassador Jules Lukasiewicz to the Polish Foreign Office, Paris, February 1939. *Ibid.*, pp. 43–45. In his comments upon the American attitude towards the approaching struggle in Europe, Lukasiewicz remarks as follows: "It must not be overlooked that British prestige has suffered a severe setback in American public opinion as a result of events in the Far East and owing to the results of the Munich Conference. . . . It is of course the weak side of the United States that they already today have determined their attitude in case of eventual conflict, but at the same time are unable to take an active part in bringing about positive solution of European problems."

1. *Hitler Takes the Czechs under Protective Custody*

Perhaps these indirect assurances from Ambassador Bullitt of American
intervention on the side of the democracies in the event of World War
II may have strengthened the optimism of Chamberlain with regard
to the situation in Europe. At any rate, he continued to cling to his hope
that war could be averted by a policy of appeasement, and he closed his
eyes to the evident signs that Hitler would soon liquidate Czechoslovakia.

With the British Prime Minister in this bemused condition, Hitler
moved rapidly to carry out his objectives. On January 21 he had a significant conversation with M. Chvalkovsky, the Czech Foreign Minister,
who had been summoned to Berlin. Chvalkovsky was informed that
first of all his country must immediately leave the League of Nations.
Then she should be at all times ready to mold her foreign policy in
accordance with Nazi desires. As a final item in this program of subjection, the Czech Army should be materially reduced.[58]

Paris and London learned of these harsh conditions from a dispatch
sent by the French Minister in Prague.[59] But even this ominous news
did not destroy British hopes for the continuance of peace. On March 1
the British Ambassador conveyed to Sumner Welles a special message
from Lord Halifax to the President. The latest information in England
was to the effect that "Herr Hitler has for the time being abandoned
the idea of precipitating an immediate crisis such as he seemed to be
contemplating at the beginning of the year." There were no "preliminary signs of impending mobilization" in Germany. Sir Nevile Henderson had gained the impression that Hitler "was at present planning no
immediate adventure."[60] Chamberlain was still wearing his cloak of
confidence and on March 9 had assured the representatives of the press
that "Europe was settling down to a period of tranquility."[61]

But in Prague there were no false hopes. Ruthenia and Slovakia were
giving indisputable signs of secessionist desires. On March 6, President

[58] Notes on the discussion between Foreign Minister Ribbentrop and the Czech
Foreign Minister, Chvalkovsky, in Berlin, January 21, 1939; Report on the reception
of the Czech Foreign Minister, January 21, 1939. *Nazi Conspiracy and Aggression*,
V, P-S 2795, 2796, 2906, pp. 430, 571. There had been a previous significant conversation between Ribbentrop and Chvalkovsky in Berlin, October 13, 1938, and between Hitler and Chvalkovsky, October 14, 1938. *Documents on German Foreign
Policy, 1918–1945*, IV, 60–63, 69–72.

[59] Minister M. V. de Lacroix to the French Foreign Office, Prague, February 18,
1939. *French Yellow Book*, pp. 60–61.

[60] Viscount Halifax to President Roosevelt, March 1, 1939. 740.00/597½, *Confidential file*, MS, Department of State.

[61] London *Times*, March 10, 1939.

Hácha dismissed the Ruthenian Government and three days later he took similar action against the government of Slovakia. The Slovak Premier, Monsignor Tiso, fled to Berlin where he had an interview with Hitler on March 13. The Führer demanded that he issue at once a proclamation of Slovak independence. Armed with this mandate, Tiso went to Bratislava where on March 14 he issued the required proclamation. Ruthenia quickly followed suit and this action dissolved what was left of the Czech State.[62]

After German troops had massed along the Czech border in a menacing manner, Hitler sent a summons to President Hácha to visit Berlin for a significant conversation. Upon his arrival on the evening of March 14 he was accorded the honors due to the head of an important state, and the Führer added a grotesque touch to the occasion by sending a box of chocolates to Hácha's daughter. But these favors did not mean that the Czech President would not have to undergo an extended exercise in humiliation. He was permitted to have merely a brief rest in his hotel rooms before being conducted to the Chancellery to see Hitler. He was plainly unnerved and tried to curry favor with the Führer by making critical comments upon the government of Beneš. The regime of his predecessor in office had been "alien" to him and the only time he had met Beneš some misunderstandings had immediately arisen. He now realized that the fate of Czechoslovakia was in Hitler's hands but he retained the hope that her independence was safe.

The Führer was pleased with this cringing, compliant spirit. It made it easier for him to announce that he intended to take the provinces of Bohemia and Moravia under protective custody. The Czechs had merely two alternatives. They could resist and suffer dreadful punishment, or they could submit gracefully and be given a measure of autonomy.

After setting forth these harsh conditions, Hitler signed the documents necessary to carry out his objectives and then left Hácha to the brutalities of Göring and Ribbentrop. Finally, after several fainting spells induced by exhaustion, Hácha signed the Statute of the Protectorate. As he left the Chancellery at 4:30 in the morning, Chvalkovsky, who accompanied him, exclaimed with deep emotion: "Our people will curse us, and yet we have saved their existence. We have preserved them from a horrible massacre."[63]

On March 15, Hitler and his legions entered Prague in triumph. On

---

[62] Conference between the Führer and the Slovak Prime Minister, Tiso, Berlin, March 13, 1939. *Nazi Conspiracy and Aggression*, V, P-S 2802, pp. 443–46.

[63] Ambassador Coulondre to Georges Bonnet, Berlin, March 17, 1939. *French Yellow Book*, pp. 96–97. Sir Nevile Henderson, *Failure of a Mission* (New York, 1940), pp. 217–18; Conferences between the Führer and President Hácha, Berlin, March 15, 1939. *Nazi Conspiracy and Aggression*, V, P-S 2798, pp. 433–40.

this same day, Chamberlain told the House of Commons that the "situation has radically altered since the Slovak Diet declared the independence of Slovakia. The effect of this decision put an end by internal disruption to the State whose frontier we had proposed to guarantee. His Majesty's Government cannot accordingly hold themselves any longer bound by this obligation."[64] On the following day Sir John Simon developed the Prime Minister's reasoning with regard to the obligation to defend Czechoslovakia. It was difficult to guarantee something which no longer existed. It was indeed impossible "to suppose that in these circumstances the guarantee to maintain the State of Czechoslovakia can have any meaning."[65]

But this policy of appeasement was suddenly thrown overboard by the Prime Minister under pressure from Lord Halifax. On the morning of March 17, the American chargé d'affaires saw Halifax who informed him that Chamberlain would deliver a speech which would be a "rather stiff one." He was not prepared to say "that they would or would not go to the rescue of Rumania or Poland at this time. They are going to start educating public opinion as best they can to the need of action. They are suspicious that Hitler will keep on moving and that rather quickly."[66]

That night (March 17), the Prime Minister made a speech in Birmingham which sounded a note of sharp criticism of Hitler's absorption of Czechoslovakia. While he felt bound to repeat that he was

not prepared to engage this country by new unspecified commitments operating under conditions which cannot be foreseen, yet no greater mistake could be made than to suppose that, because it believes war to be a senseless and cruel thing, this nation has so lost its fibre that it will not take part to the uttermost of its power in resisting such a challenge if it were made.[67]

On the following day Ambassador Kennedy talked with Halifax who expressed the opinion that if Hitler moved into Rumania, England could not "wait any longer. Halifax says that they must determine at once one of two things: first, whether Hitler is bluffing, and if so his bluff should be called; if he is not bluffing, the sooner they take him on the better it will be. He thought that the Prime Minister's speech last night very definitely committed them to action if Hitler started for Rumania. My hunch is that if Chamberlain opposes that idea very

64 *Parliamentary Debates*, House of Commons, March 15, 1939, col. 437.
65 *Ibid.*, March 16, 1939, cols. 546, 554.
66 Chargé Johnson to Secretary Hull, London, March 17, 1939. 740.00/628, *Confidential file*, MS, Department of State.
67 London *Times*, March 18, 1939.

strongly there may be a break between the Prime Minister and Hali-fax."[68]

m. *Reaction in the U.S. to German Absorption of Czechoslovakia*

The news of the German absorption of Czechoslovakia came to Secretary Hull while he was enjoying a vacation in Florida. He immediately telephoned to Sumner Welles, the Acting Secretary of State, and dictated a statement to be given to the press. After some emendations by the President, this statement was released on March 17. It emphasized the viewpoint that the American Government, founded upon the principles of human liberty and democracy, could not refrain from expressing its "condemnation of acts which have resulted in the temporary extinguishment of the liberties of a free and independent people with whom . . . the people of the United States have maintained specially close and friendly relations."[69]

The word "temporary," the Department of State later explained, meant that the American Government did not recognize the legality of the establishment of a German protectorate over Czechoslovakia. Vladimír Hurban would still be recognized as the Czech Minister in Washington. Exports from Bohemia, Moravia, and Slovakia, however, would be treated by the United States customs officers as German products and high countervailing duties would be levied upon them. On March 23, the trade agreement that had been negotiated with Czechoslovakia was suspended by Presidential proclamation.[70]

Six weeks after the destruction of the Czech Republic, a World's Fair was opened in New York City. In anticipation of this event the Czech Government had erected a building in which would be displayed some exhibits that would impress friendly eyes with the development of industries in the land of Masaryk. On the façade was an inscription taken from the words of Comenius, seventeenth-century educator and patriot:

> After the Tempest of Wrath Has Passed
> The Rule of Thy Country Will Return to Thee
> O Czech People

Under the ruthless rule of Russia it will be many decades before this prophecy will come true.

---

[68] Ambassador Kennedy to Secretary Hull, London, March 18, 1939. 740.00/630, *Confidential file*, MS, Department of State.

[69] *Peace and War: United States Foreign Policy, 1931–1941* (Washington, 1943), pp. 454–55.

[70] Hull, *op. cit.*, pp. 614–15.

XX

Russia Instigates War in the Far East;
Roosevelt Blames Japan

DURING THE long months that Hitler devoted to redrawing the frontier lines in Europe, Joseph Stalin was preparing to change the map of the Far East. Chiang Kai-shek, as his chief cartographer, would unwittingly splash Red across the chart of eastern Asia all the way from Outer Mongolia to Mukden and then draw back in sudden alarm at the implications of his handiwork. His task could best be done in the atmosphere of armed conflict, and this was produced by Russian agents who blew sparks of friction in North China into the wild flames of an undeclared Sino-Japanese war.

a. *Communist Instigation of War in the Far East*

Communist instigation of the outbreak of the undeclared war of July 7 is indicated in some revealing remarks of the Chinese Ambassador in Moscow. During a conversation with the American diplomatic representative he confessed that he had arrived in Moscow in November 1936 as a "firm supporter of Chinese-Soviet friendship." One of the main purposes of his mission had been "to obtain assurances from the Soviet Government that *if China pushed Japan so far as to make war inevitable, the Soviet Union would support China with supplies and armed forces.*"[1] Shortly after his arrival in Russia he had questioned Litvinov on this point but had received the answer that the Soviet Government would prefer to have this matter settled at Nanking. In this regard it was significant that during the spring and summer of 1937 the Russian Ambassador at Nanking had endeavored to "make the Chinese Government believe that if it would undertake to offer armed resistance to Japan it would confidently expect the armed support of the Soviet Union."[2]

Communist instigation and continued support of the conflict between Chinese and Japanese armed forces in July 1937 were further illustrated by the evident reluctance of the Kuomintang to agree to a formula of accommodation. To do so would mean an open break with the Com-

---

[1] The italicizing of this part of the quotation is the author's.
[2] Mr. Henderson to Secretary Hull, December 21, 1937. 793.94/11763, Moscow, MS, Department of State.

munists, who since the Sian agreement, had worked for a common front between themselves and the Nationalists against Japan. This situation is well described in a dispatch from Nanking:

Competent observers here consider the situation as one moving toward war; they point out that if the National Government should hold to the former plan of surrendering North China rather than resist Japanese aggression there, the National Government's existence would be seriously jeopardized because it is believed to have pledged resistance to Japan as part of the settlement of the Sian revolt and non-resistance would cause the alienation of the Communist forces in the northwest who are about to be incorporated into the Government's armies.[3]

Japanese military authorities did not at first appear to realize the strength of this tie between the Communists and the Nationalists, and they hoped for an early settlement of the clash on the night of July 7. Some of them were inclined to believe that "the firing by Chinese troops which started the incident was not premeditated."[4] This conciliatory attitude led to the agreement of July 11 which was formally signed by General Chang on the nineteenth. Its terms were mild. There would be an apology and some punishment for the Chinese captain responsible for the outbreak of hostilities. There would also be assurances for the future which provided for the voluntary retirement of Chinese officials in North China who impeded Sino-Japanese co-operation and the expulsion of the communistic elements from the Peiping district.[5]

On July 12 the Japanese Ambassador (Saito) had a long conversation with Secretary Hull during the course of which he explained the policy of the Foreign Office. At the conclusion of Saito's remarks, Hull expressed his approval of Japanese efforts "to work out a friendly settlement" of the incident.[6] On the following day Ambassador Grew informed the Department of State that he believed that "if some way of avoiding general hostilities without losing face could be found, the Japanese Government might possibly still be pleased to find this way."[7]

It seemed to Mr. Hornbeck that the Japanese Foreign Office was taking the position that conversations should not be held by representatives of the Chinese and Japanese governments "but between Japanese officials in North China and the local Chinese officials on the theory

[3] Mr. Peck to Secretary Hull, Nanking, July 12, 1937. 793.94/8715, MS, Department of State.

[4] Walter H. Mallory, "Japan Attacks, China Resists," Foreign Affairs, XVI (1937), 129–33.

[5] Memorandum by the ambassador in Japan (Grew), Tokyo, July 22, 1937. United States and Japan, 1931-1941, I, 333–34.

[6] Memorandum by Secretary Hull, July 12, 1937. Ibid., pp. 316–18.

[7] Ambassador Grew to Secretary Hull, Tokyo, July 13, 1937. Ibid., pp. 319–20.

that North China is a political entity separate from the authority and control of the Chinese (Nanking) Government." It was his opinion that the American Government should "make no approach to either the Chinese or the Japanese authorities and make no public comment."[8]

Secretary Hull followed this advice. On the evening of July 13 he summoned Ambassador Saito to his apartment in the Carlton Hotel and frankly informed him that the American Government was "paramountly concerned in the preservation of peace." Because of this fact it would confine its utterances "to phases entirely within range of its impartial, friendly attitude towards all alike." Its action would "stop entirely short of any question or phase of mediation."[9]

This "hands off" attitude would continue to be observed by the Department of State if no general war followed the clash at Peiping. In the event of long-continued hostilities tremendous pressure would be exerted upon Secretary Hull to undertake some form of mediation. But in the early days of July 1937 there still seemed some hope for peace. It was true, however, that the action of the Chinese Nationalist Government in disavowing the agreement of July 11 was causing deep concern in the minds of many observers. When this disavowal was followed by the dispatch of "a large body of troops" to the Peiping area, it was obvious that a crisis had arrived.[10]

On July 15, Ambassador Grew was still hopeful that the Peiping Incident could be peacefully settled. Japan had sent to China only a small army to reinforce existing Japanese garrisons and he had received assurances that there was no intention to set up "any independent country" in North China. The main point at issue was the validity of the agreement of July 11 between the Chinese and Japanese military authorities. It was also significant that communist agitators were "active in disseminating misinformation with regard to the concentration of both Chinese and Japanese troops."[11] The Kremlin was bitterly opposed to any peaceful settlement of the dispute between China and Japan.

b. *Secretary Hull Makes a Statement on U.S. Policy*

The approach of a general war between China and Japan was viewed with open dismay by the British Foreign Office. As early as May 1937,

[8] Memorandum by Mr. Hornbeck, July 13, 1937. 793.94/8737, 8922, MS, Department of State.

[9] Memorandum by Secretary Hull, July 13, 1937. *United States and Japan, 1931–1941*, I, 320–22.

[10] Ambassador Grew to Secretary Hull, Tokyo, July 13, 1937. 793.94/8741, MS, Department of State.

[11] Ambassador Grew to Secretary Hull, Tokyo, July 14–15, 1937. *United States and Japan, 1931-1941*, I, 322–23.

Prime Minister Chamberlain had expressed great concern about the situation in the Far East and had proposed an exchange of views between the Foreign Office and the Department of State with reference to various means whereby Anglo-American-Japanese relations could be improved. On June 1, Secretary Hull handed to Sir Ronald Lindsay his reply to this British proposal. It had been intimated to the Department of State that Japan might be ready to adopt a policy of "co-operation with her neighbors in the Far East and with the Powers that had great interests there." This intimation had been received by Secretary Hull with great interest. He believed that "there were forces within and between Japan and China working toward peace." In the event, however, that war would break out in the Far East the American Government would follow traditional procedures with reference to the situation. It would not enter into any alliance to preserve peace, but, through frequent consultations, would hope to work out and follow a parallel policy with Britain and the other powers that were parties to the Four-Power and Nine-Power treaties.[12]

This encouraging note from Secretary Hull was undoubtedly shared with the French Foreign Office which suggested to Ambassador Bullitt the invocation of Article 7 of the Nine-Power Treaty which provided for a consultation of the signatory powers whenever a situation arose "which in the opinion of any one of them involves the application of the stipulations of the present Treaty." Léger expressed to Bullitt his fears that any call upon the League of Nations "to attempt to settle this dispute would be extremely damaging to the League which once again would prove to be impotent." French Foreign Office officials were insistent that "it would be absolutely essential to get the United States into the discussion."[13]

The British Foreign Office favored a "combined Anglo-American démarche" in Tokyo and Nanking rather than an invocation of the Nine-Power Treaty, and Foreign Secretary Eden suggested this to Ambassador Bingham. From Tokyo, Ambassador Grew expressed a strong dissent from this view. He could see "no reason why we should take action."[14] He also indicated that in Japan the unanimity of opinion relative to the situation in North China was "striking." It was not "a case of unwilling deference by the Government to military initiative. The Cabinet enjoys high prestige, is wholly in command and lends full support to steps recently taken by the Japanese Army in North China. . . .

[12] Cordell Hull, *Memoirs* (New York, 1948), I, 530-33.
[13] Ambassador Bullitt to Secretary Hull, Paris, July 13, 1937. 793.94/8748, MS, Department of State.
[14] Ambassador Grew to Secretary Hull, Tokyo, July 13, 1937. 793.94/8742, MS, Department of State.

At no time during the period of my assignment at this post have I observed indications of so strong and unanimous a determination on the part of the Japanese Government to resist even at the cost of extensive hostilities any movement which might tend to weaken the position of Japan in North China." Mr. Grew also remarked that there was not sufficient evidence to justify the hypothesis that "either the Japanese Government or the Army deliberately engineered the incident in order to force a 'show down.' "[15]

On the following day Ambassador Grew sent a long dispatch to Secretary Hull which stated that the British Embassy in Tokyo was opposed to any precipitate action on the part of Secretary Eden. A strong suggestion along this line had been sent to London. As far as American action was concerned, Grew advised that "the American Government refrain from offering its good offices toward settlement of the North China incident." One of the principal objectives of Japanese foreign policy was "the elimination of the influence of western powers as a factor in Far Eastern politics." There was no reason, therefore, for any belief that Japan would look with favor upon any attempt at American mediation. In conclusion Grew emphasized the fact that the recent improvement in Japanese-American relations had resulted from the fact that the Department of State had transferred the stress of its representations to Japan from an "endeavor to restrain the use by Japan of force to the laying down of reservations of American rights in China."[16]

Under the impact of all this advice, Secretary Hull informed the British Foreign Office that it was felt that "co-operation on parallel but independent lines" would be the best policy for the Department of State to follow.[17] This note had been given to the British Ambassador after long consultations between Secretary Hull, Sumner Welles, Mr. Hornbeck, Norman Davis, and the President. The reaction of the ambassador to this note is interestingly told in a memorandum by Mr. Hornbeck:

The British Ambassador read the memorandum very carefully. He then remarked: "This means, I would understand, that the American Government is not prepared to join in representations at Tokyo and at Nanking." Under instruction, Mr. Hornbeck explained to the British Ambassador that it was fully the desire of this Government to co-operate with the British Govern-

[15] Ambassador Grew to Secretary Hull, Tokyo, July 13, 1937, 793.94/8745, MS, Department of State.

[16] Ambassador Grew to Secretary Hull, Tokyo, July 14, 1937. 793.94/8766, MS, Department of State.

[17] Secretary Hull to the American Embassy in London, July 14, 1937. 793.94/8777, MS, Department of State.

ment in the effort to discourage entry by the Japanese and Chinese upon serious hostilities, . . . that this Government has already urged upon both the Japanese and the Chinese the importance of maintaining peace; that we hoped that the British Government would do likewise; that we intended to continue our efforts; and that we felt that co-operation on parallel but independent lines would be more effective and less likely to have an effect the opposite of that desired than would joint or identical representations. . . . The Ambassador then read the memorandum again, maintained silence for some time, and then, with a smile, said that he understood.[18]

After Secretary Hull had made it clear to the British Foreign Office that he preferred to follow a policy along independent rather than joint lines, he issued (July 16) a public statement indicating the attitude of the Department of State with reference to the situation in the Far East. He began by expressing a viewpoint which had become quite familiar: "There can be no serious hostilities anywhere in the world which will not in one way or another affect interests or rights or obligations of this country." American policy, therefore, strongly accented the importance of settling international disputes by peaceful means. Other items in the American creed were then cited: "We advocate national and international self-restraint. We advocate abstinence by all nations from use of force in pursuit of policy and from interference in the internal affairs of other nations."[19]

It was significant that this statement was in general and not in regional terms. There was no mention of the basic principles that had controlled American policy in the Far East: the Open Door and the maintenance of Chinese territorial integrity. It was evident that Secretary Hull was feeling his way with great care and still hoped for a peaceful settlement of the Peiping Incident. On July 21 he repeated to Ambassador Saito his earnest desire for peace in the Far East and gave further assurances of his "impartial" attitude towards both nations.[20] When Ambassador Grew communicated to the Japanese Foreign Minister these sentiments of Secretary Hull, Hirota replied that he was still hopeful for peace. Everything depended upon the execution of "the agreement drawn up on July 11 and signed on July 19 by General Chang." Japan was not asking Nanking to recognize the agreement "but only that it shall withhold obstruction."[21]

[18] Memorandum by Mr. Hornbeck, July 14, 1937. 793.94/8786, MS, Department of State.

[19] Statement of Secretary Hull, July 16, 1937. *United States and Japan, 1931-1941,* I, 325–26.

[20] Memorandum by Secretary Hull, July 21, 1937 *Ibid.,* pp. 330–32.

[21] Memorandum by Ambassador Grew, July 22, 1937. *Ibid.,* pp. 333–34.

c. *The Situation in North China Becomes Ominous*

When the Peiping Incident was only a week old, Mr. Hornbeck cherished hopes for a maintenance of peace. He felt that "unless the Chinese press too hard, diplomatically and militarily, from Nanking, there would appear to be substantial likelihood that an adjustment will be arrived at without the matter going to the point of military operations."[22] One straw in the wind in this regard was the fact that General Chang Tzu-chung (also the mayor of Tientsin), who had signed the agreement of July 11, had suddenly become ardently pro-Japanese and would "assist them in effecting autonomy in Hopei province."[23]

Other important persons in the Far East were inclined to become pro-Japanese. The French Ambassador in Tokyo was firmly opposed to any action that would indicate pressure upon Japan. He was "convinced that the Japanese did not premeditate or commence the incident and he believes that they are anxious to avoid war."[24] Japanese explanations of the origin of the Peiping Incident carried conviction to other minds. At Nanking, the counselor of the Japanese Embassy made a long statement to Mr. Peck, the American chargé. He insisited that "first firing positively was by the Chinese. The only ammunition carried by [Japanese] troops in maneuvers consists of one cartridge per soldier and these are in possession of the commanding officer. Firing began again while two Japanese officers were in Wanping and obviously was started by the Chinese because the Japanese would not willingly endanger lives of these emissaries."[25]

On July 16, Ambassador Grew reported from Tokyo that "the steady development of plans of the Chinese Government to mobilize its forces and to concentrate them in North China was the principal cause for the decision taken yesterday by the Japanese Government to send reinforcements from Japan to North China." In this connection, the Ho-Umedzu Agreement of July 6, 1935, was of prime importance. In accordance with the terms of this instrument Chinese troops would be withdrawn from Hopeh Province. If they were sent into that province during the present difficulty, war pressures might quickly develop.[26] On July 19 the

[22] Memorandum by Mr. Hornbeck, July 15, 1937. 793.94/9010, MS, Department of State.

[23] Ambassador Johnson to Secretary Hull, Peiping, July 15, 1937. 793.94/8775, MS, Department of State.

[24] Ambassador Grew to Secretary Hull, Tokyo, July 15, 1937. 793.94/8781, MS, Department of State.

[25] Mr. Peck to Secretary Hull, Nanking, July 15, 1937. 793.94/8788, MS, Department of State.

[26] Ambassador Grew to Secretary Hull, Tokyo, July 16, 1937. 793.94/8789, MS, Department of State.

Chinese Foreign Office sent a note to Japan offering an armistice and further diplomatic negotiations designed to find some formula of settlement. This proposal was obviously unsatisfactory to the Japanese Government which adhered to the viewpoint that the Peiping Incident had been settled by the agreement of July 11. The matter was one that concerned only the local authorities. It was essential, therefore, that the agreement of July 11 be carried out without any obstructions from Nanking. The fact that the Chinese military commander in North China had permitted his troops to cross the Ho-Umedzu line was an indication that he was looking for trouble.[27]

There was another factor in this grave Far Eastern equation. The Communists were evidently pushing for a clash between the Nationalist armies and the Japanese. On July 16 the counselor of the Japanese Embassy in Nanking (Hidaka) complained to the Chinese Foreign Office that "an additional and very important element of danger has been injected into the situation by the Communists (he implied that he meant the Comintern and the Soviet Government) who 'are attempting to aggravate the trouble between China and Japan.' " Hidaka also let it be known that he had been told by "a high Chinese official" that the "Chinese Government had been intercepting telegrams from Moscow to agents in China which revealed these activities."[28]

d. *The Department of State Insists upon an Independent Policy*

In London, Anthony Eden felt increasing concern over the developments in the Far East. On July 20 he had a talk with Ambassador Bingham and expressed the view that the "situation" in North China "had taken a grave turn for the worse." He felt "himself barren of ideas, [but] said he would welcome any suggestions from the American Government as to any action which might tend towards appeasement. . . . He understood and fully agreed with the Secretary of State's position that American action and British action should be along parallel lines, and was confident that separate action by the two Governments with the same objective would have . . . greater weight than any action by his Government alone."[29]

On the evening of July 20, Eden suddenly reverted to his former be-

---

[27] Ambassador Grew to Secretary Hull, Tokyo, July 20, 1937. 793.94/8863, MS, Department of State.

[28] Mr. Peck to Secretary Hull, Nanking, July 17, 1937. 793.94/8812, MS, Department of State.

[29] Ambassador Bingham to Secretary Hull, London, July 20, 1937. 793.94/8875, MS, Department of State.

lief in the efficacy of Anglo-American joint action and inquiry was made whether the Department of State would agree to this approach.[30] Secretary Hull promptly replied that he believed "the course of action thus far pursued" by both governments had "been truly co-operative and that . . . [they] should again, each in his own way, urge upon the Japanese and Chinese Governments the importance of maintaining peace."[31]

After the Department of State had carried out this item, word came from China that Chiang Kai-shek had indicated to the British Ambassador at Nanking that he was willing to carry on negotiations with the Japanese Government but this information could best be imparted to Tokyo by some neutral nation with large interests in the Far East. Britain had indicated to Chiang that this task could not be undertaken by any British diplomat.[32] Chiang then told Ambassador Johnson that "the Central Government of China, out of a sincere desire for peace, had acceded to Japanese demands and had withdrawn its opposition to a local settlement of the Marco Polo Bridge Incident . . . along the lines of the three points covered by the settlement of July 11."[33]

This apparently pacific disposition on the part of Chiang Kai-shek was reassuring to many persons interested in Far Eastern development, and they felt even more optimistic when they read in the Paris *Soir* the following statement by the Japanese Ambassador in Paris: "I do not look for anything grave. To people who ask whether we want to go to war with China, I simply reply: 'We are really not so stupid.' "[34]

But Japan could be pushed into war through Chinese intransigence. On July 27 the situation in North China took a definite turn for the worse. According to Japanese accounts, Chinese troops attacked a Japanese force at Lanfang and then entrapped a "Japanese force at the southwest gate of Peiping."[35] This news led Secretary Hull to cable to the American ambassadors in Peiping and Tokyo and instruct them "to confer immediately with the British Embassies and in their discretion to take action on lines parallel with the British action toward dissuading the Japanese authorities from proceeding with any plan for military

[30] Ambassador Bingham to Secretary Hull, London, July 21, 1937. 793.94/8877, MS, Department of State.

[31] Secretary Hull to the American Embassy in London, July 21, 1937. 793.94/8920, MS, Department of State.

[32] Ambassador Johnson to Secretary Hull, Peiping, July 23, 1937. 793.94/8936, MS, Department of State.

[33] Ambassador Johnson to Secretary Hull, Nanking, July 25, 1937. 793.94/8980, MS, Department of State.

[34] Paris *Soir*, July 26, 1937.

[35] Memorandum of a conversation between Mr. Suma and Mr. Hornbeck, July 27, 1937. 793.94/9309, MS, Department of State.

operations which would be likely to endanger the lives of American nationals."[36]

Mr. Hornbeck was not inclined to believe that such action would prove helpful:

Nothing short of a definite indication on the part of one or more of the great foreign Powers that it would be prepared to throw some type of *force* into the equation would appreciably affect the play of forces which is now taking place on the Chinese-Japanese diplomatic and military battlefield. . . . We have spoken on behalf of peace and we probably should continue to do so. . . . In whatever we say we should take great care to say only those things which may tend to pacify and to avoid saying those things which may tend to inflame the parties directly in conflict.[37]

Ambassador Grew supported the cautious policy suggested by Mr. Hornbeck. He did not "think that co-operative action by the United States and Great Britain along lines more vigorous than had hitherto been attempted, or in fact any foreign diplomatic representation would favorably affect developments."[38]

The British chargé d'affaires in Tokyo agreed with Ambassador Grew in this regard, but Anthony Eden in London thought otherwise. During a conversation with Ambassador Bingham he suggested that the "United States Government and ourselves should put forward proposals in an attempt to end existing deadlock."[39] On that same day (July 28) in Tokyo, Ambassador Grew and the British chargé had visited the Foreign Office, separately, and left strong notes that emphasized the importance, during military operations, of providing adequate protection for the lives and property of American and British nationals.[40] Hirota had given Grew "explicit assurances" that every effort would be made to safeguard all American interests in China in the area of hostilities. A few days later he repeated his statement that "Japan does not want war with China. If the Chinese Central troops which have come up to Hopeh Province will withdraw there will be no more fighting."[41]

36 Secretary Hull to Ambassador Bingham, July 27, 1937. 793.94/8993, MS, Department of State.

37 Memorandum by Mr. Hornbeck, July 27, 1937. 793.94/9080, MS, Department of State.

38 Ambassador Grew to Secretary Hull, Tokyo, July 27, 1937. 793.94/9007, MS, Department of State.

39 Ambassador Bingham to Secretary Hull, London, July 28, 1937. 793.94/9043, MS, Department of State.

40 Ambassador Grew to Secretary Hull, Tokyo, July 28, 1937. *United States and Japan, 1931-1941,* I, 337-38.

41 Memorandum by Ambassador Grew, August 6, 1937. *Ibid.,* pp. 338-39.

Secretary Hull was interested in the type of proposals that Secretary Eden wished to place before Japan. On July 29 he forwarded this question to Eden who had no ready answer. The French Foreign Office was equally devoid of ideas. When Bullitt paid a visit to the Quai d'Orsay, Delbos declined "to discuss the position in the Far East. He said that in fact China was isolated though he was definitely opposed to an appeal by China to the League of Nations. The League . . . today was a cipher and the only result of a Chinese appeal would be [that] the cipher would become the shadow of a cipher. . . . He favored . . . an appeal by China to the signatories of the Nine-Power Pact. . . . He was certain that at the present moment the Soviet Union would do nothing to aid China. Indeed, he had just received a telegram from the French Ambassador in Nanking stating that Chiang Kai-shek was furious with the Russians. The Russians had led him to believe that they would support him and now had told him that they would do nothing."[42]

After having induced Chiang Kai-shek to follow a policy that would lead to war with Japan, Russia then promptly betrayed him. On July 30, Ambassador Bullitt talked to the Russian representative in Paris who "expressed the opinion that his government would do nothing whatsoever to assist China at the present time."[43] Chiang then turned to the United States. The Chinese Ambassador in London strongly pushed the matter of an invocation of the Nine-Power Pact, but he soon conceived the idea that the American Government was holding Britain back. When this viewpoint was presented to Mr. Hornbeck, assurances were immediately given that the Department of State had been "constantly in consultation" with the British Foreign Office and was "neglecting nothing" that would help to settle the situation in the Far East.[44]

In accordance with these assurances the Department of State continued to look to London for suggestions. On August 3, Vansittart saw Ambassador Bingham and strongly stressed the importance of an offer of good offices.[45] In reply, Secretary Hull remarked that the British and American governments had already made advances that amounted to a proposal of mediation, but the Japanese Government had "clearly indicated that it is not responsively disposed toward these approaches . . . and will not tolerate interference by other countries." But even in the

[42] Ambassador Bullitt to Secretary Hull, Paris, July 30, 1937. 793.94/9097, MS, Department of State.

[43] Ambassador Bullitt to Secretary Hull, Paris, July 30, 1937. 793.94/9098-99, MS, Department of State.

[44] Memorandum of a conversation between the Chinese Ambassador (C. T. Wang) and Mr. Hornbeck, July 31, 1937. 793.94/9312, MS, Department of State.

[45] Ambassador Bingham to Secretary Hull, London, August 3, 1937. 793.94/9151, MS, Department of State.

face of this unresponsive attitude the Department of State had sent an inquiry to Ambassador Grew with reference to a new offer of mediation.[46] Grew reported that in view of the "extreme importance" of leaving no stone unturned to avoid war he could not "conscientiously recommend against a final effort by the American and British Governments in offering their good offices."[47]

On August 6, J. L. Dodds, the British chargé d'affaires in Tokyo, and Ambassador Grew had a conference concerning the situation in Japan and came to the conclusion that an offer of mediation should be extended to the Chinese and Japanese governments. The chances of acceptance were "small but not necessarily hopeless."[48] Grew thought that the offer to the Japanese Government should take the form of an "oral, confidential, semi-informal and exploratory conversation with the Minister for Foreign Affairs." The Department of State agreed with this suggestion and authorized him, when the British chargé was ready to take action, to approach the "Japanese Minister for Foreign Affairs along the lines indicated."[49]

While this instruction was en route to Tokyo, Ambassador Bullitt talked with H. H. Kung in Paris about the Far Eastern crisis. In answer to a question concerning the possibility of a large-scale war, Kung replied that "General Chiang personally wished to fight but that there was much opposition to fighting in the most influential circles in Nanking." Kung then soberly added: "I'm afraid he [Chiang] will fight." In discussing China's finances, Kung said that he "considered it of the utmost importance that the $50,000,000 loan with regard to which he had talked with the President, Jesse Jones, and Pierson, should go through. . . . He had talked with Maisky, Soviet Ambassador in London, who had assured him that if the United States, England and France would make a joint protest against Japan's action and would offer mediation, and if Japan should reject the offer, the Soviet Union would go to war on the side of China."[50]

It is evident that Chiang Kai-shek, under the impact of continued Russian promises of armed assistance, "personally wished to fight." There was little chance that any offer of mediation would be accepted. But the Department of State knew little of the real situation in Nan-

[46] Secretary Hull to Ambassador Bingham, August 5, 1937. 793.94/9141, MS, Department of State.

[47] Ambassador Grew to Secretary Hull, Tokyo, August 6, 1937. 793.94/9216, MS, Department of State.

[48] Joseph C. Grew, *Ten Years in Japan* (New York, 1944), pp. 214–16.

[49] Secretary Hull to Ambassador Bingham, August 7, 1937. 793.94/9217, MS, Department of State.

[50] Ambassador Bullitt to Secretary Hull, Paris, August 6, 1937. 793.94/9220, MS, Department of State.

king: peace seemed just around the corner of a friendly conference. On August 10, Grew informed Hirota that he had been instructed to present a "definite offer of good offices" in an "informal, confidential and exploratory way." If a meeting could be arranged between "Japanese and Chinese plenipotentiaries" at some convenient neutral spot, some formula of peace might be worked out. Hirota expressed his appreciation of this offer of mediation but he added that negotiations were in progress between Ambassador Kawagoe and Mr. Kao, of the Chinese Foreign Office. War might "still be avoided if Chiang Kai-shek would respond with some 'proposal' which could serve as a basis for negotiations."[51]

There was little hope that Chiang would make such a proposal. On August 12, Ambassador Johnson reported that he had been

reliably informed that Chu Teh and Mao Tze Tung, military leaders of the Communistic forces in Shensi, visited Nanking within past few days as sequel to an earlier visit by Chou En-lai, Secretary-General of the Communistic regime at Yennan, Shensi, and that an agreement was reached for the co-operation of the Communistic forces with Government troops against the Japanese.[52]

e. *The Scene Shifts to Shanghai*

While diplomats talked, the armies of Japan moved ahead in Manchuria. By August 1, Tientsin had fallen and Chinese troop concentrations in the Peiping area had been bombed by the active Japanese air force. Soon Japanese troops occupied the entire Hopeh Province, and the American public was shocked by stories of rape and looting. When the scene shifted to Shanghai there were detailed accounts of Japanese brutality that made an indelible impression upon Secretary Hull. The city did not fall to the Japanese until November 9, and during this long period of military activity there were many incidents that disturbed the Department of State.

Before heavy fighting started in the Shanghai area, Sumner Welles submitted to Secretary Hull a memorandum which emphasized the opinion that Japan would "neither be deterred from fighting China by financial considerations nor, if the two countries fight, find herself hamstrung and compelled to forego her objectives in consequence of financial exhaustion."[53]

[51] Memorandum by Ambassador Grew, August 10, 1937. *United States and Japan, 1931–1941,* I ,339–41.

[52] Ambassador Johnson to Secretary Hull, Nanking, August 12, 1937. 793.94/9297, MS, Department of State.

[53] Memorandum of Sumner Welles for Secretary Hull, August 10, 1937. 793.94/9487, MS, Department of State.

On the same day, Mr. Hornbeck submitted a memorandum which dealt specifically with Shanghai. He thought the Secretary of State might "reasonably suggest to and even urge upon the Chinese Government that it withdraw troops which it apparently has introduced . . . into the area around Shanghai which falls within the so-called 'demilitarized zone' which was set up by agreement between the Japanese and the Chinese in 1932 . . . . Regardless of reasons or rights, those [Chinese] troops are not needed there for purposes of maintaining order; . . . they serve as an irritant to the Japanese."[54]

When Japanese marines landed in Shanghai on August 11 this question of the "demilitarized zone" immediately arose. But the Chinese mayor of the city stated that he and the local garrison commander had "no control over the Chinese troops of 88th Division arriving in the area." Their commander was "somewhere in the rear."[55] On August 13 large Japanese reinforcements arrived in Shanghai and during the next ten days there was severe fighting with large casualties. The inevitable "incidents" now occurred. On August 14 the Commander in Chief of the United States Asiatic Fleet sent to the American Embassy in Nanking a telegram requesting him to make a "vigorous protest to Chinese Government of bombing American vessel Shanghai by Chinese planes. Two bombs dropped within 20 yards of *Augusta*. . . . In case any further bombing of U. S. vessels will use anti-aircraft battery in self-defence."[56] This telegram was supported by a similar message from Consul General Gauss to Secretary Hull: "Repeated and increasingly heavy bombing by Chinese planes is continuing. Several bombs have dropped within area of foreign refuge near waterfront. . . . Chinese planes are not respecting Settlement or area of refuge. I urge strongest representations to the Generalissimo."[57] On August 15 the chairman of the Shanghai Municipal Council sent an urgent message to the "Consul General for Norway and Senior Consul" asking him to convey "to the Chinese Authorities the most solemn protest against the tragic and unpardonable bombing yesterday of part of the International Settlement, which was known to be entirely free of belligerent troops."[58] Three days later, Consul General Gauss informed Secretary Hull that "despite

[54] Memorandum of Mr. Hornbeck for Secretary Hull, August 12, 1937. 793.94/9940, MS, Department of State.

[55] Consul General Gauss to Secretary Hull, Shanghai, August 12, 1937. 793.94/9305, MS, Department of State.

[56] Commander in Chief of the United States Asiatic Fleet to the American Embassy in Nanking, August 13, 1937. FW 793.94/9351, MS, Department of State.

[57] Consul General Gauss to Secretary Hull, Shanghai, August 14, 1937. 793.94/9348, MS, Department of State.

[58] C. S. Franklin, chairman of the Shanghai Municipal Council, to the consul general for Norway, August 15, 1937. 793.94/10595, MS, Department of State.

fact that Chinese have been informed officially that American tenders carrying women and children would leave Shanghai at a stated hour on yesterday, Chinese planes appeared over the area precisely at the hour of departure resulting in Japanese anti-aircraft fire until they were driven away."[59]

In order to check this lawlessness and find some path to peace, the British chargé d'affaires (August 18) presented to the Japanese Foreign Office a proposal that if both the Chinese and Japanese governments would agree to withdraw their armed forces from the Shanghai area and would agree that the protection of Japanese nationals in the International Settlement be entrusted to foreign authorities, His Majesty's Government would be "prepared to undertake this responsibility if other Powers will join them in doing so."[60] The Japanese Foreign Office did not accept this suggestion. When Secretary Hull heard from Ambassador Grew to this effect, he informed the British Foreign Office that there was no use in having the Department of State support the British proposal.[61]

As the clash between Chinese and Japanese forces at Shanghai continued, Chinese planes seemed unable to avoid bombing American ships. Even the Chinese shore batteries were careless in directing their fire. On the evening of August 20 a shell exploded on the deck of the United States Cruiser *Augusta,* killing one seaman and wounding eighteen others.[62] Three days later two "air bombs," believed to be of "Chinese origin," were dropped in the International Settlement, seriously injuring an American citizen.[63] But Secretary Hull was far more interested in reports of Japanese bombing of Nanking than in Chinese bombing of the International Settlement in Shanghai. On September 1, Ambassador Grew called at the Foreign Office to present a protest against Japanese bombing operations "in various parts of China." Hirota replied that "it was the intention of the Japanese forces in China to attack only military establishments but that mistakes were unfortunately inevitable." He then reported to Mr. Grew the lawless situation in Tsingtao since the removal of Japanese nationals. He thought it might be expedient for the powers to "make representations in Nanking" with regard to this situation. Turning to the matter of Sino-Soviet relations he remarked that the recent conclusion of a pact between China

[59] Consul General Gauss to Secretary Hull, Shanghai, August 18, 1937. 793.94/9467, MS, Department of State.

[60] Ambassador Grew to Secretary Hull, Tokyo, August 18, 1937. 793.94/9470, MS, Department of State.

[61] Secretary Hull to Ambassador Grew, August 19, 1937. 793.94/9470, MS, Department of State.

[62] Consul General Gauss to Secretary Hull, Shanghai, August 21, 1937. 793.94/9565, MS, Department of State.

[63] Ambassador Johnson to Secretary Hull, Nanking, August 27, 1937. 793.94/9746, MS, Department of State.

and Russia might have unfortunate results. There was "grave danger of the communists getting control in China." The communist menace was "very real" because their actual aim was "to take over eventual complete control of the Government and country." With reference to peace in the Far East, the Chinese could have it on three conditions: (1) good relations with Manchuria; (2) withdrawal of Chinese troops from North China; (3) the cessation in China of anti-Japanese activities and propaganda.[64]

The communist menace in China gave Secretary Hull little concern. He was now thoroughly aroused over reports of indiscriminate bombings in China by the Japanese. In a long instruction to Ambassador Grew he spoke his mind very plainly. It appeared to him that Japanese unresponsiveness to American protests against bombings showed that the Japanese Government did not set a high value upon American efforts "to cultivate good will, confidence, and stability in general." If the Japanese Government would just follow the high principles enunciated by the American Government on July 16 the situation in the Far East would probably improve. While the American Government had endeavored to follow an "absolutely impartial course" during the current crisis in China, the actions of the Japanese armed forces had shocked American opinion. It would be expedient for the Japanese Government to keep in mind that their course in China was looked upon in America with the same degree of disapproval that it had evoked in Britain. American public opinion "has been outraged by the methods and strategy employed by the combatants, particularly by the Japanese military, and has become gradually more critical of Japan." It was high time the Japanese Government gave heed to the principles so often expressed by the Department of State.[65]

It is evident that the statement of American principles by Secretary Hull on July 16 was a verbal bombshell directed against Japan. All talk of an "absolutely impartial course" towards China and Japan during the July crisis was mere diplomatic eyewash which no realistic statesmen took seriously. Hull was definitely antagonistic towards Japan, and his statement of July 16 was a prelude to the quarantine speech of President Roosevelt on October 5.

f. *China Appeals to the League*

On July 16 when Secretary Hull was giving sharp expression to the principles of international conduct advocated by the United States, the

---

[64] Ambassador Grew to Secretary Hull, Tokyo, September 1, 1937. 793.94/9835; memorandum of Ambassador Grew, September 1, 1937. 793.94/10157, MS, Department of State.

[65] Secretary Hull to Ambassador Grew, September 2, 1937. *United States and Japan, 1931–1941*, I, 361–64.

Chinese Government issued an appeal to the signatories of the Nine-Power Treaty against Japanese "aggression" in North China.[66] The American and British governments had endeavored to mediate in this conflict between China and Japan, but the Japanese Government had not accepted these offers of good offices. When the fighting broke out in the Shanghai area the need for mediation grew more acute, but nothing was accomplished by the Nine-Power signatories. On August 12 the Chinese Ambassador (C. T. Wang) had a talk with Mr. Hornbeck with reference to the invocation of the Nine-Power Treaty. Hornbeck immediately made it clear to him that Article 7 of that treaty contained no directives that specified "what action, if any, is to be taken in case one or more of the signatory Powers disregard the pledges which they have made in the treaty." The ambassador then meekly stated that what he wished to know was "what courses of action were being discussed in course of consultations between and among the American and the British and the French Governments." He received no light from Mr. Hornbeck in this regard, so the conversation was concluded.[67]

On August 20 the Chinese Ambassador had another conversation with Mr. Hornbeck who, on this occasion, was flanked by Secretary Hull. When the ambassador inquired about the invocation of the Nine-Power Pact, Secretary Hull mumbled some generality and referred him to Mr. Hornbeck. Mr. Hornbeck was equally vague. He wondered "what the Chinese Government would estimate as likely to be the concrete effect of action such as it was suggesting." The ambassador replied that "one effect at the outset might be the moral effect." The conversation made no progress and soon closed with the ambassador and Secretary Hull exchanging "expressions of serious solicitude over the gravity of the situation."[68] On the following day Mr. Hornbeck sent a memorandum to Secretary Hull advising against "making any commitment" with reference to taking the initiative in an invocation of the Nine-Power Pact.[69]

In Britain the Foreign Office was more responsive to the pressures exerted in favor of a positive policy in the Far East. On August 26 the London *Times* complained that the situation was a difficult one but it could be remedied by closer Anglo-American co-operation. This statement disturbed the American Embassy in London. American sensitive

[66] *New York Times,* July 17, 1937.

[67] Memorandum by Mr. Hornbeck concerning a conversation with the Chinese Ambassador, August 12, 1937. 793.94/9649, MS, Department of State.

[68] Memorandum by Mr. Hornbeck of a conversation among Secretary Hull, the Chinese Ambassador, and Mr. Hornbeck, August 20, 1937. 793.94/9752, MS, Department of State.

[69] Memorandum by Mr. Hornbeck on Far Eastern situation, August 21, 1937. 793.94/9938, MS, Department of State.

nerves were calmed by a note from the Foreign Office which criticized the paragraph in the London *Times* as an example of "irresponsible journalism."[70]

The British Foreign Office now evinced a spirit of sweet reasonableness. During a conversation with one of the Chinese representatives in London, Mr. Eden remarked that the "British Government was prepared to support any course of action which the American Government might choose to embark upon." When this observation was conveyed to Secretary Hull by the Chinese Ambassador in Washington, it brought forth the inevitable question: Did the ambassador think "that any course of action not involving force would be effective?" The ambassador admitted that "he thought that for effectiveness force would be essential."[71] This frank answer disclosed the essential difficulty in securing any invocation of the Nine-Power Pact. The signatory nations were not ready to supply the force that would be essential to any successful action against Japan.

These difficulties in securing an invocation of the Nine-Power Pact led the Chinese Government to turn to the League of Nations. On August 30 a note was addressed to M. Joseph Avenol, Secretary-General of the League, which reviewed the incidents connected with the Marco Polo Bridge clash between Chinese and Japanese armed forces. M. Avenol was then requested to communicate this statement to the members of the League and to the Advisory Committee set up under the resolution adopted on February 24, 1933.[72]

This action by the Chinese Government spurred the British Foreign Office to inquire if the United States contemplated "being represented at Geneva in any way" in the event that the League would give a hearing to China's appeal.[73] Secretary Hull replied that America might be represented on the Advisory Committee if the League decided that the Advisory Committee was still in existence.[74]

While the Chinese Foreign Office was making preparations for a formal appeal to the League of Nations, Chiang Kai-shek had a long talk with Ambassador Johnson. He remarked that he was "puzzled over American policy in the present Far Eastern situation, particularly as regards our [America's] unwillingness to associate ourselves with

[70] Johnson to Secretary Hull, London, August 26, 1937. 793.94/9711, MS, Department of State.

[71] Memorandum of a conversation among Secretary Hull, the Chinese Ambassador, and Mr. Hornbeck, August 28, 1937. 793.94/9831, MS, Department of State.

[72] Hoo Chi-tsai to M. Joseph Avenol, Geneva, August 30, 1937. 793.94/9951, MS, Department of State.

[73] *Aide-mémoire* from the British Embassy, August 31, 1937. 793.94/9941, MS, Department of State.

[74] Secretary Hull to the American consul at Geneva, September 3, 1937. 793.94/9941, MS, Department of State.

Great Britain in attempting to restrain Japan." He questioned the word "parallel" and "asked why it was that we had not been willing to take joint action with the British." Johnson told him that the Department of State "preferred to act in consultation" with Britain, and when "in agreement, independently." He also stated that he had not been aware of "any difference of opinion or purpose as between the two Governments."[75]

The next complaint filed against American apparent indifference to the cause of China came from Madame Chiang Kai-shek. She felt outraged that the American Government had refused "passports to American instructors in aviation whom the Chinese Government had invited to come to China even before the present conflict began." She hoped that America would really "be neutral in this matter and not place any obstacles in China's way when it is fighting for its very life."[76] Secretary Hull immediately replied that there was a strong feeling in the United States that American citizens "should not participate or become involved in fighting which may be taking place in any foreign country." Such a belief was held "irrespective of the foreign country where such fighting is occurring." The attitude of the government "must be responsive to the beliefs of the American people."[77]

The Department of State was more co-operative with regard to action in concert with the League. On September 12, China formally appealed to the League under Articles 10, 11, and 17 of the Covenant. This appeal was referred to the Far-East Advisory Committee. The American Government was invited to appoint a representative on the committee, and on September 20 the Department of State accepted the invitation by appointing Leland Harrison to serve without any voting privileges. Mr. Harrison was also the American Minister to Switzerland. In its communication to the Secretary-General of the League, the Department of State emphasized the fact that the American Government would not take upon "itself those responsibilities which devolve from the fact of their membership upon members of the League." It would be prepared, however, to "give careful consideration to definite proposals which the League may address to it."[78]

On October 5 the Far-East Advisory Committee adopted two reports and laid them before the League Assembly. The first of these reviewed the situation in the Far East and concluded that the "military operations

[75] Ambassador Johnson to Secretary Hull, Nanking, September 1, 1937. 793.94/9862, MS, Department of State.

[76] Ambassador Johnson to Secretary Hull, Nanking, September 1, 1937. 793.94/9873, MS, Department of State.

[77] Secretary Hull to Ambassador Johnson, September 7, 1937. 793.94/9922, MS, Department of State.

[78] Department of State, *Press Release,* September 21, 1937.

carried on by Japan against China by land, sea and air" could be justified "neither on the basis of existing legal instruments nor on that of the right of self-defense." It was obvious that they were "in contravention of Japan's obligations" under the Nine-Power Pact and the Pact of Paris.[79]

g. President Roosevelt Proposes a Quarantine

There is no doubt that the speedy action of the Far-East Advisory Committee was prompted by the belief that the American Government would support a policy of sharp denunciation of Japanese military operations in China. At Geneva it had long been realized that America was viewing Japan with increasing coolness. Hull's statement of the principles of international conduct on July 16 had evoked within a month favorable replies from more than fifty nations. A moral sanitary cordon was being drawn around Japan. Moreover, there were certain points of friction that developed between Japan and the United States as a result of the conflict in China. On August 25 the Japanese Government announced a blockade of China's coast from Shanghai southward; ten days later the blockade was extended to the entire coast of China. Although it was limited to Chinese shipping, Japan reserved the right to stop merchant vessels of other nations for the purpose of ascertaining their identity.[80] Inasmuch as Japan had not declared war on China, this blockade was not legal as applied to American vessels, and Secretary Hull instructed the United States Consul General at Shanghai that there was no need to give "affirmative assent to measures which may be taken by the Japanese naval authorities in their enforcement of their blockade." American vessels should show "to Japanese naval authorities evidence of nationality but permit further investigation only under express protest."[81]

This dangerous situation in the Far East gave Ambassador Grew deep concern. He was particularly anxious to avoid any break with Japan. In a long dispatch to Secretary Hull he frankly gave his views as to the best policy for America to pursue. Up to this time the Department of State had shown an attitude of impartiality in its relations with China and Japan. He ardently hoped that this attitude would be maintained. While he believed that it was important to continue concerted action with Britain, yet there were certain limitations connected with such a policy. British methods were not "always best calculated to

[79] League of Nations Official Journal, Special Supplement No. 177, pp. 37–42.
[80] Department of State, Press Release, September 10, 1937.
[81] Secretary Hull to American Consul General at Shanghai, September 22, 1937. United States and Japan, 1931–1941, I, 371–72.

achieve desired results." There was at times "an ineptitude in their methods, and especially in the tone and language and timing of their official communications." He thought that the Department of State should aim to "avoid unnecessarily sacrificing our present relations" with Japan. There was nothing to be gained by hampering America's "future interests, and perhaps our own future helpfulness in working for peace by creating among the Japanese people a renewed antagonism against the United States."[82]

This feeling of impartiality towards the combatants in the Far East seemed to color the opinions expressed by Under Secretary Sumner Welles in a conversation with M. Oumansky, the Soviet chargé d'affaires. The Russian representative quickly showed that he was deeply dissatisfied with the cautious attitude of the Department of State in the China conflict. He wished to know if the American Government intended to co-operate with other governments in connection with the possible imposition of "military or economic sanctions" upon Japan. Welles made the chilling reply that M. Oumansky appeared to have "completely misunderstood the whole basis of the United States policy ... of taking no sides in the present conflict." Oumansky mumbled that such a policy was a "very discouraging one" and hurriedly left the Department of State.[83]

But this impartial attitude towards China and Japan was completely abandoned by President Roosevelt in his address in Chicago on October 5. He was strongly in favor of a quarantine against aggressor nations.[84] His words of criticism and warning were directed chiefly against Japan and their baleful effect was all that Grew had feared. It was really big talk in a high key. He was far more worried about party reverses at home than about Japanese movements in Manchuria. An economic recession in the United States had made it clear that the ballyhoo of New Deal politicians had struck some very sour notes that greatly annoyed the ears of American workers who were out of jobs. The Morgenthau *Diaries* give indisputable proof of the deep concern the Administration felt over the wide break in the economic structure of the nation.[85]

Joined with this bad news from the economic front was the hostile reaction in the press over the appointment of Senator Hugo Black to the Supreme Court. In September it was made known that Mr. Black

[82] Ambassador Grew to Secretary Hull, Tokyo, September 15, 1937. 793.94/10697, MS, Department of State.

[83] Memorandum of Sumner Welles of a conversation with M. Oumansky, Soviet chargé d'affaires, October 2, 1937. 793.94/10630, MS, Department of State.

[84] *United States and Japan, 1931–1941,* I, 379–83.

[85] "The Morgenthau Diaries," *Collier's,* CXX (October 4, 1947), 20; *ibid.,* CXX (October 25, 1947), 85.

had once hidden his face under the wide hood of a Klansman. In dismay he fled to Europe and President Roosevelt found it convenient to make a hurried trip to the Far West. It was highly expedient for him to make some address that would divert public attention from the widespread effects of economic recession and to cover the flight of the nimble Justice Black. A sharp denunciation of the Japanese advance in North China would draw a big herring across a noisome trail.

The quarantine speech of October 5 had many macabre overtones designed to frighten the American people. It indicated that large portions of the world were experiencing a "reign of terror," and that the "landmarks and traditions which have marked the progress of civilization toward a condition of law, order and justice" were being "wiped away." "Innocent peoples and nations" were being "cruelly sacrificed to a greed for power and supremacy" which was "devoid of all sense of justice and humane consideration." If this sad condition of affairs existed in other parts of the world it was vain for anyone to "imagine that America will escape, that it may expect mercy, that this Western Hemisphere will not be attacked, and that it will continue tranquilly and peacefully to carry on the ethics and the arts of civilization."

Newspapers of a one-world persuasion sprang to the President's support. The *New York Times* and the *World-Telegram* promptly attacked the "unrealities of isolation,"[86] while the *New York Daily News* suggested a long-range Anglo-American naval blockade of Japan if that nation were to overrun China and threaten the interests of the Western powers.[87]

Some papers advocated an economic boycott as a means to bring Japan to reason. The *Washington Post* urged that America "immediately cease to buy Japanese goods,"[88] and this opinion was strongly seconded by the *Washington Evening Star*[89] and the Rochester *Democrat and Chronicle*.[90] The *Atlanta Constitution* expressed the emphatic opinion that "war-diseased nations must be quarantined,"[91] and the *Birmingham News*[92] and the Raleigh *News and Observer*[93] joined this chorus. In the Middle West the *Chicago Daily News*,[94] the *St. Louis Globe-Democrat*,[95] and the *Cincinnati Enquirer*[96] expressed agreement with the "general principles" of the President's address. On the Pacific Coast the *San Francisco Chronicle*,[97] the *Los Angeles Times*,[98] and the Portland *Morning Oregonian*[99] adopted a favorable attitude.

[86] October 6, 8, 1937.
[87] October 3, 7, 1937.
[88] October 8, 1937.
[89] October 6, 7, 1937.
[90] October 6, 1937.
[91] October 7, 1937.
[92] October 6, 11, 1937.
[93] October 6, 8, 1937.
[94] October 6, 8, 1937.
[95] October 15, 1937.
[96] October 7, 8, 1937.
[97] October 6, 1937.
[98] October 6, 7, 1937.
[99] October 6, 1937.

But there was a large legion of newspapers that rejected any thought of economic sanctions against Japan. Such action would lead to war. The *New York Herald-Tribune* believed that the President's speech had been based upon the "identical sands of confusion, emotion and wishful thinking which so tragically engulfed Mr. Wilson's great vision."[100] The New York *Sun* warned the President that American public opinion would not approve any policy of "pulling chestnuts out of the fire for any association of foreign nations."[101] The *Boston Herald* boldly declared that "Americans must not embark on another costly attempt to reform the world,"[102] while even the stanchly Democratic *Boston Post* cried out in protest: "He [the President] must know that the American people are in no mood for a crusade."[103]

The *Chicago Tribune* was openly hostile to any threat of a boycott against Japan. Economic sanctions would lead America down the road to war.[104] The *Detroit Free Press* voiced the opinion that there was no "adequate reason for remarks that were evangelistic rather than statesmanlike, and were manifestly designed to stir emotions rather than provoke careful thought."[105] The *Milwaukee Journal* remarked that a boycott is a "first cousin to outright war,"[106] and the Spokane *Spokesman-Review* stated ominously that the President's Chicago address "approximated a declaration of war."[107]

The columnists were divided in their opinions of the Chicago address. Boake Carter was fearful that the President suffered from the "disease of moral fervor for reform."[108] Paul Mallon regarded the address as a clever move to divert attention from the unfortunate appointment of Hugo Black to the Supreme Court,[109] while General Hugh S. Johnson was worried that America, as in 1917, would play the role of "sucker."[110]

On the other hand, David Lawrence hailed the address as the "speech the whole world has been waiting for several months to hear";[111] Dorothy Thompson was delighted that she could now envisage the end of American "neutrality,"[112] and Walter Lippmann praised the President

[100] October 6, 8, 1937.
[101] October 6, 7, 1937.
[102] October 6, 7, 1937.
[103] October 11, 1937.
[104] October 6, 1937.
[105] October 7, 1937.
[106] October 10, 1937.
[107] October 6, 7, 1937.
[108] *Boston Daily Globe*, October 8, 1937.
[109] *Boston Herald*, October 8, 1937.
[110] *New York World-Telegram*, October 6, 1937.
[111] *Chicago Daily News*, October 7, 1937.
[112] *New York Herald-Tribune*, October 10, 1937.

for a much-needed clarion call to the democracies to resist aggressor nations.[113]

The Catholic press had few words of praise for the President's Chicago challenge. *America* flatly stated that the "people of the United States positively are opposed to foreign imbroglios";[114] the *Ave Maria* was filled with misgivings,[115] while Father Gillis, in the *Catholic World,* was sharply critical of any pressure in favor of American intervention in the Far East.[116]

It is interesting to note that the *Christian Century,* which reflected the Protestant viewpoint, was distinctly suspicious of the Chicago speech. In a forecast of the future it warned that if America went to war on behalf of China the result would be a victory for Russia.[117]

This Russian angle of the situation in the Far East was clearly perceived by many observers. On October 12 the Division of Far Eastern Affairs prepared a memorandum for the use of Secretary Hull. With reference to possible economic sanctions, the memorandum asks the question whether the United States should take the lead in such a movement. In answer to this question it remarks: "It is believed that the assuming of such a position by any country would bring that country face to face with a very real hazard. . . . It seems to me [Mr. Hamilton, chief of the Division] that public opinion in the United States is definitely opposed to the United States assuming a position of leadership in the imposing of restrictive measures directed at Japan. Moreover it should be borne in mind that if restrictive measures should take the form of economic 'sanctions,' the United States would be called upon to carry the heaviest burden.[118] . . . If some program could be worked out which would give Japan a reasonable prospect of economic security and which would remove Japan's fear of Communism and attack from the Soviet Union, there would be removed some basic elements in the situation responsible for Japan's present imperialistic program."[119]

[113] *New York Herald-Tribune,* October 16, 1937.

[114] October 16, 1937.

[115] October 23, 1937, pp. 534–35.

[116] December 1937, pp. 257–65. On October 9, 1937, Senator David I. Walsh wrote a note to Secretary Hull in which he inclosed a telegram from the Maryknoll Fathers in Japan. They deeply regretted the "recent change official attitude towards Sino-Japanese trouble," and urgently requested his influence "towards restoring previous attitude impartial tolerance as most practical policy." 793.94/10546, MS, Department of State.

[117] October 20, 1937, pp. 1287–88.

[118] In a letter to Mr. Hornbeck, Mr. Taneo Taketa, a representative of the South Manchuria Railway, points out the close economic ties between the United States and Japan. The South Manchuria Railway alone had purchased "far more than $100,000,-000 worth of equipment from the United States." Other firms had purchased large amounts. 793.94/10708, MS, Department of State.

[119] Memorandum prepared by the Division of Far Eastern Affairs, October 12, 1937. 793.94/10706, MS, Department of State.

From Tehran there came a message that confirmed Japan's fear of the rising tide of bolshevism in China. On October 14 the American Minister in Tehran had a conversation with the newly arrived Japanese Minister who "predicted that the next upheaval in China would proceed along Bolshevistic lines and he felt that the great tragedy in the present situation was that England and America were by their attitude unconsciously pushing China nearer the abyss."[120]

There was no doubt about the increasingly intimate relations between the Chinese Nationalists and the Communists under Mao Tse-tung. By 1937, Russia had practically detached Outer Mongolia from China and Chinese representatives endeavored to hide this fact while pressing their attack upon Japan for expansion in North China. On October 14, Secretary Hull had a conversation with the Chinese Ambassador (Dr. C. T. Wang). He inquired "very confidentially as to Russia's attitude towards Outer Mongolia and with respect to observing the integrity of China generally." The ambassador was careful not to "undertake to give an opinion, except to minimize the influence and attitude of Russia with respect to Outer Mongolia at this time, adding that Outer Mongolia continues to claim herself as a part of China and to assert Chinese sovereignty."[121]

In the face of a great deal of information available in the Department of State showing communist control over Outer Mongolia, it is hardly likely that Secretary Hull gave much credence to this observation by the Chinese Ambassador. It is certainly true, however, that the Secretary closed his eyes to the rapid Red advance in many parts of China and he certainly did not understand the implications of the close tie between Chiang Kai-shek and the communist armies. There was a world of truth in the statement of the Japanese Minister to Tehran: "The next upheaval in China will proceed along Bolshevistic lines." Few persons in the Department of State realized the accuracy of this prophecy or gave it any real consideration. Since the recognition of Russia in 1933, bolshevism appeared to many Americans as a challenge to our social order rather than as a military threat.

[120] Mr. Engert to Secretary Hull, Tehran, October 14, 1937. 793.94/10660, MS, Department of State.

[121] Memorandum of a conversation between Secretary Hull and the Chinese Ambassador, October 14, 1937. 793.94/10791, MS, Department of State.

XXI

Japan Proposes a Joint Search for World Peace but Hull Declines

a. *Germany Views with Evident Dissatisfaction the Outbreak of War between China and Japan*

THE OUTBREAK of war between China and Japan aroused the deep concern of all the Western powers that had financial interests in the Far East. Even Germany, whose sphere of influence in Shantung Province had been lost as a result of the World War, took an active interest in the undeclared war in China. In an instruction to various German diplomatic missions, the Foreign Office stressed the fact that a policy of "strict neutrality" would be followed. An early peaceful settlement of the difficulties was strongly desired for the sake of German "economic interests in the Far East and in view of our anti-Comintern policy. A military showdown between China and Japan would benefit the Soviet Government which has an interest in engaging Japan elsewhere and weakening her by military operations."[1]

The German Ambassador in Rome reported that the official Italian point of view on the Far Eastern conflict was identical with that of the German Foreign Office. The main question in Rome was with reference to the retention of the Italian military mission in China.[2] Germany also had a military mission in China together with expanding economic interests. Oskar Trautmann, the German Ambassador in Nanking, was strongly pro-Chinese and he deeply regretted the adverse impact of the outbreak of war upon German commercial aspirations. He believed that Chiang Kai-shek was determined to have a "military showdown" with the Japanese, and he regarded the outlook for China as "not at all unfavorable." It was essential that German military leaders like Marshal von Blomberg should realize that a Japanese victory was by no means "certain."[3]

Under pressure from Japan, Germany stopped the shipment of arms to China, but she hesitated about recalling the German military mission

[1] The German Foreign Ministry to various German diplomatic missions, July 20, 1937. *Documents on German Foreign Policy, 1918–1945,* Series D (Washington, 1949), I, 733–34.

[2] The German Ambassador in Rome (Hassell) to the German Foreign Office, July 21, 1937. *Ibid.,* p. 735.

[3] The German Ambassador in China (Trautmann) to the German Foreign Office, July 21, 1937. *Ibid.,* p. 736.

from Nanking.[4] The Foreign Office also informed Japan that it would be useless to ask for an invocation of the anti-Comintern Pact against China "since the Pact does not have for its object the combating of Bolshevism on the territory of a third State."[5] The Foreign Office then sent a long instruction to the Embassy in Tokyo. Regret was expressed at the outbreak of a war that would "prevent the consolidation of China" and thereby "further the spread of Communism in China." Moreover, it was feared that such a conflict might "drive the Chinese into the arms of Russia." It would be unwise at this time to recall the German military mission from Nanking. Their places would probably be filled with Russian advisers, and this might lead to an "undesirable result for the Japanese."[6]

On July 28 the Japanese Ambassador in Berlin paid a visit to the Foreign Office to file a complaint that "Japan felt the lack of a complete understanding of the anti-Communist achievement inherent in the Japanese action against China." He thought that the German Government should understand the fact that Japan was "performing an anti-Communistic task" that would benefit in an important way the Third Reich.[7] As the ambassador grew more heated in his denunciation of communist activities in China, Weizsäcker tried the expedient of "laughing off" some of his vehement remarks. But this resort to humor made no impression upon the diplomat from Nippon who kept insisting that "behind the Nanking Government stands Communism," and therefore it would be "in the interest of general peace not to encourage the Nanking Government." This insistence finally led to the issuance of instructions to the German military mission in China "not to take part in military operations."[8]

On July 31 the German Foreign Office sent pointed inquiries to its ambassadors in China and Japan with reference to the verity of Japanese reports that communist activity was behind the Peiping Incident. Trautmann, from Nanking, replied that the Japanese statements were mere propaganda "which no one in the Far East believes. On the other hand, I consider it quite possible that China is being driven by Japanese action into the arms of Soviet Russia."[9]

[4] The German Ambassador in Japan (Dirksen) to the German Foreign Office, July 27, 1937. *Ibid.*, p. 740.

[5] The German Foreign Ministry to the German Embassy in China, July 28, 1937. *Ibid.*, p. 742.

[6] The German Foreign Ministry to the German Embassy in Japan, July 28, 1937. *Ibid.*, pp. 742–44.

[7] Memorandum by Weizsäcker, German Foreign Office, of a conversation with the Japanese Ambassador, July 28, 1937. *Ibid.*, pp. 744–45.

[8] Foreign Office memorandum, July 30, 1937. *Ibid.*, pp. 745–47.

[9] Ambassador Trautmann to the German Foreign Office, Peking, August 1, 1937. *Ibid.*, p. 748.

From Tokyo, Ambassador Dirksen reported in a very different vein. Hirota had informed him that he had "unimpeachable evidence of intensified Communist activity in China on the part of the Chinese Communists as well as of the Comintern and the Soviet Government."[10] Some weeks later Dirksen indicated that there was growing resentment in Japan relative to the retention of the German military mission in Nanking.[11] This fact was freely admitted by the chief of the Far Eastern Division of the German Foreign Office in a talk with the American chargé d'affaires. The anti-Comintern angle of the situation was also discussed by this Foreign Office official:

I [Prentiss Gilbert] may say that it appears rather evident here that Germany finds herself caught between her special relations with Japan under the anti-Communist treaty and her interests in China. . . . Von Schmieden said that the Japanese were making a great propaganda effort out of Russian aid to China but that this effort was aimed chiefly at influencing Germany and that as far as he could ascertain Russian material assistance was, if it existed at all, extremely limited. . . . He said that the eventuality least to be desired was either a decisive Japanese or Chinese victory. Of the two a Japanese victory was more to be feared as he believed that Japan in such a case would act to eliminate Western interests from China and in general from the Far East. . . .

The Military Attaché informs me in regard to Germany's maintenance in Nanking of a "Military Attaché's office" said to comprise over one hundred officers who have been advising Chiang Kai-shek. . . . The Japanese Military Attaché here recently took up with the War Ministry the question of the withdrawal or at least the reduction in number of these officers. . . . The War Ministry declined on the ground that it would be dishonorable in view of the long and friendly relations which had existed between the Nanking office and Chiang Kai-shek.[12]

On August 28, Gilbert reported that he had learned that the acting head of the German Foreign Office had expressed himself "heatedly respecting Japanese action and policy." He feared that "Japan's entanglement in China . . . would be indefinitely protracted" and would therefore nullify "the value to Germany of the German-Japanese understanding respecting Russia which received a form of outward expression in the anti-Communist agreement."[13]

[10] Dirksen to the German Foreign Office, Tokyo, August 3, 1937. *Ibid.*, pp. 748–49.
[11] Dirksen to the German Foreign Office, Tokyo, August 23, 1937. *Ibid.*, pp. 754–55.
[12] Prentiss Gilbert to Secretary Hull, Berlin, August 26, 1937. 793.94/9753, MS, Department of State.
[13] Prentiss Gilbert to Secretary Hull, Berlin, August 28, 1937. 793.94/9755, MS, Department of State.

But notwithstanding this hostility in some quarters of the German Foreign Office with reference to Japanese expansion in North China, the policy of the German Government towards Japan remained conciliatory. Taking advantage of these gestures of friendship, the Japanese Foreign Office, on September 22, requested the recall of Trautmann from Nanking. When von Neurath sharply replied to the Japanese Ambassador that Trautmann would "remain in Nanking,"[14] Japan merely took this rebuff quietly. She was sure that she could use Germany to advance her interests and could afford to overlook occasional slights. In November 1937 she once more turned to the German Foreign Office and made use of it to launch a peace offensive. The terms of peace offered to China were regarded by Herr von Dirksen as "very moderate" and could be accepted by Nanking "without loss of face."[15] When these terms were made known to Chiang Kai-shek he remarked that the "Chinese Government would be swept out by the tide of public opinion" if it accepted them.[16] The Generalissimo stated that he was ready to open peace negotiations on a more favorable basis, but he insisted that the whole transaction be kept secret.[17] Hope for the success of these negotiations grew more slender after Japanese military successes in North China. Moreover, it now seemed to Hitler that Japan would be victorious in the struggle in China. He favored this result because he believed that "Communism existed to a menacing extent in China." But in many circles in Germany there was a definite pro-Chinese slant. The Foreign Office, the Economics Ministry, and the War Office were reported to be "pro-Chinese together with a majority of German editors." But Ribbentrop was definitely pro-Japanese and there were many other important Nazis who supported this viewpoint.[18]

[14] Memorandum by the German Foreign Minister (von Neurath), September 22, 1937. *Documents on German Foreign Policy, 1918–1945*, I, p. 760.

[15] The German Ambassador in Japan (Dirksen) to the German Foreign Ministry, November 3, 1937. *Ibid.*, pp. 778–79. The terms of peace offered to China by Japan were as follows: (1) in Inner Mongolia there would be established an autonomous government corresponding to the status of Outer Mongolia; (2) in North China a demilitarized zone would be created along the border of Manchukuo to a point south of the Peiping-Tientsin line; (3) in Shanghai a demilitarized zone would be set up which would be more extensive than the existing one and would be under the control of an international police force; (4) the Chinese Government would cease its present anti-Japanese policy; (5) China and Japan would make a common fight against communism; (6) there should be a reduction of customs duties upon Japanese goods; (7) in China the rights of aliens would receive adequate protection.

[16] German Ambassador in China to the Foreign Ministry, November 5, 1937. *Ibid.*, pp. 780–81.

[17] German Ambassador in China to the German Foreign Ministry, December 3, 1937. *Ibid.*, pp. 787–89.

[18] Prentiss Gilbert to Secretary Hull, Berlin, October 20, 1937. 793.94/10783, MS, Department of State.

Ribbentrop and his circle were counting upon a succession of Japanese victories in North China and their expectations were justified. As the Japanese armies continued their steady advance, the peace terms offered China became increasingly stiffer. In December when Madame Chiang Kai-shek read the new Japanese terms she was filled with "the deepest consternation."[19] They could not be considered for one moment. Finally, on January 16, 1938, the Japanese Foreign Office declared that its peace offensive had failed and that all negotiations were terminated.[20] German mediation between China and Japan had been a total failure.

The German Foreign Office was now ready to adopt a more pro-Japanese attitude. The more important items in this program of conciliation were: (1) German recognition of Manchukuo; (2) the recall of German military advisers from China; (3) the discontinuance of the export to China of munitions of war.[21] The long arguments and fervid pleas of Trautmann in Nanking had failed in the face of Hitler's desire to make the Rome-Berlin-Tokyo Axis a dominant force in world politics.

b. *The Abortive Brussels Conference, November 3–24, 1937*

While Germany was trying to effect through mediation some solution to the impasse in North China, the Brussels Conference was working along the same line. On October 5 the Far-East Advisory Committee suggested that the signatories of the Nine-Power Treaty meet in conference to decide upon a policy that should be pursued relative to the conflict in China.[22] Secretary Hull immediately took the cue and issued a statement that the government of the United States had been "forced to the conclusion that the action of Japan in China is inconsistent with the principles which should govern relationships between nations and is contrary to the provisions of the Nine Power Treaty . . . and to those of the Kellogg-Briand Pact."[23] The Japanese Foreign Office countered with a statement which blamed China for the incident leading to the outbreak of the undeclared war. The "subsequent development of the

[19] German Ambassador in China to the German Foreign Ministry, December 26, 1937. *Documents on German Foreign Policy, 1918–1945*, I, 809.

[20] German Ambassador in Japan to the German Foreign Ministry, January 16, 1938. *Ibid.*, pp. 819–20.

[21] Memorandum of a conversation between the German Foreign Minister and the Japanese Ambassador, Berlin, May 20, 1938. *Ibid.*, pp. 867–68.

[22] Second report of the subcommittee of the Far-East Advisory Committee adopted by the committee on October 5, 1937. 793.94/10668, MS, Department of State.

[23] Press release issued by the Department of State, October 6, 1937. *United States and Japan, 1931–1941*, I, 396–97.

Japanese military action has been but the unavoidable consequence of the hostile operations of China."[24]

On October 12, President Roosevelt announced that the American Government was willing to "attend a conference of the parties to the Nine Power Treaty," and three days later Ambassador Grew endeavored to persuade the Japanese Foreign Minister (Hirota) to accept an invitation to this proposed conference. Hirota returned a polite negative. He believed that this meeting of the powers would "merely result in bolstering up China and in prolonging rather than shortening the warfare."[25]

This negative Japanese attitude indicated the real futility of holding a conference dealing with Far Eastern problems, but Belgium was finally prevailed upon to stage the meeting at Brussels. The instructions to the American delegation pointed out that the purpose of the conference was to "study peaceable means of hastening the end of the regrettable conflict" which prevailed in the Far East. Particular attention should be paid to "the rights and interests of the United States under the Nine Power Treaty." Stress was placed upon the fact "that the first objective of the foreign policy of this country is national security." The delegates should constantly keep in mind "that public opinion in the United States has expressed its emphatic determination that the United States keep out of war."[26]

The caution that was evident in these instructions was probably induced by the knowledge that Japan was in no mood to respond to pressure. This fact was confirmed by a dispatch from Tokyo. Ambassador Grew warned Secretary Hull that in Japan "all classes of the people feel that the security and future existence of the nation are involved in the present situation and that there can be no turning back no matter what pressure be brought by other Powers."[27]

Although the conference had no program for exerting pressure upon Japan, it did not hesitate to declare that the "Japanese concept of the issues and interests involved in the conflict under reference is utterly different from the concepts of most of the other nations and the governments of the world." It was apparent that direct negotiations between China and Japan would not lead to "any solution which would give promise of peace between those two countries." Therefore, inasmuch

[24] Ambassador Grew to Secretary Hull, October 9, 1937. 793.94/10524, MS, Department of State.

[25] Memorandum by Ambassador Grew, October 15, 1937. 793.94/11026, MS, Department of State.

[26] Secretary Hull to Norman H. Davis, October 18, 1937. *Peace and War: United States Foreign Policy, 1931–1941* (Washington, 1943), pp. 389–90.

[27] Ambassador Grew to Secretary Hull, Tokyo, November 2, 1937. 793.94/10946, MS, Department of State.

as the conflict in China was the concern of all nations interested in the preservation of world peace, it was the duty of the signatories of the Nine-Power Pact to consult with reference to finding a formula that would put an end to the conflict in China.[28]

Norman H. Davis, the head of the American delegation at Brussels, had taken such an active role since the conference convened that many rumors arose to the effect that the United States had been principally responsible for the calling of the conference and for the preparation of its agenda. On November 16 the Japanese Foreign Minister expressed to Ambassador Grew his deep concern that the Japanese public would regard the United States as the "real leader" in the work of the conference. Up to this time Japanese public opinion had regarded Britain as the country that had been "foremost in endeavoring to develop a solid front against Japan." He would deplore any shift of this onus to America. "Good relations with the United States" was the cardinal point in his foreign policy and he was greatly concerned lest it might be endangered by the proceedings of the Brussels Conference.[29]

When Grew reported this conversation to the Department of State he was instructed by Secretary Hull to present supplementary information to Hirota. On November 18, Grew went to the Foreign Office and assured Hirota that the American Government had not taken the initiative in calling the Brussels Conference. He also read that portion of Hull's instruction that referred to American efforts to maintain and develop good relations between Japan and the United States. At the conclusion of the instruction there was an expression of apprehension that the situation in the Far East might "injure those relations."[30]

It was evident that the Department of State was unusually careful not to offend Japanese sensibilities. This was further indicated in the declaration adopted by the conference on November 24. This statement placed a strong accent upon certain basic principles: respect for the sovereignty of other nations; abstention from interference in the internal affairs of other nations; and a determination to refrain from seeking political or economic domination over them. After this introductory statement, the declaration then expressed the view that "whenever armed force is employed in disregard of these principles the whole structure of international relations . . . is disturbed." After stating that force could not provide a "just and lasting solution" for disputes between nations, the declaration finally asserted that a satisfactory settle-

---

[28] Declaration adopted by the conference at Brussels, November 15, 1937. *Peace and War,* pp. 390–92.

[29] Memorandum of Ambassador Grew, Tokyo, November 16, 1937. 793.94/11672, MS, Department of State.

[30] Memorandum of Ambassador Grew, Tokyo, November 18, 1937. *Ibid.*

ment of the war in the Far East could be achieved only through friendly consultation between the signatories of the Nine-Power Pact.[31]

This quiet and nonexplosive declaration indicated that the powers were not ready to apply any sanctions against Japan. It was merely a pious admonition that expressed a hope for Japanese restraint. There was no thought of compelling that restraint by collective action.

c. *The* Panay *Incident*

The *Panay* Incident was a direct result of the Japanese offensive against Nanking. In the latter part of November 1937 the Chinese Foreign Office was removed to Hankow and this necessitated a change of residence on the part of the representatives of foreign powers. Some Americans refused to leave Nanking, so the gunboat *Panay* was stationed at that city with orders to give them needed protection. On December 8, the Japanese Consul General in Shanghai urged the foreign consuls resident in the city to request their nationals to evacuate Nanking without delay. On the morning of the following day the officer in charge of the American Embassy sent from the *Panay* a radio reply advising the Japanese authorities of the names of eighteen Americans planning to remain in Nanking.

On December 10 the Japanese launched a sharp offensive against Nanking. As a measure of protection the position of the *Panay* was communicated to the Japanese Consul General at Shanghai with a request "that he notify Japanese forces so that ship might not be endangered by their military activities."[32] As the Japanese increased their offensive on December 11, "shells began falling on the near shore not far up river from *Panay*." The *Panay* delayed moving up the river "until shells were falling in the water ahead and on the opposite bank." It dropped anchor twelve miles from Nanking and the officials still left in the American Embassy sent a naval radiogram asking the Department of State to make their position known to the Japanese since bombing planes were constantly in the air above the position of the *Panay*.[33]

On December 12, while flying a large American ensign and with two newly painted American flags on her top deck, the *Panay* was repeatedly bombed by Japanese planes. After severely damaging the gunboat, the planes then bombed three vessels of the Standard Oil Company, setting

31 Declaration adopted by the conference at Brussels, November 24, 1937. *Peace and War*, pp. 393–94. See also, *The Conference of Brussels, November 3–24, 1937, Convened in Virtue of Article 7 of the Nine-Power Treaty of Washington of 1922* (Washington, 1938).

32 Consul General Gauss to Secretary Hull, Shanghai, December 10, 1937. 793.94/11569, MS, Department of State.

33 Atcheson to Secretary Hull, Nanking, December 11, 1937. 793.94/11583, MS, Department of State.

fire to two of them and causing the other to be beached. Two members of the crew of the *Panay* died from their wounds, while Lieutenant Commander Hughes and ten of the officers and crew were seriously injured.[34]

On the following morning, before any protest could be received from Ambassador Grew, Foreign Minister Hirota called at the Embassy. He said that the Japanese naval commander at Shanghai had accepted full responsibility for the incident, and then expressed the profound apologies of his government.[35] At twelve-thirty on that day (December 13), the President handed to Secretary Hull a memorandum requesting him to inform the Japanese Ambassador, when he called at the Department of State, that the American Chief Executive was "deeply shocked and concerned by the news of indiscriminate bombing of American and other non-Chinese vessels on the Yangtse," and that he expected "full expressions of regret and proffer of full compensation."[36]

That evening Secretary Hull sent an instruction to Ambassador Grew which embodied the items in the President's memorandum. He then stressed the importance of assurances that in the future "American nationals, interests and property in China" would not be "subjected to attack by Japanese armed forces."[37]

At first Grew feared that the bombing of the *Panay* might "result in a breach of diplomatic relations and that Saito would be given his passports and that I would be recalled." His apprehensions were relieved by Hirota's apology, a promise of indemnity, and by the conciliatory actions of Japanese naval authorities.[38] It was apparent that throughout Japan there was deep concern over the *Panay* Incident. By December 16, Grew was reporting to Secretary Hull that cash donations were pouring into the Embassy and into newspaper offices for eventual transmission to the Embassy.[39]

On December 18 the Division of Far Eastern Affairs prepared a memorandum which recited the fact that the *Panay* Incident had "not inflamed public opinion in the United States," and that the "firm position adopted by this Government seems to have satisfied public opinion."[40] The way was open for a settlement of the incident. On Decem-

---

[34] Navy Department, *Press Releases*, December 24, 25, 1937.

[35] Memorandum by Secretary Hull, December 13, 1937. *United States and Japan, 1931–1941*, I, 522–23.

[36] Memorandum of President Roosevelt, December 13, 1937. *Ibid.*, p. 523.

[37] Secretary Hull to Ambassador Grew, December 13, 1937. *Ibid.*, pp. 523–24.

[38] Joseph C. Grew, *Ten Years in Japan*, pp. 234–35.

[39] Ambassador Grew to Secretary Hull, Tokyo, December 16, 1937. *United States and Japan, 1931–1941*, I, 528.

[40] Memorandum of the Division of Far Eastern Affairs, December 18, 1937. 793.94/11741, MS, Department of State.

ber 24, Hirota sent the expected note containing a reference to the apology expressed in his previous communication of December 14. As to the future he stated that the strictest orders had been issued to the military and naval forces so as to prevent a recurrence of the *Panay* Incident.[41] On the following day (Christmas), Secretary Hull sent an instruction to Grew accepting the explanations and promises of Hirota. When Grew presented this note, Hirota exclaimed: "I heartily thank your Government and you yourself for this decision. I am very, very happy."[42]

The *Panay* Incident was formally closed by the acceptance of an indemnity of $2,214,007.36. The whole matter had been handled with admirable restraint by the officials of both countries. It is greatly to be regretted that this pacific spirit soon faded away.

d. *The Mission of Admiral Ingersoll to London*

The *Panay* Incident was not settled by the conciliatory letter of Foreign Minister Hirota (December 24). The attack on the American gunboat had deepened the distrust in the President's mind that had been given explosive expression in the quarantine speech of October 5. In December he began to give earnest consideration to the matter of arranging a closer understanding with Great Britain with reference to the Far East. He was well aware of the fact that increasing tension in Europe kept the British Foreign Office from exerting strong pressure upon Japan. On December 15, Pertinax, in the *Echo de Paris,* gave a terse description of the situation:

The worst would be that Great Britain, under the pretext of supporting the United States and of gaining the United States for a permanent co-operation, should let herself go in a dangerous counter-stroke in the China Sea. In the condition of Europe today, British forces should not be withdrawn from the principal task, which consists of holding in check the two totalitarian states which are our neighbors. It is not by action in the Far East but by action in Europe that British prestige may be reestablished.

It was evident to most statesmen that Britain could exert pressure upon Japan only in close concert with the United States. In order to prepare the way for that concert, Sir Robert Craigie, British Ambassador in Tokyo, kept hammering upon this theme in his conversations with

---

[41] Ambassador Grew to Secretary Hull, December 24, 1937. 394.115 Panay/196, MS, Department of State.

[42] Ambassador Grew to Secretary Hull, Tokyo, December 26, 1937. 394.115 Panay/200, MS, Department of State.

Ambassador Grew. He insisted that the United States "should stand shoulder to shoulder with Great Britain in opposing Japanese depredations because injury to British interest in the Far East would automatically injure the interests of the United States." Grew realized the danger that attended the proposed close concert with Britain, and feared that America would have to pay the price "of British ineptitudes, both of action and of statement, which have contributed their full measure toward the developing of the feeling of exacerbation now prevailing between Great Britain and Japan." Moreover, he did not "altogether share" Craigie's views "that a lowering of British prestige and influence in the Far East must necessarily injure American interests." He thought that the American policy of moving along parallel rather than joint lines with Britain had been "sound and sane."[43]

But President Roosevelt was now convinced that we should move closer to Britain, and with this thought in mind he decided to send Admiral R. E. Ingersoll to London to explore the situation. Ingersoll arrived in the British metropolis in January 1938. The "primary purpose" of his mission was

to investigate and to talk with the British Admiralty officials as to what we could do if the United States and England would find themselves at war with Japan in the Pacific, to explore all the means, what means could be used, what arrangements it would be necessary to make in regard to command relationships, in regard to communicating with each other, of establishing liaison officers and preparing certain codes and ciphers, and so forth.

After extensive conversations with the officials in the War Plans Division of the British Admiralty it was arranged that there should be a "distribution of codes and ciphers." There was no definite agreement based upon these conversations, but the exploration of the *probability* of Anglo-American joint action was significant. As Admiral Ingersoll frankly stated: "Everybody knew as indicated by this trip that I made to London in 1938, that sooner or later, we were all going to be involved in a war in the Pacific which would include the Dutch, the Chinese possibly, the Russians, the British, and ourselves, and we had to make preliminary arrangements to explore what could be done to arrange for a means of communicating with each other."[44]

If "everybody" in the Roosevelt circle knew that "sooner or later"

[43] Ambassador Grew to Secretary Hull, Tokyo, December 11, 1937. 793.94/11841, *Strictly Confidential*, MS, Department of State.

[44] Testimony of Admiral R. E. Ingersoll, February 12, 1946. *Hearings Before the Joint Committees on the Investigation of the Pearl Harbor Attack* (Washington, 1946), IX, 4273–78.

we would intervene in World War II, the pointed Roosevelt protestations in 1940 to the contrary would indicate how he became a master of mendacity.

e. Japan Establishes a Series of Puppet Governments in China

It was apparent to Japan after the undeclared war had extended several months that the Nationalist Government under Chiang Kai-shek would continue to fight for an indefinite period. Therefore, it might be good strategy to set up a series of puppet governments that would be responsive to Japanese desires. On December 14, 1937, the "Provisional Government of the Chinese Republic" was proclaimed in Peiping. Several months later (March 28, 1938) the "Reformed Government of the Chinese Republic" was erected in Nanking. These rival puppet governments lasted until March 30, 1940, when the Provisional Government in Peiping disappeared and the "Reorganized National Government" was established at Nanking.[45]

In order to secure economic concessions from these puppet governments, Japan created the North China Development Company and the Central China Development Company. Within the areas controlled by Japanese troops, the currency systems were revised and tariff schedules on Japanese manufactures were reduced. A Federal Reserve Bank was established and the puppet regime at Peiping decreed that its issues should be the only currency that could circulate within its jurisdiction.[46] On May 31, Peiping officials announced that the North China tariff duties would be extended to Central China.[47] The Open Door in China was fast becoming a mere phrase.

The British Foreign Office watched these Japanese moves with rapidly increasing concern because of their effect upon British trade with China. On February 14, Sir Alexander Cadogan sent to Mr. Hornbeck a memorandum containing the outline of a settlement of the situation in the Far East which Foreign Office officials regarded as "reasonable." To impose this settlement upon Japan would require close Anglo-American concert. The governments of the two powers should inform Japan that their interests in the Far East were suffering serious damage through the failure of the Japanese Government "to

[45] *Japan Year Book, 1939–1940*, p. 1085.
[46] Memorandum by Ambassador Grew, Tokyo, April 12, 1938. *United States and Japan, 1931–1941*, I, 762–63; *Far Eastern Survey*, VII, 55–56, 83–84, 89–90, 99, 107; *Journal of Commerce*, March 16, 1938.
[47] *New York Herald-Tribune* June 1, 1938. For an extended account of this Japanese drive to dominate the economic life of North China see William C. Johnstone, *The United States and Japan's New Order* (New York, 1941), chap. 11.

observe the terms of Article 1 of the Nine Power Treaty." It should then be plainly stated that the two governments did not "intend to acquiesce in any further or continuing breach of the terms of the Treaty." After these bold words, the note of the two governments should then deal with the question of Shanghai. It should be obvious that China could hardly "develop the effective and suitable Government contemplated in the Nine Power Treaty so long as Chinese authority is in any degree excluded from Shanghai. . . . The traditional aim of American and British policy . . . has been to encourage China to develop into a modern State. But this aim has been to a large extent frustrated by inability to break away from the older tradition of imposing tutelage and protecting foreign interests by armed force." It was doubtful whether security could "be obtained for foreign interests by the old methods of foreign administered areas and foreign garrisons." Moreover, China was becoming increasingly reluctant to "accept a situation in which one-half the population of their greatest city is withdrawn from Chinese control." The best solution would probably be to ask Japan to surrender what other powers would also surrender. "The only alternative to maintaining the International Settlement by force is to surrender all foreign control and restore complete Chinese control." The existing municipal administration of the Settlement should be "merged into a larger body which, while remaining a Chinese authority, would contain a foreign element with full representation of Japanese, British and other foreign interests."[48]

After studying this far-reaching proposal of Cadogan for two months, Hornbeck replied in a letter that amounted to a flat rejection. He thought that Japan would in due time be brought to see the error of her ways through the pressure "of the moral indignation of other nations and her own economic difficulties." There was also the possibility that the American Government might employ some form of economic reprisal against Japan in order to induce her to change her policy.[49]

Before the Department of State gave any serious thought to planning economic reprisals against Japan, Secretary Hull thought it expedient to reiterate the principles that guided his policy. In an address at the National Press Club (March 17, 1938), he threw a direct challenge in the face of Japan. America would not withdraw from the Far East because of Japanese pressure in that area:

[48] Sir Alexander Cadogan to Stanley K. Hornbeck, London, February 14, 1938. 793.94/12855⅕, *Confidential file,* MS, Department of State.

[49] Sir Alexander Cadogan to Stanley K. Hornbeck, London, May 23, 1938. 793.94/12855⅗, *Confidential file,* MS, Department of State.

To waive rights and to permit interests to lapse in the face of their actual or threatened violation—and thereby to abandon obligations—in any important area of the world, can serve only to encourage disregard of law and of the basic principles of international order, and thus contribute to the inevitable spread of international anarchy, throughout the world. For this country, as for any country, to act in such manner *anywhere* would be to invite disregard and violation of its rights and interests *everywhere,* by every nation so inclined, large or small.[50]

Some two months later (May 31), a vehement protest was sent to Tokyo against the continued exclusion of American businessmen from their places of business and missionaries from work in areas where hostilities had ceased and where Japanese nationals were busily plying their trades.[51] When the Japanese Government failed to take any steps to remedy this situation, the American Chamber of Commerce and the American Community Committee sent a cablegram to Secretary Hull urging the Department of State to take a firm stand against Japanese practices.[52] Secretary Hull responded with another pointed protest to Japan. After citing a list of Japanese discriminatory practices like currency manipulation, trade controls, tariff preferences, and monopolies that worked to the exclusion of foreign trade, Hull observed that these policies indicated a purpose "to establish in areas which have come under Japanese military occupation general preferences for, and superiority of, Japanese interests, an inevitable effect of which will be to frustrate the practical application of the principle of the Open Door."[53]

f. *The Far East after Munich*

The Anglo-French capitulation at Munich gave the Japanese Government a signal to go ahead in the Far East without any apprehension of serious interference on the part of Britain or France. Even before Munich the British Government had abdicated as far as China was concerned. In the first week in September 1938, Sir Robert Craigie, British Ambassador at Tokyo, informed Grew that "owing to the crisis in Europe he had been directed by his Government to avoid a showdown

---

[50] Address of Secretary Hull at the National Press Club, March 17, 1938. *Documents on American Foreign Relations, January 1938–June 1939,* ed. S. Shepard Jones and Denys P. Myers (Boston, 1939), pp. 6–17.

[51] Ambassador Grew to Japanese Minister for Foreign Affairs, Tokyo, May 31, 1938. *United States and Japan, 1931–1941,* I, 764–66.

[52] *New York Times,* September 3, 1938.

[53] Ambassador Grew to Japanese Prime Minister and Minister for Foreign Affairs, (Prince Konoye), October 6, 1938. *United States and Japan, 1931–1941,* I, 785–90.

with the Japanese Government at present and to carry on as best he could."[54]

Knowing that Britain was helpless in the Far East, Japan prepared another military drive to conquer China. On October 12 a Japanese expeditionary force of 30,000 troops was landed near Hong Kong and began its advance upon Canton. In less than ten days (October 21), Canton fell before the invaders, and on October 26, Japanese troops entered Hankow. The government of Chiang Kai-shek had hurriedly evacuated Hankow and moved 800 miles up the Yangtze to Chungking. After this impressive military success, the Japanese Government issued a statement which proclaimed a new order in eastern Asia—the complete political, economic, and cultural co-ordination of China and Manchukuo with the Japanese system. The object of this new order was to "secure international justice, to perfect the joint defence against Communism, and to create a new culture and realize a close economic cohesion throughout East Asia." Japan was confident "that other Powers will on their part correctly appreciate her aims and policy and adapt their attitude to the new conditions prevailing in East Asia."[55]

On the following day Secretary Hull showed that he did not correctly appreciate the aims of Japan in East Asia. In a statement to the press Hull remarked that the attitude of the American Government towards the situation in Asia was still governed "by the generally accepted principles of international law, by the provisions of treaties to which the United States and numerous countries—among them China and Japan—are parties, and by principles of fair dealing and fair play between and among nations."[56] The Japanese answer to Hull's statement was given on November 18 with distinct overtones of defiance. It attempted to deny that there had been any real discrimination in Japanese-controlled China against the business interests of foreign nationals. Restrictions had been imposed for the purpose of preserving peace and order. Normal conditions would be restored as soon as circumstances would permit. It should be clearly understood, however, that "any attempt to apply to the conditions of today and tomorrow inapplicable ideas and principles of the past would neither contribute toward the establishment of a real peace in East Asia nor solve the immediate issue."[57]

---

[54] Ambassador Grew to Secretary Hull, Tokyo, September 8, 1938. 793.94/13837, *Confidential file*, MS, Department of State.

[55] Statement by the Japanese Government, November 3, 1938. *United States and Japan, 1931–1941*, I, 477–78.

[56] Statement of Secretary Hull, November 4, 1938. *Ibid.*, pp. 481–82.

[57] Department of State, *Press Release*, November 19, 1938. See also, Foreign Minister Arita to Ambassador Grew, November 18, 1938, Tokyo. *United States and Japan, 1931–1941*, I, 797–800.

On December 19, Foreign Minister Arita once more referred to the new order in the Far East. In a statement to foreign correspondents in Tokyo he insisted that the formation of a Japanese-Manchurian-Chinese bloc was politically necessary as a measure of defense against communism and economically necessary because the rest of the world was erecting higher and higher tariff walls and resorting to other measures in the direction of economic self-sufficiency. In this new order the three countries would maintain their independence and individuality. Also the new regime would not aim at "excluding European and American economic activities from East Asia" although the "requirements of national defence and of economic security might make it necessary to impose certain restrictions on the activities of third powers."[58]

This indirect way of denouncing the Nine-Power Treaty did not please Secretary Hull who replied that the "people and the Government of the United States could not assent to the establishment, at the instance of and for the special purposes of any third country, of a régime which would arbitrarily deprive them of the long established rights of equal opportunity and fair treatment which are legally and justly theirs along with those of other nations."[59]

g. *Chiang Kai-shek Suggests Another Washington Conference*

It was evident to most observers in the Far East that Japanese-American relations in the fall of 1938 had reached an impasse which might be difficult to break. To Chiang Kai-shek it seemed a golden opportunity for an invitation to another Washington Conference. On October 8 he sent an impassioned plea to President Roosevelt along this line. While the President's notes to European nations had contributed greatly towards quieting the situation on that continent,

the resort to brutal force and slaughter still prevail in the Far East and world peace is still far from realization. I am confident that you, Mr. President, who have already done so much in the past for peace, surely will not ignore the problem of peace in the Far East. . . . It is said that, owing to heavy human losses and economic difficulties, Japan is beginning to realize that force solves no problem. More than once she has sought mediation for peace by Germany and Italy. But Mr. President, my people feel that they can only look to your Government for leadership in the active search for peace because we have complete faith that the kind of peace the American Government is inspired to sponsor will be a just peace.

[58] *New York Times,* December 20, 1938. See also, statement of the Japanese Minister for Foreign Affairs (Arita), December 19, 1938. *United States and Japan, 1931–1941,* I, 816–18.
[59] Department of State, *Press Release,* December 31, 1938.

Now that the European situation is settling down, may it not be possible for the American Government to initiate a move for the peace of the Far East by inviting all the Governments interested to attend a Conference, stipulating a general cessation of hostilities as a pre-condition and aiming at seeking a lasting settlement through calm and fair-minded deliberation?[60]

When Mr. Hornbeck, the adviser on Political Relations, was shown this plea from Chiang Kai-shek he prepared a memorandum for the guidance of Secretary Hull. He thought that the reply of the President to this communication should consist of "little more than a polite acknowledgment with an assurance of interest and attention." He believed that an attempt to call a conference at this time with regard to the Far Eastern situation would produce far more of harm than it could possibly "produce of good. It is believed that the same would be true of any attempt which might be made by the American Government to say anything at this time on the subject of mediation in relation to that situation. It is believed, however, that it would be inadvisable and inexpedient to say either of those things to Chiang Kai-shek." The reply should be "noncommittal."

The reply drafted under this Hornbeck prescription was so cool and colorless that the President sent it back to Sumner Welles with the notation: "Can you make this message to Chiang Kai-shek a little more personal and a little warmer?" A new note from the President to Chiang was drafted and, on October 19, Hornbeck handed it to the ambassador from China. It indicated that the American Chief Executive was "giving close and sympathetic attention to the situation . . . and that he was observing every development with a desire so to act as to contribute . . . toward an alleviation of the distress, destruction and suffering which are inherent in and produced by the Chinese-Japanese hostilities."[61] The Chinese Ambassador accepted this brush-off with Oriental calm and the incident was closed. Subsequently, Chinese pressure upon the President would elicit a more prompt and satisfactory response.

h. *The Economic Ties That Failed to Bind Japan Closely to the United States*

American relations with China have given eloquent disproof of the theory of economic determinism. Despite the fact that American investments in Japan and American trade with that country have been

---

[60] Chiang Kai-shek to President Roosevelt, October 8, 1938. 793.94/14047½, *Confidential file*, MS, Department of State.

[61] Memorandum of Mr. Hornbeck, October 19, 1938. 793.94/14047½, *Confidential file*, MS, Department of State.

many times larger than our economic interests in China, American policy towards China has been distinctly more friendly that it has been towards Japan. In 1938 it was estimated that our investments in China (exclusive of mission property) were approximately $132,000,000, as compared with $387,000,000 in Japan.[62] Our trade with Japan was considerably greater than that with China:

	U.S. Exports to China	U.S. Exports to Japan	U.S. Exports to Russia	U.S. Exports to all South America
1928	$137,661,000	$288,158,000		
1930	89,600,000	164,700,000		
1932	56,200,000	134,500,000		
1934	68,667,000	210,000,000	$15,011,000	
1936	46,819,000	204,348,000	33,427,000	$204,222,000
1937	49,697,000	288,378,000	42,903,000	318,384,000

These statistics give a significant picture of our rapidly growing trade with Japan and our relatively small trade with China.[63] The China market had always been a disappointing one and continued so down to the outbreak of World War II. But the dream of 450,000,000 Chinese customers clamoring for American goods kept haunting millions of Americans who conveniently forgot that China had little to exchange for the products of this country.

The importance of Japan as America's third best customer is well described by John W. Masland:

Between 1931 and 1941 the outstanding fact is the number one position held by Japan both as buyer and seller. Between 1931 and 1940, inclusive, American exports to Japan averaged 48% of total exports to the Far East, and imports from Japan averaged 21 per cent of total imports to us. During this period Japan was America's third best foreign customer, outranked only by Great Britain and Canada, and we were her best customer. . . . American-Japanese trade, moreover, was mutually profitable and satisfactory, based upon an exchange of goods and commodities required by each but unavailable at home. . . . Among a large proportion of American exporting and importing firms doing business with all or several of the Far Eastern countries, Japan was the best customer or the chief source of supply, whichever the case. . . . American business men were usually well pleased by their

[62] A. Whitney Griswold, *The Far Eastern Policy of the United States* (New York, 1938), pp. 468–69.
[63] Ralph Townsend, *The High Cost of Hate* (San Francisco, 1939), pp. 23, 39, 48; Miriam S. Farley, "America's Stake in the Far East, I: Trade," *Far Eastern Survey*, V (July 29, 1926), 161–70; C. F. Remer, *Foreign Investments in China* (New York, 1933), chap. 15; Ethel B. Dietrich, *Far Eastern Trade of the United States* (New York, 1940).

contacts with Japan. They found that the Japanese were prompt in meeting their obligations and that Japanese goods kept up to quality standards.[64]

It should also be kept in mind that Japanese domination over a large portion of China and her exchange controls and other devices that deeply worried Secretary Hull did not seriously affect American trade with China. Indeed, quite the reverse. American exports to China in 1939 were $55,614,000 as compared with $46,819,000 in 1936, and this export trade in 1940 was $77,590,000 as compared with $49,697,-000 in 1937. These welcome returns from trade caused commercial groups to look "with considerable disfavor upon the use of embargoes and other strong measures against Japan. . . . It was not until 1941, as the war crisis approached, that trading groups accepted drastic economic pressures."[65]

But commercial pressure groups had little influence in the shaping of American policy in the Far East. A far more vocal and influential pressure group was composed of missionaries to China and their ardent supporters in the United States. In 1937 there were fifty societies and boards in the United States interested in Chinese missions. There was a $50,000,000 investment in these missions with an annual outlay of $4,000,000. In China there were some 2500 Protestant missionaries. The cause of these missions was ardently espoused by such organizations as the Rockefeller Foundation, the Y.M.C.A., the Y.W.C.A., the Associated Board of Christian Colleges in China (13 of them), and by groups representing twenty-seven colleges and universities in the United States.

Propaganda in favor of China was spread through the numerous contacts between the administrative officials of these missionary boards and societies, and officials in the Federal Government. Dr. A. L. Warnshuis, of the Foreign Missions Conference, was particularly active and successful in influencing the minds of many government officials. Propaganda was also circulated by letters from missionaries in China and from mission boards to churches and foundations. Some of these letters which were bitterly critical of Japan were distributed in America in very large numbers.

This American missionary propaganda in favor of China had a very important influence in molding the American mind against Japan. It also prepared a climate of opinion favorable to embargoes and trade restrictions that would seriously affect Japanese-American commerce.

[64] John W. Masland, "Commercial Influence Upon American Far Eastern Policy, 1937–1941," *Pacific Historical Review*, XI (1942), 281–83.
[65] *Ibid.*, p. 297.

It was significant that one of the important pressure groups that called
for economic reprisals against Japan was the Committee on Non-Participation in Japanese Aggression with Henry L. Stimson as the chairman.[66] Stimson had pressed Japan to the wall at Geneva in 1933 and as
a member of the Roosevelt Cabinet in 1940–1941 was strongly inclined
towards war with Japan. He welcomed the moral imperatives of the
missionaries in their criticisms of Japan, and they hardly realized that
he was a real war hawk whose shrill cries for economic restrictions
would become a summons to war.

i. Secretary Hull Rejects a British Suggestion for Exerting Economic Pressure upon Japan

In the early months of 1939 there was increasing pressure upon Secretary Hull in favor of economic reprisals against Japan. On December
31, 1938, the British Ambassador in Tokyo submitted to Ambassador
Grew a long memorandum which outlined in detail an economic offensive against the Japanese Empire. First of all, emphasis was placed upon
Japanese needs for certain essential raw materials—mineral oil, ores
and metals, cotton, wool, rubber, wood pulp, and heavy chemicals. The
principal sources for these materials were the United States and the
British Empire. In order to create exchange for the purchase of these
much-needed products, Japan could sell to foreign nationals merchandise, shipping services, and gold. But "her sales of all three . . . did not
provide sufficient funds to pay for what she bought from abroad during
the years of industrial and military and naval development previous to
1937. . . . Since the beginning of 1937 . . . Japan's difficulties in finding
funds to pay for her necessary imports from abroad have greatly increased. She has not been able to borrow money abroad since 1932 . . .
and there is no likelihood of her being able to borrow abroad in the
near future." Her receipts from shipping services had been greatly reduced since July 1937, and her sales of merchandise had not brought in
the hoped-for revenues. In the period from January to November 1938,
she paid in foreign currencies for merchandise alone 2058 million
yen and received from her "sales of merchandise in foreign currencies,
1636 million yen, so that her debit balance in foreign exchange was
422 million yen." In order to offset the debit balances in foreign exchange of 961 million yen in 1937 and 422 million yen in January–

    [66] John W. Masland, "Missionary Influence Upon American Far Eastern Policy,"
Pacific Historical Review, X (September 1941), 279–96. See also, Johnstone, *op. cit.*,
chaps. 14–15.

November 1938, Japan exported to the United States gold to the value of 876 million yen in 1937 and 670 million yen in 1938.

In view of these facts, it seemed apparent that if "there were to be imposed even a relatively small restriction on Japan's exports of merchandise or gold and if credits and loans were simultaneously to be withheld, Japan's economic situation would immediately become critical. If an embargo were to be placed on Japan's exports to the British Empire, the United States and France (thus affecting 70% of her total foreign exchange producing trade), the effect would set in motion a process which must rapidly prove disastrous for Japan's economy."[67]

On January 7, 1939, Grew sent this memorandum to Secretary Hull with some observations of his own. He did not discount the impact of an embargo upon Japan which he was sure would at least reduce the standard of living in that country, but he stressed certain psychological factors that helped to balance this uncertain equation. The Japanese were

a hardy race, inured to personal and national sacrifice; they have been accustomed throughout their history to meeting catastrophe and disaster; in them the "do or die" spirit is more deeply ingrained than in almost any other people. . . . For Japan to admit defeat in the present hostilities after pouring out so much blood and treasure in China . . . is an hypothesis which we in this Embassy find it very difficult to entertain. To support if not to prove this thesis by quoting figures and statistics is simple enough, and it is on the basis of figures and statistics that my colleagues rest their opinions concerning the effectiveness of economic sanctions. I should add, parenthetically, that these colleagues had been confidently predicting for the past two years that the economic collapse of Japan was about to occur.[68]

On February 3, Mr. V. A. L. Mallet, the British chargé d'affaires, had a conversation with Mr. Welles concerning the views of Ambassador Craigie. After a brief exchange of views, Mr. Welles bluntly remarked that the American Government "would not consider for the time being undertaking retaliatory measures against Japan." In the event that the Department of State wished to "consider the matter further," it would "inform the British Government accordingly and discuss further with them some of the issues involved."[69]

Within the Department of State there was a considerable amount of

[67] Ambassador R. L. Craigie to Ambassador Grew, Tokyo, December 31, 1938. 793.94/14671, *Strictly Confidential*, MS, Department of State.

[68] Ambassador Grew to Secretary Hull, Tokyo, January 7, 1939. *Ibid.*

[69] Memorandum of a conversation between Sumner Welles and Mr. V. A. L. Mallet, February 3, 1939. 793.94/15197, MS, Department of State.

further discussion with reference to opening an economic offensive against Japan. On February 11, Mr. Hornbeck prepared a memorandum on the subject. Up to the turn of the twentieth century the Japanese were looked upon as "a comparatively amiable, artistic and art loving and peaceful people who needed to be taught and could be patronized." But Japan's character was "not what it was thought before 1895 to be," and her "strength is not what it has been thought since 1905 to be." Over and over since 1905 the world has, because of "fear of Japan, acquiesced in aggressive predatory activities on Japan's part. . . . Step by step Japan has moved forward. . . . There are three methods by which . . . nations may offer resistance: by moral opposition, by economic opposition, and/or by military opposition." For many years the United States had tried moral opposition to Japan's unlawful progress, but it had not effectively protected American rights. Proposals had been made to try economic opposition but objections had been promptly made that the Japanese are a "militant and powerful people" who might retaliate "by an appeal to arms." Thus, "moral opposition not sufficing and economic opposition being not even tried," the prospect is that in the long run "the situation will so develop that military opposition by this country will *have to be* offered."[70]

Herbert Feis, the adviser on International Economic Affairs, was not so military-minded as Mr. Hornbeck. He was impressed with some of the arguments presented by Sir Robert Craigie with reference to the effect upon Japan of increasing economic pressure exerted by Britain, France, and the United States. He was certain that this pressure would mean much more than a mere lowering of the standard of living in Japan. But he did "not wish the foregoing criticism of the economic analysis of the American Ambassador to be interpreted as an argument in favor of imposing sanctions on Japan." After some criticisms of the Craigie memorandum relative to the exhaustion of Japan's gold reserves, he discusses the effect of an embargo upon the sales of gold by the Japanese Government:

I am dubious of the conclusion that "the simplest and most effective first step would appear to be for Great Britain, the United States of America and France to refuse to purchase any further gold from Japan." Since the United States holds so much of the world's gold, it would not be to its interest to take action which would make it less desirable for other nations to hold gold as an emergency measure. Hence I do not believe that an embargo on gold exports from Japan should be undertaken unless extremely drastic measures are contemplated, and the embargo on gold is undertaken simultaneously

[70] Memorandum by Stanley K. Hornbeck, adviser on Political Relations, February 11, 1939. 793.94/14671, *Confidential file,* MS, Department of State.

with an embargo on exports of goods from Japan. Before such drastic action as this is undertaken it would appear to me more logical to try less extreme measures such as denunciation of our existing commercial treaty with Japan.[71]

In a memorandum on the feasibility of exerting strong economic pressure upon Japan, the Division of Far Eastern Affairs agreed with Mr. Feis that no action should be taken relative to refusing to buy Japanese gold. It also agreed with him that an embargo upon commerce with Japan, undertaken by Britain, France, and the United States, would "bring chaos to Japan's economy and soon reduce drastically the effectiveness of her military forces."[72]

When these memoranda were sent to Ambassador Grew he was not deeply impressed with them. He particularly disagreed with the memorandum prepared by Herbert Feis. It was entirely possible that the impact of economic sanctions might overthrow the existing capitalistic system in Japan, but Mr. Feis overlooked the fact that "a new economic system might be devised to meet a condition of extreme emergency." It was also true that Mr. Feis did not go into the question "of the uses to which Japan could put new resources available in the occupied areas in China." Attention should be called to the fact that Japan was "self-sufficient in the matter of food supplies." It should also be remembered that for several years the Japanese Government had been building large reserves of "military raw materials." This being true, it could not be said with authority that an embargo upon the commerce of Japan would seriously affect her military operations or her political program. The elements in power in Japan had "repeatedly declared their intention to evolve, if necessary, a new economic system which would enable Japan, notwithstanding the restrictions imposed in the matter of sanctions, to continue her present program in China." The question whether the Japanese people would accept and support this new system "is a political and not an economic one."[73]

Mr. Feis had the last word in this argument, which he answered by stating that it was not at all clear to him that "some type of socialism or fascism will enable the Japanese to acquire necessary raw materials or to avoid the drastic physical overhauling and rebuilding of their economy which would follow the application of sanctions. . . . No mere alteration of the social or political framework within which the Japa-

[71] Memorandum by Herbert Feis, February 15, 1939. 793.94/14671, *Confidential file*, MS, Department of State.

[72] Memorandum by the Division of Far Eastern Affairs, February 15, 1939. *Ibid.*, MS, Department of State.

[73] Memorandum by Ambassador Grew, Mr. Dooman, and Mr. Coville, Tokyo, March 13, 1939. 793.94/14818½, *Confidential file*, MS, Department of State.

nese economy operates would necessarily solve the basic economic problems that would follow from effective sanctions."[74]

j. *China Anticipates War in Europe and Asks Britain and France to Consult with Her with Regard to a Common Front against Japan*

It is apparent that during the spring of 1939 there was a great deal of talk concerning economic sanctions against Japan. They could be effective, it was widely believed, if several of the great powers took concerted action. On April 4, the Chinese Ambassador (Wellington Koo) handed to M. Léger, Secretary-General of the Ministry for Foreign Affairs (France), a memorandum containing proposals for action against Japan. It proposed, in view of the threat of war in Europe, that there should be "immediate practical consultation between the French, British and Chinese Governments for joint action in the Far East against Japanese aggression and offers to collaborate fully in the preparation of a plan [involving] military and economic measures." Later, the "Soviet Union should be asked to join them, and the United States should be asked to take parallel action." China should agree "to supply all the man-power including military effectives and materials at her disposal and the French and British Governments should send to the Far East all available air and naval forces for the joint prosecution of the war. . . . China, England and France should . . . apply jointly to Japan economic and financial sanctions."[75]

The British Government answered this Chinese proposal by saying

that they would be unwilling to enter into any agreement now with the Chinese Government based on the hypothesis that if Great Britain should become involved in war in Europe, Japan would attempt to seize British possessions in the Far East. The British Government stated further that they had hopes that the presence of the American fleet in the Pacific might prevent a Japanese attack on British possessions in the Far East. In case Japan should attack British possessions in the Far East and in case no assistance from the United States should be forthcoming, the British Government had decided that they could bring no assistance to their possessions in the Far East until the successful conclusion of war in Europe.[76]

[74] Memorandum by Herbert Feis, April 5, 1939. 793.94/14818½, *Confidential file*, MS, Department of State.

[75] Ambassador Bullitt to Secretary Hull, Paris, April 18, 1939. 793.94/14901, *Confidential file*, MS, Department of State.

[76] Ambassador Bullitt to Secretary Hull, Paris, April 18, 1939. 793.94/14902, *Confidential file*, MS, Department of State.

The French Government was not so immediate and so explicit in their answer to China. After waiting a considerable time the French Foreign Office replied that the Chinese proposal was "most interesting but that it seemed premature to give consideration at the present time to entering into any such agreement." The chief of the Far Eastern Division of the French Foreign Office informed Ambassador Bullitt that he thought it would be "unwise to reply to the Chinese proposal by a categorical refusal" and thereby drive Chiang Kai-shek into Japanese arms. It would be expedient to "keep the Chinese 'dangling.' "[77]

k. *Japan Asks Secretary Hull for a Joint Japanese-American Effort to Find Some Formula of Peace for Europe*

While Chinese statesmen were endeavoring to build up a tripartite front against Japanese attacks when World War II broke out in Europe, the Japanese Foreign Office was seeking feverishly for some formula that would preserve the peace of Europe. Japan did not relish her ties with Nazi Germany and she was profoundly worried about intimations that Hitler was seeking some accord with Stalin. Communism had long been recognized as a dire threat to the Japanese position in the Far East. Any understanding between Hitler and Stalin would help undermine Japanese security.

The German Foreign Office tried to divert suspicion from their overtures to Russia by warning the Japanese diplomats about the sinister moves of Britain in the direction of Moscow. On April 27, Lord Halifax told Ambassador Kennedy that he had just assured the Japanese Ambassador that "any talks they had with Russia did not presuppose any mixing up in the Japanese proceedings at all, and that the British were inclined to confine themselves wholly to the situation in Europe provided the Japanese behaved themselves reasonably well."[78]

These crosscurrents in diplomacy led the Japanese Foreign Office to seek an intimate association with the United States in a search for a formula that would scatter the clouds of war that were gathering along the European horizon. It was evident that she could no longer trust any European associates.

The first move in the direction of a Japanese-American accord came on May 16 at a luncheon given in honor of Ambassador Grew "by a Japanese who, while holding no official position, is a close friend and confidant of high officials at the Court." At the conclusion of the lunch-

[77] Ambassador Bullitt to Secretary Hull, Paris, May 3, 1939. 793.94/14946, *Confidential file*, MS, Department of State.

[78] Ambassador Kennedy to Secretary Hull, London, April 27, 1939. 740.00/1192, *Confidential file*, MS, Department of State.

eon, this Japanese host who enjoyed court favor, had a confidential
conversation with Grew. He pointed out that strong pressure was being
exerted by Germany and Italy and "by reactionary groups in Japan,"
towards "entering into some arrangement . . . which would reaffirm
the solidarity among the nations whose policies were opposed by Democratic nations." The group to which the host belonged "had succeeded
in defeating the proposal to conclude the alliance and are now doing
their best to defeat the 'strengthening of the Anti-Comintern Pact.' "
This same group was evidently in favor of a closer association with the
United States. Grew responded to this overture by stating that it should
be "obvious that the restoration of peace and good relations between
Japan and China must be a condition precedent to the restoration of
good relations between Japan and the United States."

On the following day (May 17), Grew attended another luncheon
given in his honor by Foreign Minister Arita. Grew had instructed the
American chargé d'affaires, Eugene H. Dooman, to sound out Arita on
the conversation of the previous day. Dooman found out that Arita
knew all about the talk between Grew and his important Japanese host.
The conversation then passed on to the topic of Japan entering into a
more comprehensive anti-Comintern pact with Germany and Italy.
Arita remarked that while Japan was "very anxious to avoid involvement in the affairs of Europe," yet it could not ignore the fact that "Russia straddled Europe and Asia and that whether Japan liked it or not,
its policies and actions form a bridge by which events in the Far East
and in Europe act and react on each other." He was glad, however, to
give an assurance that the new proposed Anti-Comintern pact "would
contain no military, political or economic clauses."

These diplomatic conversations were resumed on May 23 when Mr.
Dooman had dinner with Baron Hiranuma, the Prime Minister. Hiranuma confided to Dooman his "horror" over the possibility of a second
world war which he feared would "result in the total destruction of
civilization." He believed that dreadful contingency might best be prevented by Japan acting as the middleman between the dictatorships and
the democratic nations. In the Far East he had sought to stabilize the
situation by following the course of "moral diplomacy." The sphere of
this line of policy could be widened. Japan, like the United States, "was
not directly involved in the troubles of Europe, and it was his thought
that these two nations . . . were in a position to exercise a moderating
influence on Europe." Dooman answered this lead by stating that the
principal difficulty "in the way of collaboration was . . . Japan's policies
and actions in China." The Prime Minister observed that he was well
aware of the fact that Americans assumed "that Japan had deliberately

provoked the conflict in China with a view to seizing the more populated and productive parts of the country, but he felt confident that the American Government realized that it had not been the original intention or desire of Japan to do anything more than to protect its rights in North China." If Secretary Hull would insist that a "settlement of the China conflict" should be a condition precedent "to joint American-Japanese efforts to moderate the situation in Europe, . . . the course which he had in mind would have to be abandoned."[79]

The reply of Secretary Hull to these Japanese "feelers for peace" was cool and discouraging. It would be best for Japan to work for peace in Europe by exerting pressure upon the European governments with which it had "special relations." If Japanese statesmen were anxious to "see a true world peace established and maintained," it would be expedient for them to take effective action towards putting an end to existing hostilities in the Far East. In the meantime, the Department of State was "sincerely interested" in the proposed Japanese-American search for a formula for preserving European peace and would be glad to receive further communications in that regard.[80]

Dooman, in Tokyo, thought that this reply was a little unconciliatory, and delayed its presentation. During this interval the President decided to take some definite action against Japan. In this regard he was partly influenced by the advice of Stanley K. Hornbeck who had strongly advised that the Department of State adopt a more positive policy.[81] He was also influenced by the fact that on July 18, Senator Vandenberg had introduced a resolution requesting the President to give the required notice to Japan of the termination of the treaty of 1911 in six months.[82] On July 26, Secretary Hull sent a note to Ambassador Horinouchi informing him that the treaty of February 21, 1911, contained provisions which needed "new consideration." Towards preparing the way for such consideration and with a view to a better "safeguarding and promoting [of] American interests," the American Government decided to give a formal notice that the treaty of 1911 would terminate on January 26, 1940.[83]

As Frederick Moore aptly remarks, this note of July 26 sounded a

---

[79] Eugene H. Dooman, chargé d'affaires at Tokyo, to Secretary Hull, June 7, 1939. 740.00/1812, Confidential file, MS, Department of State. See also, Dooman to Secretary Hull, May 23, 1939. 740.00/1565, Confidential file, MS, Department of State.

[80] Secretary Hull to the Japanese Prime Minister (Hiranuma), July 8, 1939. United States and Japan, 1931–1941, I, 5–8.

[81] Memorandum by Stanley K. Hornbeck, March 8, 1939. 793.94/14922, MS, Department of State.

[82] S. Res. 166.,

[83] Secretary Hull to the Japanese Ambassador (Horinouchi), July 26, 1939. United States and Japan, 1931–1941, II, 189.

definite note of casuistry. The American Government had hitherto "been pretty frank in its dealing with Japan. But this Note seemed to me to lack frankness. The Treaty was being abrogated because of Japanese actions in China for which the American Government could not obtain redress, and because of the widespread American demand upon the Government that we stop supplying the Japanese with war materials. Yet the Note gave as the reason that 'changes may need to be made toward better serving the purposes for which such treaties are concluded.' When the Japanese pointed this out to me I could only reply that in my opinion this was casuistry, that the Department could not fail to know that once the Treaty with Japan were terminated it could not possibly obtain ratification of another from the Senate in its present mood towards Japan. I was annoyed with the Department for resorting to what seemed diplomatic evasion. Had the Japanese done that, we would have put it down as another act of duplicity."[84]

The termination of the treaty of 1911, together with the refusal of Secretary Hull to give any serious consideration to the Japanese proposal for a joint effort to discover some formula that would preserve the peace of Europe, was a clear indication to the Japanese Foreign Office that America was adopting a new policy in the Far East. It would be a more positive one with Japan feeling the brunt of the new pressure. In Tokyo the American chargé d'affaires (Dooman) felt this at once and he advised Secretary Hull that he was "strongly impressed by the primary significance which is generally attached in Japan to the fact that notice of termination of the commercial treaty was given by the United States without prior intimation as there would have been had the action been motivated in large part by economic considerations. The deduction that the motivating considerations were political in character is confirmed by noting American press and other popular reaction to the notice of termination."[85]

Few Americans realized that through hostile press comments a climate of opinion was being created that was so hostile to Japan that a war psychosis would eventually develop. Hull's casuistry in the note of July 26 helped to produce in Japan a feeling that America had begun to move down the road to war under the banner of mendacity. That banner came more and more to the front as the Roosevelt Administration moved towards the tragedy of Pearl Harbor.

[84] Frederick Moore, *With Japan's Leaders* (New York, 1942), pp. 111–13.

[85] E. H. Dooman to Secretary Hull, Tokyo, August 3, 1939. *Hearings Before the Joint Committee on the Investigation of the Pearl Harbor Attack* (Washington, 1946), XX, 4196–97.

XXII

Europe Moves towards War

WITH RUSSIA pushing China into conflict in the Far East it was soon evident to some observers that no armistice was in sight. If Chiang Kai-shek grew tired of pulling hot Soviet chestnuts out of the fires of war he would at once be smeared as a traitor to Chinese unity and communist agents throughout eastern Asia would clamor for his exile or execution. Peace would have to bear a communist tag.

a. *Chamberlain Makes a Momentous Pledge to Poland*

While Stalin was blowing upon the embers of war in the Far East, Hitler began to implement plans for expansion that would soon lead to conflict in Europe. As early as October 24, 1938, Ribbentrop suggested to Lipski, the Polish Ambassador in Berlin, that the Polish Government should agree to a "reunion of Danzig with the Reich," and should also consent to the building of "an extra-territorial motor road and railway line across Pomorze." In return Poland would be assured the "retention of railway and economic facilities" in Danzig, and Germany would guarantee the Polish-German frontiers. Lipski was not enthusiastic about these proposals,[1] and the Polish Foreign Office returned a polite negative.[2]

Further conversations were held on November 19 when Lipski frankly informed Ribbentrop with disturbing candor that "any tendency to incorporate the Free City [of Danzig] in the Reich must inevitably lead to conflict." The Foreign Minister promptly gave assurances, "in a very friendly tone," that he felt so close to Poland that he did not wish to carry on relations with Lipski in a "formal diplomatic manner" but on a friendly plane, "frankly and openly." After this cordial gesture he stressed his anxiety to find some solution of the Danzig problem that would be mutually satisfactory. With regard to a motor road across the Corridor, Lipski thought it might "be possible" to arrive at some understanding.[3]

The next scene in this drama of Danzig was staged at Berchtesgaden. Hitler was not inclined to accept the negative answer of Beck. As a

[1] M. Lipski to Foreign Minister Beck, Berlin, October 25, 1938. *Polish White Book* (London, 1939), pp. 47–48; *Documents on the Events Preceding the Outbreak of the War. German White Book* (New York, 1940), pp. 199–201.

[2] M. Beck to M. Lipski, October 31, 1938. *Polish White Book,* pp. 48–50.

[3] M. Lipski to Foreign Minister Beck, Berlin, November 19, 1938. *Ibid.,* pp. 50–52.

realist in world politics he knew very well that Poland did not have the
military strength to resist German demands and he was certain that no
power or combination of powers could lend Poland sufficient assistance
to repel a German attack upon Warsaw. But Hitler did not wish war
with Poland. He could use her as a bulwark to neutralize any Russian
threat to a vastly expanded Third Reich or perhaps as an ally in future
aggressive actions against the Soviet Union. If Poland would accept
the role of chief satellite in the Nazi orbit her expansion was guaranteed. Germany and Poland could dominate Europe and Hitler's word
would be law from Warsaw to Lisbon.

Beck, however, was not greatly attracted by the political possibilities
that lay along the path of German-Polish co-operation. He preferred
to nurse the hope of continued Polish independence in the face of overwhelming German strength. At the greatest cross roads in all history he
rejected a ride in the German war machine along a path that promised
Poland power and plunder as a satellite state. Instead, he and the Polish
Cabinet followed the counsel of Chamberlain and chose the road that
led to war with Germany and the consequent destruction of the Polish
State. The British-Polish understanding in the spring of 1939 led Hitler to turn to Stalin in search of the alliance that was an incitement to
a conflict that eventually brought Red domination over a beaten and
dismembered Poland. Polish diplomacy in 1938–1939 was a design for
disaster.

In the early days of 1939, Hitler believed that Beck was so well
versed in the principles of *Realpolitik* that he would be glad to go hand
in hand with the Nazi leaders in a joint search for plunder that was
weakly guarded by the broken-down states of Europe. For this chance
to hunt with Hitler he would have to pay a definite price. On January 5,
1939, at Berchtesgaden, this matter was bluntly placed before Beck.
With reference to the questions of Danzig and the Corridor it was
necessary to get "out of the old grooves and seek a solution on completely novel lines." This would mean a solution whereby "Danzig would
return to Germany politically, but would remain with Poland economically." As for the Corridor, a connection "with East Prussia was as vital
a matter for the Reich as the connection with the sea was for Poland."
In return for these concessions Germany would give Poland a "definite
guarantee of her frontiers . . . including the boundaries of the Corridor." Beck had no glib answer for these proposals. The Danzig question was an "extraordinarily difficult" one, "but he was quite ready to
think the matter over."[4]

4 Conversation between Hitler and Beck at Berchtesgaden, January 5, 1939. *German White Book*, pp. 205–7.

On January 6 at Munich, Ribbentrop proposed and Beck once more discussed the Danzig and Corridor questions. Ribbentrop proposed the "reunion of Danzig with Germany," and in return all Polish economic interests in that territory would be "guaranteed in the most generous manner." If Poland would consent to an "extra-territorial motor-road and railway across the Corridor," Germany would then "guarantee the Corridor and all Poland's present possessions." Beck remained cool to these proposals and gloomily confided to von Ribbentrop that he saw "no possibility whatever of agreement" on these matters.[5]

Further conversations between Beck and Ribbentrop in Warsaw on January 25–27 led to no important results.[6] In March 1939, Ribbentrop began to lose patience with Poland. On March 21 he rehearsed the Danzig and Corridor questions with Ambassador Lipski and remarked that the Führer was "increasingly surprised at the Polish attitude" with regard to them. He believed that a further attempt should be made to "put German-Polish policy on the right track," and he hoped that Beck would soon visit Berlin for the purpose of seeking a solution of problems that demanded a speedy solution. With particular reference to the Corridor the Führer recognized the "justice of the Polish demand for free access to the sea," and was willing "to renounce possession of the Corridor for once and for all."[7]

It is apparent that Hitler thought he was going very far in his offers to Poland. The truculent tone so evident in his relations with Austria and Czechoslovakia was missing in his overtures to the Polish Foreign Office. But Beck was prompt in rejecting these conciliatory gestures. Poland could not agree to any extraterritorial road across the Corridor. With regard to Danzig the Polish Government thought it might be possible to solve that question by a "joint Polish-German guarantee" of the continued status of a "free city."[8]

In taking this determined stand against concessions to Germany, Beck was embarking upon a desperate gamble which he eventually lost. He had decided to attempt to balance Britain against Germany even though he was uncertain as to the course the British Government might follow. He aimed to pay a visit to London early in April, but he was apprehensive lest Britain might try "to capitalize his visit in potential ne-

---

[5] Conversation between Ribbentrop and Beck, Munich, January 6, 1939. *German White Book*, pp. 207–9; *Polish White Book*, p. 54.

[6] Conversations between Ribbentrop and Beck, Warsaw, January 25–27, 1939. *Polish White Book*, p. 56.

[7] Conversation between Ribbentrop and Ambassador Lipski, Berlin, March 21, 1939. *German White Book*, pp. 210–12.

[8] Foreign Minister Beck to Ambassador Lipski, Warsaw, March 25, 1939. *Polish White Book*, pp. 64–66.

gotiations with Berlin" rather than endeavor to work out a basis for "constructive collaboration" with Poland.[9]

But Chamberlain had no intention of turning to Hitler. He suddenly produced a formula whereby four important powers—Britain, France, Poland, and Russia—would sign a declaration that they "would act together in the event of further signs of German aggressive ambitions."[10] In a dispatch to Secretary Hull, Ambassador Bullitt described the fate of this proposal:

I discussed the situation with Léger this morning. With regard to the British proposal, France, of course, accepted [it] and the Soviet Union accepted unconditionally. The key to the situation, however, is Poland. Yesterday morning it had been Chamberlain's opinion that the Poles would not accept. The Poles had asked the British Government a large number of questions with regard to the exact aid which Great Britain would bring to Poland in case of a German attack. . . . Léger went on to say that in his opinion Beck would not dare to reject flatly the British proposal because the responsibility would be terrible if . . . later Germany should attack Poland.[11]

Beck did reject this British proposal, but he was careful to explain that he did so because he feared that it would not be "adequate" to meet the existing emergency. He greatly preferred a bilateral agreement between Britain and Poland.[12] Chamberlain gave this suggestion prompt consideration and on March 27 the British Foreign Office informed Beck that if the Poles "would defend themselves if they are attacked," Britain would make a statement pledging "all her forces and resources" to their assistance. But despite these bold words, Britain could not possibly send to the Corridor any effective fighting forces in case Germany launched an attack upon Poland. On March 27, Lord Halifax told Ambassador Kennedy that even in the face of possible conflict with Germany no move would be made down the road to conscription. The Chamberlain Government realized that Britain did not have the military equipment to arm prospective conscripts and they also feared that the trade unions were "prepared to upset the industrial program" if there was any serious attempt "to force conscription."[13]

[9] Ambassador Biddle to Secretary Hull, Warsaw, March 18, 1939. 740.00/631, *Confidential file,* MS, Department of State.

[10] Keith Feiling, *The Life of Neville Chamberlain* (New York, 1946), pp. 402–3.

[11] Ambassador Bullitt to Secretary Hull, Paris, March 24, 1939. 740.00/676, MS, Department of State.

[12] Beck to Count Raczynski, Warsaw, March 23, 1939. *Polish White Book,* pp. 70–71.

[13] Ambassador Kennedy to Secretary Hull, London, March 27, 1939. 740.00/690, *Confidential file,* MS, Department of State. Despite this lack of military preparedness, many Britishers talked very boldly about what Britain could do in the event of war with Germany. In August 1938 the British military mission in Portugal made some

Notwithstanding this impasse as far as military preparedness was concerned, Chamberlain went ahead and on March 31 announced in the House of Commons that if any action were taken in Europe that "clearly threatened Polish independence, and which the Polish Government accordingly considered it vital to resist with their national forces," His Majesty's Government would feel "bound at once to lend the Polish Government all support in their power."[14]

When one keeps in mind the fact that the British Government could not put one soldier in the Polish Corridor in the event of war between Poland and Germany, the dubious quality of this Chamberlain assurance is clearly evident. The inevitable question then arises: Why did Beck seek so anxiously for a promise of aid that was of no real value? By turning his back upon Hitler he invited a swift destruction that no European power could avert. Perhaps he felt that Hitler was merely bluffing and therefore it would be safe for him to assume the role of a Polish Ajax boldly defying the Nazi lightning!

Daladier seemed to share this opinion because he confided to Ambassador Bullitt that he was "especially delighted by the strong and courageous stand the Poles had taken."[15] But he was deeply concerned by the fact that Britain was not pushing a program of conscription. If a European war broke out Britain would be forced to play a minor role "except on the sea." France, therefore, would have to bear a burden that "would be terrible." In the back of Daladier's mind there lingered the suspicion that Poland would be a weak ally. Although Beck would probably sign some type of alliance with Britain during his visit to London, there was always the possibility that the "Poles would find one excuse or another to wriggle out of their obligations to fight on the side of France and England."[16]

Chamberlain did not have this distrust of Poland and he continued to hope that war was around such a distant corner that he would not have to worry about conscription for a long time. He was somewhat im-

interesting comments which may have impressed the Poles. Lieutenant Chamberlain was particularly verbose: "We know that Germany and Italy are bluffing. Together with the younger officers of our staff I am of the opinion that we should start war immediately." In this war he was certain that Britain could count upon the "close cooperation of the United States." In this connection, Commander Gade, United States naval attaché at Lisbon, made a pertinent observation: "At present the possibilities for speedy aid to Great Britain and France are being studied in America. One must conclude that help shall not be sent as in the World War, only after one year, . . . but in the course of seven to ten days." Letter from the Polish General Staff in Warsaw to the Foreign Minister, August 8, 1939. *German White Paper*, pp. 14–16.

[14] Feiling, *op. cit.*, p. 403.

[15] Ambassador Bullitt to Secretary Hull, Paris, March 31, 1939. 740.00/715, *Confidential file*, MS, Department of State.

[16] Ambassador Bullitt to Secretary Hull, Paris, April 3, 1939. 740.00/735, *Confidential file*, MS, Department of State.

pressed by a statement Hitler had made to him at Godesberg: "I have
won more with words than I have with bayonets." To Ambassador
Kennedy this remark seemed to indicate that Chamberlain, and the
English people generally, were indulging in wishful thinking. But
Chamberlain was enough of a realist to admit that Hitler was "definitely aware that the longer he permits England and France to arm the
less likely he is to win with one decisive blow."[17]

The importance of an early blow against Britain was emphasized in
the German press. The British Embassy in Berlin warned Lord Halifax
that these press comments reflected accurately the growing hostility of
Hitler to the Chamberlain policy of "encirclement." Halifax, in turn,
informed President Roosevelt that the British fleet might at any moment be the object of a Nazi "lightning attack."[18]

Despite Hitler's hatred of the British policy of encirclement, Chamberlain went ahead and on April 6 he had the Foreign Office issue a
statement that Britain and Poland were "prepared to enter into an agreement of a permanent character" that would be reciprocal in its application. Until the signature of this permanent agreement, Poland was
ready to give an assurance to Britain that it would render assistance to
His Majesty's Government under the same conditions as those contained in the British assurance of March 31.[19] Beck had now pushed
Poland far down the road to war and national destruction. Such a policy
pointed directly to disaster.

b. *Lord Halifax Tries to "Work Something Out" with the Duce*

While Chamberlain was moving towards closer relations with Poland
he was also endeavoring to drive a wedge between Hitler and Mussolini. On March 20 he wrote a personal letter to the Duce in which he
stressed the dangers that attended Hitler's plans for German expansion.
If Italy allied herself with the Western democracies the peace of Europe
would be preserved and definite advantages would be secured. Ambassador Kennedy learned of this letter from Lord Halifax who endeavored to keep him abreast of the more important aspects of British policy.
When Kennedy inquired if Britain would be inclined to "pay a big
price" for Italian co-operation, Halifax replied that he "thought so but
would not want to deliver until he saw Mussolini's performance."[20]

17 Ambassador Kennedy to Secretary Hull, London, April 4, 1939. 740.00/736,
Confidential file, MS, Department of State.
18 Lord Halifax to President Roosevelt, London, April 5, 1939. 740.00/887½,
Confidential file, MS, Department of State.
19 Polish-British communiqué, April 6, 1939. *Polish White Book*, p. 74.
20 Ambassador Kennedy to Secretary Hull, London, March 20, 1939. 740.00/638,
Confidential file, MS, Department of State.

Joseph Davies, American Ambassador in Brussels, agreed with Chamberlain in thinking that the moment was ripe for a deal with Mussolini. He greatly feared that the peace of Europe was "tottering." It was important, therefore, for the President to make some move to stave off a war. He believed that Mussolini was the key figure in Europe. It was essential for the Duce to realize that Italy's "present and future interests" were tied closely to the Western democracies. If Europe should become involved in a major conflict the dictatorships were bound to lose. The Duce should "go slow and not precipitate a crisis now by demands which French pride cannot accept."[21]

While President Roosevelt was giving careful consideration to these suggestions from Davies, Lord Halifax still hoped that he would be able to "work something out" with Mussolini.[22] But Chamberlain began to doubt that his Foreign Secretary could do much with the Duce. He remarked to Kennedy that Mussolini, as a dictator, had to "keep on moving." His next adventure might be in Albania. When Kennedy inquired what action the British Government would take if the Duce moved in that direction, Chamberlain glumly muttered that it would be a "terrible calamity as far as England is concerned because he would not want to get into a war over Albania."[23]

c. *Mussolini Moves into Albania*

The terrible calamity feared by Chamberlain was soon precipitated by Mussolini. Italian troops marched into Albania and had no trouble in taking over the entire country. This move had been planned for many months, and the *Ciano Diaries* are filled with references to the probable invasion of that country. The Duce's desire to acquire Albania was greatly strengthened by Germany's absorption of Czechoslovakia. The reasons presented by Germany for this bold action were so specious that Ciano was disgusted with their transparent character: "Such pretexts may be good for Goebbels propaganda, but they should not use them when talking with us." To Mussolini it seemed imperative that Italy should take Albania as a counterbalance to German acquisitions.[24]

Ciano was deeply angered by the cavalier attitude assumed by Hitler in conveying to the Duce the news of the seizure of Czechoslovakia. To

[21] Ambassador Davies to Secretary Hull, Brussels, March 21, 1939. 740.00/646, *Confidential file*, MS, Department of State.

[22] Ambassador Kennedy to Secretary Hull, London, March 27, 1939. 740.00/690, *Confidential file*, MS, Department of State.

[23] Ambassador Kennedy to Secretary Hull, London, April 4, 1939. 740.00/736, *Confidential file*, MS, Department of State.

[24] *The Ciano Diaries, 1939–1943*, ed. Hugh Gibson (Garden City, 1947), March 15, 1939, pp. 42–43.

his diary he confided the belief that the Führer was "unfaithful and treacherous." He then noted that the King had denounced the Germans as "rascals and beggars," while Marshal Balbo had vehemently expressed his disgust at the Duce's acquiescent attitude. At the close of one of Mussolini's ardent speeches in favor of collaboration with Germany, Balbo had acidly remarked: "You are shining Germany's boots." But the Duce continued to cling to Hitler and addressed to his critics the querulous comment: "We can't be political whores."[25]

King Zog of Albania thought this was a colossal understatement when he learned on April 7 that Italian troops were attacking Durazzo. On the following day Tiranë was occupied by the Duce's military forces and the fighting was over. On April 16 an Albanian delegation paid a visit to Rome to offer the crown to the King of Italy. Ciano noted that the leader of this delegation (Verlaci) appeared very "depressed" and delivered his speech with a "tired air" that betrayed no enthusiasm.[26] The requirements for a Roman holiday were very exhausting.

d. *American Reaction to the Seizure of Albania*

American reaction to Italian absorption of Albania was immediate and hostile. The old friendship that had marked Italian-American relations during the early years of the Mussolini regime had been shattered by the Duce's alignment with Hitler. In 1937 the Italian Government had been greatly disappointed at the tardiness which attended the negotiations for a new treaty of friendship, commerce, and navigation between the two countries, and efforts had been made to push the Department of State along the path to an early conclusion of the pact.[27] Ambassador Philipps was apprehensive that this continued American delay would push Italy firmly into the eager arms of Hitler, but Secretary Hull insisted that it was "unwise to bind our hands" by entering into a most-favored-nation treaty with Italy "at least for the present." It would be best to let matters "hang fire" and await a clarification of the international situation. A policy of delay should be continued and American replies to Italian notes should be "more deliberate than usual."[28]

This developing coolness between Italy and the United States led Ambassador Kennedy to leave London for a brief visit to Rome. He discovered that the Countess Ciano deprecated the disappearance of cor-

---

[25] *Ibid.*, March 19–21, 1939, pp. 48–50.

[26] *Ibid.*, April 16, 1939, pp. 66–67.

[27] Ambassador Phillips to Secretary Hull, Rome, February 8, May 14, June 8, June 19, 1937. 711.652/85–102, MS, Department of State.

[28] Francis B. Sayre to Ambassador Phillips, November 19, 1937. 711.652/119, MS, Department of State.

diality that had marked the relations between the two countries at the beginning of the Mussolini regime. She expressed the opinion that the policy of the democracies had made it necessary for her father to "play along with Hitler for his own protection."

Kennedy had some furtive admiration for Countess Ciano but his dispatches express only contempt for her flirtatious husband. After meeting Ciano at a tea he sent to Secretary Hull one of his most pungent dispatches:

I also met Ciano. . . . I have no idea how able he is in his office, but I have never met a more pompous ass in my life. He spent most of his time rushing girls into a corner for conversation, and at the dinner he would not talk seriously for five minutes for fear that the two or three girls who were invited in order to get him to come, might get out of sight. . . . I came away with the belief that we would accomplish much more by sending a dozen beautiful chorus girls to Rome than a flock of diplomats and a fleet of airplanes. . . . The President's speeches drive them absolutely crazy. . . . Every time the President says anything, nobody in the Cabinet or Government in Rome is fit to talk with for the rest of the day.[29]

After the Department of State received this dispatch, Secretary Hull and President Roosevelt seemed to take a definite delight in making speeches or issuing statements that would keep Mussolini and his Cabinet in a state of high nervous excitement. On April 8, Hull denounced the Italian invasion of Albania as an "additional threat to the peace of the world,"[30] while, on the same day, at Warm Springs, the President voiced the opinion that the continued independence of small nations everywhere had a definite bearing upon American safety and prosperity.[31]

On Easter Sunday (April 9), as he was leaving Warm Springs for Washington, the President turned to the small crowd that had pressed close to his private car and significantly remarked: "I'll be back in the fall if we don't have a war."[32] To Walter Lippmann this statement seemed a plain intimation to Hitler and Mussolini that the United States would not remain indifferent if the dictators kept undermining the independence of small nations.[33]

When the President reached Washington on April 10 he read a confidential dispatch from Ambassador Bullitt which contained strong

[29] Ambassador Kennedy to Secretary Hull, London, March 17, 1939. 865.00/1805, *Confidential file,* MS, Department of State.

[30] *Peace and War: United States Foreign Policy, 1931–1941* (Washington, 1943), p. 455.

[31] *New York Times,* April 9, 1939.

[32] *Ibid.,* April 10, 1939.

[33] *New York Herald-Tribune,* April 14, 15, 1939.

hints of impending war: "I talked with Bonnet briefly tonight. He asked me to inform my Government that 'it was five minutes before twelve.' There might be war at any moment."[34] Two days later, Bullitt talked with Premier Daladier who believed that Hitler and Mussolini would probably "make war within the next week or two. . . . He was utterly unable to understand the reasons which at this moment led Chamberlain to be optimistic. He felt that Chamberlain was either misled or criminally weak."[35]

While Daladier was talking war to Bullitt, Lord Halifax was talking peace to Kennedy. On April 11, Halifax had a long conversation with Kennedy and appeared "strangely optimistic." He expressed the opinion that he did "not expect war. He said he hesitates always to tell me this because he feels I think he is 'burying his head in the sand' and he admits that up to date he has been a little bit wrong." This optimism Kennedy ascribed in part to reassurances from the Duce: "Mussolini's attitude as expressed to the Government over the Albanian matter has not increased their concern. It has rather made them feel that the situation is not as hopeless as everybody else seems to think it is."[36]

It was obvious to Bullitt that the British Foreign Office was being led astray by rose-colored reports from Lord Perth, the British Ambassador in Rome. Bonnet told Bullitt that he had learned from François-Poncet, the French Ambassador in Rome, that Mussolini had recently sent "a warm personal message to Chamberlain assuring him that he desired the most friendly relations with England and that he intended to respect fully the Anglo-Italian pact with regard to the Mediterranean." Lord Perth had further informed François-Poncet that Ciano "had promised him that Italy positively would not attack Greece." He had also promised Perth that "the Italian troops would be withdrawn from Spain immediately after the victory parade in Madrid on May 2." To Bullitt these statements of Lord Perth proved him to be "just as great an ass as he had been all his life and that Mussolini was playing the British for 'suckers.' " The British Ambassador in Paris agreed that Bullitt's characterization of Perth was entirely just.[37]

On the basis of this false hope that Mussolini was really on the side of the democracies, Chamberlain felt strong enough to develop his policy of reassurance to nations threatened by German aggression. On April 13, he made another one of his momentous announcements. The

[34] Ambassador Bullitt to Secretary Hull, Paris, April 9, 1939. 740.00/754, *Confidential file,* MS, Department of State.

[35] Ambassador Bullitt to Secretary Hull, Paris, April 11, 1939. 740.00/772, *Confidential file,* MS, Department of State.

[36] Ambassador Kennedy to Secretary Hull, London, April 11, 1939. 740.00/774, *Confidential file,* MS, Department of State.

[37] Ambassador Bullitt to Secretary Hull, Paris, April 12, 1939. 740.00/787, *Confidential file,* MS, Department of State.

House of Commons was informed that any action that menaced the independence of either Greece or Romania would cause the British Government to extend to those countries all the assistance within its power.[38]

While Chamberlain was busily engaged in extending promises of aid that he could not possibly deliver, Hitler was preparing for war. On April 12 the chief of the German General Staff had a talk with the American chargé d'affaires in Berlin. He was not backward in intimating that "unless fewer obstacles were placed in the way of Germany's eastern expansion it would be necessary for Hitler to end the opposition . . . in the West."[39]

With this feeling of war in the European atmosphere, President Roosevelt made an address on April 14 to the Governing Board of the Pan-American Union which everyone realized was really beamed at European dictators. He challenged Hitler's complaint of encirclement by stating that there was "no such thing as encircling . . . any peaceful nation by other peaceful nations." And then as a direct thrust at Nazi and Fascist methods of expansion, he asked a question that was topped with a sharp barb: "Do we really have to assume that nations can find no better methods of realizing their destinies than those which were used by the Huns and Vandals 1500 years ago?"[40]

As a postscript to this critical and provocative address, he sent by cable an appeal to Hitler and Mussolini requesting them to make no further moves that might lead to a European war. He also asked them to give assurances that their armed forces would "not attack or invade" for a period of at least ten years the territory or possessions of a long list of nations. It should be clear, even to dictators, that "international problems" could best be solved "at the council table."[41] At this point he must have pushed his tongue hard upon his cheek because he was well aware of the fact that none of the European nations that had profited by the Treaty of Versailles was willing to give up one crumb of the spoils of war. The injustices of that treaty could be rectified only through war.

The British and French governments knew this was true and their fears of eventual conflict made them welcome the President's intervention in the affairs of Europe. Ambassador Kennedy sent word of Chamberlain's "great appreciation" of the message from the White House, but he noted that the Prime Minister had "failed more in the past week than he has in the past year. He walks like an old man and yes-

[38] *Parliamentary Debates,* House of Commons, April 13, 1939, CCCXLVI, 13.

[39] Chargé d'Affaires Geist to Secretary Hull, April 13, 1939. 740.00/794, *Confidential file,* MS, Department of State.

[40] Department of State, *Press Release,* April 15, 1939, XX, 294–96.

[41] *Peace and War,* pp. 455–58.

terday talked like one."[42] He was beginning to realize the complete failure of his policy.

In France, Daladier and Bonnet were outspoken in their praise of the President's challenge to the dictators. Daladier assured Ambassador Bullitt that he regarded the message as a "historic act of the first importance," and then he remarked with reference to the President: "He is the last of the Mohicans."[43] The symbolism was ominous. Would the Americans, like the Mohicans, be a vanishing race because of the impact of devastating wars?

e. The Dictators' Reply to the President's Criticism

The President's denunciation of the dictators as modern "Huns and Vandals" was bound to evoke a bitter reply. In order to raise the pitch of their anger and make their replies so extreme in language that the American public would become increasingly war-minded, the President held a press conference on April 15 and took advantage of his gifts as a showman to impress his audience with the manner in which he had verbally spanked Hitler and Mussolini.[44]

Mussolini made an indirect reply on April 20 at a meeting of influential Fascists who had assembled to discuss the holding of a World's Fair in Rome in 1942. The fact that such a fair was being planned was a clear demonstration, according to the Duce, of his pacific purposes. With specific reference to the President's message he contemptuously remarked that he was not greatly impressed "by Messiah-like" communications.[45]

Hitler's reply was a more formidable affair. On April 28 he delivered an address to the Reichstag during which he played the dual role of Führer and court jester. The words he directed to European listeners carried a covert menace. The nonaggression pact with Poland had been terminated by Polish adherence to the encirclement policy sponsored by Britain and France. This same policy carried such a strong note of hostility towards Germany that it had automatically invalidated the Anglo-German Naval Pact of 1935 and the consultative agreement Hitler had concluded with Chamberlain at Munich.

After this defiant introduction, Hitler answered President Roosevelt's message in a series of questions and answers. The answers were couched in a serio-comic style that revealed the bright glow of anger

[42] Ambassador Kennedy to Secretary Hull, London, April 17, 1939. 740.00/908, Confidential file, MS, Department of State.

[43] Ambassador Bullitt to Secretary Hull, Paris, April 15, 1939. 740.00/820–823, Confidential file, MS, Department of State.

[44] The Public Papers and Addresses of Franklin D. Roosevelt, ed. Samuel I. Rosenman (New York, 1938), pp. 205–17.

[45] New York Times, April 21, 1939.

beneath the thin fabric of forced humor.[46] He rejected any thought of acceptance of the President's proposals and in Washington the heralds of war began to blow a muted message that troubled the anxious ears of millions of Americans. Senator Borah believed that Hitler had closed the door on further discussions of peace proposals, and Senator Nye expressed the opinion that the President had invited "at least in part" the sharp words of the Führer.[47] There was little doubt that the provocative words of the President's message had provided additional tinder that awaited the sparks of war.

f. The Role of Russia Becomes Increasingly Important

As Chamberlain's dreams of co-operation with Hitler and Mussolini began to fade he slowly turned in the direction of another dictator, Joseph Stalin. In the third week in March he had devised a four-power formula that might stop Hitler, but the Polish Government had objected to any association with Russia. Chamberlain did not blame the Poles for their suspicious attitude because he himself had long cherished a "most profound distrust of Russia."[48] The British Foreign Office shared this viewpoint and was ready to "relegate Russia to a second line of defence not only because of the practical difficulties of including her in any agreement reached with the Poles but also because they have little confidence in Russia's reliability."[49]

Lord Halifax, however, cautiously kept the line to Moscow open, and on April 11, he had a conference with Maisky, the Soviet Ambassador in London. He found Maisky "cynical about the whole situation and rather of the opinion that the fat is in the fire as far as everybody is concerned with Russia sitting on the side lines." This candid cynicism caused Halifax "completely to distrust" Maisky and led him to refrain from telling the ambassador anything of importance for fear that it might be passed on to possible enemies.[50]

French officials felt much the same way. Bonnet informed Bullitt that the Soviet Government had "replied evasively" to French proposals for military conversations between French and Russian staff officers. He found the Russians were "much stronger in their speeches and statements than they were when it came to negotiation."[51] But Bonnet had persisted in asking the Russians for a "unilateral guarantee" of Ro-

[46] *Ibid.*, April 29, 1939.
[47] *Ibid.*, April 29, 1939.
[48] Feiling, *op. cit.*, p. 403.
[49] Ambassador Kennedy to Secretary Hull, London, March 28, 1939. 740.00/696, *Confidential file*, MS, Department of State.
[50] Ambassador Kennedy to Secretary Hull, London, April 11, 1939. 740.00/774, *Confidential file*, MS, Department of State.
[51] Ambassador Bullitt to Secretary Hull, Paris, April 12, 1939. 740.00/787, *Confidential file*, MS, Department of State.

manian frontiers in the event of German aggression against that country. He had also suggested that the Soviet Union seriously consider the negotiation of an "agreement with France for immediate assistance in case of war similar to the Anglo-Polish Agreement."[52]

It is evident that despite the distrust that both Britain and France had for Russia, they still tried to extract from the Russian Foreign Office some promises of aid if Hitler made another step along the road to German expansion. On April 15, Sir William Seeds, at Moscow, presented to Litvinov a suggestion that his government, following British and French action, should make upon its own initiative a public declaration that "in the event of any act of aggression against any neighboring State to the Soviet Union which that State were to resist, the assistance of the Soviet Government would be given, if the desire for it were expressed."[53]

Bonnet told Bullitt that the Soviet Government had rejected this British proposal and had suggested instead that "Great Britain, the Soviet Union and France should conclude accords for immediate military support in case of aggression similar to the pact recently concluded between Great Britain and Poland."[54] Apparently the Russian proposals also included suggestions that British assistance to Poland should be restricted to the contingency of German aggression and that any Polish-Romanian alliance should apply to *all* States and not merely to Russia. According to the Polish Ambassador at Moscow, Grzbowski, the terms of the Russian proposals included permission for Soviet troops to enter Poland by northern and southern routes and for a declaration by Britain that her guarantee of Poland applied only to her *western* frontier.[55] Jules Lukasiewicz, Polish Ambassador at Paris, adds that Russia also wished a free hand in the Baltic states and a Polish-Russian treaty with far-reaching implications.[56]

But even though Polish officials knew of these Russian hopes to control her future, they continued to reject any German proposal for an understanding. On March 26, Ribbentrop once more pressed upon Ambassador Lipski an agreement that would include the "reunion of Danzig with the Reich and the construction of an extra-territorial motor-road and railway connection between the Reich and East Prussia." Lipski curtly countered with the remark that "any further pursu-

52 Ambassador Bullitt to Secretary Hull, Paris, April 15, 1939. 740.00/821, *Confidential file*, MS, Department of State.

53 G. Gafencu, *Derniers Jours de l'Europe* (Paris, 1946), p. 140.

54 Ambassador Bullitt to Secretary Hull, April 19, 1939. 740.00/1001, *Confidential file*, MS, Department of State.

55 R. Umiatowski, *Russia and the Polish Republic, 1918–1941* (London, 1945), p. 130.

56 Max Beloff, *The Foreign Policy of Soviet Russia, 1929–1941* (New York, 1949), II, 235.

ance of these German plans . . . meant war with Poland."[57] By May 2 the Polish press had proceeded to the point where a demand was made that "Danzig become Polish."[58] With Warsaw expressing a rising sentiment of Polish nationalism there was little prospect for a German-Polish agreement.

g. *Pope Pius XII Makes a Plea for Peace*

As the clouds of misunderstanding gathered along the German-Polish frontier, Pope Pius XII made an important move in the direction of peace. On May 5 the Papal Nuncio in Paris called on Foreign Minister Bonnet to inform him that the Pope had decided to summon "immediately a peace conference to consist of representatives of France, Italy, Germany, Great Britain and Poland." Bonnet conveyed this news to Daladier who promptly advised the Nuncio that France "would not participate in any conference held under the threat of German guns." Such a conference would be "foredoomed to failure." When the Nuncio remarked that it was "too late to change this project," Daladier said he regretted this fact because His Holiness "would destroy by such action the immense influence in the world which had been obtained for the Church by the last Pope." It would be "clear to everyone that the Pope would be engaged merely in pulling Italian chestnuts out of the fire and preparing a new Munich."

These words of warning made a deep impression upon the Nuncio who later returned to see Daladier and assured him that the decision of the Pope with regard to the proposed conference was "not irrevocable and the opinion of the French Government would have great weight in the Papal decision."[59]

On May 8, Bonnet told Bullitt that he had learned that the Pope had information which he regarded "as positive that Hitler would attack Poland in the near future. This was the reason why he wished to call a conference of the leading European powers in order to seek a formula of peace." The Nuncio then assured Bonnet that His Holiness had "not consulted Mussolini nor had he been inspired by Mussolini."[60]

On the following day Bullitt talked with Alexis Léger, the Secretary-General of the French Foreign Office, who said that he had discussed with Bonnet and Daladier the Pope's proposal for a conference of powers with regard to peace and it had been decided to reject it. If such a

---

[57] Conversation between Ribbentrop and Ambassador Lipski, March 26, 1939. *German White Book*, pp. 214–15.

[58] German chargé d'affaires in Warsaw to the Foreign Office, May 2, 1939. *Ibid.*, pp. 229–30.

[59] Ambassador Bullitt to Secretary Hull, Paris, May 6, 1939. 740.00/1355, *Confidential file*, MS, Department of State.

[60] Ambassador Bullitt to Secretary Hull, Paris, May 8, 1939. 740.00/1370, *Confidential file*, MS, Department of State.

conference were held "both France and Poland would be expected to make concessions to Germany and Italy with the Pope as arbitrator and Great Britain as super-arbitrator." The French Government held to the belief that any establishment of "good relations between France and Italy could be achieved only by direct negotiations." The Foreign Office was certain that Poland "would not accept the arbitration of any foreign Power in the matter of Germany's demands." At this point Léger expressed the suspicion of Britain that seemed always to lie at the back of French minds. He believed that the British Government had "sensed that at such a conference German demands for British colonies might be brought up. Halifax therefore had replied to the Papal Nuncio in London that he believed the French Government would not accept such a conference and that in consequence, Great Britain would not favor it." Halifax had then made a "counterproposal which showed clearly that once all question of discussions of British colonies should be eliminated, Great Britain would be very glad to arbitrate away the possessions and interests of her associates, France and Poland." Léger informed Bullitt that he was then preparing the draft of a note to Britain saying that Halifax's proposal would be "just as inacceptable to the French Government as the Pope's proposal."[61]

From Warsaw came word that the Papal Nuncio in that city had broached the matter of a five-power conference to the Polish Foreign Office. Beck was fearful that such a conference would deal mainly with French concessions to Italy and would then turn to the matter of Polish concessions to Germany. Poland did not wish to participate in a second Munich conference in which she would be one of the chief victims.[62] It was the opinion in Warsaw that the Papal proposal could be traced "indirectly to Mussolini."[63]

On May 9 the Papal Secretary of State, Maglione, confided to the French Ambassador to the Vatican that "in view of the replies the Pope had received which seemed to indicate that there was no immediate danger of war, the Pope had decided to withdraw his suggestion." Bonnet expressed to Bullitt his great relief at "this conclusion of the affair as he considered it most important not to offend the Pope, and he felt that the Pope had not had his feelings hurt in any way."[64] To Bonnet the ceremonies of diplomacy were more important than the substance.

61 Ambassador Bullitt to Secretary Hull, Paris, May 9, 1939. 740.00/1404, *Confidential file,* MS, Department of State.

62 Ambassador Biddle to Secretary Hull, Warsaw, May 8, 1939. 740.00/1372, *Confidential file,* MS, Department of State.

63 Ambassador Biddle to Secretary Hull, Warsaw, May 10, 1939. 740.00/1418, *Confidential file,* MS, Department of State.

64 Ambassador Bullitt to Secretary Hull, Paris, May 10, 1939. 740.00/1416, *Confidential file,* MS, Department of State.

XXIII

Stalin Lights the Fuse to World War II

a. *Britain Is Reluctant to Regard Russia as an Ally*

BEFORE THE PAPAL interlude in favor of world peace had even been set in motion, Russia had already made her first overtures to Germany for an accord. On April 17, 1939, Merekalov, the Soviet Ambassador in Berlin, paid a visit to the German Foreign Office and frankly informed Weizsäcker, State Secretary, that he saw no reason why relations between Germany and Russia should not be on a "normal footing." Indeed, from this normal footing they might become "better and better."[1]

On this same day, as the Germans and the Russians were putting out cautious feelers for a possible understanding, Prime Minister Chamberlain had a talk with Ambassador Kennedy and remarked with easy confidence that he felt he could "make a deal with Russia at any time now." He would delay action, however, until he had gotten the "Balkan situation straightened away."[2]

It is evident that he feared that any intimate understanding between Britain and Russia might "divide the Balkan resistance to Germany and that, if it drove Spain over to the Axis, we might thereby lose more in the West than we should gain in the East." There was also the constant factor of Chamberlain's deep-seated suspicion of Russia and her aims: "I can't believe that she has the same aims and objects as we have, or any sympathy with Democracy as such. She is afraid of Germany and Japan, and would be delighted to see other people fight them." He would postpone as long as possible any negotiations with Russia which looked towards a close political connection.[3]

The American Ambassador in Brussels (Davies) thought this policy of delay in dealing with Russia was a mistake and he made an appeal to Secretary Hull for immediate action. He was convinced that the

decisive factor in Hitler's determination will be whether or not Russia will support Britain and France wholeheartedly. From personal knowledge I know that the Soviets did mistrust Britain and France; both their purposes and their performances. They do trust you [Secretary Hull]. They also believe in me.

[1] Memorandum by Weizsäcker, April 17, 1939. *Nazi-Soviet Relations, 1939–1941* (Washington, 1948), pp. 1–2.

[2] Ambassador Kennedy to Secretary Hull, London, April 17, 1939. 740.00/908, *Confidential file*, MS, Department of State.

[3] Keith Feiling, *The Life of Neville Chamberlain* (New York, 1946), pp. 408–9.

I am impelled, therefore, to suggest that if you considered it advisable I could go to Moscow on the pretext of cleaning up personal affairs for a few days ... and can personally, and if need be unofficially, see Litvinov, Kalinin and Molotov, and I am quite sure, Stalin also, with the object of aiding in securing a quick and speedy agreement with Britain against aggression. Neither the French nor the British, in my opinion, can personally reach the highest authorities there. . . . I am confident that I not only can see the proper people, otherwise unreachable, but that they have confidence in my good judgment and sincerity. . . . Speed is vital.[4]

The Department of State was not ready to authorize this special mission to Moscow, so the British and French governments continued in their own confused way to seek some basis for an accord. But the Soviet Government was not making this task an easy one. On April 20, London and Paris received from Moscow a proposal that the "three countries guarantee not only to fight at once in case of direct attack on any one of the three, but also that all three countries should guarantee to go to war in case of an aggression against any other country in Europe." Bonnet at once objected that guarantees of this kind would not carry "conviction." It would be "totally impossible" to get "French soldiers to march in case of a German attack on Estonia unless such an attack should first involve Poland."[5]

While Britain and France were trying to find some alternative formula that would be agreeable to Moscow, the Baltic countries were showing a definite suspicion of Russian proposals to defend their integrity. In the third week in April 1939, Estonia and Latvia sent notes to the Russian Foreign Office which emphatically stated that they were in no danger of war and therefore did not need any Russian assistance. Two weeks later they announced their readiness to "sign a non-aggression pact with Germany."[6]

Romania was also deeply suspicious of Russia. On April 25, Gafencu, the Romanian Foreign Minister, had a talk with Ambassador Kennedy in London. He confided to him that he had strongly urged the British Foreign Office "not to have anything to do with Russia . . . because Russia does not think the same way and is not really interested in peace as the rest of the world understands it." He was convinced that Hitler did not want war but would seek to win "Danzig and the colonies with

[4] Ambassador Joseph Davies to Secretary Hull, Brussels, April 18, 1939. 740.00/934, Confidential file, MS, Department of State.

[5] Ambassador Bullitt to Secretary Hull, Paris, April 21, 1939. 740.00/1068, Confidential file, MS, Department of State.

[6] David J. Dallin, Soviet Russia's Foreign Policy, 1939–1942 (New Haven, 1942), p. 23; Ambassador Bullitt to Secretary Hull, Paris, April 21, 1939. 740.00/1072, Confidential file, MS, Department of State.

a battle of words." But nevertheless, as a former soldier, he had stressed to Chamberlain the importance of immediate conscription in case his prophecy went wrong.[7] It was apparent to him that the "policy of the Soviet Union was to become involved as little as possible in any European war in the hope that at the end of such a war . . . the Red army might sweep the Continent in the interest of Bolshevism."[8]

The British Foreign Office shared some of Gafencu's suspicions of Russia and could not be hurried into any close relationship with the Soviet Government. On April 24, Halifax sent instructions to the British Ambassador in Moscow directing him to ask the "Soviet Government immediately to issue a [unilateral] guarantee of Rumania and Poland on all fours with the British guarantees. . . . The French Government . . . considered this new British démarche extremely stupid and refused to order the French Ambassador in Moscow to join his British colleague in the démarche." If the Soviet Government would issue the statement the only result "would be to enrage the Poles and the Rumanians." As an alternative the French Foreign Office proposed that the Soviet Union be requested "to guarantee to give support to France and England in case either one should become involved in war due to promises to protect States in Eastern Europe. Similarly, France and England should agree to give support to the Soviet Union in case the Soviet Union should become involved in war due to assistance to France and England."[9]

While this matter was being discussed, Daladier was "increasing to the greatest possible extent French military preparations." An imposing armament would have far more effect upon Hitler than fair words. The British Ambassador at Paris had expressed the belief that Hitler's speech of April 28 had "left the way open for fruitful negotiations." This viewpoint was regarded by Daladier as "dangerous nonsense." There should be no pressure upon Poland to accept German proposals for an understanding.[10]

In many other respects the British attitude of mind disturbed Daladier. Lord Halifax was showing definite reluctance to accept the latest French proposals to Russia.[11] The British Foreign Office was most

[7] Ambassador Kennedy to Secretary Hull, London, April 25, 1939. 740.00/1160, *Confidential file*, MS, Department of State.

[8] Ambassador Bullitt to Secretary Hull, Paris, April 28, 1939. 740.00/1218, *Confidential file*, MS, Department of State.

[9] Ambassador Bullitt to Secretary Hull, Paris, April 25, 1939. 740.00/1154, *Confidential file*, MS, Department of State.

[10] Ambassador Bullitt to Secretary Hull, Paris, April 28, 1939. 740.00/1230, *Confidential file*, MS, Department of State.

[11] These proposals included the following points: (1) if France should become involved in war because of military assistance given to Poland or Rumania, the Soviet Union would support France immediately with all her military forces; (2) if the

anxious not to provoke the "susceptibilities of Poland and Rumania where Russia was concerned." Moreover, it did not wish to forfeit the "sympathy of the world at large by giving a handle to German anti-Comintern propaganda," nor did it wish to "jeopardize the cause of peace by provoking violent action by Germany."

After giving this situation mature consideration, Lord Halifax sent to France this alternative proposal: the Soviet Government should make a public declaration on its own initiative which should make some reference to the new obligations assumed by Britain and France relative to certain eastern European countries. It should then state that in the event that Britain or France became involved in hostilities in fulfillment of these obligations, the assistance of the Soviet Government would be available *if desired* and would be afforded *in such manner as might be most convenient*. This cautious language, it was believed, would not offend in any way the susceptibilities of either Poland or Romania.[12]

It is apparent that the wary attitude of the British Foreign Office gave offence to Stalin. Payart, the French chargé d'affaires in Moscow, said that Halifax's proposals had "enraged Stalin" who regarded them as an effort to relegate Russia to the role of a third-rate power. At any rate, on May 3, Litvinov suddenly resigned his office as Foreign Commissar and was succeeded by Molotov. In London, Sir Robert Vansittart, the chief diplomatic adviser to the Government, expressed to Bullitt his fears that the dismissal of Litvinov meant the adoption by the Soviet Government of a policy of isolation. If this were true it soon led to the "collapse of resistance to Hitler in Western Europe and the Balkans." When Bullitt inquired if Litvinov's resignation had been occasioned by the "dilatory and almost insulting policy which the British Government had pursued vis-à-vis the Soviet Union since Hitler's invasion of Czechoslovakia," Vansittart answered that he "feared that British policy might have contributed to Stalin's attitude."

Bullitt pursued his conversation with Vansittart and suddenly received the surprise of his diplomatic career. To his question as to why the British Government had refused to accept the French proposals relative to action in concert with Russia, Vansittart frankly replied that "no French proposals had yet reached the British Government." Sir Eric Phipps, in Paris, had apparently not considered them important

Soviet Union should become involved in war because of assistance given to Poland or Rumania, France would support the Soviet Union immediately with all her military forces; (3) conversations should take place at once "for the purpose of concerting measures to make the assistances envisaged effective." Ambassador Bullitt to Secretary Hull, Paris, April 29, 1939. 740.00/1235, *Confidential file*, MS, Department of State.

[12] Ambassador Kennedy to Secretary Hull, London, May 1, 1939. 740.00/1256, *Confidential file*, MS, Department of State.

enough to rush to the Foreign Office. After recovering from his astonishment, Bullitt gave to Vansittart an outline of the French proposals which the British diplomat at once pronounced to be "far superior" to the ones sponsored by Lord Halifax. Without wasting any time, Bullitt now hurried to Paris and persuaded Daladier to telephone to Ambassador Corbin, in London, and direct him to present the French proposals to the British Foreign Office.[13]

But the British Foreign Office paid little attention to this pressure. On May 8 the British reply to the Soviet proposals of April 17 was delivered to Molotov by the British Ambassador in Moscow. In substance, the new British proposal contained the following items: (1) the Soviet Government should announce its willingness to assist Poland and Romania should those countries become the victims of aggression; (2) this assistance should be given in suitable form *only if requested* and only *if Britain and France, in pursuance of the guarantee which they have given to Poland and Romania, had already moved to implement these guarantees.*[14]

On May 11, in the columns of *Izvestia*, the Russian attitude towards these proposals was clearly expressed:

Great Britain's suggestions avoid the subject of a pact of mutual assistance between France, Great Britain, and the U.S.S.R. and consider that the Soviet Government should come to the immediate aid of Great Britain and France should they be involved in hostilities as a result of the obligations they have assumed in guaranteeing Poland and Roumania.

Great Britain says nothing about the aid which the U.S.S.R. should naturally receive on the principle of reciprocity from France and Great Britain should it be involved in hostilities owing to the fulfilment of the obligations it may assume in guaranteeing any of the States of Eastern Europe.

It thus follows that under this arrangement, the U.S.S.R. must find itself in a position of inequality.[15]

Daladier sympathized with this Russian criticism of the attitude of the British Foreign Office and he did not blame the Soviet Government for its rejection of the British proposals. In commenting upon the existing diplomatic deadlock he confided to Bullitt that he would insist that the French proposals be made the basis of any further negotiations with Russia. All that the British had accomplished by their "dilatory and half-hearted proposals was to make the Russian terms stiffer." He had

[13] Ambassador Bullitt to Secretary Hull, Paris, May 5, 1939. 740.00/1351, *Confidential file*, MS, Department of State.

[14] Chargé d'Affaires Grummon to Secretary Hull, Moscow, May 9, 1939. 740.00/1385, *Confidential file*, MS, Department of State. The italics are the author's.

[15] Max Beloff, *The Foreign Policy of Soviet Russia, 1929–1941* (New York, 1947), II, 244–45.

"few illusions" about the Soviet Union but he believed that it was "essential" to have Russia in the concert of nations against Hitler.[16]

Under strong pressure from France, the British Foreign Office receded from its uncompromising attitude towards Russia. On May 24, Lord Halifax instructed Sir Ronald Lindsay, in Washington, to the effect that the Soviet Government had been informed that Britain was "now disposed to agree that effective co-operation between the Soviet, French and British Governments against aggression in Europe might be based on a system of mutual guarantees in general conformity with the principles of the League of Nations." This co-operation would cover direct attacks on any of the three governments by a European state and cases where any of them was engaged in hostility with such a state "in consequence of aggression by the latter upon another European country."[17]

But these British proposals made no reference to any assistance that might be given to Estonia, Latvia, or Finland in case these Baltic countries should become the victims of aggression. In a speech on May 31, Molotov called attention to the dangers of German infiltration into the states bordering upon Soviet Russia, and he expressed the opinion that the British Government had not as yet envisaged a system of real reciprocity in its proposed concert of powers. On June 3 the Russian reply to the latest British proposals was received in London. It emphasized the necessity of a definite guarantee of Estonia and Latvia even though those states were opposed to such an arrangement. On June 7, Prime Minister Chamberlain informed the House of Commons of the strong distaste of the Baltic countries for any guarantee of their status. On this very day Estonia and Latvia gave expression to their suspicions of Russia by signing nonaggression treaties with Germany.[18]

In the *Morning Post,* June 8, Winston Churchill made an attack upon the attitude of the Chamberlain Government towards Russia and attempted to justify the demands of the Soviet Government for the inclusions of the Baltic states in the proposed system of guarantees. In order to meet this criticism and to quiet public sentiment in this regard, Chamberlain announced that William Strang, chief of the European Department of the Foreign Office, would be sent on a special mission to Moscow. But he felt that his hand had been forced in this whole Russian matter and he poured out his feelings in a conversation with Ambassador Kennedy:

[16] Ambassador Bullitt to Secretary Hull, Paris, May 16, 1939. 740.00/1500, *Confidential file,* MS, Department of State.

[17] Lord Halifax to Sir Ronald Lindsay, May 24, 1939. 740.00/1670, *Confidential file,* MS, Department of State.

[18] Dallin, *op. cit.,* pp. 41–42; *German White Book,* pp. 367–69.

He [Chamberlain] said that he does not regard the situation in a favorable light at all. . . . He regards the most important thing that could be done would be for the French to make some gesture to the Italians on the question of their demands. . . . The Russian situation is most annoying to him. He is not at all sure that the Russians have the slightest idea of concluding the pact and if they do not accept the latest proposition, he is not at all sure that he will not call the whole thing off.[19]

It is obvious that Chamberlain was dragging his feet along the unwelcome path to a possible accord with Russia. Under the impact of the pressure of public opinion he had arranged for Strang to go to Moscow but this special mission would amount to nothing because Strang's instructions were so uncompromising that they could not lead to an understanding with the Soviet Government. With reference to the Baltic states and to Belgium, the Netherlands, Poland, Romania, and Switzerland he held out strongly against the "imposition of a guarantee on Powers unwilling to receive it." Inasmuch as His Majesty's Government had no intention of proposing a guarantee of Poland against Russia, "they feel that Great Britain should not guarantee or be guaranteed by Russia against a Polish attack." In conclusion, His Majesty's Government was not ready to make a "tripartite agreement not to conclude a separate peace . . . before objectives of peace had been decided upon."[20]

Armed with these instructions, Strang began his diplomatic conversations with Molotov on June 15. Apparently, the Russian Foreign Commissar was willing "temporarily to shelve" proposals relative to a guarantee of the Baltic states if British objections were "insuperable." According to his prescription the proposed tripartite pact would be a "guarantee against direct aggression" and would exclude the contingency "of an attack upon one of the signatories resulting from assistance given by the latter to a third Power." This suggestion did not please Mr. Strang who pointed out that Britain was anxious to have Russian help in the event she became involved in hostilities arising out of assistance to Poland. Molotov, however, held his position strongly and also insisted upon the inclusion of a "no separate peace" clause in the proposed arrangement.[21]

Molotov seemed particularly concerned about the possibility of German infiltration of the Baltic states and a subsequent *coup d'état* which

[19] Ambassador Kennedy to Secretary Hull, London, June 9, 1939. 740.00/1684, *Confidential file*, MS, Department of State.

[20] Lord Halifax to Sir Ronald Lindsay, June 12, 1939. 740.00/1797, *Confidential file*, MS, Department of State.

[21] Lord Halifax to Sir Ronald Lindsay, June 17, 1939. 740.00/1799, *Confidential file*, MS, Department of State.

would install officials friendly to German designs. For this reason he stressed the importance of an "undertaking to give assistance in the case of indirect as well as of direct aggression." He also demanded that the proposed political agreement should go hand in hand with a military convention of a detailed nature. His demands were strongly contested by the British and French delegations at Moscow.[22]

b. *Chamberlain Begins to Pursue the Russian Phantom*

British opposition to Russian demands became weaker as the European situation grew more grave. By the last of June the British Foreign Office was ready to go to great lengths to appease Russia. This story was told very frankly by Daladier to Ambassador Bullitt:

Daladier said that the British were now falling over themselves to accede to the Russian demands. Two texts for submission to the Soviet Government had been prepared today. The first contained no specific mention of the Baltic States, the Netherlands, Belgium and Switzerland, but would be accompanied by a secret memorandum covering them. The second contained a complete acceptance of the Russian demands. Strang in Moscow would be instructed tonight or tomorrow to present these two texts to the Soviet Government and to state that the British and French preferred the first text but were ready to accept the second if the Russians should insist.

I asked Daladier if he believed that this would conclude the negotiations or if he believed the Russians would insist upon subjecting this political accord to the conclusion of a future military agreement. He said that he had urged the British to take up the question of a military agreement with the Russians before taking up the matter of the political agreement but the British had refused to do this. He was by no means certain that the Russians would surrender this demand and feared that the negotiations might be dragged out indefinitely. . . . He added that the Soviet Government had repeatedly assured the French and British Governments that it was not negotiating in any way with the German Government.[23]

c. *Germany Seeks an Accord with Russia*

These assurances were only partly true. The basis for a German-Russian accord had already been laid. On May 30 the German State Secretary in the Foreign Office wrote to the German Ambassador in Moscow an instruction which contained a revealing paragraph: "Contrary to the

[22] Beloff, *op. cit.*, II, 254; L. B. Namier, *Diplomatic Prelude, 1938–1939* (New York, 1948), pp. 186–89.

[23] Ambassador Bullitt to Secretary Hull, Paris, June 28, 1939. 740.00/1822, *Confidential file*, MS, Department of State.

policy previously planned, we have now decided to undertake definite negotiations with the Soviet Union." Astakhov, the Russian chargé d'affaires in Berlin, was called to the Foreign Office for a conversation with Weizsäcker who referred to the remarks of the Russian Ambassador in April relative to an "improvement of Russo-German political relations." He then stated that he did not know "whether there was still room for a gradual normalization [of relations] after Moscow had, perhaps, already given ear to the enticements of London." Astakhov cautiously replied that he would await instructions from Moscow before discussing the matter any further.[24]

Russia made the next move through the Bulgarian Minister in Berlin. On June 15 he called at the Foreign Office and had a talk with Dr. Woermann, head of the Political Division. He stated emphatically to Woermann that if "Germany would declare that she would not attack the Soviet Union or that she would conclude a non-aggression pact with her, the Soviet Union would probably refrain from concluding a treaty with England."[25]

On the basis of this intimation, Schulenberg called at the Russian Foreign Office on June 29 and had a long conversation with Molotov. He gave an assurance that "we would welcome a normalization of the relations between Germany and Soviet Russia. . . . For this we had furnished a number of proofs, such as reserve in the German press, conclusion of the non-aggression treaties with the Baltic countries and desire for resumption of economic negotiations. . . . We . . . would continue to take advantage of any opportunity to prove our good will." Molotov replied that the foreign policy of the Soviet Government was "aimed at the cultivation of good relations with all countries and this of course applied, providing there was reciprocity, to Germany too." He finally remarked that "normalization of relations with Germany was desirable and possible."[26]

d. Britain and France Make New Overtures to Russia

The Western democracies were ignorant of the secret negotiations that were being carried on between Nazi Germany and Soviet Russia. Daladier had some doubts about Russian assurances, but he had no idea that the Nazi-Soviet accord was really moving towards an early conclusion. Léger expressed to Bullitt the opinion that "there were eighty chances

[24] Weizsäcker to Schulenberg, Berlin, May 30, 1939. *Nazi-Soviet Relations, 1939–1941*, pp. 15–17.
[25] Foreign Office memorandum by Dr. Woermann, June 15, 1939. *Ibid.*, pp. 20–21.
[26] German Ambassador in Moscow (Schulenberg) to the German Foreign Office, June 29, 1939. *Ibid.*, pp. 26–27.

in a hundred" that the Anglo-French conversations with Molotov in Moscow "would be concluded successfully in the near future." But there were other difficulties:

Relations between Poland and France had again become extraordinarily unpleasant. At a moment when it was absolutely essential for the French Government to know the exact thoughts of the Polish Government with regard to Danzig, the Polish Ambassador in Paris was so nervous and irritable that it was impossible to have any really intimate conversation with him. He had insulted both Daladier and Bonnet so grossly that Daladier would no longer see him and Bonnet could get nothing out of him. Similarly, Beck in Warsaw had no relations of an intimate nature with the French Ambassador. As a result, all the French Ministers from Daladier down were reluctant to do anything of a concrete nature for Poland. He [Léger] believes that both France and England should give loans to Poland and send airplanes to Poland at once in order to convince the Germans that France and England are determined to support Poland if Poland should become involved in war with Germany. The Polish Ambassador was entirely right in his demands for such assistance; but his manner of presentation . . . was such that he killed his own case.[27]

Léger's optimism concerning the satisfactory progress of the Anglo-French negotiations with the Soviet Government was distinctly premature. The matter of guarantees caused serious concern because some of the states that would be covered by these proposed pledges were openly against them. Finland, the Netherlands, and Switzerland strongly voiced their objections in the first week in July,[28] and this fact forced Britain and France to seek desperately for some formula that would be generally satisfactory. On June 30 the British Ambassador was directed to submit to the Soviet Government a proposal which placed "all States who might receive assistance on the same footing." It also gave to the Soviet Government the right to "decide upon the need" for giving assistance to one of the guaranteed states. Assurances would also be given to Moscow of "Anglo-French aid once hostilities had started." The British Ambassador in Moscow was also instructed to indicate the "prejudicial effect on the peace front (in view of public or private objection by Baltic States and Rumania and the unknown attitude of Holland to a Soviet or tripartite guarantee) of Russian demands for publication in treaty of a list of States guaranteed against aggression." He should express British preference for the enumeration of these guaranteed states in a secret supplementary agreement. It was also important

[27] Ambassador Bullitt to Secretary Hull, Paris, June 30, 1939. 740.00/1840, *Confidential file*, MS, Department of State.
[28] *Bulletin of International News*, XVI, pp. 721, 736–37, 741.

to include the Netherlands, Switzerland, and possibly Luxemburg in the list of states whose protection would be guaranteed.[29]

Molotov was willing to have the list of guaranteed states extended so as to include Belgium, Estonia, Finland, Greece, Latvia, Poland, Romania, and Turkey, but he strongly objected to the addition of the Netherlands and Switzerland unless pacts of mutual assistance between the U.S.S.R. and Poland and Turkey be immediately concluded. He also wished the term "indirect aggression" to be defined as "an internal coup d'état or a reversal of policy in the interest of an aggressor."[30] There were several alternative formulas dealing with "indirect aggression," but none of them was satisfactory and conversations continued. Agreement upon the matter of a military convention was also difficult. On July 7, Lord Halifax was ready to make further concessions to the Soviet Government. He would accept the following definition of indirect aggression: "Action accepted by State in question under threat of force by another Power and involving abandonment of its independence or neutrality." The British Ambassador in Moscow was directed to endeavor to include "consultation in case of aggression against Holland, Switzerland or Luxemburg." If agreement was impossible on this suggestion then he was to try to secure a "limited tripartite agreement susceptible of extension and providing for consultation in the event of aggression against another Power." It was made clear that the Foreign Office would not "agree to make entry into force of agreement depend on conclusion of military conversations."[31]

On the same day that Lord Halifax sent these instructions to Moscow, Ambassador Bullitt had a conversation with the French Foreign Minister. The difficulty of finding some acceptable definition of "indirect aggression" once more came to the front:

This afternoon Bonnet said to me that instructions had now been sent to the British and French Ambassadors in Moscow ordering them to say to the Soviet Government that the Soviet definition of "indirect aggression" was totally inacceptable to the French and British Governments. He said that the portion of the Soviet note which had especially shocked the French and British was the phrase that "any change in the makeup of the Government of any of the Baltic States which tended to favor an aggressor must lead to immediate military action by the Soviet Union, France and England." Bonnet

---

[29] Lord Halifax to Sir Ronald Lindsay, June 30, 1939. 740.00/1895, *Confidential file*, MS, Department of State.

[30] Lord Halifax to Sir Ronald Lindsay, July 4, 1939. 740.00/1897, *Confidential file*, MS, Department of State. See also, Georges Bonnet, *Défense de la Paix: De Washington au Quai d'Orsay* (Geneva, 1946), p. 193; G. Gafencu, *Derniers Jours de l'Europe* (Paris, 1946), pp. 217–23.

[31] Lord Halifax to Sir Ronald Lindsay, July 7, 1939. 740.00/1958, *Confidential file*, MS, Department of State.

added that this phrase, if accepted, would make it possible for the Soviet Union to invade any of the Baltic States at any minute on any flimsy pretext with the armed support of France and England. It was obvious that neither France nor England could accept such a proposal.

Bonnet added that the French and British Ambassadors in Moscow had been given a large number of alternative definitions of aggression which they would propose to Molotov. . . . They had also been ordered to inform the Soviet Union that France and England were ready to adjourn immediate signature of an agreement with regard to Switzerland and Holland provided the Russians would agree to discuss the matter later.

I [Bullitt] asked Bonnet if he still thought the negotiations with the Soviet Union could be brought to a successful conclusion. He replied that he really had no idea. The Russian demands had been so extraordinary that he was no longer certain that the Soviet Government really desired to reach an agreement.[32]

Some two weeks later [July 19], the British Foreign Office made another concession but would not accept the entire Russian program. The situation was tersely described to Ambassador Kennedy by Lord Halifax:

Halifax said that their final words to the Russians now is that they will accept the military pact but will not accept the Russians' definition of indirect aggression and if the Russians insist on it the English are going to call the whole deal off.[33]

The following day Kennedy had a talk with Prime Minister Chamberlain. Although he was fairly optimistic about the general outlook for the next thirty days, he was

sick and disgusted with the Russians and while he believes that the Russians are willing to continue talking without accomplishing anything, his patience is exhausted. He told me he had a conversation with Prince Paul, of Jugoslavia, and Prince Paul was definitely of the opinion that if England did not consummate a deal with the Russians, Germany would. The Prime Minister said he does not feel there is any danger of that.[34]

On August 5, Lord Halifax sent to Sir Ronald Lindsay, in Washington, a brief notation: "At interview on August 2nd, Molotov again re-

[32] Ambassador Bullitt to Secretary Hull, Paris, July 7, 1939. 740.00/1887, *Confidential file*, MS, Department of State.
[33] Ambassador Kennedy to Secretary Hull, London, July 19, 1939. 740.00/1931, *Confidential file*, MS, Department of State.
[34] Ambassador Kennedy to Secretary Hull, London, July 20, 1939. 740.00/1936, *Confidential file*, MS, Department of State.

fused to accept our definition of indirect aggression."[35] The game was just about up and Molotov was almost ready to show his hand. The farce of further conversations continued on August 12 when the British and French military missions arrived in Moscow. Voroshilov promptly asked the highly embarrassing question whether Poland and Romania would permit the passage of Russian troops through their territories in the event of German aggression. General Doumenc telegraphed to Paris and urged the Daladier Government to accept the Soviet viewpoint and exert pressure upon Poland in favor of concessions to Russia.[36]

e. *Germany Signs an Important Treaty with Russia*

While the British and French governments were anxiously seeking some formula of accommodation with Russia, the German Government was making successful efforts to establish a rapprochement with its eastern neighbor. On the evening of July 26, Dr. Carl Schnurre, head of the Eastern European Division of the Foreign Office, invited to dinner Astakhov, the Soviet chargé d'affaires, and Barbarin, the chief of the Soviet Trade Mission to Germany. Astakhov referred to the close community of interests in foreign policy that had formerly existed between Germany and Russia. Dr. Schnurre quickly took up this theme and indicated that the old friendly relations could be restored by adopting the following program: (1) the re-establishment of collaboration in economic affairs; (2) the normalization and improvement of political relations; (3) a new arrangement which would take account of the vital political interests of both parties. Astakhov concurred with this view but cautiously advised that the movement towards this accord should be "very slow and gradual."[37]

But Germany was in a hurry to push to completion this understanding with Soviet Russia. On August 2, Ribbentrop had an important conversation with Astakhov during which he stressed the opinion that the German Government was "favorably disposed toward Russia." If Moscow had a similar disposition there was "no problem from the Baltic to the Black Sea that could not be solved between the two of us."[38]

[35] Lord Halifax to Sir Ronald Lindsay, August 5, 1939. 740.00/2044, *Confidential file*, MS, Department of State. The British viewpoint on indirect aggression was clearly set forth by Lord Halifax on July 24. "The State in question must be acting under threat of force and its action must involve abandonment of its independence and neutrality." 740.00/2018, *Confidential file*, MS, Department of State.

[36] Namier, *op. cit.*, pp. 206–8; Georges Bonnet, *Fin d'une Europe*, pp. 275–94.

[37] German Foreign Office memorandum, July 27, 1939. *Nazi-Soviet Relations, 1939–1941*, pp. 32–36.

[38] Ribbentrop to Ambassador Schulenburg, August 3, 1939. *Ibid.*, pp. 37–38.

In Moscow, Schulenburg discussed the situation with Molotov who frankly admitted that his government "desired normalization and improvement" of relations with Germany. But this admission was guarded and Molotov was so cautious in his admissions that it seemed evident to the German Ambassador that it would take "considerable effort on our part to cause the Soviet Government to swing about."[39] It was soon evident that Ribbentrop was ready to make this effort. On August 14, Schulenburg was instructed to see Molotov and emphasize the opinion that the period of opposition between Soviet Russia and Nazi Germany could be "brought to an end once and for all" by a frank appraisal of mutual interests. There were no "real conflicts of interest between Germany and the U.S.S.R." Indeed, there was distinctly lacking any "cause for an aggressive attitude on the part of one country against the other." It should be obvious that "German-Soviet policy today has come to an historic turning point." The situation in Europe called for German-Soviet co-operation, not conflict. It would be fatal "if through mutual lack of views and intentions, our peoples should be finally driven asunder." The existing crisis was of so grave a nature that von Ribbentrop himself was ready to visit Moscow to present the German viewpoint to both Molotov and Stalin.[40]

Molotov assured Schulenburg that he "warmly welcomed German intentions of improving relations with the Soviet Union" but he insisted that "adequate preparation" for a discussion of outstanding problems in German-Soviet relations was "indispensable." During the conversation Molotov seemed so "unusually compliant" that Schulenburg was of the opinion that the Soviet Foreign Office regarded the suggestion of a German visit to Moscow a "very flattering" testimonial of an ardent desire for Nazi co-operation with Russia. The situation was improving so rapidly that it appeared as though the Reich would "achieve the desired results" in the pending negotiations.[41]

With negotiations moving rapidly towards a favorable conclusion, the German Foreign Office accelerated the tempo of its efforts. Schulenburg was instructed to assure Molotov that Germany was ready for the signature of a nonaggression pact. Moreover, the Reich would guarantee the Baltic states jointly with the Soviet Union and would exercise her influence "for an improvement of Russian-Japanese relations." In order to speed the signature of a treaty covering these points, von Rib-

---

[39] Schulenburg to Ribbentrop, Moscow, August 4, 1939. *Ibid.*, pp. 39–41.

[40] Ribbentrop to Schulenburg, August 14, 1939. *Ibid.*, pp. 50–52.

[41] Schulenburg to the German Foreign Office, Moscow, August 16, 1939; Schulenberg to the State Secretary in the German Foreign Office, Moscow, August 16, 1939. *Ibid.*, pp. 52–57.

bentrop indicated that he was prepared to take a plane to Moscow any time after August 18.[42]

Molotov welcomed the proposed visit of von Ribbentrop to Moscow as an indication that the German Government valued more highly co-operation with Russia than did the Chamberlain Government of Britain which had sent to Moscow merely a chief of one of the divisions of the Foreign Office (Strang). But he wished to make it clear that Russia desired the conclusion of an economic agreement before the establishment of a political understanding.[43] This wish was easily fulfilled by the signature, at Berlin, of a convention that dealt exclusively with economic matters. On August 20, Hitler himself sent a telegram to Stalin in which he expressly accepted the draft of a nonaggression treaty which Molotov had prepared. He then requested that Stalin receive Foreign Minister von Ribbentrop on August 22 or 23.[44] Stalin made a favorable reply and the stage was prepared for a German-Soviet accord that ushered in World War II.[45]

Meanwhile, conversations continued between Voroshilov and the members of the Anglo-French military mission. The demands of Voroshilov were purposely inacceptable. Not only did Russia insist upon the right of Russian troops to enter Polish and Romanian territory but also to occupy the principal ports of the Baltic states and the main islands near their coasts if she thought such measures were necessary to forestall German aggression. These demands made a very unfavorable impression upon Polish statesmen who were fearful of Russian good faith. When the French Ambassador asked for acquiescence in the Russian request for the right to send troops across Polish soil, Foreign Minister Beck replied: "We concede to no one, under any form, the right to discuss the use of any part of our territory by foreign troops."[46] On August 21, according to Daladier, he overcame Polish objections in this regard and authorized General Doumenc to sign with Russia the proposed military convention. M. Bonnet and M. Lukasiewicz, the Polish Ambassador in Paris, gave different versions,[47] but the matter is of no great importance because the announcement of the Ribbentrop mission to Moscow sounded the death knell of any rapprochement between Russia and the Western democracies.

[42] Ribbentrop to Schulenburg, August 16, 1939. *Ibid.*, pp. 58–59.
[43] Schulenburg to Ribbentrop, Moscow, August 18, 1939. *Ibid.*, p. 58.
[44] Hitler to Stalin, August 20, 1939. *Ibid.*, pp. 66–67.
[45] Stalin to Hitler, August 21, 1939. *Ibid.*, p. 69.
[46] Namier, *op. cit.*, pp. 207–9; Léon Noël, *L'Aggression Allemande contre la Pologne* (Paris, 1946), p. 423.
[47] Édouard Daladier, "Le Procès de Nuremberg et le Pacte Germano-Russo," *Minerve*, April 5, 1946; General Maurice Gamelin, *Servir* (Paris, 1936), II, 444, contends that Daladier first telegraphed to General Doumenc and then secured Polish consent.

On the afternoon of August 23, Ribbentrop arrived in Moscow. That evening he had a long conference with Stalin who burst out into bitter criticisms of Britain. Ribbentrop sounded the same note and acidly complained that Britain had always sought to "disrupt the development of good relations between Germany and the Soviet Union." She was obviously weak and "wanted to let others fight for her presumptuous claim to world domination." Stalin agreed with this indictment. He had not liked the attitude of the British military mission which "had never told the Soviet Government what it really wanted." There was no doubt in his mind that Britain, in a military sense, was distinctly weak. Her domination of the world in spite of this fact was "due to the stupidity of the other countries that always let themselves be bluffed." After appropriate toasts, the signature of the German-Soviet nonaggression treaty was hailed as the dawn of a new political day in world politics.[48] To millions of fearful persons in panic-stricken lands from the Baltic to the Mediterranean, it was the beginning of night over Europe.

f. *The Duce Tries to Sit on a Slippery Diplomatic Fence*

During the fateful month of August, Mussolini tried desperately to maintain a dignified position on a very slippery diplomatic fence. As early as July 7 he had told the British Ambassador (Loraine) that "if England is ready to fight in defense of Poland, Italy will take up arms with her ally Germany." But he became exceedingly vacillating as the crisis deepened. On August 10 he instructed Ciano frankly to "inform the Germans that we must avoid a conflict with Poland since it will be impossible to localize it and a general war would be disastrous for everybody."[49] Ribbentrop resented this policy of caution: "The decision to fight is implacable." After talking to Hitler, Ciano realized that there was "no longer anything that can be done. He [Hitler] has decided to strike, and strike he will."[50]

Ciano returned to Rome "completely disgusted with the Germans, with their leader, with their way of doing things. They have betrayed us and lied to us." Mussolini, after considering the reports of Ciano, decided (August 15) that Italy should "not march blindly with Germany.... He wants time to prepare the break with Germany."[51] On the

---

48 Memorandum of a conversation between Ribbentrop and Stalin, August 23–24, 1939. *Nazi-Soviet Relations, 1939–1941*, pp. 72–78.

49 *The Ciano Diaries, 1939–1943*, ed. Hugh Gibson (Garden City, 1947), pp. 109, 118.

50 *Ibid.*, p. 119.

51 *Ibid.*, p. 120–21.

eighteenth, however, the Duce's doubts reappeared and he remarked to Ciano that "Germany might do good business cheaply." Moreover, he feared "Hitler's rage." On the twenty-first the Duce announced to Ciano that he had decided to go along with the Germans, but after much argument he consented to a conference between Ciano and Ribbentrop. He agreed that Ribbentrop should be informed that Italy would "not intervene if the conflict is provoked by an attack on Poland."[52] But the Nazi-Soviet Agreement of August 23 upset Ciano's calculations and the proposed meeting with the German Foreign Minister was abandoned.

g. *Chamberlain Expands His Pledges to Poland*

While the Duce was endeavoring to squirm into a favorable position on a precarious perch, Chamberlain was still trying to reason with Hitler. On August 22 he sent to Berlin a warning that, despite the announcement of the Nazi-Soviet Agreement, Britain would still carry out her obligation to defend Polish independence.[53] When Nevile Henderson went to Berchtesgaden to deliver this communication he found Hitler in a mood of "extreme excitability." During a second interview the Führer was more composed although sharply critical of British policy. No longer did he "trust Mr. Chamberlain" who had given a "blank check to Poland."[54] In a letter to the British Prime Minister he strongly asserted his constant desire for peace with Britain and he complained that his pacific advances had always been rejected. With reference to the questions of Danzig and the Corridor he observed that he had been ready to settle them "on the basis of a proposal of truly unparalleled magnanimity." But Poland, acting upon assurance of armed assistance from Britain in case of conflict with Germany, had refused to accede to a German request for the return of Danzig to the Reich and for a railway and a motor road across the Corridor. Also, Britain and France were mobilizing their armed forces as a threat to compel Germany to recede from her firm stand with reference to Poland. This action would force Germany to answer mobilization with mobilization.[55]

This diplomatic impasse made European statesmen realize that World War II was just around the corner of tomorrow. In order to avert such a dread contingency, King Leopold of Belgium, speaking for the so-called "Oslo Powers" (Belgium, Denmark, Finland, Luxemburg,

[52] *Ibid.*, pp. 123–25.
[53] *British Blue Book,* p. 97.
[54] Sir Nevile Henderson, *Failure of a Mission* (New York, 1940), pp. 269–70.
[55] Chancellor Hitler to Prime Minister Chamberlain, August 23, 1939. *British White Paper,* p. 10.

the Netherlands, Norway, and Sweden), broadcast an appeal to "those in whose hands rests the fate of the world," to avoid "the catastrophe which threatens humanity." With prophetic vision this appeal stressed the fact that the impact of a second world war would destroy "the spiritual and material values created by centuries of civilization"; no nation would emerge as a "victor."[56]

This appeal by King Leopold was followed by one from Pope Pius XII (August 24), who admonished European rulers that "nothing is lost with peace; all may be lost with war."[57] On the previous day, President Roosevelt had sent an urgent message to King Victor Emmanuel of Italy exhorting him to "formulate proposals for a pacific solution of the present crisis."[58] Ciano thought that the President's appeal did not "make much sense,"[59] and after waiting several days the King replied that "there has been done and there is being done by us whatever is possible to bring about peace with justice."[60] Without waiting for this reply, the President also sent appeals to President Móscicki, of Poland, and Chancellor Hitler (August 24), urging them to try to settle their differences by direct negotiation or by arbitration.[61]

Móscicki replied at once (August 25) that he strongly favored direct negotiations. When no answer came from Hitler, President Roosevelt (August 25) sent him a second message alluding to the readiness of the Polish Government to try to find some path to peace through direct negotiations.[62] In response to this pressure, Hitler answered that he had "left nothing untried for the purpose of settling the dispute between Germany and Poland in a friendly manner. Even at the last hour he accepted an offer from the Government of Great Britain to mediate in this dispute. Owing to the attitude of the Polish Government, however, all these endeavors have remained without result."[63]

While the second Roosevelt message was en route to Hitler, the Führer sent a message to Mussolini in which he intimated that action against Poland would begin "in a short time." He then asked for "Italian understanding" of his position. The Duce replied that Italy was "not ready to go to war." Ciano, in order to implement this reply, began to make out a long list ("enough to kill a bull—if a bull could read") of military needs essential to any Italian war effort.[64]

While Ciano was making these calculations, Hitler summoned Nev-

[56] British Blue Book, pp. 185–86.
[57] Ibid., pp. 191–92.
[58] Peace and War: United States Foreign Policy, 1931–1941 (Washington, 1943), p. 475.
[59] Gibson, op. cit., p. 127.
[60] Department of State, Bulletin, I, pp. 159–60.
[61] Ibid., pp. 157–59.   [63] Ibid., p. 483.
[62] Peace and War, pp. 479–80.   [64] Gibson, op. cit., pp. 128–29.

ile Henderson to the Chancellery. He emphasized the importance of an early settlement of the dispute between Germany and Poland and then made an offer of friendship and eventual alliance between Germany and Britain. Speaking with "calm and apparent sincerity," he described his efforts as a "last effort, for conscience' sake, to secure good relations with Great Britain."[65] He could have saved his breath because on this very day (August 25) Chamberlain had entered into a far-reaching treaty with Poland. It provided that if "one of the Contracting Parties become engaged in hostilities with a European Power in consequence of aggression by the latter against the Contracting Party, the other Contracting Party will at once give the Contracting Party engaged in hostilities all the support and assistance in its power." The treaty then obligated Britain and Poland to maintain the *status quo* in vast areas in Eastern Europe.[66]

This action of Chamberlain is as difficult to understand as his pledges to Poland in March and April. If he had been willing "to write off eastern Europe as geographically indefensible, to let Hitler move eastward, with the strong probability that he would come into conflict with Stalin," such a policy would have been "the sanest and most promising course western diplomacy could have followed."[67] Instead, the British Prime Minister assumed a series of obligations he could not possibly fulfill, and to make sure this was so he failed to expedite the matter of building up the British Army. Although the House of Commons approved a bill for conscription on April 27, the first contingent of British recruits was not called to the colors until July. No troops could be rushed to Poland and a pitifully small force would be ready for service in France. It is evident that André Géraud *(Pertinax)* should write a book on the "grave-diggers of Britain."

h. *Hitler Sends a Warning to France*

After sending Nevile Henderson to London with another note to Chamberlain, Hitler turned to France. On August 25 he called the French Ambassador (M. Coulondre) to the Chancellery and submitted a statement that was to be forwarded to Daladier. He disclaimed any wish for war with France, particularly on account of Poland. In the spring of 1939, he had made "extremely fair proposals to Poland, demanding the return of Danzig to the Reich and of a narrow strip of territory leading from this German city to East Prussia." But the Poles had not only rejected these "proposals" but had also subjected the Ger-

[65] Henderson, *op. cit.*, p. 272.

[66] The text of the treaty is contained in the *Polish White Book*, pp. 100–102.

[67] William H. Chamberlin, *America's Second Crusade* (Chicago, 1950), p. 51.

man minority "to the worst possible treatment." To make matters much worse the Polish Government had decreed general mobilization and were shooting at German planes crossing the Corridor. Such actions were intolerable. If Germany took suitable action against them, and if France gave support to Poland in this event, war between Germany and France would be inevitable.[68]

The reply of Daladier was dignified and able: "Unless you attribute to the French people a conception of national honour less high than that which I myself recognize in the German people, you cannot doubt that France will be true to her solemn promises to other nations, such as Poland, which, I am perfectly sure, wants also to live in peace with Germany." He was confident that there was no real barrier to a pacific solution of the existing crisis if the will for peace existed "equally on all sides." As for himself, there should be no doubt in anyone's mind that he was ready to make all the efforts "an honest man" could make "to ensure" the success of any real step towards a just settlement of differences.[69]

When he presented this note to Hitler, M. Coulondre begged him "in the name of history and for the sake of humanity, not to thrust aside this last chance." He remarked that the Führer's prestige was great enough "outside Germany to remain undiminished even after a gesture of appeasement." Hitler quickly replied that the decision was really up to Poland. If she would make concessions there would be peace, but "Poland's mind was set in morbid resistance." Therefore, if she evinced an apparent willingness to "talk matters over it would, doubtless, be in order to gain time for her mobilization."[70]

On August 27, Hilter sent his formal reply to Daladier's letter. After repeating his desire for peace with France he referred to increasing Polish provocations and alleged brutal treatment of the German minority under Polish control. This "Macedonian situation must be liquidated on our eastern frontier." It was now necessary to formulate a precise prescription for peace: "Danzig and the Corridor must return to Germany."[71] Such terms were equivalent to a declaration of war.

i. The Führer Turns Once More to Britain

But despite the fact that his demands were equivalent to a declaration of war, Hitler still harbored some hope that Chamberlain would break

[68] M. Coulondre to M. Georges Bonnet, Berlin, August 25, 1939. *French Yellow Book*, pp. 302-5.

[69] M. Georges Bonnet to M. Coulondre, Paris, August 26, 1939, inclosing the communication from Daladier to Hitler. *Ibid.*, pp. 311-12.

[70] M. Coulondre to M. Georges Bonnet, Berlin, August 27, 1939. *Ibid.*, pp. 317-18.

[71] Chancellor Hitler to Premier Daladier, August 27, 1939. *Ibid.*, pp. 321-24.

at the last moment and prepare the way for a new Munich. It is evident from the Nürnberg documents that "some time . . . after signing of the treaty with Soviet Russia [August 23, 1939]," Hitler issued the "order for the campaign against Poland." The beginning of this campaign was "ordered for 25 August but on 24 August, in the afternoon, it was postponed until 1 September in order to await the results of new diplomatic maneuvers with the English Ambassador."[72]

This testimony of General Göring was confirmed by Ribbentrop: "Hearing that military steps had been taken against Poland, I asked him [the Führer] to withdraw it and stop the advance. The Fuehrer at once agreed to do it. . . . This was the 25th of August, 1939, and then negotiations with Mr. Henderson in Berlin started. . . . The Fuehrer made again an offer of friendship and of close collaboration with Great Britain. When this didn't come off, the Fuehrer decided to treat directly with the Poles."[73]

On August 26, Henderson arrived in London with this latest Hitler proposal. After two days of careful consideration the British Cabinet sent Henderson back to Berlin with a lengthy answer. It was agreed that there should be a prompt settlement of the "differences between Germany and Poland," but "as a prerequisite to this settlement the German Government should clearly understand that His Majesty's Government had obligations to Poland by which they are bound and which they intend to honor." It should, however, be entirely possible that a "reasonable solution of the differences between Germany and Poland could be effected by an agreement . . . which would include the safeguarding of Poland's essential interests." This agreement should then be "guaranteed by other Powers." If desired, His Majesty's Government "would be ready to make their contribution to the effective operation of such a guarantee." In order to arrive at this meeting of minds between Germany and Poland, direct discussions between the two powers should be promptly initiated. Failure to reach a "just settlement" of existing difficulties would "ruin the hopes of better understanding between Germany and Great Britain," and would "bring the two countries into conflict."[74]

This last sentence has a definite ominous ring which indicated that as Hitler became more conciliatory after August 25, the British Cabinet became more fixed in its determination to stand behind Poland. With

[72] The testimony of General Göring, Nürnberg, August 29, 1945. *Nazi Conspiracy and Aggression,* VIII, TC–90, 534–35.
[73] The testimony of Herr von Ribbentrop, August 29, 1945, Nürnberg. *Ibid.,* TC–91, pp. 535–36.
[74] Reply of His Majesty's Government to Chancellor Hitler, August 28, 1939. *British Blue Book,* p. 126 ff.

reference to the reasons why Hitler pursued this policy of conciliation, Henderson has some pertinent observations. He had "reason to believe . . . that the order for the German Army to advance into Poland was actually issued for the night of August 25th–26th. It is difficult otherwise to find justification for the various orders and arrangements which came into force on August 26th and 27th. . . . The fact may well be . . . that Hitler had had in consequence of the Prime Minister's letter one last hesitation and countermanded the orders to his army. . . . His hesitation was due . . . to one final effort to detach Britain from Poland."[75]

The Nürnberg documents show that Henderson's "hunch" concerning the sudden switch in Hitler's plans with reference to Poland was remarkably correct. After issuing orders to the German Army to move against Poland he lost his nerve and made a last attempt to induce the British Government to write another chapter of appeasement. He knew that the German and Russian armies would crush Poland in the matter of a few weeks, and that Britain could interpose no barrier to impede their progress. But this Polish campaign aroused many misgivings in his mind. In the end, how big a price would he have to pay Stalin for his assistance? Would it not be possible to drive a better bargain with the credulous Chamberlain?

At any rate, Hitler once more tried conciliation. When Henderson arrived in Berlin on the evening of August 28 with the reply of the British Government to Hitler's latest proposal, he went at once to the Chancellery. He found the Führer "once again friendly and reasonable and appeared to be not dissatisfied with the answer which I had brought to him. He observed . . . that he must study it carefully and would give me a written reply the next day. . . . Though he had been noncommittal, he had been calm and even conciliatory."[76]

But on August 29 the situation changed for the worse. The Polish Government decreed a general mobilization of their armed forces and this word reached Berlin within a few hours. The British Government had sent a warning to Warsaw that such a step "would create the impression all over the world" that Poland was "embarking on war." For this reason the Polish Government postponed the public announcement of mobilization "for several hours."[77] But the news was soon in Hitler's hands and it greatly disturbed his uneasy nervous balance.

Henderson quickly discovered this fact when he was summoned to the Chancellery at 7:15 on the evening of the twenty-ninth. Hitler immediately launched into an excited denunciation of the atrocities com-

75 Henderson, op. cit., pp. 270–72.
76 Ibid., pp. 275–77.
77 Minute of Count Szembek's conversation with Sir Howard Kennard and M. Noël, Warsaw, August 29, 1939. Polish White Book, p. 108.

mitted upon German nationals in Poland. This ghastly state of affairs was "unbearable for a Great Power." He now insisted upon "the return of Danzig and the Corridor to Germany, and the safeguarding of the existence of the German national group in the territories remaining to Poland." While the British Government apparently believed that these grave differences between Germany and Poland could be settled by "direct negotiations," the German Government did not share this viewpoint. But as a proof of the sincerity of its intentions "to enter into a lasting friendship with Great Britain," it would accept British mediation on the basis of "securing the despatch to Berlin of a Polish Emissary with full powers." It was expected that this emissary would arrive on Wednesday, August 30.[78]

The time limit fixed for the arrival of this proposed Polish plenipotentiary seemed to Henderson to have the "ring of an ultimatum." Hitler emphatically denied this implication: he wished merely to stress the urgency of the situation. He then terminated the interview with a brief but "quite honest" assurance of his "liking for Englishmen generally and his constant endeavor to win Britain's friendship."[79]

j. Zero Hour in Europe

Although Henderson discounted some of these protestations of friendship for Britain, he promptly informed the Foreign Office of the contents of Hitler's note. A few hours later he received a reply which expressed the view that it was unreasonable to expect that His Majesty's Government could produce a Polish plenipotentiary in Berlin within twenty-four hours. Moreover, it would be more in accord with usual diplomatic practice for the German Government to send to Warsaw, through the Polish Ambassador in Berlin, an outline of the proposals to be discussed by the Polish plenipotentiary and the German Foreign Office.[80]

It is significant that although the British Foreign Office opposed the hurried dispatch of a Polish emissary to Berlin to discuss German proposals for a settlement of existing differences, the French Ambassador in Berlin held quite a different viewpoint. He thought that the "Polish Government should agree to appoint a plenipotentiary since, after all, the German Chancellor accedes to the suggestion made to him by Britain and France for direct contact between Berlin and Warsaw."

[78] British Blue Book, pp. 135–37.
[79] Henderson, op. cit., pp. 278–79.
[80] British Blue Book, pp. 139–42.

This plenipotentiary should be M. Lipski, the Polish Ambassador in Berlin.[81]

In the meantime, Nevile Henderson waited during the afternoon and evening of August 30 for some further communication from the German Foreign Office. In the note that Hitler had handed to him on August 29 it had been stated that the Foreign Office would immediately draw up proposals which, "if possible," would be "placed at the disposal of the British Government before the arrival of the Polish negotiator." It soon became apparent to Henderson that Ribbentrop would not find it "possible" to send these proposals to the British Embassy, so he tried to stave off war by imploring the Polish Ambassador in Berlin "to urge his Government to nominate without delay someone to represent them in the proposed negotiations."[82]

But Poland refused to be moved by this pressure, so at midnight (August 30) Henderson called at the German Foreign Office to discuss the situation with von Ribbentrop. When he suggested that the Polish Ambassador be invited to the Foreign Office, von Ribbentrop indignantly replied that such a course would be "utterly unthinkable and intolerable." Henderson noticed that the Foreign Minister appeared to be in a state of "great excitement" and kept "leaping from his chair and . . . asking if I had anything more to say." Henderson insisted upon reading the entire British note and when he had concluded, Ribbentrop produced the promised German proposals which he "gabbled through . . . as fast as he could in a tone of the utmost annoyance. . . . When he had finished, I accordingly asked him to let me see it." But the Foreign Minister "refused categorically, threw the document with a contemptuous gesture on the table and said that it was now out of date since no Polish Emissary had arrived in Berlin by midnight."[83]

The German proposals were surprisingly moderate and some arrangement for preserving peace might have been concluded if a Polish plenipotentiary had arrived in Berlin on August 30. The proposals provided for the return of Danzig to the Reich, but the fate of the Corridor was to be decided by a plebiscite of its inhabitants. The "exact frontiers" of the Polish port of Gdynia were to be determined by discussions between Germany and Poland, and, if necessary, were to be delimited by an international committee of arbitration.[84]

Although Henderson returned to the Embassy feeling that the German Army would invade Polish territory at any moment, a new respite

81 M. Coulondre to M. Georges Bonnet, Berlin, August 30, 1939. *French Yellow Book*, pp. 341–42.

82 Henderson, *op. cit.*, p. 281.

83 *British White Paper*, p. 17.

84 *German White Book*, pp. 485–88.

was gained through the intervention of Mussolini. On August 31, Count Ciano called Halifax on the telephone "to tell him that the Duce can intervene with Hitler only if he brings a fat prize: Danzig. Empty-handed he can do nothing. . . . After a while Halifax sends word that our proposal regarding Danzig cannot be adopted." Ciano then had a hurried conference with the Duce who agreed to a new proposal which favored the calling of a five-power conference "with the object of reviewing clauses of the Treaty of Versailles which are the cause of the present disturbance in the life of Europe." The British and French ambassadors welcomed this proposal with enthusiasm, and in his telephone conversation with Halifax, Ciano insisted upon a "quick answer." But the day passed without any word from the British Foreign Minister and at 8:20 P.M. the telephone central office informed Ciano that "London has cut its communications with Italy."[85]

While this attempt of Mussolini to preserve peace was breaking down, the French Ambassador in Berlin went to the Polish Ambassador (M. Lipski) and entreated him to get in touch with Ribbentrop. Lipski was impressed with this advice and telephoned to Warsaw for instructions. At 2:00 he received instructions that the Polish Foreign Office favored "the establishment of contact" with the German Government.[86] After a telephone conversation with the German State Secretary of the Foreign Office (Weizsäcker), a conference between Lipski and Ribbentrop was arranged for 6:30. When Lipski called at the Foreign Office, Ribbentrop immediately inquired if he had "special plenipotentiary powers to undertake negotiations." When Lipski answered in the negative, Ribbentrop seemed taken aback and closed the conference with the remark that he would inform the Führer of the situation.[87]

According to his instructions from the Polish Foreign Office, Lipski was merely to "establish contact and to discuss where and how negotiations could be opened."[88] It should have been apparent to the Polish Foreign Minister that the tides of war were moving too rapidly to be stopped by a mere point of contact in Berlin and an inquiry concerning future negotiations. Colonel Beck missed the bus to Berlin and Poland paid in terms of a fourth partition.

While the Polish Foreign Office still expected to discuss proposals for the settlement of differences between Germany and Poland, the

[85] Gibson, *op. cit.*, pp. 134–35.

[86] M. Léon Noël to M. Georges Bonnet, Warsaw, August 31, 1939. *French Yellow Book*, pp. 349–50.

[87] M. Lipski to the Polish Ministry for Foreign Affairs, Berlin, August 31, 1939. *Polish White Book*, pp. 119–20.

[88] M. Corbin to M. Georges Bonnet, London, September 1, 1939. *French Yellow Book*, pp. 358–59.

Polish War Office pushed its plans for general mobilization. When Hitler heard of these plans he decided to strike early on the morning of September 1. As a background for this military advance an official German communiqué was issued at 9:00 P.M. on August 31. After referring to the failure of Poland to send to Berlin by the evening of August 30 a plenipotentiary invested with the authority to engage in direct conversations, the communiqué stated that instead of talking terms of peace, Poland had speeded preparations for war. Such preparations had forced Germany to strike in self-defense.[89]

In the early morning of September 1, German troops crossed the Polish frontier at several points and German planes began to bomb Polish airdromes and lines of communications. At 10:30, on the same morning, Hitler addressed the Reichstag. During the preceding night Polish soldiers had "fired the first shots" across the German frontier. Bullets were now being answered with bullets, bombs with bombs. This crisis would make it necessary for the Führer once more to "put on that uniform which was always so sacred and dear to me. I shall not take it off until after the victory—or I shall not live to see the end."[90] After he had completed this address, he sat for several minutes "with bowed head." It had been noticeable that his delivery "did not have quite the customary fire and vehemence, and the speech sounded less cohesive and well prepared."[91]

In summing up responsibility for the September outbreak, Ulrich von Hassell made the following entry in his diary:

My final conclusions about the week's events up to September 1 are as follows: Hitler and Ribbentrop wanted war with Poland and knowingly took the risk of war with the Western Powers, deluding themselves to varying degrees up to the very last with the belief that the West would remain neutral after all. The Poles, for their part, with Polish conceit and Slavic aimlessness, confident of English and French support, had missed every remaining chance of avoiding war. The government in London, whose ambassador did everything to keep the peace, gave up the race in the very last days and adopted a kind of devil-may-care attitude. France went through the same stages, only with much more hesitation. Mussolini did all in his power to avoid war. His mediation proposal of September 2 offered no more hope of success because England no longer could or would back down. The attitude of France on this day is not quite clear.[92]

[89] Official German communiqué, August 31, 1939. *German White Book*, pp. 489–90.
[90] Address by the Führer to the Reichstag, September 1, 1939. *Ibid.*, pp. 498–504.
[91] Chargé d'Affaires Kirk to Secretary Hull, Berlin, September 1, 1939. 740.0011 EW./1939/10, *Confidential file*, MS, Department of State.
[92] September 1, 1939, pp. 72–73.

In taking the momentous step of September 1, Hitler apparently believed that his military preparations would command success. It is estimated that he had spent some forty billion dollars on armaments, excluding the weapons he had seized in Austria and Czechoslovakia. The German military machine had a minimum of 160 divisions of which at least 100 were fully equipped with modern weapons. Several of these divisions were armored. Hitler could also count upon at least 1,000 aircraft assigned to tactical units. But this air force was too weak to blast Britain into submission, and the German Navy was not strong enough to insure a landing of sufficient German troops to conquer the poorly prepared British Isles. Without a chance of defeating Britain, "let alone the British Empire, Germany could not win the war; at best a stalemate would have ensued which, however, would have made it impossible for Hitler to attain his more distant, major objectives."[93]

k. *Roosevelt Makes an Appeal for Civilian Populations*

On September 1, President Roosevelt issued an appeal to Britain, France, Germany, and Poland to refrain from bombing civilian populations in unfortified cities. Unless such a procedure were followed, thousands of innocent human beings "who have no responsibility for the hostilities which have broken out will lose their lives."[94] Hitler immediately replied that he "unconditionally endorsed" the President's plea, and this action was followed by Poland on the same day.[95] On September 2 the British and French governments issued a declaration stating that they were "entirely in sympathy with the humanitarian sentiments" which inspired the President's appeal.[96]

l. *Last-Minute Attempts at Mediation*

Pope Pius XII was not satisfied with merely softening the asperities of war. It was far more important to prevent the outbreak of World War

[93] Robert Strausz-Hupé and Stefan T. Possony, *International Relations* (New York, 1950), pp. 648–53; N. M. Sloutski, *The World Armaments Race, 1919–1939* (Geneva, 1941), p. 23; Asher Lee, *The German Air Force* (New York, 1946), p. 274. It should also be remembered that Russia was a most uncertain ally. According to the Yugoslav Ambassador to the United States, Oumansky, the Soviet Ambassador at Washington told him that "the aim of Soviet policy was not to be involved in the present conflict. Thus, when the time came for peace negotiations, the Soviets, as the strongest European power, would play a decisive role in the shaping of the new map of Europe." Constantin Fotitch, *The War We Lost: Yugoslavia's Tragedy and the Failure of the West* (New York, 1948), pp. 35 ff.

[94] Appeal of President Roosevelt to Britain, France, Germany, Italy, and Poland, September 1, 1939. *French Yellow Book*, p. 364.

[95] *Polish White Book*, p. 129.

[96] *New York Times*, September 3, 1939.

II. On August 31 he sent an urgent appeal to Germany and Poland to do "everything within their power to avoid any incident and to abstain from taking any measure likely to aggravate the existing tension."[97]

The powers paid little attention to this Papal plea but a suggestion from Count Ciano for a conference attracted more attention. After Hitler had indicated to the Italian Foreign Minister that he would not "reject the proposal completely," Ciano called Bonnet and Halifax on the telephone and once more proposed a conference to discuss the bases of a possible settlement of the existing emergency. Bonnet welcomed the suggestion, but Halifax, after a Cabinet meeting, stated that the proposal could be accepted only if Germany would first agree to evacuate the Polish territory they had invaded. This was an impossible condition; for a second time Britain defeated Italian attempts to find some formula of peace.[98]

In Berlin, Nevile Henderson was deeply dejected. During a conversation with the American chargé d'affaires he remarked that "if the Polish Government had agreed to direct negotiations and had appointed a plenipotentiary, precipitate action by Germany might have been prevented or at least delayed. The statement made by the Polish Ambassador to Ribbentrop was not . . . sufficiently comprehensive."[99]

In Paris, on the morning of September 2, the Polish Ambassador called on Foreign Minister Bonnet and insisted that the "French alliance with Poland obliged France to give immediate and automatic military assistance to Poland." Bonnet replied that no ultimatum could be sent to Germany until after the meeting of the Chamber of Deputies on that afternoon. The German Government would then have forty-eight hours in which to reply. The Polish Ambassador became so excited at this remark that he rushed to Daladier to complain of the seeming indifference of the Foreign Office to the treaty engagements of France. He stated that the British Government was "intensely disturbed by the delays of the French Government." Daladier quickly caught this infection of excitement and burst out: "It is clear that in spite of all reverence for warnings, that box (meaning the Quai d'Orsay) has not yet learned its duty." He assured the Polish Ambassador that he "would send for Bonnet at once and would take the direction of foreign affairs into his own hands."[100]

[97] M. Charles-Roux, Ambassador to the Holy See, to M. Georges Bonnet, Rome, August 31, 1939. French Yellow Book, p. 351.

[98] Gibson, op. cit., pp. 136–37; see also, Ambassador Philipps to Secretary Hull, Rome, September 2, 1939. 740.0011 EW./1939/53, MS, Department of State.

[99] Chargé d'Affaires Kirk to Secretary Hull, Berlin, September 1, 1939. 740.0011 EW./1939/29, Confidential file, MS, Department of State.

[100] Ambassador Bullitt to Secretary Hull, Paris, September 2, 1939. 740.0011 EW./1939/51, Confidential file, MS, Department of State.

He found this easier to say than do. Bonnet remained as Foreign Minister and he continued to plague the Polish Ambassador. On the afternoon of September 2, after the meeting of the Chamber of Deputies, the ambassador called at the Foreign Office and inquired if "the French Government intended to order the French Ambassador in Berlin to demand an immediate reply to his *démarche* of yesterday." Bonnet blandly replied that this question would be discussed at a Cabinet meeting which might be held that evening or on September 3. After this meeting "an ultimatum of 48 hours probably would be sent to Germany." Bonnet's unruffled manner once more caused the Polish Ambassador to lose his temper and he demanded the issuance of "an immediate ultimatum to Germany." As a result of this pressure, it was decided to "propose to the British Government that the British and French Ambassadors in Berlin should be instructed tonight to call at the German Foreign Office tomorrow morning and state that they could not wait longer than seven o'clock tomorrow evening for a reply to their démarches of yesterday."[101]

At 9:00 on the morning of September 3, Nevile Henderson paid a visit to the German Foreign Office and delivered an ultimatum to the effect that unless assurances were given before 11:00 of the suspension of hostilities and the withdrawal of German troops from Poland, Great Britain would be at war with the Reich from that hour.[102] When Paul Schmidt, Hitler's interpreter, translated this ultimatum to the Führer and to Ribbentrop, there was

complete silence. Hitler sat immobile, gazing before him. He was not at a loss, as was afterwards stated, nor did he rage as others allege. He sat completely silent and unmoving. After an interval . . . he turned to Ribbentrop: ". . . What now?" asked Hitler with a savage look, as though implying that his Foreign Minister had misled him about England's probable reaction. Ribbentrop answered quietly: "I assume that the French will hand in a similar ultimatum within the hour." As my duty was now performed, I withdrew. To those in the anteroom pressing around me I said: "The English have just handed us an ultimatum. In two hours a state of war will exist between England and Germany." . . . Goering turned to me and said: "If we lose this war, then God have mercy on us." Goebbels stood in a corner, downcast and self-absorbed. Everywhere in the room I saw looks of grave concern.[103]

At 12:00 the French Ambassador presented the expected ultimatum with a time limit fixed at 5:00. For a second time in the twentieth cen-

[101] Ambassador Bullitt to Secretary Hull, Paris, September 2, 1939. 740.0011 EW./1939/63, MS, Department of State.
[102] Henderson, *op. cit.*, pp. 298–99.
[103] Paul Schmidt, *Hitler's Interpreter* (London, 1950), pp. 157–58.

tury diplomacy had failed to avert a world war. The old myth of successful Anglo-French diplomatic formulas faded before the lurid realities of a world conflict that would reduce both Britain and France to second-rate powers.

In London, Lord Halifax confided to Ambassador Kennedy that the outbreak of war

reminded him of a dream he once had in which he was being tried for murder. When he was finally convicted and found guilty he was surprised what a feeling of relief came over him. It was very much the same now; he had planned in all ways to keep away a World War and had worked himself into a sad state of health and now that he had failed he found himself freshened up for the new struggle. . . .

It became more and more apparent to one as Halifax talked . . . that what Britain depends on more than anything else to end the war before the world collapses, is the internal collapse inside of Germany. They had definite confidence in their secret service reports that the oil and gasoline supply is definitely not over four months and that there is a definite feeling in Germany against war and if it got too tough economically, Hitler would be out.[104]

The reports of British intelligence experts were as inaccurate in military matters as they were with reference to gas and oil supplies in the Reich. General Ironside informed the British Cabinet, on the basis of a series of reports, that German strategy was based upon a quick campaign. Some of the terrain leading into Polish territory was quite rugged. If the Poles made it "tough" for the invading Germans "so that it required a couple of months to make any headway," Hitler's "hordes would have great difficulty in retreating or advancing."[105]

The American military attaché in Berlin was equally optimistic with regard to checking the progress of the German military machine. The Poles were following a preconceived plan that envisaged "delaying the German advance with covering forces and stubbornly holding fortified areas. . . . They are making the Germans pay dearly for every kilometer gained and are exhausting the best German divisions." The Polish defense was "being carried out as planned by the Poles and the French and British missions, and appears to be succeeding."[106]

These dispatches from Berlin read like chapters from *Alice in Wonderland,* and in 1939 it appeared as though Neville Chamberlain was assuming the role of the Mad Hatter when he could not send even token assistance to the hard-pressed Poles. Nowadays it seems evident that

[104] Ambassador Kennedy to Secretary Hull, London, September 4, 1939.
[105] *Ibid.*
[106] Chargé d'Affaires Kirk to Secretary Hull, Berlin, September 5, 1939. 740.0011 EW./1939/150, *Confidential file,* MS, Department of State.

the real Mad Hatter was Franklin D. Roosevelt who pressed Chamberlain to give promises to the Poles when there was no possibility of fulfilling them. According to some reports, it was William C. Bullitt who cast Roosevelt in this grotesque role.

I recently received from Mr. Verne Marshall, former editor of the *Cedar Rapids Gazette,* a letter in which he made the following significant statements:

President Roosevelt wrote a note to William Bullitt [in the summer of 1939], then Ambassador to France, directing him to advise the French Government that if, in the event of a Nazi attack upon Poland, France and England did not go to Poland's aid, those countries could expect no help from America if a general war developed. On the other hand, if France and England immediately declared war on Germany [in the event of a Nazi attack upon Poland], they could expect "all aid" from the United States.

F.D.R.'s instructions to Bullitt were to send this word along to "Joe" and "Tony," meaning Ambassadors Kennedy, in London, and Biddle, in Warsaw, respectively. F.D.R. wanted Daladier, Chamberlain and Josef Beck to know of these instructions to Bullitt. Bullitt merely sent his note from F.D.R. to Kennedy in the diplomatic pouch from Paris. Kennedy followed Bullitt's idea and forwarded it to Biddle. When the Nazis grabbed Warsaw and Beck disappeared, they must have come into possession of the F.D.R. note. The man who wrote the report I sent you, saw it in Berlin in October, 1939.[107]

After receiving this letter from Mr. Marshall I wrote at once to Mr. Bullitt and inquired about this alleged instruction from the President. He replied as follows: "I have no memory of any instruction from President Roosevelt of the nature quoted in your letter to me and feel quite certain that no such instruction was ever sent to me by the President."[108]

Mr. Joseph Kennedy sent to me a similar negative answer with reference to this alleged instruction from the President, but the *Forrestal Diaries* would indicate that Bullitt did strongly urge President Roosevelt to exert pressure upon Prime Minister Chamberlain and that Roosevelt responded to this pressure. The following excerpt has far-reaching implications:

27 December 1945: Played golf today with Joe Kennedy (Joseph P. Kennedy, who was Roosevelt's Ambassador to Great Britain in the years immediately before the war). I asked him about his conversations with Roosevelt

[107] Mr. Verne Marshall to the author, September 25, 1951. See also the special article in the *Washington Times-Herald,* November 12, 1941 by Arthur Sears Henning.

[108] William C. Bullitt to the author, November 10, 1951.

and Neville Chamberlain from 1938 on. He said Chamberlain's position in 1938 was that England had nothing with which to fight and that she could not risk going to war with Hitler. Kennedy's view: That Hitler would have fought Russia without any later conflict with England if it had not been for Bullitt's (William C. Bullitt, then Ambassador to France) urging on Roosevelt in the summer of 1939 that the Germans must be faced down about Poland; neither the French nor the British would have made Poland a cause of war if it had not been for the constant needling from Washington. Bullitt, he said, kept telling Roosevelt that the Germans wouldn't fight; Kennedy that they would, and that they would overrun Europe. Chamberlain, he says, stated that America and the world Jews had forced England into the war. In his telephone conversations with Roosevelt in the summer of 1939 the President kept telling him to put some iron up Chamberlain's backside. Kennedy's response always was that putting iron up his backside did no good unless the British had some iron with which to fight, and they did not. . . .

What Kennedy told me in this conversation jibes substantially with the remarks Clarence Dillon had made to me already, to the general effect that Roosevelt had asked him in some manner to communicate privately with the British to the end that Chamberlain should have greater firmness in his dealings with Germany. Dillon told me that at Roosevelt's request he had talked with Lord Lothian in the same general sense as Kennedy reported Roosevelt having urged him to do with Chamberlain. Lothian presumably was to communicate to Chamberlain the gist of his conversation with Dillon.

Looking backward there is undoubtedly foundation for Kennedy's belief that Hitler's attack could have been deflected to Russia.[109]

Mr. Kennedy is known to have a good memory and it is highly improbable that his statements to Secretary Forrestal were entirely untrustworthy. Ambassador Bullitt was doing a lot of talking in 1939 and he was regarded as the mouthpiece of the President. In January 1939 he had a long conversation with Count Jerzy Potocki, the Polish Ambassador in Washington, and left him with the impression that "he [Bullitt] had received from President Roosevelt a very detailed definition of the attitude taken by the United States towards the present European crisis. He will present this material at the Quai d'Orsay. . . . The contents of these directions . . . were: (1) The vitalizing foreign policy, under the leadership of President Roosevelt, severely and unambiguously condemns totalitarian countries; . . . (2) it is the decided opinion of the President that France and Britain must put [an] end to any sort of compromise with the totalitarian countries."[110]

In February 1939, Bullitt had a conversation with Jules Lukasiewicz,

109 *The Forrestal Diaries*, ed. Walter Millis and E. S. Duffield (New York, 1951), pp. 121–22.
110 Count Jerzy Potocki to the Polish Foreign Office, Washington, January 16, 1939. *German White Paper*, pp. 32–34.

the Polish Ambassador in Paris, and once again he seemed to speak with authority. He confided to Lukasiewicz that Washington official circles were greatly concerned about the outbreak of war in Europe. If Britain and France were defeated, Germany "would become dangerous to the realistic interests of the United States on the American continent. For this reason, one can foresee right from the beginning the participation of the United States in the war on the side of France and Britain. . . . One thing . . . seems certain to me, namely, that the policy of President Roosevelt will henceforth take the course of supporting France's resistance . . . and to weaken British compromise tendencies."[111]

These excerpts from the dispatches of the Polish ambassadors in Washington and in Paris afford a clear indication of the fact that President Roosevelt, through Bullitt, was exerting steady pressure upon Britain and France to stand up boldly to Nazi Germany. When this policy led to a war in which Nazi armed forces easily crushed French resistance, it is easy now to understand the poignancy of Premier Reynaud's pleas to Roosevelt for prompt assistance. He and Daladier had taken the assurances of Bullitt seriously and the hysterical tone of Reynaud's repeated wires to the White House indicates a feeling of betrayal. From the battered walls of Warsaw there were loud murmurs about broken British promises. When their muted echoes reached London, Neville Chamberlain must have remembered the constant "needling from Washington" in favor of a more resolute stand against Hitler, and Joseph Kennedy must have had reluctant recollections of the many occasions when the President "kept telling him to put some iron up Chamberlain's backside." Germany had been baited into a war with Britain and France when she would have preferred a conflict with Russia over the Ukraine. Chamberlain got plenty of iron up his backside, but it was Nazi hot metal that seared him and all Britain and helped to break into bits a proud empire that all the King's horses and all the King's men can never put together again.

[111] Ambassador Jules Lukasiewicz to the Polish Foreign Minister, Paris, February 1939. *Ibid.*, pp. 43–45.

XXIV

Roosevelt Adopts a More Positive Policy
towards the War in Europe

a. *The President Promises Peace for the U.S.*

IMMEDIATELY after the outbreak of World War II, President Roosevelt made a radio address in which he reminded the American people that they should master "at the outset a simple but unalterable fact in modern foreign relations. When peace has been broken anywhere, peace of all countries everywhere is in danger." This theme of a "one world" he emphasized again and again: "Passionately though we may desire detachment, we are forced to realize that every word that comes through the air, every ship that sails the sea, every battle that is fought does affect the American future." In order to relieve the apprehensions that millions of Americans must have felt as a result of this stress upon the one-world concept, he then glibly gave the following assurance: "Let no man or woman thoughtlessly or falsely talk of America sending its armies to European fields. At this moment there is being prepared a proclamation of American neutrality." This assurance was followed by a reference to the "historic precedent that goes back to the days of the administration of President George Washington." America would remain "a neutral nation." But he closed his address with a curtain line that had an ominous implication: *"As long as it remains within my power to prevent,* there will be no blackout of peace in the United States."[1]

b. *The Mission of William Rhodes Davis to Berlin*

One way to prevent a blackout of peace in the United States was to bring the war in Europe to a close. This might be effected through American mediation. In the early part of September 1939, William Rhodes Davis, an independent oil operator of large wealth, decided to ask President Roosevelt to approve a mission to Berlin and Rome for the purpose of arranging American mediation. Davis was a close friend of John L. Lewis who had bought Roosevelt's good will by a half-

---

[1] Radio Address delivered by President Roosevelt from Washington, September 3, 1939. *Peace and War: United States Foreign Policy, 1931–1941* (Washington, 1943), pp. 483–86.

million dollar contribution to the campaign fund of 1936. Davis himself had made a modest contribution of $300,000 to the same fund.

Through his intimate connections with Dr. Hertslet, representing German banking and industrial interests, and with President Cárdenas of Mexico, Davis had arranged large sales of oil to Germany. Inasmuch as a European war would put an end to these sales, Davis was extremely anxious to promote peace. After the outbreak of the war he hurried to Washington where, with the assistance of John L. Lewis, he arranged for a conference with President Roosevelt. On September 15 a meeting was held in the White House with the President, "Steve" Early, John L. Lewis, Adolf Berle, Cordell Hull, and Mr. Davis in attendance. It was decided to send Davis to Rome and Berlin in order to see if there was any possibility of arranging terms for American mediation in the war that had just broken out.

After some difficulty at Bermuda which required State Department intervention to permit him to continue on his trip, Davis finally arrived in Berlin for some important conferences with General Göring. At the first conference he made the following statement to Göring.

It is my opinion that immediate settlement would return to Germany . . . Danzig, the Corridor and the former provinces in Poland which were taken away from Germany by the Treaty of Versailles, and that the question of the colonies formerly owned by Germany, prior to 1914 . . . could be compromised. If Mr. Hitler would set forth a reasonable basis of settlement and the assistance of Mr. Roosevelt requested as mediator, he would give it serious consideration. The President, I am sure, believes that a new economic arrangement should be arrived at by the contesting nations which would provide each nation with raw materials, goods and commodities essential to maintain its economic integrity and well-being.

The Field Marshal replied: "These statements are very surprising as the impression in Germany is that Mr. Roosevelt's feelings are now against Germany and that he is sympathetic to England and France." . . . Regarding the question of peace, the Field Marshal stated: "Germany is and always has been ready to work for peace in Europe on sound equitable lines. The views . . . which you have conveyed to me correspond substantially to the views of Mr. Hitler and his Government. A world conference appears under the circumstances to be the only practical medium through which these mutual hopes for peace can be achieved. Germany will welcome the aid of Mr. Roosevelt in bringing about such a conference. . . . The fundamental and motivating purpose of such a conference must be to establish a new order in the world designed to secure an enduring peace. A pre-requisite to that aim is the complete liquidation of the Versailles system. . . . Germany is prepared to accept any method and to welcome any suggestion, consistent with its inalienable

right as a nation to live on a basis of equality with other nations, which will
guarantee enduring peace for itself and the smaller European nations."

On October 3, Davis had another meeting with Göring who remarked:

You may assure Mr. Roosevelt that if he will undertake mediation, Germany
will agree to an adjustment whereby a new Polish State and a new Czechoslovakian independent government would come into being. However, this
information is for him alone and to be used by him only if necessary to bring
about a peace conference. . . . As for myself and my Government, I would be
glad to attend and in the event of such a conference I would represent Germany. I agree that the conference should be in Washington.

In conclusion, Göring informed Mr. Davis that Hitler would speak
on October 6 and his remarks would, in spirit and content, "be of a
nature which impartial analysis must accept as a basis for negotiation."[2]
    After these conferences with Mr. Davis, Göring talked with Chan-
cellor Hitler concerning this proposed American mediation. The Chancellor apparently took the matter very seriously and on October 6 he
made a speech which he thought would lay the basis for a world conference. He emphasized the importance of an early calling of a conference
of the "leading nations" on the European continent. It should be held
"before millions of men are . . . uselessly sent to their death and billions
of dollars' worth of property destroyed. The continuation of the present
state of affairs in the West is unthinkable. Each day will soon demand
increasing sacrifices."
    After this introduction Hitler indicated the bases of an enduring
peace: (1) the foreign policies of European states should frankly recognize the liquidation of the Treaty of Versailles; Germany's colonial
possessions before 1914 should be returned to her; (2) there should be
a reorganization of the international economic system which would include a new system of markets and a final settlement of currencies;
(3) the most important item in a program for the abolition of future
wars was "the establishment of an unconditionally guaranteed peace

    2 This account of the Davis mission to Berlin is based upon a letter from Mr. Verne
Marshall, former editor of the *Cedar Rapids* (Iowa) *Gazette*, in which the background
of the mission is given in detail. See Verne Marshall to Charles C. Tansill, April 11,
1951. Mr. Marshall was kind enough to supply me with the letters that Mr. Davis
wrote to President Roosevelt on October 11, 12, 1939. These letters fully describe the
conversations between Mr. Davis and General Göring and indicate his evident anxiety
to place this information before the President. I asked ex-Senator Burton K. Wheeler
many questions concerning the correspondence between Mr. Davis and President
Roosevelt and he assured me that it was authentic. For further data on this matter see
the *Des Moines Register*, October 31, 1946.

and of a sense of security on the part of individual nations. . . . An essential part of this necessary sense of security, however, is a clear definition of the legitimate use and application of certain modern armaments which can at any given moment strike straight at the heart of every nation and hence create a permanent sense of insecurity."[3]

While Hitler was presenting to the world this sane and moderate program, Davis was flying back to Washington with a record of the conciliatory conversations with Göring. At this same time Roosevelt commenced his momentous correspondence with Winston Churchill.[4] Its influence cannot be judged until it has been carefully read and all the implications given extended consideration. But at any rate, something did change Roosevelt's mind in October 1939. When Mr. Davis returned to Washington he phoned to Miss LeHand and indicated his readiness to report to the President on his Berlin trip. After a brief pause she informed him that "the Chief" was "in conference" and could not be disturbed. When this conference continued indefinitely, Davis wrote a long letter to the President (October 11) and told him in detail of his conferences with Göring and the fact that Hitler's address on October 6 had been conciliatory in tone and an indirect assurance that the Führer would support the idea of American mediation. He received no answer to this letter and there was no invitation to the White House. A mission that seemed so bright with promise had suddenly ended in a dismal failure. Did one of the famous "sealed letters" from Winston Churchill to Franklin Roosevelt cause a rejection of this Hitler "feeler" for American mediation? Did American foreign policy thereafter follow British suggestions?

c. *The Barriers Preserving Neutrality Are Broken Down*

Two days after Britain and France declared war against Germany, the President (September 5) issued two proclamations. The first closely followed the language of the neutrality proclamation issued by President Wilson after the outbreak of World War I. It emphasized the role America would play as a neutral, reminded American citizens of their duties under international law, and warned the belligerents against infringing upon American rights. The second proclamation implemented the Neutrality Act of 1937 and imposed an embargo upon the export of arms, ammunition, and implements of war to belligerent powers.[5]

---

[3] Address of Chancellor Hitler, October 6, 1939. Text given in Friedrich Stieve, *What the World Rejected, Hitler's Peace Offers, 1933–1939* (Berlin, 1939), pp. 13–16.
[4] Winston S. Churchill, *The Gathering Storm* (Cambridge, 1948), pp. 440–41.
[5] Department of State, *Bulletin*, I, September 9, 16, 1939, pp. 203–11, 246–49.

This embargo checked the shipment to Britain and France of some
$79,000,000 worth of war materials for which export licenses had al-
ready been issued. Allied victory, as in World War I, depended upon
an uninterrupted flow of munitions to British and French ports. Would
the President be able to secure amendments to the Neutrality Law that
would permit these shipments?

His first step in this direction was to issue on September 13 a summons to Congress to meet in special session on the twenty-first. When
they met they listened to a Presidential message that was filled with in-
accuracies designed to justify some radical changes in neutrality legislation. He contended that existing legislation altered the foreign policy
of the nation in such a way as to impair peaceful relations with other
nations. Our policy with respect to belligerent countries had, with one
notable exception, been "based upon international law." The exception
had been the non-intercourse and embargo laws of the Napoleonic
period and their effect upon the economy of the nation had been disastrous. These economic limitations had been the prelude to war. The
Neutrality Act of 1935 had been another lamentable exception because
some of its provisions had been "wholly inconsistent with ancient pre-
cepts of the law of nations." He regarded the ban on arms shipments
as "most vitally dangerous to American neutrality, American security
and American peace." In the proposed new legislation he wished provisions that would (1) forbid war credits to belligerents; (2) prohibit
travel by American citizens on belligerent vessels; (3) provide for a
license system for the import and export of munitions of war; (4) restore the cash-and-carry provision which had expired on May 1; (5)
authorize the exclusion of American shipping from combat areas.[6]

The President's message aroused a tremendous debate in the press,
over the radio, and in Congress. According to a poll conducted by the
Christian Science Monitor, editorial opinion in the country was strongly
in favor of the repeal of existing neutrality legislation.[7] But letters and
telegrams soon began to pour into the offices of senators and representatives in a veritable deluge. In these communications the ratio *against*
repeal was reported to be five to one.[8] Under the impact of this pressure
a bill was reported on September 30 from the Senate Committee on
Foreign Relations. Its provisions reflected much isolationist sentiment:
(1) when the President or Congress found a state of war existing between foreign countries, the President was required to name the belligerents and apply the act; (2) no United States vessel could lawfully

[6] *Ibid.,* September 23, 1939, pp. 275–80.
[7] September 20, 1939.
[8] *New York Times,* September 21, 1939.

carry passengers or goods to any port of the belligerent nations; (3) the cash-and-carry system was restored and made mandatory for all goods. They could be shipped only after the title and interest of American citizens had been extinguished; (4) a ban was placed upon the arming of merchant vessels of the United States; (5) the prohibition of travel by American citizens on belligerent ships was continued; (6) the President was authorized to forbid the entry of American ships into combat areas; (7) the President might bar the entry of foreign submarines or armed merchantmen into American ports; (8) belligerents were limited to ninety-day credit transactions with reference to the purchase of American goods.[9]

Before the debate in the Senate began on this proposed legislation, Senator Borah made a careful study of every aspect of neutrality legislation. As the outstanding member of the Senate Committee on Foreign Relations, his viewpoint was of great importance. Since 1933 he had paid particular attention to the European picture with an emphasis upon Germany. In 1938 he expressed a strong desire to visit Germany and have a talk with Chancellor Hitler with reference to the plight of the Jews and many other topics connected with world peace. Through William K. Hutchinson, a prominent newspaperman, the German Government learned of Borah's desire to visit the Third Reich. On November 28 the German Foreign Office sent an invitation to Borah to spend some time in Germany and have extended conferences with Ribbentrop and Hitler. Borah was anxious to accept this invitation but decided to place the matter before Secretary Hull. When Hull returned from the Pan-American Conference at Lima, our relations with Germany had grown more strained, and Borah realized that Hull would strenuously oppose any visit to Germany. The President was also hostile to such a move, so Borah finally postponed his trip indefinitely. The outbreak of war in September 1939 put an end to such dreams, but to the historian the incident has definite importance. In his conversations with William Rhodes Davis, Göring was distinctly conciliatory. The same conciliatory attitude towards Borah might have had significant consequences.[10]

While Borah was studying the situation after September 3, 1939, he began a correspondence with Professor Edwin M. Borchard, of Yale University. Borchard was an eminent professor of international law and was an able critic of the Roosevelt foreign policy. Borah had indicated his opposition to any lifting of the arms embargo after the outbreak of World War II. Such action seemed to him to be an infraction

[9] Allen W. Dulles, "Cash and Carry Neutrality," *Foreign Affairs*, XVIII (1940), 179–95.

[10] William K. Hutchinson, *William E. Borah, Late Senator From the State of Idaho* (Washington, 1940), pp. 29–40.

of international law. In support of this viewpoint Professor Borchard
wrote to Borah on September 20. He firmly believed that "the changing
of a neutrality law to *relax* a country's neutrality with the motive or even
with the effect of aiding one belligerent, is a distinct violation of international law. Changes may be made in neutrality during war, but only
in the direction of tightening or safeguarding a country's neutrality,
and not in the direction of relaxing it. . . . I cannot escape the unfortunate belief that whatever we do or do not do to the Neutrality
Act, the proposal and its dramatic submission indicate the Executive
mood. . . . I fear that excuses for intervention may readily be found."[11]
On the following day, in a letter to the *New York Times,* Professors
Philip C. Jessup and Charles C. Hyde of Columbia University confirmed the position of Professor Borchard.[12]

On September 23, Professor Thomas H. Healy, of Georgetown University, sent to Borah a long memorandum in answer to several questions. He indicated that the President's viewpoint that an arms embargo
was against the principles of international law was quite incorrect. Such
embargoes had long been a part of international practice. He then emphasized the fact that the embargoes and non-intercourse acts that preceded the War of 1812 had not caused that war. Finally, he expressed
the opinion that the arms embargo could be abandoned only if it could
be proved that such action was necessary for American interests and
safety and not for the benefit of one set of belligerents.[13]

Acting upon this advice, Borah led the fight in the Senate against any
repeal of the arms embargo which he was certain was designed to aid
Britain and France. Transport of troops would eventually follow the
shipment of arms. After supplying them with arms and ammunition,
"can we, if the hour of greater need should occur, refuse to send our
armies? . . . The only way I see in which we can stay out of this war,
having taken the first step for the reasons for which we are asked to
take it, is for the war to end before we get in." He was not impressed
with the popular thesis that the Allies were fighting a crusade for
democracy. To him the war was "nothing more than another chapter
in the bloody volume of European power politics."[14]

Professor Borchard warmly praised this speech of Borah. He had put
his "finger on the real issue" and it should "not be lost from view." It
might be, "of course, that in the present temper many men will not be

11 Edwin M. Borchard to Senator William E. Borah, September 20, 1939. Borah
Papers, Library of Congress.
12 September 21, 1939.
13 Memorandum by Professor Thomas H. Healy, September 23, 1939. Borah Papers, Library of Congress.
14 *Congressional Record,* October 2, 1939.

impressed, but will merely be irritated by the fact that the proposed change violates international law. Given the motive and the effect, nothing could in my mind be clearer."[15]

During the debate in the Senate, Mr. Lundeen, from Minnesota, argued in favor of a prompt demand for Allied payment of war debts. If they did not comply with this demand he thought the British and French West Indies should be seized "in accordance with the Jacksonian theory, expounded in the days of good, strong, red-blooded, affirmative democracy. . . . Let us show that there is some red blood in us. . . . Now is the time to acquire them."[16]

Outside the Senate the debate was carried on by numerous speakers who adopted widely different viewpoints. Former President Hoover believed that the Allies did not require the assistance of the United States to win the war. With their vast economic resources, combined with the pressure of a tight blockade, it would be impossible for Germany to win. He was opposed to any outright repeal of the arms embargo. It should be modified to permit the sale of "defensive weapons."[17] Colonel Lindbergh agreed with this Hoover viewpoint. In addition he avowed a warm attachment to isolationism which led him to chide Canada for staying within the British Commonwealth of Nations. "Sooner or later we must demand the freedom of this continent and its surrounding islands from the dictates of European power."[18]

Dorothy Thompson grew so hysterical over the remarks of Colonel Lindbergh that she poured out her wrath in three long installments in the *New York Herald-Tribune*.[19] These articles opened the eyes of Mrs. Franklin D. Roosevelt who had "sensed" some Nazi ideal in the Lindbergh speech which she had not been able to bring herself "to believe was really there."[20]

Colonel Stimson now leaped into the fray to joust with Colonel Lindbergh, and along the college front Presidents Butler, of Columbia, and Conant, of Harvard, lent their assistance to the movement to repeal the neutrality law. As a result of all this sound and fury and persistent pressure from the Administration, a new neutrality law passed both houses of Congress on November 3.[21] On the following day the President signed the bill and at once issued two proclamations to implement it. One delimited the waters off the British Isles and the coasts of Western

[15] Professor Edwin M. Borchard to Senator Borah, October 3, 1939. Borah Papers, Library of Congress.
[16] *Congressional Record*, October 14, 1939.
[17] *The United States in World Affairs, 1939* (New York, 1940), p. 174.
[18] *New York Times*, October 14, 1939.
[19] *New York Herald-Tribune*, October 18, 20, 23, 1939.
[20] *New York World-Telegram*, October 19, 1939.
[21] *Congressional Record*, November 3, 1939.

Europe as a combat area which no American vessel could enter "except under such rules and regulations as may be prescribed." Under the law they could not carry cargo or passengers to any of the belligerent ports in Europe and Africa as far south as the Canary Islands, and under the proclamation they were prohibited from entering the neutral ports of Ireland, Sweden, Denmark, Belgium, the Netherlands, and Norway south of Bergen.[22]

On September 5 an embargo was applied to the shipment of munitions of war and military equipment to belligerents except on a cash-and-carry basis. This restriction did not seriously affect the exports of war matériel to the Allies. In September 1939 the shipments of arms, ammunition, and implements of war to France amounted to $4,429,323; in December the value of these shipments rose to $17,857,281. The value of shipments to Britain did not rise so abruptly. In September 1939 they amounted to $1,422,800; in December they rose to $4,184,377.[23] It should be remembered that the title, right, and interest in this war matériel had to be extinguished before it could be exported. During the period from 1914–1917 there were no restrictions on belligerent borrowing. Loans to the Allied governments had financed huge shipments of munitions of war to their ports. Under the Neutrality Act of November 4 belligerent borrowing was prohibited.

d. A Safety Belt for the Western Hemisphere

In September 1939 the foreign ministers of the American Republics met in Panama and adopted a large number of resolutions the most significant of which was the Declaration of Panama (October 3, 1939).[24] Under the terms of this resolution a "safety belt" was drawn around the Americas south of Canada varying in width from 300 to 1000 miles. Belligerents were warned against committing any hostile action within this zone whether by land, sea, or air. This declaration was an interesting demonstration of collective Pan-American action, but it had little validity because the American Republics did not provide any force to maintain the neutrality of the zone.

In December 1939 the German pocket battleship *Graf von Spee* engaged in a running naval battle with three British cruisers and was

---

[22] Proclamation of November 4, 1939. Department of State, *Bulletin*, I, 455–56. The Neutrality Act of November 4 and the accompanying proclamations are given in Denys P. Myers and S. Shepard Jones, *Documents on American Foreign Relations, July 1939–June 1940* (Boston, 1940), pp. 656–97.

[23] *The United States in World Affairs, 1939*, p. 341.

[24] Samuel F. Bemis, *The Latin American Policy of the United States* (New York, 1943), pp. 363–66.

finally blown up by order of its captain (December 17) near the port of Montevideo, Uruguay. The twenty-one American Republics sent a prompt protest to the governments of Britain, France, and Germany against this violation of the safety zone.[25] Britain and France rejected any thought of compliance with the provisions of the Declaration of Panama unless an adequate naval force of the American Republics patrolled the safety zone and insured its neutrality.[26] The German Government made the point that it was futile for it to take any affirmative action with regard to the safety zone because the British and French governments had already taken adverse action.[27] When the American Government took no step to establish a naval patrol in the safety zone to make the provisions of the Declaration of Panama dangerous for belligerents to violate, the declaration became a mere pious aspiration. Pan-American collective action was a mere stuffed club without the armed support of the United States.

e. *Secretary Hull Engages in a Battle of the Books*

At the very opening of World War II, American attention was attracted to the implications of submarine warfare by the sinking of the S. S. *Athenia* (September 3) ten miles off the north Irish coast. Nearly one hundred persons lost their lives, including some thirty Americans.[28] The German Government denied that the *Athenia* had been a victim of a German submarine; it had probably struck a mine. The American press was remarkably restrained in its comments upon the *Athenia* incident. There was no loud clamor for immediate reprisals.

The reprisals were taken by the British and French governments which on September 8 announced a long-range blockade of Germany. Germany responded by declaring a counterblockade against British and French coasts (September 11). In Britain a Ministry of Economic Warfare was hurriedly established which worked in conjunction with the French Ministry of Blockade. Long lists of contraband were published and British naval vessels were stationed in the North Sea near the Skagerrak to intercept merchant ships en route to the Baltic. Other patrols were established at Gibraltar and Suez. Contraband control bases were set up in the ports of Kirkwall, Weymouth, and the Downs in Britain; Dunkerque, LeHavre, and Marseilles in France; at Gibral-

[25] Jones and Myers, *op. cit.*, pp. 121–22.
[26] *Ibid.*, pp. 122–27. See also, Philip M. Brown, "Protective Jurisdiction," *American Journal of International Law*, XXXIV (1940), 112–16.
[27] Jones and Myers, *op. cit.*, pp. 127–30.
[28] Report of American Minister to Eire (Cudahy), September 5, 1939. *Ibid.*, pp. 698–99.

tar, Malta, Oran, Port Said, and Haifa. Ships sailing for Germany or for neutral ports from which goods could be conveniently transported to that country, were urgently "advised" to call at one of these control bases for search. Otherwise they might be hailed upon the high seas and compelled to enter a base.[29] Shipowners could escape this irritating practice if they secured from British consuls at the home ports "navi-certs" or certificates which testified as to the innocent character of the cargo.

This pattern of British procedure had been established during the years from 1914 to 1917 and history was merely repeating itself.[30] This was also true with regard to the treatment of neutral mails. In the British control ports, neutral mail bags were examined with great care for con-traband which included money and securities, and letters might be cen-sored. Up to the middle of November 1939 the British had detained thirty-three American ships for examination, and had removed cargoes, wholly or in part, from seven of them.[31] After November 4, under the terms of the Neutrality Act, American ships were forbidden to carry cargoes in combat areas in European waters. It was expected in Wash-ington that British detentions would sharply decrease after this date. But the British Government, with the same irritating unconcern for American feelings that it showed during the years 1914 to 1917, con-tinued the practice of detention and even compelled American ships to proceed to control ports within the combat area which was closed to them by the express terms of the Neutrality Act.

After invoking the doctrine of continuous voyage against shipments of goods from neutral ports to Germany, the British Government adopted another item from its practice of 1915. On November 27 an Order in Council was issued which provided that after December 4 any neutral vessel sailing from a neutral port, but having on board "goods which are of enemy origin or are enemy property," might be required to go to an Allied port and there discharge that portion of her cargo.[32] To implement this order in an effective manner a joint organization of British and French officials was established in London, while British

---

[29] C. H. McLaughlin, "Neutral Rights Under International Law in the European War, 1939–1941," *Minnesota Law Review*, XXVI (1941–1942), 1–49, 177–222.

[30] Charles Callan Tansill, *America Goes To War* (Boston, 1938), pp. 516–85.

[31] Department of State, *Bulletin*, I, 461, 557–60. With regard to these British in-terceptions of American vessels and the removal of part of the cargoes of some of them, it should be noted that American trade with some neutrals adjacent to Germany had shown some significant increases after the outbreak of the war. For the full year 1938 the value of American exports to Norway was $22,567,000; in 1939 it increased to $32,100,000. For Sweden during the same period the increase was from $64,227,000 to $96,661,000.

[32] British Order in Council, November 27, 1939. Jones and Myers, *op. cit.*, pp. 705–7.

liaison officers were sent to Paris to work with the French blockade and naval ministries.[33] Allied naval vessels were then instructed to intercept German exports on all the seven seas so that goods that had been smuggled through the naval cordon in the combat area might be seized before reaching their destination.

These measures, which were palpable infractions of international law, were justified on the ground that they were necessary reprisals against German violations of the law of nations. The old arguments of 1914–1917 were dusted off by the British Foreign Office and used with the same cool insolence. In reply Secretary Hull, with his tongue in his cheek, sent to London the usual protests. On December 8, 1939, he specifically objected to the Order in Council of November 27 because it unlawfully interfered with the "legitimate trade" of American nationals. There could be no justification "for interfering with American vessels or their cargoes on grounds of breach of blockade." Likewise, the question of contraband could "not arise with respect to goods en route from Germany to the United States."[34] On December 14 another note filed a sharp protest against the British practice of compelling American vessels to proceed to ports within the combat area for detailed examination of their cargoes. Such actions were "without regard to the municipal law of the United States or the rights, obligations, and liabilities of American vessels under that law."[35] Some two weeks later (December 27), a third protest was made in connection with the British treatment of American mails. The Foreign Office was warned that the American Government could not admit the right of the British authorities "to interfere with American mails on American or other neutral ships on the high seas nor can it admit the right of the British Government to censor mail on ships which have involuntarily entered British ports." It felt compelled, therefore, to "make a vigorous protest against the practices outlined above."[36]

British expansions of the contraband list and British black lists gave further cause for American protests but notes from Secretary Hull were regarded in London as mere exercises in diplomatic double talk. The Foreign Office was well aware of American practices after April 1917. From American intervention in 1917 to the close of the war in November 1918 the Department of State had sanctioned some of the infrac-

[33] *New York Times,* December 5, 1939.

[34] The United States Embassy at London to the Foreign Office of the United Kingdom, December 8, 1939. Department of State, *Bulletin,* I, 651.

[35] Secretary Hull to the British Ambassador (Lord Lothian), December 14, 1939. Department of State, *Bulletin,* II, 4.

[36] The United States Embassy at London to the Foreign Office of the United Kingdom, December 27, 1939. Department of State, *Bulletin,* II, 3.

tions of international law against which it had previously protested. It was difficult for Secretary Hull to press the Allies too sharply with reference to practices which the American Government had adopted when it entered the World War against Germany.[37] Like a model watchdog, the conscience of Secretary Hull barked only at strangers.

f. Hitler Adopts a Conciliatory Policy towards the U.S.

The outbreak of World War II came as an unpleasant surprise to the German Admiralty which had hoped the conflict might be postponed until 1944. Admiral Raeder promptly advised an all out war against Britain in the form of unrestricted submarine warfare, but Hitler immediately rejected this counsel. He was deeply shocked at the news of the sinking of the *Athenia,* and upon the advice of the Naval Staff he denied German responsibility. Later when it was learned that the U-30 had torpedoed the liner, the commander, Lieutenant Lemp, was severely reprimanded.[38]

On September 7, during a conference with Admiral Raeder, Hitler insisted that "in order not to provoke neutral countries, the United States in particular, it is forbidden to torpedo passenger steamers, even when sailing in convoy. Warfare against French merchant ships, attacks on French warships and mine laying off French ports is prohibited."[39] These orders were partially modified on September 10 so that mixed British-French convoys, if escorted by French or French and British forces, might be attacked north of Brest. On October 16 there was a further modification: "All merchant ships definitely recognized as enemy ones (British or French) can be torpedoed without warning. Passenger steamers *in convoy* can be torpedoed a short while after notice has been given of the intention to do so." Passenger ships were already being torpedoed when "proceeding without lights."[40]

Hitler now made a conciliatory gesture towards the United States. On October 9, the American freight steamer, *City of Flint,* bound for a British port, was captured by the German pocket battleship, *Deutschland.* After a brief visit to the Norwegian port of Tromsö and the Russian port of Murmansk, the *City of Flint* with a German prize crew put into another Norwegian port where the authorities interned the

[37] Thomas A. Bailey, *Policy of the United States Toward the Neutrals, 1917–1918* (Baltimore, 1942).

[38] Anthony Martienssen, *Hitler and His Admirals* (New York, 1949), pp. 22–23.

[39] Conference of commander in chief, Navy, with the Führer, September 7, 1939. *Fuehrer Conferences on Matters Dealing with the German Navy* (Washington, 1947), pp. 3–5.

[40] Report of Commander in Chief, Navy, to the Führer, October 16, 1939. *Ibid.,* p. 21.

German crew and returned the vessel to its American commander. On November 10, Admiral Raeder submitted a report to which Hitler agreed: "The *City of Flint* case has been mismanaged. . . . It appears advisable to allow the *City of Flint* to return to the United States unmolested. . . . The Fuehrer agrees with the Commander in Chief, Navy; no further action is to be taken against the *City of Flint*."[41]

At the end of December 1939 the rules controlling submarine activity were formulated as follows: "The following ships are subject to submarine attack without warning: (1) All merchant ships recognized as enemy; (exceptions are passenger ships sailing alone which are definitely unarmed); (2) all neutral ships sailing in enemy convoy; (3) all ships sailing without lights; (4) all ships refusing to stop or making use of radio telegraph; (5) American crews are [to be] treated with the greatest consideration."[42]

Thus, at the close of four months of warfare on the high seas, German anxiety to conciliate America had resulted in exceptional treatment of United States vessels. Ninety ships carrying neutral flags had been sunk but not one of the ninety had flown American colors. Only four American ships had been stopped at sea by German naval vessels; none had been compelled to enter a German port for search and none had been attacked by commerce raiders. Thanks to pressure from the Führer the German Navy was on its good behavior.

g. *Finland Goes Down Fighting Soviet Aggression*

While Hitler was making conciliatory gestures towards France and the United States, Soviet Russia was showing to all the world how well founded the fears had been of Russian aggression on the part of the small Baltic states. With the large slice of Poland acquired under agreement with Germany the Russian appetite was stimulated to further seizures. On September 29, Estonia was forced to sign a mutual assistance pact which permitted the Soviet Union to establish naval and air bases within its territory and to maintain garrisons to protect them. On October 5, Latvia was compelled to sign a similar pact, and on October 16, Lithuania followed suit. In *Izvestia* this highhanded procedure was delicately described as a means of showing how the "Soviet government respects the rights of small nations."[43] The same solicitude was soon shown towards Finland.

[41] Report of Commander in Chief, Navy, to the Führer, November 19, 1939. *Ibid.,* p. 36.
[42] Report of the Commander in Chief, Navy, to the Führer, December 30, 1939. *Ibid.,* pp. 66–67.
[43] *New York Times,* October 7, 1939.

Relations between Finland and Russia had long been based upon the Treaty of Tartu (October 14, 1920) which had established the boundaries between the two countries. Russian acceptance of the terms of this treaty was confirmed by the nonaggression treaty of January 21, 1932.[44] This was followed by a treaty of conciliation (April 22, 1932) under whose terms the high contracting parties agreed to submit to a conciliation commission for the amicable settlement of all disputes which could not be handled satisfactorily through diplomatic channels.[45] On April 7, 1934, the formal nonaggression treaty was extended to December 31, 1945.[46]

During the summer of 1939, while Britain and France were vainly endeavoring to reach some agreement with Soviet Russia concerning the building of a barrier against German aggression, the Kremlin kept insisting that the negotiations should include a guarantee of Finnish independence. The Finnish Government strenuously objected to any such arrangement on the ground that it would give Russia an excuse for quartering soldiers in Finland. The Soviet pact with Nazi Germany put an end to these negotiations and provided the impetus that pushed Europe into war. Shortly after the outbreak of war (September 17) the Soviet Government gave to the Government of Finland an assurance that she would "pursue a policy of neutrality" in her relations with her neighbors at Helsinki. But this policy of neutrality had a Russian twist that was given an ominous illustration with regard to Estonia, Latvia, and Lithuania. In order to save Finland from a similar fate, President Roosevelt sent a message to President Kalinin (October 11), the head of the Supreme Council of the Soviet Union, calling attention to the "long-standing and deep friendship which exists between the United States and Finland," and expressed the hope that no demands would be made upon that country which would be inconsistent with its independence. Kalinin's reply was the usual Soviet exercise in mendacity. The "sole aim" of Russia was to strengthen "friendly co-operation between both countries" and to effect a guarantee of the "security of the Soviet Union and Finland."[47]

Soviet friendly co-operation now took a strange turn. On October 14 the Kremlin demanded the cession of an area on the Cape of Hanko, a large number of islands in the Gulf of Finland, and a portion of the Karelian Isthmus. Molotov then made a speech (October 31) in which he intimated that Finland would be wise not to expect any help from

---

[44] *The Finnish Blue Book*, published for the Ministry for Foreign Affairs of Finland (New York, 1940), pp. 23–26.
[45] *Ibid.*, pp. 27–31.
[46] *Ibid.*, pp. 36–37.
[47] Department of State, *Bulletin*, I, 395.

foreign countries like the United States.[48] This threat was followed on November 26 by a charge that Finnish troops had attacked some Russian forces along the border. On November 28, Moscow denounced the nonaggression treaty with Finland, and on the following day severed diplomatic relations. It was apparent to the Department of State that a crisis had been reached in the relations between Finland and Russia so mediation was offered by Secretary Hull.[49] This was abruptly rejected by the Kremlin and on November 30, Soviet armed forces launched an attack upon Finland by sea, air, and land. This brutal aggression caused the Council of the League of Nations (December 14) to adopt a resolution declaring that "the Union of Soviet Socialist Republics is no longer a Member of the League."[50]

In the United States the action of Soviet Russia evoked intense indignation. On December 1, at a press conference, President Roosevelt denounced the invasion of Finland as "a wanton disregard for law."[51] The American press echoed this indictment. The *New York Times* scored Soviet aggression as "the most flagrant example to date of a completely unjustifiable attack."[52] The *Atlanta Constitution* condemned the assault upon Finland as a demonstration of "ruthless savagery";[53] the *Dallas Morning News* was shocked at the "murderous and unprovoked attack";[54] the *Cleveland Plain Dealer* was nauseated at the "sheer brutality of the Soviet action";[55] while the *Washington Evening Star* was aghast at the "peculiarly revolting lust of Stalin."[56]

Encouraged by these strong expressions of sympathy for Finland, President Roosevelt (December 6) instructed the Secretary of the Treasury to set aside in a separate account Finland's annual debt installment ($234,693), with a thought of eventual repayment. On December 10 it was announced that through the agencies of the Reconstruction Finance Corporation and the Export-Import Bank, credits amounting to $10,000,000 had been opened to make it possible for the Finnish Government to purchase agricultural surpluses and supplies in the United States.[57] But Finland needed arms and munitions of war rather than plows and pious platitudes. It was not long before the Russian steam roller crushed all signs of Finnish resistance, and when

[48] *The Finnish Blue Book,* pp. 56–60.
[49] Department of State, *Bulletin,* I, 609.
[50] *The Finnish Blue Book,* p. 111.
[51] *New York Times,* December 2, 1939.
[52] *Ibid.,* November 30, 1939.
[53] December 1, 1939.
[54] December 2, 1939.
[55] December 1, 1939.
[56] December 1, 1939.
[57] *New York Times,* December 7–11, 1939.

the Finns in 1941, with Hitler's help, once more waged war against
the Soviet armed hordes, American opinion suddenly changed to warm
support of Stalin. A break had occurred in the relations between the
German and Russian dictators. Instead of welcoming war between these
enemies of democracy and sitting on the side lines with cheers for their
mutual destruction, America, led by the Roosevelt Administration, espoused the cause of Russia and started the flow of lend-lease goods to
that country that eventually transformed her into the Frankenstein that
now menaces the world. After June 1941, "brave little Finland" was
attacked in many American quarters as the ally of the hated Nazis and
some Americans looked at Helsinki through the eyes of the editors of
the *New Masses* and the *Daily Worker*.

h. *The Mission of Sumner Welles*

The heroic struggle of Finland against Soviet aggression evoked warm
admiration in Italy and was one of the many indications that seemed to
point to the possibility of driving a wedge between Italy and Germany.
Since the Nazi-Soviet Pact of August 1939 there was a growing feeling
in Italy that the Rome-Berlin Axis was out of date. Count Ciano was
constantly pouring this viewpoint into the ears of the Duce, and on
December 16, in an address to the Grand Council, he boldly expressed
his opinions to an important group of leading Fascists. He proclaimed
the fact that the Nazi-Soviet treaty had been negotiated without any
prior understanding with Italy. The vain attempts of the Duce to find
a formula of peace in August–September 1939 were impressively rehearsed and the attitude of Germany was depicted in a none-too-friend-
ly spirit. In Italy, Ciano himself said that his address was widely regarded as a funeral oration over the death of the Axis.[58]

Ciano's address was followed by a significant letter from Mussolini
to Hitler. After describing the strong sympathy felt in Italy for the
fighting Finns, the Duce then told how British propaganda was successful in pointing out the ominous aspects of Nazi-Soviet collaboration. Because of the friendship that had existed between Poland and
Italy he urged the creation of a Polish national state under the aegis of
Germany. With reference to a spring offensive against Britain and
France he questioned whether it was wise to beat the Allies to their
knees at the expense of the "flower of Germany's youth." The democracies bore "within themselves the seeds of their inevitable decay." Let
time work its inevitable course with them. The real foe to be taken care

---

[58] *The Ciano Diaries, 1939–1943*, ed. Hugh Gibson (Garden City, 1947), December 19, 1939, p. 180.

of was Russia: "The solution of your Lebensraum is in Russia alone."[59]

The Italian Ambassador in Berlin (Attolico) took this letter to Hitler on January 8, 1940. The Führer read it with great care and clearly understood all its implications. With Ribbentrop and Göring he discussed every aspect of German-Italian relations and then decided to postpone an answer until he had the situation in better shape. Moreover, the suspense would arouse profound concern in the Duce's mind and make him feel that he must conciliate the Führer.

In this period of the Duce's indecision the moment seemed opportune for an attempt to drive a wedge between Germany and Italy. In the early days of January 1940, President Roosevelt sent for Sumner Welles and discussed with him the advisability of sending a representative to Europe to canvass the "possibilities of concluding a just and permanent peace." The President had no interest in a "temporary or tentative armed truce." Something more fundamental would have to be achieved. Perhaps Welles himself would be the man of the hour who could open the portals of peace. At any rate, in February 1940 the President decided to send him to Rome and Berlin, and from there to Paris and London. Conversations with Mussolini and Hitler might offer some hint as to peaceful procedures that would prevent the dreaded spring offensive. From Germany there had come certain whispers of a desire for peace. Under the proper encouragement these whispers might gain significant volume.

Welles arrived in Rome on February 25 and had an interview with Ciano on the following day. He found Ciano "always cordial and entirely unaffected," with an evident desire to be helpful.[60] In the *Ciano Diaries,* Welles is described as "distinguished in appearance and manner," and the tone of the conference was "very cordial."[61] Ciano made no attempt to conceal his detestation of von Ribbentrop and his "underlying antagonism toward Hitler." When Welles brought up the matter of a "just and permanent peace," Ciano outlined the terms that Hitler would have accepted in October 1939, but he was uncertain about the Führer's present viewpoint.[62]

The interview with Mussolini was quite a different affair and Ciano regretted its "icy atmosphere." The Duce appeared to Welles as a man laboring "under a tremendous strain." He was "ponderous and static rather than vital," and during the interview sat most of the time with

[59] Elizabeth Wiskemann, *The Rome-Berlin Axis* (New York, 1949), pp. 187–88. For an important insight into the relations between Rome and Berlin, 1939–1943, see L. Simoni, *Berlino—Ambasciata d'Italia, 1939–1943* (Rome, 1946).

[60] Sumner Welles, *The Time for Decision* (New York, 1944), p. 78.

[61] Gibson, *op. cit.,* p. 212.

[62] Welles, *op. cit.,* p. 82.

his eyes closed. As soon as the formalities of introduction were completed, Welles handed to Mussolini a letter from President Roosevelt.
It was an interesting missive which emphasized the "satisfaction which
the United States government would derive from a continuation of
Italian neutrality," and which indicated the President's strong desire
"to meet personally with the chief of the Italian government." In the
event of such a meeting the President believed he could "persuade Mussolini that the best interests of Italy could be served only if he refused
to prostitute the Italian people to the greater glory of Hitler."

The Duce seemed pleased with the suggestion of a meeting with
Roosevelt. He had hoped for a long time that "this meeting . . . would
really take place." When he remarked that there were so many miles
of ocean between Italy and America that it would be difficult to arrange
for a conference, Sumner Welles quickly interjected with the statement:
"There are halfway points which would halve that distance." The Duce
responded: "Yes, and there are ships to take us both there."[63] But no
plans were actually made for this meeting which might have changed
the history of the world. Instead, Welles and the Duce merely talked
of the importance of breaking down economic barriers between countries and the necessity for a program of real disarmament. The conversation then shifted to the terms of peace Germany might accept and
concluded with a direct question from Welles: "Do you consider it
possible at this moment for any successful negotiations to be undertaken
between Germany and the Allies for a lasting peace?" "Yes," answered
the Duce with emphasis, and Welles was now ready for his journey to
Berlin.[64]

The interview with Ribbentrop was in sharp contrast to the encouraging talks with Ciano and the Duce. The Foreign Minister received
Welles "without even the semblance of a smile, and without even a
word of greeting." After a moment's pause, Welles spoke a few words
in English because he knew that Ribbentrop had spent some time in the
United States and spoke English fluently. Instead of responding to this
overture, Ribbentrop barked at Dr. Paul Schmidt the German word
"interpret," and the conversation began its uneasy course. After Welles
indicated that he had been sent to Europe to canvass the possibility of
establishing a permanent peace, Ribbentrop took his cue and commenced a turgid oration that lasted over two hours. In conclusion, he
insisted that Germany wanted peace but only on condition that "the
will on the part of England to destroy Germany is obliterated once

[63] *Ibid.*, p. 85.
[64] *Ibid.*, p. 88.

and for all." The only way that objective could be accomplished was "through complete and total Germany victory."

The interview with Hitler on March 2 was less of an ordeal. He greeted Welles "pleasantly" and was "dignified, both in speech and in movement." When Welles remarked that his conversation with Mussolini had instilled the hope that the "foundations of a durable peace might still be laid," Hitler began to discuss the basic importance of some general agreement upon a program of disarmament. He had long been in favor of disarmament but had received no encouragement from Britain or France. He agreed with Welles that "a liberal, unconditional most-favored-nation international trade relationship" was an ideal "toward which the nations of the world should strive." Under "more normal conditions Germany would gladly co-operate toward that end." He then outlined Germany's objectives. They were historical, political, and economic. Germany had no aim other than the return of the "German people to the territorial position which historically was rightly theirs." Germany's political aims emphasized national security. There was no real desire to dominate non-German peoples. If such peoples adjacent to her boundaries did not constitute a threat to German security, there was no intention to interfere with their independence. From the economic standpoint Germany claimed the right to profit through trade with the nations close to her in central and southeastern Europe. She would no longer permit the Western powers of Europe to infringe or impair her preferential position in that respect. Germany would also insist that "the colonies stolen from her at Versailles be returned to her." In conclusion, he repeated the words of Ribbentrop: "I can see no hope for the establishment of any lasting peace until the will of England and France to destroy Germany is itself destroyed. I feel that there is no way by which the will to destroy Germany can itself be destroyed except through a complete German victory."[65]

Welles now clearly realized that his mission to Germany was in vain, but he felt obliged to have a frank talk with General Göring at Karinhall. Göring's manner was "simple, unaffected and exceedingly cordial." He quickly assured Welles that Germany had "no ambitions of any kind . . . which could affect the Western Hemisphere," and he challenged the assertion that a war in Europe would profoundly affect America. Welles then shifted the conversation to the topic of German discriminations against the Jews. This evoked the reply that racial discriminations were in effect in a large portion of the United States with regard to Negroes. In conclusion, Göring repeated the comments of Ribbentrop and Hitler with special reference to the desire of Britain

[65] *Ibid.*, pp. 104–9.

and France to destroy Germany. If they succeeded in that objective they would create a community of "Bolsheviks and Communists."[66]

From Berlin, Welles went at once to Paris for conversations with important French officials. He regretted that President Lebrun did not have the driving force of Poincaré who had guided French destinies during World War I. While talking with Senator Jeanneney, President of the French Senate, he was reminded of a trenchant saying of Clemenceau anent the Germans: "There is only one way in which to deal with a mad dog. Either kill him or chain him with steel chains which cannot be broken." But France lacked both the will and the ability to forge those chains.

In England he found the will to forge chains that would keep Germany in subjection for a long period. This will was vehemently expressed by Winston Churchill. He was certain that no solution of the European crisis would be found "other than outright and complete defeat of Germany, the destruction of National Socialism, and the inclusion, in the new peace treaties, of provisions which would control Germany's course in the future in such a way as to give Europe and the world peace and security in the days to come, at least for a hundred years."[67] He still adhered to the pattern of Versailles.

It is significant that Churchill had no words of criticism of Russia even though it was apparent that Hitler could not have gone to war in 1939 without some assurance of Soviet support. The menace of bolshevism gave Churchill little concern in 1940. In the following year when Hitler attacked Russia, Churchill worked feverishly to send her armed assistance. A real statesman would have recognized the dual threat of both nazism and communism and would have welcomed them with bloody hands to hospitable graves.

Sumner Welles apparently agreed with this British viewpoint. The "pencil with two ears"[68] made no adverse comment upon such dangerous blindness. To him, as well as to Churchill, the only real enemy was Nazi Germany. This made it all the more necessary for him to hurry back to Rome and try to separate Mussolini from Hitler. But Ribbentrop had preceded him with a long letter from Hitler. The Führer insisted that Italy would have a glorious future only if she worked in close collaboration with Germany. He was confident that the Duce saw this unmistakable fact: "I . . . believe that the destinies of our two States, of our two Peoples, of our two revolutions, and of our two regimes are indissolubly linked."[69]

66 *Ibid.*, pp. 113–18.
67 *Ibid.*, pp. 132–33.
68 Paul Schmidt, *Hitler's Interpreter* (London, 1950), p. 169.
69 Wiskemann, *op. cit.*, pp. 196–97.

Ribbentrop was not as successful as he had hoped he would be in his conversations with Mussolini. The Duce was still opposed to a German spring offensive against Britain and France, and it would take a personal conference between the two dictators to change Mussolini's mind. This should be held, according to Ribbentrop, at Brenner Pass on the morning of March 18.

While Ribbentrop was making these preparations for the meeting at Brenner Pass, Welles arrived in Rome on March 16 and had conferences with both Ciano and Mussolini. Ciano frankly informed him that from Ribbentrop he had learned that "Germany was determined to undertake an all-out military offensive in the near future." She was "not considering any peace solution short of a military victory." This it was believed could be accomplished "within five months. . . . France would crumble first and England shortly after." Ciano himself was by no means convinced of a German victory. If the Allies could prevent a break-through of their defensive positions it was quite possible that victory might be theirs.

On the evening of March 16, Welles saw Mussolini and noted at once that he seemed to have shed the worries that had tormented him a few weeks before. When Welles brought up the matter of laying the basis of a permanent peace, the Duce promptly remarked that Ribbentrop had "insisted that Germany would consider no solution other than a military victory, and that any peace negotiations were impossible." He also informed Welles that he had learned that Germany was ready to start "an immediate offensive." In Germany it was expected that France would fall "within three or four months."

In view of these German expectations it would be necessary for the Allies to bait their hooks of peace with juicy concessions. Germany must have adequate *Lebensraum*. With reference to the independence of the Polish people he believed that "in any determination of new boundaries for Poland the transfer of populations recently carried out by the Germans must be regarded as definitive." Moreover, the just claims of Hungary should be taken into account and "all of the claims of Italy" must be given a "satisfactory solution."

These terms were so far-reaching that Welles remarked that he would have to telephone to President Roosevelt and ask for specific instructions. He would communicate the President's decision to Count Ciano that evening. When he put through a long distance telephone call to Washington the President shied away from any discussion of the political bases of the proposed peace. He expressed the opinion that "the problem of security was the fundamental issue," but he offered no solution of this problem. He was extremely cautious in his comments, but he did make the observation that neither Britain nor France wished "to destroy either Germany or the German people."[70] To Hitler this assurance would appear as either naïve or disingenuous.

It was evident to Mussolini that President Roosevelt was not able to outline any bases for peace that would prove inviting to Hitler. He would have to attend the conference at Brenner Pass without any ammunition that might induce the Führer to abandon a spring offensive in favor of peace proposals. On March 18 he listened to Hitler's long presentation of the thesis that the destinies of Germany and Italy were indissolubly joined. Italian intervention in the war was inevitable. It was noticeable that the Führer gave no details of his planned spring offensive. He still harbored a definite suspicion of Italian trustworthiness. But this long "Brenner Monologue" had its effect upon the Duce who finally cast aside all his apprehensions and emphatically asserted his intention of entering the war on the side of Germany.[71]

On March 19, Ciano was back in Rome and assured Welles there was "no threat of an immediate military clash." The President would have time "to study Welles's reports and perhaps to take some peace steps." Welles was so pleased with the prospect that he talked of a possible meeting between Mussolini and the President in the Azores. He also remarked to Blasco d'Aieta that "even without undertaking any offensive, Germany will be exhausted within a year." He considered "the war already won by the French and English."[72] After other conversations equally fatuous, Welles returned to Washington with a full budget of misinformation for the President.[73]

i. *Britain and Germany Flout the Neutrality of Norway*

While Sumner Welles was making ready to visit Rome and Berlin in February 1940 the first signs of the spring military offensive were becoming evident. The German ship *Altmark* had taken refuge in a Norwegian fiord with several hundred British sailors on board as prisoners. A search by Norwegian gunboats had failed to disclose the presence of these sailors, but the British Admiralty had information concerning their detention on the *Altmark*. On February 16, Winston Churchill,

[70] Welles, *op. cit.,* pp. 140–41.

[71] Schmidt, *op. cit.,* pp. 172–73.

[72] Gibson, *op. cit.,* March 20, 1940, pp. 224–25.

[73] The background of the Welles mission is told by Secretary Hull, *Memoirs* (New York, 1948), I, 737–40: "Some time later the President expressly stated to me that Welles had come to him secretly on several occasions and pleaded to be sent abroad on special missions. . . . I feel satisfied that Welles had requested the President to send him on the trip in 1940. . . . I myself would not have considered sending Welles or anyone else of his official position to Europe on such a mission at that stage in the war."

as First Lord of the Admiralty, ordered Captain Vian to proceed in H.M.S. *Cossack* to Norwegian waters and liberate the prisoners. In effecting this rescue Captain Vian deliberately violated the neutrality of Norwegian coastal waters and the Norwegian Government sent a prompt protest to London. The Prime Minister excused this violation on the ground that previous German infractions of international law had compelled the British to take similar action.[74]

This *Altmark* incident was merely one expression of the intention of the British Government repeatedly to violate the neutrality of Norwegian waters for the purpose of adversely affecting the German war effort. As early as September 19, 1939, Winston Churchill, after consulting the British War Cabinet, brought to the notice of the First Sea Lord and others the importance of stopping the transportation of Swedish iron ore from Narvik to Germany. Inasmuch as the German ore ships kept within the Norwegian three-mile limit the only way they could be stopped would be by mining those marginal waters. In 1918 this had been done and Churchill suggested that Britain "should repeat this process very shortly."[75] The first German memorandum with reference to action in Norwegian waters was written on October 3, 1939. Thus, as Lord Hankey clearly shows, "the British Government began to plan their major offensive in Norway a fortnight before the Germans." It is significant that the Nuremberg Tribunal purposely overlooked the memorandum of Winston Churchill and contended that the idea of attacking Norway "originated with Raeder and Rosenberg. . . . The omission to mention this part of the story in the Judgement is the more inexplicable because the whole story was told to the House of Commons by Mr. Churchill in April 1940, and it was a matter of public knowledge."[76]

On December 16, 1939, Mr. Churchill prepared another memorandum which he presented to the Cabinet six days later. The subject was once more the stoppage of iron ore from Narvik to Germany. He regarded such a stoppage as "a major offensive operation of war," and it could be accomplished by laying "a series of small minefields in Norwegian territorial waters at the two or three suitable points on the coast, which will force the ships carrying ore to Germany to quit territorial waters and come onto the high seas." This action would compel Germany to "undergo a severe deprivation, tending to crisis before the summer." This mining of Norwegian waters was a mere technical infringement of international law. No evil effect would be produced in

[74] Churchill, *op. cit.*, pp. 561–64.
[75] *Ibid.*, pp. 533–34.
[76] Lord Hankey, *Politics, Trials and Errors* (Chicago, 1950), pp. 73, 72, 74.

the United States by such an infringement where it would be looked
upon "in the way most calculated to help us."[77]

As Lord Hankey points out, the judgment at the end of the Nuremberg Trial made much of German plans against Norway in mid-Decem-
ber 1939, but it did "not contain a word of Mr. Churchill's Memorandum to the War Cabinet dated December 16. . . . Any detached person
would think this is a supremely important piece of evidence for the
Tribunal, for it places the British plan on the same level of importance
as the German plan, which is so severely condemned as a crime in law
in the Judgement." Although the War Cabinet refused to accept the
reasoning of this Churchill memorandum, it did permit "the preparation of plans for landing a force at Narvik for the sake of Finland. . . .
These proceedings also show the pressure the War Cabinet was under
from their most powerful colleague . . . to persuade them to a technical
act of aggression liable to set all Scandinavia ablaze—a 'crime,' to use
Nuremberg's extravagant language, for which the Germans were des-
tined to be so severely condemned by the Tribunal. Not a single word
of it appears in the Nuremberg Judgment."[78]

The judgment is completely silent on the action of the Supreme War
Council of the Allies when (on February 5, 1940) it "approved plans
for the preparation of three or four allied divisions for service in Finland, and for persuading Norway and Sweden to permit the passage of
supplies and reinforcements to the Finns and 'incidentally to get hold
of the Gallivare ore field.' From then on the preparations for despatch
of allied troops to Norway were intensified." By the beginning of April
1940 the preparations "for the major offensive in Norway had been
completed by both camps. . . . The actual landing, that is to say the
German major offensive did not take place until April 9. *Twenty-four
hours before that, namely* between 4:30 and 5 A.M. on April 8, the
British minefields had been laid in the West Fjord near Narvik!"[79]
Needless to say, these facts were not given any place in the Nuremberg
Judgement.

While the Norwegian Foreign Office was drafting a note of protest
to London, word came that German warships were approaching Oslo.
On the following day Norwegian batteries sank the German heavy
cruiser *Blücher* and seriously damaged the cruiser *Emden*. This spirited
defense merely postponed the fall of Oslo.

A German attack upon the iron ore port of Narvik was successful in
spite of heroic resistance by Norwegian warships, and Hitler's plans

[77] Churchill, *op. cit.,* pp. 544–47.
[78] Hankey, *op. cit.,* pp. 74–76.
[79] *Ibid.,* p. 78. See also, *Britain's Designs on Norway, German White Book No.
4,* (New York, 1940), pp. 60–68.

for the occupation of Norway proceeded according to schedule. British plans for the stoppage of ore shipments to Germany were completely defeated. At the same time (April 9), German troops crossed the Danish frontier and thus another northern neutral came under Nazi control.

j. *Greenland Is Placed under the Monroe Doctrine*

When the news came to Washington that German troops had occupied Denmark and Norway, President Roosevelt (April 10) issued a proclamation extending the combat zone (closed to American ships) northward along the entire Norwegian coast and eastward along the Russian Arctic coast to a point 200 miles east of Murmansk.[80] He also issued an executive order "freezing" Danish and Norwegian holdings of securities and other property in the United States in order to prevent their use by German authorities. As a result of the German invasion of Denmark, the Parliament of Iceland adopted a resolution declaring that the "government of Iceland, for the time being," was no longer shared with the King [of Denmark]. The Parliament then took over the control of foreign relations. Prime Minister Hermann Jónasson now opened negotiations with Secretary Hull looking towards the establishment of a legation in Washington and a Consulate General in New York City. In return, the American Government would open a consular office in Reykjavík, capital of Iceland.[81]

On April 12, Secretary Hull had a conversation with the British Ambassador (Lord Lothian) in which he stressed the view that the Monroe Doctrine covered the Western Hemisphere "without qualification." It was obvious that Greenland came within the scope of that doctrine. After discussing the situation with Canadian officials, an American Consulate was established at Godthaab and Coast Guard cutters were sent to patrol the waters around Greenland. It was not long before the Department of State took more decisive action.

[80] For documents printed in the *Norwegian White Book*, see Jones and Myers, *op. cit.*, pp. 398–408. The reactions of President Roosevelt and Secretary Hull are shown in *ibid.*, pp. 408–15.

[81] Hull, *op. cit.*, pp. 752–54.

XXV

Roosevelt Seeks a Pretext for War
with Germany

a. *Hitler Launches a Blitzkrieg along the Western Front*

BEFORE THE NAZI armed forces had scored an important success in
the Norway campaign, President Roosevelt began a series of endeavors
to keep Italy out of the war. On April 29 he sent a telegram to Mussolini in which he expressed his deepest satisfaction with reference to
"the policy of the Italian Government in exerting every effort to prevent war from spreading to southern and southeastern Europe." A
further extension of the area of hostilities would bring into the war
"still other nations which have been seeking to maintain their neutrality." He could see "no reason to anticipate that any one nation or any
one combination of nations" could successfully "dominate either the
continent of Europe . . . or a greater part of the world." He earnestly
hoped that the powerful influence of Italy would continue to be exercised "in behalf of the negotiation of a just and stable peace."[1]

When Ambassador Phillips conveyed this message to Mussolini he
was informed that "Italy, Germany and Russia did not desire an extension of the war." The Duce then expressed the opinion that "Germany could not be beaten" and that an Allied naval blockade would be
"completely ineffective." The President should realize that the political
system created by the Treaty of Versailles had been liquidated. In the
new system Germany "would willingly permit a new independent
Polish State" to be erected but it would not have the "old boundaries
which were completely without justification." Germany was "also willing that a new Czechoslovakian state be reestablished." Last, but not
least, certain important concessions should be given to Italy.

Throughout this conversation Mussolini appeared to go "out of his
way to be friendly." He requested Ambassador Phillips to "thank President Roosevelt cordially" for his message and he seemed to be "extremely appreciative of it."[2]

In his diary, Count Ciano had a somewhat different story to tell. He
noted that the Duce received the Roosevelt message with "ill grace"

---

[1] President Roosevelt to the Premier of Italy (Mussolini), April 29, 1940. *Peace
and War: United States Foreign Policy, 1931–1941* (Washington, 1943), pp. 519–20.
[2] Ambassador Phillips to Secretary Hull, Rome, May 1, 1940. *Ibid.*, pp. 520–22.

and that he said "little or nothing to the American Ambassador."[3] Mussolini then sent a brief note to the President in which he argued that responsibility for World War II did "not fall upon Germany but upon the initiatives of the Allies." As far as he knew, Germany was "opposed to a further extension of the conflict, and Italy likewise." With reference to the President's belief that "an extension of the war fronts" might have a serious effect upon the Western Hemisphere, he called attention "to the fact that Italy has never concerned itself with the relations of the American republics with each other and with the United States (thereby respecting the Monroe Doctrine), and might therefore ask for 'reciprocity' with regard to European affairs."[4]

Ciano regarded this note as "cutting and hostile."[5] It was certainly not conciliatory. The Duce was "literally exalted" by the news of Hitler's victories in Norway. In a letter describing his successes the Führer complained that the "excessive rapidity" of the advance of his troops had not "permitted his involving the English forces more effectively" so as to "destroy them completely." He intimated that he would have to "obtain a victory in the West as soon as possible" because of "hidden threats of American intervention."[6]

On this same day (May 4) the German General Staff issued a statement that awakened instant apprehensions in Belgium and the Netherlands. The charge was made that those countries had not maintained an impartial neutrality. It was also alleged that on January 12, 1940, some extended discussions had taken place in Breda "between Dutch, Belgian, French and British staff officers." These discussions were supposed to have been for the purpose of aiding British and French forces to launch an "attack on the Ruhr."[7]

Alleging the necessity of anticipating this Anglo-French invasion, the German Government began a blitzkrieg upon the Western Front. News of this attack came to President Roosevelt early on the morning of May 10 when Ambassador Cudahy telephoned the White House to report that a large German air force was already over Luxemburg en route to Belgium and the Netherlands. Later during the morning "President Roosevelt and Secretary Hull called from time to time asking for latest developments." Cudahy replied that the news was "en-

[3] *The Ciano Diaries, 1939–1943*, ed. Hugh Gibson (Garden City, 1947), May 1, 1940, pp. 241–42.

[4] The Premier of Italy (Mussolini) to President Roosevelt, May 2, 1940. *Peace and War*, p. 522.

[5] Gibson, *op. cit.*, p. 242.

[6] *Ibid.*, May 4, 1940, p. 243.

[7] "Allied Intrigue in the Low Countries," *German White Book* No. 5 (German Library of Information, New York, 1940), pp. xi–xxii, xxiii–xxxix. See also, Eelco Nicolaas van Kleffens, *Juggernaut over Holland* (New York, 1941).

tirely reassuring."[8] But King Leopold, of Belgium, was not so confident about the situation. Fearful of the outcome of the German invasion he sent a hurried telegram to President Roosevelt expressing the ardent hope that he would support with all his "moral authority the efforts which we are now firmly decided to make in order to preserve our independence." The President could only reply that he and the American people cherished the strong desire that "policies which seek to dominate peaceful and independent peoples through force and military aggression may be arrested, and that the government and people of Belgium may preserve their integrity and freedom."[9]

In Rome, Ambassador Phillips told Ciano that the German blitzkrieg was "bound to stir America profoundly." It had already stirred the Pope who had sent telegrams to the "rulers of the three invaded states." This act had incensed Mussolini who blurted out to Ciano that the Papacy was "a cancer which gnaws at our national life." If necessary he would "liquidate this problem once and for all." Later the Pope evidenced a "clear-cut intransigency" and remarked that he was "even ready to be deported to a concentration camp."[10]

Into this tense and ominous atmosphere in Rome the President once more intervened by sending another note to Mussolini. Rumors that the Duce was "contemplating early entry into the war" had given him "great concern." Most Americans believed that the whole world faced a "threat which opposes every teaching of Christ, every philosophy of all the great teachers of mankind over thousands of years." Therefore, as the President of the United States he made "the simple plea that you, responsible for Italy, withhold your hand, stay wholly apart from any war and refrain from any threat of attack."[11]

Ciano noted that the new communication from the President was not in a "covertly threatening style." It was rather a "discouraged and conciliatory message." Allusions to the "Gospel of Christ" would have "little effect upon the mind of Mussolini," who was convinced that Germany would win the war. As an ally of Hitler, Italy could secure rich spoils of war.[12]

b. *Roosevelt Regards Neutrality as an Outmoded Concept*

While the President was pleading with Mussolini to remain neutral in the great conflict that was wrecking Europe, he himself was pushing

8 John Cudahy, *The Armies March* (New York, 1941), pp. 80–81.
9 Department of State, *Bulletin*, II, May 11, 1940, 492–93.
10 Gibson, *op. cit.*, May 10–May 13, pp. 247–49.
11 President Roosevelt to Premier Mussolini, May 14, 1940. *Peace and War*, p. 526.
12 Gibson, *op. cit.*, p. 250.

America down the road to war. On April 16 it was reported that the Anglo-French Purchasing Commission could obtain planes of almost any type then being produced for the armed forces of the United States.[13] This news encouraged the French Premier, Paul Reynaud, to send to Washington (May 14) the startling request that the American Government arrange for the "sale or lease of old destroyers."[14] On the following day Winston Churchill, who displaced Chamberlain as Prime Minister on May 10, sent a more ambitious request that was quite breath-taking:

All I ask now is that you [President Roosevelt] should proclaim non-belligerency, which would mean that you would help us with everything short of actually engaging armed forces. Immediate needs are: First of all, the loan of forty or fifty of your older destroyers; . . . Secondly, we want several hundred of the latest types of aircraft; . . . Thirdly, anti-aircraft equipment and ammunition. . . . Fourthly, the fact that our ore supply is being compromised from Sweden, from North Africa and perhaps from Northern Spain, makes it necessary to purchase steel in the United States. . . . I should like to feel reasonably sure that when we can pay no more, you will give us the stuff all the same. Fifthly, . . . the visit of a United States Squadron to Irish ports . . . would be invaluable.[15]

The President replied that he could not make a deal concerning the destroyers "without authorization from Congress." Moreover, America "needed the destroyers" for its "own defences."[16] Churchill greatly regretted this negative answer but he still hoped to get "at the earliest possible date" the "largest possible number of Curtiss P-40 fighters." In conclusion he sounded a loud note of alarm that he knew would profoundly affect the President. If Britain were "left by the United States to its fate," there was a definite danger that the British fleet might be turned over to the Germans as a bargaining point.[17]

We have already noted[18] that in 1939, while Chamberlain was still Prime Minister, Churchill began his momentous personal correspondence with President Roosevelt. It has been stated that one of the first cablegrams sent by Churchill to Roosevelt was phrased in a most grandiloquent manner. The gist of it has been given as follows: "I am half American and the natural person to work with you. It is evident we see

[13] *New York Times*, April 16, 1940.
[14] *F. D. R.: His Personal Letters*, ed. Elliott Roosevelt (New York, 1950), II, 1036.
[15] Winston S. Churchill, *Their Finest Hour* (Boston, 1949), pp. 24–25.
[16] Roosevelt, *op. cit.*, p. 1036.
[17] Churchill, *op. cit.*, pp. 56–57.
[18] See *ante*, p. 561.

eye to eye. Were I to become Prime Minister of Britain we could control the world."[19]

Churchill states that he sent "nine hundred and fifty" of these cablegrams to the President and received "about eight hundred in reply." His relations with the American Chief Executive "gradually became so close that the chief business between our two countries was virtually conducted by these personal interchanges between him and me. . . . As head of the State as well as Head of the Government, Roosevelt spoke and acted with authority in every sphere."[20]

It is obvious that Churchill regarded Roosevelt as an American dictator who had little concern for the opinions of Congress and the American people. With reference to the matter of war the Churchill cablegrams reveal that he believed that Roosevelt could plunge America into the conflict in Europe at any time he desired. The French Cabinet apparently had the same viewpoint.

The urgency of Churchill was translated into hysteria by Premier Reynaud. On May 18, Bullitt was informed by Alexis Léger, Secretary-General of the French Foreign Office, that Reynaud was about to request President Roosevelt to ask Congress for a declaration of war against Germany. Bullitt frankly informed Léger that such a request would be worse than useless: Congress would almost unanimously vote against such a declaration. The President then talked to Bullitt over the telephone and instructed him to say that "anything of this nature was out of the question." But Reynaud continued to press for the impossible. On May 22 he told Bullitt that the German tide was growing more menacing every minute. There was grave danger that the French public would insist upon a separate peace with Germany. In that event a German victory over Britain "would follow in a few weeks." After this dire event the Panama Canal would be destroyed by air bombardment and the "American Army would be able to offer little resistance." Prompt action by the American Government was "the only real guarantee that Hitler would not some day be in the White House."[21]

A week later the Reynaud appeals grew more frantic. On May 28 he warned Bullitt that he had convincing evidence that "if France and England were conquered, Hitler would move almost immediately against the United States." The American fleet should be sent at once to the Mediterranean so as to exert pressure upon Mussolini to stay out of the war.[22]

The President did not send the fleet to the Mediterranean but he

[19] John H. Snow, *The Case of Tyler Kent* (New York, 1946), p. 6.
[20] Churchill, *op. cit.*, p. 23.
[21] Cordell Hull, *Memoirs* (New York, 1948), I, 766–73.
[22] *Ibid.*, p. 773.

decided to permit American pilots to fly planes, ordered by the Allies, to Halifax and other ports in the Canadian maritime provinces. Before this decision the Dominion had been designated as a combat area and American nationals had not been allowed to enter it in aircraft belonging to belligerent nations. The President then urged Churchill to send additional planes to France but he was told that Britain needed all available aircraft for defense against expected German attack. Ambassador Bullitt became furious over this negative reply from Britain and he confided to Secretary Hull his belief that the British Cabinet "might be conserving their air force and fleet so as to use them as bargaining points in negotiations with Hitler."[23]

Both the President and Secretary Hull discounted these observations of Bullitt. They were certain that while France "was finished," Britain, with the aid of American supplies, could withstand a German assault. It was imperative, therefore, that these supplies be rushed at once to British ports. Joseph C. Green, chief of the Division of Controls, brought to Secretary Hull's attention an old statute of May 12, 1917. The language of this statute could be interpreted so as to authorize the exchange of army and navy aircraft for new models of a more advanced type. Arrangements were made with a Buffalo concern to deliver to them fifty planes belonging to the Naval Reserve squadrons in exchange for planes of a "superior type." These planes were then rushed to Britain. But Churchill wanted more than planes. In order to meet his importunate requests, the President turned to the Acting Attorney General, Francis Biddle, who conveniently ruled that the Secretary of War had the right to sell surplus war supplies to "any corporation or individual upon such terms as may be deemed best."[24]

General George C. Marshall, as Chief of Staff, now came to the front and directed his chief of Ordnance and his Assistant Chief of Staff to survey the entire list of American reserve ordnance and munitions stocks. On June 3 he approved these lists. The first list was a lengthy one:

It comprised half a million .30 calibre rifles out of two million manufactured in 1917 and 1918. . . . For these there were about 250 cartridges apiece. There were 900 soixante-quinze field guns with a million rounds, 80,000 machine guns and various other items. . . . On June 3 all the American Army depots and arsenals started packing the material for shipment. . . . By June 11 a dozen British merchant ships moved into the bay [Raritan] and anchored, and loading from lighters began.[25]

23 *Ibid.*, pp. 774–75.
24 *New York Herald-Tribune*, June 8, 1940.
25 Churchill, *op. cit.*, p. 142. See also, House Document No. 288, 78 Cong., 1 sess., p. 3.

But this flood of war matériel reached the Allies too late to stop the rapid German advance. On May 15, General Winkelman, the Dutch Commander in Chief, signed articles of capitulation. German pressure upon Belgium rapidly mounted. When General Giraud's Army in Holland was completely crushed and the French Ninth Army collapsed on the Mézières-Dinant front, it was evident that a crisis had arisen. After the news of the British retreat to Dunkerque was brought to King Leopold he realized that the situation had become critical. On May 27 the demoralization of the French military forces was so rapid and complete that he decided the time had arrived to ask the German High Command to state its terms for a suspension of hostilities. The blunt answer called for unconditional surrender. The King felt compelled to comply with this grim demand, and at 4:00 A.M. on the following day the Belgian Army obeyed a cease fire order from headquarters.[26]

c. *The President Makes a Third Plea to Mussolini to Stay Out of the War*

Before the bad news from Belgium was received in the United States, the President decided to make another plea to Mussolini to stay out of the war. In this third communication to the Duce, Roosevelt offered to act as a mediator between Hitler and the Allies. Ambassador Phillips was instructed to deliver this message to Mussolini personally, but Count Ciano bluntly informed him that this was not possible. When Ciano finished reading the President's plea he was asked by Phillips as to the nature of the reply: "He said with conviction—'it would be a no' and he went on to explain that Mussolini's position was not merely a question of securing Italy's legitimate aspirations but that the Duce was determined to carry out his obligations under his alliance with Germany." Later in the day Ciano sent for Ambassador Phillips and confirmed the statements he had made during the morning meeting. Mussolini desired to preserve his "freedom of action" and was not disposed to "enter into any negotiations which . . . would not be in the spirit of Fascism."[27]

Although to Sumner Welles the "horizon looked extremely dark,"[28] Roosevelt thought that the clouds might take on a silver lining if he could persuade Mussolini to stay out of the war. On May 30 he made his fourth appeal to the Duce. Ambassador Phillips was instructed to

---

[26] Cudahy, *op. cit.*, pp. 97–116.

[27] Ambassador Phillips to Secretary Hull, Rome, May 27, 1940. 740.0011 EW./1939/2691¾, MS, Department of State.

[28] Conversation between Sumner Welles and the British Ambassador, May 27, 1940. 740.0011 EW./1939/3124, *Confidential file*, MS, Department of State.

call upon Count Ciano and once more emphasize the fact that the entrance of Italy into the war would "immediately and prejudicially affect" the interests of the United States. While the American Government had never "asserted any political interests in Europe," it had "asserted its clearly defined interests of an economic and property character. Through the extension of the war to the Mediterranean region and the inevitable destruction of life and property . . . the legitimate interests of the American people will be gravely curtailed." Inasmuch as the relations between the Italian and American peoples had always been particularly close, it was hoped that nothing would be done adversely to affect them.[29]

On June 1, Ciano informed Ambassador Phillips that the Duce did not agree "with the point taken by the President with regard to the interests of the United States in the Mediterranean" and he maintained that the United States had the same interest in that area as Italy had, for example, "in the Caribbean Sea." The decision had "already been taken to enter the war."[30]

d. Reynaud Makes a Last Appeal to Roosevelt for Immediate Military Assistance

It had long been realized in Paris that Italy would probably enter the war as soon as Hitler's armies had gained important successes. The early collapse of the Netherlands and Belgium had made a deep impression upon the mind of Mussolini who was intent upon securing some of the spoils of war. Ambassador Bullitt knew this fact only too well and for this reason he begged the President to consent to the delivery of some old destroyers that would strengthen French naval forces in the Mediterranean. The President's reply remained negative: "Any exchange for American destroyers probably inacceptable because of enormous sea area which must be patrolled by us and would require Congressional action which might be very difficult to get. Our old destroyers cannot be sold as obsolete as is proved by fact. All of them are now in commission and in use or are in process of being commissioned for actual use."[31]

Churchill was critical of the President's continued refusal to send old destroyers to the Allies. On June 5 he remarked to Mackenzie King that although the American Chief Executive was an excellent friend he had

[29] Secretary Hull to Ambassador Phillips, May 30, 1940. 740.0011 EW./1939/ 2691⅜, *Confidential file*, MS, Department of State.

[30] Ambassador Phillips to Secretary Hull, Rome, June 1, 1940. 740.0011 EW./ 1939/2691¼, *Confidential file*, MS, Department of State.

[31] President Roosevelt to Sumner Welles, June 1, 1940. Roosevelt, *op. cit.*, p. 1036.

sent "no practical help" to Britain. He had not expected any military aid from the Americans "but they have not even sent any worthy contribution in destroyers or planes." It would be expedient "not to let Americans view too complacently prospect of a British collapse, out of which they would get the British Fleet and the guardianship of the British Empire."[32]

On the day that Churchill sent this letter to Mackenzie King, the Germans began the final phase of the Battle of France. In five days they blazed a path to Paris. With a crushing defeat staring him in the face, Reynaud sent another plea to President Roosevelt. Its tone was quite epic but there was a strong feeling that the French Premier was like some frightened boy whistling loudly as he walked down a very dark alley: "For six days and six nights our divisions have been fighting without one hour of rest against an army which has a crushing superiority in numbers and material. Today the enemy is almost at the gates of Paris. We shall fight in front of Paris; we shall fight behind Paris; we shall close ourselves in one of our provinces to fight and if we should be driven out of it we shall establish ourselves in North Africa to continue the fight and if necessary in our American possessions." To make matters even worse, at this tragic hour Italy had "stabbed France in the back." The Allies were in desperate straits and required at once all the material support of the United States "short of an expeditionary force."[33]

Reynaud's allusion of Italy's entrance into the war was turned by Roosevelt into a sharp thrust at Mussolini. That evening, in an address at Charlottesville, Virginia, the President alluded to the sweep of the tides of war across the Continent of Europe and the consequent menace to America of such a martial flood. Then, adopting a graphic phrase from Reynaud's plea earlier in the day, he suddenly remarked with dramatic intensity: "On this tenth day of June, 1940, the hand that held the dagger has struck it into the back of its neighbor."[34] This unexpected interpolation directed at the Duce indicated the President's bitterness towards a dictator to whom he had made four futile pleas for nonintervention.

But Reynaud needed more than bitter allusions. Churchill rushed to France and tried to recall to Marshal Pétain the glorious stand of the Allied armies in the spring of 1918. The Marshal replied very quietly "that in those days he had a mass of manoeuvre of upwards of sixty

[32] Prime Minister Churchill to Mackenzie King, June 5, 1940. Churchill, *op. cit.*, pp. 145–46.

[33] Premier Reynaud to President Roosevelt, June 10, 1940. *Peace and War*, pp. 549–50.

[34] *Ibid.*, pp. 545–49.

divisions; now there was none." In 1918 there had been "sixty British divisions in the line." In 1940 the story was tragically different and Pétain was "haunted" by the grief he felt "that Britain, with her forty-eight million population had not been able to make a greater contribution to the land war against Germany."[35]

The remarks of Marshal Pétain irritated Churchill considerably. On June 12 he sent to President Roosevelt the latest news from the French front and in this communication he permitted his resentment to color his message: "The aged Marshal Pétain, who was none too good in April and July, 1918, is, I fear, ready to lend his name and prestige to a treaty of peace for France." This was the moment for the President to "tip the balance in favour of the best and longest possible French resistance."[36] In the White House it was believed that Reynaud's arm might be strengthened by brave words and bright promises. The Premier was assured that the American Government was "doing everything in its power" to make available to the Allied powers the war matériel they so urgently needed. The "magnificent resistance of the French and British armies" had profoundly impressed the American people.[37]

When Ambassador Kennedy brought to Churchill a copy of this Presidential salute to Allied courage, the Prime Minister pressed for its immediate publication. It could play a "decisive part in turning the course of world history." At the very least it would "decide the French to deny Hitler a patched-up peace with France."[38] In a hurried note to Reynaud, Churchill indicated the compromising character of the Roosevelt message. If France, on the basis of this assurance from the American Chief Executive, would continue in the war, it should be obvious that the United States was "committed beyond recall to take the only remaining step, namely, becoming a belligerent in form as she has already constituted herself in fact."[39]

The President realized the truth of this Churchill statement. He had already committed beyond recall the United States to take part in the war then raging in Europe but he could not afford in the summer of 1940 to let this fact become known. His campaign for re-election as President would soon take shape and he knew he could not hope for success if the voters knew that he was secretly putting America into World War II. He quickly sent word to Churchill explaining that he

[35] Churchill, op. cit., pp. 155–56.

[36] Churchill to Roosevelt, June 12, 1940. Ibid., p. 178.

[37] President Roosevelt to Premier Reynaud, June 13, 1940. Peace and War, pp. 550–51.

[38] Churchill to Roosevelt, June 13, 1940. Churchill, op. cit., p. 185.

[39] Churchill to Premier Reynaud, June 13, 1940. Ibid., p. 185.

could not agree to the publication of his message to Reynaud. The Department of State saw in such publication the "gravest dangers." Churchill would not take this "disappointing telegram" as a final answer from the White House. On June 15 he frankly told the President that events in Europe were moving "downward at a pace where they will pass beyond the control of American public opinion." Eventually America would enter the struggle; why not now? It would be expedient to remember that if the Churchill Government fell a new cabinet might give the British fleet to Hitler. What would the United States do in that event? There was desperate need for the delivery of thirty-five destroyers at once. This matter should not be delayed.[40]

Reynaud realized that he could not wait for several months until American assistance reached France. It was now or never. On June 14 he sent a message to Roosevelt that plumbed the depths of despair. German troops had just burst into Paris. Would it pay France to "continue to sacrifice her youth in a hopeless struggle?" Unless America could rush to France's aid with armed force she would "go under like a drowning man and disappear after having cast a last look towards the land of liberty from which she awaited salvation."[41] When Roosevelt replied with a warm encomium upon the "resplendent courage" of the French armies but with no promise of immediate military aid, Reynaud requested Churchill to release his Government from its obligations not to negotiate a separate peace. The Prime Minister hastened to France in a vain effort to save the situation, but Reynaud had resigned by the time he reached Bordeaux. Marshal Pétain now assumed the burden of leadership and forwarded to Berlin a request for an armistice.[42]

On June 18, Ambassador Biddle was assured that the French fleet would "never be surrendered to the enemy."[43] After receiving this comforting news Secretary Hull instructed the American representatives in Berlin and Rome that the government of the United States "would not recognize any transfer, and would not acquiesce in any attempt to transfer any geographic region of the Western Hemisphere from one non-American power to another non-American power."[44] Germany would not be permitted to occupy any French islands in the Caribbean.

[40] Churchill to Roosevelt, June 14–15, 1940. *Ibid.*, pp. 188–89.

[41] Premier Reynaud to President Roosevelt, June 14, 1940. *Peace and War*, pp. 551–52.

[42] Churchill, *op. cit.*, pp. 200–15.

[43] Ambassador Biddle to Secretary Hull, Bordeaux, June 18, 1940. *Peace and War*, p. 554.

[44] Department of State, *Press Release*, June 19, 1940.

e. *The Destroyer Deal*

The fall of France imparted a sense of urgency to the Administration's program for aiding Britain by the sale or lease of war matériel. The President's qualms about constitutional limitations slowly disappeared under the drumfire of repeated requests from Churchill. Moreover, he brought into his Cabinet certain new members who were not averse to a prowar inclination. This was particularly true of the new Secretary of War, Henry L. Stimson, who was a notorious war hawk. It is apparent that after June 1940 the Administration embarked upon a phony bipartisan policy that pointed directly to American intervention in the European conflict.

This policy was given a green light on June 10 when Senator Sheppard offered an amendment to a pending defense bill authorizing the War Department to exchange unserviceable or surplus materials for others of which there was a scarcity. Senator Clark, of Missouri, declared that the purpose of the amendment was "an evasion of international law and of the Neutrality Act."[45] But the amendment was adopted by a large majority and the measure finally became law on July 2, 1940.

In the meantime Senator David I. Walsh had sponsored legislation that would provide against any "limitation or reduction in the size of our Navy."[46] The Act of June 28, 1940, embodied the ideas of Senator Walsh. It was not long, however, before the fertile mind of Benjamin Cohen, special assistant to the Attorney General, found several loopholes in this act. The President still had wide powers he could use without previous consultations with Congress. This opinion of Mr. Cohen was shrewdly argued but the Chief Executive "frankly doubted" if it would "stand up." He also feared that Congress was "in no mood at the present time to allow any form of sale."[47]

These doubts were dissolved under the impact of pressure from Churchill. On June 24 he wrote to Mackenzie King and once more emphasized the danger that if England fell there was the possibility that Hitler would get the British fleet.[48] Four days later, in a letter to Lord Lothian in Washington, he repeated this disturbing thought which should be repeated to Roosevelt. He also complained that Britain

[45] *Congressional Record*, June 11, 1940, pp. 12041–42.
[46] *Ibid.*, June 21, 1940, p. 13314.
[47] President Roosevelt to Secretary Knox, July 22, 1940. Roosevelt, *op. cit.*, pp. 1048–49.
[48] Churchill to Mackenzie King, June 24, 1940. Churchill, *op. cit.*, p. 227.

had "really not had any help worth speaking of from the United States so far."[49] After more than a month of silence he wrote again to the President (July 31) to inform him that the need for destroyers had "become most urgent." The whole fate of the war might rest upon the speed with which these destroyers were delivered. He was confident that the President would not "let this crux of the battle go wrong" for want of the much-needed warships.[50] When Lord Lothian spoke of an exchange of naval bases for destroyers, Churchill indicated his preference was for an indefinite lease and not an outright sale.[51]

Churchill's cablegram to the President (July 31) had led to a Cabinet meeting in the White House on August 2. There was immediate agreement that "the survival of the British Isles under German attack might very possibly depend on their getting these destroyers," but there was also recognition that legislation would be "necessary" to authorize any deal concerning the destroyers. If the British Government would give positive assurances that the British fleet "would not under any conceivable circumstances fall into the hands of the Germans," the opposition in Congress would be "greatly lessened." Perhaps William Allen White would work upon Wendell Willkie, Joseph Martin, and Charles McNary and thus divide the Republican ranks! When the President talked with White over the telephone he elicited a promise from the famous editor to get in touch with Willkie at once.[52]

There was no doubt in Churchill's mind that any transfer of American destroyers to Britain would be a "decidedly unneutral act by the United States." It would justify a declaration of war by Hitler.[53] Such action would be eminently agreeable to Churchill who would ardently welcome American help in the struggle against the dictatorships. But the situation had to be handled carefully. When Lord Lothian (August 6) cabled that the President was exceedingly anxious for a pledge that the British fleet would not be turned over to the Germans in the event that Britain fell, Churchill refused to give one. The British nation would "not tolerate any discussion of what we should do if our island were overrun." It would be best to couple the transfer of destroyers with the lease of naval and air bases in Newfoundland and on some British islands in the Caribbean.

On August 13 the essential paragraphs in this agreement were worked out during a conference between the President, Secretaries

[49] Churchill to Lord Lothian, June 28, 1940. *Ibid.,* pp. 228–29.

[50] Churchill to President Roosevelt, July 31, 1940. *Ibid.,* pp. 401–2.

[51] Churchill to Lord Lothian, August 3, 1940. *Ibid.,* 402–3.

[52] Memorandum of President Roosevelt, August 2, 1940. Roosevelt, *op. cit.,* pp. 1050–51.

[53] Churchill, *op. cit.,* p. 404.

Knox, Morgenthau, and Stimson, and Sumner Welles.[54] In the meantime William Allen White had received assurances from Wendell Willkie that he would "not make a campaign issue of the transfer." The services of General Pershing were next enlisted. The old warrior warned the American public in a broadcast that Britain needed immediate aid. This could best be given by placing at the disposal of the British and Canadian governments "at least fifty over-age destroyers which are left from the days of the World War."[55] Admirals Yarnell, Standley, and Stirling supported this viewpoint.

On August 16, President Roosevelt issued a statement that he was negotiating with the British Government for the acquisition of naval and air bases.[56] Nothing was said about a deal for destroyers. Senator David I. Walsh was still showing strong opposition to such a transaction. With the hope of changing the Senator's opinion in this regard the President wrote him a letter with the familiar salutation, "Dear Dave." He assured the Senator that the British islands were "of the utmost importance to our national defence as naval and operating bases." After reminding him that Jefferson in 1803 had purchased Louisiana "without even consulting Congress," the President then expressed the hope that there would be no further opposition to a deal that would be the "finest thing for the nation that has been done in your lifetime and mine."[57]

"Dear Dave" did not fall for this bait so he was later smeared as a loose character. But even so stanch a New Dealer as Secretary Hull had doubts about a destroyer deal and he regretfully informed Lord Lothian that in order "to meet the wishes of your Government an amendment to these provisions of law [the United States Code and the Act of June 28, 1940] may be necessary."[58] But this would take time and Britain's need was immediate. In the meantime Churchill on August 20 had announced in Parliament that negotiations were in progress for leasing air and naval bases in Newfoundland and on

[54] Memorandum of President Roosevelt, August 13, 1940. Roosevelt, *op. cit.*, p. 1052. The proposed agreement with Britain concerning the destroyers in exchange for naval and air bases upon British territory read as follows: "1. Assurance on the part of the Prime Minister that in the event that waters at G. B. become untenable for British ships of war to remain, they would not be turned over to the Germans or sunk but would be sent to other parts of the Empire. 2. Agreement that G. B. will authorize use of Newfoundland, Bermuda, Bahamas, Jamaica, St. Lucia, Trinidad and Brit. Guiana as naval and air bases by the U. S. in the event of an attack in the Am. Hemisphere by any non-American nation. . . . Land necessary for above to be bought or leased for 99 years."

[55] *New York Times*, August 5, 1940.

[56] *Ibid.*, August 17, 1940.

[57] President Roosevelt to Senator David I. Walsh, August 22, 1940. Roosevelt, *op. cit.*, pp. 1056–57.

[58] Hull, *op. cit.*, p. 833.

British islands in the Caribbean to the United States. Two days later he explained to President Roosevelt the difficulties that would attend any exchange of letters that would admit "in any way that the munitions which you send us are a payment for the facilities." The dispatch of war matériel to Britain should seem to be "a separate spontaneous act on the part of the United States, arising out of their view of the world struggle."[59] But Sumner Welles informed Lord Lothian that under existing legislation it was "utterly impossible" for the President to send destroyers to Britain as a spontaneous gift; they could be sent only as a *quid pro quo.*

On August 23 the President confessed to Secretary Hull that the negotiations with Britain "on the bases and destroyers have bogged down. Please see what you can do."[60] In an extended conference among the President, Secretary Hull, and Lord Lothian the matter was further explored. Secretary Hull made it clear to the British Ambassador that the President "had no authority whatever to make a gift of public property to any Government or individual." But Attorney General Jackson had no trouble finding convenient loopholes in existing legislation. His assistant, Ben Cohen, had also discovered them some months previously. The Act of June 15, 1917, made it unlawful to send any ship out of the United States that was "built, armed or equipped as a vessel of war, with any intent or under any agreement or contract . . . that such vessel shall be delivered to a belligerent nation." This restriction did not apply "to vessels like the over-age destroyers which were not built, armed, equipped as, or converted into, vessels of war with the intent that they should enter the service of a belligerent."[61]

Mr. Jackson blandly pushed aside the pertinent provisions of the Treaty of Washington (May 8, 1871) and Article 8 of the Hague Convention XIII of 1907 which required that a neutral government take measures to prevent the departure from its jurisdiction of any vessel intended to engage in belligerent operations, if the vessel was specially adapted within the neutral's jurisdiction to warlike use. The one precedent that Mr. Jackson adduced to support his contention concerning the transfer of destroyers was a most dubious one. Indeed, the opinion of the Attorney General was distinctly "phony" and was based upon the familiar dictum: "What's the Constitution between friends."

The way was now prepared for the destroyer deal. On September 2

---

[59] Churchill to President Roosevelt, August 22, 1940. Churchill, *op. cit.,* pp. 409–10.

[60] Hull, *op. cit.,* p. 834.

[61] Department of State, *Bulletin,* III, September 7, 1940, 206–7.

notes were exchanged between Secretary Hull and Lord Lothian which first recited that the British Government, freely and without consideration, granted to the United States a lease for the "immediate establishment and use of naval and air bases and facilities" on the Avalon Peninsula and on the southern coast of Newfoundland, and on the east coast and on the Great Bay of Bermuda. The second item dealt with the establishment by the United States of air and naval bases on certain British territory in the Caribbean (Bahamas, Jamaica, Saint Lucia, Trinidad, Antigua, and British Guiana) in exchange "for naval and military equipment and material which the United States Government will transfer to His Majesty's Government." The leases would run for a period of 99 years.[62] At the same time Churchill also gave an assurance that the British fleet would not be scuttled or surrendered. This assurance was not to be published.

From the viewpoint of international law the destroyer deal was definitely illegal. As Professor Herbert Briggs correctly remarks: "The supplying of these vessels by the United States Government to a belligerent is a violation of our neutral status, a violation of our national law, and a violation of international law."[63] Professor Edwin Borchard expressed a similar opinion: "To the writer there is no possibility of reconciling the destroyer deal with neutrality, with the United States statutes, or with international law."[64] The whole matter was correctly described by the *St. Louis Post-Dispatch* in a pertinent headline: "Dictator Roosevelt Commits an Act of War."[65]

f. *Propaganda Pushes America towards Intervention*

During the years 1914 to 1917, British propaganda played a significant part in preparing the American mind for intervention in the World War. In the period prior to American intervention in World War II the British Government did not have to bear a heavy burden of propaganda: there were thousands of Americans who eagerly assumed this responsibility. The colorful story of these merchants of death has been told in such detail that it will be given merely a brief mention in these pages.[66]

Rev. Harry Emerson Fosdick gave Roosevelt an excellent cue when

---

[62] *Peace and War*, pp. 564–68.

[63] "Neglected Aspects of the Destroyer Deal," *American Journal of International Law*, XXXIV (October 1940), 587.

[64] "The Attorney General's Opinion on the Exchange of Destroyers for Naval Bases," *ibid.*, p. 697.

[65] September 4, 1940.

[66] Harold Lavine and James Wechsler, *War Propaganda and the United States* (New Haven, 1940).

he remarked that "of all the ways for Christians to make a war seem holy, the simplest way is to get Jesus into it."[67] The President followed this tip on January 4, 1939, when he addressed Congress on the state of the nation. Storms from abroad were challenging three institutions "indispensable to Americans, now as always. The first is religion. It is the source of the other two—democracy and international good faith. . . . We have learned that God-fearing democracies of the world which observe the sanctity of treaties and good faith in their dealings with other nations cannot safely be indifferent to international lawlessness anywhere. They cannot forever let pass, without effective protest, acts of aggression against sister nations."[68]

The belligerent implications of these words were not lost upon members of Congress who fully realized the dangers and futility of embarking upon a holy war. Their fears were heightened when the President enlarged upon the same theme in an international broadcast under the auspices of the Christian Foreign Service convocation: "Today we seek a moral basis for peace. . . . It cannot be a moral peace if freedom from invasion is sold for tribute. . . . The active search for peace which the early Christians preached meant meeting and overcoming those forces in the world which had set themselves against the brotherhood of man and which denied the equality of souls before the throne of God."[69]

Catholic leaders did not respond to this summons to enlist the churches in a movement towards intervention. Catholic cardinals like O'Connell and Dougherty were strongly opposed to America's entry into World War II, and the Catholic press was outspoken in its criticism of the implications in the President's policy. The *Catholic World* thought Americans "were in no position to save anyone. We shall be lucky to save ourselves. . . . What kind of madness has got hold of those who advocate our settling the quarrels of the world, changing the habits of nations that have been fighting for the last thousand years? Who do we think we are?"[70] The *Ave Maria* was equally opposed to intervention: "The people of this country do not want war at this moment; they can see no transgression against our safety or honor to justify a war. . . . They have no commission, human or divine, to challenge aggression not directed against them."[71]

The *Ave Maria* was particularly sharp in its criticism of William Allen White, famous Kansas editor, who was "doing everything humanly possible to get us into the European conflict." It was certainly

[67] *Ibid.*, p. 62.
[68] *Peace and War*, pp. 447–48.
[69] Lavine and Wechsler, *op. cit.*, p. 62.
[70] June 1940, p. 264.
[71] "Notes and Remarks," October 29, 1940, p. 517.

true that White had been very busy in the fight against fascism. He was a member of the Union for Concerted Peace Efforts, the American Committee for Non-participation in Japanese Aggression, the National Refugee Service, the Council Against Intolerance, and the Non-partisan Committee for Peace through the Revision of the Neutrality Law. This last organization was an active pressure group in favor of sabotaging existing neutrality legislation.

After this work had been carried to a successful conclusion, White helped to launch the Committee to Defend America by Aiding the Allies. The implications of this movement should have been evident to him. In December 1939, Robert Sherwood wrote to White to express the view that "it was necessary for the United States to intervene in a military way to check aggression by dictators." In his reply White remarked that he had always stood with Sherwood "in spirit" but had been constrained "by an old man's fear and doubt when it comes to lifting my voice for war."[72]

In the spring of 1940 after this new organization had begun its activities, White became feverish in his anxiety to speed the gift of munitions of war to the hard-pressed Allies. In July he and the members of the Committee to Defend America by Aiding the Allies bent every effort to secure "the release of fifty or sixty over-age but recently reconditioned American destroyers to England." When the President failed to show any great enthusiasm to push through a destroyer deal, White felt that "he had, as it were, lost his cud."[73] Contact was made with large numbers of influential persons throughout the United States and they were urged to exert pressure upon the Chief Executive. The committee with its six hundred local chapters and thousands of volunteer workers was able to inundate the Capitol in Washington with a flood of letters and telegrams favoring the destroyer deal. The President owed a big debt to White who was so naïve as to believe that America could walk halfway down the road to war and then stop.

This naïveté was clearly indicated on December 20, 1940, in a letter he wrote to Roy Howard of the Scripps-Howard newspaper chain. He assured Howard that "the only reason in God's world" he was a member of the Committee to Defend America by Aiding the Allies was to keep America "out of war."[74] Some of the war hawks on the committee deeply resented White's letter to Howard. When Frederick McKee flew to Emporia to persuade White to issue a statement that he was "not for peace at any price," he was met with a flat refusal. But White

[72] Walter Johnson, The Battle Against Isolation (Chicago, 1944), pp. 60–61.
[73] Ibid., pp. 99–100.
[74] Ibid., p. 181.

then showed his mental confusion by signing a round-robin letter to
the President urging him to do "everything that may be necessary to
insure defeat of the Axis powers." This letter, as the committee recognized, had "more warlike implications than the repeal of the neutrality
law or the convoy issue."[75] But there were still some lingering doubts
in the mind of Clark Eichelberger who wired White on December 26
about the "unfortunate repercussions" of the letter that had appeared
in the Scripps-Howard newspapers. It was at last apparent to White
that he had failed to understand the real intentions of the Committee
to Defend America by Aiding the Allies. Its real drive was towards
war, not peace. In his letter of resignation he confessed that he was
"amazed" that he was "so far behind the procession," but he would go
"no faster nor no further."[76] He had been used as a convenient façade
by an organization that had talked of peace while rushing down the
road to war. He was the symbol of millions of Americans.

g. Lend-Lease—Back Door to Intervention in World War II

It was entirely fitting that lend-lease legislation should have a prelude
of promises by the President that American boys would not be sent
abroad to die along far-flung frontiers. It had been evident to the President in the summer of 1940 that American involvement in World War
II might be just around the corner of the next year. Senator Wheeler
had read between the lines of the President's pronouncements and
when he saw the word *war* written in bold letters he tried to block such
a contingency by a strongly-worded plank in the Democratic platform.
But the pledge to keep out of "foreign wars" was nullified by the preg-
nant phrase—"except in case of attack."[77] It would not be difficult for
an Administration seeking war to push one of the Axis powers to the
point where an attack was inevitable.

But the American people, like William Allen White, had to be
fooled by pacific phrases. When the election currents in the fall of
1940 appeared to be making a turn towards Wendell Willkie, the
President made some new pledges at Philadelphia on October 23: "To
every man, woman and child in the nation I say this: Your President
and your Secretary of State are following the road to peace. . . . We

[75] *Ibid.*, pp. 189–90.
[76] *Ibid.*, pp. 193–94.
[77] Charles A. Beard, *American Foreign Policy in the Making, 1932–1940* (New
Haven, 1946), pp. 282–94.
[78] *New York Times*, October 24, 1940.

are arming ourselves not for any purpose of conquest or intervention in foreign disputes."[78] A week later, in Boston, his pledge became more specific: "While I am talking to you mothers and fathers, I give you one more assurance. I have said this before, but I shall say it again and again and again: Your boys are not going to be sent into any foreign wars."[79]

Robert Sherwood who helped to prepare this Boston speech had some qualms of conscience in later years: "For my own part, I think it was a mistake for him [the President] to go so far in yielding to the hysterical demands for sweeping reassurance, but, unfortunately for my own conscience, I happened at the time to be one of those who urged him to go the limit on this. . . . I burn inwardly whenever I think of those words 'again—and again—and again.' "[80]

In the spring of 1941 these fires of conscience were burning very low in the President's entourage. Under the impact of appeals from Churchill in England the entire structure of American neutrality was finally demolished by the legislative bomb of lend-lease. This bomb was many months in the making. On November 6, 1940, Churchill wrote to Roosevelt to express his profound relief at the election results: "I feel you will not mind my saying that I prayed for your success and that I am truly thankful for it. . . . I must avow my sure faith that the lights by which we steer will bring us all safely to anchor."[81] Those lights would lead America into the war.

On December 8, 1940, Churchill sent another long letter in which he outlined in great detail the pressing needs of Britain. In Churchill's eyes these needs were also America's needs because Britain was fighting our war as well as hers. The safety of the United States was "bound up with the survival and independence of the British Commonwealth of Nations." Therefore, America should rush to Britain war matériel of specified kinds together with the gift or loan "of a large number of American vessels of war." It was useless to expect Britain to pay for these loans. The moment was approaching when the British Government would "no longer be able to pay cash for shipping and other supplies." The few dollars Britain had left were badly needed for domestic requirements. It would be wrong "in principle" for Britain to be "divested of all saleable assets, so that after the victory was won with our blood, civilisation saved, and the time gained for the United States to be fully armed against all eventualities, we should stand

[79] *Ibid.*, October 31, 1940.
[80] Robert E. Sherwood, *Roosevelt and Hopkins: An Intimate History* (New York, 1948), p. 201.
[81] Churchill, *op. cit.*, pp. 553–54.

stripped to the bone." America should bear a large part of the financial burden for a new crusade in Europe.[82]

Roosevelt received this communication while he was cruising in the Caribbean. When he returned on December 16 he signified his ardent approval of aid to Britain at America's expense. On the following day, at a press conference, he recited an interesting parable:

Suppose my neighbor's house catches fire and I have a length of garden hose four or five hundred feet away. If he can take my garden hose and connect it up with his hydrant, I may help him to put out the fire. Now what do I do? I don't say to him before that operation, "Neighbor, my garden hose cost me fifteen dollars; you have to pay me fifteen dollars for it." No! What is the transaction that goes on? I don't want fifteen dollars—I want my garden hose back after the fire is over. . . . What I am trying to do is to eliminate the dollar sign.[83]

What he really meant to say was that he was trying to eliminate the dollar sign so far as Britain was concerned. The American taxpayers would have it before their anxious eyes for the next generation. But before they had time to make any estimates, a lend-lease bill was introduced in the House of Representatives. It bore the significant number H.R. 1776. In that year we declared our independence from Britain; in 1941 we put it into grave peril by giving Britain a blank check which Churchill filled in with great gusto and then sent back to Washington for Roosevelt's indorsement. Harry Hopkins was the contact man in this regard and while still in Britain he heard Churchill's famous broadcast in which the following dangerous nonsense was beamed to rapt American listeners:

It seems now to be certain that the Government and the people of the United States intend to supply us with all that is necessary for victory. In the last war the United States sent two million men across the Atlantic. But this is not a war of vast armies, firing immense masses of shells at one another. We do not need the gallant armies which are forming throughout the American Union. We do not need them this year, nor next year, nor any year that I can foresee.[84]

These assurances of Churchill were of the same stripe as the Roosevelt assurances during the last days of his campaign for re-election. He probably remembered Lord Northcliffe's sharp indictment of the

[82] *Ibid.*, pp. 558–67.
[83] *New York Times*, December 18, 1940.
[84] Sherwood, *op. cit.*, pp. 261–62.

American masses during the World War: "What sheep!" They could be sheared once more for British benefit by constant repetition of the old propaganda line about Britain fighting America's fight. Roosevelt repeated this line on December 29 in a "fireside chat" to the American people. Aid to Britain was now a question of "national security." If Britain were conquered, "all of us in the Americas would be living at the point of a gun."[85]

On the following day the President summoned to the White House, Secretary Morgenthau and Arthur Purvis, head of the Anglo-French Purchasing Commission, to discuss the details of lend-lease legislation. On January 2, 1941, Edward Foley, Morgenthau's general counsel, and his assistant, Oscar Cox, began the arduous task of drafting the bill. When opposition to the bill developed in certain circles in the State Department, Secretary Knox remarked to Morgenthau in his best serio-comic manner: "Let's organize a hanging bee over there someday and hang the ones that you and I pick out."[86] Some of the clique around the President probably would have regarded the matter of a hanging bee very seriously when Senator Wheeler began a series of blasts against lend-lease legislation. On January 4, 1941, he asked some very pertinent questions: "If it is our war, how can we justify lending them stuff and asking them to pay us back? If it is our war, we ought to have the courage to go over and fight it, but it is not our war."[87] A week later, in a radio broadcast, he feathered a shaft that evoked an immediate cry of pain from the sensitive President. He regarded the lend-lease program as "the New Deal's 'triple A' foreign policy—to plow under every fourth American boy."[88] The President deeply resented these prophetic words and denounced the Wheeler comment upon lend-lease as the "rottenest thing that has been said in public life in my generation."[89]

Although Admiral Stark expressed on January 13 the opinion that "we are heading straight for this war,"[90] the lend-lease program was sold to the American people as a form of peace insurance.[91] On March 11, 1941, the lend-lease bill was signed by the President, and it was not long before a forecast of Senator Taft was proved correct: "I do

[85] *Peace and War*, pp. 599–601.

[86] Charles A. Beard, *President Roosevelt and the Coming of the War*, 1941 (New Haven, 1948), p. 19.

[87] *New York Times*, January 5, 1941.

[88] *Congressional Record*, January 12, 1941, 77 Cong., 1 sess., pt. 10, pp. 178–79.

[89] *New York Times*, January 15, 1941; *The Public Papers of Franklin D. Roosevelt: 1940*, p. 712.

[90] Beard, *op. cit.*, p. 19.

[91] See the lengthy analysis of Congressional comment in Beard, *ibid.*, pp. 24–68.

not see how we can long conduct such a war [undeclared war] without actually being in the shooting end of the war."[92]

h. *Hitler Is Anxious to Avoid Conflict with the United States*

This "shooting end of the war" was greatly feared by Hitler who strove in every way to avoid any incident that might lead to war with the United States. In order to conciliate public opinion in neutral countries, submarine commanders, from the very beginning of the war, had been directed "to conform to the Hague Convention." Passenger lines were not to be torpedoed even when under escort.[93]

In September and October 1939, Hitler had high hopes that America might be induced to accept the role of mediator and thus bring to an early close a war that he had entered with many misgivings. In a previous chapter we have dealt with the mission of William Rhodes Davis to Berlin for the purpose of arranging mediation.[94] It is apparent that Berlin took this mission quite seriously. In Hitler's speech of October 6 there were evident indications of his readiness to accept Roosevelt as mediator, and on the following day Mr. Kirk, American chargé d'affaires in Berlin, cabled to Secretary Hull that "someone close to Hitler had conveyed the thought that the President might use Hitler's speech as the occasion to send a confidential message to him endorsing his 'efforts toward peace.' "[95] On October 9, Kirk cabled that a German press spokesman informed him that Germany "would certainly accept from the President a suggestion for a truce and negotiations toward peace and intimated that Germany might take part in a conference somewhere far removed from the war theater—which some interpreted to mean Washington."[96]

The terms of peace that Germany would present to such a peace conference were made known to the President and Secretary Hull through the long letter that William Rhodes Davis had sent to the Chief Executive. General Göring had spoken to Mr. Davis (October 3) in the following terms:

You may assure Mr. Roosevelt that if he will undertake mediation, Germany will agree to an adjustment whereby a new Polish State and a new Czechoslovakian independent government would come into being. . . . As for myself and my Government, I would be glad to attend and in the event of such

[92] *Congressional Record,* 77 Cong., 1 sess.
[93] *Ante,* pp. 570–71.
[94] *Ante,* pp. 558–61.
[95] Hull, *op. cit.,* p. 710.
[96] *Ibid.,* p. 711.

a conference I would represent Germany. I agree that the conference should be in Washington.[97]

At this time Germany was already profoundly disturbed by the way the Russians were acting in Poland. During the meetings of a peace conference in Washington there would be an opportunity to focus the eyes of the world upon the ills of Europe and attempt to remedy them. If the President had possessed real courage and vision he would have welcomed these German overtures and staged a peace conference that would have saved both Poland and Czechoslovakia. But he and Secretary Hull were fearful that a move towards peace might benefit Hitler and discourage the Allies so they rejected the German peace feelers[98] and thus prepared the way for eventual Red domination over both those countries. In the long chapter of historical might-have-beens, Roosevelt plays a prominent and dismal part.

Roosevelt's rejection of the idea of a peace conference in Washington did not put an end to Nazi efforts to conciliate the United States. Hitler was exceedingly anxious not to have war with America. This fact is clear in the testimony given during the Nürnberg trials. Ribbentrop insisted upon the pacific disposition of the Führer concerning the United States,[99] and Weizsäcker confirmed this fact: "No German desired to be at war with the United States or looked for trouble in that direction. . . . We were not to let ourselves be provoked to be the ones who bring the conflict to the open daylight. Wherever there would be unfriendly acts, . . . we would not be the ones who start."[100]

The German press, under strict instructions, stopped its sharp criticism of the United States and of prominent American officials. Nazi officials became increasingly careful about any statements that might offend American sensibilities, and the German chargé d'affaires in Washington (Dr. Hans Thomsen), in a press release, went so far as to call President Roosevelt "high-minded" and to praise his admonitions of neutrality.[101] In April 1940, General Walther von Brauchitsch assured representatives of the press that he had always admired the youthful strength of the United States and its people to which he attributed the "gigantic success of the new continent."[102]

The new American neutrality law (November 4, 1939) gave certain satisfaction to Hitler who assured leading Nazis that it would

[97] *Ante*, p. 560.
[98] Hull, *op. cit.*, pp. 710–12.
[99] *Nazi Conspiracy and Aggression*, Supplement B, pp. 1194 ff.
[100] H. L. Trefousse, *Germany and American Neutrality, 1939–1941* (New York, 1951), p. 27.
[101] *Facts in Review*, September 14, 1939.
[102] Trefousse, *op. cit.*, p. 34.

render the United States harmless.[103] Under this law the waters around
the British Isles and the entire European coast from Bergen to the
Spanish border were closed to American ships.[104] These restrictions
pleased the Führer who decreed on December 30, 1939, that American
crews were to be treated "with the greatest consideration."[105] In this
same spirit Admiral Raeder issued instructions that American ships
were not to be pursued or sunk in order that "all difficulties which
might result from trade war between the United States and Germany
might be avoided at the very beginning."[106] But this German policy of
conciliation was sorely tried by incidents arising out of the establishment of a neutrality zone announced by the Panama Conference, October 3, 1939. This safety belt around the Americas south of Canada
varied in width from 300 to 1000 miles. Belligerents were warned to
refrain from naval action within that area, but no armed forces were
stationed along the safety belt to enforce this regulation.

In order to conciliate America the German Admiralty issued orders
designed to prevent naval engagements within this safety belt.[107] When
the Admiralty wished to recede from this position, Hitler refused to
permit any change of orders.[108] Moreover, the Führer adhered to this
conciliatory policy even when American vessels adopted a course that
must have enraged him. In December 1939 the German liner *Colum-
bus* left Veracruz and was closely trailed by the U.S.S. *Tuscaloosa* which
constantly broadcasted her position. This action compelled the Nazi
captain to scuttle his ship some 450 miles east of Cape May.[109] The
same tactics were pursued by the U.S.S. *Broome* in trailing the *Rhein,*
which also was scuttled by her captain.[110] The freighter *Idarwild* was
followed by the *Broome* until it was destroyed by H.M.S. *Diomede*
(November 1940), with the *Broome* standing by to watch the result
of her pursuit.[111] The German Government refrained from filing any
protest at these actions.

At a naval conference on March 18, Admiral Raeder was finally able
to secure an important concession from the Führer. This took the form
of a new blockade order (March 25, 1941) which not only included

---

103 *International Nuremberg Trial,* XXVI, Document 789-PS, 327–36.
104 See the excellent map in Samuel F. Bemis, *A Diplomatic History of the United
States* (New York, 1950), pp. 840–41.
105 *Fuehrer Conferences on Matters Dealing with the German Navy, 1939,* p. 66.
106 *International Nuremberg Trial,* XL, Document Doenitz-86, March 5, 1940, 99.
107 Trefousse, *op. cit.,* p. 41; *Fuehrer Conferences on Matters Dealing with the
German Navy, 1940,* I, 13.
108 *Ibid.,* II, 37–55; *ibid., 1941,* I, 50–56, 62–67.
109 *New York Herald-Tribune,* December 21, 1939.
110 Trefousse, *op. cit.,* p. 42.
111 *New York Times,* November 30, 1940.

Iceland but went as far as the waters of Greenland.[112] The first naval incident in the North Atlantic would soon take place.

The background for such an incident had been carefully filled in by President Roosevelt. In August 1940 he had sent Admiral Robert L. Ghormley, Major General D. C. Emmons, and Major General George V. Strong to London for exploratory conversations concerning eventual "armed co-operation with the British Commonwealth." After some months of conversations with important officers in the British armed services, Admiral Ghormley, in October 1940, sent to Admiral Stark a full report on his mission. Stark, in turn, presented to Secretary Knox on November 12 a memorandum on national objectives. One of the most important items in this memorandum was "the prevention of the disruption of the British Empire." In order to achieve this objective, in January 1941 a series of secret staff conversations began in Washington. Two months later (March 27, 1941), the ABC-1 Staff Agreement was consummated which envisaged a "full-fledged war co-operation when and if Axis aggression forced the United States into the war."[113]

One of the sections of this agreement was aimed at creating an incident that would "force the United States into the war." It contained the following explosive phraseology: "Owing to the threat to the sea communications of the United Kingdom, the principal task of the United States naval forces in the Atlantic will be the protection of shipping of the Associated Powers." In order to carry out this task the Royal Navy hastened to give the United States Navy the "benefit of its experience, and of the new devices and methods for fighting submarines that had already been evolved." The responsibility "now assumed by the United States Navy meant the organization of a force for escort-of-convoy." On February 1, 1941, this patrol force was given "the new and appropriate designation of Atlantic Fleet," and its commander, Rear Admiral Ernest J. King, was promoted to the rank of Admiral and designated Commander in Chief Atlantic Fleet.[114] The first naval incident was almost at hand.

On April 10, 1941, the destroyer *Niblack* (Lieutenant Commander E. R. Durgin), in the waters off Iceland, picked up three boatloads of survivors from a torpedoed Netherlands freighter. As the last men were being pulled aboard, the sound operator made contact on a submarine. The division commander, D. L. Ryan, immediately assumed that the submarine was approaching for an attack so he ordered Mr.

[112] *Fuehrer Conferences on Matters Dealing with the German Navy, 1941*, I, 29. See map in Bemis, *op. cit.*, p. 858.

[113] Samuel E. Morison, *The Battle of the Atlantic, September 1939–May 1943* (Boston, 1947), pp. 38–47.

[114] *Ibid.*, pp. 49–52.

Durgin to drop some depth charges which caused the submarine to retire. This was the first action between United States and German armed forces.[115]

As the system of convoy escorts developed in accordance with Anglo-American plans, other incidents were bound to occur. On April 17, John O'Donnell, well-known newspaper commentator, published a statement that "battlecraft" of the American Navy and Coast Guard were "giving armed escort to munition-laden British merchantmen leaving American ports." The President, through his secretary, Mr. Early, replied that American naval forces were merely on "neutrality patrol" in the Atlantic. He then charged that Mr. O'Donnell was guilty of a "deliberate lie."[116] On April 25, during a press conference, the President expressly denied that naval escorts were being provided for fleets carrying lend-lease goods, and he developed at great length the difference between patrolling and convoying.[117] A month later (May 27), in a national broadcast, he insisted that the delivery of war matériel to Britain was "imperative" and then stated that he had extended "our patrol in north and south Atlantic waters."[118]

It was evident to Senator Taft that the President's broadcast disclosed "an intention on his part to push further and further toward war without consulting the people. . . . His speech contains vague threats of aggressive, warlike action to be undertaken in his sole discretion."[119] Two weeks later the *Washington Post* printed a story by two columnists, Alsop and Kintner, to the effect that more than a month earlier there had been an encounter between American and German vessels of war and this had been followed by offensive operations on the part of an American destroyer.[120] The columnists were making a specific reference to the *Niblack* incident which had been kept very quiet by navy authorities. Secretary Knox promptly denounced this story but failed to confirm or explicitly deny it.[121] In further statements he was purposely vague.[122]

While these exercises in double talk were being carried on, the President was taking active measures to see that Greenland did not fall into German hands. On January 9, 1941, the Department of State issued a

[115] *Ibid.*, p. 57.
[116] *New York Daily News*, April 17, 1941; *New York Times*, April 18, 1941.
[117] *New York Times*, April 26, 1941.
[118] *Documents on American Foreign Relations, July 1940–June 1941*, ed. S. Shepard Jones and Denys P. Myers (Boston, 1941), III, 48–57.
[119] *New York Times*, May 28, 1941.
[120] *Washington Post*, June 9, 1941.
[121] *New York Times*, June 12, 1941.
[122] *Ibid.*, July 3, 11, 12, 1941.

release indicating that an American consulate had been established at Godthaab, and that provision had been made for the purchase in the United States of small arms for the Greenland police.[123] These steps were followed by the signature (April 9, 1941) of an agreement authorizing the United States to occupy Greenland for defensive purposes. Inasmuch as the Danish Minister in Washington (Henrik Kauffmann) had no authority to conclude such an agreement, he was recalled by the Nazi-controlled Danish Foreign Office. He preferred to remain in Washington and was recognized by Secretary Hull as the regularly accredited minister.[124] Needless to say, from the viewpoint of international law, this whole transaction was legally indefensible.[125]

In the meantime the Führer was showing a strong determination to adhere to his policy of keeping out of war with the United States. In May 1941 the German attitude was summed up at a meeting between Hitler and his naval advisers:

Whereas up to now the situation confronting submarines and naval forces on operations was perfectly clear, naval warfare in the North Atlantic is becoming increasingly complicated as the result of the measures taken by the U.S.A. In order to help Britain, the American neutrality patrol, which was hitherto confined to the area within the American neutrality zone, has been reinforced and considerably extended toward the east to about 38° W., i.e. as far as the middle of the Atlantic. The true character of the American neutrality patrol is shown by the fact that vessels on patrol have also been instructed to report by radio any battleships encountered. . . .

We have laid down the following rules for naval warfare in order to comply with German political aims with regard to the U.S.A.:

No attack should be made on U.S. naval forces and merchant vessels.

Prize regulations are not to be applied to U.S. merchant ships.

Weapons are not to be used, even if American vessels conduct themselves in a definitely unneutral manner.

Weapons are to be used *only if U.S. ships fire the first shot.*

As a result of these instructions and of the constant endeavors on the part of Germany not to react to provocation, incidents with the U.S.A. have been avoided up to the present time.

It is unmistakable that the U.S. Government is disappointed about this cautious attitude on the part of Germany, since one of the most important factors in preparing the American people for entry into the war is thus eliminated. The U.S. is therefore continuing its attempt to obliterate more and more the boundary line between neutrality and belligerency, and to stretch

---

[123] Jones and Myers, *op. cit.*, II, 87.

[124] *Ibid.*, III, 230–35.

[125] H. W. Briggs, *American Journal of International Law*, XXXV (1941), 506–13.

the "short of war" policy further by constantly introducing fresh measures contrary to international law.[126]

The next naval incident involving German-American relations was the sinking of the American merchant ship (May 21, 1941) *Robin Moor,* New York to Cape Town, by a German submarine. There was no visit or search but the crew and passengers were allowed to take to open lifeboats.[127] As the sinking occurred outside the blockade zone it is evident that the submarine commander disregarded orders concerning American ships. Admiral Raeder immediately issued orders to prevent further incidents of this nature, and Hitler, after confirming these instructions, remarked that he wished to "avoid any incident with the U.S.A."[128] On June 20 the President sent a message to Congress in which he bitterly criticized Germany as an international outlaw.[129] He followed this message with another move in the direction of war. On July 7 he ordered American occupation of Iceland. Two days later Secretary Knox gave a statement to the press which implied that the American patrol force in the North Atlantic had the right to use its guns when the occasion arose.[130]

This occasion arose on September 4, 1941, when the destroyer *Greer,* bound for Iceland, was informed by a British plane that a submerged U-boat lay athwart her course some ten miles ahead. The *Greer* at once laid a course for the reported submarine, and after having made sound contact with it, kept it on her bow for more than three hours. During this period a British plane dropped four depth charges in the vicinity of the submarine without effect. Finally, the submarine commander grew tired of this game of hide-and-seek and launched a torpedo which the *Greer* was able to dodge. When the *Greer* counterattacked with depth charges, the submarine launched another torpedo which was avoided. When sound contact with the submarine could not be re-established, the *Greer* resumed course for Iceland.[131]

On September 11 the President gave a broadcast which presented a distorted version of the *Greer* incident. He conveniently forgot to tell that the initiative had been taken by the *Greer:* "She [the *Greer*] was flying the American flag. Her identity as an American ship was unmis-

---

[126] *Fuehrer Conferences on Matters Dealing with the German Navy, 1941,* I (May 22, 1941), 68–69.

[127] *Documents on American Foreign Relations, 1940–1941,* III, 417–19.

[128] *Fuehrer Conferences on Matters Dealing with the German Navy, 1941,* II (June 21, 1941), 1.

[129] *Documents on American Foreign Relations, op. cit.,* pp. 58–60.

[130] *New York Times,* July 10, 1941.

[131] Morison, *op. cit.,* pp. 79–81; *Congressional Record,* 77 Cong., 1 sess., pt. 8, 8314.

takable. She was then and there attacked by a submarine. Germany admits that it was a German submarine. . . . We have sought no shooting war with Hitler. . . . The aggression is not ours. Ours is solely defense."[132] American vessels would now shoot at sight.

In the face of this serious incident that clearly showed the aggressive character of American naval patrolling, Hitler maintained his policy of avoiding difficulties with the United States. On September 17 orders concerning American merchant vessels exempted them from attack, even when in convoy, in all zones except that immediately surrounding the British Isles. In the Pan-American safety belt "no warlike acts" were to be carried out on German initiative.[133]

The American answer to these pacific gestures was to authorize escort duty for American destroyers. It was arranged that an American escort group, based on Argentia, should take over from a Royal Canadian Navy escort at a designated place off Newfoundland and hand over the convoy to a Royal Navy escort at an agreed mid-ocean meeting place. Convoying was now an established practice, and it should be kept in mind that Secretary Knox, during the lend-lease hearings, had frankly admitted that he regarded convoying as an "act of war."[134]

This *de facto* war in the Atlantic soon produced another incident. On October 16 five American destroyers rushed from Reykjavik, Iceland, to the help of a convoy that was being attacked by submarines. On the following day, while in the midst of the fighting, the destroyer *Kearny* was struck by a torpedo and slowly made its way back to Iceland.[135] It had deliberately moved into the center of a pitched battle between German submarines and British and Canadian warships and had taken the consequences. It was not long before President Roosevelt gave to the American people a twisted account of the incident. On October 27 he recounted the happenings on October 16 and 17 and asserted that he had "wished to avoid shooting." America had "been attacked. The U.S.S. *Kearny* is not just a Navy ship. She belongs to every man, woman, and child in this Nation. . . . Hitler's torpedo was directed at every American." In order to give additional overtones of villainy to his description of Nazi wickedness he then stated that he had a secret map made in Germany which disclosed Hitler's plan to put all the continent of South America under his domination. But that was not all. He had in his possession another document made in Germany that revealed Hitler's intention, if he was victorious, to "abolish all existing religions."

132 *Peace and War*, pp. 737–43.
133 *Fuehrer Conferences on Matters Dealing with the German Navy, 1941*, II, 44.
134 *Hearings* Before the Senate Committee on Foreign Relations, Lend-Lease Bill, 1941, pt. 1, p. 211.
135 Morison, *op. cit.*, pp. 92–93.

It should be evident that the "forward march of Hitlerism" should be stopped. . . . We are pledged to pull our own oar in the destruction of Hitlerism." The American Navy had been given orders to "shoot on sight." The Nazi "rattlesnakes of the sea" would have to be destroyed.[136]

This declaration of war was confirmed by the *Reuben James* incident. On October 31, while the *Reuben James* was escorting a convoy to Iceland, some German submarines were encountered about 600 miles west of that island. The American destroyer was struck by a torpedo and rapidly sank. Only 45, out of a crew of about 160, were saved. When the news of the sinking of the *Reuben James* reached Germany, Hitler remarked: "President Roosevelt has ordered his ships to shoot the moment they sight German ships. I have ordered German ships not to shoot when they sight American vessels but to defend themselves when attacked."[137] On November 13, 1941, the directives for conduct of German warships when encountering American naval vessels remained pacific: "Engagements with American naval or air forces are not to be sought deliberately; they are to be avoided as far as possible. . . . If it is observed before a convoy is attacked that it is being escorted by American forces, the attack is not to be carried out."[138]

Germany was trying desperately to stay out of war with the United States. America's attitude was clearly stated by Sumner Welles at Arlington on November 11: "Beyond the Atlantic a sinister and pitiless conqueror has reduced more than half of Europe to abject serfdom. It is his boast that his system shall prevail even unto the ends of the earth. . . . The American people after full debate . . . have determined upon their policy. They are pledged . . . to spare no effort and no sacrifice in bringing to pass the final defeat of Hitlerism and all that which that evil term implies. . . . We cannot know, we cannot yet foresee, how long and how hard the road may be which leads to that new day when another armistice will be signed."[139]

To the mind of Welles and to others in the White House group it was obvious that America was really in the war. But the American people did not realize that momentous fact, nor did they know that they were pledged "to spare no effort and no sacrifice in bringing to pass the final defeat of Hitlerism." It was easy for Mr. Welles to speak glibly of sacrifice. He had long enjoyed wealth and high social position. The word "sacrifice" had always been excluded from his dictionary. As the

---

[136] *Peace and War*, pp. 767–72.

[137] Trefousse, *op. cit.*, p. 122.

[138] *Fuehrer Conferences on Matters Dealing with the German Navy, 1941*, II, 66–67.

[139] *Peace and War*, pp. 784–87.

spokesman for the President he was suddenly breaking to the American people the dread news that they had become involved in a war they had ardently wished to avoid. The war hawks of 1941 were never tired of sneering at the majority of Americans as benighted isolationists who had tried to build a Chinese wall around the United States and thus cut it off from all foreign contacts. They knew their sneers were patent lies. America had never been isolated from the social, economic, religious, and cultural forces that shaped the modern world. Thanks to its geographical position it had escaped the recurring tides of conflict that had crumbled the walls of ancient civilizations and washed away the heritage men had earned through dauntless courage and high endeavor. Americans had been isolationists only against war and its evident evils, and their country had grown prosperous beyond the dreams of the founding fathers. But in 1915, President Wilson began to nurse the thought of sharing America's ideals and wealth with the rest of the world, and two years later he led us into a foreign war that he hoped would make the world safe for democracy. But this theme song turned sour in American ears when it led to the great parade of 1917 which ended for many men in the vast cemeteries in France. It gained new popularity after 1933, and with Roosevelt as maestro, the old macabre accents began to haunt every home. In 1941 his orchestra of death was anxiously waiting for the signal to begin the new symphony. He had hoped for a German motif but Hitler had refused to assist with a few opening martial notes. Perhaps some Japanese statesman would prove more accommodating! At any rate, after the *Reuben James* incident had fallen flat he turned his eyes towards the Orient and sought new inspiration from the inscrutable East. He found it at Pearl Harbor when Japanese planes sounded the first awesome notes in a chorus of war that is still vibrating throughout the world. The story of how the first notes in the script of that chorus were written in by President Roosevelt is told in the next chapter.

XXVI

Japan Is Maneuvered into Firing the First Shot at Pearl Harbor

WHEN THE PRESIDENT perceived that Hitler would not furnish the pretext for a war with Germany, he turned to the Far East and increased his pressure upon Japan. The path to Pearl Harbor had already been pointed out by Mr. Hornbeck in February 1939. After discussing how the American Government had tried to restrain the Japanese advance in North China by "moral and economic opposition," he stated his belief that in the long run the situation would so "develop that military opposition by this country will have to be offered."[1]

But Herbert Feis, the adviser on International Economic Affairs, still favored economic pressure, so on July 26, 1939, Secretary Hull sent a note to Ambassador Horinouchi informing him that the Treaty of February 21, 1911, would terminate on January 26, 1940. The way was thus prepared for an all out economic offensive against Japan. But before this could be launched, several incidents arose which further disturbed the course of Japanese-American relations.

a. *Japanese Bombings of Chungking*

On July 10 the American chargé d'affaires in Tokyo called on the Minister of Foreign Affairs and made "the strongest possible representation with regard to the recent bombings at Chungking." Mr. Arita said that he was "distressed" to learn that Ambassador Johnson and his staff "had been put in jeopardy," but it was "impossible for him to promise that the bombing of Chungking would cease." Attack from the air was an important phase of the military operations in that area.[2] On this same day the President informed Secretary Hull that he desired to receive "without delay a statement from the Japanese Government in regard to the matter."[3] On July 20 the Japanese Ambassador had a conference with Secretary Hull. When the Ambassador explained that military necessities dictated the bombings, Hull sharply rebuffed him by remarking that if the bombings continued "something very serious

---

[1] *Ante,* pp. 502.

[2] Eugene Dooman to Secretary Hull, Tokyo, July 10, 1939. 793.94/15187, MS, Department of State.

[3] Secretary Hull to American Embassy in Tokyo, July 10, 1939. 793.94/15201A, MS, Department of State.

was liable to happen." When the Ambassador murmured that he hoped the American Government would urge its nationals to "keep away from places of danger," Hull acidly replied that the United States did not "concede the right of any other outside country to a monopoly of highways or streets or other localities in China."[4]

b. *The Tientsin Affair*

It was soon apparent that the Department of State was adopting a far more aggressive attitude towards Japan than was the British Foreign Office. This fact was given a convincing demonstration in the Tientsin affair. During the World War the Chinese liquidated the Austrian and German concessions in this city, and in 1920 the Russian concession was taken over. British investment in its concession in Tientsin was estimated at $46,000,000; French investment in the French concession was considerably less. In the British concession banks held silver to the value of $50,000,000 in the name of the Chinese Nationalist Government. When they refused to turn this over to Japanese authorities, reprisals were ordered against the British and French concessions. Barricades and wire entanglements were erected around them and they were subjected to a rigorous blockade. As a result of this pressure Sir Robert Craigie, the British Ambassador in Tokyo, consented to sign a far-reaching agreement (the Craigie-Arita Agreement) on July 21. Under the terms of this formula the British Government fully recognized that as long as large-scale military operations were in progress in China, the Japanese forces there would insist upon "special requirements for the purpose of safeguarding their own security and maintaining public order in the regions under their control, and that they have to suppress or remove any such acts or causes as will obstruct them or benefit their enemy."[5]

The Department of State had no intention of following the British policy of appeasement. Although the Japanese had been unusually conciliatory towards the Americans and had given assurances that their goods would be permitted to move through the embargoes around the British and French concessions, the Department of State was disposed to challenge the Japanese program in Tientsin. Its attitude was reflected in a memorandum prepared in the Division of Far Eastern Affairs:

If Great Britain should give way at Tientsin and substantially meet Japanese demands there, that surrender would signal to Japan Great Britain's vulner-

---

[4] Memorandum of conversation between Secretary Hull and the Japanese Ambassador, July 20, 1939. 793.94/15253, MS, Department of State.

[5] *New York Herald-Tribune,* June 20, July 6; *New York Times,* June 22, July 15, 1939; *Parliamentary Debates,* House of Commons, CCCL, July 24, 992.

ability to further demands and would be the beginning of abandonment by the Powers of the National Government of China. If Great Britain and France were driven, through pressure . . . to close the French Indochina and Burman routes, the United States would be unable, in defense of its own interests, to afford China any further material assistance in the latter's resistance to Japanese aggression. . . . If the United States does not make an effort at this point, the assistance of Great Britain and France may well be lost to any later efforts that developments may require the United States to make.[6]

The outbreak of World War II eliminated any possibility that either Britain or France could give any real assistance to the United States in the Far East. It also occasioned a careful survey by the Japanese of the impact of the war upon its program. The Nazi-Soviet Pact had deeply disturbed Japanese statesmen who had welcomed ties with Germany as one means of blunting any Soviet thrust in the Far East. The international situation had to be restudied and a policy of caution was an imperative. From the American Embassy in Tokyo came a report that "the immediate effects of a European war should bring about a sharp increase in the demand for American goods, particularly cotton, wood pulp, machinery and other industrial equipment, nonferrous metals, iron and steel and chemicals." Without these imports from America, "Japan's industrial expansion program would completely break down."[7] America would have to be conciliated.

c. *Chiang Kai-shek Asks that Roosevelt Mediate in Sino-Japanese War*

While European statesmen were having a case of war jitters, Chiang Kai-shek suddenly asked for Roosevelt mediation in the Sino-Japanese War. On September 1 the Chinese Ambassador in Paris called on Bullitt and gave him the substance of some long telegrams he had received from Chiang Kai-shek. The Generalissimo hoped that President Roosevelt could "take action immediately to put an end to the war between China and Japan." He did not want the public to know "that this initiative had come from him." It should appear as "a purely American initiative." With regard to the Soviet Union the Generalissimo wanted the President to realize that he (the Generalissimo) retained "absolute freedom of action." He had "no pacts with the Soviet Union binding him in any way." There was need to take action before Japan established "a so-called Chinese Government under Wang Ching-wei." It

[6] Memorandum of the Division of Far Eastern Affairs, July 6, 1939. 793.94/15241, MS, Department of State.

[7] Eugene Dooman to Secretary Hull, Tokyo, September 1, 1939. 894.00/873, MS, Department of State.

would be best to have Britain and France associated in this move towards mediation.[8]

The President was aware of the difficulties of proposing mediation at that time, and any inclination he might have had was checked by the news from China. After the outbreak of war in Europe, Britain was anxious to remove her troops from the Far East. To accelerate this movement, Japan addressed a note to Britain and France pointing to the importance of this action. This step was resented by Secretary Hull who frankly informed the Japanese Ambassador he regarded the move as an indication that Japan was anxious to push the Western powers out of China.[9] The British Foreign Office welcomed these stern words to Japan but doubt was expressed that any real support would be given to British interests in the Tientsin concession where it was greatly needed. It would probably be expedient to remove British troops and thus avoid a clash with Japanese forces.[10] In France the Foreign Office had been fearful that "the Soviet Union might send bombing planes to assist the German army in attacking France." They desired, therefore, "to placate Japan" even though this might injure China.[11] This appeasement policy on the part of France would soon be put into effect.

d. *The President's Attitude towards Japan Becomes Increasingly Belligerent*

While Britain and France were making plans to appease Japan, President Roosevelt was giving extended consideration to a program of pressure upon that country. He knew from the dispatches from Tokyo that Japan would be increasingly dependent upon imports of certain basic commodities from the United States. The time had arrived when he could use to advantage this economic club. In his talks with the President in September (1939), Ambassador Grew had stressed the fact that sanctions against Japan might lead to war. If an embargo were placed upon American oil exports to Japan the result could well be a Japanese thrust in the direction of the Netherlands East Indies in order to control the rich petroleum resources of Borneo. The President's answer to these fears indicated that he was thinking in terms of war with Japan: "We could easily intercept her fleet."[12]

[8] Ambassador Bullitt to the Secretary of State (Secret for the President), Paris, September 1, 1939. 793.94/15333, *Confidential file,* MS, Department of State.

[9] Memorandum of conversation between Secretary Hull and the Japanese Ambassador, September 7, 1939. *Japan: 1931–1941,* II, 12–14.

[10] Ambassador Bullitt to Secretary Hull, Paris, September 11, 1939. 793.94/15369, *Confidential file,* MS, Department of State.

[11] Ambassador Bullitt to Secretary Hull, Paris, October 20, 1939. 793.94/15426, *Strictly Confidential,* MS, Department of State.

[12] Herbert Feis, *The Road to Pearl Harbor* (Princeton, 1950), p. 41.

But Grew wished to prevent rather than provoke war with Japan. While the President was uttering this belligerent bombast, Grew was confiding to his diary that Secretary Hull should "offer the Japanese a *modus vivendi*" and then commence negotiations for a new commercial treaty. In Japan the Shidehara policy of conciliation "has existed. It can exist again."[13] To Grew the Japanese program with its insistence upon "strategic protection against a future attack by Soviet Russia" did not appear too unreasonable. If America wished to change this program it should not try to do so through the employment of sanctions: "There must be no tone of threat in our attitude."[14]

It is evident that Grew did not appreciate the fact that the President's dislike of Japan had gone very deep and spread very far. He was inclined to discount all Japanese gestures for an understanding. In Japan, Grew had some friendly talks with the Foreign Minister who gave repeated assurances that "the Japanese forces in China have not the slightest intention to drive out American interests and that they have the strictest orders to the contrary." Measures were being taken "to facilitate American commerce." Indeed, certain "positive measures were being taken in line with the valuable suggestions" which Grew had recently made.[15]

These Japanese gestures of conciliation were answered by a White House press release which called for a moral embargo upon the shipment to Japan of "airplanes, aeronautical equipment and materials essential to airplane manufacture."[16] Japan was being penalized for her bombing operations in China. To make these penalties more effective a press release was issued by the Department of State on December 20 containing the significant statement that "national interest suggests that for the time being there should be no further delivery to certain countries of plans, plants, manufacturing rights, or technical information required for the production of high quality aviation gasoline."[17]

These measures were merely the prelude to a subsequent program of economic pressure upon Japan. Senator Pittman had introduced a resolution which authorized the President to forbid the export of specified war matériel whenever he found that any signatory of the Nine-Power Treaty was endangering the lives of American citizens or depriving them of their lawful rights. But the Department of State was not ready to push this legislation. A new ministry was about to take office

[13] *Ibid.*, p. 42.
[14] Joseph C. Grew, *Ten Years in Japan* (New York, 1944), pp. 296–303.
[15] Ambassador Grew to Secretary Hull, Tokyo, December 4, 1939. *Japan: 1931–1941*, II, 40–43.
[16] *Ibid.*, p. 202.
[17] *Ibid.*, pp. 203–4.

in Japan and it would be given an opportunity to show its hand. On January 17 the newly appointed Minister of Foreign Affairs (Arita) issued a statement which spoke of the efforts he would make to "normalize" relations with the United States. He was referring particularly to the fact that treaty relations with the United States would expire on January 26. After that date there would be no legal barrier to legislation or to Presidential proclamations imposing severe restrictions upon exports to Japan.

e. *Japan Establishes a New Central Government in China*

Japan's program for expansion in China made it impossible to "normalize" relations with the United States. On March 15, 1940, the Japanese Prime Minister issued a statement which called for the creation of "a new international relationship between Japan, Manchukuo and China." This would necessitate the establishment of "a new Central Government of China" to be headed by Wang Ching-wei.[18] On March 30, at Nanking, this puppet government was formally proclaimed. It was immediately noted, however, that the three important northern provinces of Hopeh, Shansi, and Shantung, including such key cities as Peiping, Tientsin, and Tsingtao, were not placed under the control of the Wang regime.

Secretary Hull's answer to this Japanese action was immediate and forceful: "The Government of the United States has ample reason for believing that the Government [of Chiang Kai-shek] with capital now at Chungking, has had and still has the allegiance and support of the great majority of the Chinese people. The Government of the United States of course continues to recognize that Government as the Government of China."[19]

The language of the Department of State was significantly different from that employed by Sir Robert Craigie, the British Ambassador in Tokyo. On March 28, Craigie delivered an address to the Japanese-British Society in which the note of conciliation was strongly accented. He believed that Britain and Japan were "striving for the same objective, namely, a lasting peace and the preservation of our institutions from extraneous, subversive influences."[20] This friendly gesture towards Japan was favorably regarded by the London *Times* which spoke of the proposed establishment of the Wang regime as "an offer of peace to the Chinese people."[21]

[18] *Japan: 1931–1941*, II, 56–57.
[19] *Ibid.*, 59–60.
[20] London *Times*, March 29, 1940.
[21] *Ibid.*, March 25, 1940.

f. *Japan Compels Both Britain and France to Adopt a Policy of Appeasement*

The British Foreign Office quickly changed its tune when the Japanese Foreign Minister (Arita) announced on April 15 that the economic ties that bound Japan to the Netherlands East Indies were particularly important. For that reason the government of Japan could not but be "deeply concerned over any development accompanying the aggravation of the war in Europe that may affect the *status quo* of the Netherlands Indies."[22] The Netherlands Minister in Washington (Dr. Loudon) immediately issued a statement that his government would resist any "preventive protection" of its colonial possessions.[23] Secretary Hull was equally quick to announce the attitude of the Department of State: "Intervention in the domestic affairs of the Netherlands Indies or any alteration of their *status quo* by other than peaceful processes would be prejudicial to the cause of stability, peace and security not only in the region of the Netherlands Indies but in the entire Pacific area." He then alluded to the provisions of the Root-Takahira Agreement of 1908 and the Four-Power Treaty of 1921 with reference to "the maintenance of the existing *status quo* in the region of the Pacific Ocean."[24] President Roosevelt was about to leave for a vacation at Warm Springs, Georgia, when the Hull statement was given to the press. He remarked that the Secretary of State had spoken "right to the point," and then significantly added: "I'll be right back if another country is invaded."[25]

Japan did not take this threat very seriously and immediately inaugurated a policy of pressure upon France. On June 17 the Japanese Government presented to the Pétain regime a series of demands which were aimed at stopping all shipments of supplies to Chungking through Indochina. Three days later these demands were complied with and the government of Chiang Kai-shek received a severe setback.

On June 19 another Japanese victory was recorded. For a year pressure had been applied to British and French banks in Tientsin to compel them to turn over to Japanese authorities a large amount of silver that belonged to the Nationalist Government of China. These banks finally yielded to Japanese demands and also agreed to permit Japanese-sponsored paper currency to circulate in the British and French concessions.

The British Foreign Office resented this Japanese pressure and on June 10 made inquiries through Lord Lothian as to the possibility of

[22] *New York Times,* April 16, 1940.
[23] *New York Herald-Tribune,* April 19, 1940.
[24] Department of State, *Bulletin,* II, April 20, 1940, 411.
[25] *New York Times,* April 18, 1940.

Anglo-American fleet movements in the Atlantic and Pacific. When Hull gave a negative answer, Lothian, accompanied by the Australian Minister, pointedly asked Hull on June 27 "whether Japan should be opposed or appeased." A stringent economic embargo could be imposed upon Japan and warships could be sent to Singapore as a demonstration of naval unity. These measures might compel the Japanese Government to adopt a less aggressive policy. If appeasement appealed to the Department of State, Britain was ready to make further concessions. On June 28, Hull vetoed the idea of an embargo and refused to consider the dispatch of any American warships to Singapore. He was equally opposed to a policy of appeasement. It would be best to let things drift along and let Japan take the initiative.[26]

Japan was not backward in this regard. After securing from France an agreement to stop the shipments of war matériel to Chiang Kai-shek through Indochina, the Japanese Government persuaded Britain (July 17) to close the Burma Road for a period of three months. Munitions of war, gasoline, motor trucks, and railway materials could no longer reach China by this route.[27] Secretary Hull, although he had refused to make any promise of support to Britain, announced that the United States had a "legitimate interest in keeping open the arteries of commerce in every part of the world." The closing of the routes to China through Burma and Indochina had been "unwarranted interpositions of obstacles to world trade."[28]

g. The President Orders a Cautious Economic Offensive against Japan

While Secretary Hull was following a policy of watchful waiting, the President favored more forceful measures. Under the recently enacted National Defense Act authority was granted for a rigid control over exports from the United States. Secretary Morgenthau was eager to have the Treasury Department take over this job of export control, while Secretary Hull was exceedingly anxious that the task be given to another department. He was fearful that Morgenthau's crusading fervor against the dictatorships might lead to a clash in the Pacific. The President finally decided to appoint a single administrator of export control who would be directly under White House supervision. Actually, the control of policy and the issuance of licenses remained in State Department hands.

[26] Feis, *op. cit.*, pp. 69–71.
[27] *Documents on American Foreign Relations, 1940–1941*, III, 270–71.
[28] Department of State, *Bulletin*, III, July 20, 1940, 36.

The basic differences of opinion between the State and Treasury departments were highlighted by what occurred the last week in July 1940. On the evening of July 18, Secretaries Stimson, Knox, and Morgenthau dined with Lord Lothian and the Australian Minister. After the conversation had centered upon the impact of an oil embargo upon Japan, Lothian suddenly suggested that it might be possible for Britain to arrange for the destruction of the oil wells in the Dutch East Indies. If these two sources of supply were cut off from Japan her war machine would come to an abrupt stop.[29]

When this matter was discussed at the White House, the President seemed deeply interested in this program of pressure but Sumner Welles promptly asserted that an embargo against Japan would lead to a Japanese attack upon British or Dutch colonial possessions. This viewpoint was sharply challenged by Knox, Morgenthau, and Stimson who advised bold measures to curb Japan. Morgenthau, realizing that he "spoke to the President's nature and inclination," drew up a proclamation that placed the export of *all* kinds of oil and *all* scrap metals under control. This was signed by the President who sent it to Welles for countersignature. Under the excited insistence of Welles the President discarded the proclamation he had signed and substituted one that dealt only with aviation motor fuel and lubricants, and No. 1 heavy melting iron and steel scrap.[30]

The Japanese Embassy, seeing the newspaper accounts that spoke of total embargo upon oil and scrap metals, hurriedly made inquiries at the Department of State. Welles gave comforting reassurances as to the real scope of the President's proclamation and asserted that the action was not aimed at any particular country. The Japanese Government assailed this position in three long diplomatic notes but Welles, with his tongue in his cheek, held his ground.[31] Lord Lothian, fearing that Roosevelt had tipped his hand, counseled greater prudence in the future, and this advice was strongly seconded by the Dutch representative.

This policy of prudence, however, received a sharp and unexpected attack from Ambassador Grew. He had long been opposed to sanctions against Japan because he believed they would be the prelude to war. But in a long dispatch of September 12, 1940, he reversed his opinions:

If we conceive it to be in our interest to support the British Empire in this hour of her travail, and I most emphatically do so conceive it, we must strive by every means to preserve the status quo in the Pacific at least until the

[29] Feis, *op. cit.*, pp. 89–91.
[30] *Ibid.*, p. 93. The text of this Presidential proclamation of July 26, 1940, is given in *Japan: 1931–1941*, II, 216–18.
[31] *Ibid.*, pp. 93–94.

European war has been won or lost. In my opinion this cannot be done . . .
by merely registering disapproval and keeping a careful record thereof. . . .
Until such time as there is a complete regeneration of thought in this country
[Japan], a show of force, together with a determination to employ it if need
be, can alone contribute effectively to the achievement of such an outcome
and to our own future security.[32]

This dispatch from Grew confirmed the President's desire to exert
more economic pressure upon Japan. The Japanese thrust southward
gave him increasing concern. On September 23, Japanese soldiers
moved into Indochina and soon took over Tonkin Province. When this
news reached the White House, together with reports that Japan was
about to conclude an alliance with Germany, it was decided to place
an embargo upon the shipment of all grades of iron and steel scrap to
Japan.[33] This was a step Japanese statesmen had anticipated by building
up a large stockpile for immediate needs.[34] The President's action was
a challenge instead of a bombshell.

h. *Japan Concludes an Alliance with the Rome-Berlin Axis*

The alliance with the Rome-Berlin Axis was long in the making. The
most important Japanese promoter of this agreement was General Hiroshi Oshima, the Japanese military attaché and subsequently the Ambassador in Berlin. He and Ribbentrop were particulary intimate. In
the summer of 1938, during the Sudeten crisis, Ribbentrop inquired if
Japan would be willing to sign a treaty aimed at all the potential enemies of the proposed Rome-Berlin-Tokyo triangle.[35] Tokyo rejected
this proposal[36] and in February 1939, Prince Ito was sent to Berlin to
acquaint Ribbentrop with the decision that Japan wished to limit the
proposed treaty to action against Russia alone.[37] In April 1939, Ribbentrop redoubled his efforts to reach an intimate accord with Japan. He
insisted that such an arrangement would be a warning to Washington
to remain neutral in the event of an outbreak of war in Europe. But
Japan remained cold to these suggestions,[38] and after the signature

[32] *Pearl Harbor Attack*, pt. 2, p. 637.

[33] Department of State, *Bulletin*, III, September 28, 1940, 250.

[34] For a detailed study of Japanese planning relative to iron and steel shortages,
see J. B. Cohen, *Japan's Economy in War and Reconstruction* (Minneapolis, 1949).

[35] Interrogation of General Oshima, February 4, 1946. *Record of Proceedings, International Military Tribunal for the Far East*, Exhibit No. 497, pp. 6050–54.

[36] *Ibid.*

[37] *Ibid.*, pp. 6063–71.

[38] Ribbentrop to General Eugen Ott, March 15, April 26, 1939, and General Ott
to Ribbentrop, May 4, 1939. *Ibid.*, Exhibit No. 486-K, p. 6115; Exhibit No. 502, p.
6098; and Exhibit No. 503, pp. 6103–6.

of the Nazi-Soviet Treaty in August 1939 this frigidity definitely increased.

But Ribbentrop never lost hope that he could induce Japan to enter into closer political relations with Germany, and through the agency of the I. G. Farben Chemical Trust large sums of money were spent in Japan for propaganda purposes.[39] On June 12, 1940, Ambassador Ott reported that he was "still endeavoring to stir up Japanese ill-feeling against America by influencing the press and leading political personalities."[40] On July 8, Naotake Sato arrived in Berlin for a conference with Ribbentrop. He remarked that Japan had drawn the attention of the United States "to herself since the beginning of the Chinese war, and that she tied up the American fleet in the Pacific Ocean." When the Nazi Foreign Minister inquired as to the fundamental differences between Japan and the United States, Sato pointed to the Nine-Power Pact. It seemed evident to Ribbentrop that Japan could soon be brought into intimate association with the Rome-Berlin Axis.[41]

On July 12 a conference was held in Tokyo between representatives of the ministries of War, Navy, and Foreign Affairs with reference to the signature of a tripartite pact.[42] In order to hasten their decision, Heinrich Stahmer hurried to Tokyo. The conversations between Stahmer and Matsuoka began on September 9 with Stahmer always emphasizing the fact that Germany's prime purpose in seeking the alliance with Japan was to keep America out of the war.[43] By September 16 the opposition in Japan had been largely silenced, and on September 27 the pact was signed with great pomp in Berlin.[44] Article 3 was phrased in language that pointed straight at the United States: "Japan, Germany and Italy . . . undertake to assist one another with all political, economic and military means when one of the three Contracting Parties is attacked by a power at present not involved in the European War or in the Sino-Japanese Conflict."[45]

There is evidence to show that Japan extracted from Stahmer a secret oral understanding that she retain for herself the right to decide whether the *casus foederis* existed in any situation that might

---

[39] Ambassador Ott to the Foreign Ministry, September 19, 1939. United States Military Tribunal, Case VI: *The United States of America Against Krauch, et al.*, p. 1823.

[40] Ambassador Ott to the Foreign Ministry, June 12, 1940. *Far-Eastern Military Tribunal*, Exhibit No. 516, pp. 6152–53.

[41] Interview between Ribbentrop and Sato, July 8, 1940. *Ibid.*, Exhibit No. 524, pp. 6179–84.

[42] *Ibid.*, Exhibit No. 527, pp. 6191–6212.

[43] *Ibid.*, Exhibit Nos. 549, 550, 552, 553, pp. 6323–93.

[44] William L. Shirer, *Berlin Diary* (New York, 1941), pp. 532–37.

[45] *Japan: 1931–1941*, II, 165–66.

arise.[46] There is further evidence to indicate that Japan signed the tripartite pact primarily to deter the United States from entering the war. In the instructions from the Japanese Foreign Minister to Admiral Nomura on October 8, 1941, it was repeatedly stated that one of the reasons why Japan entered into the alliance with Germany and Italy was to maintain "amicable relations with America."[47] Matsuoka made a similar statement to Masuo Kato in 1941.[48] In September 1940 it was difficult for the Department of State to appreciate this viewpoint.

i. *America Draws Closer to Britain*

To the Roosevelt Administration it seemed obvious that the new Rome-Berlin-Tokyo Axis was a design for war. In order to sound a note of defiance to this menacing political alignment, the President, on October 12, boldly declared that the "Americas will not be scared or threatened into the ways the dictators want us to follow. . . . No combination of dictator countries of Europe and Asia will stop the help we are giving to almost the last free people fighting to hold them at bay."[49] In order to implement these bold words, the President had already instructed the Department of Agriculture to cease paying subsidies for wheat exports to the Far East since much of this grain was being purchased by Japan. At the same time Prime Minister Churchill announced in the House of Commons that the Burma Road would be opened on October 8.

Throughout November and December 1940, Lord Lothian continued to push for joint talks and joint action in the Far East. The conference between Secretary Hull and the British Ambassador on November 25 was typical:

The British Ambassador came in at his request, having just returned from London. He referred to the Far Eastern situation with apprehension, saying that he believed the Japanese were likely soon to attack Singapore. . . . The main point the Ambassador raised was that there should be conferences between the naval experts of our two Governments with respect to what each would or might do in case of military outbreaks on the part of Japan. I [Hull] said that, of course there could be no agreement entered into in this respect, but there should undoubtedly be collaboration with the view of making known to each other any and all information practicable in regard to what both might have in mind to do, and when and where, in case of a military movement by Japan in the South or in some other direction.

[46] H. L. Trefousse, *German and American Neutrality, 1939–1941* (New York, 1951), p. 71.

[47] *Pearl Harbor Attack*, pt. 12, pp. 56–60.

[48] Masuo Kato, *The Lost War, A Japanese Reporter's Inside Story* (New York, 1946), p. 20.

[49] *New York Times*, October 13, 1940.

The Ambassador said that the information he had gathered in London was that, while our Naval Attaché, Admiral Ghormley, was a good man, he consistently declined to discuss possible future plans on the ground that he had absolutely no authority. . . . He said he hoped there would be discussion between his and our high naval officials with respect to all phases of the Pacific situation.[50]

We have already seen how these conversations between Hull and Lord Lothian resulted in the Joint Staff conferences that began in Washington in the last week of January 1941.[51] These conferences paralleled a drive to put into effect an embargo upon exports to Japan. On December 10 the White House issued a statement announcing that after December 30 new licensing restrictions would apply to exports of iron ore, pig iron, ferroalloys, and "certain iron and steel manufactures and semi-manufactures."[52] On December 20 restrictions were placed upon the export of bromine, ethylene, abrasives, hydraulic pumps, and equipment for the production of aviation lubricating oil.[53] Three weeks later (January 10, 1941) this economic offensive shifted to restrictions upon the export of copper, brass, zinc, nickel, and potash.[54] These proclamations were followed by a series of others that seemed to touch everything from radium to kip skins—that is everything but oil.

j. Matsuoka and Prince Konoye Are Willing to Sacrifice Japan's Position in China for the Cause of Peace

While the President was preparing this new economic offensive against Japan, Matsuoka was prepared to sacrifice Japan's position in China for the cause of peace. In November 1940, Matsuoka asked Bishop James E. Walsh, Superior General of the Catholic Foreign Mission Society of Maryknoll, New York, and Father J. M. Drought, of the same order, to undertake a special mission to Washington in order to impress upon the President the fact that the Japanese Government "wished to negotiate a peace agreement: (1) An agreement to nullify their participation in the Axis Pact . . . (2) a guarantee to recall all military forces from China and to restore to China its geographical and political integrity." Other conditions bearing upon the relations of Japan and the United States were to be explored and agreed upon "in the conversations that it was hoped would ensue."

[50] Conversation between Secretary Hull and Lord Lothian, November 25, 1940. 740.0011 P.W./40, MS, Department of State.
[51] Ante, pp. 609.
[52] Japan: 1931–1941, II, 232–35.
[53] Ibid., pp. 236–37.
[54] Ibid., pp. 238–40.

Bishop Walsh and Father Drought then had a conference with General Muto, the director of the Central Bureau of Military Affairs, who assured them that "he and his associates in the Japanese Army were in accord with the efforts to reach a peace agreement."

Bishop Walsh and Father Drought hurried to Washington where (on January 23, 1941) they placed the whole matter before President Roosevelt and Secretary Hull during a long conference of more than two hours. They were told that the matter would be "taken under advisement,"[55] and thus ended an anxious effort on the part of the Japanese Government to find a path to peace even though this path led to a renunciation of Japan's objectives in China and a tremendous loss of face. It seems quite possible that the Far Eastern Military Tribunal brought to trial the wrong persons. It might have been better if the tribunal had held its sessions in Washington.

k. *An Informal Negotiation Looking towards an Improvement in Japanese-American Relations*

Just before Bishop Walsh and Father Drought placed their peace proposal before the President, an informal Japanese peace delegation began some fruitless conversations with officials in the Department of State. This delegation was headed by S. Hashimoto, once a member of the Amur Society and more recently connected with Shi-Un-So, the Purple Clouds Society.[56] Mr. Hashimoto was devoted to the cause of peaceful relations between the United States and Japan and he had connections with important members of the Japanese Government.

In lengthy conversations with Mr. Hornbeck, Mr. Hamilton, and Mr. Ballantine[57] he explored every phase of the difficulties between Japan and the United States. To Mr. Hashimoto it appeared obvious that the best way to improve Japanese-American relations was for the Department of State to convince Prince Konoye of the "desirability of pursuing a new course." If America would help to secure for Japan "an open door to trade in the colonial possessions of various countries throughout the world," Prince Konoye might have the courage of his real convictions. This friendly gesture would be of enormous value.

Mr. Hornbeck had no use for friendly gestures towards Japan. Japan should be chided, not conciliated. His answer to Hashimoto's plea for new efforts towards a friendly understanding was a gruff negative:

---

[55] *Far Eastern Military Tribunal*, Exhibit No. 3441, pp. 32979–85.

[56] Other members of the delegation were Mr. Sato and Mr. Toda.

[57] Stanley K. Hornbeck was adviser on Political Relations, Maxwell M. Hamilton was chief of the Far Eastern Division, and Joseph W. Ballantine was a Foreign Service officer.

It is Japan, not the United States, that has been the aggressor: Japan, not the United States, has disregarded law, violated treaties, killed and injured persons, created fear, destroyed property, discriminated, necessitated evacuations, piled up armaments, seized territory and threatened to seize more, *et cetera*. . . . It is Japan, not the United States, that has made threats and talked of war.[58]

l. *Blueprint for Anglo-American Co-operation*

While informal negotiations looking towards an improvement in Japanese-American relations were reaching an impasse, the formal Joint Staff conferences between the American delegation and representatives of Britain, Canada, Australia, and New Zealand finally resulted in the ABC-1 Staff Agreement. During the sessions the British had ardently argued that the defense of Singapore was so essential that the United States should be willing to divide the Pacific fleet for that purpose. This proposal was rejected by the American delegation. In the ABC-1 Staff Agreement, in the event of American intervention in the war, the main task assigned to the American fleet was a defensive one (the protection of our island possessions). But it was also to undertake diversions in the direction of the Marshall and Caroline Islands and to attack Japanese communications and shipping. The plan, therefore, provided for connected but not joint naval operations.

After an extended consideration of all the factors involved, the plan was endorsed by the Secretaries of the Navy and War; the President gave it no explicit approval.[59] It was soon apparent, however, that American military plans were profoundly affected by it.[60] The changes made in them were far more than mere technical details: they indicated a close community of thought between important representatives of America and Britain. They were additional bonds drawing the two countries closer together and all their dangerous implications were not lost upon the President. A blueprint had been drawn for Anglo-American co-operation. It would be implemented as soon as the Chief Executive could find a pretext for doing so.

m. *Japan Seeks Peace, Not War, with the United States*

As Hitler moved towards war with Russia he began to think more and more of Japanese assistance in this projected struggle with the Soviets.

---

[58] Memorandum by Mr. Hornbeck, January 15, 1941. 711.94/2206, MS, Department of State.

[59] Testimony of Admiral Stark. *Pearl Harbor Attack*, pt. 5, p. 2391.

[60] Admiral H. R. Stark to the Commanders in Chief of the U.S. Pacific fleet, the Asiatic fleet, and the Atlantic fleet, April 3, 1941. *Ibid.*, pt. 17, pp. 2462–63.

During a conference with his military leaders on January 8–9, 1941, Stalin was denounced as a "cold-blooded blackmailer" who would, if he found it expedient to do so, repudiate "any written treaty at any time." In any contest with Russia, Germany could receive vital help from Japan.[61] Japanese assistance against Britain was equally important. When General Oshima returned to Germany in 1941 he hurried to Fuschl to see his old friend, Ribbentrop. The Nazi Foreign Minister had a great deal to say. Japan, in its own interest, should enter the war "as soon as possible." This intervention would destroy England's key position in the Far East. It was also "bound to keep America out of the war."[62]

On March 3, Ribbentrop renewed his pressure upon Oshima in favor of an early entry into the war by Japan. He again advised that no action be taken against the United States. Two days later (March 5), Hitler issued a secret order to the German armed forces which summarized the Ribbentrop viewpoint:

It must be the aim of the collaboration based on the Three Power Pact to induce Japan as soon as possible to take active measures in the Far East. Strong British forces will thereby be tied down, and the center of gravity of the interest of the United States of America will be diverted to the Pacific. . . . The common aim of the conduct of the war is to be stressed as forcing England to the ground quickly and thereby keeping the United States out of war.[63]

On March 26, Matsuoka, now serving as the Japanese Foreign Minister, arrived in Berlin. On the following day Ribbentrop plied him with the usual arguments. It would be "very advantageous if Japan would decide as soon as possible to take an active part in the war upon England." Japanese intervention would be "most likely to keep America out of the war." When Matsuoka was taken into the presence of Hitler he heard a repetition of Ribbentrop's remarks, but he refused to commit himself. On March 28, Ribbentrop continued the conversations with Matsuoka and the war in the Pacific was discussed from all angles. Finally the Japanese Foreign Minister bluntly inquired about the attitude of Germany towards America after Britain was defeated. Ribbentrop quickly answered that "Germany did not have the slightest interest in a war against the United States." Matsuoka closed the con-

---

[61] *Fuehrer Conferences on Matters Dealing with the German Navy, 1941,* I, 4.

[62] *Nazi Conspiracy and Aggression,* IV, 1834-PS, 469–75.

[63] *International Nuremberg Trial,* XXXIV, Hitler's Order, March 5, 1941, 075-C, 302–5; also, *Nazi Conspiracy and Aggression,* VI, 906–8.

ference with the expression of a wish that America might be converted to "our way of thinking."[64]

Matsuoka moved from Berlin to Moscow where on April 13 he signed with Molotov a neutrality pact. It is possible that Hitler welcomed this pact as a part of his scheme to lull Russian suspicions with reference to the approaching Nazi offensive,[65] but it is certain that it aroused apprehensions in many minds in Berlin.

n. *Admiral Nomura Strives to Improve Japanese-American Relations*

The appointment of Admiral Nomura as ambassador to the United States was another friendly gesture on the part of the Japanese Government. The new ambassador had been the naval attaché in Washington during the World War where he formed a friendly acquaintance with Franklin D. Roosevelt then serving as the Assistant Secretary of the Navy. He had also been a member of the Japanese delegation to the Washington Disarmament Conference, 1921–1922. His reception at the White House (February 14) was cordial but the President frankly referred to the fact that relations between Japan and the United States were steadily "deteriorating."[66] At the State Department he discovered a studied "policy of coolness toward the Japanese."[67]

On March 8, Hull and Nomura had their first conversation on Japanese-American relations. Subsequently they met more than forty times in vain endeavors to find some firm ground on which to build a new structure of friendship. Hitler viewed these negotiations with frank alarm. As Ribbentrop later remarked:

The Fuehrer . . . saw the attitude of the United States "short of war" and he was worried . . . about groups in Japan who wanted to come to an arrangement with America. He was afraid that if an arrangement would be made between the United States and Japan, this would mean, so to speak, the back free for America and the expected attack or entry into the war by the United States would come quicker.[68]

Ribbentrop, in the spring of 1941, exerted strong pressure upon the German Ambassador in Tokyo with reference to the Hull-Nomura talks. Japan should insist upon the abandonment of unneutral policies

---

[64] Memorandum of a conversation between Ribbentrop and Matsuoka, March 28, 1941. *Nazi-Soviet Relations, 1939–1941*, pp. 298–303.

[65] Elizabeth Wiskemann, *The Rome-Berlin Axis* (New York, 1949), p. 258.

[66] Memorandum by Secretary Hull, February 14, 1941. *Japan: 1931–1941*, II, 387.

[67] Frederick Moore, *With Japan's Leaders* (New York, 1942), p. 171.

[68] Testimony of Ribbentrop at Nürnberg, September 10, 1945. *Nazi Conspiracy and Aggression*, Supplement B., pp. 1200–1201.

on the part of the United States. The ambassador, in turn, emphasized to the Japanese Foreign Office the importance of being firm with the United States. That was the only way to keep America neutral.[69]

o. *Matsuoka Advises a Policy of Delay*

In the spring of 1941 before he left for Berlin, Matsuoka wrote to Thomas Lamont a "passionate plea" for the promotion of better understanding between Japan and the United States. When he reached Rome, en route to Berlin, he received a message from the Japanese Embassy in Washington that "a specially chartered airplane was waiting for him at Lisbon to take him to America for a confidential meeting with the President. This had been arranged by Roy Howard, Matsuoka's intimate friend." But Matsuoka would first have to go to Berlin and Moscow to complete the important items in his program. In Moscow he talked freely with Ambassador Steinhardt in an effort to prepare the way for conversations in Washington.[70] When he arrived in Dairen on April 21 he received a call from Konoye who asked him to fly at once to Tokyo. He returned to the capital to find an American proposal that Nomura had just cabled from Washington.[71]

At this point, according to the story as related by Toshikazu Kase, Matsuoka found that negotiations in Washington were being conducted on the basis of a series of "informal" conversations between two American Catholic priests "and an ex-official of the Japanese Treasury Department whose integrity was rather dubious." For this reason, Matsuoka asked for a halt in the negotiations.[72] As a matter of fact, Mr. Kase is badly confused in this matter of the negotiations. As the deposition of Bishop Walsh clearly shows, Matsuoka himself asked Bishop Walsh and Father Drought to go on a special mission to Washington, and their program was worked out in a series of conferences among Foreign Office officials, General Muto, and Prince Konoye.[73] It is certainly incorrect to state that this mission had "been inaugurated without the knowledge of the foreign minister."[74]

p. *Secretary Hull and Ambassador Nomura Search in Vain for a Formula of Peace*

During the spring and summer of 1941, through more than forty conversations between Hull and Nomura, the search for a formula of peace

---

[69] *Far Eastern Military Tribunal,* pp. 24721–25.

[70] Toshikazu Kase, *Journey to the Missouri* (New Haven, 1950), p. 44. See also, Ambassador Steinhardt to Secretary Hull, Moscow, March 24, 1941. *Japan: 1931–1941,* II, 143–45.

[71] Kase, *op. cit.,* p. 45.

[72] *Ibid.,* p. 45.

[73] *Ante,* pp. 628–29.

[74] Kase, *op. cit.,* p. 45.

was carried on in vain. The story of these negotiations is told in great detail in the memoirs of Prince Konoye[75] and in the documents published by the Department of State.[76]

The Japanese Government was willing to give two important pledges: (1) to use only peaceful measures in the southwest Pacific; (2) to go to the support of Germany only in the event she was the object of aggression. In return for these pledges Japan wished America (1) to restore normal trade relations between the two countries; (2) to assist Japan to secure access to basic raw materials in the southwest Pacific area; (3) to exert pressure upon Chiang Kai-shek so that he would consent to certain peace terms; (4) if Chiang refused to yield to this pressure the American Government would withdraw support from his regime; (5) and finally, to lend friendly diplomatic assistance aimed at the removal of Hongkong and Singapore as doorways "to further political encroachment by the British in the Far East."

Secretary Hull countered with a memorandum emphasizing the following points: (1) respect for the territorial integrity and the sovereignty of each and all nations; (2) support of the principle of noninterference in the internal affairs of other countries; (3) support of the principle of equality, including equality of commercial opportunity; (4) nondisturbance of the status quo in the Pacific except as the status quo may be altered by peaceful means.[77]

The discussion of these bases for a friendly accord was not helped by occasional verbal pyrotechnics on the part of Matsuoka. On May 14 he had a conversation with Ambassador Grew during the course of which he sharply criticized the attitude of the United States towards Germany. American attacks upon German submarines might bring into action Article 3 of the Tripartite Pact of September 27, 1940.[78]

This conversation was the subject of comment by Sumner Welles during a conference with the British Ambassador. Lord Halifax inquired as to the progress of the Hull-Nomura talks. Was there any chance that they would have a successful outcome? Welles thought that the "chances might not be better than one in ten." He then handed to Halifax a copy of a letter Matsuoka wrote to Grew immediately after their conversation on May 14. It was written in such a rambling style that Halifax thought it "bore evidence of lunacy." Welles shared this impression but finally came to the conclusion that it "might be due to the fact that Mr. Matsuoka was understood to be drinking extremely

[75] *Pearl Harbor Attack,* pt. 20, pp. 3985–4029.
[76] *Japan: 1931–1941,* II, 325–795.
[77] *Ibid.,* p. 407.
[78] Ambassador Grew to Secretary Hull, May 14, 1941. *Ibid.,* pp. 145–48.

heavily at this time and the mental state apparent in the writing of this letter might be momentary rather than permanent."[79]

It is obvious that Matsuoka's belligerent state of mind was a result of the pressure from Berlin. Hitler would soon launch his attack upon Russia and he was particularly anxious that America remain neutral. But this Japanese threat failed to restrain Roosevelt. On June 20 an announcement was made in Washington that no more oil would be exported from American eastern ports (including the Gulf of Mexico) except to the British Empire and the Western Hemisphere. Two days later, Hitler's armies crossed the Russian frontier and the German offensive began to roll. When the news reached Tokyo, Matsuoka rushed to the Emperor and vehemently argued that Japan should support Germany by immediately attacking Russia. He readily admitted that his program implied possible war with the United States.[80]

Although Konoye wished to apply a brake to the forward tactics of Matsuoka, the Japanese army leaders were restive and liaison conferences on June 25 and July 2 mapped a new and dangerous program: (1) Japan should not rush into a conflict with the Soviets; (2) the tripartite pact should not be abandoned; (3) Japan should move south into Indochina.[81] Knowledge of this decision reached Washington during the first week in July. The Japanese code had been broken and from July to December 1941 the President and the Secretary of State could read the instructions from the Japanese Foreign Office to Ambassador Nomura.[82] The projected Japanese drive to the South was soon familiar in all its details.

q. *Matsuoka Is Dropped but Roosevelt Grows More Belligerent*

Prince Konoye reluctantly accepted the decisions of the liaison conferences but he was determined not to endure the constant arguments of Matsuoka for a bolder policy towards the United States. During the new liaison conferences of July 10 and 12, Matsuoka led a bitter attack upon the United States and even asked for a termination of the Hull-Nomura conversations. But the Army and Navy representatives in the conference were strongly in favor of the continuation of the talks, so Matsuoka's proposal was quickly defeated. It was evident that the Foreign Minister was quite unpopular with his colleagues who decided to

---

[79] Memorandum of a conversation between Sumner Welles and Viscount Halifax, May 17, 1941. 711.94/2207, MS, Department of State.

[80] "Memoirs of Prince Konoye," *Pearl Harbor Attack*, pt. 20, p. 3993. See also the diary of the Marquis Koichi Kido, in *Far Eastern Military Tribunal*, Exhibit No. 635.

[81] "Memoirs of Prince Konoye," *op. cit.*, pp. 4018-19.

[82] These intercepted decoded messages from Tokyo to Washington are given in detail in *Pearl Harbor Attack*, pt. 12, pp. 1-316.

get rid of him by indirection. On July 16 the whole Cabinet resigned. Konoye was then asked to form a new cabinet, and when it was organized, Admiral Toyoda was given the post of Foreign Minister.

This significant cabinet change made little impression upon the President and several of his advisers who had been pushing for sanctions against Japan. One of the most active of these was Secretary of War Henry L. Stimson. As early as December 16, 1940, he confided to his diary that eventually America would be drawn into the war.[83] During the spring and summer of 1941 he was constantly pressing the President to take stronger measures against the Germans.[84]

Some of the instructions sent by Tokyo to Nomura strengthened the Stimson counsel. These intercepted messages were placed before the President and influenced his decisions. On July 14 a particularly important message was decoded. It clearly outlined Japanese objectives: "The immediate object of our occupation of French Indochina will be to achieve our purposes there. Secondly, its purpose is, when the international situation is suitable, to launch therefrom a rapid attack. . . . In the main, through the activities of our air arm . . . we will once and for all crush Anglo-American military power and their ability to assist in any schemes against us."[85] A week later the Foreign Office sent an ominous instruction to Ambassador Nomura:

Should the U.S. . . . take steps at this time which would unduly excite Japan (such as . . . the freezing of assets), an exceedingly critical situation may be created. Please advise the United States of this fact, and attempt to bring about an improvement in the situation.[86]

The very step that the Japanese Foreign Office greatly feared was then being seriously discussed by American cabinet officials. The Navy Department counseled caution, the Treasury Department was anxious for prompt action against Japan, while the Department of State vacillated from day to day. On July 24 the President had a conference with Ambassador Nomura and talked with brutal frankness. He said that he had not shut off oil supplies from Japan because such action would have furnished a pretext for "moving down upon the Netherlands East Indies." But in view of the oil shortage in the eastern part of the United States there were many persons who were asking why further oil shipments to Japan were permitted while she was following a policy

[83] Henry L. Stimson and McGeorge Bundy, *On Active Service in War and Peace* (New York, 1948), p. 366.

[84] *Ibid.*, pp. 367–76.

[85] Intercepted Japanese message from Canton to Tokyo, July 14, 1941. *Pearl Harbor Attack*, pt. 12, pp. 2–3.

[86] Japanese Foreign Office to Ambassador Nomura, July 23, 1941. *Ibid.*, pp. 4–5.

of aggression. In the event that Japan did move upon the Netherlands East Indies she could be certain that Britain would rush to the assistance of the Dutch, and this, in turn, might involve the United States in hostilities. The President then stated that he had a proposal to make to the Ambassador:

If the Japanese Government would refrain from occupying Indochina with its military and naval forces, or, had such steps actually been commenced, if the Japanese Government would withdraw such forces, the President could assure the Japanese Government that he would do everything within his power to obtain from the Governments of China, Great Britain, the Netherlands, and of course the United States itself a binding and solemn declaration . . . to regard Indochina as a neutralized country.[87]

On the following day (July 25) Colonel Iwakuro had a long talk with Mr. Ballantine and expressed the hope that an understanding with the United States could be effected. As far as Japan was concerned this could be achieved in a satisfactory manner if the American Government "did not take measures in the nature of embargoes or freezing of assets against Japan."[88] The President was not impressed with this gesture of good will. On the following day (July 26) an order was issued freezing Japanese funds in the United States. When Ambassador Nomura called at the Department of State to inquire as to the administration of this order, he was received in a definitely cold manner by Sumner Welles. He expressed the hope that the measure would not mean any "further deterioration in the relations of our two countries," but Welles parried the indirect query by remarking upon the "extraordinary patience which the United States had demonstrated in its relations with Japan during recent years." Nomura quietly stated that he believed the best thing to do under the circumstances was to adopt some "compromise solution which would prove acceptable to both sides." Welles crisply replied that he did not see "that there was the slightest ground for any compromise solution."[89] It was evident that Welles was thinking of war.

This feeling of a deadlock was deepened during a conversation between Welles and Mr. Wakasugi, the Japanese Minister to the United States. Wakasugi was about to return to Tokyo to report to his Govern-

[87] Memorandum of a conversation between President Roosevelt and the Japanese Ambassador, July 24, 1941. *Japan: 1931–1941,* II, 527–30.

[88] Memorandum of a conversation between Colonel Iwakuro and Mr. Ballantine, July 25, 1941. *Ibid.,* pp. 530–32.

[89] Memorandum of a conversation between Sumner Welles and Ambassador Nomura, July 28, 1941. *Ibid.,* pp. 537–39. For Nomura's story of the negotiations with the United States see his article "Stepping-Stones to War," *Proceedings* of the United States Naval Institute, LXXVII, No. 9 (September 1951), 927–30.

ment on the actual state of Japanese-American relations. He wanted a
frank statement from Mr. Welles in this regard. The Acting Secretary
of State was glad to respond in his usual cold, detached manner. Japan
should always keep in mind the basic principles of American foreign
policy:

The maintenance of peace in the Pacific; the renunciation by all of the powers interested in the Pacific of force and of conquest as their national policy;
the recognition of the rights of independent and autonomous peoples of the
Pacific to independence and integrity; and equal opportunity and fair treatment for all. . . . If Japan continued on an aggressive policy of force and
undertook moves of expansion . . . I thought it necessary at this stage to say
that in my judgment such a situation as that would inevitably be regarded as
intolerable by the United States and . . . would inevitably result in armed
hostilities in the Pacific.[90]

This threat of war was very discouraging to Wakasugi who clearly
realized that Japanese-American relations had reached an impasse that
had very dangerous implications. On the following day (August 5) he
received an instruction from Tokyo that gave ample evidence of the
deep concern the Foreign Office felt with regard to the situation: "We
are convinced that we have reached the most important, and at the same
time the most critical, moment of Japanese-U.S. relations."[91] In order
to improve these strained relations the Japanese Government was willing to pledge that it would "not further station its troops in the Southwestern Pacific areas except French Indo-China and that the Japanese
troops now stationed in French Indo-China will be withdrawn forthwith on the settlement of the China Incident." Japan would gladly
guarantee the neutrality of the Philippine Islands if the United States,
in turn, would suspend its military measures in the southwestern Pacific
areas, would help Japan to secure access to the important natural resources of these areas, and would also restore normal trade relations
between Japan and the United States. In answer to an oral statement by
the Japanese Ambassador, Hull replied that he felt "very discouraged
indeed" about future relations between the two countries.[92]

Similar discouragement in Tokyo led the Konoye Ministry to send
instructions to Nomura to sound out Secretary Hull about a joint meeting between the Prime Minister and President Roosevelt.[93] When the
Japanese Ambassador handed to Hull this proposal for a conference

[90] Memorandum of a conversation between Sumner Welles and Mr. Wakasugi,
August 4, 1941. *Ibid.*, pp. 540–46.

[91] Japanese Foreign Office to Ambassador Nomura, August 5, 1941. *Pearl Harbor
Attack,* pt. 12, pp. 10–11.

[92] Memorandum of a conversation between Secretary Hull and Ambassador Nomura. *Japan: 1931–1941,* II, 546–50.

[93] Japanese Foreign Office to Ambassador Nomura, August 7, 1941. *Pearl Harbor
Attack,* pt. 12, pp. 12–13.

between Prince Konoye and President Roosevelt, the reply came in the form of a written memorandum which rejected the Japanese proposals of August 6 as "lacking in responsiveness."[94] It was evident that Hull thought no purpose would be served by a Konoye-Roosevelt meeting. This fact was clear to Nomura who cabled the Foreign Office that he greatly feared "that even the offer of the Prime Minister to personally come here would not move the United States to any perceptible degree." He could only report that he saw "dark clouds over the world."[95]

r. *The Atlantic Conference Pushes America Closer to a Break with Japan*

For Japan there were very dark clouds along the Newfoundland horizon. On the evening of August 9, in the Newfoundland harbor of Argentia, Roosevelt and Churchill had their first conference. The British were particularly concerned about the danger of a Japanese thrust into the southwest Pacific area, and Sir Alexander Cadogan had drafted parallel Anglo-American declarations designed to halt this possible advance. America was to state very frankly that "any further encroachment by Japan in the Southwestern Pacific" would compel the United States to take measures that might lead to war. In order to implement this declaration the President was to "seek authority from Congress" to employ American armed forces as he thought best. The President at once rejected any thought of consulting with Congress. On his own initiative and responsibility he would let the Japanese Government know that if her armed forces moved southward, "various steps would have to be taken by the United States notwithstanding the President's realization that the taking of such further measures might result in war between the United States and Japan." But Sumner Welles thought that the United States should play the role of policeman in a much wider area than the southwest Pacific. America should be ready to repel any Japanese thrust whether it was directed "against China, against the Soviet Union or against the British Dominions or British colonies, or the colonies of the Netherlands in the Southern Pacific area." Churchill and Roosevelt were in hearty agreement with this wider formula,[96] but the President was too cautious to broadcast it to the American public. It had better remain a secret understanding.

Churchill had failed to secure a parallel declaration that pointed

[94] Memorandum of a conversation between Secretary Hull and Ambassador Nomura, August 8, 1941. *Japan: 1931–1941*, II, 550–53.

[95] Ambassador Nomura to the Japanese Foreign Office, August 9, 1941. *Pearl Harbor Attack*, pt. 12, p. 15.

[96] Memoranda of conversations at Argentia among President Roosevelt, Prime Minister Churchill, Sir Alexander Cadogan, Harry Hopkins, and Sumner Welles. *Ibid.*, pt. 4, pp. 1784–92.

straight to war, but the Roosevelt pledges of support relieved most of his fears. This fact was revealed in his speech to Parliament on January 27, 1942: "The probability, since the Atlantic Conference . . . that the United States, even if not herself attacked, would come into a war in the Far East, and thus make final victory sure, seemed to allay some of these anxieties. . . . As time went on, one had greater assurance that if Japan ran amok in the Pacific, we should not fight alone."[97]

s. *Roosevelt Refuses to Meet Prince Konoye*

In a statement he handed to the Japanese Ambassador on August 17, Roosevelt carried out his pledge to Churchill. It was phrased in language that was not unduly provocative, but its meaning was very clear:

If the Japanese Government takes any further steps in pursuance of a policy or program of military domination by force or threat of force of neighboring countries, the Government of the United States will be compelled to take immediately any and all steps which it may deem necessary toward safeguarding the legitimate rights and interests of the United States and American nationals and toward insuring the safety and security of the United States.

With reference to a meeting between Prince Konoye and President Roosevelt, the Japanese Ambassador was informed that if his Government was ready "to suspend its expansionist activities" and embark upon a "peaceful program for the Pacific," the government of the United States "would be glad to endeavor to arrange a suitable time and place to exchange views."[98]

Before this Roosevelt statement could reach Tokyo, Foreign Minister Toyoda had a conference with Ambassador Grew and once more strongly pushed the idea of a meeting at Honolulu between Konoye and Roosevelt. He ardently hoped that at such a meeting it would be possible "to reach a just and equitable agreement."[99] Grew was so deeply impressed with the sincerity of Toyoda's plea that he immediately sent a dispatch to Secretary Hull and urged, "with all the force at his command, for the sake of avoiding the obviously growing possibility of an utterly futile war between Japan and the United States, that this Japanese proposal not be turned aside without very prayerful consideration. . . . The opportunity is here presented . . . for an act of the highest statesmanship . . . with the possible overcoming thereby of apparently insurmountable obstacles to peace hereafter in the Pacific."[100]

On August 28, Ambassador Nomura delivered to President Roose-

[97] Winston S. Churchill, *The End of the Beginning* (Boston, 1943), p. 33.
[98] *Japan: 1931–1941*, II, 556–59.
[99] Memorandum by Ambassador Grew, August 18, 1941. *Ibid.*, pp. 560–64.
[100] Ambassador Grew to Secretary Hull, Tokyo, August 18, 1941. *Ibid.*, p. 565.

velt a personal message from Konoye pleading for a meeting which could "explore the possibility of saving the situation."[101] In his remarks to Nomura with reference to a possible meeting with Konoye, the President appeared to think that it would be difficult for him to go as far as Hawaii. Possibly Juneau, Alaska, would be more suitable.[102]

As the President vacillated as to what course to pursue about this proposed meeting with Konoye, an Imperial conference was held on September 6. It was finally decided that Japanese preparations for war would have to be continued so "that they be completed approximately toward the end of October." At the same time, the Foreign Office should "endeavor by every possible diplomatic means to have our demands agreed to by America and England." If these negotiations did not lead to favorable results by the early part of October, then the government should "get ready for war against America."[103]

The position of Japan was very clear. It was insisting upon American recognition of Japan's dominance in the Far East. In the Root-Takahira Agreement of November 30, 1908, we had given Japan a green light to move ahead in Manchuria.[104] Japan had taken advantage of President Theodore Roosevelt's friendly suggestions and had strongly intrenched herself in large areas in North China. In the face of rapidly expanding Russian power in the Far East, this action had been regarded as a national imperative. In the Far East the future belonged either to Japan or Russia, not to a China that had been exhausted by an endless cycle of war, revolution, and war. The policy of President Franklin D. Roosevelt and Secretary Hull in giving strong support to a gravely weakened China was highly unrealistic, and the later collapse of the American position in China stems straight back to the decisions taken in September and October 1941.

During the eventful weeks of September, President Roosevelt seemed unable to make up his mind concerning a meeting with Konoye. In order to dispel this sense of uncertainty, the Division of Far Eastern Affairs (Mr. Ballantine) prepared a long memorandum which was highly critical of Japan. In conclusion, Mr. Ballantine remarked: "The holding of the meeting between the President and the Japanese Prime Minister on the basis of the present status of the discussions between this country and Japan would result in more of disadvantage than of advantage as regards this country's interests and policies."[105] From

---

[101] Prince Konoye to President Roosevelt, August 27, 1941. *Ibid.*, pp. 572–73.

[102] Memorandum by Secretary Hull of a conference between the President and Ambassador Nomura, August 28, 1941. *Ibid.*, pp. 571–72.

[103] "Memoirs of Prince Konoye," *Pearl Harbor Attack,* pt. 20, pp. 4004–5.

[104] See *ante*, pp. 4–5.

[105] Memorandum by the Division of Far Eastern Affairs, September 23, 1941. 711.94/2344, *Strictly Confidential,* MS, Department of State.

Tokyo, Ambassador Grew spoke from an entirely different angle. He would not stand inflexibly upon certain principles and demand that Japan agree to accept every one of them. Political differences can be expressed in subtle shades that need not affront nations involved in serious controversy; one does not have to insist upon the conventional pattern of black and white. If America would show some slight spirit of compromise, this concession might evoke concessions on the part of Japan and some path to understanding might be found. There was no real point in insisting that Konoye agree in advance to a long agenda which would awaken instant opposition in Japan. During the sessions of a conference between Konoye and Roosevelt it was highly possible that a spirit of reciprocity might arise which would turn thoughts from war to peace. The situation required statesmanship of the highest order. There seemed no reason to doubt that it could be found in Washington.[106]

Unfortunately, at this time of national crisis, President Roosevelt did not measure up to the demands of the hour. Without the courage to make a decision in the matter of meeting Konoye, he pushed the responsibility upon the shoulders of Secretary Hull. Hull did not hesitate. He was always "wound-up" for such occasions. On October 2 he handed to Ambassador Nomura a statement that contained all the Hull clichés about high moral principles being the directing force in international relations. Dubious American practices in the Caribbean were not mentioned. After a long rehearsal of the reasons why the Hull-Nomura conversations had been a flat failure, he sonorously remarked that before there could be a meeting between the President and Prince Konoye, there would first have to be an agreement upon basic principles of policy.[107] He knew that such an agreement was not possible. He had cleared the decks of the American ship of state for war at any time. It would not be long in coming.

t. *General Marshall and Admiral Stark Oppose an Ultimatum to Japan*

The Hull note of October 2 did not kill all Japanese hopes for an adjustment of difficulties with the United States. Konoye retained a faint belief that through indirect channels he still might find a means of convincing President Roosevelt of his sincerity. Through August and September 1941 he had worked through Bishop Walsh, of the Mary-

106 Ambassador Grew to Secretary Hull, September 29, 1941. *Japan: 1931–1941*, II, 645–50.

107 Oral statement handed by Secretary Hull to Ambassador Nomura, October 2, 1941. *Ibid.*, pp. 656–61.

knoll mission, who sent many messages to Father Drought in New York. These messages, which revealed a strong desire for accommodation, were "concealed under missionary phraseology." Father Drought conveyed the messages to Washington, but to no avail. Finally, on October 14, Walsh was commissioned by Konoye to hurry to Washington and tell the President that "the pressure of events on the Japanese Government was such that it would not be able to negotiate much longer."[108] The Konoye Ministry fell long before Walsh reached Washington.

In the meantime, Foreign Minister Toyoda had turned to the British Ambassador in Tokyo and requested his help with regard to the Konoye-Roosevelt meeting. Craigie at once cabled to London his view of the situation. It was decidedly critical of the Hull policy:

By pursuing a policy of stalling, the United States is arguing about every word and every phrase on the grounds that it is an essential preliminary to any kind of an agreement. It seems apparent that the United States does not comprehend the fact that by the nature of the Japanese and also on account of the domestic conditions in Japan, no delays can be countenanced. It would be very regrettable indeed if the best opportunity for the settlement of the Far Eastern problems since I assumed my post here, were to be lost in such a manner. . . . Both the U.S. Ambassador in Japan and I are firmly of the opinion that it would be a foolish policy if this superb opportunity is permitted to slip by by assuming an unduly suspicious attitude.[109]

On October 7, in a final bid for an understanding with the United States, Toyoda told Grew that it seemed apparent that the United States "wished the Japanese Government to revert at once and unqualifiedly to the *status quo* which had prevailed four years ago. . . . The Japanese Government was willing and prepared to return to the situation prevailing four years ago but it was essential that the Government of the United States should understand that to undo virtually at a moment's notice the work of the past four years is an undertaking of tremendous scope." It would take time on the part of the Japanese Government and understanding on the part of the American.[110]

But these gestures of conciliation failed to evoke the hoped-for response from Washington, so on October 16 the Konoye Cabinet resigned.[111] In the new Cabinet, General Hideki Tojo assumed the post of Prime Minister, with Shigenori Togo as the new Minister of Foreign

108 Affidavit of Bishop Walsh, *Far Eastern Military Tribunal*, Exhibit No. 3441, pp. 32985–90.

109 *Pearl Harbor Attack*, pt. 12, p. 51.

110 Joseph C. Grew, *Ten Years in Japan*, pp. 451–52.

111 "Memoirs of Prince Konoye," *Pearl Harbor Attack*, pt. 20, pp. 4007–11. See also, *Far Eastern Military Tribunal*, Exhibit No. 2250.

Affairs. The story of the attempts of the Tojo Cabinet to find some formula of accommodation with the United States is a twice-told tale that does not have to be repeated here.[112] The hopelessness of the situation was apparent to Ambassador Grew who warned Secretary Hull that "action by Japan which might render unavoidable an armed conflict with the United States may come with dangerous and dramatic suddenness."[113]

The Army feared this sudden Japanese attack upon an American outpost, and they were deeply disturbed during a meeting of the Army-Navy Joint Board when Mr. Hornbeck, representing the Department of State, advocated a firm stand against Japan.[114] The armed forces were not ready for war with Japan, and they resented the pressure of Chiang Kai-shek for assistance that might lead to American intervention. On November 2 the Generalissimo wrote to Roosevelt that a new Japanese offensive against Yunnan might shake the morale of the Chinese Army and the Chinese people "to its foundation." For the "first time in this long war a real collapse of resistance would be possible" if the Japanese drive succeeded in taking Kunming.[115] General Marshall and Admiral Stark were extremely anxious that these appeals from Chiang should not push the President to some rash act. On November 5, after a review of the situation in the Far East, they strongly recommended that "no ultimatum be delivered to Japan."[116]

This blunt recommendation temporarily slowed the President's progress down the road to war. On the following day (November 6) he had a talk with Secretary Stimson with reference to the pressing need for time to complete American military preparations. It might be well for the Department of State to arrange for a truce "in which there would be no movement or armament for six months." Stimson opposed such a truce. It was still "very important to keep the Chinese in the war, and I believed that they would feel that such a truce was a desertion of them, and that this would have a very serious effect on Chinese morale." On November 7 the President polled the Cabinet on the question of whether he would receive popular support "if it became necessary to strike at Japan in case she should attack England in Malaya or the Dutch in the East Indies. The Cabinet was unanimous in the feeling that the

---

112 Herbert Feis, *The Road to Pearl Harbor* (Princeton, 1950), pp. 282–325; Charles A. Beard, *President Roosevelt and the Coming of the War 1941* (New Haven, 1948), pp. 496–516; Frederic R. Sanborn, *Design for War* (New York, 1951), pp. 377–425.
113 Ambassador Grew to Secretary Hull, November 3, 1941. *Japan: 1931–1941*, II, 704.
114 *Pearl Harbor Attack*, pt. 14, pp. 1062–65; pt. 5, pp. 2085–86.
115 Chiang Kai-shek to President Roosevelt, November 2, 1941. *Ibid.*, pt. 15, pp. 1476–78.
116 *Ibid.*, pt. 14, pp. 1061–62; pt. 16, pp. 2222–23.

country would support such a move."[117] This unanimity was not as genuine as Secretary Stimson's diary would indicate. Hull thought that there was definite need for numerous speeches throughout the country which would prepare the people for the possibility of war.[118] The tragedy of the situation was that America was really at war without any clear perception of that fact by the popular mind. As Admiral Stark wrote to Admiral Hart on November 7: "The Navy is already in the war of the Atlantic, but the country doesn't seem to realize it. Apathy, to the point of opposition is evident in a considerable section of the press. . . . Whether the country knows it or not, *we are* at war."[119]

u. *Japan Is Maneuvered into Firing the First Shot at Pearl Harbor*

In the second week in November 1941 tension began to mount in Tokyo. On November 10 the Japanese Foreign Minister expressed to Grew the opinion that the "preliminary and exploratory conversations" in Washington had proceeded long enough. It was time for both countries to "enter into formal and official negotiations." The Japanese Government had "repeatedly made proposals calculated to approach the American point of view, but the American Government . . . had taken no step toward meeting the Japanese position."[120] On this same day (November 10), Ambassador Nomura presented to President Roosevelt a further explanation of his Government's proposals. In the meantime the Japanese Foreign Office instructed Nomura that November 25 was the deadline. All negotiations would have to be concluded by that date.[121] This deadline was repeated from Tokyo on November 11.[122] Under pressure from the Foreign Office, Nomura was extremely anxious to secure an early answer to the Japanese proposals of November 7 and 10. While he was awaiting this answer, he noted the military preparations that were being rushed by the Roosevelt Administration: "They are contriving by every possible means to prepare for actual warfare."[123] Tokyo replied to this cablegram by insisting that the deadline of November 25 was "an absolutely immovable one."[124]

[117] Henry L. Stimson's *Diary*, November 6–7, *Pearl Harbor Attack*, pt. 11, p. 5420.
[118] Secretary Hull to Justice Roberts, December 30, 1941. *Ibid.*, pt. 20, p. 4112.
[119] Admiral Stark to Admiral Hart, November 7, 1941. *Ibid.*, pt. 5, p. 2121.
[120] Memorandum by Ambassador Grew, November 10, 1941. *Japan: 1931–1941,* II, 710–14.
[121] Japanese Foreign Office to Ambassador Nomura, November 5, 1941. *Pearl Harbor Attack,* pt. 12, p. 100.
[122] Japanese Foreign Office to Ambassador Nomura, November 11, 1941. *Ibid.,* pp. 116–17.
[123] Ambassador Nomura to Japanese Foreign Office, November 14, 1941. *Ibid.,* pt. 12, p. 127.
[124] Japanese Foreign Office to Ambassador Nomura, November 15, 1941. *Ibid.,* p. 130.

Secretary Hull knew of this deadline through intercepted Japanese instructions to Nomura, so on November 15 he handed to Nomura a long oral statement setting forth the bases of an agreement. He knew they would not be acceptable to Japan. Complete control over "its economic, financial and monetary affairs" should be restored to China, and Japan should abandon any thought of preserving in China, or anywhere else in the Pacific area, a "preferential position."[125]

The abrupt tone of this note was a challenge that could easily lead to a break in diplomatic relations. Japan had long feared that such a break was inevitable, but in a final attempt to stave off such an emergency it had been decided to send to Washington another diplomat who would assist Nomura in the delicate negotiations that were hanging by a very slender thread. The new appointee, Saburo Kurusu, had served as consul in Chicago and New York and had recently been in Berlin as ambassador. His happy marriage to an American girl gave him a personal interest in maintaining friendly relations between Japan and the United States.[126]

On November 17, Nomura and Kurusu had a talk with President Roosevelt, and then long, inconclusive conversations with Hull were carried on. To Kurusu it seemed that the President was "very much in earnest in regard to effecting an understanding between Japan and the United States." With Hull, little progress was made. This was particularly true with reference to a solution of the difficulties between China and Japan. Roosevelt seemed to have taken a liking to his old naval acquaintance, Nomura, and was not ready to push things. One day Lowell Mellett and Max Lowenthal paid a visit to the office of Senator Burton K. Wheeler to convey the information that "the President does not want to push America into the war." The Senator took this statement with a large grain of salt, but he remembered that at times Secretary Hull had been more belligerent than the President. This fact had been particularly evident during the sessions of the Democratic National Convention in 1940. When Wheeler was putting up a strong fight to write an antiwar plank in such specific terms that the President could not disregard it, "Jimmy" Byrnes confided to him that Hull was strongly against such a plank. It would prevent him from exerting maximum pressure upon Japan.[127]

In November 1941 the Hull policy of pressure upon Japan was being implemented at full strength. On November 20, Kurusu discussed with Hull the matter of bringing to a close the hostilities between China and

---

[125] Oral statement handed by Secretary Hull to Ambassador Nomura, November 15, 1941. *Japan: 1931–1941*, II, 734–37.

[126] "The Career of Saburo Kurusu," November 19, 1941. Co-ordination of information, Far Eastern Section, 711.94/2529, MS, Department of State.

[127] Conversation between the author and Senator Burton K. Wheeler.

Japan. The Japanese Foreign Office believed this could be arranged if the United States would stop sending supplies to China. After stressing this point, Nomura then remarked: "If the tension between Japan and the United States can be relaxed, be it ever so little, particularly in the southwestern Pacific, and quickly clear the atmosphere, then I think we could go on and settle everything else." Kurusu pushed the idea of a *modus vivendi*,[128] and President Roosevelt responded by outlining one that might be accepted. The fourth item in this Presidential proposal read as follows: "U.S. to *introduce* Japs to Chinese to talk things over but U.S. to take no part in their conversations. Later on Pacific agreements."[129]

Japan met this show of conciliation with a concession of her own. The deadline in the negotiations was now extended from November 25 to November 29. But this was the final concession: "This time we mean it, that the deadline absolutely cannot be changed. After that things are automatically going to happen."[130]

On the same day that this deadline was extended (November 22), Nomura and Kurusu once more met Hull in conference. It was soon apparent from his tone that there was small chance that Japanese conditions for a truce would be accepted: (1) a revocation of the American order of July 26 freezing Japanese credits in the United States and thereby stopping all shipments of oil from American ports; (2) American consent to a program aimed at increasing the export of oil and other commodities from the Netherlands East Indies to Japan; (3) American mediation between China and Japan so as to initiate negotiations between the two powers and the cessation of American assistance to Chiang Kai-shek. American consent to these conditions was out of the question even if Japan made far-reaching concessions in return.

During the conference on November 22, Hull acidly complained of the "threatening tone" of the Japanese press and then asked why some Japanese statesman did not start "preaching peace?" When Nomura remarked that he "did not have the slightest doubt that Japan desired peace," Hull scoffed at this statement and lamented that it was a pity that Japan "could not do just a few small things to help tide over the situation." He was particularly critical of the Japanese attitude towards Chiang Kai-shek.[131]

Two days later (November 24), Hull had a conference with the

---

[128] Memorandum of a conversation among Secretary Hull, Ambassador Nomura, and Mr. Kurusu, November 20, 1941. *Japan: 1931–1941*, II, 753–56; Sanborn, *op. cit.*, pp. 463–64.

[129] *Pearl Harbor Attack*, pt. 14, pp. 1108–9.

[130] Japanese Foreign Office to Nomura and Kurusu, November 22, 1941. *Ibid.*, pt. 12, p. 165.

[131] Memorandum of a conference among Secretary Hull, Ambassador Nomura, and Mr. Kurusu, November 22, 1941. *Japan: 1931–1941*, II, 757–62.

diplomatic representatives of Australia, Britain, China, and the Netherlands. He quickly discovered that the Chinese Ambassador, Dr. Hu Shih, was not enthusiastic about a three months' truce with Japan.[132] But Hull went ahead and drafted a *modus vivendi* which President Roosevelt regarded as a "fair proposition" but he was "not very hopeful" and thought there might be "real trouble very soon."[133]

On the following morning (November 25), Hull showed to Secretaries Knox and Stimson this draft that provided for a three months' truce with Japan. But its terms were so drastic that Stimson believed that Japan would not accept it. That afternoon Secretaries Hull, Knox, and Stimson, along with General Marshall and Admiral Stark, went to the White House for a long conference with the President. From intercepted Japanese cablegrams to Nomura, the President knew that the Japanese deadline for an end to the current negotiations was on November 29. He expressed a fear that Japanese armed forces might make an attack "as soon as next Monday." The main question was "how we should maneuver them into the position of firing the first shot without allowing too much danger to ourselves."[134]

When Hull returned to the Department of State he had a long talk with the Chinese Ambassador who handed him a telegram from Chungking: "After reading your [Hu Shih's] telegram the Generalissimo showed rather strong reaction. He got the impression that the United States Government has put aside the Chinese question in its conversations with Japan instead of seeking a solution and is still inclined to appease Japan at the expense of China." This impudent telegram placed Hull on the defensive. He frankly admitted that the conversations he had been carrying on with the Japanese envoys was merely a delaying action: "The official heads of our Army and Navy for some weeks have been most earnestly urging that we not get into war with Japan until they have an opportunity to increase further their plans and methods and means of defense in the Pacific area."[135]

On the afternoon of November 25 there were more cablegrams from China. Mr. T. V. Soong handed Secretary Stimson another cablegram from Chiang Kai-shek in which the Generalissimo urged the United States to be "uncompromising" in its attitude towards Japan.[136] This pressure was increased by a communication from Owen Lattimore, the American adviser of Chiang Kai-shek, to Lauchlin Currie, administrative assistant to President Roosevelt: Any *"modus vivendi"* arrived at

[132] *Pearl Harbor Attack*, pt. 14, pp. 1138–41.
[133] *Ibid.*, pp. 1142.
[134] Henry L. Stimson's *Diary*, November 25, 1941. *Ibid.*, pt. 11, p. 5433.
[135] Memorandum of a conversation between Secretary Hull and the Chinese Ambassador, Dr. Hu Shih, November 25, 1941. 711.94/2479, MS, Department of State.
[136] *Pearl Harbor Attack*, pt. 14, pp. 1161.

with Japan "would be disastrous to Chinese belief in America."[137] For a week Currie was "terribly anxious" because he feared that "Hull was in danger of selling China and America and Britain down the river."[138] In Chungking, Madame Chiang Kai-shek became "unrestrainedly critical" of the American Government for its failure to "plunge into the war" and thus aid China.[139]

On the morning of November 26, Hull saw a telegram from Churchill to the President: "There is only one point that disquiets us. What about Chiang Kai-shek? Is he not having a very thin diet?"[140] It was not long before Hull was nearly hysterical. During a telephone conversation with Secretary Stimson he remarked that he had just about made up his mind about the *modus vivendi*—he "would kick the whole thing over."[141] A few moments later Stimson phoned to the President and informed him that a Japanese expeditionary force was moving south from Shanghai. The President promptly "blew up" and exclaimed that this fact "changed the whole situation because it was an evidence of bad faith on the part of the Japanese."[142] But the leading officers of the American armed forces still counseled caution. On this same morning (November 26) there was a meeting of the Army-Navy Joint Board and Admiral Ingersoll presented a series of arguments "why we should not precipitate a war."[143]

But Hull was tired of carrying on negotiations with Japan. He was not a master of diplomatic double talk and he squirmed under the direct questions of the Japanese envoys. As far back as January 23, 1941, he had listened without any real interest to the proposals that Bishop Walsh and Father Drought had brought from Matsuoka: "(1) an agreement to nullify their [Japanese] participation in the Axis Pact; (2) a guarantee to recall all military forces from China and to restore to China its geographical and political integrity."[144] If he had rejected these unusually conciliatory proposals why should he be deeply concerned about recent ones that did not go nearly so far!

On the afternoon of November 26 he abandoned all thought of a truce with Japan and put into final shape a ten-point proposal. Both he and the President knew this program would be rejected by Japan.

[137] *Ibid.*, p. 1160; also the *Hearings* Before the Sub-Committee to Investigate the Administration of the Internal Security Act and Other Internal Security Laws of the Committee on the Judiciary, United States Senate, 82 Congress, 1 sess., pt. 1, pp. 153–58.

[138] *Ibid.*, p. 158.

[139] Ambassador Gauss to Secretary Hull, Chungking, December 3, 1941. 711.94/2600, MS, Department of State.

[140] *Pearl Harbor Attack*, pt. 14, p. 1300.

[141] Henry L. Stimson's *Diary*, November 26, 1941. *Ibid.*, pt. 11, p. 5434.

[142] *Ibid.*

[143] *Ibid.*, pt. 9, p. 4259.

[144] See *ante*, pp. 628–29.

There was no thought of compromise or conciliation: "The Government of Japan will withdraw all military, naval, air and police forces from China and from Indochina." When Kurusu read the ten-point proposal of Secretary Hull he immediately inquired if this was the American answer to the Japanese request for a *modus vivendi* or truce. Was not the American Government interested in a truce? Hull merely replied that "we have explored that" but had arrived at no real decision. Kurusu could only reply that the Secretary's attitude "could be interpreted as tantamount to meaning the end."[145] It was obvious that the next step was war.

On the morning of December 4, the Navy radio receiving station at Cheltenham, Maryland, intercepted a Japanese overseas news broadcast from Station JAP in Tokyo, in which there was inserted a false weather report, "east wind rain." On November 19 the Japanese Government had instructed its ambassador in Washington that such a weather forecast would indicate imminence of war with the United States.[146] After intercepting this Japanese instruction the radio receiving stations of the American armed forces were on the alert for the "east wind rain" message. As soon as it was translated, Lieutenant Commander Kramer handed it to Commander Safford with the exclamation: "This is *it*." Safford got in touch immediately with Rear Admiral Noyes who telephoned the substance of the intercepted message "to the naval aide to the President."[147]

According to the testimony of Captain Safford [in 1941 a Commander], the

"winds" message and the change of the [Japanese] naval operations code came in the middle of the week: two days to Saturday and three days to Sunday. It was unthinkable that the Japanese would surrender their hopes of surprise by delaying until the week-end of December 13–14. This was not crystal-gazing or "intuition"—it was just the plain, common sense acceptance of a self-evident proposition. Col. Sadtler saw it, and so did Capt. Joseph R. Redman, U.S.N., according to Col. Sadtler's testimony in 1944. ... The Japanese were going to start the war on Saturday, December 6, 1941, or Sunday, December 7, 1941.[148]

For the next three days Commander Safford and Lieutenant Commander Kramer tried in vain to get some action out of their superior officers with regard to the implications of the "east wind rain" message.

145 Oral statement handed by Secretary Hull to Ambassador Nomura and Mr. Kurusu, November 26, 1941. *Japan: 1931–1941*, II, 766–70.

146 Japanese Foreign Office to Ambassador Nomura, Tokyo, November 19, 1941. *Pearl Harbor Attack*, pt. 12, p. 154.

147 George Morgenstern, *Pearl Harbor* (New York, 1947), p. 206.

148 *Ibid.*, p. 211. The testimony of Captain Safford is given in detail in *Pearl Harbor Attack*, pt. 8, pp. 3555–3814.

When they induced Captain McCollum to exert some pressure upon Admiral Stark he was given a sharp rebuke which so infuriated him that he later poured the whole story into the receptive ears of Admiral Kimmel. This disclosure led Kimmel to press for the Pearl Harbor investigations.

The unaccountable failure of high naval officers to convey a warning to Honolulu about the imminence of war was given additional highlights on the evening of December 6 when the Japanese reply to the American note of November 26 was sent secretly to Ambassador Nomura. It was intercepted by Navy receiving stations and decoded. When the President read this message to Nomura he at once exclaimed: "This means war!" He tried to get in touch with Admiral Stark but was informed that the chief of naval operations was at the National Theatre enjoying the delightful strains of *The Student Prince*.[149] The next day the Admiral's ears would be assailed by the crashing echoes of the attack upon Pearl Harbor.

It would ordinarily be assumed that the President, after reading this intercepted Japanese message, would hurriedly call a conference of the more important Army and Navy officers to concert plans to meet the anticipated attack. The testimony of General Marshall and Admiral Stark would indicate that the Chief Executive took the ominous news so calmly that he made no effort to consult with them.[150] Did he deliberately seek the Pearl Harbor attack in order to get America into the war? What is the real answer to this riddle of Presidential composure in the face of a threatened attack upon some American outpost in the faraway Pacific? This problem grows more complicated as we watch the approach of zero hour. At 9:00 A.M. on December 7, Lieutenant Commander Kramer delivered to Admiral Stark the final installment of the Japanese instruction to Nomura. Its meaning was now so obvious that Stark cried out in great alarm: "My God! This means war. I must get word to Kimmel at once."[151] But he made no effort to contact Honolulu. Instead he tried to get in touch with General Marshall, who, for some strange reason, suddenly decided to go on a long horseback ride. It was a history-making ride. In the early hours of the American Revolution, Paul Revere went on a famous ride to warn his countrymen of the enemy's approach and thus save American lives. In the early hours of World II, General Marshall took a ride that helped prevent an alert from reaching Pearl Harbor in time to save an American fleet from serious disaster and an American garrison from a bombing that cost more than two thousand lives. Was there an important

149 In this regard the testimony of Commander Lester B. Schulz is pertinent and colorful. *Ibid.*, pt. 10, pp. 4662–63.

150 *Ibid.*, pt. 3, pp. 1049–1541; pt. 5, pp. 2096–2477.

151 Morgenstern, *op. cit.*, p. 269.

purpose behind this ride? This question looms constantly larger as we look further into the Pearl Harbor hearings.

When Colonel Bratton, on the morning of December 7, saw the last part of the Japanese instruction to Nomura he realized at once that "Japan planned to attack the United States at some point at or near 1 o'clock that day."[152] To Lieutenant Commander Kramer the message meant "a surprise attack at Pearl Harbor today."[153] This information was in the hands of Secretary Knox by 10:00 A.M., and he must have passed it on to the President immediately.

It was 11:25 A.M. when General Marshall returned to his office. If he carefully read the reports on the threatened Japanese attack (on Pearl Harbor) he still had plenty of time to contact Honolulu by means of the scrambler telephone on his desk, or by the Navy radio or the FBI radio. For some reason best known to himself he chose to send the alert to Honolulu by RCA and did not even take the precaution to have it stamped, "priority." As the Army Pearl Harbor Board significantly remarked: "We find no justification for a failure to send this message by multiple secret means either through the Navy radio or the FBI radio or the scrambler telephone or all three."[154] Was the General under Presidential orders to break military regulations with regard to the transmission of important military information? Did he think that the President's political objectives outweighed considerations of national safety? Was the preservation of the British Empire worth the blood, sweat, and tears not only of the men who would die in the agony of Pearl Harbor but also of the long roll of heroes who perished in the epic encounters in the Pacific, in the Mediterranean area, and in the famous offensive that rolled at high tide across the war-torn fields of France? New cemeteries all over the world would confirm to stricken American parents the melancholy fact that the paths of military glory lead but to the grave.

But the President and Harry Hopkins viewed these dread contingencies with amazing equanimity. In the quiet atmosphere of the oval study in the White House, with all incoming telephone calls shut off, the Chief Executive calmly studied his well-filled stamp albums while Hopkins fondled Fala, the White House scottie. At one o'clock, Death stood in the doorway. The Japanese had bombed Pearl Harbor. America had suddenly been thrust into a war she is still fighting.

---

[152] *Ibid.*, p. 275. See also the testimony of Colonel Rufus S. Bratton in *Pearl Harbor Attack*, pts. 9–10, pp. 4508–4623.

[153] *Ibid.*, p. 276.

[154] *Pearl Harbor Attack*, pt. 39, p. 95; Robert E. Ward, "The Inside Story of the Pearl Harbor Plan," United States Naval Institute *Proceedings*, LXXVII, No. 12 (December 1951), 1271–83.

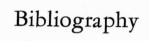

Bibliography

BIBLIOGRAPHY

I. Manuscript Sources

Official Papers

STATE DEPARTMENT CATEGORIES OF DIPLOMATIC CORRESPONDENCE

033.1140 Stimson, Henry L.
033.6511 Grandi, Dino
123   Bullitt, William C.
150.01
462.00R293
462.00R294
500.A15A5
500.A4B
611.6231
611.94231
693.002
693.002 Manchuria
701.6511
702.6211
711.00111 Armament Control
711.62
711.652
711.94
711.942
711.945
740.00
740.0011 European War—1939
740.0011 Mutual Guarantee—
  Locarno
740.0011 Pacific War
741.00
741.52
751.6111
751.62
751G.94
756.94
761.9411
763.7219

765.84
793.94
793.94 Commission
793.9411
800.51 W89 France
811.00 Nazi
811.20 (D) Regulations
811.34
811.4611
811.607
811.659 Helium-American Zeppelin
  Transport, Inc.
840.48 Refugees
862.00
862.002
862.002 Hitler, Adolf
862.014
862.20
862.4016
862.406
862T.01
863.00
865.00
884.6363 African Exploitation and
  Development Co.
893.00
893.00 P.R./Hankow
893.00 Tsinan
893.01 Manchuria
893.102 Tientsin
893.51
894.002
894.51

Private Papers

(In MSS Division, Library of Congress, unless otherwise noted)

Borah, William E.
Coolidge, Calvin
House, Edward M., Yale University
   Library
Knox, Philander C.
Lansing, Robert

Marshall, Verne, Cedar Rapids, Iowa
Roosevelt, Theodore
Root, Elihu
Taft, William H.
Wilson, Woodrow

II. Printed Sources

Official Documents

A. United States:
  Congress:
    The Congressional Record, 1900–1941.
    Pearl Harbor Attack, Hearings before the Joint Committee on the Investigation of the Pearl Harbor Attack, 79th Congress, Second Session, 39 parts. Washington, D. C., 1946.
  Department of State:
    Bulletins, 1933–1941.
    Documents on German Foreign Policy, 1918–1945, Series D:
      I. *From Neurath to Ribbentrop, 1937–1938.* Washington, D.C., 1949.
      II. *Germany and Czechoslovakia, 1937–1938.* Washington, D.C., 1949.
      IV. *The Aftermath of Munich, 1938–1939.* Washington, D. C., 1951.
    Papers Relating to the Foreign Relations of the United States, 1900–1934.
    Papers Relating to the Foreign Relations of the United States, Japan: 1931–1941, 2 vols. Washington, D. C., 1943.
    Nazi-Soviet Relations, 1939–1941. Washington, D. C., 1948.
    Peace and War: United States Foreign Policy, 1931–1941. Washington, D. C., 1943.
    Press Releases, 1933–1941.
  International Military Tribunal: *Trial of the Major War Criminals Before the International Military Tribunal, Nuremberg, 14 November, 1945–1 October, 1946.* 42 vols. Nürnberg, 1947–49.
  International Military Tribunal for the Far East: *Record of Proceedings* (mimeographed).
  Navy Department:
    Office of Naval Intelligence: *Fuehrer Conferences on Matters Dealing with the German Navy, 1939–1941,* 5 vols. Washington, D.C., 1947.

Office of the United States Chief Counsel for Prosecution of Axis Criminality: *Nazi Conspiracy and Aggression,* 11 vols. Washington, D. C., 1946–48.

B. Great Britain:

British Blue Books:

Documents Concerning German-Polish Relations and the Outbreak of Hostilities Between Great Britain and Germany on September 3, 1939. Cmd. 6106. Miscellaneous No. 9. London, 1939.

Protocols Determining the Frontiers between Germany and Czechoslovakia, Berlin, November 20–21, 1938. Cmd. 5908. Miscellaneous No. 11. London, 1938.

British Foreign Office Documents:

Documents on British Foreign Policy, 1919–1939, Third Series, Vols. I–II, 1938. London, 1949.

British White Papers:

Correspondence Respecting Czechoslovakia, September, 1938. Cmd. 5847. Miscellaneous No. 8. London, 1938.

Further Documents Respecting Czechoslovakia, Including the Agreement Concluded at Munich on September 29, 1938. Cmd. 5848. Miscellaneous No. 8. London, 1938.

Agreement Between the Government of the United Kingdom and the Polish Government Regarding Mutual Assistance, London, August 25, 1939. Cmd. 6616. Poland No. 1. London, 1945.

C. Finland:

Finnish Blue Book: The Development of Finnish-Soviet Relations in the Light of Official Documents, Including the Peace Treaty of March 4, 1940. New York, 1940.

D. France:

French Yellow Book. New York, 1940.

E. Germany:

Documents on the Events Preceding the Outbreak of the War. New York, 1940.

German White Paper of Polish Documents. New York, 1940.

Verhandlungen zur Lösung der sudetendeutschen Frage. Berlin, 1938.

F. Poland:

Polish White Book: Official Documents Concerning Polish-German and Polish-Soviet Relations, 1933–1939. London, 1940.

G. League of Nations:

Official Journal, 1929–1939.

Report of the Commission of Enquiry (with annexes), Document C. 663. M. 320, 1932, Vol. VII. Geneva, 1932.

Unofficial Collections of Documents, Letters, Speeches

Arms and the Covenant: Speeches by the Rt. Hon. Winston S. Churchill, 1929–1938, compiled by Randolph S. Churchill. London, 1939.

Documentary Background of World War II, 1931–1941, ed. James W. Gantenbein. New York, 1948.

Documents and Materials Relating to the Eve of the Second World War, 2 vols. New York, 1948.

Documents on American Foreign Relations, 1938–1941, ed. S. Shepard Jones and Denys P. Myers and published annually by the World Peace Foundation. Boston.

Documents on International Affairs, ed. John W. Wheeler-Bennett and published for the Royal Institute of International Affairs. London, 1930–39.

Hitler's Speeches, 1922–1939, ed. Norman H. Baynes, 2 vols. Oxford, 1942.

My New Order: Speeches by Adolf Hitler, 1922–1941, ed. Count Raoul de Roussy de Sales. New York, 1941.

Roosevelt, Franklin D. *F.D.R., His Personal Letters, 1928–1945,* ed. Elliott Roosevelt, 2 vols. New York, 1950.

Public Papers and Addresses of Franklin D. Roosevelt, ed. Samuel I. Rosenman, 13 vols. New York, 1938, 1941, 1950.

Roosevelt's Foreign Policy, 1933–1941, Franklin D. Roosevelt's Unedited Speeches and Messages. New York, 1942.

Speeches on Foreign Policy: The Rt. Hon. Viscount Halifax, 1934–1940. Oxford, 1940.

The Struggle for Peace: Speeches by the Rt. Hon. Neville Chamberlain, 1937–1939. London, 1939.

III. NEWSPAPERS AND PERIODICALS

Newspapers

A. AMERICAN
  Birmingham, Ala.
    Age-Herald
    News
  Los Angeles, Cal.
    Examiner
    Times
  Montrose, Cal.
    Ledger
  San Francisco, Cal.
    Chronicle
    Examiner

Washington, D. C.
  News
  Post
  Star
  Times-Herald
Jacksonville, Fla.
  Florida Times-Union
Atlanta, Ga.
  Constitution
  Journal
Boise, Idaho
  Idaho Statesman

Chicago, Ill.
Daily News
Tribune
Indianapolis, Ind.
News
Star
Des Moines, Iowa
Register
Emporia, Kansas
Gazette
Topeka, Kansas
State Journal
Louisville, Ky.
Courier-Journal
New Orleans, La.
Times-Picayune
Baltimore, Md.
American
Sun
Boston, Mass.
Christian Science Monitor
Globe
Herald
Post
Transcript
Springfield, Mass.
Republican
Detroit, Mich.
Free Press
Kansas City, Mo.
Journal
Star
St. Louis, Mo.
Globe-Democrat
Omaha, Nebr.
World-Herald
Reno, Nev.
Nevada State Journal
Albuquerque, N. Mex.
Journal
Brooklyn, N. Y.
Eagle
Buffalo, N. Y.
Express
News

New York, N. Y.
Daily News
Evening Post
Herald-Tribune
Journal
Sun
Times
Wall Street Journal
World-Telegram
Rochester, N. Y.
Democrat and Chronicle
Raleigh, N. C.
News and Observer
Grand Forks, N. Dak.
Herald
Cincinnati, Ohio
Enquirer
Post
Cleveland, Ohio
News
Plain Dealer
Oklahoma City, Okla.
Daily Oklahoman
Portland, Ore.
Oregonian
Philadelphia, Pa.
Evening Bulletin
Inquirer
Public Ledger
Record
Pittsburgh, Pa.
Post-Gazette
Providence, R. I.
Journal
Nashville, Tenn.
Banner
Dallas, Texas
News
Salt Lake City, Utah
Deseret News
Richmond, Va.
Times-Dispatch
Seattle, Wash.
Times

Spokane, Wash.
  Spokesman-Review
Milwaukee, Wis.
  Journal
  Sentinel
B. BRITISH
  Liverpool
    Daily Post
  London
    Daily Herald
    Daily Mail
    Daily Telegraph
    News Chronicle
    Observer
    Times
  Manchester
    Guardian

C. FRENCH
  Paris
    L'Oeuvre
    Le Figaro
    Le Soir
    Le Temps
D. GERMAN
  Berlin
    Berliner Allgemeine Zeitung
    Berliner Tageblatt
  Cologne
    Koelnische Zeitung
E. ITALIAN
  Rome
    Giornale d'Italia
    L'Osservatore Romano

Periodicals

A. AMERICAN
  America
  American Historical Review
  American Journal of
    International Law
  Bradstreet's
  Catholic World
  Christian Century
  Collier's
  Commonweal
  Commercial and Financial
    Chronicle
  Current History
  Far Eastern Review

  Foreign Affairs
  Journal of Commerce
  Journal of Modern History
  Minnesota Law Review
  Nation
  New Republic
  Pacific Historical Review
  Political Science Quarterly
  Proceedings of the United
    States Naval Institute
  Yale Review
B. ENGLISH
  Contemporary Review
  Nineteenth Century and After

IV. DIARIES, MEMOIRS, MISCELLANEOUS

Bonnet, Georges. *Le Défense de la Paix, de Washington au Quai d'Orsay.*
  Geneva, 1946.
Bono, General Emilio de. *Anno XIII.* London, 1937.
Churchill, Winston S. *The End of the Beginning.* Boston, 1943.
Churchill, Winston S. *The Gathering Storm.* Boston, 1948.
Churchill, Winston S. *Their Finest Hour.* Boston, 1949.

Churchill, Winston S. *The Grand Alliance.* Boston, 1950.

Ciano Diaries: Personal Diaries of Count Galeazzo Ciano, 1939–1943, ed. Hugh Gibson. Garden City, 1947.

Davies, Joseph E. *Mission to Moscow.* New York, 1941.

Dodd, William E. *Diary, 1933–1938,* ed. William E. Dodd, Jr. and Martha Dodd. New York, 1941.

Farley, James A. *Jim Farley's Story: The Roosevelt Years.* New York, 1948.

Forrestal, James A. *Diaries,* ed. Walter Millis and E. S. Duffield. New York, 1951.

François-Poncet, André. *The Fateful Years: Memoirs of a French Ambassador in Berlin, 1931–1938.* New York, 1949.

Gafencu, Grigore. *Last Days of Europe: A Diplomatic Journey in 1939.* New Haven, 1948.

Gamelin, General M.-G. *Servir.* Paris, 1946:
    Vol. I: *Les Armées françaises en 1940.*
    Vol. II: *Le Prologue du Drame, 1930–1939.*

Gisevius, G. B. *Bis zum bitteren Ende.* Zurich, 1946.

Goebbels, Joseph. *Diaries,* ed. Louis P. Lochner. Garden City, 1948.

Graves, General William S. *America's Siberian Adventure.* New York, 1931.

Grew, Joseph C. *Ten Years in Japan.* New York, 1944.

Hassell, Ulrich von. *Diaries, 1938–1944.* Garden City, 1947.

Henderson, Sir Nevile. *Failure of a Mission.* New York, 1940.

Hitler, Adolf. *Mein Kampf.* Munich, 1926.

Hoover, Herbert. "Communism Erupts in Europe," *Collier's,* CXXVIII (September 8, 1951), 26–27, 68–71.

Hull, Cordell. *Memoirs,* 2 vols. New York, 1948.

Ishii, Kikujiro. *Diplomatic Commentaries,* trans. and ed. W. R. Langdon. Baltimore, 1936.

Kase, Toshikazu. *Journey to the "Missouri."* New Haven, 1950.

Kato, Masuo. *The Lost War: A Japanese Reporter's Inside Story.* New York, 1946.

Konoye, Prince. *Memoirs,* in *Pearl Harbor Attack,* pt. 20, pp. 3985–4029.

Lansing, Robert. *War Memoirs.* Indianapolis, 1935.

Lloyd George, David. *Memoirs of the Peace Conference.* New Haven, 1939.

Lochner, Louis P. *What About Germany?* New York, 1943.

Miller, David H. *My Diary at the Conference of Paris,* 21 vols. New York, 1924.

Moley, Raymond. *After Seven Years.* New York, 1939.

Morgenthau, Henry. "The Morgenthau Diaries," *Collier's,* CXX (October 4, 1947), 20–21, 45, 48–49; (October 11), 20–21, 72–79; (October 18), 16–17, 71–75; (October 25), 24–25, 83–86.

Nicolson, Harold. *Peacemaking 1919.* Boston, 1933.

Noël, Léon. *L'Aggression allemande contre la Pologne.* Paris, 1946.

Perkins, Frances. *The Roosevelt I Knew.* New York, 1946.

Reinsch, Paul. *An American Diplomat in China.* New York, 1922.

Reynaud, Paul. *La France a sauvé l'Europe.* Paris, 1947.

Rothermere, Viscount. *Warnings and Predictions.* London, 1939.

Russell, William. *Berlin Embassy.* New York, 1941.

Schmidt, Paul. *Hitler's Interpreter.* London, 1950.

Schuschnigg, Kurt von. *Requiem in Rot-Weiss-Rot.* Zurich, 1946.

Seymour, Charles, (ed.). *The Intimate Papers of Colonel House,* 4 vols. Boston, 1926.

Shirer, William. *Berlin Diary.* New York, 1941.

Shotwell, James T. *At the Peace Conference.* New York, 1937.

Stimson, Henry L. *The Far Eastern Crisis: Recollections and Observations.* New York, 1936.

Stimson, Henry L. *Diary* [November–December 1941], in *Pearl Harbor Attack,* pt. 11, pp. 5431–39.

Stimson, Henry L., and McGeorge Bundy. *On Active Service in War and Peace.* New York, 1947.

Tolischus, Otto. *Tokyo Record.* New York, 1943.

Weizsäcker, Ernst von. *Memoirs,* trans. John Andrews. Chicago, 1951.

Welles, Sumner. *Memoranda of Conversations* [at Argentia, Newfoundland], *August 10–11, 1941,* in *Pearl Harbor Attack,* pt. 4, pp. 1784–92.

Welles, Sumner. *Time for Decision.* New York, 1944.

Wilson, Hugh. *Diplomat Between Wars.* New York, 1941.

V. BIOGRAPHIES, HISTORIES, SPECIAL STUDIES, ARTICLES

Alsop, Joseph, and Robert Kintner. *American White Paper: The Story of American Diplomacy and the Second World War.* New York, 1940.

Bailey, Thomas A. *Woodrow Wilson and the Lost Peace.* New York, 1944.

Bailey, Thomas A. *The Man in the Street: The Impact of American Public Opinion on Foreign Policy.* New York, 1948.

Baker, Ray S. *Woodrow Wilson and World Settlement,* 3 vols. New York, 1922.

Barmine, Alexander. *One Who Survived.* New York, 1945.

Beard, Charles A. *American Foreign Policy in the Making, 1932–1940.* New York, 1948.

Beard, Charles A. *President Roosevelt and the Coming of the War, 1941.* New Haven, 1948.

Beer, George L. *African Questions at the Paris Peace Conference,* ed. L. H. Gray. New York, 1923.

Beloff, Max. *The Foreign Policy of Soviet Russia, 1929–1941.* New York, 1929.

Bemis, Samuel F. *The Latin American Policy of the United States.* New York, 1945.

Benson, Oliver E. *Through the Diplomatic Looking Glass: Immediate Origins of the War in Europe.* Norman, Okla., 1939.

Birdsall, Paul. *Versailles Twenty Years After.* New York, 1941.

Blum, Léon. *Peace and Disarmament*. London, 1932.

Bonn, M. J. "How Sanctions Failed," *Foreign Affairs*, XV (1937), 350–61.

Borchard, Edwin M. "The Multilateral Treaty for the Renunciation of War," *American Journal of International Law*, XXIII (1929), 116–20.

Borchard, Edwin M. "The Arms Embargo and Neutrality," *American Journal of International Law*, XXVII (1933), 293–98.

Borchard, Edwin M., and William P. Lage. *Neutrality for the United States*. New Haven, 1937.

Borchard, Edwin M., and Phoebe Morrison. *Legal Problems in the Far Eastern Conflict*. New York, 1941.

Borg, Dorothy. *American Policy and the Chinese Revolution, 1925–1928*. New York, 1947.

Briggs, Herbert. "Neglected Aspects of the Destroyer Deal," *American Journal of International Law*, XXXIV (1940), 569–87.

Briggs, Herbert. "Non-Recognition of Title by Conquest," *Proceedings of the American Society of International Law* (May 13–15, 1940), pp. 79–81.

Burnett, Philip M. *Reparation at the Paris Peace Conference*. New York, 1940.

Buss, Claude A. *War and Diplomacy in Eastern Asia*. New York, 1941.

Cave, Floyd A., *et al. The Origins and Consequences of World War II*. New York, 1948.

Chamberlin, William H. *Japan Over Asia*. Boston, 1937.

Chamberlin, William H. *America's Second Crusade*. Chicago, 1950.

Commager, Henry S. *The Story of the Second World War*. Boston, 1945.

Cooper, Russell M. *American Consultation in World Affairs*. New York, 1934.

Dallin, David J. *Soviet Russia's Foreign Policy, 1939–1942*. New Haven, 1942.

Dallin, David J. *Soviet Russia and the Far East*. New Haven, 1948.

Davies, Lord. *The Problem of the Twentieth Century: A Study in International Relationships*. London, 1934.

Davis, Forrest, and Ernest K. Lindley. *How War Came*. New York, 1942.

Dietrich, Ethel B. *Far Eastern Trade of the United States*. New York, 1940.

Donald, Sir Robert. *The Polish Corridor and the Consequences*. London, 1929.

Dulles, Allen W. *Germany's Underground*. New York, 1947.

Farley, Miriam S. "America's Stake in the Far East," *Far Eastern Survey*, V (July 29, 1926), 161–70.

Fay, Sidney B. *Origins of the World War*, 2 vols. New York, 1929.

Feiling, Keith. *Life of Neville Chamberlain*. London, 1946.

Feis, Herbert. *The Road to Pearl Harbor*. Princeton, 1950.

Ferguson, John H. *American Diplomacy and the Boer War*. Philadelphia, 1939.

Field, Frederick V. *American Participation in the China Consortium*. Chicago, 1931.

Flynn, John T. *Country Squire in the White House.* New York, 1940.

Flynn, John T. *The Roosevelt Myth.* New York, 1948.

Friedman, Irving S. *British Relations with China, 1931–1939.* New York, 1940.

Friters, George. *The International Position of Outer Mongolia.* Dijon, 1939.

Gedye, George E. R. *The Revolver Republic.* London, 1930.

Gedye, George E. R. *Betrayal in Central Europe.* New York, 1939.

Géraud, André (Pertinax). "France and the Anglo-German Naval Treaty," *Foreign Affairs,* XIV (1935), 51–61.

Géraud, André (Pertinax). *The Gravediggers of France.* New York, 1944.

Griswold, A. Whitney. *The Far Eastern Policy of the United States.* New York, 1938.

Haines, C. Grove, and Ross J. S. Hoffman. *Origins and Background of the Second World War.* New York, 1943.

Hall, Walter P. *Iron out of Calvary: An Interpretative History of the Second World War.* New York, 1946.

Hankey, Lord. *Politics, Trials and Errors.* Chicago, 1950.

Harris, C. R. S. *Germany's Foreign Indebtedness.* London, 1935.

Hart, B. H. Liddell. *The German Generals Talk.* New York, 1948.

Hasluck, E. L. *The Second World War.* London, 1948.

Hedin, Sven. *The Silk Road.* New York, 1938.

Heiden, Konrad. *Adolf Hitler, eine Biographie.* Zurich, 1944.

Hornbeck, Stanley K. *The United States and the Far East.* Boston, 1942.

Hutton, Graham. *Survey After Munich.* Boston, 1939.

Johnson, Allen C. *Viscount Halifax.* London, 1941.

Johnson, Walter. *The Battle Against Isolation.* Chicago, 1944.

Johnstone, William C. *The United States and Japan's New Order.* New York, 1941.

Kaeckenbeeck, Georges. *The International Experiment of Upper Silesia.* London, 1942.

Kawakami, Kiyoshi. *Japan in China.* New York, 1938.

Keith, Arthur B. *The Causes of the War.* London, 1940.

Koenig, Louis W. *The Presidency and the Crisis: Powers of Office from the Invasion of Poland to Pearl Harbor.* New York, 1944.

Langer, William L. *Our Vichy Gamble.* New York, 1947.

Langer, William L., and S. Everett Gleason. *The Challenge to Isolation, 1937–1940.* New York, 1952.

Lavine, Harold, and James Wechsler. *War Propaganda and the United States.* New Haven, 1940.

Lawrence, F. W. *This Gold Crisis.* London, 1931.

Lee, Dwight E. *Ten Years.* Boston, 1942.

Lennhoff, Eugene. *The Last Five Hours of Austria.* New York, 1938.

Lennox, Victor G. "Anthony Eden," *Foreign Affairs,* XVI (1938), 691–703.

Lewis, Cleona. *America's Stake in International Investments.* Washington, 1938.

Luckau, Alma. *The German Delegation at the Paris Peace Conference.* New York, 1941.

Lyons, Eugene. *Assignment in Utopia.* New York, 1938.

Macartney, Maxwell H. H., and Paul Cremona. *Italy's Foreign and Colonial Policy, 1914–1937.* New York, 1938.

Mackintosh, John. *The Paths That Led to War, Europe 1919–1939.* London, 1940.

McLaughlin, C. H. "Neutral Rights Under International Law in the European War, 1939–1941," *Minnesota Law Review,* XXVI (1941–42), 1–49, 177–222.

McNair, Harley F. *China in Revolution.* Chicago, 1931.

Martel, René. *The Eastern Frontiers of Germany.* London, 1930.

Martienssen, Anthony. *Hitler and His Admirals.* New York, 1949.

Masland, John W. "Missionary Influence Upon American Far Eastern Policy," *Pacific Historical Review,* X (1941), 279–96.

Masland, John W. "Commercial Influence Upon American Far Eastern Policy, 1937–1941," *Pacific Historical Review,* XI (1942), 281–99.

Maugham, Viscount. *The Truth About the Munich Crisis.* London, 1944.

Maurois, André. *Tragedy in France.* New York, 1940.

Mendelssohn, Peter de. *Design for Aggression.* New York, 1946.

Miller, David H. *The Peace Pact of Paris.* New York, 1928.

Millis, Walter. *This Is Pearl!: The United States and Japan, 1941.* New York, 1947.

Moore, Frederick. *With Japan's Leaders.* New York, 1942.

Moore, Harriet L. *Soviet Far Eastern Policy, 1931–1945.* Princeton, 1945.

Moore, John Bassett. "An Appeal to Reason," *Foreign Affairs,* XI (1933), 547–88.

Moore, John Bassett. "The New Isolation," *American Journal of International Law,* XXVII (1933), 607–29.

Morgenstern, George. *Pearl Harbor: The Story of the Secret War.* New York, 1947.

Morison, Samuel E. *The Battle of the Atlantic, September 1939–May 1943.* Boston, 1947.

Morrow, I. F. D. *The Peace Settlement in the German-Polish Borderlands.* London, 1936.

Namier, L. B. *Diplomatic Prelude, 1938–1939.* London, 1948.

Namier, L. B. *Europe in Decay, 1936–1940.* London, 1950.

Nevins, Allan. *Henry White: Thirty Years of American Diplomacy.* New York, 1930.

Nickerson, Hoffman. *The New Slavery.* Garden City, 1947.

Nicolson, Harold. *Why Britain is at War.* London, 1939.

Norins, Martin R. *Gateway to Asia: Sinkiang.* New York, 1944.

Perkins, Dexter. *America and Two Wars*. Boston, 1944.
Pollard, Robert T. *China's Foreign Relations, 1917–1931*. New York, 1933.
Powell, E. Alexander. *Thunder Over Europe*. New York, 1931.
Price, Ernest B. *The Russo-Japanese Treaties of 1907–1916 Concerning Manchuria and Mongolia*. Baltimore, 1933.
Rauch, Basil. *Roosevelt, From Munich to Pearl Harbor*. New York, 1950.
Reid, John G. *The Manchu Abdication and the Powers*. Berkeley, Cal., 1935.
Remer, C. F. *Foreign Investments in China*. New York, 1933.
Remer, C. F. *A Study of Chinese Boycotts*. Baltimore, 1933.
Rey, Charles F. *The Real Abyssinia*. Philadelphia, 1935.
Rothfels, Hans. *The German Opposition to Hitler*. Chicago, 1948.
Rudin, Harry R. *Germany in the Cameroons*. New Haven, 1938.
Rudin, Harry R. *Armistice, 1918*. New Haven, 1944.
Sanborn, Frederic R. *Design for War*. New York, 1951.
Schwarz, Paul. *This Man Ribbentrop: His Life and Times*. New York, 1943.
Scott, Arthur P. "George Louis Beer," in *Marcus W. Jernegan Essays in American Historiography*, ed. W. T. Hutchinson. Chicago, 1937.
Sering, Max. *Germany Under the Dawes Plan*. London, 1929.
Sharman, Lyon. *Sun Yat-sen: His Life and Its Meaning*. New York, 1934.
Sherwood, Robert E. *Roosevelt and Hopkins*. New York, 1948.
Simoni, L. *Berlino-Ambasciata d'Italia, 1939–1943*. Rome, 1946.
Simpson, Sir John H. *Refugees*. New York, 1938.
Sokolsky, George. *The Tinder Box of Asia*. New York, 1932.
Sokolsky, George. "These Days," Washington *Times-Herald* (March 14, 1951).
Stieve, Friedrich. *What the World Rejected: Hitler's Peace Offers, 1933–1939*. Berlin, 1939.
Takeuchi, Tatsuji. *War and Diplomacy in the Japanese Empire*. New York, 1935.
T'ang Leang-li. *Suppressing Communist Banditry in China*. Shanghai, 1934.
T'ang Leang-li. *The Puppet State of Manchukuo*. Shanghai, 1935.
Tansill, Charles Callan. *America Goes to War*. Boston, 1938.
Tansill, Charles Callan. *Canadian-American Relations, 1875–1911*. New York, 1944.
Trefousse, H. L. *Germany and American Neutrality, 1939–1941*. New York, 1951.
Tyau, M. T. Z. *China Awakened*. New York, 1922.
United States in World Affairs, annual, ed. Whitney H. Shepardson and William I. Scroggs. 1933–41.
Veblen, Thorstein. *The Nature of Peace*. New York, 1917.
Ware, Edith. *Business and Politics in the Far East*. New Haven, 1932.
Wheeler-Bennett, John W. *Disarmament and Security since Locarno*. London, 1932.
Wheeler-Bennett, John W. *The Wreck of Reparations*. London, 1932.
Wheeler-Bennett, John W. *Hindenburg: Wooden Titan*. London, 1936.

Wheeler-Bennett, John W. *Munich: Prologue to Tragedy.* New York, 1948.

White, John A. *The Siberian Intervention.* Princeton, 1950.

Willoughby, Westel W. *The Sino-Japanese Controversy and the League of Nations.* Baltimore, 1935.

Winkler, Max. *Foreign Bonds: An Autopsy.* Philadelphia, 1933.

Wolfers, Arnold. *Britain and France between Two Wars.* New Haven, 1940.

Woolbert, Robert. "Italy in Abyssinia," *Foreign Affairs,* XIII (1935), 499–508.

Woolf, Leonard. *Empire and Commerce in Africa.* New York, 1920.

Woolsey, Lester H. "The Porter and Capper Resolutions against Traffic in Arms," *American Journal of International Law,* XXIII (1929), 379–83.

Zabriskie, Edward H. *American-Russian Rivalry in the Far East.* Philadelphia, 1946.

Zernatto, Guido. *Die Wahrheit ueber Oesterreich.* London, 1938.

Index

INDEX

ABC-1 Staff Agreement, 609, 630
Abyssinia. *See* Ethiopia
Addis, Sir Charles, 61
Addis Ababa, 184, 194, 205, 318;
  capture of, 255; Treaty of, 166
Aduwa, 166, 179
African Exploration and Development Company, 184
Aglen, Sir Francis, 71
Albania, 231, 515, 516–17
Albuquerque Journal, 293, 302, 349
Algeciras Conference, 166
Allen, Gen. Henry T., 22
Allen, Senator, 232
Allenstein, 19
Almería, 338
Aloisi, Baron Pompeo, 188, 230, 254
Alsace-Lorraine, 274
Alsop, Joseph, 610
Altmark incident, 580–81
Amau, 133–34, 136, 157, 158
Amba Aradam, 250
America (national weekly), 315, 346, 479
American Army of Occupation (1923), payment of costs for, 26
American Aviation (periodical), 353
American Commission of Inquiry, 16
American Jewish Congress, 332
American Standard Vacuum Oil Company, 142
American Zeppelin Transport, Inc., 351
Anglo-American policy in 1898, 3
Anglo-French Purchasing Commission, 587
Anglo-German Naval Agreement, 301–2, 303, 520
Anglo-Italian Agreement, 260, 261
Anglo-Japanese alliance of 1902, 3

Der Angriff, 333–34
Anschluss. See Austria
Anti-Comintern Pact, 156, 320, 444, 506
Antigua, 599
Anti-Semitism, 25, 40, 49, 266, 268, 273, 275, 278, 282–84, 306, 385, 387, 433–37, 439, 577
Antung-Mukden Railway, 94 n.
Aoki, Lieut.-Col. Seiichi, 138
Argentina, 213, 441
Arita, Japanese Foreign Minister, 158
Arms embargo, 219, 220, 221, 222, 236, 237, 238, 245–47, 561–66
Arms Reduction Conference, 193 n.
Assab, 165
Associated Board of Christian Colleges in China, 499
Astakhov, Russian chargé d'affaires, 533, 537
Astor, Viscountess, 394
Athenia, (S.S.), 567, 570
Atlanta Constitution, 39, 105, 279, 296, 320, 338, 429, 430, 477, 573
Atlantic Conference of Roosevelt and Churchill, 639–40
Augusta (U.S.S.), 469
Auslandsorganization, 357
Australia, 259, 630
Austria, 187, 231, 235, 330, 331; conquest of approved by Mussolini, 382–83; debts of, 358, 438–39; independence of, 331; occupied by Germany, 359–61, 383; plebiscite on independence of, 378; relations of with Germany, 371–88
Ave Maria (magazine), 346, 479, 600
Avenol, Joseph, 473